The Bengal Native Army

The Bengal Native Army

F. G. Cardew

The Bengal Native Army
by F. G. Cardew

Originally published in 1903 under the title
A Sketch of the Services of the Bengal Native Army to the Year 1895

Leonaur is an imprint of Oakpast Ltd

Text in this form and material original to this edition
copyright © 2008 Oakpast Ltd

ISBN: 978-1-84677-560-4 (hardcover)
ISBN: 978-1-84677-559-8 (softcover)

http://www.leonaur.com

Publisher's Notes

The opinions expressed in this book are those of the author
and are not necessarily those of the publisher.

Contents

Preface	7
Memorandum	9
The Conquest of Bengal	11
The Mysore War	45
The Mahratta War	83
Gurkhas & Mahrattas	129
The First Burma War	158
Afghanistan & Scinde	184
The Sikh Wars	222
The Great Mutiny	286
The Northwest Frontier	328
The Afghan War	358
Egypt & Burma	403
Tribesmen	436
Appendices	459

Preface

It is hoped that these pages may form a suitable introduction to the regimental histories of the Bengal Army, filling up gaps in the military history of Northern India as told by them, recording actions and achievements of corps which now no longer exist, and giving a general view of events common to many regiments, which, if repeated at length in the record of each, would extend the succeeding volumes to an unnecessary degree.

Many of the periods dealt with are too much neglected in the histories available to the general reader; the details for these have been collected from contemporary magazine literature, while the more important authorities are quoted at the heads of chapters.

F. G. C.

Memorandum

This book was originally compiled by Lieutenant F. G. Cardew in 1890-91; it was afterwards revised in the Military Department by Mr. G.W. deRhé-Philipe, but, owing to a variety of circumstances, its publication has been delayed and it has only now been found practicable to put it through the press.

In the course of revision, advantage has been taken of the opportunity to make the work more complete by, first, the insertion of accounts of many little-known operations which had been omitted from the original compilation; secondly, by the introduction of more detailed and particular accounts of the more important campaigns; and, finally, by bringing it up to the abolition of the Presidency armies in 1895.

In carrying out the revision of this compilation, a large number of works and periodicals of various descriptions, and of varying degrees of authority, have been consulted, and a list of these is appended, but it is to be understood that the revision is based essentially on official records.

Military Department
Calcutta
21st March 1903

CHAPTER 1

The Conquest of Bengal

Although the record of British progress in India has been essentially a military history, yet nearly a century elapsed after the first establishment of English traders in the country before the formation of an armed force for their defence.

The East India Company was formed in 1599 by an association of merchants, who established their first factory at Surat in 1612, and in 1640 erected Fort St. George. In the same year was despatched from England the first expedition to Bengal: this consisted of two ships, of which the crews were so well received by the Nawab of those provinces that the Company decided to prosecute the trade, and finally established a factory at Hooghly.

The Bengal settlements, however, remained dependent on that of Fort St. George, while their trade was subject to the control of the native government of Bengal, by whom they were forbidden to entertain any military strength, beyond "an ensign and thirty men" to do honour to the principal agents.

In 1681 Bengal became independent of Madras, Mr. Hedges being sent from the latter place as the Company's "Agent and Governor in the Bay of Bengal and the factories subordinate." The first Governor took with him from Madras a party of a corporal and twenty soldiers, which little band was increased in 1683 by a company of soldiers, together with arms and accoutrements sufficient for another company, Meanwhile the traders at Hooghly had been for many years subject to the jealous repression and exactions of the native government, and, being unable owing to the smallness of their numbers to enforce their claims, their ventures had been thwarted and their trade impoverished to such a degree that the Company at length decided to equip an expedition of sufficient strength to assert the rights of their agents and to make definite terms with the Emperor Aurangzeb and Nawab Sha-istah Khan, the Governor of Bengal. This expedition consisted of a fleet of ten ships bearing six complete companies of infantry, which were augmented by the seamen to ten companies, or 1000 men. It was further increased by a force of 400 men from Madras, and a company of Portuguese infantry (called Topasses, from the hats which they wore) raised by Job Charnock, the chief agent at Hooghly. But when the expedition arrived at the mouth of the Hooghly the fleet had already lost a third of its strength through contrary winds and bad weather. Several months were passed in desultory fighting and negotiations, until the British forces were reduced to the utmost straits by the effects of the climate, and at length found themselves hemmed in by overwhelming numbers and obliged to make their last stand on the fever-stricken island of Ingelli. At this crisis an offer of further negotiations was gladly accepted by Charnock, and in August 1687 a treaty was finally concluded with Nawab Sha-istah Khan, by which the English regained their former rights and received assurances for the future.

A year had not passed, however, before the oppressions of the Nawab recommenced. Charnock again had recourse to negotiations; but while these were in progress there arrived from England, under the command of Captain Heath, an armed frigate bearing 160 men, sent out by the Court of Directors to carry into execution the orders which had been given to the leaders of the former expedition. Heath, an impatient and hot-tempered man, immediately had recourse to hostilities, seized and pillaged Balasore, made a demonstration before Chittagong, and at length, finding that neither his violence nor his negotiation were of much avail, he carried off the whole of the Company's troops, servants and portable property to Madras.

In August 1690, terms having been again agreed on with the Emperor, and Sha-istah Khan having been succeeded by Ibrahim Khan as Nawab of Bengal, Mr. Charnock, with the Company's servants, returned to the Hooghly and established themselves at Sutanati. For some years the settlement continued to increase rapidly without further molestation from the native government, until in 1695 occurred the rebellion of Suba Singh, a Hindu *zemindar* of Burdwan, who, having attracted considerable numbers to his cause, threatened the safety of the Company's settlements. On this the local government enlisted native soldiers for the protection of their property, and putting their factories info a state of defence originated the fortifications of Chinsura, Chandernagore, and Calcutta.

In 1699 Bengal was raised by the Court to the rank of a Presidency. Sir Charles Eyre was appointed President; and the fort at Calcutta, which was being rapidly pushed on, was named Fort William, in honour of King William III. In this year also was started the new 'English Company,' which, after several years of rivalry with the old or 'London Company,' was finally united to the latter in 1708. The military force at this time amounted to some 130 men, exclusive of a small party of artillerymen called "the Gunner and his Crew."

For many years the trade and prosperity of Calcutta continued to increase rapidly; and although the military establishment appears to have kept pace with that of other branches of the service, yet no serious danger threatened the settlement until the year 1742, when the Mahrattas devastated the whole province and sacked the town of Hooghly. At this juncture the European and Armenian inhabitants were, for the first time, regularly embodied into a militia; a number of lascars were entertained to help the gun-room crew in working the guns, and the so-called Mahratta Ditch was commenced round the settlement: however, the Mahrattas did not advance, and the latter work was abandoned.

In 1754 the first legislative enactment for the regulation of the Company's military force was passed, and under it Articles of War were framed which, with slight modification, continued to guide the service for many years. The regular military establishment at this time appears to have consisted of five companies of infantry and one of artillery.

In 1756 the Nawab Siraj-ud-Daulah succeeded to the Government of Bengal, and with this event opened the first great epoch of British progress in India, which, beginning in massacre, reverse, and almost extermination, finally ended in the subjugation of the whole Empire to British rule.

The Nawab had only assumed the government for a few weeks when he allowed himself to be carried away by his deep-rooted hatred of the English into open hostilities against the Company's settlements. Having attacked and taken the factory of Kasimbazar, with its little garrison of two officers (Lieutenant Elliot and Surgeon Forth) and forty-two regular soldiers, of whom less than half were Englishmen, he advanced on Calcutta with his whole army, and crossed the Hooghly on the 15th of June. Within the capital consternation reigned among the inhabitants; confusion and timidity paralysed the leaders; the fort was ill-arranged and its defences decaying; the ammunition was scanty and inferior; the guns dismounted and useless, and the garrison amounted only to some 500 men, of whom but 174 were Englishmen. Hostilities were commenced by a slight success of the British, who seized the fort of Tannah on the opposite side of the river; but they were soon driven back and closely blockaded in Calcutta. At the first reverse the whole of the native soldiers deserted; and in the course of the five days' defence which ensued, their conduct was surpassed in baseness by the headlong and selfish flight of the Governor, the Commandant and a great number of the officers of militia, who, embarking in the only available boats, went on board a Company's ship which was lying in the river and dropped down to Govindpur, leaving the unfortunate remnant of the garrison to their fate.

On the 20th of June the fort was taken, and on that night occurred the horrible incident of the "Black Hole", the story of which is too well known to need repetition.

The survivors of the British inhabitants, together with a reinforcement of three ships from Bombay, took refuge at Palta: here they were joined in August by some 230 men from Madras under Major Kilpatrick, while a volunteer company was also formed, including a number of civil servants, among whom was the future Governor-General, Warren Hastings. Further reinforcements were solicited from Madras, but, owing to delays and indecision, the whole of these, under Lieutenant-Colonel Robert Clive, did not reach Palta until December the 20th.

The expedition now comprised 250 of His Majesty's 39th Regiment, 570 of the Madras European infantry, 1,200 Madras sepoys, some details of artillery, 230 Bengal European infantry, and 70 volunteers, making a total of about 2,400 men.

Clive advanced from Palta on December 27th, and, after some sharp fighting, took the fort of Budge-Budge on the 29th. The forts of Tannah and Aligarh were abandoned by the Nawab's troops without a shot being fired, and on January 2nd Fort William was again in the hands of the British. Hooghly was re-taken on January 17th by a force detached under Major Kilpatrick; and on the 12th a large body of about 5,000 of the enemy was defeated at Gongi, near Bandel, by 50 British soldiers and 100 sepoys under Captain Eyre Coote.

Whilst these expeditions were in progress, Clive turned his attention to the means at hand of securing the footing just regained by the English in Bengal. He found his small army confronted on the one side by the forces of the Nawab, with whom all attempts at negotiation proved useless, and on the other, by the French settlers of Chandernagore, whom the events occurring in Europe, where war had lately been declared between England and France, would certainly range amongst his enemies. He determined to supply his pressing need for reinforcements by the formation of a battalion of sepoys. The native troops (called *Buxarries*, and in Madras, *Telingas* or *Peons*) which had hitherto been employed as occasion required, were wholly undisciplined, and were armed and equipped in native style: even the more carefully trained Madras and Bombay sepoys adhered to native dress and equipment. Clive, however, determined to try the experiment of assimilating them as nearly as possible to European troops. Having raised some three or four hundred picked men, he furnished them not only with arms but also with dress of European pattern, drilled and disciplined them as regular troops, and appointed a British officer and non-commissioned officers to command and instruct them. This, the earliest Bengal Native regiment, was for many years known as the *Lal Paltan*[1] on account of its equipment, but later it went by the name of *Gillis-ki-paltan*, from Captain Primrose Galliez, who obtained command of it in 1763 and held that post for many years: it became the 2nd Battalion of the 12th Bengal Native Infantry in 1796.

Recruits for Clive's native battalion were easily obtained. The Musalman conquest of Bengal and the general disturbances in the governments of Northern India brought numbers of the fighting races down to the lower provinces in search of service, or enrichment by other means, and in the corps then raised around Calcutta were to be found Pathans, Rohillas, Jats, Rajputs, and even Brahmans.[2]

At the end of January reinforcements arrived in Bengal of artillery and stores: and on the 5th of February Clive attacked and defeated the Nawab's army, which had advanced within the Company's territory, near Cossipore. The British loss (Royal Navy included) was 57 killed and 117 wounded, of whom 18 of the killed and 35 of the wounded were sepoys; that of the enemy was reckoned at 1,300. A treaty of peace with Siraj-ud-Daulah was the result of the battle. The total casualties in action up to this period, in the army, appear to have amounted to forty-one Europeans (including six officers) and eighteen natives killed, and 78 Europeans (including nine officers) and 55 natives wounded,—192 in all.

---

1. *Paltan* is derived from the English, platoon, which is itself a corruption of the French *peloton*.
2. The first regiments of the Bengal Native Army having been raised in Bengal, both Hamilton *(Geographical, Statistical and Historical Description of Hindustan)* and Bishop Heber *(Indian Journal)* take it for granted that these corps were composed of native Bengalis,—a ridiculous error out of which the Bengali press has made much capital of late years.

Clive's next object was the attack of the French settlement of Chandernagore. Reinforcements reached him from Bombay early in March, and, notwithstanding the opposition of the Nawab, hostilities were begun before Chandernagore on the 14th of that month. A combined attack by the troops and fleet was made on the fort on the 23rd, and the place surrendered on the same day. The casualties amongst the troops on this occasion were about forty killed and wounded: in the fleet the losses were more severe, amounting to thirty-two killed and 99 wounded, including several officers.

This success induced great numbers of natives to apply for service in Clive's army, and his newly raised battalion of sepoys was largely augmented. Meantime, while perfecting the drill and discipline of these troops, Clive was also occupied in negotiations with Mir Jafar Khan, the Nawab's principal officer in Bengal, and this with so much success that an advantageous treaty was concluded early in June. By this an agreement was made for mutual support, and besides the advantages already ceded by Siraj-ud-Daulah in February, all the lands lying south of Calcutta were granted to the Company and a pledge was exacted that the Nawab would erect no fortifications below Hooghly. These negotiations did not check the advance of the troops, who were at length, by Mir Jafar Khan's aid, enabled to make preparations for an attack on the Nawab.

On the 16th of June the army reached Path, and on the 18th Major Eyre Coote, with a force of 200 Europeans and 500 sepoys, attacked and captured Katwa.

At this juncture suspicions began to be entertained of the sincerity of Mir Jafar Khan in his promises of support to the English, and Clive called a council of war to decide the question of immediate action or delay until after the monsoon. Though the majority of votes—his own amongst them—were for the latter course, Clive's final decision was for active measures. He advanced from his position on the 22nd of June and arrived at Plassey on the morning of the 23rd.

The following, according to Broome, was the actual strength of the forces engaged: British artillery, including 50 sailors, 150 men, with eight six-pounder guns and two small howitzers; British infantry (detachments of the 39th Foot, and of the Bengal, Madras and Bombay European infantry), 750; Topasses, 200; native infantry, Madras and Bengal, 2,100. The Nawab's army is said to have numbered 50,000 foot and 18,000 horse, with a very powerful train of artillery.

The battle was begun about 8 a.m. by artillery fire from both sides, the English force being drawn up in line in front of a mango grove. After half an hour's firing, Clive, finding that his exposed position was causing a loss of valuable lives, retired into the grove, the bank round which served as a breastwork for his men. The British artillery kept up a smart and effective fire from behind this shelter, which played havoc amongst the masses of the Nawab's army, while the guns of the latter were not only badly served, but their ammunition rendered useless by a heavy shower of rain. Soon after noon the Nawab was much disheartened by the news of the death of his most trusted General, Mir Madin. Once aroused, his fears continued to increase every moment; he eagerly adopted the advice of those around him to return to his capital; orders were hastily given for the troops to retire to their fortified camp; the Nawab mounted a fast *sowari* camel, and, escorted by 2,000 horsemen, fled precipitately to Murshidabad.

Clive, seeing the turn which affairs were taking, advanced with his whole force and cannonaded the enemy's entrenchments, upon which their troops again turned out and came into action; but the dispositions of the English general were well made: his infantry were lodged close to the enemy's entrenchment, and their hot musketry fire, coupled with a heavy cannonade from the guns, quickly threw the troops of the Nawab into confusion. By 5 p.m. the whole enormous mob was scattered in headlong flight, and the camp, with all its baggage and stores, was in the hands of the English. The pursuit was kept up until 8 p.m., when Clive halted for the night at Daudpur.

Our loss in the battle was extremely small, amounting (exclusive of any casualties that may have occurred amongst the seamen) to only five Europeans and thirteen natives killed, and eighteen Europeans (including three officers) and thirty natives wounded.[3] Of the officers wounded on this memorable occasion two were of the Bengal Army, Lieutenant Cassells of the artillery and Lieutenant De Lubers of the European infantry: the name of the third officer (a lieutenant of the Madras artillery) has unfortunately not been preserved. Among the wounded, too, was Midshipman Richard Shorediche, of the *Kent*. Many years after, in 1829, the surviving corps of the Bengal Army received authority to inscribe the word "Plassey" on their colours. Siraj-ud-Daulah arrived at Murshidabad at midnight on the 23rd. Throughout the 24th, as news reached him of the advance of the English,.his terror hourly increased, and he fled at night from the city,

---

3. These figures are taken from Clive's official returns. They differ materially from those given in Broome's History and other publications.

almost alone. Clive entered Murshidabad on the 29th and placed Mir Jafar Khan on the *masnad*. On the 3rd of July Siraj-ud-Daulah was brought back a captive to Mir Jafar, and on the same night was ruthlessly murdered by order of Miran, the son of the new Nawab.

For two months after the victory of Plassey, Clive was occupied in exacting from Mir Jafar Khan the indemnity previously agreed upon, and in settling the disputes which arose amongst the British officers, military and naval, over the partition of the same. At the same time he turned his attention to the increase of the military force of Bengal, and to this end he enlisted men for a second regular battalion of sepoys, and formed the corps on drafts from the old battalion. Meanwhile a small force of French under Monsieur Law, which had marched from Bhagalpur to the assistance of Siraj-ud-Daulah, on hearing of the overthrow of that prince, made towards Patna with the intention of joining the Rajah Ram Narayan. In order to prevent his junction, a detachment was despatched under Major Coote, on the 6th of July, consisting of 220 British troops and 500 sepoys, with a detail of artillery.

On their march occurred the first recorded instance of a native court-martial in Bengal, when a sepoy was tried for conniving at the escape of a prisoner, and sentenced, by a court composed of *Subadars* and *Jemadars* of the detachment, to receive 500 lashes and be dismissed the service.

Alter many difficulties and hardships at the most unhealthy season of the year, Coote's detachment reached Patna on the 26th of July, Only to find that Law had escaped them and was now on the borders of Oudh where he could take refuge at any moment. For many days great discontent had existed among the troops: the British soldiers were in a mutinous state, and the Madras sepoys declared that they would go no further into the interior. However, expostulations and persuasions prevailed on them to advance again; and they continued in push on as far as Chapra (2nd August), whence a despatch from Clive recalled the detachment to Patna, and eventually to Murshidabad, where it arrived on September the 13th.

During this autumn a slight disturbance occurred amongst the Nawab's troops at Kasimbazar; and a revolt took place at Dacca, whin a company of the 1st Native Battalion was sent to assist the Nawab of that place.

On the 17th of November Clive marched from Calcutta, and joined the Nawab at Murshidabad; with him was a force of 550 British, some details of artillery, and 1,500 sepoys; while the Nawab was in accompanied by a force of 40,000 men. Following the route by which Coote had advanced in July, the combined force arrived at Patna on the 4th of February, 1758. Here some months were passed in discussing the settlement of the country; while Clive also occupied himself in raising a third battalion of sepoys, composed, for the most part, of men enlisted in the Bhojpur district.

On Clive's return to Murshidabad in May, news reached him of the increased strength of the French on the Madras coast. He Immediately returned to Calcutta, and pushed on the completion of the new fort at Govindpur, the present Fort William. In July he accepted the post of President of the newly re-organised local Government, and forthwith set about measures of considerable importance to the military strength of Bengal. Instead of sending back to their presidencies the British detachments from Madras and Bombay, all who volunteered for service in Bengal were formed into a Bengal European battalion,[4] into which also were received a number of volunteers, both officers and men, from His Majesty's 39th Regiment; the artillery was re-organised and formed into two companies; and a fourth battalion of sepoys was raised at the same time. The command of this corps was soon afterwards conferred upon Lieutenant Hugh Grant, from whom it became known as *Grant-ki-paltan:* in the re-organisation of 1796 it became the 1st battalion of the 2nd Regiment.

Meanwhile, the French successes in the Carnatic were becoming more and more pronounced, and the Madras Government appealed to Bengal for assistance. On the 12th of October, 1758, a strong detachment was sent by Clive under Lieutenant-Colonel Francis Forde, the Commandant in Bengal, with orders to proceed by sea to Vizagapatam, and, by creating a diversion there, to render assistance to the Madras Government. With this detachment were five companies of the Bengal European Battalion, the 2nd Artillery Company, the 1st and 2nd Bengal Native Battalions, and a battalion of Madras sepoys who had come round to Bengal in 1756. This was the first occasion on which Bengal sepoys were sent by sea on active service.

Colonel Forde met the French Army of the Northern Circars, under the Marquis de Conflans, on the 8th of December at Condore, about forty miles from Rajahmundry, and inflicted on them a signal

---

4. Both Broome and Innes assign a much earlier date to the formation of the Bengal European Battalion (now the 1st Battalion of the Royal Munster Fusiliers), but the exact date is really a matter of conjecture, and probably they are both wrong. Innes' statements on this point are, indeed, disproved by Clive's returns.

defeat: as his force advanced to the attack, the two Bengal Native battalions, which were on the flanks, were fully exposed to view, while the European Battalion, which formed the centre, was completely concealed by high standing crops: the French, moving obliquely to their right to attack the native battalion forming the left of the British line, exposed their left flank to the British centre; thrown into great confusion by a deadly volley from the British battalion, they fell back hastily, and the volley being succeeded by a charge, they were, after a short but severe combat, driven from the field with loss. Our loss was Captain Adnet, and fifteen British and 100 native soldiers killed; four officers and twenty British and 100 native soldiers wounded. The enemy lost six officers and 120 killed and wounded of the French troops, and a large number of sepoys.[5] No honorary distinction for this engagement was given until 1841, when, under some misapprehension, the Madras Government authorised the 1st Madras European Regiment, of which corps not a man was present in the action, to inscribe the word "Condore" on its colours. The distinction has recently been placed on the colours of the Royal Munster Fusiliers, the only corps now existing which is, as representing the 1st Bengal European Regiment, entitled to wear it.

Colonel Forde advanced on the 9th, accompanied by the Rajah Anandiraj of Vizianagram; while a detachment sent on in advance under Captain Knox seized the town and fort of Rajahmundry, on the Godaveri, on the 10th. Here a delay of six weeks took place, owing in the failure of Anandiraj to fulfil his engagements, and it was not until the 6th of February that the English force occupied Ellore. After seizing the French factory of Narsipur, Forde advanced and stormed the fort of Konkale on the 3rd March, and thence continuing his march to Masulipatam, arrived there on the 6th.

The fort of Masulipatam was a position of great natural strength, surrounded on three sides by a swamp of considerable extent. Almost at the outset of the siege the English found themselves in a most critical position; their treasure chests were empty; their retreat by the road by which they had come was cut off by the recapture of Rajahmundry by the French under du Rocher; and, the siege of Madras having been raised, a powerful army under General Lally was marching thence to the relief of Masulipatam. At this critical moment the European troops broke into open mutiny, but were pacified and re-assured by Colonel

---

5. Cambridge says—"We had forty-four Europeans killed and wounded, among which were two captains and three lieutenants; and the French 156, officers included."

Forde, and the preparations for the assault pushed on with vigour. At length at midnight on the 7th of April the attempt was made; Captain Knox led the 1st Bengal Battalion in a false attack, while the remainder of the force was formed in three divisions for the real assault. The plan was completely successful, and, the principal defences having been carried by storm, on the morning of the 8th of April, de Conflans surrendered. The conduct of the Bengal troops on this occasion was excellent, and they emulated the Europeans in their gallantry. Our loss was three officers, twenty-two British and fifty native soldiers killed; 62 British and 150 sepoys wounded. The enemy lost of Europeans alone 113 killed.

The effect of this success was to damp the ardour of the Nizam, who had previously been lending aid to the French, and he opened negotiations with Colonel Forde: meeting, however, with but indifferent success, he at length in disgust withdrew his force towards Hyderabad. The expected French reinforcements arrived off Masulipatam a week after its capture, and being apprised of that event, sailed for Ganjam, which place they fortified. In October Colonel Forde, accompanied by Captain Knox, returned to Calcutta, leaving Captain Fischer in command of the detachment, now reduced to some 1,100 men, of whom 300 were Europeans. The latter was ordered to return by land to Calcutta: marching by the route by which they had advanced in the preceding year, news reached Fischer at Rajahmundry that the French from Ganjam had occupied Coconada. He reached that place on the 28th December, and the fort was surrendered on the following day without a struggle.

Thus terminated the efforts of the French on the east coast, and by the success of Forde's expedition in the face of great difficulties those districts were acquired for England which had formerly constituted the most valuable possession of France in Hindustan.

Captain Fischer continued his march with the two Bengal battalions of his detachment, sending the Europeans and artillery by sea; and arrived at Calcutta in March, 1760.

Meanwhile the past year had been a busy one in Bengal. To make up, in some degree, for the absence of such a large detachment in the Northern Circars, a fifth battalion of sepoys was raised at the end of 1758, the command of which was given to Lieutenant George Wilson, whose name it bore. In the midst of the work of organising recruits and strengthening the defences of Fort William, Clive's attention was called to fresh danger threatening from the north. Since the death of

Aurangzeb the power of the Delhi dynasty had been rapidly decreasing: internal strife and external reverses had sapped the strength of the once all-powerful empire; and the time now under review found the reigning Emperor Alam Gir Sani a mere puppet in the hands of his favourite minister, Ghazi-u-din Khan, commonly called Umed-ul-Mulk. Early in 1759 the Emperor's eldest son, Shahzada Ali Gohar, who subsequently ascended the throne as Shah Alam, impatient of the control of his father's minister, raised the standard of revolt in Rohilkhand and, prompted by the interested counsels of the chiefs who joined him, marched, in the first instance, towards Patna, with the intention of seizing the rich provinces of Bengal and Bihar. Clive, who saw the motives for, and the instability of, the support accorded to the Shahzada, declared his intention of suppressing the rebellion against the emperor, and marched towards Patna with a force of 450 British and 2,500 sepoys, comprising the 3rd and 4th Battalions, and part, of the 5th. In company with Miran, the son of the Nawab Mir Jafar Khan, he reached Patna on April the 8th, where he found that the Rajah Ram Narayan had already successfully repelled the attack of the Shahzada's force, and that the latter had, as Clive had conjectured, fallen to pieces at the first sign of a reverse. The Shahzada himself took refuge with Monsieur Law in the French station of Chatarpur, and Clive, having spent some weeks in quieting the surrounding districts and strengthening the defences of Patna, where he left a detachment of European troops and five companies of sepoys, returned to Calcutta in June, 1759

Scarcely had he arrived there when rumours of yet another enemy retched him. For some time past the Dutch stations in Bengal had viewed with apprehension and jealousy the growing influence of the English. Encouraged, doubtless, by the attitude of Mir Jafar Khan, who was faithless and ungrateful enough to side against his foreign allies at any moment when it seemed to his advantage to do so, the Dutch brought matters to a head in October, 1759, when a fleet of seven vessels full of troops arrived in the Hooghly; while in the meantime their forces at Chinsura had been strengthened by the enlistment of sepoys and the arrival of European recruits. The English strength was inferior both by sea and land. Three Indiamen comprised the whole of their fleet, while their army was weakened by detachments at Patna, Midnapore, Vizagapatam and several other stations. Clive, however, was not shaken by the difficulties of the situation from the customary firmness of his attitude. Hostilities were commenced by the Dutch in November, when their ships seized several trading vessels bearing the

English flag, and the factories of Palta and Raipur were destroyed. On this Clive ordered Captain Wilson, who acted an commodore of the English fleet, to engage the enemy immediately: a hard-fought action ensued on November the 24th, which ended In the complete discomfiture of the Dutch and the capture of every one of their ships.

On the same day the British Army under Colonel Forde, who had arrived opportunely from Vizagapatam and assumed command, engaged the Dutch force from Chinsura at Chandernagore, and drove them back on their base with great loss. On the following day he again gave them battle at Badara and, after half an hour's sharp fighting, completely defeated and dispersed them. The loss of the English was trifling, while that of the Dutch amounted to 320 killed, 300 wounded, and upwards of 600 prisoners. The 3rd and 4th Bengal Native Battalions were engaged in this action.

After these reverses the Dutch were only too eager to come to terms, and a treaty was shortly agreed on, by which they acknowledged themselves the aggressors, promised to pay ten *lakhs* indemnity, and disavowed the conduct of their fleet; receiving back in return the ships and prisoners' which had been taken by the English.

The close of the year was occupied by Clive in finding fit successors to himself in the command of the army and in the post of Governor of Bengal, with a view to his own departure for England: for the former post he chose Major Caillaud and for the latter Mr. Vansittart, both of the Madras service. He also gave his attention to obtaining recruits for the Bengal European Battalion, and to raising the strength of the five native battalions to 1,000 men each; the complement of officers allowed to each of these battalions was one captain, one lieutenant and one ensign, with four European non-commissioned officers. Finally, he organised an expedition under Major Caillaud against the Shahzada, who was again threatening the Northern Provinces, and accompanied it in person as far as Murshidabad. This done, he took his departure from India on the 25th of February, 1760.

Major Caillaud's force, with the troops of Mir Jafar Khan under the command of Miran, left Murshidabad on the 18th January, 1760, on their way to Patna. But news now reached them which considerably altered the aspect of affairs and the position of the Shahzada himself. The old Emperor was put to death at the end of 1759 by his minister Umed-ul-Mulk (Ghazi-u-din), who forthwith proclaimed a younger son, under the title of Shah Jahan Sani, as Emperor. On this news reaching the Shahzada he immediately assumed the emblems of royalty, caused himself to be proclaimed emperor under the name of Shah Alam, and demanded acknowledgement of his title from all rulers of provinces. As the eldest son of the late emperor and the rightful heir, numbers flocked to support him, and he became a much more powerful enemy than when merely an outlawed and needy adventurer. These facts did not, however, alter the determination of the English and Mir Jafar, who, having for years regarded the sovereignty of Delhi as an. empty name, were not inclined to suffer its encroachments quietly. This being so, the force hastened on to the support of their frontier ally, the Rajah of Patna. As in the former expedition, however, Shah Alam arrived at Patna before the English Army, but, although Ram Narayan, less successful than on the previous occasion, was completely defeated,[6] the emperor neglected to follow up his victory, and was found by Major Caillaud still investing Patna. In the action which ensued (Sirpur, 22nd February, 1760) the emperor's army was completely broken and dispersed, a result to which the steady firing and determined bayonet charge of the sepoy battalions largely contributed.

But the obstinacy and indolence of Miran wasted the advantages which might have been the result of this victory: until the 29th of February he refused to move from Patna, and was only induced to some show of energy by the news that the emperor, having recovered from his reverse, was marching boldly on Burdwan. For a whole month the allied forces of Major Caillaud and the young Nawab prosecuted a stern chase after the emperor through a difficult and almost unknown country; and it was only by the extraordinary indecision of the latter that they were finally enabled to come up with him. Meanwhile the news of the emperor's advance on Burdwan had thrown Mir Jafar and the authorities at Calcutta into the greatest alarm, which was not decreased by the appearance of a Mahratta force, threatening the capital from the direction of Midnapore. While endeavouring to make terms for himself with the emperor, Mir Jafar marched with his whole force towards Burdwan, whither a part of his army, assisted by 300 of the Company's troops under Captain Speir, had already been sent; on the 23rd of March this force was augmented by Captain Fischer with 500 more men, while the two battalions

---

6. In this action, which was fought at Masimpur on the 9th February, 1760, the British detachment which had been left at Patna by Clive was almost annihilated. The only officer who survived was the Surgeon, William Fullarton, who was also, some years later, the sole survivor of the atrocious Patna massacre.

of sepoys from the Northern Circars under Captain MacLean were advancing through Midnapore to effect a junction with the army. On the 1st of April Shah Alam was within a few miles of the Nawab's camp, but hesitated to attack him, and on the 4th the Nawab was joined by his son and Major Caillaud. Still the emperor refused to give battle, which Major Caillaud, being without cavalry was unable to force on him, and the apathy of the Nawab, only equalled by that of the enemy, denied the British commander assistance. At length Shah Alam entirely abandoning the object of his march, returned by the route he had come and hastened against Patna.

The garrison of that place was in a precarious condition; the defences were weak and the force behind them consisted of only Ram Narayan's troops, with a small detachment of sepoys and no officer but Dr. Fullarton. The emperor's army was joined at Bihar by Monsieur Law and a small force of French, whence the whole proceeded to invest Patna. The defence was a most gallant one, but the little garrison was all but at its last stand when it was relieved on the 28th of April by a detachment under Captain Knox, of which the 1st Native Battalion from the Northern Circars formed a part.

On the following day a sally by Knox compelled the emperor to retire, and drove his army back to Gaya Manpur; while a fortnight later a large force under the Nawab of Purnea, who was marching to join the emperor, was encountered and completely dispersed by the English—an engagement (Birpur, 16th June, 1760) in which the 1st Native Battalion greatly distinguished itself.

Major Caillaud joined the force at Patna within a few days, but, after chasing the Nawab of Purnea into the district of Bettiah,[7] again left for Calcutta on the 31st August, having been summoned to meet Mr. Vansittart, the new Governor. One of the first of his acts on return to headquarters was to endeavour to raise some cavalry, the want of which he had felt so much during his past campaign. With this view he caused two troops of European dragoons and one of hussars to be raised from the European infantry; while a short time previously he had succeeded in raising two *rissalahs* of cavalry, called the Moghul Horse, composed of, and officered entirely by, natives, who provided their own horses, arms and accoutrements, and received Rs. 50 a month pay.

The greater part of the autumn was occupied in settling the

---

7. It was during this expedition that Miran, the son of Mir Jafar and the commander of his forces, was struck dead by lightning, 3rd July, 1700—three years, to the day, after he had procured the murder of Siraj-ud-Daulah.

internal affairs of Bengal which had been thrown into confusion by the misgovernment of Mir Jafar: to this end Mir Muhammad Kasim Ali Khan, his son-in-law, was appointed the Nawab's deputy, and invested with the administration, while Mir Jafar himself was removed from Murshidabad to Calcutta, and retained there under British protection.

In November, Lieutenant-Colonel Caillaud was appointed to command the Madras Army, and Major Carnac arrived in Calcutta to relieve him: he remained, however, for some time longer in Bengal.

The last two months of the year were occupied in settling the provinces of Midnapore, Burdwan, Birbhum and Monghyr, all of which had been disturbed by the emperor's invasion and the subsequent changes of Government. In the attack on, and defeat of, the rebellious Rajah of Kharakpur, near Monghyr, a detachment of sepoys showed great gallantry, carrying the rajah's positions and dispersing the enemy at the point of the bayonet.

At the beginning of 1761, Major Carnac assumed command of the Bengal Army, and immediately resumed hostilities against the Emperor Shah Alam: the latter had profited by his long rest, and had considerably increased his influence and strength; his headquarters were established at Bihar, and towards that place Carnac marched in the first days of January. The emperor met him at Suan, about three *kos* west of Bihar, on the 15th of the month, and was defeated and his army dispersed. The English, following up the flying enemy, came in contact with Monsieur Law and his party, who were endeavouring to cover the retreat; these after some resistance were thrown into disorder and Law, with about fourteen officers and fifty men, surrendered.

The English continued a harassing pursuit of Shah Alam until the 19th of January, when the latter, finding his followers deserting him and his position daily becoming more precarious, opened negotiations with Carnac, and all hostilities ceased.

It had by this time become apparent that the Bengal Army was insufficient to meet the increasing demands on its services. Accordingly two more battalions of sepoys were raised, one at Patna by Captain Stibbert and one at Chittagong by Lieutenant Mathews. They were numbered, respectively, the 6th and 7th Battalions; the former became the 1st Battalion of the 8th[8] in 1796, and the latter, after most distinguished service, was disbanded for mutiny in 1784.

---

8. Having been stationed at Jellasore for some time this battalion acquired the designation of *Jallasur-ki-paltan*.

The total strength in Bengal now amounted to 200 British and 200 native cavalry, 200 artillery, and 900 British and 8,400 native infantry, including local companies.

In April, 1761, Captain Champion, who had been left with a detachment at Gaya, attacked and defeated Kamgar Khan, Nawab of Tirhut, who had formerly been Shah Alam's chief adviser.

Two months later, the emperor determined to make an effort to seize the throne of Delhi, and set out for this purpose, escorted to the frontier in great state by a British force.

In April Lieutenant-Colonel Coote arrived in Bengal, and assumed the post of Commander-in-Chief; he shortly afterwards proceeded to Patna to take command of the army in the field, but such were the disputes which immediately arose between him and the new Nawab, Mir Muhammad Kasim, that both he and Carnac were recalled to Calcutta by the Governor, leaving at Patna, under Captain Carstairs a detachment consisting of one company of artillery, four companies of the European Battalion, and the 2nd and 3rd Native Battalions.

Nor were matters improved during the remainder of 1761 or in the following year: several changes occurred in the Council, and the party which had the ascendancy in all matters were men who at every turn increased the growing hostility of the Nawab to the English. Thus, affairs went from bad to worse, until in June, 1763 it was evident to all parties that a crisis was at hand.

At this time the army of Mir Muhammad Kasim was in a state of efficiency and discipline very different from the disorganised rabble of his predecessors. The cavalry were well organised and mounted; the infantry, divided into *najibs* and *telingas,* of whom the latter were modelled on the pattern of the Bengal sepoys, were excellently equipped and armed; and the artillery, also organised on the European model, was in no way inferior to that of the English, as far at least as their weapons and ammunition were concerned.

In the Bengal Army, on the other hand, various changes were introduced, as a collision with the Nawab became more and more a matter of the immediate future. During 1762, the independent companies at Burdwan were increased to a battalion, whose number in order of raising was the 8th, but which was always known as the *Burdwan-ki-paltan..* Early in 1763 a second Burdwan Battalion, the 9th, was raised, commonly known as the *Chota Burdwan-ki-paltan.* These two corps were commanded, respectively, by Captains MacLean and Smith, and became, in 1796, the first battalions of the 1st and 9th Regiments.

The independent companies at Midnapore were also formed into a battalion (the 10th,—afterwards the 1st battalion of the 6th) under Lieutenant Archibald Swinton;[9] a local battalion, the 11th, was raised at Chittagong by Lieutenant Lewis Brown; and about April, 1763, a 12th Battalion was raised at Calcutta, the command of which was at a later period given to Captain John Trevanion; this in 1796 became the 2nd Battalion of the 7th Regiment[10].

These additions to the army raised the total force in Bengal to about 1,500 Europeans and 10,000 natives: of these, four companies of British infantry, 220 in all, and one of artillery, 40 strong, with the 2nd, 3rd and 5th Native battalions, 2,500, were at Patna, under the command of Captain Carstairs; at Burdwan were two native battalions; in Midnapore three companies of Europeans, some artillery, and a troop of native cavalry; at Chittagong two native battalions; and the remainder of the force at the Presidency.

In accordance with the expectations of all concerned, hostilities between Nawab Mir Muhammad Kasim and the English began towards the end of June 1763. On the 24th of that month, Mr. Ellis, the Agent at Patna, hearing that reinforcements of the Nawab's troops were coming from Monghyr to strengthen the garrison of the former place, determined to seize the city before their arrival. The plan was carried into execution in the early morning of the following day, but the victors did not even complete their success to the extent of possessing themselves of the citadel, and gave themselves up to unbridled license and plunder. Within a few hours the Nawab's troops arrived from Monghyr, and, after a very short resistance, completely turned the tables on the British force, which retreated in confusion to the factory. The loss in the taking of the place was as follows:—killed, four officers and eight other Europeans: wounded, five officers, ten European soldiers, and 100 sepoys. Finding himself hard-pressed, Mr. Ellis attempted to retreat into Oudh, but after a harassing march of two days the force was completely surrounded by the enemy and the whole either killed or taken prisoners; all the Europeans who were taken prisoners were carried to Patna and there massacred three months later, with the exception of Dr. Full-

---

9. From a corruption of this officer's name this battalion acquired the name of *Sooltern-ki-paltan*.— P.
10. At one time known in the native army as *Teerbanis-ki-paltan;* at a later period, however, it was called *Duffal-ki-paltan,* from Captain Duffield, who commanded it for some years.

arton, who was spared, and of four sergeants who escaped. Captain Carstairs was killed at Manji, where the force made their last stand (1st July, 1763).

War was declared at Calcutta against Mir Muhammad Kasim on the 7th of July, and Mir Jafar Khan was restored to power and proclaimed *Subadar* of Bengal; but before the main army under Major Adams[11] could move from the Presidency, the Nawab had reached Kasimbazar, the factory at which place he attacked and captured without difficulty.

On July the 17th, a brilliant combat was fought by a detachment composed of the 2nd Burdwan Battalion, who were escorting treasure and supplies from Burdwan for the main army. Near the Adji river the battalion, under Lieutenant Glenn, was attacked by overwhelming forces of the enemy, who, encouraged by the hopes of rich plunder, returned again and again to the onslaught, but were finally driven off with enormous loss, and Glenn, with his convoy, reached Katwa the same evening. Here he found the fort defended by a weak and dispirited detachment of the enemy; notwithstanding his previous hard work, he boldly attacked the place, which, after a feeble, resistance, was evacuated. Glenn, with his little force, joined the main army, under Major Adams, on the following day.

On the 19th of July, the first general engagement took place between Major Adams' force and the army of the Nawab under Muhammad Takki Khan opposite Katwa and close to the field of Plassey. The English gained a complete victory, though with considerable loss, and, following up their success on the 23rd, marched to Murshidabad, which was abandoned by the enemy after the loss of the outlying entrenchments at Motijhil.

On the 25th, Jafar Khan made a triumphant entry into the city, and took his seat on the *masnad*.

On the 2nd of August, Major Adams' army was again in the presence of the enemy, who were drawn up on the plains of Gheriah to the number of nearly 40,000 men, of whom 12,000 were cavalry: confident in their own strength, the enemy advanced to the attack, and in the battle which ensued the British position was several times in danger, but the steadiness and gallantry of the English and native infantry at length bore down all opposition, and after a hard-fought action Adams remained master of the field, having gained a brilliant victory and captured the whole of the enemy's artillery (seventeen

---

11. Major Thomas Adams, His Majesty's 84th Regiment.-P.

guns) and large quantities of stores. Among the killed on this occasion were Lieutenant Kaylor, of the Artillery, and the gallant Lieutenant Glenn above-mentioned.

On the 5th of August, Major Adams resumed his march, and on the 11th encamped nearly parallel to the enemy's fortified lines at Udwah-nala. The latter position was a very strong one, and it was not until September the 5th that the assault was attempted. At daybreak on that day the place was carried with but small loss on our side, though it included Captain John Broadbrook[12] who had for many years commanded the 1st Battalion of Sepoys. The enemy fled to Monghyr, which place was invested by Major Adams and surrendered to him on the 22nd of October.

The fall of Monghyr was the death-knell of the unfortunate persons whom the Nawab had captured in their retreat from Patna at the beginning of the war. Hitherto Mir Muhammad Kasim had been content to keep them as hostages, and near his own person; now, overcome with blind fury, he ordered their execution, which was carried out in the most brutal manner on the 5th of October.

Meanwhile Adams advanced on Patna and commenced the siege on the 28th of October, the Nawab having fled at his approach and established himself at the village of Bakrim, about twenty miles distant. Seven days were occupied in breaching the defences, and on the 6th of November the place was carried by assault after a stubborn resistance on the part of the garrison, and with considerable loss to the British force. Major Irving, a very gallant officer, who had recently been transferred to the Company's service from the 84th Foot, was mortally wounded in the assault.

Major Adams, with his victorious army, continued to pursue Mir Muhammad Kasim until early in December, when he took refuge with the Nawab of Oudh. The campaign was thus brought to a successful termination, the whole of Bengal and Bihar having been reduced in the short space of four months, four strong positions captured by assault, and the enemy, with vastly superior numbers, defeated in two hard-fought battles.

The commander, Major Adams, who had thus so well performed the work assigned him by the Government, returned to Calcutta with the intention of proceeding to England. But his health, which

---

12. There appears to have been considerable doubt as to what this officer's name really was,—see *Broome*, 204. When he was in the 39th he appeared in the War Office Army List as "John Bradbridge."

was completely shattered by the fatigues and exposure of the past months, gave way as he was about to embark, and he died in Calcutta on the 16th of January, 1764, deeply regretted by the army and the Government.

The past year had seen a great increase in the native army of Bengal. Besides the battalions, from the 8th to the 12th, raised early in the year, several additions had been made during the autumn campaign. In August, the 13th and 14th Battalions were raised at Kasimbazar and Calcutta, respectively, by Captain Robert Campbell and Captain Gilbert Ironside; these became in 1796 the 1st Battalions of the 3rd and 5th, respectively.[13] In October was raised the 15th Battalion by Captain John White at Monghyr, which afterwards became the 1st Battalion of the 12th, or *Hote-ki-paltan* (a corruption of White). The 16th was formed in Midnapur in October, and the command subsequently given to Captain Hampton; it became the 2nd Battalion of the 1st in 1796.[14] About the same time, another corps, the 17th, was raised at Burdwan by Captain Witchcot, which afterwards became the 1st Battalion of the 4th.[15] The commencement of 1764. saw yet further additions to the army. In January, on the removal of the 13th Battalion from Murshidabad, another corps was raised there by Captain Goddard; this was the 18th (afterwards the 1st Battalion of the 7th, or *Gaurud-ki-paltan):* while the warlike rumours which reached Calcutta two months later, relative to the movements of the Nawab of Oudh and the Emperor, in support of Mir Muhammad Kasim, caused orders to be issued in March for the raising of two more corps, the 19th and 20th Battalions, the former at Murshidabad by Captain Dow (afterwards the 1st Battalion of the 11th,—*Doo-ki-paltan),* the other at Jellasore by Captain Scotland (afterwards the 1st Battalion of the 10th,—*Escotten-ki-paltan).* Finally, at the end of the same month, the 21st Battalion was raised at Patna by Captain James Morgan: this corps, after a very distinguished career of service as *Morgan-ki-paltan,* was incorporated with the 10th Bengal Native Infantry in 1796.

In the same month attention was paid to the provision of an efficient cavalry force for the army. The three weak and expensive troops of European cavalry were formed into one troop of serviceable

---

13. The native names of these corps were *Gowan-ki-paltan* (derived from Captain Clotworthy Gowan) and *Ranseet-ki-paltan* (a corruption of Ironside).
14. *Bailun-ki-paltan,*—from Captain Robert Blane, who was appointed to the command about 1773.
15. *Crawford-ki-paltan,*—from Captain James Crawford senior), appointed to the command in 1768.

strength, and, after a good deal of discussion, the irregular Moghul Horse was increased to 1,200 men, each *rissalah* under native officers, with a few Europeans attached to the whole. The Council at Calcutta had been desirous of forming a body of regular native cavalry on the European system, but was dissuaded by Major Carnac, who declared that "the Moguls, who are the only good horsemen in the country, can never be brought to submit to the ill-treatment they receive from gentlemen wholly unacquainted with their language and customs."

In the following month, April, 1764, the eighteen existing battalions (the 2nd, 3rd and 5th having been destroyed at Patna in the preceding year), which had previously taken rank according to the dates of their captains' commissions, were definitely numbered according to the rank of their then captains.

The following list gives the names of the commanding officers in their order, with the original numbers of the battalions according to the dates of their raising:

		Order of Raising
1	Captain Giles Stibbert	6
2	Captain Lachlan MacLean	8
3	Captain Hugh Grant	4
4	Captain Robert Campbell	13
5	Captain Thomas Witchcot	17
6	Captain John Trevanion	12
7	Captain Lewis Brown	11
8	Captain William Smith	9
9	Captain Primrose Galliez	1
10	Captain Gilbert Ironside	14
11	Captain James Morgan	21
12	Captain John White	15
13	Captain Archibald Swinton	10
14	Captain Samuel Hampton	16
15	Captain John Stables	7
16	Captain James Scotland	20
17	Captain Thomas Goddard	18
18	Captain Alexander Dow	19

At this period the establishment of a battalion consisted of three

British officers, a native, commandant, and a native adjutant. There were ten companies (two of which were grenadiers), with each of which was a *subadar* and three *jemadars*: each company had a stand of colours attached to it, of the same colour as the men's facings, in the centre of which was the *subadar*'s device, such as a sabre, a dagger, or a crescent: the grenadier companies bore the British Union, in the upper corner, as a distinction. The dress of battalions and the colour of their facings were at this time regulated by commanding officers, but when once fixed, could not be altered without permission from the Board : thus, the Morgan Battalion when first raised had white facings, white turbans with red ends, and white *kamarbands* with a red cross; its colours were the flag of St. George. It would seem from this description that the head-dress of the men resembled to some extent a native *pagri*.

The beginning of 1764 found the greater part of the army in camp at Sarwant on the Dargauti, near the then boundary of the dominions of the Nawab-Wazir of Oudh, the various provincial posts being held by the new battalions which were just in process of being raised.

On his departure to Calcutta, Major Adams handed over the command of the army to Major Knox; but that officer was himself in such a bad state of health that he had in turn to resign the command to Captain Jennings, and followed Major Adams to the Presidency, where he too died soon afterwards. Captain Jennings found the command to which he had temporarily succeeded a task of great difficulty and danger. The late Nawab, Mir Muhammad Kasim, from the security of Oudh, occupied himself in tampering, by the aid of his emissaries, with the fidelity of the British troops, European and native, especially with the French and Germans, who composed a large proportion of the former. Disaffection gradually spread throughout the army, until in February, 1764, the Europeans broke out into open mutiny, and 160 of them deserted and marched to Allahabad, where they took service in various native armies. The example of mutiny was followed by the native corps on the 13th of February, and the danger was only avoided by the tact and coolness of Captain Jennings. However, tranquillity was shortly restored by the distribution of a money donation presented by the Nawab Mir Jafar Khan, and the commanding officer, deeming it advisable to keep the men employed, broke up the camp at Sarwant and marched to Sasaram, and thence on the 5th of March to Hariharganj. Here on the following day Major Carnac and Major Champion joined the army, and the former assumed command.

Meanwhile Mir Muhammad Kasim, after his expulsion from Bengal, had joined the Nawab of Oudh (Shuja-ud-Daulah) and the Emperor Shah Alam at Allahabad, and their allied forces were now marching towards Benares with the intention of reducing Bihar. Accordingly, on March 13th—17th, Major Carnac marched to Buxar, where he took up and strengthened a defensive position. Want of supplies, however, compelled him to retire again to Patna in April; and here the English force was attacked by the whole strength of the enemy on the 3rd of May. The battle was stubbornly contested, but the superior numbers of the enemy could make no impression on the steady ranks of the British and sepoys, and the assailants were compelled to retire, having suffered very heavy loss. Unfortunately Major Carnac stopped all pursuit, so that the victory was not as decisive as it might otherwise have become; and the enemy, retiring unmolested took up a position at Buxar at the end of the month. Major Carnac, in his despatch to the Council, reporting this battle, remarks—"I cannot say too much of the good behaviour of the army in general, and in particular of the sepoys, who sustained the brunt of the attack."

On the retreat of Shuja-ud-Daulah a detachment under Major Champion crossed the Ganges, wasted the Ghazipur district, and advanced as far as the banks of the Ghagra, when the approach of the monsoon compelled them to return. Meanwhile Major Carnac continued to pursue an inactive and dilatory course, notwithstanding repeated orders from the Council that he should take more forward measures. At length, on the 28th of June, letters arrived from the Court of Directors ordering his dismissal from the service, in consequence of disagreements with Mr. Vansittart, the Governor, in the previous year, and he was succeeded in the command by Major Munro,[16] who arrived on the 13th of August. The long period of inaction had been most prejudicial to the discipline of the troops, and a spirit of disaffection was rife amongst the sepoys; this developed into open mutiny in the case of the 9th Battalion *(Gillis-ki-paltan)* in the 8th of September. The whole of the mutineers were captured by the Marines[17] and Trevanion's battalion on the 11th of that month, and Munro, thinking an example necessary, ordered twenty-four of the ring-leaders to be

---

16. Major Hector Munro, of His Majesty's 89th Regiment (Gordon Highlanders). Afterwards General Sir Hector Munro, K.B., Commander-in-Chief in Madras, and Colonel of the 42nd Regiment (Royal Highlanders.) Died on the 26th December, 1805.
17. Captain Maurice Wemyss' company of the Marines, which had been landed from the squadron when the mutinies of March, 1764, occurred, and afterwards sent up the country to join the army in the field.

tried by drum-head general court-martial. These were sentenced to death and were blown away from the guns, the grenadiers amongst the condemned claiming (according to Captain Williams) to be tied to the guns on the right, as the right had been their place in action.

Major Munro now made preparations for prosecuting the campaign against the Nawab Wazir of Oudh and Mir Muhammad Kasim, and, assuming the offensive, marched from Bankipore on the 9th of October. His force consisted of 900 Europeans of all arms[18] and eight battalions of Native Infantry, selected for their efficiency; these were the 1st, 2nd, 3rd, 6th, 8th, 11nth, 13th, and 15th; and in addition 1,000 Moghul Horse. Besides the above, Captain Goddard, with the 17th Battalion, was sent on an expedition against Rhotasgarh, which place he occupied without resistance.

Major Munro's force met the enemy in a skirmish at Kalwarghat, on the banks of the Son, on the 10th, and again in a severe cavalry affair near the Bunas Nala on the 13th of October, where our loss was fourteen Europeans and sixty of the Moghul Horse killed and wounded. On October the 23rd a pitched battle was fought at Buxar, when the sepoy troops behaved with the greatest gallantry, and steadily repelled the furious charges of the enemy's cavalry. At length Munro ordered a general advance of his line, when, after a faint resistance, the whole of the enemy's force broke up and fled in disorder; the Nawab Shuja-ud-Daulah, having retreated across the Torah Nala, destroyed the bridge by which he had crossed, and the remnants of his retreating army, finding the bridge broken, threw themselves into the stream, where thousands were drowned or suffocated in the mud in their attempts to cross. The loss of the British force amounted to 825 killed and wounded, of whom 205 sepoys were killed, 414 wounded, and 58 missing. The Moghul Horse, 1,000 strong, lost forty-five killed and twenty-two wounded.[19] The only officers who were killed were Lieutenant Francis Spilsbury of the 96th Foot, and Ensign Richard Thompson of the Bengal European Battalion. In 1829 the surviving corps which shared in this important victory were granted authority to inscribe "Buxar" on their colours.

---

18. The European infantry was composed of the Bengal European Battalion, two weak companies of the Bombay European Battalion, and small detachments of Marines and of His Majesty's 84th, 89th and 96th Regiments.
19. The losses of the British Army at the battle of Buxar are somewhat differently stated in *Broome's History* and other publications. The figures given in the text are taken from Major Munro's official return, published in the *London Gazette* of the 18th June, 1765.

It may here be mentioned that on the day before the battle of Buxar Mir Muhammad Kasim, robbed and deserted by his immediate followers, was ignominiously driven from the camp of his so-called ally, Shuja-ud-Daulah. He escaped into Rohilkhand, and eventually, after experiencing many vicissitudes of fortune, died, in extreme indigence, at Delhi, in 1777.

On the 24th, Major Sir Robert Fletcher joined the army with reinforcements, including the 10th (Ironside's) Battalion, and on his arrival Major Champion was sent to the Midnapore frontier, which was threatened by the Mahrattas, taking with him two recently formed companies of the European battalion, a detail of artillery, and two battalions (the 14th and 16th) of Native Infantry.

The whole army crossed the Ganges on the 27th of October, and on the 8th November advanced to Benares, from which place a ransom of four *lakhs* of rupees was exacted. Meanwhile the Emperor Shah Alam had been making overtures to the English, representing himself as merely a state prisoner in the hands of Shuja-ud-Daulah; eventually he came to the English camp, and pitched his own close to it for security. Authority having been received from the Council, measures were taken for his protection, and a treaty was signed. The following curious order was published on this occasion:

> Such of the officers as will be off duty tomorrow, who choose to wait on the King and wish him Joy of being put in possession of Sujah-ud-Dowlah's country by the English, are desired to meet at the headquarters at 9 o'clock tomorrow morning; it is necessary to acquaint them that it is customary to make him a *salam* on the occasion, and the least that should be given by a captain is five gold *mohurs* and three by a subaltern.

Two more companies of Europeans from Patna reinforced the army, and an expedition was despatched under Major Pemble to lay siege to the fort of Chunar: this detachment consisted of the European grenadiers, three battalions of sepoys, the company of pioneers, a company of cadets, and fifty artillery-men. Two assaults were made on the fortress on the 2nd and 4th of December, but, although the behaviour of the troops was excellent, both attacks were repulsed with loss. On the 5th of December, the detachment was recalled, and Major Munro fell back on Benares, where he took up a position covering the city. The remainder of December was passed in unavailing negotiations with Shuja-ud-Daulah.

Early in January Major Munro left the army to proceed to England, and Major Carnac, having been re-instated in the army with the rank of Brigadier-General, was appointed to succeed him; meantime the command temporarily devolved on Major Sir Robert Fletcher.

In the same month the Nawab Mir Jafar Khan died, and his eldest surviving son, Najm-ud-Daulah, was appointed his successor by the Government at Calcutta, in supersession of the direct heir, who was a child of Miran, Mir Jafar's eldest son.

On the 14th January, Sir Robert Fletcher recommenced active operations against Shuja-ud-Daulah, and advanced towards Allahabad, driving the enemy's army before him. Meanwhile he sent Major Stibbert to command at Benares, with instructions to again attempt the capture of Chunar; this fortress surrendered on the 8th of February, and on the 11th Allahabad was surrendered to Sir Robert Fletcher after a feeble resistance.

Brigadier-General Carnac arrived in camp at Chunar on the 13th of February and assumed command of the Field Force, which was at this time divided as follows:

Main force at Allahabad, under Sir Robert Fletcher
- 14 companies of European infantry (about 700)
- 1 company of artillery
- 1 company of European pioneers (60 men)
- 1 troop of European cavalry (60 men)
- 4 squadrons of Moghul Horse (800 men)
- 8 battalions of sepoys

Brigade at Benares and Chunar, under Major Stibbert
- 6 companies of European infantry (300 men)
- 1 company of artillery (a large proportion of lascars)
- A detail of pioneers
- 2 squadrons of Moghul Horse (400 men)
- 6 battalions of sepoys

On joining the army Brigadier-General Carnac; issued orders for the concentration of the whole force at Allahabad, with the exception of two native battalions left to garrison Benares and Chunar. On the junction being effected, one native battalion was left to garrison Allahabad, and a small brigade was left near that place under Sir Robert Fletcher, while Carnac and the main army advanced into Oudh, occupied the principal towns, collected revenue, and finally pushed on with all the cavalry and one sepoy battalion to Fyzabad, the old capital, where he remained during the greater part of April, regulating the affairs of the province and receiving the submission of the various chiefs and *zemindars*. Meanwhile Shuja-ud-Daulah had gained the support of the Mahrattas, and was preparing for an advance from Rohilkhand upon the Lower Doab. General Carnac re-united his army at Sujapur, in the Doab, on the 2nd of May, and on the 3rd met the enemy near Korah, where a skirmish with the Mahratta Horse took place, resulting in the flight of the latter. On the 11th of May, a detachment under Major Stibbert was despatched with orders to reduce the Khairabad district, which duty was successfully accomplished, and Stibbert cantoned his force at Lucknow during the rains. Meanwhile the Mahrattas, who had retired across the Jumna after the affair at Korah, re-entered the Doab and advanced close up to the British camp at Jajmau: on the 16th of May the force advanced to attack them, and on the 20th encamped on the bank of the Jumna, opposite to Kalpi, in the neighbourhood of which place the enemy had taken up a position. On the 22nd a strong detachment, under Sir Robert Fletcher, crossed the river, and attacked the enemy; an action ensued, which after an hour resulted in the complete defeat and dispersion of the Mahrattas, who made the best of their way towards Gwalior. The Doab was thus freed from any immediate prospect of attack, and the army returned to Allahabad, where it arrived on the 25th of June.

General Carnac returned in advance of the army, to prosecute negotiations with Shuja-ud-Daulah and the Emperor. The former, finding the Mahrattas unreliable and the Rohillas very lukewarm in supporting him, had early in May sought to arrange terms with the English; in this he had been so far successful that he now joined General Carnac, and, under the auspices of the latter, a reconciliation took place between him and the Emperor at the end of June, when all three proceeded to Allahabad, and afterwards to Benares, there to await the arrival of Lord Clive from Calcutta.

Clive had been appointed Governor and Commander-in-Chief and had arrived in Calcutta in May: the business of the civil administration had, however, detained him at the Presidency, and it was not until August the 1st that he joined General Carnac at Benares. Thence a few days later they proceeded to Allahabad, where the conditions of the treaties between the Company, the Emperor, and Shuja-ud-Daulah were agreed on. These were in the main the restoration of all his possessions to the Nawab-Wazir with the exception of Chunar, which was retained by the English, and the provinces of Korah and Allahabad, which were ceded to the Emperor, a British force being stationed at Allahabad for the protection of the Emperor; while on the British side the most important item of the treaty was the grant to the Company, by the Emperor, of the Dewani of Bengal, Bihar, and Orissa.

Lord Clive had, immediately on his arrival, turned his attention to the army, an extensive re-distribution and re-organisation of which was now arranged.

Towards the end of the previous year another battalion of Bengal infantry had been raised at Calcutta under Captain Douglas Hill, so that there were at this time nineteen battalions in existence. According to Clive's organisation, the army was to be divided into three brigades of similar strength and composition, namely,—one company of artillery, one regiment of European infantry (for which purpose the Bengal European Regiment was now re-organised as three distinct regiments or battalions), one *rissalah* of native cavalry, and seven battalions of sepoys. For this object, the troop of European cavalry was disbanded, and the men transferred to the infantry and artillery, only a small body-guard for the Governor being retained; the Moghul Horse was dismissed, with the exception of 300; and two more battalions of sepoys were raised. Of these, one was formed at Allahabad under the superintendence of Colonel Smith, and its command given to Captain David Scott; it was raised during the month of Moharram, and hence obtained the name of *Husseini-ki-paltan;* it was numbered the 20th Battalion, and posted to the second brigade. The 21st Battalion was raised at Bankipore by Colonel Sir Robert Barker, whose name it bore. These two corps, in the re-organisation of 1796, became, respectively, the 2nd Battalion of the 10th and the 2nd Battalion of the 11th Bengal Native Infantry. The three brigades were now formed and stationed as follows:

First Brigade: Headquarters, Monghyr
Lieutenant-Colonel Sir Robert Fletcher, Commanding
1st European Regiment, Major Alexander Champion
1st Company of Artillery, Major William Jennings
1st *Rissalah* of Cavalry, Lieutenant James Skinner

Native Infantry

2nd Battalion	Captain Christian Fischer
3rd Battalion	Captain Arthur Achmuty
4th Battalion	Captain Robert Campbell

5th Battalion	Captain Wm. MacPherson
10th Battalion	Captain Gilbert Ironside
15th Battalion	Captain Benjamin Wilding
17th Battalion	Captain Thomas Goddard

Second Brigade: Headquarters, Allahabad

Colonel Richard Smith, Commanding the Brigade
2nd European Regiment, Lieutenant-Colonel Joseph Peach
2nd Company of Artillery, Captain Ralph Winwood
2nd *Rissalah* of Cavalry, Lieutenant George Bolton Eyres

Native Infantry

1st Battalion	Captain Arthur Forbes Achmuty
7th Battalion	Captain Lewis Brown
8th Battalion	Captain William Smith
15th Battalion	Captain James Nicol
16th Battalion	Captain James Scotland
18th Battalion	Captain Alexander Dow
20th Battalion	Captain David Scott

Third Brigade; Headquarters, Bankipore

Colonel Sir Robert Barker, Commanding the Brigade
3rd European Regiment, Lieut.-Colonel Charles Chapman
3rd Company of Artillery, Captain Nathaniel Kindersley
3rd *Rissalah* of Cavalry, Lieutenant John Mair

Native Infantry

6th Battalion	Captain Vernon Duffield
9th Battalion	Captain Primrose Galliez
11th Battalion	Captain James Morgan
12th Battalion	Captain John White
14th Battalion	Captain Samuel Hampton
19th Battalion	Captain Douglas Hill
21st Battalion	

The Corps of Engineers had been fixed by an order of October 2nd, 1764, at the following establishment:

One Chief Engineer, to rank as Captain
Two Sub-Directors, to rank as Captain-Lieutenants
Four Sub-Engineers, to rank as Lieutenants
Six Practitioner Engineers, to rank as Ensigns

A fourth company of artillery was reserved for duties at Fort William and the redoubts at Palta and Budge-Budge.

The native cavalry *rissalahs* consisted of one British officer, one sergeant-major and four sergeants, four native officers, two trumpeters, six *daffadars*, and one hundred privates.

The native infantry establishment was fixed at one captain, two lieutenants, two ensigns, three sergeants, three drummers, a native commandant, and forty native officers, a native adjutant, ten trumpeters, thirty *tom-toms* (drummers), 130 non-commissioned officers, and 690 privates. To each battalion were attached two 3-pounder field pieces.

The close of the year saw the enforcement by Lord Clive of a measure which was destined within a few months to imperil the safety and indeed the very existence of the Company in India. This was the abolition of double field batta, with regard to which orders had previously been several times received from the Court of Directors. In the course of the discussion on the subject, two senior captains of the Presidency had, by orders of the Council, drawn up an estimate of such extraordinary monthly expenses as they considered necessary on field service; the list of these is curious and includes the following items:

	R	a
Madeira wine, 30 bottles at R 1-8 each	45	0
Beer, 30 bottles at R 0-12 each	22	8
Arrack, 15 bottles at R 0-4 each	3	12
	71	4

The above monthly allowance is headed as "necessary for a captain during a campaign."

However, notwithstanding all protests, the Court was determined, and, in December, 1765, orders were issued by Clive that at the Presidency or in its immediate neighbourhood troops in garrison should receive no batta; in cantonments half batta; in the field single batta; but that beyond the Karamnasa river troops in the field should receive double, and in cantonments single, batta.

These arrangements came into force in January, 1766, without any apparent demur on the part of the officers; and Clive, congratulating himself on the peaceable operation of his measures, turned his attention to another matter deeply concerning the officers of the Company's service. This was the disposition of a legacy of five *lakhs* of rupees bequeathed to him personally by the late Nawab Jafar Khan. Although nothing in the covenants lately framed by the

Court of Directors prohibited the acceptance of such a legacy, yet Lord Clive determined not to appropriate the money to his own use, but to apply it to the formation of an invalid pension fund for the Company's military servants. On being informed of his intentions, the Council expressed their "lively sense of his generous and well-placed donation," and, after preliminary reference to the Court of Directors, an indenture was eventually drawn up, by the terms of which Lord Clive hands over in trust to the Company the sum of "three *lakhs* of rupees, R.50,000 in money, R.50,000 in jewels and one *lakh* in gold *mohurs*, in all five *lakhs* of rupees of the value of £62,833-6-3," the interest of which is to be paid yearly for the benefit of the Company's military servants and their families.

While Lord Clive was thus occupied in promoting the interests and welfare of the service, the officers of the Company's Army were busy with secret preparations for a movement which they hoped and expected would force the Council to rescind the obnoxious new batta rules. It was agreed throughout the three brigades that all the captains and subalterns in the service should resign their commissions on the 1st of May. This step was actually carried out by the first and third brigades, the former of which was throughout the movement the most violent and mutinous : indeed all discipline was relaxed in this command, and the European soldiery followed the disgraceful example of their officers. Clive was in complete ignorance of the storm which was brewing until the end of April, when the magnitude of the danger was suddenly revealed to him with a clearness that would have terrified a weaker man. He saw clearly that to yield would be to show the army its power, and so to sap the foundations of all discipline and order in the Company's territories. He determined to hold out inflexibly, unless the mutinous officers should cause the men to join them in obtaining their demands, in which case no course seemed to be open but to yield. However, any organised resistance by force on the part of the troops was in no case attempted; and the vigorous and determined measures with which Clive met the difficulties of the situation soon convinced the malcontents of the rashness with which they had acted. By the end of May the disturbance in all three brigades was quelled, and a number of officers having been sent down to Calcutta for trial, the remainder hastened to tender their submission. A number of court-martials were held in the following months for the trial of the principal offenders: among these the most interesting was that of

Sir Robert Fletcher, who, in command of the First Brigade, had not only encouraged the officers in their mutinous conduct, but even seems to have been the originator of the whole combination. He was found guilty of mutiny, was cashiered, and proceeded to England: but within a few years his commission was restored to him by the Court of Directors, and he was sent out as commander-in-chief to Madras.

Meanwhile the difficulties of Lord Clive had been greatly increased by the attitude of the Mahrattas, who throughout the year had been threatening the frontiers of Allahabad and Korah: and the necessity of keeping a strong brigade in those provinces made the fact evident that the existing battalions were not sufficient for the requirements of Bengal. Orders were therefore issued for the raising of six new corps, which were designated Parganna Battalions, and were employed under the Revenue Department in the districts: for this same purpose three battalions of sepoys (the 2nd, 7th, and 14th) had already been told off, but they were found quite inadequate for the work. The six new corps were numbered from 22nd to 27th, and were attached two to each brigade—the 22nd and 25th to the First Brigade, the 23rd and 26th to the Second, and the 24th and 27th to the Third: two more battalions (the 28th and 29th) of a similar nature were raised shortly after, and attached, respectively, to the First and Second Brigades, and in the following year another was raised and attached to the Third Brigade, thus bringing the number of Bengal battalions up to thirty.

At the same time various internal reforms and improvements were introduced in the regular brigades of the army, including the framing and publishing of a code of regulations, together with a fixed standard of staff, contract, and contingent allowances.

These were the last measures of Lord Clive for the advantage of the Bengal Army. The dangers and abuses, to meet and reform which had been his special mission from the Court of Directors when he accepted the Government two years before, had all been averted and restrained. Fresh and unforeseen difficulties had arisen, and these too had been successfully surmounted: peace and order had been restored where the British influence had been threatened with blight and extinction: in the army, an efficient and well regulated force had been created, where all had been insubordination, corruption, and extravagance. At the moment little remained to be done which ordinary capacity and firmness could not undertake.

Clive found his health daily breaking, and determined to depart in the beginning of the year: Mr. Verelst was nominated to succeed him as Governor, and Colonel Richard Smith as Commander-in-Chief in succession to Brigadier-General Carnac, who was also going home. On the 29th of January, 1767, he left India, and with his departure "closes the first, and not the least eventful epoch in the History of the Bengal Army."

CHAPTER 2

The Mysore War

In the year 1767, the only occurrence of note in Bengal was the despatch by sea of a detachment from the First Brigade, under Lieutenant-Colonel William Smith, to assist the Government of Fort St. George in the Northern Circars on the outbreak of the war with Haidar Ali. This force consisted of 350 European infantry, fifty artillerymen (with five guns), and three native battalions, *viz.*, the 3rd, 4th, and 13th. It remained on this service for two years, during which Colonel Smith died and was succeeded by Lieutenant-Colonel Peach of the 1st European Regiment. The 3rd Battalion, commanded by Captain A. F. Achmuty, proceeded to Madras, and was actively employed under Brigadier-General Joseph Smith, during the operations in the Baramahal and Mysore, in 1768-69. The remainder of the detachment landed at Masulipatam and marched into the Nizam's Dominions, and was instrumental in bringing the Nizam to submission and procuring the cession to the Company of the Northern Circars (February, 1768). In May and June, 1768, the detachment was actively employed, in the districts of Chicacole and Kimedi, against an insurgent chief, named Narayan Deo, who was defeated near the fort of Jalumur on the 24th May, and that place itself was captured on the 30th of the same month. In 1769, the detachment (now completed by the junction of the 3rd Battalion) was actively employed in the Ganjam district. In the early part of 1770 the whole of these troops returned to Bengal, a part by sea, but the greater portion by land, marching through Cuttack. Of the former, the two grenadier companies of the 4th (or Gowan's) Battalion were lost at sea, the ship on which they were embarked never having been heard of again,—an unfortunate occurrence which made a fatal impression on the mind of the Bengal sepoys in regard to sea voyages, and was afterwards a fruitful source of trouble.

About this time the Saniyasis, who are described by Williams as "religious plunderers," became very troublesome in Northern Bengal, moving about the country in large bands, plundering, burning, and destroying. Some of the Parganna battalions were employed against them, but with small success, as they almost invariably misbehaved when brought into contact with the enemy. It thus happened that no less than three detachments were disgracefully defeated and almost destroyed by these plunderers; one, under Lieutenant Keith at Rangpur, in January, 1770; a second, under Captain Thomas, in December, 1772; and a third, under Captain Edwards, in March, 1773. In consequence of their misconduct, all the Parganna battalions, with the exception of the 24th, were broken up in 1773, the three regular battalions employed on Parganna duty being at the same time returned to their respective brigades.

Against these insurgents was engaged, for the first time, the new native Body-Guard, called "The Governor's troop of Moguls," which brings us for the first time to a corps which survives at the present day. It was raised and disciplined by Captain Sweny Toone in 1773, to act as a Body-Guard to the governor-general in time of peace, and to accompany the commander-in-chief on campaigns. It was commanded by a captain, with a subaltern and four sergeants under him, and there were no native officers. It served afterwards in the Rohilla campaign under Colonel Champion.

In 1772 the Bhutiahs descended from their mountains and overran operations the province of Cooch-Behar. The 6th Battalion, under the command of Captain John Jones, was sent up from the Presidency to expel them, and was engaged in some arduous operations. On the 21st December, Captain Jones stormed the fort of Cooch-Behar, not without considerable loss, he himself and Lieutenant Dickson being amongst the wounded. During the following months he succeeded in driving the Bhutiahs out of the province, and even carried the war into their own country, taking Dhalimkot by storm in April, 1773.

About this time the number of subalterns in sepoy battalions was increased by two, making a total of three lieutenants and three ensigns. The company colours were also abolished, and only two stand allowed to each battalion, as in the Company's European regiments, and all the *tom-toms* and trumpeters were dismissed, and fifes and drums substituted.

Meanwhile, in 1771, the Emperor Shah Alam, notwithstanding the failure of his efforts to gain English aid, determined to march to Delhi, there to regain his father's throne: he left Allahabad in December and placed himself under the protection of the Mahrattas, thereby, as the Court of Directors declared, forfeiting his right to the provinces of Allahabad and Korah, which had been ceded to him by the English. Having entered Delhi in state, he found that his turbulent supporters were eager only for fresh lands to plunder: the Rohilla country was their first object of attack, and having forced their way in, they overran a great part of Rohilkhand, and threatened the territory of the Nawab-Wazir of Oudh.

Fearing an invasion of his own territories, the Nawab-Wazir advanced to the frontiers of Oudh, with some British troops under the command of Sir Robert Barker, then Commander-in-Chief. Here he was visited by Hafiz Rahmat Khan, Chief of the Rohillas, and in June, 1773, a treaty was agreed upon between the Nawab-Wazir and Hafiz Rahmat Khan, in which the former undertook to drive the Mahrattas out of Rohilkhand, and to do so again if they invaded the country after the rainy season, in return for which the Rohillas promised to pay the Nawab-Wazir forty *lakhs* of rupees. The Mahrattas had in the meantime retired from Rohilkhand, but in November, 1773, they attempted a fresh invasion, which was defeated by the Oudh troops, aided by a British detachment. Hafiz Rahmat Khan, who, in order to avoid paying the subsidy of forty *lakhs* had entered into treacherous correspondence with the Mahrattas, now that their expulsion from Rohilkhand was accomplished, shuffled and hesitated in making payment of the sum due under the treaty, until at length the Nawab-Wazir determined to take possession of the province as a recompense for the Rohilla breach of faith. To effect this he asked for British support and assistance, which, after some hesitation on the part of Warren Hastings, who had come out in 1772 as the first Governor-General, was conceded by the Select Committee.

In January, 1774, therefore, the Second Brigade, under Colonel Champion, received orders to join the Nawab-Wazir, and marched accordingly from Dinapore. The force was composed of the 2nd Company of Artillery the "Select Picket,"[1] the 2nd European Regi-

---

1. During the period .from 1772 to 1775 there was a great dearth of vacancies in the commissioned ranks of the Bengal Army. Accordingly the gentlemen cadets arriving from Europe were formed into a separate company, and carried arms until vacancies occurred. This company was called "The Select Picket," and was posted on the right of the advanced guard of the army in the field. Sir Henry White, Sir Gabriel Martindell, and other distinguished officers carried arms, as cadets, in "The Select Picket."

ment, a battalion of Sepoy Grenadiers (probably formed from the flank companies of the native battalions of the brigade), and the 1st, 8th, 10th, 15th, 16th, 18th and 20th Battalions of Bengal Native Infantry. With these troops Colonel Champion, on the 24th February, joined the Nawab-Wazir, and on the 17th April the united armies entered the Rohilla country. On the 23rd April the rival forces met in a pitched battle on the Baighul river, between Miranpur-Katra and Tissua, twenty-three miles to the south-east of Bareilly,—an engagement, from the day on which it was fought, long known as "the battle of St. George." In this the Rohillas were defeated, though they fought with great gallantry, and their brave leader Hafiz Rahmat Khan himself fell. No sooner was the fighting over than the Nawab's cavalry proceeded to plunder the Rohilla camp, in which they found much booty, and it was this that led our own troops to observe—"We have the honour of the day, and these banditti the profit." The British losses were 39 killed and (including two officers) 93 wounded. The losses of the Nawab's troops amounted to 80 killed and 174 wounded.

In 1775, the then Commander-in-Chief, Sir John Clavering, ordered a complete re-numbering of the sepoy battalions. There existed at this time twenty-one regular battalions and one Parganna Battalion (the 24th), and it was directed that all the regular battalions should be numbered consecutively by brigades, beginning with the First Brigade, which was to have the first seven numbers, down to the Third Brigade, which was to have the last seven: the 7th Battalion was made independent and localised at Chittagong, while its place in the line was taken by the 24th, which then became the 14th. By this scheme the number of every battalion, except the 21st, was altered.

On the 10th June, 1776, was fought the brilliant action of Korah. Battle of In the preceding month Lieutenant-Colonel Parker had been detached from Belgram, in Oudh territory, with part of the 2nd Company of Artillery and the 15th and 16th Battalions of Native Infantry, to watch the motions of one Mahbub Khan, a disaffected officer in the service of the Nawab-Wazir, who was posted at Korah, about twenty-five miles below Cawnpore, with a force of seven battalions and nineteen guns. It being an object to gain possession of these guns, Colonel Parker marched on Korah, and demanded their surrender. Mahbub Khan himself was not present, but the demand was resisted by the next in command, upon which Colonel Parker moved forward to enforce it: a sharp conflict ensued, resulting in the complete defeat and dispersion of Mahbub Khan's troops and the capture of the whole of his guns. The loss sustained by Colonel Parker's detachment is not recorded, but it appears to have been considerable: Captain Gravely, commanding the 15th Battalion, was dangerously wounded and subsequently died of his wounds; Lieutenant Erskine, of the 16th, was killed. In 1829, the two corps engaged (which had then become the late 1st and 10th Regiments of Bengal Native Infantry) received permission to inscribe "Korah" on their colours. The latter half of 1777 saw another important addition to the native army.

In 1776, the Nawab-Wazir of Oudh agreed to keep up a mixed force of all arms, which should be disciplined by British officers: in the following year, however, when the numbers agreed upon were not yet completed, and the troops were only partially disciplined and organised, a Minute of Council, dated 4th August, 1777, ordered the transfer of the whole to the Company's service. The force at this time consisted of two regiments of cavalry, three companies of *golandáz* or native artillery (their first employment by the British) and nine battalions of infantry.

The infantry battalions were brought down to the strength of those in the Company's service, were numbered from the 22nd to the 30th, and three posted to each brigade. Of these only the 23rd, 26th, 27th and 30th survived the re-organisation of 1796, becoming then respectively the 2nd Battalion of the 6th, the 2nd of the 3rd, the 2nd of the 5th and the 2nd of the 9th; the last-mentioned battalion still survives as the 1st Bengal Infantry.[2]

The two cavalry regiments were reduced to a strength of 400 men each, and with a third regiment, which was now raised, a brigade was formed under Colonel Stibbert. The new regiment was raised, as far as possible, on the *silladar* system, the men furnishing their own horses.

Early in 1778, at the request of the Bombay Government, who were hard-pressed by the Mahrattas, six battalions of sepoys from the First Brigade (numbering 5,400 men), a regiment of native cavalry (600 strong), a company of native artillery, and a body(500) of so-called "Kandahar Horse" were assembled at Cawnpore under Lieutenant-Colonel Matthew Leslie, and subsequently marched across India to the Bombay Presidency, where they served with distinction against the Mahrattas until 1784. The battalions of infantry sent on this expedition were the 1st, 2nd, 4th, 5th, 6th and 7th.

---

2. The native names of these corps were, in order, *Rajek-ki-paltan, Ung-ki-paltan* (from Captain George Young), *Baillie-ki-paltan* (from Captain, afterwards Lieutenant-General Sir Ewen Baillie), and *Neelwar-ki-paltan* (from Captain Thomas Naylor).

The Kandahar Horse was a body of cavalry in the service of the Nawab-Wazir of Oudh, by whom they were lent to the Company for this service. They were entirely Pathans, and distinguished themselves greatly during their service in the Bombay Presidency.

To make up for this loss of strength in Bengal, nine more battalions of infantry were raised during 1778, of these, the first three were raised at Cawnpore in July, and were numbered from the 31st to 33rd; the next six, numbered from the 34th to the 39th, were also raised in July, mostly about Benares. These latter were ordered to be raised at the expense of Chet Singh, Rajah of Benares. (G.O.C.C., 15th, 26th and 30th July, 1778). Of these nine battalions only the 32nd and the 34th survived the re-organization of 1796, when they became respectively the 2nd of the 2nd and the 2nd of the 8th.[3]

The force under Colonel Leslie commenced its march in the hottest month of the year, an urgent message having been received from Bombay desiring its immediate despatch. It crossed the Jumna at Kalpi on the 19th of May, not without opposition, and advanced as far as Chatarpur, in Bundelkhand. Here Colonel Leslie remained for a month carrying on fruitless and unauthorised negotiations with the neighbouring rajahs; he subsequently moved on to Rajgarh, on the Kân River, and again halted; so much, indeed, did he delay that, after one or two warnings, orders were at length despatched by the Council directing his supersession and appointing Colonel Goddard to command the expedition. However, on the 3rd October, before the arrival of this order, Colonel Leslie died.[4] During this detention, Colonel Goddard took the town of Mau by storm, with a loss on our side of six killed and twenty wounded, and frequent skirmishes took place with the Mahratta horsemen.

On the 8th October, Goddard moved forward from the Kân, and after a trying march, during which the detachment was continually harassed and annoyed by the enemy's cavalry and rocketeers, reached Hoshangabad, on the Nerbudda, on the 1st December. Here he halted,

---

3. The native names of these two corps *(Bule-ki-paltan* and *Dabie-ki-paltan)* were derived from Captain Charles Bowles and Captain William Davis.
4. Lieutenant-Colonel Matthew Leslie had been for many years an officer of the 48th Foot, with which he served in North America during the Seven Years' War, He was Assistant Quarter Master General of Braddock's force in the disastrous expedition to Fort du Quesne, and was wounded in the battle of the Monongahela River (9th July, 1755), in which Braddock himself fell. He was afterwards Assistant Quarter Master General of the force which, under the Karl of Albemarle, besieged and captured the Havannah, in 1762.

awaiting orders from Calcutta, until the 16th January, 1779, when he again moved forward, and reached Burhanpur on the 30th. At this place he was detained for a week by contradictory orders from the Government of Bombay, whose forces had during that month made an advance on Poona, been worsted, and compelled to agree to the disgraceful convention of Wargaum, one of the terms of which was that the force under Goddard should be sent back to Bengal. Having received accurate information regarding these events, Goddard, disregarding the convention, left Burhanpur on the 5th February, and directed his course for Surat, where he arrived on the 25th. At this place the force remained for the remainder of the year, while various negotiations with the Mahratta powers were being carried on, and during this period Goddard was granted the rank of Brigadier-General, and invested by the Supreme Council with certain political powers that rendered him, to a considerable extent, independent of the Government of Bombay.

The negotiations with the Mahratta powers produced no result, and, on the 1st January, 1780, Goddard once more took the field. Crossing the Tapti, he proceeded to the northward, and on the 19th captured Dabhoi after a trifling resistance. He next marched against Ahmedabad, which was, after a siege of five days, taken by storm on the 15th February, with a loss on our side of 106 killed and wounded, including amongst the former Captain Gough, commanding the 5th Battalion, who fell in the breach. About the end of the month Goddard marched to the southward in pursuit of Sindhia and Holkar, the two principal Mahratta chiefs, who were ravaging the country near Baroda, and some fighting took place at Pawangarh on the 17th, 18th, and 19th March, but the enemy declined a decisive engagement, though they kept hovering round the British force. However, finding a favourable opportunity, Goddard succeeded in surprising Sindhia and Holkar before daylight on the morning of the 3rd April, captured their camp, and for the time dispersed their troops. About the middle of May he was reinforced by a detachment from Madras, consisting of a company of artillery, with six guns, a battalion of sepoys, and a battalion of the Madras European Regiment, and shortly after the advent of the rainy season necessitated the suspension of further operations.

In the meantime reinforcements for Goddard's army (a company of artillery and 2,400 native infantry drafts, organised in four battalions) had been prepared in Bengal and placed under the command of Captain Popham, but at the last moment it was decided to employ them in creating a diversion on the Northern Mahratta borders. The energy of Captain Popham effected more than the most sanguine could have expected from so small a force; for, having driven back a plundering horde of Mahrattas from Gohad, he besieged and carried by assault the fortress of Lahar on the 20th of April 1780.[5] But the most brilliant and unlooked-for success of this little army was that of the 3rd of August, when he stormed and captured, almost without a shot being fired, the celebrated fortress of Gwalior, which had always been regarded as impregnable.

On the termination of the rainy season, Goddard, who had been appointed Commander-in-Chief of the Bombay Army, once more took the field, but the campaign in the west of India opened under circumstances of great difficulty. Bombay was quite unable to support the expense of the war, and even Bengal, whose efforts had been more limited, was at a loss for money; while the troops of Goddard's army were clamouring for the payment of their arrears. Madras, too, was in great straits by reason of the hostilities which had just commenced with Haidar Ali. However, the first military event of the campaign was an important success,—namely, the surrender, on the 11th December, after a month's siege, of the strong fortress of Bassein.

About this time, Goddard, under the authority of the Council, proposed terms of peace to the Mahrattas, but the latter knew very well the straits to which the English were reduced, and looked for more advantage from a prosecution of hostilities than from any treaty which should terminate them; they therefore treated all Goddard's overtures with silence and contempt.

About the middle of January, 1781, Goddard captured the fort of Arnalla, and this was followed, in February, by his forcing the Bhor Ghaut and advancing on Poona, a measure which he conceived would prove more effectual in bringing the war to a conclusion than the reduction of the numerous forts scattered over the country. But in this he committed a mistake: the force under his command (about 6,000, of whom only 640 were Europeans) was not strong enough for the purpose, and in April he was forced back and compelled to retreat down the Ghaut with heavy loss, not the least item of which was the

---

5. The loss of Popham's detachment, at the storming of Lahar, was two British officers (Lieutenant Logan and Ensign Gardiner), one native officer and nineteen men killed, and two British and seven native officers and 94 men wounded, making a total of 125.

fall of the gallant Lieutenant-Colonel Parker, who had commanded at the battle of Korah in 1776. He eventually retired to Kalyan, where he took up quarters for the monsoon.

Towards the end of 1780, Major Popham was relieved in his command by Lieutenant-Colonel Camac, who brought considerable reinforcements with him. The force under Camac amounted to about 5,000 men, and being intended for operations against Sindhia, it marched to the southward, took the fort of Sipri, and reached Sironj in February, 1781.

Here he was greatly harassed by the enemy, and his supplies being cut off, he was reduced to great distress and compelled to call for reinforcements. These were despatched under the command of Lieutenant-Colonel Muir, but before they could arrive Camac found himself under the necessity of retreating. Halting at Mahatpur he was followed by Sindhia, of whom he finally relieved himself by a daring night attack (24th March), resulting in the total defeat of the enemy and the capture of all his guns, camp equipage, elephants, and stores.

For some months longer the war languished, but Sindhia was beginning to desire an end of the contest; he received with favour overtures which were made to him in August by Colonel Muir, who was now in command, and at length in October a treaty was concluded. The news of this event decided, if it did not hasten, the Poona Government to come to an arrangement with the English; and a cessation of hostilities was effected early in March, 1782. A treaty was concluded on the 17th of May, but it was not ratified until February, 1783. The Bengal troops in the west of India returned to their own presidency by the route taken by them when proceeding towards Bombay in 1778, and reached Cawnpore in April 1784, reduced in numbers to about half their original strength. Their services were warmly acknowledged in General Orders by the Governor-General, medals and other rewards were conferred upon the officers and men, and in 1829 the corps engaged in these operations, from 1778 to 1784, were authorised to inscribe the word "Guzerat" on their colours.[6]

Before detailing the other operations of the Bengal Army during the years 1781 and 1782, it will be necessary to notice the great changes which, in the former year, took place in its constitution and

---

6. By some extraordinary mistake the Bengal European Regiment, which had absolutely no part in General Goddard's operations in the west of India, was included in the grant of this honour, and it is still borne on the colours of the Royal Munster Fusiliers.

numbers. In November, 1780, the four battalions of sepoy drafts which had been under the command of Major Popham, and which had, later on, been re-organised in three battalions, were constituted regular battalions and numbered the 40th, 41st, and 42nd, and the command conferred, respectively, on Captains Clode, M'Clary, and Bruce. Of the forty-two battalions of Bengal infantry now existing, the six in Bombay were regarded as not on the Bengal establishment, and the period of their return being quite indefinite, they were left outside of the new organisation now introduced. At the same time the 20th Battalion, which had exhibited a mutinous spirit in connection with the distribution of the prize taken on the occupation of Chandernagore, when war with France broke out in 1778, was broken up. This left thirty-five battalions on the Bengal establishment, and these by Minutes of Council dated 26th December, 1780, and G.O.C.C, dated 10th January, 1781, were augmented to 1,000 rank and file each, and formed into thirty-five regiments of two battalions of 500 men each. The regiments so formed were each commanded by a major commandant, and each battalion by a captain. Another regiment (the 36th) was raised soon after at Berhampore, and the command given to Major John Fullarton.

At the same time the Bengal European infantry, which had, in 1779, been formed into three double battalion regiments, was once more re-organised in three regiments of a single battalion each.

Shortly before these changes (G. O. C. C, 30th October, 1780) a detachment, the command of which was conferred upon Colonel T. D. Pearse, of the Bengal Artillery, was ordered to assemble at Midnapore to proceed by land to Madras to the assistance of the Army of that Presidency, which was hard-pressed by Haidar Ali, the ruler of Mysore: at the same time, the Commander-in-Chief, Sir Eyre Coote, proceeded to Madras by sea, taking with him two companies of artillery, with 630 lascars and 350 men of the 2nd Battalion of the 1st Bengal European Regiment. The force under Colonel Pearse consisted of one company of artillery, six companies of lascars, and five regiments of Bengal Native infantry completed to the new establishment, *viz.,* the 12th, 13th, 24th, 25th, and 26th: the 20th had also been detailed for this service, but, as already stated, this corps was disbanded before the detachment marched. The detachment left Midnapore early in the year, but was much delayed on the march, especially at Ganjam, where it arrived towards the end of March and was detained by the violence of an infectious disease; this, together with numerous desertions, considerably thinned the ranks of the battalions before a junction was effected with Sir Eyre Coote and the Madras Army, which was not accomplished until the 3rd of August, 1781, at Pulicat. At this place the detachment was broken up, and the several regiments distributed amongst the brigades of Coote's army, the orders with regard to which had been published as early as January, 1781. By this arrangement the 12th and 25th were posted to the 2nd Brigade, commanded by Colonel Ross Lang; the 13th was in the 3rd Brigade, under Colonel Pearse; the 24th was in the 4th Brigade, commanded by Lieutenant-Colonel Owen; and the 26th in the 5th Brigade, of which the brigadier was Lieutenant-Colonel George Brown. This mixture of Bengal and Madras troops does not, however, seem to have answered well, judging from the following General Order, dated the 22nd September, 1781:

> The General is much concerned to have so many reports daily of disputes between the Bengal and Coast sepoys. The appellation 'Bengalee' made use of by the Coast sepoys should be particularly explained to their men by the officers commanding the Bengal Native corps, as the general designation by which the sepoys of this country know those of the other establishment, and without attaching to it the same meaning as it has in Bengal.

Yet throughout the campaigns in the Carnatic, the Bengal troops acquitted themselves honourably. Prior to the arrival of Pearse's detachment, the Bengal troops which had accompanied Sir Eyre Coote to the coast had been engaged at the capture of Karanguli, the relief of Wandiwash, the attack on Chilambram, and the great battle of Porto Novo. The first action in which they were engaged after the junction of Pearse's force was that fought on the 27th August at Pollilur. on the very ground on which Haidar Ali had, in the preceding year, cut off and destroyed Colonel Baillie's detachment. The position taken up by Haidar was a strong one, the advance against him being rendered peculiarly difficult by the number of water-courses which cut up the ground; the British force was indifferently handled, but eventually the enemy was forced out of his position, and during the night Haidar retreated to Conjeveram, leaving the English masters of the field. On the 27th of the following month, Coote came up with Haidar at Sholingarh, and inflicted on him a severe defeat, the Bengal troops (especially the 13th Regiment) taking a prominent share in the victory. On the 23rd October, the grenadier company of the 1st Bengal European Regiment and the 24th Bengal Native Infantry, forming part of a detachment under Lieutenant-Colonel Owen, took part in an action near Virakandalur. On this occasion the grenadiers greatly distinguished themselves, re-capturing a gun which had fallen into the enemy's hands. In November, the army retired in the direction of Madras, and was cantoned at Poonamallee.

In January, 1782, an advance was again made towards Vellore, which was in need of provisions, and that place was relieved on the 11th. Subsequently the Bengal troops took part in many important operations. In September of this year, Sir Eyre Coote went to Bengal on account of his failing health; he returned in the spring of 1783, but died at Madras (27th April 1783) before he could resume command of the army, which was now held by Major-General Stuart.[7]

Early in the summer of 1783, preparations were made for the recovery of Cuddalore, which had been taken in April, 1782, by the French, who had for some time been actively assisting Haidar Ali: an attack was made on the 13th June, 1783, on the entrenched position held by;the French outside the fort; from various causes it was only partially successful, but it ended in the enemy abandoning their position and withdrawing into the fort. They made a vigorous sortie on the 24th, but were repulsed. The conduct on this occasion of the 24th Bengal Native Infantry, under Captain Williamson, was very distinguished: they met the French with the bayonet, defeated them, and drove them out of the trenches, taking several prisoners, including the Chevalier de Damas, who led the attack, and Bernadotte, afterwards king of Sweden, then a sergeant in the French Army.[8] Among the Bengal officers who were killed during the operations at Cuddalore were Captain Durey, 25th, and Lieutenant Grueber, 24th Regiment.

The position of the English was at this time very critical, diminished as their forces were by casualties and disease. Fortunately at this juncture news was received of peace having been concluded between France and England, and hostilities ceased. A treaty with Tippoo (Haidar having died in December, 1782) followed in March 1784.

Throughout this campaign the hardships of the army were great

---

7. Major-General James Stuart of Torrance. This officer, when Lieutenant-Colonel of the old 90th Regiment, commanded the storming party at the capture of Fort Moro, Havannah, in 1762.

8. In some places this exploit is ridiculously attributed to the late 7th Bengal Native Infantry, a regiment which was at that time serving in the west of India under General Goddard. The error probably originated in the fact that the 24th Regiment was, under the re-organization of 1796, incorporated with the old double-battalion 7th Native Infantry, which afterwards, in 1824, became the late 10th and 13th Native Infantry.

from the scarcity of money and supplies. The consequence was that desertions were constant, and in this respect the Bengal troops, who were in a foreign country and therefore doubtless suffered more than the Madras sepoys, unfortunately set a prominently bad example.

On the 19th of April, 1784, the Bengal troops received orders to march for their own Presidency, where they arrived in January, 1785, reduced in numbers from over 5,000 to less than 2,000 men. The force was visited at Ghiretti by the governor-general, and thanked in General Orders; honorary standards were granted to each battalion; *subadars* and *jemadars* received gold and silver medals, respectively, and non-commissioned officers and sepoys similar medals of inferior value. In 1829, the surviving corps were authorised to inscribe "Carnatic" on their colours.

In Bengal itself the three years during which Colonel Pearse's detachment was fighting in Madras had been comparatively uneventful ones from a military point of view. The only important event near the Presidency was the revolt of Chet Singh, the Rajah of Benares, and its subsequent suppression by a force under Major Popham. As has too often been the case in Indian history, the outbreak of the revolt was marked by circumstances of great barbarity. In consequence of continued signs of disaffection, orders were issued for the arrest of the Rajah in his palace at Benares: this was effected on the morning of August 16th, 1781, and he was left in the charge of Lieutenant Stalker, 27th Native Infantry, under a guard, consisting of two companies of grenadiers of Major Popham's regiment (the 35th Native Infantry), commanded by Lieutenants Scott and Symes. Unfortunately, through some mistake, the party had left camp in the morning without any ammunition. As soon as the omission was discovered, reinforcements were sent by Major Popham, but before these could arrive, the two defenceless companies at the palace were attacked by a multitude of the Rajah's followers and massacred, almost to a man, among the slain being Lieutenants Stalker, Scott, and Symes. The Rajah immediately fled to Latifpur, a strong fort belonging to him about ten miles southeast from Chunar. On the 19th a considerable body of his forces occupied Ramnagar, on the right bank of the Ganges opposite Benares, and on the following day a rash and ill-judged attack was made on this place by some detachments under Captain Mayaffre, of the Artillery, who paid for his foolhardiness with his life, Captain Doxat, commanding the company of "Foreign Rangers," and a number of men being also killed. This defeat further inflamed the rebellion, and the governor-general, who was at Benares at the time, was obliged to retreat to Chunar. Reinforcements, however, soon appeared on the scene and further operations followed, the regiments employed being the 1st Battalion of the 6th, and the 7th, 19th, 30th and 35th. On September 4th, Captain Blair, with a detachment of 550 men and two guns, attacked the enemy at Patita, seven miles from Chunar: the Rajah's troops (4,500 men with six guns) fought with great steadiness, but an opportune and gallant attack made on their guns by the grenadier companies of the 35th compelled them to retire with considerable loss, leaving four guns in the hands of the victors. Shortly after a combined attack on Patita and Latifpur, by two columns, was organised. Major Popham commanded the first of these columns and seized the fort of Patita after a faint resistance. Major Crabb, who commanded the other column, experienced more opposition. A powerful body of the Rajah's troops met him at Lora on the 20th September, but they were defeated after a sharp action and driven with loss through the pass of Sukrut to Latifpur. On hearing of this double disaster, the Rajah fled to Bijaigarh, in the Kaimur Hills, which was his last resource, and the whole of his army dispersed. Major Popham advanced rapidly on Bijaigarh, when the Rajah again fled, and the place was taken (10th November), and found to contain treasure to the amount of twenty-five *lakhs* of rupees, which was immediately distributed to the troops.

We have now reached a period of several years' peace, during which the Bengal Army was reduced as much as possible, and every effort made to lessen the drain on the impoverished exchequer.

As early as the middle of 1783, reductions had been made in the army which remained in Bengal. In accordance with the Minutes of Council of the 28th August, 1783, a general reduction of the army to peace establishment took place. Regiments of infantry were reduced from 1,000 to 700 men, battalions being divided into five companies of seventy men each.

The first point to be noticed in the changes which now took place is the further re-numbering of the infantry regiments.

In 1782, the regiments of the line, exclusive of the six corps in Bombay, were reduced to thirty-five in number by the mutiny of the 35th (Major Popham's) Regiment at Berhampore. This corps was ordered on service to the Northern Circars early in 1782; but a rumour getting abroad that they would be sent by sea, the men refused to go, and declared that they would prevent the advanced party from marching. This was one of the results of the unhappy loss at sea, in 1770, of the grenadier companies of the then 4th Battalion, already mentioned. The 4th, 15th and 17th Regiments at Barrack pore, which had also been ordered on this service, shared in a lesser degree in the insubordinate conduct of the 35th. For this offence two *subadars* and two sepoys were executed by being blown away from guns, in accordance with the sentence of a court-martial, and the 35th Regiment was disbanded and "dismissed the service in a public and ignominious manner" (G. O. C. C. 20th March, 1782). The number of the disgraced regiment was given to the 36th.

On the return of the Bombay detachment it became necessary to give the six infantry battalions included in it places amongst the brigade regiments. "In order to effect this without increase of the establishment, six of the present brigade regiments are to be reduced, *viz.*,-the 33rd, 34th, and 35th (being the youngest regiments), and the 4th,[8] 15th, and 17th on account of their unsoldierlike conduct when ordered on service in March, 1782,"—(Minutes of Council, 19th January, 1784). The returned regiments were brought on to the establishment with their original numbers, and the thirty-five regiments were accordingly numbered as follows:

Previous to 1781.	1781.	1784.	REMARKS.	Previous to 1781.	1781.	1784.	REMARKS.
1st	...	1st	In the detachment to Bombay.	5th	...	5th	In the detachment to Bombay.
2nd	...	2nd	Ditto.	6th	...	6th	Ditto.
3rd	1st	3rd	......	7th	...	7th	Ditto.
4th	...	4th	In the detachment to Bombay.	8th	2nd	8th	
				9th	3rd	9th	
11th	5th	10th		27th	20th	23rd	
12th	6th	11th		31st	24th	24th	In the detachment to Madras.
18th	12th	12th	In the detachment to Madras.	32nd	25th	25th	Ditto.
19th	13th	13th	Ditto	33rd	26th	26th	Ditto.
13th	7th	14th		28th	21st	27th	
14th	8th	15th		29th	22nd	28th	
15th	9th	16th		30th	23rd	29th	Now the 1st Bengal Infantry.
16th	10th	17th		34th	27th	30th	
17th	11th	18th		35th	28th	31st	
21st	14th	19th		36th	29th	32nd	
23rd	16th	20th		37th	30th	33rd	
25th	18th	21st		38th	31st	34th	
26th	19th	22nd		39th	32nd	35th	

8. This was the celebrated *Matthews-ki-paltan*, one of the most distinguished corps of the Bengal Native Army. It was raised in 1761, and had served with much distinction under Adams and Munro, especially at the battles of Gheriah and Buxar.

The history of the native cavalry during the preceding twenty years had been a rather varied one, and requires some special notice. The three *rissalahs* of Clive's organisation of 1765 were not, as might have been expected, a very efficient force; and they were criticised as follows, about 1770, by General Smith, the Commander-in-Chief, previous to his resigning his command:

> The black cavalry are at present of no further use than to attend the commander-in-chief and colonels of brigades, and are too inconsiderable to be of service in time of war; for I know by experience it is impossible, from the viciousness of the horses, to discipline cavalry here to any tolerable degree of perfection, and castrating the horses ruins their spirit. On the commencement of a war, the best cavalry in Indostan may be procured within six weeks, either Durannees, Tartars, Persians, or Mahrattas. Subalterns at present command the three troops and enjoy the emoluments of them, which, together with the clothing, is said to amount to little less than R.820,000 a year.

In consequence, apparently, of these strictures, the whole body of cavalry was disbanded in 1772, and not a single mounted man remained in the service of the Company in Bengal. However, in the following year, 1773, the Body-Guard, was raised, and in 1776 the Nawab-Wazir agreed to keep up a contingent of six cavalry regiments, officered by Englishmen, and did actually raise two, which were transferred to the Company in the following year; and these, with a third, raised at that time, were formed into a brigade under Colonel Stibbert. One of these regiments has been mentioned as forming part of Colonel Goddard's detachment, employed against the Mahrattas in the west of India. The other two were now (Minute of Council, 5th May, 1783) entirely reduced, the horses sold, and the men discharged, except such as might be selected for infantry service. On the return of the Bombay detachment, we find the order recorded (Minute of Council, 19th January, 1784) that "the two *rissalahs*" of cavalry included in that force are to be retained in the Company's service for the present. This, apparently, refers to the regiment of Bengal Native cavalry and the Kandahar Horse.

In the course of the following year, a considerable further reduction was made in the infantry, the 31st, 32nd, 33rd, 34th and 35th Regiments being reduced and also several of the then existing independent (i.e., local) corps.—(Minutes of Council, dated the 27th January and 15th February, 1785).

This was followed, in 1786, by the disbanding of the Chittagong Independent Regiment (Minutes of Council, dated the 22nd March, 1786). The disbandment of the Ramgarh Light Infantry was also ordered, but before it could be carried into execution, a letter arrived from Europe which led to the retention of the regiment By the same Minutes of Council the double battalion organisation was abandoned, and the native infantry was re-organised in thirty single battalion regiments of ten companies each, styled "battalions." These arrangements had not yet been completely carried into effect when the letter mentioned above (dated 21st September, 1785) arrived from the Court of Directors ordering the adoption of a somewhat similar measure and directing in addition that the existing native infantry was to be re-organised in thirty-six battalions, each of a strength of 640 natives of all ranks, with ten European officers and eight European sergeants,—(Minutes of Council, 22nd May, 1786). This was done; the Ramgarh Light Infantry was brought into the line as the 31st Battalion,[9] the 32nd Battalion was formed of drafts from four battalions at Fatehgarh, the 33rd and 34th by drafts from seven battalions at Cawnpore and Fatehgarh, the 35th by drafts from four battalions at Chunar, and the 36th by drafts from seven battalions at Barrackpore, Dacca, and Midnapore, and from the Ramgarh Light Infantry,—(G. O. C. C, 18th May, 1786). The five regiments formed from drafts were popularly known as the "Chari Yari," or "Four Friends," in allusion, it is said, to the supposition that they had each been formed from drafts of four regiments.

The strength of the single battalion regiments now formed was eight companies of eighty all ranks, and the peace establishment for Bengal was fixed (Minutes of Council, 22nd May, 1786) as follows:

- 3 battalions of European artillery
- 6 battalions of European infantry
- troops of native cavalry
- 36 battalions of native infantry
- 30 companies of lascars
- 1 corps of engineers (consisting of 22 officers only)

The army was divided into six brigades of sepoy regiments, with one European battalion in each.

---

9. In 1796 this battalion became the 2nd of the 4th. Its native designation *(Chota Crawford-ki-paltan)* was derived from Captain James Crawford, junior.

The two existing *rissalahs* of cavalry were reduced to troops of eighty each of all ranks, and stationed one at Cawnpore, the other at Fatehgarh. This order, however, only remained in force for one year, when each troop was augmented by one native officer and fifty-three men,—(Minutes of Council, 2nd July and G. O. C. C, 21st October, 1787). Towards the end of the year a further augmentation was made, each corps being formed into a regiment of three troops, each troop consisting of one British and two native officers and fifty-five men. These corps were now designated "the 1st and 2nd Regiments of Cavalry," and a captain was appointed to the command of each.—(Minutes of Council, 7th December, and G. O. C. C, 14th December, 1787.)

Some short notice is here necessary also of the artillery, in-which the changes since 1777 had been frequent. In that year, it will be remembered, the first companies of *Golandaz* were received into the Company's service from that of the Nawab-Wazir of Oudh. Their strength was three British and four native officers, three British and sixteen native non-commissioned officers and eighty men to each company, while the whole three were commanded by a major (Patrick Duff), with a staff of an adjutant, a quarter-master and a sergeant-major. Six companies of lascars were attached to each *Golandaz* company. In 1778, on the advice of Colonel Pearse, three battalions of *Golandaz* were raised, the men for them, besides two of the existing companies, being selected from the companies of lascars. The third original *Golandaz* company had meanwhile accompanied Brigadier General Goddard's expedition to the west of India. The artillery was now formed into a separate brigade of one European and three native battalions. Notwithstanding the success of this experiment and the efficiency of the native artillery so formed, the *Golandaz* battalions were reduced in 1779, and the old system of lascars revived: and, though a company was raised from the old material to accompany Colonel Pearse to Madras in 1780, yet, in 1784-85, both this company and the one which had rendered such excellent service with Brigadier-General Goddard in the west of India were reduced.

In 1787, Lord Cornwallis (who came out as Governor-General and Commander-in-Chief in September, 1786) inspected all the corps of the army, and placed on record that he "viewed with no less admiration than astonishment the very high military condition and proficiency of the native corps in Bengal."

Of the interior economy, etc., of corps, the following details are gleaned from General Orders and other sources. The recruiting ground for the infantry at this time, and for many subsequent years, was principally about the Ganges in Bihar and Oudh. A general officer, writing in 1809,[10] says:

> During the last forty years the native army has been almost entirely recruited from the countries extending on both sides of the Ganges, from Patna or Dinapore up to Anoopsheher and Rohilcund. The tract which has furnished the greatest number of recruits for the native infantry in that period is included between the Ganges and the Gogra, from the junction of these rivers near Manjee to Shahjehanpore, on the eastern confines of Rohilcund. The *zemindars* throughout this tract are almost entirely Bramins and Rajpoots, and are a brave, manly race of people.

The establishment of a native infantry battalion by the organisation of 1786 was as follows:

Staff	Two companies of grenadiers
Commandant	and six battalion companies
Adjutant	of the following strength
Surgeon Assistant	1 Subaltern
Black doctor	1 Sergeant
Non- effective	1 *Subadar*
Sergeant-Major	1 *Jemadar*
Quarter-master Sergeant	4 *Havildars*
Drill *Havildar*	4 *Naiks*
Drill *Naik*	1 Drum
Drum and Fife Major	1 Fife
	68 Privates

The old appointment of Native Commandant was abolished in 1781, and the pay of battalions was drawn in one abstract by the commanding officer, and ordered to be issued to the men in the presence of company commanders.

In a General Order dated 18th July, 1778, we find, with reference to the training of the men, that ten rounds of ammunition are to be allowed per man yearly for musketry practice:

> .... the targets are to be made of painted canvas, and a butt of earth erected behind them to preserve the balls.

---

10. *East India U. S. Journal,* July 1834, p. 15.

In the cavalry, at the same time, the staff allowance for field officers, for horses and regimental furniture, is fixed at R150, and for captains and for subalterns at R100. And a little later (G. O. C. C, 9th November, 1780), commanding officers of the native cavalry regiments are directed to send to the Presidency one *daffadar* and twelve troopers to be instructed in military riding, training, and breaking horses.

In 1787, a scale of camp equipage was laid down, that for a sepoy battalion being as follows:—seven marquees for the officers and surgeons, three private tents for the sergeants and quarter guard, eleven bell tents (probably for the sepoys' arms, who at this time had no shelter for themselves), and three necessary tents.

The Bengal continued on a peace establishment until the outbreak of the Mysore War in 1790, the only important event in the meantime being the despatch in 1789 of a detachment of native infantry to reinforce the Company's settlement at Fort Marlborough, Bencoolen, on the north-west coast of Sumatra, where disturbances were threatened. One object held in view by Lord Cornwallis in despatching these troops was to overcome the aversion of the Bengal sepoys to service beyond sea, against which the disaster of 1770, already related, had deeply prejudiced them. Volunteers were called for from the 1st, 30th, and 32nd Battalions, and a bounty of R10 per man was offered. The detachment (of the strength of four companies) was completed in a few days, notwithstanding that two subadars of the 32nd tried to deter the men from volunteering, for which offence they were publicly discharged from the service with ignominy. The promised bounty was paid to the volunteers before they started, and not a single desertion occurred. On the voyage every care was taken of the men, but during their stay at Bencoolen they suffered much from sickness, and many deaths occurred. The detachment returned to Calcutta in December.

In order that the narrative of the war in Mysore may not be interrupted, it is convenient to mention in this place that in January, 1791 two companies of the 30th Battalion were detached on service to Prince of Wales' Island (Penang). In the following April these companies were employed in some operations in Quedah territory, on the coast of Malacca, opposite Penang, and Lieutenant Thomas Williamson, who commanded them, was wounded in action at Point Pria Fort on the 12th of that month.

The outbreak of war with Tippoo Sultan in the beginning of 1790, and the necessity of affording aid to the Madras Presidency, led to the augmentation of Bengal infantry battalions to ten companies and the addition of a *daffadar* and twenty troopers to each troop of cavalry,—(Minutes of Council, 1st February, 1790). Lord Cornwallis, who was determined to prosecute the war in the most vigorous manner, gave orders on the same date for the formation of a detachment for service in the Carnatic: this consisted of the 76th Foot and six battalions of Bengal Native infantry, *viz.,* the 3rd, 7th, 13th, 14th, 26th, and 28th (completed to ten companies each by drafts from the 8th, 9th, 20th, 23rd, 33rd, and 35th Battalions), with the 2nd Battalion of Artillery and twelve companies of lascars, the whole under the command of Lieutenant-Colonel Cockerell, Quarter-master General of the Army in Bengal. The detachment (except the 76th Foot and part of the artillery, which went by sea) marched to Midnapore, and thence to the southern bank of the Subanrika River, in three divisions, and proceeding onwards on the 22nd March, 1790, arrived at Conjeveram on the 1st August, where it joined a force called "the Centre Army" under the command of Colonel Kelly of the Madras Army. It was inspected by that officer on the 4th of August, and complimented on its appearance and on the small diminution in its numbers which had occurred during the long march from Bengal. It is certain, however, that numerous desertions did take place, for special General Orders on the subject were published on the 12th April and the 29th June; in the latter we find the following:—"The Commander-in-Chief has observed that by far the greatest number of men who have deserted from Lieutenant-Colonel Cockerell's detachment are natives of Oudh and the countries beyond Benares. An experience so unquestionable must satisfy every person that whatever advantages such men may possess in point of height and appearance, they are by no means so fit for soldiers in the Company's service as the natives of our own provinces. It is therefore directed that commanding officers of battalions of sepoys do receive as few men as possible from the countries to the west of Benares, but fill up all vacancies in these battalions, as far as may be practicable, with natives of the Company's provinces; and that battalion which is composed of the greatest number of men of the latter description will, in the estimation of the commander-in-chief, be the most useful corps and the most to be relied on."

On this expedition the authorities, mindful of the disturbances which had occurred eight years before, brigaded the Bengal troops separately from the Madras sepoys. The 3rd, 13th, and 26th Battalions formed, with the 74th (Highland) Regiment, the 1st Brigade of the

Centre Army, under Lieutenant-Colonel Maxwell, 74th; the 7th, 14th, and 25th Battalions, with the 76th Foot, formed the 2nd Brigade, under Lieutenant-Colonel Cockerell.

Little was effected during the remainder of 1790, and the Centre Army was not engaged with the enemy, except in a few trifling skirmishes.

At the end of the year Lord Cornwallis, being dissatisfied with the result of the campaign, determined to take the field in person, and at the same time reinforce the army in the field in the Carnatic with additional troops from Bengal. In G. O. C. C, dated 8th November, 1790, the 1st Regiment of Bengal Cavalry was ordered to be made up to six troops of regulation strength by drafts from the 2nd Regiment, and to go by sea to Madras; and, at the same time, a volunteer force of 1,400 sepoys was called for, who were also to accompany the commander-in-chief to Madras by sea. More than the required number volunteered, and proceeded to Madras, where on arrival they were formed (G. O. by Earl Cornwallis, dated 3rd February, 1791) into two battalions, the 1st and 2nd Battalions of Bengal Volunteers, the command of which was conferred upon Captains Thomas Welsh and Henry Hyndman. A reinforcement of fifty artillerymen also proceeded to Madras. It does not appear how the Bengal cavalry were employed, but they were probably used merely as a Body-Guard by Lord Cornwallis. They returned to Bengal in the autumn of 1791.

On the 29th of January Lord Cornwallis assumed command of the troops in the field, at Vellout, and having determined to carry the war into the enemy's country and assail Seringapatam, he moved forward on the 5th February. Ascending the Mugli Pass without opposition, and capturing the forts of Kolar and Uskata, he advanced on Bangalore, before which fortress he arrived on the 5th of March. On the following day a cavalry action took place, in which the British, who were at first successful, pushed their pursuit too far, and, becoming entangled in a country intersected with ravines, were driven back in confusion with a loss of twenty killed, forty-eight wounded, and three missing, Lieutenant-Colonel Floyd, commanding the cavalry, being amongst the badly wounded.

On the 7th the *pettah* (or walled town) of Bangalore was carried by assault by a detachment under Lieutenant-Colonel Cockerell, consisting of His Majesty's 36th, the 26th Bengal Battalion, a detachment of artillery, and some pioneers, supported by the 76th Foot, the 3rd Bengal Battalion and the 1st Bengal Volunteers. Later on the same day an attempt was made by Tippoo to recover the place, but this was perceived in time by Cornwallis, who reinforced the troops in the town with the 76th, which had been withdrawn in the course of the morning, and the enemy were driven back after severe fighting. The British loss on this occasion was 131 killed and wounded, out of which the Bengal battalions had three killed and eighteen wounded; the loss of the enemy was about 2,000.

The siege of Bangalore Fort was now prosecuted with as much vigour as possible, but under great difficulties, as the besiegers were constantly threatened by the whole of the enemy's very superior force. The assault was delivered on the night of the 21st of March, the 7th and 26th Bengal Battalions forming part of the storming party: it proved completely successful, though this fortunate result would have been less assured but for the hesitation and timidity of Tippoo. Hundreds of the enemy were killed, while our loss amounted to only seventeen killed and 86 wounded, of which the share of the Bengal battalions was three killed and fifteen wounded. The total British loss before Bangalore was 120 killed, 305 wounded, and eight missing,—433 in all.

Having effected a junction with the Nizam's cavalry, amounting to 10,000 men, in April, Lord Cornwallis made preparations for the siege of Seringapatam, and marched towards that place on the 3rd of May. On the 13th he received information that Tippoo, with his whole army, was encamped in a formidable position at Arikera, eight miles from Seringapatam; and determined, by making a night march, to surprise him, if possible, turn his left flank, and cut him off from his capital. This plan was frustrated by a violent storm during the night, which impeded the march of the troops; but Lord Cornwallis persevered, and at daybreak attacked Tippoo, who had now changed his front and assumed a fresh position. A severe engagement ensued, ending in the complete defeat of the enemy, who were driven under the walls of Seringapatam. The Bengal troops engaged in this action were the 2nd Battalion of artillery, the 7th, 13th, 14th, 26th and 28th Battalions of Native Infantry, the 1st Volunteer Battalion, and Lord Cornwallis' guard, which was probably a detachment from the 1st Regiment of Bengal Cavalry. Their casualties, out of a total of 426, amounted to thirty-six killed (including Ensign Ross and *Subadar* Tahir Muhammad, 13th Battalion, and *Jemadar* Dharu Singh, 26th Battalion), 141 wounded (including five British officers, of whom one, Lieutenant Duncan Macpherson, of the artillery, died), and three missing,—making 180 in all.

On the 18th Lord Cornwallis moved to Kaniyambadi, eight miles to the west of Seringapatam, in order to facilitate a junction with

Major-General Abercromby[11] and a force from Bombay, which had advanced over the Ghats from Malabar and was now at Periapatam, about forty miles to the west of Seringapatam. Owing, however, to the mortality amongst the draught cattle, the complete failure of supplies, and the incessant bad weather, combined with the non-arrival of a Mahratta Army which was to have cooperated with him, Lord Cornwallis found it impossible to prosecute the siege of Seringapatam at this juncture, and determined to retire. He accordingly directed Major-General Abercromby to retrace his steps to the Malabar coast, and after halting a few days to cover that officer's retrograde movement, he burst all his heavy guns, destroyed the stores for which carriage could not be found, and, on the 26th May, began his retreat towards Bangalore. The same day he was joined by the long-expected Mahratta Army, 40,000 strong, accompanied by two Bombay battalions under Captain Little, which had been engaged at the siege of Dharwar. The earlier arrival of this force would have completely changed the course of events, but the activity of the enemy's horse had prevented all intelligence of its approach reaching Lord Cornwallis, and thus rendered nugatory his successes up to this period. The destruction of the siege train and stores made an immediate return to Seringapatam impossible; the retirement was therefore continued, and Bangalore was reached on the 11th July.

While the preparation of a fresh siege train and other arrangements for a renewed attack on Seringapatam were in progress, a part of the army was employed in reducing Tippoo's hill forts. Of these, the first to offer any considerable resistance, was Nandidrug, built on the summit of a hill about 1,700 feet high, with precipitous and, except in one place, inaccessible sides, which rises sheer from the plain, about twenty-eight miles north of Bangalore. The village at the foot of the hill was taken on the 22nd of September, and the fort itself was carried with but small loss on the 17th of October. The 13th Bengal Battalion took part in the siege, and its flank companies were engaged in the assault.

On the 31st of October the 7th Bengal Battalion was present at the storming of Penagra, in the Baramahal, with a detached force under Lieutenant-Colonel Maxwell; and on the 8th November it took part in the unsuccessful assault of Kistnagheri, when Lieutenant Edward Bird was severely wounded. The 3rd, 13th, 14th, 26th, and 28th Battalions took part in the operations before Savandrug in December, but

---

11. This was Major-General Robert Abercromby, a younger brother of the celebrated Sir Ralph Abercromby, who fell in Egypt in 1801. He died in 1827.

not in the assault. Ramgiri and Shivanagiri surrendered to a detachment under Captain Welsh, which included the 28th Bengal Battalion. On the 24th of December the strong fort of Utradrug was stormed by a party consisting of the light infantry companies of the 52nd and 72nd Foot, and the 26th Bengal Battalion.

In the autumn of this year the battalions stationed at Barrackpore, Berhampore and Dinapore were called upon (G.O.C.C. 9th August, 1791) to furnish another body of 850 volunteers for service in the Carnatic. These were quickly forthcoming: they were despatched by sea to Madras in September, 1791, and on arrival in Mysore the men were distributed to fill vacancies in the eight Bengal battalions then with Lord Cornwallis. At the same time twenty subaltern officers were sent from Bengal for service with these battalions, and a large number of lascars were also despatched.

Towards the end of January, 1792, the confederated armies were assembled near Huliadrug, about forty miles south-west of Bangalore, and thence, on the 1st of February, they marched for Seringapatam. The strength of the British forces was—

Artillery (1,145 Europeans and 3,077 Natives)	4,222
Engineers (including 21 Natives)	41
Pioneers	1,049
British cavalry (one regiment)	404
Native cavalry (two regiments and two body-guards)	702
British infantry (seven battalions)	4,482
Native infantry (seventeen battalions)	11,133
Total	22,033

The ordnance (including the siege train) amounted to 86 pieces. The Nizam's and the Mahratta armies (18,000 and 12,000 strong, respectively) consisted entirely of Horse.

Of the Bengal troops, the 3rd, 13th and 26th Battalions and the 2nd Battalion of Volunteers formed the 3rd Brigade under Lieutenant-Colonel Cockerell, while the 7th, 14th and 28th Battalions composed the 4th Brigade under Major George Russell of the Bengal Infantry.

On the 5th of February the army arrived within six miles of Seringapatam and encamped under cover of the Kapilair Hills. The whole of Tippoo's army was posted in an enclosed and strongly fortified camp on the north bank of the Kaveri The enclosure was an irregular triangle in shape, about three miles in length and about 3,000 yards broad at the base, which was towards the west. The whole was surrounded by a strong hedge of prickly pear except towards the river; a large redoubt called the Idgah stood at the north-west angle; the apex of the triangle was flanked and protected by the defences of a rocky eminence known as Karighat hill, while the centre of the camp was strengthened by a double line of redoubts. Immediately behind the camp was the island in the Kaveri on which stood the fort and town of Seringapatam.

After carefully reconnoitring the enemy's position Lord Cornwallis decided on making an immediate attempt on Tippoo's camp without waiting for the arrival of the Bombay force, which had again ascended the Western Ghâts, and was once more moving on Seringapatam. The attack was made in three columns on the night of the 6th of February, the 3rd Brigade forming part of the right column under Major-General Medows, and the 4th being included in the centre column under Lord Cornwallis himself. As is not unusual in night assaults much confusion prevailed, and at one period the attacking forces were perilously near to repulse, but in the end the operations were completely successful, and our forces were firmly established in the position from which they had expelled the enemy. To enter a little into detail, the right column carried the Idgah redoubt and then moved down to the extreme left and reached Karighat hill. Part of the centre column, after forcing their way through the enemy s camp, crossed the river and made good their position in the island capturing several batteries which lined the bank; another portion, with which was the 14th Bengal Battalion, seized one of the large redoubts in the camp whilst the remainder, with which was Lord Cornwallis himself, was hotly engaged with a large force of the enemy, and on the repulse of the latter withdrew towards Karighat hill, and eventually joined the right column, which had wandered off in that direction in the dark, after the capture of the Idgah Redoubt. The left column, under the command of Lieutenant-Colonel Maxwell, 74th Highlanders, carried the defences of the Karighat hill without much opposition, forced its way into the entrenched camp, and eventually followed the lead of the centre column across the river.

Throughout the 7th the enemy, who were still in possession of several redoubts within the camp, made strenuous efforts to dislodge the British from the positions they had gained, but in vain; and during the night they abandoned the camp, and retired across the river into the fortress of Seringapatam.

The loss of the British in the twenty-four hours' fighting was 108 killed, 383 wounded, and four missing, making a total of 535; of this number, twenty-eight of the killed, 101 of the wounded, and eleven of the missing, 140 in all, belonged to the Bengal troops. Lord Cornwallis was slightly wounded, and Captain John Archdeacon, commanding the 14th Bengal Battalion, Lieutenant-Fireworker Alexander Buchan, Bengal Artillery, and Lieutenant Patrick Stewart, Bengal Engineers, were amongst the killed. The loss of the enemy was enormous: the killed alone were estimated at 4.000, and with wounded, prisoners and deserters the total loss was probably not less than 20,000. Seventy-six pieces of cannon were taken in the camp and on the island.[12]

On the 16th of February, Major-General Abercromby arrived with the Bombay force (about 6,000 strong, consisting of four British and seven native battalions, with a proportion of artillery), and on the 19th he crossed the river and took up a position south-west of the fort with three British and six native battalions.

After several unsuccessful attempts to dislodge the detachments on the island, and a sharp attack on the Bombay troops on the 22nd February, in which the latter sustained casualties to the extent of 104 killed and wounded, Tippoo expressed a desire to treat. Hostilities ceased on the 24th of February, and peace was concluded on the 18th of March. By this treaty the Company acquired a great accession of territory, while large portions were ceded to the Nizam and Mahrattas: an indemnity of three *crores* and thirty *lakhs* was paid by Tippoo, and a grant from this, added to the prize-money of the campaign, together with a gratuity from the Court of Directors, produced a substantial sum for all ranks. The following were the amounts received by the native ranks:—*Subadar* £27 12s., *Jemadar* £13 16s., *Havildar* £11 16s. 2d., other ranks £5 18s. 1d.

The army marched from Seringapatam on the 26th March, and in July the Bengal detachment under Lieutenant-Colonel Cockerell encamped at Nellore. It marched for its own presidency about the end of September, having received the thanks of the Madras Government for its services. Its orderly conduct on the march through the Northern Circars was brought to the special notice of the Governor-General, by whom the men were thanked on their arrival at Calcutta. (G. O. C. C, 3rd January, 1793). Honorary standards were granted to each battalion,

---

11. These figures are taken from Lord Cornwallis' despatch, published in the *London Gazette* of the 2nd July 1792. They differ somewhat from the figures given by Dirom and other writers.

and medals conferred on the native portion of the troops who had served in Mysore, and in 1829 the service was further commemorated by the grant of permission to the surviving corps to inscribe "Mysore" on their colours. The men of the two volunteer battalions returned to their respective regiments.

The close of the war was marked by the reduction of the strength of Bengal infantry battalions to the peace establishment of eight companies of 68 men each. The 1st Regiment of Native Cavalry had previously (G. O. C. C, 13th January, 1792) been reduced to its former strength of three troops.

Early in 1793, at the request of the reigning Rajah, a detachment, consisting of fifteen companies of infantry, amongst which were the 16th Battalion and a detachment of the 27th, was despatched under Captain Thomas Welsh to Assam, where it was engaged in the suppression of disturbances raised by a powerful body of rebels, who had all but overturned the Rajah's authority and had actually captured his capital, Gauhati. The rebels were routed and Gauhati recovered without difficulty, but the disturbances did not cease until the following year, and in a skirmish with some of the insurgents, in April, 1794, Lieutenant W. Cresswell, of the 27th Battalion, was killed. The troops were withdrawn from Assam in July, 1794, and the country soon relapsed into a state of anarchy.

Early in 1794, a threatened incursion by the Burmese from Arakan, into the British province of Chittagong, necessitated the assembly of a small force to protect the frontier. The 3rd European Battalion, the 34th Native Battalion, and a detachment of artillery, the whole under the command of Lieutenant-Colonel Erskine, were on the frontier for sometime, but no hostilities took place, and the troops were withdrawn in June. This was the first occasion on which we came into contact with Burma.

Sir Robert Abercromby succeeded Lord Cornwallis as Commander-in-Chief in October, 1793, and during his tour of inspection in the following year disturbances broke out in the State of Rampur, in Rohilkhand, caused by disputes regarding the succession. The commander-in-chief took the field in person at the head of an army composed of two weak regiments of cavalry, a proportion of artillery, the 2nd European Battalion, and ten battalions of sepoys, the 1st, 6th, 10th, 12th, 13th, 14th, 18th, 20th. 21st and 32nd. The infantry was divided into two brigades and a reserve, commanded, respectively, by Lieutenant-Colonel C. Ware, Lieutenant-Colonel J. MacGowan, and

Colonel G. Burrington. Marching towards Rampur, Sir Robert met the Rohilla chiefs on the 26th of October at the village of Bitaurah, nine miles to the north-west of Bareilly.[12] The enemy were strongly posted and concealed by jungle in front and on both flanks, and as they occupied a very extended front, the reserve was brought up to prolong our line to the right, the cavalry being also brought into line on the right of the whole. The enemy advanced to the attack, and our troops were fast closing with them, when, owing to some misapprehension of orders, the cavalry made a faulty movement, got into disorder, and exposed themselves to be charged in flank by the Rohilla Horse; completely routed, the two regiments fled in confusion, breaking through and disordering the 13th Battalion in their flight. The enemy's infantry followed up the charge of their cavalry, and in the hand-to-hand conflict that ensued, the right of the British line suffered most severely, every officer in the 13th being killed or wounded; however, the centre and left stood firm, and eventually the Rohillas were repulsed and put to flight. The loss sustained by the British Army on this occasion was very severe, being 352 killed (including thirteen officers), 282 wounded (including thirteen officers, one mortally), and six missing, making a total of 640. The officers killed were Colonel Burrington, commanding the Reserve; Captain Mordaunt, Lieutenant Baker and Lieutenant-Fireworker Tilfer, of the Artillery; Captain Mawbey and Lieutenant Birch, of the 2nd European Battalion; Captain Macleod, Lieutenants Hincksman, Odell, Plumer and Richardson, of the 13th Battalion; and Major Bolton and Lieutenant Cumming, of the 18th Battalion. Lieutenant Wells, Brigade-Major, died of his wounds. After the battle the Rohillas retired towards the hills, whither Sir Robert Abercromby followed them, and eventually prevailed on them to lay down their arms.

A court of inquiry was afterwards held to investigate the conduct of the cavalry, and from the evidence recorded, Sir Robert Abercromby arrived at the conclusion that the two regiments had not been guilty of any misconduct. The trial of the officer who commanded the cavalry on this occasion (Captain Richard Ramsay) was ordered in January, 1795, but he absconded rather than stand the ordeal.[13]

---

12. It is generally supposed that the battle of Bitaurah and the battle of St. George (mentioned earlier in chapter) were fought on the same or nearly the same ground. This, however, is an error. The two battle fields are thirty-two miles apart, one lying to the south-east and the other to the north-west of the city of Bareilly.

13. Captain Ramsay afterwards entered the French service, and served under Napoleon as a commissariat officer.

In 1795, to provide for the requirements of provincial garrison work, orders were given (Minutes of Council, 10th July, 1795) for the raising of two new corps. Of these, the first was the Marine Battalion, which was formed by Captain R. Hamilton for duty at Bencoolen in Sumatra, Penang, and the Andaman Islands; it consisted of twelve companies of 100 privates each, and was officered by a captain and eight subalterns. The second new corps was the Ramgarh Provincial Battalion, raised by Captain Richard Macan for duty on the Ramgarh frontier, and intended to replace the old Ramgarh Light Infantry, which had been brought into the line in 1786: it was formed on the same establishment as the regular battalions.

At the same time (Minutes of Council, 10th July, 1795) a corps of militia was raised at the Presidency for local guard and detachment duties. It was placed under the orders of the Town Major, and consisted at first of eight companies of 90 men; later it was increased to sixteen companies of 100 men each, and was found most useful in relieving the regular troops of garrison duties in time of war. This corps was brought into the line in 1861, and is now the 18th Bengal Infantry.

A few months later an unfortunate affair occurred which resulted in the disbandment of the 15th Battalion, a corps raised nearly thirty years before by Sir Robert Barker, and which had served with credit against the Mahrattas under Lieutenant-Colonel Camac. At the end of 1795 the Government contemplated sending a detachment to Malacca, and called for volunteers for that service; the 15th (then stationed at Midnapore) immediately requested that they might be sent, and were consequently complimented by Government for their zeal. At the last moment, however, apparently repenting of their determination, they refused to go, and broke into open mutiny in their lines. The 29th Battalion, then at the same station, was sent with its field pieces to restore order, and, after first being fired on by the mutineers, dispersed them with a few shots. For this serious offence the battalion was ordered (Minutes of Council, 26th October, 1795) to be disbanded with ignominy and its colours burned; while Captain Ludovic Grant, the commanding officer, to whom no blame was imputed, was directed to raise a new corps immediately, which was numbered the 37th.

Towards the end of 1795, in consequence of disturbances in the Nizam's dominions, a detachment of four battalions (the 4th, 11th, 31st and 34th) was placed under orders, under the command of Lieutenant-Colonel Erskine, for service in the Northern Circars, but was countermanded early in 1796, after some of the troops had reached Midnapore on their way to the southward. The 9th and 34th Battalions were afterwards for some months on service at Tomar.

On the 2nd of June, 1796, a G. O. C. C. was issued publishing Minutes of Council, dated the 30th May, 1796, which introduced a complete re-organisation of the Bengal Army, by which one-third of the battalions of native infantry disappeared entirely, while another third lost their independent existence and became second battalions of the remainder. The establishment was fixed, by this order, as follows:

European artillery	3 battalions of 5 companies each
European infantry	3 regiments of 10 companies each
Regular Native cavalry	4 regiments of 6 troops each
Native infantry	12 regiments of 2 battalions each

Although the establishment of cavalry ordered was four regiments, yet as the two existing regiments, which were to be converted from irregular to regular corps, were at present of only half the requisite strength, it was directed that these should first be raised to six troops, and that the two new regiments should not be formed until further orders. Eventually the 3rd Regiment was raised at Dinapore under the direction of Lieutenant-Colonel S. Black (G. O. C. C, 3rd November, 1796), and the 4th at Moneah by Captain J. P. Pigot (Minutes of Council, 20th February, 1797; G.O.C.C, 15th March, 1797). The whole four regiments, when completed, were commanded by a Colonel Commandant; each regiment was commanded by a field officer and consisted of:

2 Captains	Staff
1 Captain-Lieutenant	1 Adjutant
6 Lieutenants	1 Quarter-master
3 Cornets	1 Pay-master
2 Sergeants	1 Surgeon's Mate
6 *Subadars*	1 Sergeant Major
6 *Jemadars*	1 Quarter-master Sergeant
18 *Havildars*	1 Drill *Havildar*
18 *Naiks*	1 Drill *Naik*
6 Trumpeters	1 Trumpet Major
420 Troopers	1 Native Doctor

On the completion of the cavalry brigade the command of the

whole was given to Major-General E. Rawstorne, and then for the first time the native cavalry was separated from the infantry and declared a distinct service, its officers being promoted on a general cavalry list,— (Minutes of Council, 29th May, 1797; G.O.C.C. and June, 1797)

As regards the native infantry, the following table will show how the thirty-six battalions were disposed of in forming twelve double battalion regiments according to the new organisation:

Regiment.	Battalion.	Formed from the					
1st Regiment	1st .	1st Battn.	and the	Right Wing of the	32nd Battn.		
	2nd .	13th ,,	,,	Left ,, ,,	,,	,,	
2nd ,,	1st .	2nd ,,	,,	Right ,, ,,	28th	,,	
	2nd .	25th ,,	,,	Left ,, ,,	,,	,,	
3rd ,,	1st .	3rd ,,	,,	Right ,, ,,	27th	,,	
	2nd .	22nd ,,	,,	Left ,, ,,	,,	,,	
4th ,,	1st .	4th ,,	,,	Right ,, ,,	37th	,,	
	2nd .	31st ,,	,,	Left ,, ,,	,,	,,	
5th ,,	1st .	5th ,,	,,	Right ,, ,,	35th	,,	
	2nd .	23rd ,,	,,	Left ,, ,,	,,	,,	
6th ,,	1st .	6th ,,	,,	Right ,, ,,	36th	,,	
	2nd .	20th ,,	,,	Left ,, ,,	,,	,,	
7th ,,	1st .	7th ,,	,,	Right ,, ,,	24th	,,	
	2nd .	16th ,,	,,	Left ,, ,,	,,	,,	
8th ,,	1st .	8th ,,	,,	Right ,, ,,	33rd	,,	
	2nd .	30th ,,	,,	Left ,, ,,	,,	,,	
9th ,,	1st .	9th ,,	,,	Right ,, ,,	34th	,,	
	2nd .	29th ,,	,,	Left ,, ,,	,,	,,	
10th ,,	1st .	10th ,,	,,	Right ,, ,,	18th	,,	
	2nd .	14th ,,	,,	Left ,, ,,	,,	,,	
11th ,,	1st .	11th ,,	,,	Right ,, ,,	26th	,,	
	2nd .	19th ,,	,,	Left ,, ,,	,,	,,	
12th ,,	1st .	12th ,,	,,	Right ,, ,,	21st	,,	
	2nd .	17th ,,	,,	Left ,, ,,	,,	,,	

In carrying out these arrangements, the authorities appear to have been guided in some degree by considerations of convenience, retaining or breaking up battalions according to the accidents of their position or stations at the moment. Thus it happened that several fine old corps were broken up and ceased to exist as distinct bodies; and this was especially to be deplored in the cases of such battalions as the 18th, *Morgan-ki-paltan* a corps which had long been one of the most distinguished in the service, the 24th, whose splendid conduct at Cuddalore had conferred lasting honour on the Bengal Native infantry, and the 26th and 28th, which had rendered distinguished service in the last campaign in Mysore. By a strange coincidence, too, the oldest battalion in the Bengal Army, the old "Lal Paltan" (*Gillis-ki-Paltan*), raised by Clive in 1757, became, by this organisation, the 2nd Battalion of the 12th, the junior battalion of the line. Each of the new regiments was of the following strength:

1	Colonel Commandant
2	Lieutenant-Colonels
2	Majors
7	Captains
1	Captain-Lieutenant
22	Lieutenants
10	Ensigns
2	Sergeants
20	*Subadars*
20	*Jemadars*
100	*Havildars*
100	*Naiks*
40	Drummers and Fifers
1,600	Sepoys

Staff

1	Adjutant and Quartermaster (for the Regiment)
2	Adjutants (one for each battalion)
1	Paymaster
1	Sergeant Major
1	Quartermaster Sergeant
1	Drum Major
1	Fife Major
2	Drill *Havildars*
2	Drill *Naiks*
1	Surgeon
1	Surgeon's Mate
2	Native Doctors

The above were sub-divided into two battalions, each consisting of two grenadier and eight battalion companies.

Promotions of British officers were made regimentally up to, and including, the rank of Major. The office of Native Adjutant was abolished. The promotions in native ranks were ordered to be published in Regimental Orders, recommendations for non-commissioned ranks being sent to the commandant by officers commanding companies; those for commissioned ranks by officers commanding battalions. The payment of the men was entrusted to company commanders, and monthly muster-rolls, pay-abstracts, and acquittance rolls were introduced for the first time. The enlistment of recruits (Minutes of Council, 8th August, 1796) was vested in commanding officers of battalions, subject to the approval of the commandant of the regiment; the standard of height for infantry was fixed as over 5' 6", and that of age between sixteen and thirty years, and, as far as possible, only natives of the Company's provinces were to be entertained. The term of enlistment was three years, after which period soldiers could claim their discharge on two months' notice, except in time of war. Recruits were ordered to be sworn in after hearing certain of the articles of war, and an order was about the same time issued (G. O. C. C, 2nd June, 1796) that the articles should be read monthly on regimental parades: a revised translation of the same was prepared for that purpose. By G. O. C. G., 10th June, 1796, the dress of British officers and non-commissioned officers was ordered to be jackets, with round black hats, and the facings of the twelve regiments of the line were also laid down,—those of the 1st, 3rd, 5th and 6th to be yellow, of the 2nd, 7th, 8th and 9th white, and of the 4th, 10th, 11th and 12th buff.

These important changes form a notable epoch in the interior history of the Bengal Army. The preceding forty years had seen the rise of the force from a small handful of men employed in emergency as a tentative measure to a large, well-equipped, and well-disciplined army, constituting the greater portion of the British strength in Bengal. But the history of those years is only indirectly the history of the present Bengal Army; only three of the corps which existed in 1796 (the 1st and 18th Bengal Infantry and the Body-Guard) survive to the present time. With the struggles for existence of the old powers of India which opened with the new century commences also another chapter of Bengal Military History, and one in which the army of today is more directly concerned.

Bengal Sepoy, about 1815.

Irregular Cavalry circa 1815–1820

Skinner's Horse circa 1805–1830

A PRIEST BLESSING THE COLOURS, CIRCA 1845

CHAPTER 3

The Mahratta War

The closing years of the eighteenth century were peaceful ones in Bengal, but the rapidly increasing influence of the British in the North-West, and the responsibilities which it involved, together with indications that yet another struggle was at hand in Southern India, soon afforded proof that the strength of the army, as fixed by the re-organization arrangements of 1796, was insufficient, and that further additions must be made.

Early in 1797 a detachment, consisting of the 3rd Company of the 1st Battalion of Artillery and the 4th and 10th Regiments of Native infantry (each augmented to a strength of 1,800 privates), the whole under the command of Major-General Erskine, was despatched to the southward to relieve the Madras troops in Ganjam and at Hyderabad, which were urgently required elsewhere. The 10th Regiment and the artillery, under Major Hyndman, proceeded to Hyderabad while Major-General Erskine with the 4th marched to Chicacole whence this regiment was re-called to Bengal early in the following year. The detachment at Hyderabad, having been joined in October 1798 by a force of 4,350 men from the Madras Army, under Colonel George Roberts, shared, on the 22nd of the month, in the important service of disarming and reducing a force of about 14,000 men (officered and disciplined by Frenchmen) which had been formed for the Nizam's service by the well-known M. Raymond, and which would, it was feared, be tampered with by their countrymen in the service of Tippoo Sultan in case of renewed hostilities with the latter. The work of disarming was effected by Colonel Roberts with much judgement and without bloodshed.

About the time that Major-General Erskine's detachment marched for the Madras Presidency, the authorities in Bengal were startled with the intelligence that Shah Zaman of Kabul had entered the Punjab, and that an invasion of our North-Western Provinces was imminent. All native corps were in consequence augmented, and such troops as could be collected immediately took the field under the command of Major-General Charles Morgan. Shah Zaman, however, did not push his advance beyond Lahore, and soon after retired across the Indus, when the British troops returned to their stations. This event and the necessity of providing for the security of our northern frontier led to the addition of two regiments of native infantry to the strength of the Bengal Army in 1797. In G. O. C. C, dated the 14th November, orders for the immediate raising of these corps were issued, the 13th Regiment to be formed at Benares and the 14th at Dinapore and Buxar. In the following year, on Shah Zaman renewing his invasion (when a large force was assembled at Anupshahr, under Major-General Craig, for the protection of the British provinces), further additions were made. In G. O. C. C. 15th September, 1798, was published the Government Order (dated the 31st August, 1798) directing the formation of an additional regiment of Native Infantry to be numbered the 15th. The 1st Battalion was formed at Buxar, and the 2nd at Sasaram. The 2nd Battalion of this corps is, now the 2nd (Queen's Own) Bengal (Light) Infantry. Rather less than three months later orders were issued (Minutes of Council, 12th November, 1798; G. O. C. C, 30th November, and 5th December, 1798) for the formation of two more regiments. Of these, the 16th was raised (1st Battalion) at Jaunpur, and (2nd Battalion) at Baragaon: both these battalions have survived to the present day, and are now the 3rd and 4th Bengal Infantry. The 17th Regiment was raised at Gaya (1st Battalion) and Dinapore (2nd Battalion). The 13th, 14th and 17th were ordered to wear yellow facings, the 15th buff, and the 16th white.[1]

---

1. The native names of these ten battalions were as follow:
1st Battalion 13th,—*Poel-ki-Paltan.*—From Lieutenant-Colonel (afterwards Lieutenant-General) Peregrine Powell, who was appointed to the command in 1799.
2nd Battalion 13th,—*Martdeel-ki-Paltan.*—From Major (afterwards Lieutenant-General) Sir Gabriel Martindell, who was appointed to the corps in November 1798.
1st Battalion 14th,—*Stupper-ki-Paltan.*—From Major (afterwards Lieutenant-General) Hugh Stafford, who was appointed to the regiment on its formation.
2nd Battalion 14th,—*Cullenjun-ki-Paltan.*—From Major (afterwards Major-General) Daniel Conyngham, who was appointed to the regiment on its formation.
1st Battalion 15th,—*Makdoen-ki-Paltan.*—From Colonel (afterwards Lieutenant-General) Sir John Macdonald, who was appointed to the command of the regiment on its formation.
2nd Battalion 15th,—*Broon-ki-Paltan.*—From Major (continued on next page)

Shortly after these additions had been made to the Bengal Army, the Government of India found themselves once more involved in hostilities with the Ruler of Mysore. Since the termination of the war in 1792, Tippoo Sultan's ruling idea had been to avenge his defeat and recover the territory he had lost, and with this object in view he had for some time been engaged in intrigues with the French Government at the Mauritius, hoping with the aid of that nation, who were then at war with England, to regain his position and expel the English from Southern India. These intrigues had early attracted the attention of the Earl of Mornington (afterwards the Marquis Wellesley), who had come out as Governor-General in 1798, and who fully recognized the danger to which they exposed British interests. A peaceful solution of the difficulty failed, owing to the obstinacy and duplicity of Tippoo, and early in 1799 it became necessary to take up arms. On war being declared, the 10th Bengal Infantry and the detachment of Bengal Artillery marched from Hyderabad with the rest of the troops there, and at Ambur, on the 14th of February, joined the force there assembled for the invasion of Mysore under the command of Lieutenant-General George Harris. The army was also joined by three more companies of Bengal Artillery, and by a body of 3,000 Bengal sepoys, volunteers from every regiment of Bengal Native Infantry then existing, except the 10th, who had been formed (Minutes of Council, 29th October, 1798) into three battalions, the command of which, respectively, was conferred upon Captains John Malcolm, James Tetley, and Littellus Burrell; these troops had proceeded to Madras by sea under the command of Major-General Popham, who in the subsequent operations commanded the left wing of the army.

These Bengal troops took an active part in the operations resulting in the conquest of Mysore. The two battalions of the 10th Native Infantry were engaged in the skirmish at Malavelli, 27th March 1799,

---

(afterwards Lieutenant-General) Sir George S. Browne, who was appointed to the battalion in 1798.
1st Battalion 16th,— *Guthrie-ki-Paltan.*-From Major (afterwards Lieutenant-Colonel) John Guthrie, who was appointed to the battalion on its formation, and was mortally wounded before the fort of Thattiah in September, 1803, the first fight in which the battalion was engaged.
2nd Battalion 16th,—*Hilliard-ki-Paltan.*—From Lieutenant-Colonel John Hilliard, who was appointed to the battalion on its formation.
1st Battalion 17th,—*Bradshaw-ki-Paltan.*—From Major (afterwards General) Samuel Bradshaw, who was posted to the battalion on its formation.
2nd Battalion 17th,—*Noke-ki-Paltan.*—From Lieutenant-Colonel (afterwards Colonel) James Noke, who was posted to the battalion in January, 1799.

and had three men wounded. In the siege and capture of Seringapatam all five battalions of Bengal Native infantry were actively employed, and sustained a loss of nineteen men killed, one officer (Lieutenant G. H. Fagan, 3rd Volunteer Battalion) and forty-nine men wounded, and twenty-six men missing. The Bengal artillery had six killed and twenty-two wounded, including Lieutenant-Colonel E. Montagu, who died of his wounds. In the storming of the place on the 4th of May, 1799, the ten flank companies of these battalions formed part of the left column of attack under Lieutenant-Colonel Dunlop, 77th Foot, and sustained a loss of four men killed, ten wounded, and one missing. The native infantry corps were subsequently accorded permission to inscribe the word "Seringapatam" on their colours.

After the fall of Seringapatam, the Bengal detachment was employed under Colonel the Honourable A. Wellesley (afterwards the celebrated Duke of Wellington) in subduing refractory chiefs in the country on the northern frontier of Mysore. The whole returned to Bengal by land at the end of the year, arriving at the Presidency in May, 1800. Here they were complimented by the governor-general, and all ranks received medals and prize money. The three Volunteer Battalions were formed (Minutes of Council, 29th May, 1800, and G. O. C. C, 3rd and 4th June, 1800) into two regiments of the line, which were numbered the 18th and 19th. These corps were ordered to wear yellow facings, and in order that their honourable origin might be lastingly commemorated, they were directed to bear in the upper canton of their regimental colours an embroidered radiant star, encircled by the words "Bengal Volunteers." In the supplement to Williams' *History of the Bengal Native Infantry* it is stated that the 19th wore "a feather in their caps (turbans) as a badge of their honourable origin as Volunteers," and that "the 18th declined the option of doing so likewise."[2]

The same General Orders directed the formation of two addi-

---

2. The native names of these corps were as follow:
1st Battalion 18th,—*Markum-ki-Paltan*..—From Captain (afterwards Major) John Malcolm, who commanded the 1st Volunteer Battalion, from which this corps was formed.
2nd Battalion 18th,—*Burral-ki-Paltan*.— From Captain (afterwards Major-General) Littellus Burrell, who commanded the 3rd Volunteer Battalion, from the right wing of which this corps was formed.
1st Battalion 19th.—*Titteelee-ki-Paltan*.—From Captain (afterwards Colonel) James Tetley, who commanded the 2nd Volunteer Battalion, from which this corps was formed.
2nd Battalion 19th,—*Burral-ki-Paltan*.—From Captain Burrell named above. This corps was formed from the left wing of the 3rd Volunteer Battalion.

tional regiments of cavalry, to be numbered the 5th and 6th. Both were raised at Ghazipur. Lieutenant-Colonel Thomas Wharton was appointed to the command of the 5th, and Lieutenant-Colonel J. P. Pigot, to that of the 6th. These regiments were directed to wear, respectively, buff and orange facings.

In Northern India, during these years, nothing of much importance occurred, with the exception of the advance of Shah Zaman (already mentioned) and the disturbances caused by Wazir Ali, Ex-Nawab of Oudh. This miscreant, after his deposition, had been detained for some time at Benares, at which place, on arrangements being made for his removal to Calcutta, he broke out into open revolt (14th January, 1799), murdered Mr. Cherry, the British Resident, and others, killed Captain Conway, 1-2nd Native Infantry, and made off to Bhutwal, where he was joined by numbers of disaffected persons. Subsequently, finding himself at the head of several thousand men, he made his way into Gorakhpur and the eastern districts of Oudh, and it became necessary to send troops against him. Several skirmishes occurred, and being invariably worsted, his followers soon deserted him. He then took refuge with one of the Mahratta chiefs, who eventually delivered him up, on the condition of his life being spared. He was removed to Calcutta in 1800, and kept in close confinement until his death, which occurred in March, 1817. In February 1801, an expeditionary force was despatched by Lord Wellesley to Egypt to co-operate with the British Army sent there under Sir Ralph Abercromby, for the expulsion of the French. This expedition had originally been organized for the conquest of Java and the Mauritius, but under orders from England it was diverted to Egypt. The event is specially remarkable as being the first instance of Indian troops being employed out of Asia. The force despatched was upwards of 5,000 strong, and included an experimental troop of horse artillery commanded by Captain Clements Brown, a detachment of foot artillery under Captain-Lieutenant William Fleming, and a battalion of native infantry volunteers commanded by Major E. S. Broughton, 2nd European Regiment; the force was commanded by Major-General David Baird. Under the original project, the Bengal detachment sailed from Calcutta in November, 1800, for Trincomalee, in Ceylon, whence, on the direction of the expedition being changed, they proceeded to Bombay, where they joined the main expeditionary force. Many difficulties were met with; two transports were lost in the Red Sea, and others were damaged: eventually, it was found impossible, owing to adverse winds, to proceed up to Suez, as had been intended, and the force landed at Kosseir in detachments at various periods in May and June. From this place a long and toilsome march was performed across the desert to Keneh; thence the force marched down the left bank of the Nile to Girgeh, from which place the men were conveyed down the river in boats to Cairo, arriving there oh the 7th August. On the 28th they again embarked, and, as Walsh records, "aided by the extreme rapidity of the current," reached Rosetta on the 31st. Alexandria, however, the last stronghold of the French in Egypt, had already capitulated; the Indian detachment thus lost the chance of taking a part in the fighting, and could only join the British Army of occupation. During their stay in Egypt the smartness and high state of discipline of the Indian contingent excited general admiration and astonishment. The troops returned to India in July and August, 1802. Medals were given to all ranks employed on the expedition, in recognition of their services and of the hardships they had undergone, although they had seen no actual fighting.

Early in 1801, Lieutenant-General Gerard Lake succeeded Sir Alured Clarke as Commander-in-Chief. He arrived at Fort William and assumed the command on the 13th March.

In this year a small expedition, which included a detachment of the Bengal Marine Battalion, was despatched against Ternate, one of the Dutch Spice Islands. The fort and island surrendered on the 21st of June, after considerable resistance. In the same year both battalions of the 6th Regiment were employed under Lieutenant-Colonel Marley in suppressing disturbances in Gumsur, in the vicinity of Ganjam.

In 1801, a regular system of light infantry training was introduced for the first time in the Bengal Army. This excellent change was due to Major-General the Honourable F. St. John, who caused ten men to be selected from each company of all corps under his command, and trained as light infantry. The men so selected remained on the strength of their several companies, unless required to act separately as light infantry, when they formed an independent company.

In July of the same year orders were issued that two six-pounder field pieces called "galloper guns" were to be attached to each regiment of cavalry. On the formation of a native horse artillery, in 1817, the men who had worked these guns were drafted into that corps.

Six months later (G.O.C.C, 14th February, 1802) all recruiting was stopped, and the strength of battalions of native infantry reduced to

800 privates. On the return of the Egyptian detachment, a still further reduction of ten men per company, *i.e.*, to 700 privates per battalion, was ordered (G.O.C.C. 8th July, 1802).

Some changes were made in 1802 in the dress and equipment of *havildars* of native infantry who were directed (G.O.C.C, 20th September, 1802) to carry pikes and swords in future, instead of muskets. They were also ordered to wear pantaloons and sashes and were assimilated as much as possible to European sergeants, instead of being, as hitherto, included in the rank and file.

In May, 1802, an important change was made in the constitution of the Marine Battalion, which was now (G.G.O., 6th May; G. O. C. C., 20th May, 1802) formed into a regiment of two battalions, each consisting of ten companies of 90 privates. The officers of the lately reduced 2nd European Regiment were appointed *en bloc* to the Marine Regiment, the headquarters of which were fixed at Barrackpore.

About the same period (G.G.O., 21st April; G.O.C.C., 1st May, 1802) it was ordered that the Governor-General's Body-Guard should in future be composed, on a peace establishment, of a detail of men and horses borne in equal proportions on the establishments of the several regiments of native cavalry of the Bengal and Madras Presidencies, and to make room for the Body-Guard men on those establishments, twenty troopers were discharged from each regiment. The strength of the Body-Guard was laid down at four *subadars*, twelve *jemadars*, sixteen *havildars*, sixteen *naiks*, and 240 troopers.

In the same year, 1802, the Bengal cavalry assembled for the first time at a camp-of-exercise; this was held by orders of the commander-in-chief at Kanauj, and all the British and native cavalry, except the 3rd Native Regiment, were ordered to attend there, (G.O.C.C., 30th September, 1802)'. The camp was under Colonel St. Leger, 27th Light Dragoons, and was visited early in 1803 by the commander-in-chief, who subsequently issued an order complimenting the native regiments on their appearance and on the improvement which was observable in their efficiency.

Towards the end of 1802 began what was called the "Mud War," by which term the operations attending the reduction of certain mud forts in the Jumna Doab were long known. Some of the zemindars of this part of the country, which had recently been ceded to the Company by the Nawab-Wazir, reluctant to pay their assessments of revenue, had for some time been in a state of semi-rebellion, and one of them, Rajah Bhagwant Singh, who owned the two mud forts of

Sasni and Bijaigarh, became so defiant that it became necessary to coerce him. Accordingly, on the 12th of December a considerable force, under Lieutenant-Colonel Blair, took up a position before Sasni. This force consisted of four troops of the 3rd Native Cavalry, four battalions of Native Infantry (the 1st of the 2nd, 1st of the 8th, 2nd of the 12th, and 1st of the 15th Regiment), and some artillery. To this the 6th Native Cavalry was shortly after added. After nearly three weeks' siege operations, during which the garrison made two ineffectual sorties, an assault was attempted on the 14th of January, 1803, but owing to the depth of the fort ditch having been inaccurately calculated, and the scaling ladders proving too short, it failed, and the storming party was withdrawn after sustaining a loss of ten killed (including Captain Morrison, 2-12th Native Infantry) and twenty-nine wounded. On the 16th, the 4th Native Cavalry joined the force before Sasni, which was further strengthened a few days later by the arrival of the 27th Light Dragoons, five companies of the 76th Foot, the 2nd Battalion of the 15th Native Infantry, and two companies of the 2-8th Native Infantry; and at the same time Major-General the Honourable F. St. John arrived and took command of the force. On the 31st, the commander-in-chief himself joined the force with the 1st Native Cavalry. On the 8th of February the town adjoining the fort was taken without any loss. Later in the day the garrison made a vigorous effort to recover their position in the town, but were repulsed with heavy loss, and on the night of the 11th they evacuated Sasni and fled. They were, however, overtaken by our cavalry and dispersed, Bhagwant Singh himself barely escaping across the frontier into Mahratta territory. The force next marched against the fort of Bijaigarh, which place was besieged for some days: but when a practicable breach had been made and an assault was about to be attempted (27th February), it was found that the garrison were, as at Sasni attempting to escape: a number were cut off and killed, but all the principal leaders got clear off. In the following month the force proceeded to reduce the fort of Kachaura, belonging to another refractory *zemindar*, and here again the garrison, finding themselves hard-pressed, attempted to cut their way through the investing lines. They were pursued for several miles, and a large number cut up, but not without loss on our side. Major Nairne, 6th Native Cavalry, a very accomplished cavalry officer being among the slain. This brought the operations to a close for the time, but the country continued disaffected, and in the autumn of 1803, after the commencement of the Mahratta War, it was found necessary to send a detachment against Thattiah, a fort belonging to Rajah Chattar Sal, another rebellious *zemindar*. An attack made on the place, on the 30th September, by the 1-16th Native Infantry, under Lieutenant-Colonel Guthrie, was unsuccessful, the battalion losing the Lieutenant-Colonel, three other officers, and ninety-five men killed and wounded. Lieutenant-Colonel Guthrie died of his wounds in the following month. A complete settlement of the ceded territory was not effected until the close of the Mahratta War.

In the summer of 1803, the disturbed nature of our relations with the Mahratta powers and the probability of a general war led to a considerable increase in the strength of the Native Army of Bengal. In G.G.O., 12th July, 1803, orders were issued for the augmentation of regiments of infantry by twenty privates per company, thus bringing battalions up to a strength of 900 privates, and this was followed up (G.G.O., 13th July, 1803) by an order for the addition to the army of another regiment of native infantry of two battalions, to be numbered the 21st, the Marine Regiment being brought into the line and numbered the 20th. The 1st Battalion of the 21st was raised at Fatehgarh by Lieutenant J. Vaughan, 1-2nd Native Infantry, and the 2nd at Cawnpore by Captain J. M. Johnson, 2-15th Native Infantry; the regiment was ordered to wear yellow facings.[3] The 2nd Battalion is now the 5th Bengal (Light) Infantry. In the same month orders were issued (G.O.C.C, 28th July, 1803) for the raising at Cawnpore of a corps of Pioneers, of a strength of three companies of seventy-five men each; the command of which was given to Captain Thomas Wood, of the Engineers.

On the 31st of July, 1803, orders were issued for the raising by Major Frith of a corps of irregular cavalry, to be called the "Hindoostany Independent Regiment." It is probable that in this regiment were embodied several *rissalahs* and bodies of Irregular Horse which had been during the last few years employed by the Government for work on the frontier, and of which the history is in several instances very curi-

---

3. The native names of these battalions were derived thus:
1st Battalion 20th,—*Murriam-ki-Paltan*. From a corruption of the word "Marine,"
2nd Battalion 20th,—*Hamalteen-ki-Paltan*. From Lieutenant-Colonel Robert Hamilton, by whom it was raised.
1st Battalion 21st,—*Doobye-ki-Paltan*. From Major (afterwards Lieutenant-Colonel) Simpson Dubois, who was posted to the battalion on its formation, and served with it for some years.
2nd Battalion 21st,—*Jansin-ki-Paltan*. From Captain (afterwards Colonel) Jeremiah Martin Johnson, who raised the battalion.

ous. Besides the "Kandahar Horse" and the irregular cavalry received from Oudh in 1777, of which the remnants were for the most part included in the new regular corps of 1796, a considerable addition to the strength of this branch had also been made in February of the latter year (G. 0. C. C, 9th February, 1796). In that month the celebrated General de Boigne, who for many years had been the principal leader of Sindhia's army, arrived in British territory on his way to Europe. With him he brought his Body-Guard "a corps of 600 chosen cavaliers, of Persian nationality, superbly armed, equipped, and mounted, and attended by 100 camel-riders and four light field-pieces." This fine; body of men had been offered by de Boigne to Sindhia, who however refused to pay the price demanded, and it was ultimately acquired for the East India Company by Lord Cornwallis, who paid the general the sum of three and a half *lakhs* of rupees, and gave liberal terms of engagement to the men. This corps became afterwards Lieutenant-Colonel Brace's "Independent Regiment of Cavalry," which is mentioned in some accounts of the suppression of the disturbances created by Wazir Ali, and it seems pretty certain that it was now incorporated in the Hindustani Independent Regiment. The latter consisted of ten troops or *rissalahs*, the composition of each being one *risaldar*, two *jemadars*, ten *daffadars*, one trumpeter, and ninety privates. Their uniform was a light blue or grey *angarkha* edged with red, a crimson turban worn in the Moghul fashion, a crimson *kamarband*, white pantaloons, and boots. They were armed with "a good Hindustani cutting sword" and either a carbine, or a lance eight or nine feet long, the proportion of those carrying carbines being ten per troop.

Later in the same year a letter was received from the Court of Directors, dated 20th April, 1803, which was expressed a determination to assimilate the organisation of the regular native cavalry as much as possible to that of the infantry. For this purpose orders were issued that two regiments should constitute a brigade commanded by a colonel; at the same time a considerable addition was made to the strength of the regular regiments, which were now composed as follows:

1	Lieutenant-Colonel	1	Captain-Lieutenant
1	Major	6	Lieutenants
2	Captains	6	Cornets
6	*Subadars*	1	Sergeant-Major
12	*Jemadars*	6	*Pakhalis*
24	*Havildars*	1	Surgeon

24	*Naiks*	1	Riding Master
6	Trumpeters	1	Quartermaster Sergeant
492	Privates	1	Assistant Surgeon
6	Farriers	1	Native Doctor

One *syce* to each horse belonging to a sergeant, native officer, or native non-commissioned officer; one to each three horses of privates; a grass-cutter to every horse.

We now come to a very important epoch in the history of the Bengal Army—the Mahratta War, which began in 1803 and lasted until the end of 1805. The rapid advance of British influence in India had for some years rendered a conflict with the great Mahratta powers inevitable. threatened as they were on all sides, their jealousy of the common foe could only partially allay the ceaseless strife between the five great Mahratta chiefs: these were the Peshwa at Poona, Bhonsla in Berar, Sindhia at Gwalior, Holkar at Indore, and the Gaikwar of Baroda: the first named was the nominal head of the Mahratta nation, but at this moment he was only of importance as forming a centre of attraction for the violence of the feudatory chiefs. At length matters reached a climax in July, 1803; a powerful combination was effected between Sindhia and the Rajah of Berar, with the object of an immediate attack on the territories of the Company and of their ally the Nizam, and war was declared. The British Government, though they had striven hard to preserve peace, had for months been preparing for this contingency, and the dispositions of the various armies had already been made. They were as follows:—in the Deccan and on the western side of India about 25,000 men, with a reserve of 4,000 near Hyderabad; on the Bengal side 5,000 Bengal and Madras troops under Colonel Harcourt were detailed for the conquest of Cuttack, belonging to the Rajah of Berar; 1,300 men were placed at Midnapore, as a support to the troops engaged in the invasion of Cuttack, and 2,000 at Mirzapur for the protection of Benares; another force was assembled under Lieutenant-Colonel Broughton on the south bank of the Son; 3,500 men, under Lieutenant-Colonel Powell, were assembled near Allahabad, for the purpose of occupying Bundelkhand, which had been ceded to the Company under the treaty of Bassein; while the Grand Army, 10,500 strong, under the immediate direction of the Commander-in-Chief, Lieutenant-General Lake, was directed to rendezvous at Sikandra. The total of the British forces was about 50,000 men; those of the Mahrattas were estimated at 250,000, of whom

40,000 were organised and drilled by French officers under M. Perron. The latter was now acting as Sindhia's regent in the district belonging to the Mahratta chief between the Ganges and the Jumna, which included Delhi and Agra, and had personal charge of the old Emperor Shah Alam, who for the last five years had been a prisoner in Sindhia's power. The conquest of the above district and the destruction of the force organised by Perron for its protection was pointed out by the governor-general as the main object of the war in the north, points of lesser importance being the reduction of Bundelkhand and Cuttack.

The Grand Army was ordered to rendezvous at Sikandra in August, and when all the corps composing it had assembled (which was not until some time after the commencement of the campaign) it consisted of seven companies of artillery, the 8th, 27th, and 29th Light Dragoons, the 76th Foot, the 1st, 2nd, 3rd, 4th, and 6th Bengal Native Cavalry, and the following Bengal Native Infantry,—both battalions of the 2nd and 4th, the 2nd Battalion of the 8th, the 2nd Battalion of the 9th, both battalions of the 12th, the 1st Battalion of the 14th, both battalions of the 15th, six companies of the 2nd Battalion of the 16th, and four of the 2nd Battalion of the 17th. The newly formed Corps of Pioneers also accompanied.

General Lake left Cawnpore on the 7th of August, and on the 29th entered Mahratta territory, for the purpose of attacking a large force of the enemy drawn up at Coel, near Aligarh: the latter, however, after a brief cannonade, in which the 3rd Brigade of Cavalry (the 29th Light Dragoons and the 4th Native Cavalry) sustained a loss of one man killed and four wounded, retired without an engagement, and the general turned his attention to the capture of the fort of Aligarh. This was effected by assault on the 4th of September, when one of the gates was blown open with a twelve-pounder, and the place carried by storm after a desperate contest, and in the face of a murderous fire. The British loss, which amounted to fifty-nine killed, (including six officers,—one of whom was Lieutenant John Turton, 1-4th Native Infantry[4]) and 212 wounded (including eleven officers), occurred almost entirely in effecting an entrance into the fort, for once the gate was forced, little opposition was made, and the garrison thought only of escape. The loss of the enemy was enormous—not less than 2,000 being killed.

The Bengal troops engaged in this achievement (which the great Duke of Wellington afterwards declared to be "one of the most ex-

---

4. Among the killed also was *Subadar* Mir Karam Ali, a distinguished old native officer of the 1-4th Native Infantry.

traordinary feats" he had heard of in India) were the 1st and 2nd Battalions of the 4th and four companies of the 2-17th Native Infantry. These corps (the late 7th, 23rd and 35th Native Infantry) were, in recognition of their conduct on this occasion, each granted an honorary colour and an extra *jemadar* to carry it; and they were subsequently (in 1829) authorized to inscribe the word "Aligarh" on their colours.

Meantime, on the 2nd of September, a body of cavalry, part of the army which had retired before General Lake on the 29th of August, attacked a detachment left to garrison Shikohabad, consisting only of five companies of the 1st Battalion, 11th Native Infantry, with one gun, under Lieutenant-Colonel Conyngham. The enemy, though greatly superior in numbers, were repulsed in their first attack, but the British, having expended all their ammunition, were, on a renewal of the contest, on the 4th, obliged to capitulate, having sustained a loss of five officers and sixty-three men killed and wounded.

Before leaving Aligarh, General Lake received a letter from M. Perron, stating that he was dissatisfied with his treatment by Sindhia, and was leaving that Prince's service, and requesting a safe conduct for himself, his family, and goods through the Company's territory; this the general promptly granted. By this defection the command of Sindhia's forces in the Doab devolved upon M. Louis Bourquien.

On the same day that he received Perron's letter, General Lake commenced his march on Delhi, leaving the 1-4th Native Infantry to garrison Aligarh. On the 11th of September, at Surajpur, he heard that the enemy had crossed the Jumna to meet him, and after a march of eighteen miles he found himself (with only 4,500 men) opposed to Bourquien's whole force (19,000 men, with nearly 100 guns), drawn up in order of battle near the village of Patparganj, about eight miles to the south-east of Delhi. The position of the Mahrattas was on a rising ground and only assailable in front, each flank being protected by swamps. Lake advanced with his cavalry to reconnoitre, and when he had made himself sufficiently acquainted with the position of the enemy, which he found to be entrenched he sent orders for the artillery and infantry to move forward and join him; and while these were coming up, he resolved upon the feint of a pretended retreat to draw the enemy from the formidable position he occupied and allure him into the plain. Accordingly, as the infantry approached, the cavalry retired slowly, and the enemy, falling into the trap, left their position and advanced to pursue. As soon as the infantry had completed a junction with the cavalry, the latter opened out from the centre and allowed the infantry to pass through them to the front and, the latter having deployed, the enemy found themselves suddenly confronted by the whole of the British line. A tremendous fire was opened by the Mahrattas, but the British advanced unshaken to within a hundred paces, when they fired one volley and charged. The enemy broke and fled, on which the British infantry, breaking into columns of companies, allowed the cavalry to pass through and complete the victory, pursuing the Mahrattas to the Jumna, where large numbers of them perished in attempting to escape across the river. The loss of the latter was not less than 3,000, and 68 of their guns were captured on the field. The British loss amounted to 109 killed (including six officers,—among whom were Major Middleton, 3rd Native Cavalry, Captain McGregor, Persian Interpreter to the Commander-in-Chief, Lieutenant Hill, 2-12th, and Lieutenant Preston, 2-15th Native Infantry), 368 wounded (including Major-General Ware and ten other officers), and nine missing; total 486.

The Bengal corps engaged on this memorable occasion were the 2nd and 3rd Native Cavalry, and of the infantry both battalions of the 2nd, the 2.4th, the 2-12th, the 1-14th, both battalions of the 15th, and four companies of the 2nd Battalion of the 17th. Honorary standards were granted to all these corps,—the late 2nd and 3rd Light Cavalry, and 1st, 5th, 22nd, 23rd, 28th, 30th, 31st, and 35th Native Infantry, and they were all afterwards (in 1829) authorized to bear the word "Delhi" on their standards and colours. Of all these, only the 2-15th now survives as the 2nd Bengal (Light) Infantry.

In consequence of this defeat, the enemy evacuated the city and fort of Delhi, and on the 14th September, when General Lake crossed the Jumna, the French Commander Bourquien and four other French officers surrendered themselves prisoners. Thus, within a fortnight of his crossing the frontier, Lake had extinguished the French power in Northern India. On the 16th, the commander-in-chief entered Delhi and visited the Emperor, who placed himself under British protection.

Having appointed Lieutenant-Colonel Ochterlony Resident at the Court of the Emperor, and left the 2-4th and four companies of the 2-17th Native Infantry, with a newly raised corps of irregular infantry, to form the garrison of Delhi, Lake marched from that place on the 24th of September, and on the 4th October arrived before Agra. having been joined at Muttra on the 2nd by a strong detachment under the command of Colonel T. P. Vandeleur, consisting of the 8th and 29th Light Dragoons, the 1st and 4th Native Cavalry, and the 2-8th,

2-9th, and 1-12th, and six companies of the 2-16th Native Infantry. The enemy were found to be occupying the town and the ravines near the fort. Simultaneous attacks were made on both these points on the 10th, and were in both places successful, although the loss in the ravines was considerable. The 2nd of the 9th, the 1st of the 12th, and six companies of the 2-16th Native Infantry were engaged in the attack on the town,—the corps employed in the ravines being the 1st of the 14th, and the two battalions of the 15th Native Infantry. The British loss was one officer (Lieutenant Grant, 2-9th Native Infantry) and thirty-four men killed, seven officers (one of whom —Lieutenant Whitaker, 2-9th Native Infantry—died the same day) and 172 men wounded, and fifteen men missing.

An important result of this success was that a large number of the enemy's troops outside of the fort, amounting to 2,500 men, surrendered and marched into the British camp on the 13th of October.

Siege operations were now commenced against the fort, but before a breach could be made, the garrison capitulated, and the place with all its treasure, amounting to twenty-two *lakhs*, fell into the hands of the English on the 17th October.

Leaving the 1-2nd Native Infantry to garrison Agra, Lake marched from that place, on the 27th October, in quest of a large force (fifteen disciplined battalions) which had been detached by Sindhia from the Deccan, with the object of recovering Delhi. Having left his heavy guns and baggage at Fatehpur-Sikri, under the protection of the 2-2nd and 1-14th Native Infantry, the general executed a series of forced marches in pursuit of this force, and on the 31st arrived at Katumba within twenty-five miles of the enemy. Directing his infantry to follow three hours later, he pushed on at midnight with his cavalry, and at seven o'clock on the morning of the 1st of November overtook the Mahrattas (14,000 strong, with 72 guns) in position near the village of Laswari. Believing that they were intent only on retreating, Lake made an immediate attack with his cavalry alone, and after a severe contest, in which Colonel Vandeleur was killed, succeeded in breaking through their line, but he was met by such a heavy fire of artillery that he was forced to discontinue the action until his infantry should have arrived. These did not reach the scene of action until midday, and in the meantime the enemy had taken up a new position, in two lines, in front and rear of the village of Mahalpur, with their artillery disposed along the front, and their cavalry on the right, resting on a small but deep stream called the

Mahnus Nai. With the design of turning their right, Lake, when it was time to resume the action, directed his attack on this point, but the enemy perceived his intention, and immediately threw back the right of both lines, opening a hot fire of artillery on the foremost column, which was the right wing of the British Army, under Major-General Ware, headed by the 76th Foot. Finding that the column was suffering heavily, the General ordered the 76th, supported by the 2-12th and six companies of the 2-16th Native Infantry, to close with the enemy, and, led by Major-General Ware and by the commander-in-chief in person, these troops pressed forward to the attack in the face of a furious fire of canister shot; at a critical moment they were charged by the enemy's cavalry, but repulsed them with their fire, and a counter-charge of the 29th Light Dragoons having pierced both the enemy's lines, the infantry attack was pushed home, and the enemy driven behind the village: here they were charged by the rest of the British cavalry and utterly broken and routed; 7,000 were killed and above 2,000 taken prisoners, and Sindhia's disciplined battalions, styled "the Deccan Invincibles," ceased to exist.

Nor was this all. The whole of the enemy's guns, seventy-two in number, were taken; all their baggage and stores, together with 5,000 stand of arms, fell into the hands of the victors; and Sindhia no longer possessed an army in Hindustan.

On the other hand the loss of the British army in this great battle was not inconsiderable: the number killed amounted to 172, including Major-General Ware, Colonel Vandeleur, Major Griffith, Major Campbell, Deputy Quarter Master General, Cornet Coxwell, 1st Native Cavalry, Lieutenant Lambert, 1-15th Native Infantry, and seven other officers, while 653 (including thirty officers) were wounded.

The native regiments which were engaged on this occasion were the 1st, 2nd, 3rd, 4th, and 6th Native Cavalry, and the 2-8th, 2-9th, 1-12th, 2-12th, 1-15th and 2-15th Native Infantry, and six companies of the 2-16th. The 2-12th and 2-16th were especially thanked by the commander-in-chief for the support they afforded the 76th Foot. In the year 1829, the whole of these corps (then the late 1st, 2nd, 3rd, 4th, and 6th Light Cavalry, and the 1st, 12th, 21st, 24th, 30th, 31st, and 33rd Native Infantry) were authorized to bear the word "Laswari" on their standards and colours. Of these, only the 21st, 31st and 33rd survive to the present time as the 1st, 2nd, and 4th Regiments of Bengal Infantry.

On the 8th November, the army marched from Laswari towards

Agra, and in the neighbourhood of that place and of Bhurtpore it continued for nearly three months. At the end of November, the flank companies of the Bengal European Regiment joined the army in the field.

While these great events were in progress, the forces detailed for service in other parts of the country had also been actively engaged. The detachment assembled at Allahabad under Lieutenant-Colonel Powell (which was composed of two companies of artillery, a squadron of the 5th Native Cavalry, and the 2-11th, 1-13th, 1-18th, and 2-18th Native Infantry) crossed the Jumna and entered Bundelkhand on the 6th of September. This province had, under the Treaty of Bassein, been ceded to the Company by the Peshwa, who had instructed his officers there to surrender it to the British Government. One of these, Rajah Himmat Bahadur, readily complied, and entered into an arrangement with the British Political Agent, but another of them, Rajah Shamsher Bahadur, resisted the mandate, and prepared to hold a portion of the province by force of arms—a circumstance which rendered hostilities inevitable. As soon as Colonel Powell entered Bundelkhand, he was joined by Himmat Bahadur at the head of about 14,000 men. The combined forces crossed the Kân river on the 10th October, and on the 12th engaged Shamsher Bahadur at Kapsa, and easily defeated him. Shamsher now entered into negotiations, but he was not sincere, and in December Powell resumed offensive operations and took Kalpi after a feeble resistance. This and other successes brought Shamsher to his senses, and in January, 1804, he came into Colonel Powell's camp and made his submission.

The Bengal troops employed in reducing the province of Cuttack consisted of a company of artillery and detachments of both battalions of the 20th Native Infantry, which proceeded to Ganjam, and there joined a force consisting of the flank companies of the 22nd Foot, and some Madras troops, the whole under the command of Lieutenant-Colonel G. W. R. Harcourt, 12th Foot. At the same time the 2-7th Native Infantry, a battalion of Sepoy Volunteers, and a troop of the Body-Guard proceeded to Jellasore and Balasore, to cooperate with Colonel Harcourt's force. The latter marched from Ganjam on the 8th of September and seized Manikpatam; skirmishes afterwards took place at Ahmadpur and Birpur-Shatam-pur, but the advance on the town of Cuttack was delayed by the rains; that place was, however, reached on October the 10th, and surrendered without resistance. The adjoining fort of Barabati was a place of considerable strength: it was, however, ill-defended, and was carried by assault on the morning of October the 14th, with a loss on our side of five killed and twenty-nine wounded; its fall delivered the whole of the province of Cuttack into the hands of the English.

To the south-west of Delhi the 1-8th Native Infantry and two battalions, formed from the corps lately in Sindhia's service, were employed, under Lieutenant-Colonel George Ball, in reducing the forts of Narnaul, Kanund, etc., and establishing the authority of the British in that part of the country.

The Ramgarh Battalion was employed on the frontier toward Nagpur and took possession of Sambalpur. Lieutenant-Colonel W. Burn, with the 2nd of the 14th and some auxiliary troops, was engaged at the head of the Doab about the Karnal district.

In November, the 2-6th and two companies of the 2-13th were employed in the reduction of the fort of Chaukandi, in the Baghelkhand district, south of the Jumna, which was evacuated by the enemy after the failure of an assault in which the 2-6th lost nearly 100 men killed and wounded, including Captain Graham, who fell in the breach pierced by no less than nine bullets.

At this point it is necessary to notice that the strain of the war had rendered it necessary to make further additions to the strength of the army. Accordingly orders were issued (G. G. O., 30th September, 1803; G. O. C. C, 4th and 9th November, 1803) to raise two more regiments of Native Infantry, to be numbered the 22nd and the 23rd.[5] The former was raised at Fatehgarh by Captain John Malcolm and Lieutenant William Ball, and the latter at Cawnpore by Captains H. Cheape and William Scott; and both regiments were directed to wear yellow facings. The 1st Battalion of the 22nd still survives as the 6th Bengal (Light) Infantry.

In December, Lieutenant-Colonel Henry White, of the 2-16th, was despatched from the main army, with the detachment of his own battalion, and the 1st of the 14th, to receive possession of the fortress of Gwalior, which Ambaji Inglia, Sindhia's representative in that part of the country, had agreed to surrender. The *kiladar*, however, refused to give up the place, and Lake immediately reinforced Colonel White

---

5. The native names of these corps were derived thus:
1st and 2nd Battalions 22nd Regiment,—*Kyne-ki-Paltan*. From Colonel Francis Kyan, who commanded them both at different times.
1st and 2nd Battalions 23rd Regiment,—*Murreeroo-ki-Paltan*. A corruption of the name of Captain (afterwards Lieutenant-Colonel) John Munro, who served with both battalions.

with the flank companies of the Bengal European Regiment, the 2-9th Native Infantry, and a proportion of artillery, in view to enforcing the surrender of the place. Later on Colonel White was joined by the 2-11th and 2-18th Native Infantry from Bundelkhand. The siege of Gwalior was commenced in January, 1804, and the place surrendered on the 4th of February.

These successes, combined with those obtained in the Deccan by Major-General the Honourable A, Wellesley and in Guzerat by Colonel Woodington, broke up the Mahratta Confederacy, and compelled both Sindhia and the Rajah of Berar to sue for peace. Treaties with both were concluded early in 1804, but this was scarcely accomplished when the undisguised hostility of Jaswant Rao Holkar, the Mahratta Rajah of Indore, and the invasion by him of Rajputana, which he knew to be now under the protection of the British Government, provoked a renewal of the war.

To watch the movements of Holkar and to protect the territory of the Rajah of Jeypore, which was threatened by that Chief, Lake, on the 9th February, marched from Biana (where he had been encamped since the end of December, 1803), and after various halts reached Dausa on the 17th April. In the interval he had been joined by the flank companies of the 22nd Foot and by the troops that he had sent against Gwalior. From Dausa, on the 18th he detached Lieutenant-Colonel the Honourable William Monson, 76th Foot, with the 2-2nd, 1-12th, and 2-12th Native Infantry, to protect the city of Jeypore. Continuing his movements with the main army, the commander-in-chief reached Narwai on the 8th May, and thence sent Lieutenant-Colonel Don, with the 3rd Native Cavalry, the 2-8th and 2-21st Native Infantry, and a proportion of artillery, against Rampura, a town belonging to Holkar, situated about sixty miles south of Jeypore. This place was taken by storm on the 15th May after a smart resistance, and the season being now too far advanced for further operations and the troops suffering severely from the intense heat of the weather, Lake withdrew his army to Agra and Cawnpore, leaving Don with his two battalions and a company of artillery to occupy Rampura, and Monson reinforced by two corps of Irregular Horse under the command, respectively, of Lieutenant Lucan[6] and a chief named Bapuji Sindhia) to guard the Jeypore frontier and watch the proceedings of Holkar.

---

6. James Lloyd Lucan had been in the service of one of the Mahratta chiefs, but had resigned at the commencement of the war. Lake had gazetted him a Lieutenant in the 74th (.Highland) Regiment.

On the advance of Monson to Jeypore, Holkar had immediately fallen back, and on the capture of Rampura, he hastily crossed the Chambal and retreated to a considerable distance, followed by Monson, who, towards the end of May 1804, was encamped at Kotah, at which place he was joined, in June, by Lieutenant-Colonel Don's detachment from Rampura.

Leaving Monson in this situation for the present, it is necessary here to refer to the progress of affairs in Bundelkhand, where Lieutenant-Colonel Fawcett now commanded, Colonel Powell having left on account of severe illness, which shortly afterwards proved fatal. In May 1804, the province was invaded by Amir Khan, a soldier of fortune, at that time in the service of Holkar, who succeeded in cutting off and destroying a party of fifty artillery and two companies of the 1-18th Native Infantry then engaged in besieging the fort of Bela, near Kunch, who had unwisely been left without support. In consequence of this affair, and the general want of capacity exhibited by him, Colonel Fawcett was removed from the command in Bundelkhand, and Lieutenant-Colonel Martindell appointed in his place. This officer soon drove Amir Khan and his Pindaris out of the province; on the 2nd of July (with two squadrons of the 5th Native Cavalry, the 1-13th, 1-18th, and 2-18th Native Infantry, and two so-called "brigades" of irregular auxiliaries,) he totally defeated Rajah Ram Singh, a Bundela chief, and dispersed his forces, though not without loss, the regular troops having seven killed and nineteen wounded, while there were 121 casualties amongst the auxiliaries; and on the 28th of the same month he took Jaitpur by storm after a severe conflict. Bundelkhand, however, continued in a very disturbed state for some time.

Towards the end of June, Colonel Monson moved forward from Kotah; passing through the Mokandra Pass he arrived at Sunara on the 1st July, and on the following day a detachment under the command of Major Sinclair, consisting of the 2-2nd Native Infantry and some artillery, took the fort of Hinglasgarh by escalade.

On the 7th of July Colonel (now Brigadier-General) Monson received intelligence that Holkar, who for some time past had been encamped in Malwa, had re-crossed the Chambal river, and was advancing towards him with his whole army: at the same time he received accounts from Colonel Murray, who commanded a force advancing from Guzerat to Ujjain to cooperate with him, of his intention to fall back on the Mahi river. These circumstances placed Monson in a very critical position, for he now, in the middle of the rainy season, and in a country flooded to an extent that rendered all movements difficult and precarious, and while he was greatly straitened for supplies, found himself alone with a small army in the face of a vastly superior hostile force. He therefore determined to fall back on the Mokandra Pass, and commenced his retirement on the 8th of July, leaving his two corps of irregular cavalry behind as a rear-guard; but during the very first day's march these were attacked and defeated by Holkar's cavalry, and Lieutenant Lucan taken prisoner. The detachment continued its march to the Mokandra Pass, near the entrance to which some desultory fighting took place on the 10th. Monson, apprehensive lest the enemy should get into his rear, now determined to continue his retreat to Kotah, but when he reached that place on the 12th in torrents of rain, the Rajah refused to admit the troops or to furnish supplies. The march had therefore to be continued through a country flooded by the continuous downpour, in which the streams were unfordable, and food could only be procured with the greatest difficulty. On the 16th the guns had to be spiked and abandoned, having sunk so deep in the mud as to be inextricable. At length, after a march of great difficulty and suffering, which was increased by the harassing attacks of the Mahratta Horse and of the hill people and banditti of the country, the detachment arrived at Rampura on the 27th of July. Here Monson was joined by a detachment, under the command of Lieutenant-Colonel M'Culloch, consisting of the 2-9th and the 1-14th Native Infantry, a body of Irregular Horse under Major Frith, and six guns, together with a small supply of grain which had been despatched from Agra by the Commander-in-Chief as soon as he heard of the distressed situation of the force. As the country, however, was destitute of provisions, and Holkar was advancing in considerable force, it was decided to leave the 2-8th Native Infantry and four companies of the 2-21st, with a proportion of artillery, the whole under the command of Captain Hutchinson, Bengal Artillery, to garrison Rampura, and with the rest of the force to push on at least to Khushalgarh, from the Rajah of which place Monson expected to receive assistance. But the last days of this disastrous retreat proved even more trying than the earlier portion, for the attacks of the enemy became more vigorous and incessant, and food became daily more scarce. On the 22nd August, the detachment reached the Banas river, but the river had risen so much that it was found impossible to cross it immediately. On the 24th it became fordable, and the passage was effected in the midst of incessant attacks from the enemy, which occasioned heavy loss to the detachment—no less than twelve officers being killed, and the 2-2nd Native Infantry, commanded by Major Sinclair, who was himself amongst the slain, being almost annihilated. This battalion (the late 22nd Native Infantry), which Monson himself led in one of its charges, behaved with splendid gallantry in repelling the attacks of the enemy and covering the passage of the remainder of the troops. Monson now found himself under the necessity of abandoning his baggage, and thus lightened he reached Khushalgarh on the 25th, after defeating repeated attacks of Holkar's cavalry. Here, to add to his embarrassments, he found that Holkar's agents had tampered with the fidelity of some of the troops, of whom two companies of the 1-14th and a large portion of Major Frith's Irregular Horse deserted to the enemy. On the 26th he quitted Khushalgarh, and, still followed and incessantly attacked by the Mahratta Horse, pushed on towards Agra. On the 28th the enemy's cavalry made a last attempt to overwhelm the detachment on the plains near Hindaun, but again, as throughout the retreat, their efforts were unavailing against the steady valour of the sepoys, who reserved their fire until their assailants were within a few yards of their bayonets, and repulsed them with heavy loss. That night, however, owing to the extreme darkness, and to flying followers and such of the baggage as still remained getting intermixed with the line, the troops were thrown into a state of confusion from which it was found impossible to recover them, and in this state of disorder the straggling remnants of the ill-fated force reached Agra on the 31st, having marched 350 miles in the constant presence of an overwhelming enemy, in the midst of the greatest difficulties and hardships, through a hostile and almost impassable country, and almost without a halt.

During the march every effort was made by Holkar to shake the fidelity of the sepoys, and the greatest cruelty was shown towards any prisoners who refused to enter his service. Notwithstanding these circumstances, disaffection and desertion were far from being as extensive as might have been expected, and many of those who entered Holkar's service sent word to their officers that they had done so on compulsion, and only awaited an opportunity to escape.[6] Where so much discipline and gallantry was displayed under most trying circumstances, it is not surprising that many noticeable acts of devotion

---

6. So, at least, it was reported at the time, though it is not easily conceivable how these men contrived, under the circumstances in which they were placed, to "send word" to their officers.

should have occurred. Not the least of these was that of a native officer of the 2-2nd Native Infantry at the battle of the Banas, When that gallant corps, after the most heroic exertions in covering the passage of the river, was eventually broken by the overwhelming numbers of the enemy, this officer was seen, with the regimental colour in one hand and defending himself with the other, retiring until he reached the river bank, when he turned and plunged into the stream, and was swept away by the furious current.

As soon as he received intelligence of the disaster which had befallen Monson, Lake took measures to re-assemble his army without delay. He marched from Cawnpore, on the 3rd September, with all the disposable troops at that station, and when joined at Sikandra, at the end of the month, by the troops at Agra and those which had been at Muttra (which place Holkar had advanced to and occupied), he had with him the 8th, 27th and 29th Light Dragoons, the 1st, 2nd, 3rd., 4th and 6th Native Cavalry, the flank companies of the 22nd Foot, the 76th Foot, and the 1-2nd, 1-4th, 1-8th, 1-12th, 2-12th, 1-15th, 2-15th, 1-21st, 2-21st, and 2-22nd Native Infantry, with a proportion of artillery.

At the same time orders were issued for the immediate formation of four additional regiments of Native Infantry of two battalions each, to be numbered the 24th, 25th, 26th and 27th. The 24th and 26th were formed at Cawnpore and the 25th and 27th at Fatehgarh, principally from levies which had previously been organised at those places (G. O. C. C., 24th September and 26th October, 1804). Of these regiments none now exist, though the present 7th Bengal Infantry is considered to be in some sense the representative of the 1-24th, afterwards the 47th, to the Native designation of which it succeeded on its taking the place of that corps in the line in 1829.[7]

---

7. The native designations of these eight battalions are thus derived:
1st Battalion 24th,—*Craum-ki-Paltan*. From Captain P. Crump, 2-9th Native Infantry.
2nd Battalion 24th,—*Muttees-ki-Paltan*. From Lieutenant W. J. Matthews, 1-9th Native Infantry.
1st Battalion 25th,—*Rayle-ki-Paltan*. From Captain H. W. Royle, 1-10th Native Infantry.
2nd Battalion 25th,—*Cristeen-ki-Paltan*. From Captain C. Christie, 2-2nd Native Infantry.
The four officers named above raised the levies from which these battalions were-respectively formed.
1st Battalion 26th,—*Duberne-ki-Paltan*. From Lieutenant-Colonel P. D'Auvergne, who commanded the corps for several years.
2nd Battalion 26th,—*Hindree-ki-Paltan*. From Captain R. Henry, who was appointed to the battalion in 1805, and was for sometime in command of it.
(continued on next page)

On the 1st of October General Lake advanced towards Muttra. Holkar in the meantime had sent off his infantry and guns to attack Delhi, to the possession of which place, and of the person of the Emperor, he attached great importance; he himself remaining back with his cavalry, for the purpose of engaging the attention of the British force and of harassing it in its march, Delhi at this time, where Lieutenant-Colonel Ochterlony still held the position of Resident, was defended by a very inadequate force, but it was commanded by an officer of great energy and experience, Lieutenant-Colonel W. Burn, 2-14th Native Infantry, whom, on the approach of the Mahrattas, Colonel Ochterlony had promptly called in, with his battalion, from Saharanpur. The troops composing the garrison were the 2-4th, the 2-14th, four companies of the 2-17th, and about 1,200 irregular infantry; but the walls of the city were in a ruinous state and unfit to bear a siege, even had it been practicable to defend a place ten miles round for any length of time with rather less than 3,500 men. However, all that was possible for rendering the place secure was done on the receipt of news of Holkar's approach. The enemy's army arrived before the walls on the morning of the 8th of October, and at once began a heavy cannonade. On the next day, it being evident that a breach would soon be completed, a sortie was made by about 350 of the garrison under Lieutenant Rose, the party being made up of two companies of the 2-14th and some irregulars, with one six-pounder gun: so vigorous was their attack that in a few minutes they got possession of the batteries, spiked the guns, and threw the enemy into great confusion. On the 14th, the guns of the enemy opened a general cannonade, under cover of which an assault was made on the Lahore gate; but it was received with so much steadiness that the storming party was repulsed with considerable loss. Disheartened by these failures and hearing that General Lake was approaching, the Mahrattas raised the siege on the night of the 14th, and decamped before the next morning. Colonel Ochterlony, in his report of the siege, says that the "fatigue suffered by both officers and men could be exceeded by nothing but the cheerfulness with which it was endured." The small number of the garrison did not admit of regular reliefs or make it safe for the men to undress; to

---

1st Battalion 27th,—*Castor-ki-Paltan*. From Colonel (afterwards Lieutenant-General) H. DeCastro, who was colonel of the corps for several years.
2nd Battalion 27th.—*Mapert-ki -Paltan*. From Lieutenant-Colonel R. Mabert, who was appointed to the command in 1805.

sustain them therefore in their fatigues, provisions and sweetmeats were issued daily, "which," says Colonel Ochterlony, "had the best effect upon their spirits."

General Lake, harassed all the way from Muttra by Holkar and his cavalry, whom, however, he could not bring to action, arrived at Delhi on the 18th of October. Holkar, having sent off his infantry and guns to Deig (Deeg or Dig), now moved northwards, with his cavalry, into the Doab, which he proceeded to lay waste, and on the 30th of October, at Shamli, he surrounded and attacked Colonel Burn, who, on the commander-in-chief's arrival at Delhi, had marched from that place towards Saharanpur with the 2-14th Native Infantry, a few irregulars, and six guns. This force was hard pressed by Holkar for some days, until the approach of the British Army compelled him to retire. No sooner had Lake received intelligence of Holkar's movements, than he determined on a vigorous pursuit. Leaving Major-General Fraser[7] with all the infantry except the reserve brigade, and two regiments of native cavalry, to look after Holkar's infantry and guns, he crossed the Jumna, near Delhi (31st October) with his three regiments of light dragoons, the 1st, 4th and 6th Native Cavalry, a troop of horse artillery, and the Reserve Brigade (composed of the flank companies of the 22nd Foot and the 1-12th, 2-12th, and 1-21st Native Infantry), and proceeded in search of Holkar.

Proceeding by forced marches, Lake relieved Colonel Burn at Shamli on the 3rd November, and reached Meerut on the 8th. Leaving Colonel Burn here, reinforced by the 1-21st Native Infantry, he resumed the pursuit of Holkar, and proceeded by Hapur, Bulandshahr, Khasganj and Aliganj (where he left his infantry), to Furruckabad, under the walls of which place he found the Furruckabad, Mahrattas encamped on the morning of the 17th of November. The enemy were completely surprised, and had no time to defend themselves, as the British troops dashed into their camp without warning, cut numbers of them to pieces, and pursued the remainder for ten miles. Their loss was enormous—not less than three thousand in killed alone, while ours was only three killed and twenty-five wounded.

Meanwhile General Fraser marched down the right bank of the Battle of Deig, Jumna to near Muttra, and thence to Deig, in the Bhurtpore Rajah's territory, having been joined *en route* by the Bengal European Regiment from Muttra. At Deig he found the enemy encamped in a very strong position, their right resting on a large tank

---

7. Major-General John Henry Fraser, His Majesty's Service.

and covered by a fortified village, their front and left protected by an extensive *jhil*, with a chain of batteries in rear extending up to the walls of the fort. On the morning of the 13th of November, leaving two battalions to protect his camp, General Fraser advanced to the attack, himself leading the first line, which was the 1st (Monson's) Brigade, composed of His Majesty's 76th and the 1-2nd and 1-4th Native Infantry, which, having passed round the tank, carried the village on the enemy's right, and then, running down the hill beyond, charged the first line of guns. In this advance General Fraser's leg was shot off, and Colonel Monson succeeded to the command. The 1st Brigade, having carried the guns, continued to advance, charging the whole succession of batteries for a distance of two miles. Meanwhile the second line, which was the 2nd (Browne's) Brigade, composed of the Bengal European Regiment and the 1-15th and 2-15th Native Infantry moving towards the enemy's left, under cover of some rising ground, kept the infantry and batteries on that side in check until the arrival of reinforcements, when the enemy were obliged to retire in haste and were driven into the morass, where numbers of them perished. At the same time a body of the enemy's cavalry came up and re-took the guns lately seized by the first line and began to work them against the British: they were, however, charged and compelled to retire by Captain Norford, with a party of only twenty-eight men of the 76th Foot, but in the performance of this exploit, that gallant officer was unfortunately killed.

In this action the Mahrattas lost heavily, the killed alone being not less than 2,000: eighty-seven of their guns were captured (including six that had been presented to them by Lord Cornwallis at Seringapatam in 1792, and fourteen that had been lost in Monson's disastrous retreat), and his army was almost entirely dispersed, the shattered remains of it being forced to take shelter in the fortress of Deig.

The British loss was also severe, amounting to 148 killed (including five officers), and 479 wounded (including eighteen officers), and twenty-seven missing,—in all 654. Among the killed were Lieutenant Forbes, 1-2nd, Lieutenants Faithful and Burges, 1-4th, and Assistant-Surgeon Lyons, 2-15th Native Infantry. Lieutenants Hales and Boyd, 2-15th, died of their wounds within a few days after the battle, and Major-General Fraser succumbed to his injuries on the 25th, at Muttra.

Of the Bengal Native regiments present at the battle of Deig (the 2nd and 3rd Light Cavalry, and the 5th, 7th, 9th, 30th, 31st, and 44th

Native Infantry), all of which bore the name on their standards and colours, the 2nd (the Queen's Own) Bengal (Light) Infantry (formerly the 2-15th and the 31st), is the only one which survives.

After the action at Furruckabad General Lake, having continued his pursuit of Holkar, who fled towards Deig, rejoined the force, now under Colonel Monson, at Muttra on the 28th November, to which place it had fallen back after the battle of the 13th. Advancing from that place on the 1st December, Lake took up a position before Deig on the 13th and prosecuted the siege of that fortress with all possible vigour. A practicable breach having been made, the assault was delivered at midnight on the 23rd—24th, the force detailed for this purpose having been divided into three columns. The right and left columns stormed and captured the enemy's trenches and batteries, while the centre column entered the breach: the resistance of the garrison was desperate, but by 2 o'clock in the morning of the 24th the whole fortress, except the citadel, was in our possession: this last post was evacuated by the enemy during the following night. The loss of the British was 43 killed and 184 wounded, two of the former (Captain Young, 1-8th, and Lieutenant Bowyer, 1-12th, Native Infantry) and thirteen of the latter being British officers. The Corps of Pioneers and the 1-8th and 1-12th Native Infantry were prominently engaged in the storming of the fortress.

The shelter afforded to Holkar's troops in the fortress of Deig was sufficient evidence of the treachery towards the English of its master, Ranjit Singh, Rajah of Bhurtpore, who had hitherto been professedly on friendly terms with the British Government. The fall of Deig was a great blow, both to Holkar and the Rajah, but in order to complete the work it seemed necessary to the commander-in-chief that Bhurtpore should also be reduced. The latter was a place of exceptional strength: the town, eight miles in circumference, was thoroughly fortified and fully garrisoned, while the fort at its eastern extremity was deemed impregnable. The army marched from Deig on the 28th December, and, having been joined by Major-General Dowdeswell with the 75th (Highland) Regiment and a supply of stores arrived before Bhurtpore on January 2nd, 1805. Batteries were at once erected and the siege commenced, and after six days the breach was reported practicable; that this information was far from being founded on fact was proved by the disastrous result of the first assault, which (9th January) was, repulsed with a loss of 85 killed (including six officers) and 371 (including twenty-three officers) wounded, being nearly double that experienced at the capture of Deig. Contemporary non-official accounts seem to show that the attack was as ill-conducted as the information which led to it was inaccurate; in fact, the secret of the failure seems to have been overweening and careless confidence, the proof of which is given in the words of an eyewitness, who records the general impression of the army: "that our failure had been merely the effect of accident, and that nothing was required but a fresh breach to enable us to enter the place in triumph." No more precautions were taken to secure the success of the second assault, which took place on the 21st of January; the position of the batteries prevented any accurate view being obtained of the breach or ditch, and to remedy this, the expedient was hit upon of sending three troopers of the 3rd Native Cavalry, in the guise of deserters, who were to gallop towards the ditch, and, having taken a good look at it and the breach, were to return with their report to head-quarters. This plan succeeded so far that the garrison was deceived and allowed the troopers to approach unmolested; but the latter had not the presence of mind to profit by this circumstance, and having taken a hurried glance at the breach and ditch, they galloped back to the camp, where they pronounced the latter fordable and the breach practicable. Acting upon this very inadequate reconnaissance, an assault was ordered for the following day. The storming party advanced to the edge of the ditch under a heavy fire, when they were confronted by a sheet of water beyond the depth of a man and upwards of thirty feet wide: after being kept for nearly an hour exposed to the full violence of the enemy's fire, the column had to retire without attempting the breach, and with a loss of 74 killed and 514 wounded, making a total of 588, including nineteen British officers, of whom three were killed and sixteen wounded.

On the 9th February, Lake was reinforced by a division of the Bombay Army (which included H M.'s 65th and 86th Regiments) under the command of Major-General Richard Jones, and on the 20th and 21st a third and a fourth attempt were made to carry the town, but on each occasion the same want of judgement and the same disregard of necessary precautions were displayed, and the same disastrous results followed. The fact was that the material of which the walls were built, and which led the British officers to despise the place as "a mud fort," was the cause of the failure of their attacks, even when the ditch had been crossed and the breach attempted; the effect of artillery fire was merely to cause the walls to crumble, and not to fall in blocks; what remained was even more precipitous than before, and what fell afforded no foot-hold to the assailing parties.

At the same time it is to be observed that Lake undertook the siege with totally inadequate means, not only as regards the strength of his force generally, but also with respect to siege equipment, and the numbers of artillery men and pioneers at his disposal.

The loss in the third assault amounted to 162 killed (including one officer) and 732 wounded (including twenty-six officers). In the fourth assault we had 125 killed (including six officers) and 862 wounded (including twenty-eight officers). Our total loss before Bhurtpore thus amounted to 446 killed and 2,479 wounded, or 2,925 in all, including sixteen officers killed and ninety-three wounded. Among the former were Lieutenants Gowing and Percival, of the Bengal Artillery, Ensign Waterhouse of the 2-12th, and Lieutenants Hartley and M'Gregor of the 2-15th Native Infantry. Lieutenant Moore and Ensign Chance of the Bengal European Regiment, Lieutenant-Colonel Hammond of the 1-2nd, Lieutenant Kerr of the 1-8th, and Major Radcliffe of the 1-12th Native Infantry, died of their wounds.

Several small engagements took place in the surrounding country during the siege, in one of which near Kombhir, an attack was made by the enemy on a convoy escorted by the 1st Native Cavalry and the 1-15th Native Infantry; the escort was hard pressed and obliged to abandon part of the convoy, but the 27th Light Dragoons and the 2nd Native Cavalry arriving opportunely, the tables were turned, the convoy saved, and a great number of the enemy killed.

Skinner's Horse, afterwards so famous, distinguished themselves in several actions during the progress of the siege. They were despatched with the whole of the British Cavalry force under Major-General Smith[8] against Amir Khan, a Pindari chief, in alliance with Holkar and the Rajah of Bhurtpore, who had collected an army and made an incursion into the Company's territory in the Doab and Rohilkhand. The British force, after a hot pursuit, overtook the enemy at Afzalgarh on the 2nd of March, routed them completely, and annihilated their infantry, sustaining a loss of nine killed and forty-four (including four dragoon officers) wounded.

---

8. Major-General John Smith belonged to His Majesty's Service. He had been for twenty-five years an officer of the 1st Foot Guards, with which corps he had served during the campaign of 1793-94 in the Netherlands, He died at Muttra the 6th August, 1806.

After the failure of the fourth attempt to storm Bhurtpore, the siege was converted into a blockade, and Ranjit Singh, finding himself deprived of any efficacious support from his allies, Holkar and Amir Khan, took the opportunity of endeavouring to come to terms. Meanwhile the cavalry, having returned from the Doab, continued to harass the camp of Holkar, who remained in the neighbourhood of Bhurtpore, and, after inflicting on him one tolerably severe defeat, finally compelled him to retire beyond the Chambal river.

About the same time a force under Captain H. W. Royle, 1-10th Native Infantry, consisting of the 1-25th Native Infantry, six companies of the 2-24th, a battalion of irregular infantry and a body of horse (formerly in the service of Sindhia) commanded by Colonel Pohlman, marched from Agra on the 26th of March, against the remnant of Holkar's infantry under the Rajah Khushal Rao, which, after defeating some hostile cavalry on the 31st, it met on the 7th of April under the fortified town of Adalatnagar. The enemy were defeated with loss and all their baggage and some guns fell into the hands of the British. The casualties on our side were fourteen killed and thirty-seven wounded,—including Lieutenant W. H. Carrington, 1-25th, who lost a leg and afterwards died of his wounds.

The Rajah of Bhurtpore had for some time been negotiating with Lake; though he had thus far been successful in defending his fortress, the active preparations that he had observed to be going on for a renewal of the siege struck him with dismay, and he thought it best to come to an accommodation with his persevering foe. Accordingly, on the 10th of April, the terms of a treaty were agreed on, and on the 21st the camp was broken up and the army marched southwards across the Chambal to watch the movements of Sindhia, who, in consequence of our ill-success at Bhurtpore, was again col-leering his forces and threatening the British frontier. The army was for some time encamped at Jittor, beyond the Chambal, where it was joined by the Bundelkhand detachment under Colonel Martindell. However, no collision with Sindhia occurred, and at the end of May the encampment broke up, Martindell proceeding to Gwalior, and the Bombay Division to Rajputana, while Lake and his army marched to Agra and Muttra.

Some minor operations now claim attention, It has already been related that when Monson was retreating before Holkar he left Captain Hutchinson in Rampura with a small force. This detachment was not molested by Holkar, and remained quietly in Rampura until the cold weather set in, when Captain Hutchinson set to work vigorously to clear the surrounding country, and open the way for the Bombay Division, which was then, under Major-General Jones, on its way to join General Lake. He took Kataoli and Ramangaon, and captured Zamina, Karawal and Dhalra by storm, and by the end of March had in a great measure reduced the surrounding country to order.

During this period Colonel Burn had been actively employed in the districts to the north of Delhi, where the Sikhs were giving much trouble, ravaging the country about Saharanpur, Deoband, and Thanesar, and making incursions even as far as Shamli. He had several skirmishes with parties of these people, and on the 23rd November 1804, after a tolerably severe conflict, in which the British detachment had 124 killed and wounded, he succeeded in defeating them at Deoband and killing their leader, Sher Singh, when they retired beyond the Jumna. They returned again in March 1805, but were again driven off by this energetic officer.

In October, 1804, it became necessary to undertake operations in Cuttack, in consequence of the Rajah of Khurda, a man of considerable local influence, having thrown in his lot with the Mahrattas, and, at their instigation, cut up several small detachments which had been left in his country by Colonel Harcourt. The force employed against the Rajah included a detachment of the Bengal Artillery, and two companies of the 1-5th and four of the 2-7th Bengal Native Infantry. On the 19th October, Captain Hickland, with the two companies of the 1-5th and one six-pounder, met a portion of the Rajah's forces, upwards of a thousand strong, at Dillori, near Khurda, and routed them with great slaughter, Khurda was taken by storm on the 7th December, not without considerable loss on our side. The Rajah took refuge in the jungles, but was captured shortly afterwards, and placed in confinement at Midnapore.

In the spring of 1805, before the termination of the operations directed against Bhurtpore, and when the prospects of peace were at the least precarious, an important addition was made to the strength of the army by order of the governor-general. This was the formation of two additional regiments of regular cavalry, the 7th and 8th, the orders for which were promulgated (G. O. C. C, 5th April 1805) when Lord Lake was still before Bhurtpore. It was directed that these regiments were to be raised forthwith at Ghazipur, the 7th by Captain W. H. D. Knox and Lieutenant James Mockler, and the 8th by Lieutenants R. Pepper and S. Reid, a nucleus being afforded by the existing regiments, and the recruiting for both corps being under the superintendence of Lieutenant-Colonel T. S. Bateman.

In this place it might be mentioned that, since the commencement of the war, large bodies of irregular horse which had served under Perron in Sindhia's armies had, on their volunteering, been taken into the British service, and shared in the later operations. Amongst these were the corps under Lucan which formed part of Monson's detachment, and that under Colonel Pohlman which fought under Captain Royle at Adalatnagar in April 1805. But of all the irregular cavalry employed at this time, none attained such renown as the corps commanded by Captain James Skinner, which originally consisted of eight *rissalahs,* but which was considerably increased during the war. Captain Skinner, who was elected commandant by the men themselves, had been serving Sindhia in Perron's army, where he had already gained considerable distinction, and on joining the British Army he stipulated that he should not be employed against his old master. "Skinner's Horse" was the origin of the present 1st and 3rd Bengal Cavalry.

In the autumn of 1805, Holkar collected a numerous force and marching rapidly to the north entered the Punjab, where he hoped to induce the Sikhs to join him against the English. Lake went promptly in pursuit and chased him to the banks of the Beas, where he finally gave in and entered into a treaty, which brought this long war to an end. In this last expedition Lake had with him the Bengal Horse Artillery, the 8th, 24th (late 27th) and 25th (late 29th) Light Dragoons, the 3rd and 6th Native Cavalry, the 22nd Foot, the Bengal European Regiment, the 1-9th, 1-11th, 2-14th, 2-17th and 1-21st Native Infantry, and Skinner's and Murray's Irregular Cavalry. The army moved back to British territory in January 1806, and was broken up at Delhi in the following month.

The conclusion of peace was immediately followed by extensive reductions and retrenchments. The Body-Guard, which at the beginning of the war had been raised to a strength of 200 men, was again reduced to 100, who were moreover to be borne on the rolls of the several regular regiments. Captain Skinner's corps was entirely reduced, with the exception of his *Khas Rissalah,* which was detailed for police duty in the Delhi district. Companies of regular infantry were reduced to eighty privates each, and all the provincial battalions were disbanded, much to the disgust of the regulars, who found themselves detailed for the local duties for which the former corps had been raised.

Shortly after the return of Lord Lake from the Punjab, affairs at Gohad claimed attention. One of the articles of the treaty with Sindhia was that this fort should be assigned to him, on his providing the Rana of Gohad with an .equivalent elsewhere. The *kiladar,* however, instigated by the Rani, refused to surrender the fort, and it became necessary to coerce him. A force under the command of Lieutenant-Colonel Bowie (2-11th, 2-16th, 2-24th, 1-25th, and 2-25th Native Infantry) was accordingly despatched for this purpose in February 1806, and after a sharp conflict, in which the detachment lost five officers and about 100 men killed and wounded, the place was captured. Lieutenant W. B. Macvitie, 2-11th, and Lieutenant J. Gill, 2-25th, were killed.

In October, 1806, it was found necessary to send a detachment from Cawnpore to reduce Badekh, a small but strong fort belonging to a refractory *zemindar* named Apparbal Singh, and situated beyond the Jumna, about eighteen miles to the north-west of Kalpi. The detachment consisted of part of the 2-8th Native Infantry and two six-pounder guns, and was under the command of Captain Owen of the 2-8th; it reached Badekh on the 21st October, and the guns having failed to effect a breach, an attempt was made the same evening to carry the place by escalade, which, however, proved a failure owing to the ladders not being of sufficient length, and the storming party had to be withdrawn, having sustained a loss of twelve wounded, amongst whom was Lieutenant Payne of the Artillery.[9] On receipt of intelligence of this repulse a reinforcement was sent out consisting of a troop of the 3rd Native Cavalry, two companies of the 17th Foot and two of the 1-16th Native Infantry, with two 12-pounder and two 18-pounder guns. Before, however, this reinforcement could reach Captain Owen's camp, Apparbal Singh surrendered, and the troops returned to Cawnpore.

In January, 1807, a force (the 17th Foot, 2-1st and 1-16th Native Infantry) commanded by Lieutenant-Colonel Hawkins, took the fort of Chamir, near Kunch, in Bundelkhand, by storm, after a desperate resistance which occasioned considerable loss. Lieutenant P. M'Gregor, 17th Foot, and Lieutenant A. M'Queen, 2-1st Native Infantry, fell in the conflict.

---

9. Lieutenant Payne was carried into Cawnpore, where he died of his wound on the 25th October. In Stubbs' *History of the Bengal Artillery* (Vol. 3., p. 538) it is erroneously stated that he received his mortal wound in an attack on a fort in the Aligarh district.
10. Lord Lake was born on the 27th July, 1744, and entered the service on the 9th May, 1758, as an Ensign in the 1st Foot Guards. He served with some distinction in the American War of Independence, and in the Netherlands in 1793.94, and commanded the brigade of Guards in the brilliant action of Lincelles, 18th August. 1793. He was afterwards employed in the suppression of the rebellion of 1798 in Ireland. His career in India is briefly shown in the pre-ceding pages. He did not long survive his return to England. Having caught cold while serving as a member of the Court-Martial on General Whitelocke (of Buenos Ayres notoriety), he died on the 20th February, 1808.

In February, 1807, Lord Lake vacated the appointment of Commander-in-Chief, and returned to England.[10] He was succeeded by Lieutenant-General George Hewett.

On the 13th November, 1807, the force under Lieutenant-Colonel Hawkins, who was commanding in Bundelkhand, was employed in the reduction of the fort of Sehlehuganj, near Kaitah. After some resistance, the enemy were driven out of the place. The British force (which, besides artillery, consisted of the 2-1st, 1-16th, 1-19th, 1-26th, and 2-26th Native Infantry) sustained a loss of two men killed, and Captain-Lieutenant T. Wilson, 2-26th, and nine men wounded.

In the autumn of 1807, a large force was assembled at Aligarh, under the command of Major-General Dickens,[11] to reduce the forts of Komona and Ganauri, the strongholds of a refractory chieftain, named Dhundia Khan. The force consisted of two troops of the 24th Light Dragoons, four troops of the 3rd and five of the 6th Native Cavalry, the Corps of Pioneers, the 17th Foot, the 1-9th 1-13th, 1-23rd, 1-27th and 2-27th Native Infantry, and a battalion formed of the grenadier companies of various other native corps. Komona was invested on October 12th, 1807, and after a siege of three weeks, an assault was attempted on November 18th; the assailants were, however, driven back with great loss, but not before they had inflicted such slaughter on the enemy that the latter evacuated the fort the following night. The British casualties in the assault were 105 killed and 436 wounded, among the former being Lieutenant-Colonel William Duff, of the 1-9th Native Infantry, who commanded a brigade, Captains J. Radcliffe and W. Kirk, 17th Foot, S. Brown, 1-9th Native Infantry, and J. Robertson, 2-21st Native Infantry (Grenadiers), and Lieutenants J. M'Leod, 2-27th Native Infantry, and J. Du Feu (1-23rd), of the Pioneers; Lieutenants G. Rolland, 1-9th, and D. C. Livingstone, of the grenadiers of the 2-21st Native Infantry, died of their wounds. Lieutenant J. H. Jones, of the Engineers, was killed, and Lieutenant T. K. Ramsay (2-11th), of the Pioneers, mortally wounded during the siege.

The force afterwards marched against Ganauri, distant some seventeen miles from Komona; the place was invested on the 23rd November, and surrendered as soon as a breach was effected on the 11th December. No loss was sustained on our side.

In 1807-8, it was found necessary to send detachments against various refractory *zemindars* in Oudh. Akbarpore was taken by storm

---

11. Major-General Richard Mark Dickens (Lieutenant-Colonel of Her Majesty's 34th Foot) died at Muttra on the 29th April, 1808.

in March, 1807, by Major O'Donnell, 2-12th Native Infantry. The forts of Baddri, Samanpur and Gurha were subdued without loss by Lieutenant-Colonel Gregory,1-12th Native Infantry, in April and May, 1808; and Major O'Donnell, 2-12th, took that of Pathar-*serai* by storm after a smart resistance, in October, 1808.

In 1808, a volunteer battalion of sepoys was formed to take part in an expedition, under Captain Weguelin, to the island of Macao, the object of which was to occupy that place in order to prevent its falling into the hands of the French. The Chinese, however, did not at all understand this action, and immediately broke off all connection with the island, thus completely stopping its trade. The troops were therefore withdrawn and returned to India in February, 1809.

In 1808, an important change was introduced into the organisation of the native infantry, *viz.,* the formation of light companies. In a circular dated the 12th April the commander-in-chief directed the organisation of a light company in each battalion, and later on (G. G. O., 29th August, 1808) it was ordered that this company was in future to be considered a fixed part of each battalion, and that each battalion was thereafter to be composed of two grenadier, one light and seven battalion companies. In the following October order's were issued to assemble the several light companies (except those of the 20th Regiment) at certain stations to practise light infantry field movements, and on assembly they were organised into six battalions, which were placed under the command of selected officers. These light battalions were broken up in February, 1809, except the 4th, which, being on field service in Bundelkhand, was not broken up until May, 1811.

In 1808 Ranjit Singh, the Sikh Chief of Lahore, having extended his power over the greater part of the Punjab as well as over some of the hill states, carried his arms across the Sutlej and attacked the Sikh Chiefs under British protection. This led, early in 1809, to the assembly of a force in the vicinity of Ludhiana, for the purpose of preventing further inroads, while a mission, of which Mr. Charles Metcalfe was the head, proceeded to Amritsar to meet Ranjit Singh and endeavour to effect a peaceable settlement with him. The force concentrated on the frontier was under the command of Major-General St. Leger, and was composed, besides artillery, of the following corps:—The 8th and 24th Light Dragoons, the 4th, 5th, 6th and 8th Native Cavalry, the 17th Foot, the 2-10th, 1-23rd and 1-27th Native Infantry, and the 2nd and 3rd Light Infantry Battalions.[12] The negotiations with Ranjit Singh proved successful and a treaty of amity and alliance was entered into, under which it was agreed that the Sikh chief would not commit or suffer any encroachment on the rights or possessions of chiefs on the left bank of the Sutlej,—a treaty to which Ranjit Singh steadfastly adhered until his death thirty years later. The force under the command of General St. Leger was broken up and returned to cantonments in April and May, 1809.

It was during the negotiations at Amritsar that an incident occurred which produced a remarkable effect on the mind of Ranjit Singh. While Mr. Metcalfe was encamped near that place with his escort (two companies of sepoys taken from the 1-23rd and 2-23rd Native Infantry, under the command of Captain Popham) the festival of the Moharram occurred (10th February, 1809), which the Mahomedan sepoys of the detachment celebrated in the usual way according to their annual custom. The sight of the *taziahs,* however, inflamed the Akhalis (the most fanatical of the Sikh sects) to madness, and a body of two or three thousand of them assembled and made a furious attack on the escort. Fortunately Mr. Metcalfe and Captain Popham had had some warning, and when the Akhalis approached they found the detachment drawn up in readiness to receive them. After some firing had taken place, Captain Popham, seeing that several of his men had fallen, ordered an advance, a volley, and a charge with the bayonet. The Akhalis stood the volley without flinching, but the sight of the levelled steel was too much for them, and they turned and fled into the city, pursued by the sepoys, leaving thirty of then-number lying killed or wounded on the field. Of the escort, Captain Ferguson, 2-23rd, and sixteen men were wounded. Ranjit Singh appeared on the scene just as the affair ended, and was deeply impressed with the facility with which a couple of hundred British sepoys had discomfited and put to flight several thousands of his fiercest soldiers. He determined thenceforth to adopt European arms and discipline in his army, and thus the insignificant affray at Amritsar may be said to have been the foundation of the disciplined Sikh Army which we met in so many bloody conflicts thirty-six years later.

In January, 1809, it became necessary to send a force against Lachman Dawah, the refractory chief of Ajigarh in Bundelkhand. The detachment employed was under the command of Lieutenant-Colonel Martindell, and consisted (besides artillery) of—

---

12. The light companies of the 2-16th, 2-21st and 1-22nd Native Infantry were included in one or other of these battalions.

3rd Native Cavalry	3 squadrons
2-1st Native Infantry	4 companies
1-3rd Native Infantry	5 companies
1-4th Native Infantry	3 companies
1-18th Native Infantry	
2-26th Native Infantry	5 companies
4th Light Infantry Battalion.[13]	
Pioneers	detachment

The fortified outpost of Rajaoli was stormed on January 22nd, with a loss of twenty-eight men killed, and three officers (one, Lieutenant Jamieson, 1-19th, serving with the Light Battalion, mortally) and 112 men wounded. The detachment, reinforced by three companies of the 53rd Foot, and five of the 1-26th Native Infantry, then advanced against Ajigarh, and having carried the hill of Bahauta, which commands that place, proceeded to bombard the fort, and obliged the garrison to surrender on February 13th.

In the autumn of the same year, the settlement of the province of Hariana, lying to the west of Delhi, which had for years been in a disturbed state, necessitated the employment of military force against the turbulent Jat inhabitants. A strong detachment, under Lieutenant-Colonel George Ball, consisting of the 1st Battalions of the 9th and 22nd and the 2nd Battalions of the 18th and 23rd, with some companies of the 1st of the 10th and 2nd of the 24th, the 6th Bengal Native Cavalry, Skinner's Horse, and a strong artillery train, was accordingly sent thither. It met with no active opposition, except at the town of Bhawani, which was promptly attacked and carried by assault on the 29th of August. The garrison fought with courage, and our loss was not inconsiderable, amounting to one officer (Lieutenant O'Brien, 1-22nd) killed, and six wounded; eighteen men killed and 114 wounded. The loss of the insurgents was more than a thousand.

Later in the year a force, composed of detachments of the 2-4th, 1-9th, 2-16th, and 1-21st, was ordered against the fort of Nanpara, in Oudh, which place was occupied without opposition.

During the winter of 1809-10 the 1-9th Native Infantry, under the command of Lieutenant-Colonel McGrath, was employed in the coercion of some refractory *zemindars* in the Bahraich district,

---

13. The 4th Light Infantry Battalion was composed of the light companies of the 2-1st, 1-7th, 1-12th, 2-12th, 1-16th, 1-19th, 1-26th, and 2-26th Native Infantry.

Oudh. In the assault of the fort of Pragpur, on the 4th January, 1810, the battalion had fifty men shot down, and two of its officers, Lieutenants Woolley and Dixon, were killed. The gallantry of the battalion was specially commended by the Commander-in-Chief (G. O. C. C. 17th January 1810).

Towards the end, of 1809, in consequence of Amir Khan having attacked the Rajah of Berar, whereby many British interests were imperilled, it became necessary to move forces into Malwa. The principal force was sent from the Madras side, but a smaller one, under Colonel Martindell,—composed of the 1st, 5th, and 6th Native Cavalry, the. 53rd Foot, the 1-17th, 1-19th, 1-22nd and 1-26th Native Infantry, and the 4th Light Infantry Battalion, with a proportion of Artillery and Pioneers,—was moved from Bundelkhand to co-operate with the Madras troops, and proceeded (January 1810) to the vicinity of Sironj. Amir Khan withdrew on these movements being made; no collision took place, and in the course of the following months the troops returned to their stations.

About this time it became necessary to undertake operations in Bundelkhand against Gopal Singh. This was an adventurer who had some years before usurped the district of Kotra, but being now dispossessed of it, he took to the hills and jungles with his followers and thence began making irruptions into the various districts of Bundelkhand, carrying fire and sword wherever he appeared. Having defeated the forces of the Rajahs of Panna and Kotra, he grew so bold that it became necessary to send British troops against him. Captain E. P. Wilson, with seven companies of the 1-16th and three of the 1-7th Native Infantry, attacked him at Parari, near Kakarati, on the 18th February, 1810, but though he inflicted heavy loss on the enemy (his own being six killed and forty wounded, including four officers), the general result was indecisive, and Gopal Singh soon after descended the hills and burnt the cantonment of Tirowa. It became necessary, therefore, to adopt more vigorous measures, and reinforcements were quickly sent to the disturbed districts. On the 19th March, Lieutenant-Colonel Brown, with the 1st Native Cavalry and a squadron of the 8th, totally routed Gopal Singh at Bichaund; and soon after Captain Wilson, with his detachment above named, reinforced by a squadron of the 1st Native Cavalry and a company of pioneers, surprised and seized Gopal Singh's fortified camp at Jhargarh. The leader escaped to the jungles, but it was not long before he reappeared, and several other actions were fought. On the 19th November, Captain Watson, with a part of the 1st Native Cavalry, defeated and cut up a large body of his adherents at Bhamori. Soon after he was again defeated by Colonel Brown at Killeri, and on the 26th June and the 7th September, 1811, he sustained two more overthrows at the Dawani Pass and at Chirgaon. However, he continued the struggle until early in 1812, when convinced of the hopelessness of the contest, he proffered his submission and was pardoned by the British Government.

In August 1810, two volunteer battalions of Bengal sepoys were despatched with an expedition against the Isle of France or Mauritius. These volunteers were furnished by the 8th and 25th Regiments, the 1st of the 15th and 2nd of the 12th and 19th. The expeditionary force arrived and disembarked in Grande Baye (near the north-east extremity of the island, about fifteen miles from Port Louis, the capital) on the 29th November, 1810, and advanced on Port Louis at once. The resistance met with was feeble, and after a couple of smart skirmishes on the 30th November and the 1st December, General Decaen, the French Governor, surrendered. It is said that the feebleness of the resistance was due to the refusal of the militia (who constituted about one-third of the force at Decaen's disposal) to fight, and that these gentry, moreover, were very indignant at the employment against them of sepoys, declaring that "to have the black fellows of India sent against them was an indignity which no subject of His Majesty the Emperor and King could endure with any patience." The total loss amounted to 29 killed, 99 wounded, and 45 missing, of which the share of the two volunteer battalions was one native officer and 32 men missing.[14] A gold medal was bestowed on all commissioned officers, and a silver one on the men who served in this expedition.

In December 1810, in view of an expedition for the redaction of Java, five more battalions of volunteers were formed and designated the 3rd, 4th, 5th, 6th, and 7th (or the Light Infantry) Battalions of Bengal Volunteers. The troops detailed for this expedition were taken from the Bengal and Madras Presidencies, principally from the former. The Bengal Division, which was under the command of Colonel George Wood, consisted (besides the 14th and 59th Foot) of the following troops:

	Men
Governor-General's Body-Guard, under Captain Gall	107
Two companies of Bengal artillery	150

---

14. *London Gazette Extraordinary,* dated the 13th February, 1811.

1st and 2nd Battalions, 20th (Marine) Bengal N. I.	1,501
Four battalions of volunteers	3,592
One light infantry battalion of volunteers	576
Pioneers	361
	6,287

The troops from Bengal embarked in March 1811, and on the 1st June the whole expedition had assembled at Malacca, under Lieutenant-General Sir Samuel Auchmuty. Here considerable delay occurred, and it was not until the 2nd of August that the expeditionary force, amounting to 10,800 men, arrived off the north coast of Java. The troops landed at Chilling-Ching without opposition on the 4th and advanced to Batavia, which place was entered on the 8th. Two days later the army, having advanced, attacked and defeated a division of the enemy near Weltervreden, about two miles from the main position of the Dutch in their entrenched camp at Cornelis. The whole army did not arrive before that place until the 14th, when the enemy's forces opposed to them were estimated at 17,000 men, with about 280 guns. A fortnight was passed in making regular approaches, but, though considerable effect was produced, it soon became evident that a regular siege would be too long an undertaking, and it was resolved accordingly to make an effort to force the Dutch position by a *coup de main*. The attempt was completely successful, and on the 26th of August the place was carried by storm; the enemy made a gallant resistance, but were forced from their entrenchments, and, being driven into the open country, were pursued for several miles by the cavalry. More than 2,000 are said to have been killed, and 3,000 prisoners were taken, amongst them being three Generals, 34 field officers, 70 captains and 150 subalterns. The loss of the British force during the whole of these operations, from the date of landing, amounted to 735 British and 152 natives killed, wounded, and missing, of which the Bengal troops lost one British officer (Lieutenant-Fireworker Farnaby, Bengal Artillery) and two native officers killed, and thirteen British officers (of whom Captain Shaw, 2-13th, and Lieutenant Murrall, 2-24th, both attached to the 6th Volunteer Battalion, died of their wounds) and five native officers wounded; twenty-six non-commissioned officers and men (including two European sergeants) killed, and 108 wounded.[15] After making one more effort at Jati Ali on the 16th September, and again sustaining defeat, General Janssens, the

---

15. *London Gazette Extraordinary,* 17th December, 1811.

Dutch commander, capitulated, and the island of Java was surrendered to the English on the 17th of September.[16] On the conclusion of hostilities the Bengal troops, with the exception of some of the volunteer battalions, returned to India and received the thanks of Government in General Orders; medals were conferred on all ranks and in 1829 the Body-Guard and the two battalions of the 20th Native Infantry (the late 25th and 40th) were granted permission to wear the word "Java" on their standards, colours, and appointments. The 3rd and 4th Battalions and the Light Infantry Battalion continued serving in Java until the island was restored to the Dutch in 1816. In the interval they were not idle: in June 1812, the 4th and Light Infantry Battalions served at the storming of Yodhyakarta (usually called Jocjocarta), the palace-fort of a rebellious Sultan in the interior of Java, and in June, 1813, the 3rd Battalion shared in the reduction of Sambas, a piratical state on the western coast of Borneo. In 1815, however, the Light Infantry Battalion tarnished the fine reputation it had acquired: having been detained in the Eastern islands longer than the period for which they had volunteered, the men became discontented and insubordinate, and finally broke into open mutiny, for which crime several of the ringleaders were condemned to suffer death.

Towards the end of 1811, the 2-21st Native Infantry, under the command of Lieutenant-Colonel Tetley, was despatched from Mirzapur to coerce the Rajah of Bardhi, in Rewah, whose people had been making incursions into and plundering the Mirzapur district. The battalion was repulsed with some loss in an imprudent attempt, without guns, on the fort of Bhapawi, Colonel Tetley himself being among the wounded, but eventually the Bardhi chief's forces were dispersed, all his forts destroyed, and the country restored to order.

In January, 1812, the contumacy of the *kiladar* of Kalinjar, a strong fortress which stood twenty miles south-east of Banda in Bundelkhand, rendered it necessary to despatch a force against him. This force, which was under the command of Colonel Martindell, included both battalions of the 11th Native Infantry, the 1st Battalions of the 7th and 22nd, the 2nd Battalions of the 2nd, 5th, and 16th, and part of the Corps of Pioneers. On the 2nd of February, 1812, an attempt was made to storm the fort, but the assault was repulsed with heavy loss, two officers being killed, eleven wounded, and 210 men killed and wounded. This loss fell almost entirely on the 53rd Foot, that of the native troops being only two men killed and one

---

16. *Idem*, 21st January, 1812.

officer (Lieutenant Faithful, 2-10th, attached to the Pioneers) and 76 men wounded. The attempt, however, was so nearly successful that the *kiladar,* fearing that the next attack might be still more vigorous, surrendered on the following day.

One more small affair remains to be noted before the commencement of another general war. This was the attack and storming, at the close of 1813, of a fort named Entauri, in Baghelkhand, by a detachment under Lieutenant-Colonel J. W. Adams, consisting of details from the 1st Battalions of the 5th, 9th, and 11th Regiments, and the 2nd Battalions of the 2nd and 10th. The place was reached after a trying march, assaulted on the same day (4th December), and carried in the face of a desperate resistance by the garrison. The commander, Sarnaid Singh, a petty Rajah who had gratuitously attacked a detachment of the Company's troops, with almost all the garrison, fell in the assault.[17] The loss on our side was five killed and sixty-eight (including three British officers) wounded.

Between the close of the Mahratta war and the year 1814 but few changes of strength or constitution were made in the Bengal Army. By G. O., 29th November, 1805, orders had been issued that the Governor-General's Body-Guard should be furnished by details included in the strength of regiments of native cavalry, but in 1808 (G. G. O., 26th February) this loss of strength was counterbalanced by an increase of twelve men per troop. The uniform of the regular native cavalry at this time (G. O. C. C. 7th December, 1809) was ordered to be French grey, with red facings and white buttons and lace. In the following year, however, the facings were again changed to yellow. In this year, too, we learn that no French grey cloth arrived from England, so the uniforms had to be made of red cloth, and it was not until 1811 that the new regulation uniforms were issued complete. By G. O. C. C, 4th May, 1810, the arming of native cavalry was modified; two pistols were in future to be carried instead of one, as heretofore, and the proportion of carbines was fixed at fifteen per troop. Remounts at this time were obtained through the Government stud at Pusa, and G. O. C. C, 19th May, 1807, authorises each cavalry officer to select one horse from those sent from the Pusa stud to their regiment, the price for such chargers being R800, a tolerably large figure even in these days.

In February, 1809 (G. O. C. C, 1st February), orders were issued for the rendezvous at Sonpat and Panipat of all the irregular horse in the

---

17. *London Gazette,* 13th August, 1814.—*East India United Service Journal,* June, 1837, pages 418-27.

employ of Government; the whole to be commanded by Major James Skinner. At the same time a further enlistment for that officer's regiment was ordered. Three months later (Proclamation, G. G., 29th May, 1809) Skinner's Horse was augmented to a strength of eight *rissalahs*, with galloper guns attached. The strength and rates of pay of a *rissalah* are given as follows in the same order:

		R
	Risaldar	80
	Naib-Risaldar	50
	Jemadar	45
	Kot-Daffadar	35
5	*Daffadars*, @	28
	Nishan-bardar	28
	Nagarchi	25
100	*Sowars*, @	20
	Vakil	20
2	*Bhistis*, @	5

The uniform of the corps at this time included a yellow jacket, with red turbans and *kamarbands*.

In 1815 (G. O. C. C, 29th July) the establishment of Skinner's Horse was augmented to three corps of 1,000 *sowars* each, with the following staff and officers:

1	Captain	10	Kot-Daffadars	1	Havildar
5	Lieutenants	80	Daffadars	1	Naik
5	Cornets	10	Nishanchis	41	Sepoys above to work the galloper guns
10	Risaldars	10	Nagarchis		
10	Naib-Risaldars	10	Vakils		
10	Jemadars	100	Bhistis		

Of these corps the second is now the 3rd Bengal Cavalry.

Three corps of Rohilla cavalry, commanded by Lieutenant Roberts, Captain Cunningham and Captain Baddeley, were also placed on the above strength, with the exception of the galloper guns, while in 1809 (G. O. C. C., 12th May) another corps of irregular cavalry had been raised for provincial work in the ceded and conquered provinces, and was known as Gardner's Horse. This last is now the 2nd Bengal Lancers.

Native artillery, of which a corps had again been raised in 1797

(Minutes of Council, dated 15th October), were employed throughout the wars of these years, but instead of being formed into a separate corps, they were at first split up into small parties and attached to the British companies, of which they formed a component part,—an arrangement as faulty as it was unsuccessful. At length in 1805 they were collected into a *Golandaz* corps of five companies, while in the same year an irregular corps of *Golandaz* was formed at Delhi of men who had come over from the Mahratta service, and was gradually absorbed into the regular companies. These latter were raised to eight in number in 1808. In 1811, a troop of native horse artillery was formed for service in Java, but this was reduced on its return.

To the Bengal infantry but few additions were made up to 1814. The Pioneer corps, which had done excellent service in the sieges of the Mahratta war, was in 1808 augmented to eight companies of 90 men each, with two British sergeants per company and a detail of miners. It was placed on the same footing as other infantry corps, and denominated "the Corps of Pioneers or Sappers." By G. O. C. C, 26th February, 1808, the establishment of infantry regiments was increased by ten sepoys per company. In 1809 (G. O. C. C, 9th September) the strength of the companies of the Marine Regiment (the 20th) was increased to 16 non-commissioned officers and 130 privates each. G. O. C. C., 23rd September, 1814, orders a further increase of infantry regiments by ten men per company, in consequence of the imminence of war with Nepal, and on the 11th of January following orders were issued for the raising of three new infantry regiments, numbered from the 28th to the 30th.[18] The first of these was raised at Cawnpore, the

---

18. The native names of these corps were as follow:
1st and 2nd Battalions 28th—*Uchterlony-ki-Paltan*.—So called from Sir David Ochterlony, the first Colonel of the regiment. The name is so entered in the Army Lists, but it is worth noting that the officer referred to was not known to the sepoys as "Ochterlony," but as "Lony Aktar." The 2nd Battalion was also known as *Lambroon-ki-Paltan,* from Lieutenant-Colonel C. W. Lamborne, who was appointed to command it on its being raised.
1st Battalion 29th.—*Moira-ki-Paltan*.—So named after Lord Moira, afterwards Marquis of Hastings, in commemoration of His Lordship having presented the battalion with its first colours, and ordered the corps to be dressed and equipped like his own regiment in the King's service—the 27th Foot.
2nd Battalion 29th.—*Bisheshwar-ki-Paltan*.—The origin of this name has not been ascertained.
1st Battalion 30th—*Latter-ki-Paltan*.—From Major R. J. Latter, who was posted to the corps on its being raised, and commanded it for some years.
2nd Battalion 30th—*Carter-ki-Paltan*.—*So* named after Major H. Carter, who was appointed to the corps on its being raised.

two battalions of the 29th at Fatehgarh and Benares, respectively, and those of the 30th at Dinapore and Buxar. The 1st of the 30th, raised by Captain F. Andrei, is now the 8th Bengal Infantry. In the same year, 1815, nine provincial corps of infantry were raised, and also a "Dromedary Corps," commanded by Ensign J. W. Patton. This was found so useful that two years later its establishment of officers was increased to two lieutenants and two cornets.

In G. O. C. C, 10th November 1808, havildars of light infantry are ordered to carry muskets, instead of pikes; and, on the 22nd April, 1809, the issue is sanctioned to light companies of "two bugle-horns and five whistles." In the same year (9th January, 1809) the standard of height for light infantry was fixed at 5 feet 5 inches.

The uniform for the whole of the Bengal infantry, except the Marine Regiment and the Pioneers, was, by G. O. C. C, 8th December, 1809, ordered to be red, with yellow facings and white buttons, and lace striped red, white, and blue. These universal facings were, however, soon altered and commanding officers were allowed to select a colour for their regiments; thus we find the facings of the 28th, 29th and 30th, when they were raised, were, respectively, white, light buff, and Saxon green. The uniform of the Pioneers was green, with green facings, black buttons, and yellow lace. In the line regiments *kamarbands* of blue linen, six inches broad, were worn by all native ranks: native officers wore tight white pantaloons and half boots, and non-commissioned ranks *janghias* or short drawers; pantaloons were, however, worn in the cold weather by all ranks in some corps, and in 1813 (G. O. C. C, 2nd June) permission was given for them to be worn all the year round by such corps as might elect to do so. The head-dress of the period was a wonderful structure, called by courtesy a turban, which up to 1805 was built on an iron frame-work; but by G. O., 26th July of that year, rattan was substituted for iron, when procurable. Accoutrements up to 1810 were of black leather. On the 20th March a G. O. C. C. ordered the gradual substitution of buff leather, as the black accoutrements wore out. At the end of the Mahratta War the Bengal Army appears to have reached a higher state of efficiency than it had ever previously attained, and contemporary writers speak in the highest terms of its capabilities. The Duke of Wellington, who had gained most of his Indian experience in Madras and Bombay, and therefore judged the Bengal sepoys by what he had seen of detachments, writes:

Supposing all the consequences to be equally convenient, I acknowledge that I should wish to see the Bengal troops composing all the subsidiary forces. The men are of a better size and description, of a higher caste, and the natives have more respect for them than they have for the Coast or Bombay troops. They have proved in this campaign (Lord Lake's) that they yield to none in bravery, and I believe are tolerably disciplined, and they have long been notorious for their contempt of their enemies on horseback.

CHAPTER 4

Gurkhas & Mahrattas

For many years past the northern frontier of the Company's territories had been threatened by the constantly increasing encroachments of the Nepalese. Regardless of repeated remonstrances from the British Government, and finding that the latter, occupied with military proceedings elsewhere, were reluctant to have recourse to arms, they considered this as a sign of weakness, and increased their aggressions to such an extent that in May, 1814, war became inevitable, and an army was ordered to take the field in the autumn of that year.

This force, which, including irregulars, amounted to over thirty thousand men, was divided into four divisions, commanded and composed as follows:

1st Division, under Major-General David Ochterlony
Artillery, British and
Native   950 men
Native Infantry   2nd Bttn., 1st Regiment
                         2nd Bttn., 3rd Regiment
                         2nd Bttn., 6th Regiment
                         1st Bttn., 19th Regiment
                         2nd Bttn., 19th Regiment   6 cos
Pioneers   3rd and 4th companies   65
Native Cavalry   2nd Regiment
Skinner's Horse   1 *rissalah*

2nd Division, under Major-General Robert Rollo Gillespie
Artillery   247
Native Infantry   1st Bttn., 6th Regiment
                         1st Bttn., 7th Regiment

	1st Bttn., 17th Regiment	
	2nd Bttn., 19th Regiment	4 cos.
Light Infantry Bttn.		8 cos.
H. M.'s 8th Light Dragoons		Detachment
H. M.'s 53rd Foot		785
7th Native Cavalry		
Pioneers	5th and 6th companies	133
Skinner's Horse		1 *rissalah*

3rd Division, under Major-General John Sullivan Wood

Artillery		114
6th Native Cavalry		1 troop
H. M.'s 17th Foot		958
Native Infantry	2nd Bttn., 8th Regiment	2 cos.
	2nd Bttn., 12th Regiment	2 cos.
	1st Bttn., 14th Regiment	Left wing
	2nd Bttn., 14th Regiment	Left wing
	2nd Bttn., 17th Regiment	
Pioneers	8th company	90

4th Division, under Major-General Bennet Marley

Artillery		868
Gardner's Horse		2 *rissalahs*
H. M.'s 24th Regiment		907
Native Infantry	1st Bttn., 8th Regiment	
	2nd Bttn., 15th Regiment	
	2nd Bttn., 22nd Regiment	Left wing
	2nd Bttn., 25th Regiment	
Ramgarh Bttn.		
Champaran Light Infantry		
Pioneers	1st, 2nd, 7th companies	

Besides the above, irregular troops and native contingents joined the army to the extent of above 12,000 men, and considerable additions of regular troops were afterwards made to the 1st and 2nd Divisions.

According to the general plan of operations, the 1st Division was to attack the western extremity of the Nepal frontier; the second was to occupy Dehra Dun and besiege Jaithak; the third was to march from Gorukhpur through Bhutwal and Sheoraj to Palpa; and the fourth and strongest was to march through Makwanpur to the Gurkha capital of Khatmandu.

The history of the first campaign of this war includes a greater number of disastrous failures and of ill-arranged and worse-carried-out enterprises, due generally to an entire want of appreciation of the necessities of hill warfare than had ever before, or have ever since befallen the arms of the British in India.

Major-General Gillespie, who was the first to penetrate the enemy's frontier, entered the Dun on October the 22nd, 1814, and occupied Dehra. The Gurkha governor of the western districts was Amar Sing Thapa, who had detached a force of 600 men under Balbhadra Sing for the defence of the Dun; this leader had taken up his position in the fort of Nalapani or Kalanga, five miles from Dehra. General Gillespie resolved to carry the place by assault, and formed the attacking force into four parties, which were to advance simultaneously from different directions on the morning of the 31st October. The signal for the attack was to be the firing of a gun, but this having been done before two of the parties had reached their destinations, the assault was delivered by the other two detachments only, and the result was a failure; the attack was repelled by the garrison with considerable loss, General Gillespie himself being killed, with four other officers and twenty-seven men; while seventeen officers and 213 men were wounded. The officers killed were Lieutenant and Adjutant B. R. O'Hara, 1-6th Native Infantry, Lieutenant and Adjutant R. H. Gosling, 1st of the 27th (attached to the Light Battalion), Ensign F. Fothergill, 1st of the 17th, and Ensign R. Ellis of the Pioneers. Colonel Mawby, of His Majesty's 53rd, now took command of the Division and retired to Dehra until the arrival of a battering train from Delhi. On the 25th of November, the 1-13th Native Infantry having joined in the interval, operations were renewed, and an assault delivered on the 27th, but with no better result; the attack was completely repulsed, and with still heavier loss to us than that sustained in the first attack, four officers, fifteen British soldiers, and eighteen sepoys being killed, and eight officers and 436 men wounded. The officers of the Bengal Army killed were Captain J. Campbell, 1st of the 6th, and Lieutenant J. Cuninghame, 1st of the 13th; Lieutenant J. B. B. Luxford, Horse Artillery, died of his wounds. It was now determined to bombard the place, and measures were taken to cut off its water-supply; the result was that it was evacuated in three days, Balbhadra Sing and ninety survivors effecting their escape and joining a party of 300 men which had been sent to their relief. This party was followed and dispersed by a force under Major Ludlow, consisting of 150 men of the Light Battalion and 300 of the 1-6th Regiment.

On the 20th of December, Major-General Martindell joined the Division and assumed command. After occupying Nahan, the capital of Sirmoor, he made an attempt against Jaithak, a fort situated on the top of a lofty hill to the north of the town, and held by a body of upwards of 2,000 Gurkhas, commanded by Ranjur Sing Thapa, the son of the Gurkha Commander-in-Chief. The attack on the enemy's position was made on the 27th December by two detachments of, respectively, about 1,050 and 700 men, commanded by Major J. Ludlow, 1-6th and Major W. Richards, 1-13th Native Infantry. Major Ludlow's column came first in contact with the enemy near the village of Jampta, and there met with momentary success, but in following this up with an attack on one of the enemy's stockades, a severe repulse was experienced, ending in the complete defeat of the detachment, who retreated in confusion to Martindell's camp, having sustained a loss of one officer (Lieutenant G. M. Munt of the 1-1st, serving with the Light Battalion) killed and three wounded, and 152 men killed and wounded. Major Richards' column had in the meantime succeeded in taking up a position which cut off the water-supply of the garrison, and which, if held, must have compelled the Gurkhas to surrender, Here Richards was fiercely attacked by the enemy, and for six hours maintained his ground against all the efforts of the Gurkhas; but towards evening his ammunition began to fail, and at the same time orders to retire were received from General Martindell; a retreat was accordingly begun, but the rugged nature of the ground and the exhaustion of the men brought about confusion and ended in a defeat, in which the column sustained a loss of three officers (Lieutenant T. Thackeray and Ensign W. McM. Wilson, 2-26th, and Ensign G. Stalkart, 1-13th) and seventy men killed, and five officers and 228 men wounded, besides whom a large number of sepoys were taken prisoners. The losses of this detachment up to the commencement of its retreat had been very small, and had it not been for the failure of ammunition and the order to retire, it would have easily maintained its position. The result of these defeats was that the further advance of the division was completely checked, and though afterwards reinforced with both battalions of the 27th Native Infantry, General Martindell contented himself with simply blockading Jaithak until the spring of 1815, when the evacuation of the place was brought about by the successes of Major-General Ochterlony and the surrender of Amar Sing.

General Ochterlony, with the 1st Division, began his operations against the Gurkha General Amar Sing early in November, 1814. The principal positions occupied by the enemy were Nalagarh, Ramgarh, and Malaun. General Ochterlony, advancing with great caution, brought up his heavy guns and bombarded the first of these forts, which capitulated, together with the outpost of Taragarh, on the 5th of November. He next moved against Ramgarh, and here (26th November) a misfortune befell a detachment of his force: in a reconnaissance of the fort a small party under Lieutenant Lawtie, Bengal Engineers, was attacked and compelled to retreat by the failure of its ammunition; a reinforcement from the 2-3rd Native Infantry was involved in its flight, and Lieutenant G. T. Williams of that regiment was killed the other losses this day amounted to forty-two men killed, and thirty-four wounded. General Ochterlony now awaited the arrival of reinforcements, which reached him on the 26th of December, and consisted of the 2nd Battalion, 7th Native Infantry, and a Sikh levy. On the following day Lieutenant-Colonel Thompson was detached with fourteen companies to cut off the communications of Amar Sing with Arki and Bilaspur, from which all his supplies were drawn. This object was effected with small loss, and Amar Sing was compelled to throw back his left, still keeping his right at Ramgarh: but General Ochterlony, having threatened to cut him off from his last stronghold by turning the Malaun ridge and then marching on Bilaspur, the Gurkha general found himself obliged to fall back on the strong Malaun position, leaving small garrisons at Ramgarh and several other posts, all of which were reduced by a detachment under Lieutenant-Colonel Cooper, in February and March 1815. Meanwhile, Colonel Arnold, who had been left to watch Ramgarh during General Ochterlony's turning movement, moved round the extremity of the Malaun ridge, to cooperate with the general on its northern side. Colonel Cooper's detachment having joined the main army, on the 14th of April, all was prepared for a combined movement against the enemy's position. This consisted of a connected chain of peaks, all except two being crowned by stockades. The possession of these two points was the object of General Ochterlony's attack, and four separate columns were told off to effect that purpose, while two smaller parties were to make a diversion against the principal position of the Gurkhas at Malaun: these dispositions were made and carried out with the greatest care and skill, and with complete success; one of the heights was seized without opposition; the other, Deothal, was carried after some resistance, and the British troops, having hastily entrenched themselves, were able to repulse a furious attempt of the enemy to re-take the position on the morning of the 16th of April. The enemy in this engagement lost about 500 men, while the loss of the British on the 15th and 16th was one officer (Captain Showers, 1-19th) and 62 men killed, and 298 wounded, including five officers, of whom Lieutenant H. Bagot, attached to the Pioneers, died. General Ochterlony immediately made preparations for attacking the main position of Malaun, but, on the 11nth of May, after three days' bombardment, Amar Sing capitulated and made terms for himself and his son, Ranjur Sing, at Jaithak, by which all the provinces from Kumaon westwards were resigned to the British. Many of the Gurkhas took service with the British, and three battalions of them were at once formed.

The energetic and skilful defence by Amar Sing of his mountain positions during a space of six months, and with a force considerably less than half that of his opponents, is one of the most remarkable features of the Nepal War.

Meanwhile the 3rd Division assembled at Gorakhpur in November, 1814, but, owing to deficiency of transport and supplies, it was not until January that Major-General Wood entered the enemy's country. On the 3rd of that month an attack was made on the Gurkha post of Jitpur, which, notwithstanding extraordinary mismanagement and neglect of reconnaissance, was already an accomplished success when the general, declaring the position untenable, commanded a retreat; the British loss amounted to twenty-four men killed and five officers (of whom Lieutenant Morrieson, Bengal Engineers, died) and 104 men wounded. General Wood now declared his force to be inadequate to the task assigned to it, and confined his measures to the defence of the frontier, concentrating his force at Lautan, covering the road to Gorakhpur. Subsequently, under orders from the commander-in-chief, he made a demonstration against Bhutwal, but effected nothing, and early in May the troops were withdrawn into cantonments at Gorakhpur.

Major-General Marley's division was no more successful in carrying out the plan laid down for him. Arriving on the frontier, on December the 12th, he found that Major Bradshaw, the officer commanding on the Saran border, had already been successful in clearing the frontier posts of the Terai, having captured Barharwa, on the 25th of November, with a loss to the enemy of fifty killed, and to the British of two killed (including *Subadar* Gauhar Khan, 2-15th) and one officer and twenty men wounded of Gardner's Horse and the 2-15th Native Infantry. The defensive posts of Baragarhi, Samanpur, and Parsa were held, respectively, by Captain Hay with the head-quarters of the Champaran Light Infantry, Captain Blackney with a wing of the 2nd-22nd, and Captain Sibley with three companies of the 2nd-15th, a detachment of the Champaran Light Infantry, and a *rissalah* of Gardner's Horse. December was passed in collecting information and arranging the plan of advance on Khatmandu, during which time no precautions were taken for the permanent defence of the frontier posts. Seeing this, the Gurkhas planned simultaneous attacks on Parsa and Samanpur on the 1st of January, 1815: both were completely successful; Captain Blackney was taken entirely by surprise; himself and Lieutenant James Duncan were killed, and the detachment dispersed, with the exception of a small party kept together by Lieutenant Strettell, and led back to Gorasahan: the losses in killed, wounded, and missing amounted to 125. Captain Sibley expected an attack and asked for reinforcements, which however arrived only in time to cover the retreat of the fugitives; the detachment had made a good resistance, but was surrounded and overpowered; Captain Sibley, *Subadar* Siu Singh and *Jemadar* Shamsher Khan were killed and the detachment sustained a loss of 121 killed, 134 wounded, and three missing. These disasters had a most depressing effect on General Marley; considering his force insufficient, he hesitated to advance into the hills, and remained entirely inactive throughout January, notwithstanding the arrival of reinforcements comprising His Majesty's 14th and 17th Foot, At length, on the 10th of February, without giving notice or making any arrangements for the conduct of his duties, he departed suddenly from the camp; Colonel G. Dick assumed temporary charge of the Division, and shortly after Major-General George Wood was sent up from Calcutta to take command. On the day before the arrival of that officer (19th February) a small but brilliant success was gained through the energy of Lieutenant Pickersgill, who, having lured a body of 500 Gurkhas from the cover of the forest, charged them with a troop of Gardner's Horse under Lieutenant Hearsey, and entirely dispersed them with a loss of over 100 killed. General Wood followed the same course of procrastination as his predecessor, and declaring that the fever season was too near for operations to be possible in March, he contented himself with making a demonstration on the frontier and the season closed without his seeing an enemy.

Thus, of the four operations included in the plan of the campaign, three had proved lamentable failures, which not only frustrated the intentions of the Government, but also to a considerable extent lowered the English name and prestige throughout India.

Meanwhile an expedition into the province of Kumaon, which had been planned by the Governor-General, Lord Moira, as a diversion, had been attended with great success. This expedition was divided into two columns, commanded by Lieutenant-Colonel Gardner and Major Hearsey,—the troops with both being irregular Rohilla levies. Operations were commenced in February, 1815, and were at first successful on both sides of the province, Colonel Gardner penetrating as far as Almora, and Major Hearsey to Champawat. Here, however, the latter was defeated and himself wounded and taken prisoner; but the arrival, under Colonel Jasper Nicolls, of a reinforcement of 2,500 men, amongst which were the 1st-4th and the 2nd-5th Native Infantry and a battalion of Light Infantry, soon effected a favourable change. The Gurkhas were defeated at Sitauli, and Almora invested. Some further fighting followed, ending in the capitulation of the Gurkha commandant. The place surrendered, and a convention was signed on the 27th of April, which delivered up the whole province with its fortified places to the British. The total loss of the regular troops during the operations round Almora amounted to one officer (Lieutenant Tapley, 1-27th Native Infantry serving with the Light Battalion), and thirty-one men killed, and three officers and 123 men wounded. Colonel Gardner's irregulars lost 81 men killed and wounded.

The fall of Almora and of Malaun induced the Nepalese Government to seek to re-establish friendly relations with the British-Negotiations were begun, and a treaty was drafted, but many months were spent in the discussion of its terms, and at length, in December, 1815, it was ascertained that the government at Khatmandu refused to ratify it.

General Ochterlony, who had been gazetted a Knight Commander of the Order of the Bath and created a Baronet for his successes against Malaun, was ordered to take the field once more, and a force of nearly 17,000 men was placed at his disposal for the purpose of bringing the war to a favourable conclusion. This was arranged in three columns, as follows:

Right Column:—First Brigade, under Colonel W. Kelly, H. M.'s 24th Foot, ordered to enter Nepal by Hariharpur. Troops:—His Majesty's 24th Foot; 1st Battalion, 18th Native Infantry; right wing, 1st Battalion, and left wing, 2nd Battalion, 21st Native Infantry; the Champaran Light Infantry.

Left Column:—Second Brigade, under Lieutenant-Colonel C. Nicol, H. M.'s 66th Foot, ordered to penetrate by Ramnagar. Troops:— His Majesty's 66th Foot; the 5th and 8th Grenadier Battalions; the 1st Battalion 8th and the 2nd Battalion 18th Native Infantry.

Centre Column:—Under Sir David Ochterlony, to advance by the main entrance to Nepal through the Bichukoh or Chiriaghati Pass. 3rd Brigade,—under Lieutenant-Colonel F. M. Miller, 87th Foot. Troops:— His Majesty's 87th Foot; and the 2nd Battalions of the 12th, 22nd and 25th Native Infantry. 4th Brigade,—under Lieutenant-Colonel J. Burnett, 8th Native Infantry. Troops:—The 2nd Battalions of the 4th, 8th, 9th, and 15th, and part of the 1st-30th Native Infantry.

Details of artillery, pioneers and irregular horse with each brigade.

Sir David Ochterlony took the field early in February, 1816. To oppose the main advance over the Chiriaghati pass the Gurkhas had erected three stockades in the hills, the last of which was deemed impregnable, and had left the route through the forests of the Terai unprotected. The first of the stockades having been reconnoitred and found quite unassailable, an advance was attempted, on the 14th of February, by Ochterlony and the 3rd Brigade, through an intricate and difficult pass over the hills discovered by Lieutenant Pickersgill of the Quarter-master General's Department, by which it was hoped that the main position of the Chiriaghati pass would be turned. The experiment, which was an extremely dangerous one and in which any *contretemps* would have occasioned a serious disaster, was fortunately quite successful; and the 4th Brigade, advancing on the 17th, found that the enemy had been obliged to retire owing to their rear being threatened, and the pass was occupied without opposition. On the 27th, General Ochterlony moved against Makwanpur, and encamped about two miles from the fortified heights of that place. On the following day the post of Sekhar Khatri, which covered the left of the camp, was attacked in force by the Gurkhas: the place was gallantly defended by the small detachment there, consisting of forty men of the 87th Foot and three companies of the 2-25th Native Infantry, until reinforcements arrived, when the Gurkhas were repulsed with a loss, according to their own subsequent account, of over 800 men. Besides the 2-25th, the 2-12th was prominently engaged on this occasion, and the 2-8th, under Major Nation, distinguished itself by a bayonet charge at the close of the action. The British casualties were one officer (Lieutenant Tirrell, 1-20th Native Infantry, attached to the 2-25th), one native officer (*Subadar* Shaikh Danish, 2-25th), and 45 men killed, one officer and 176 men wounded, and two men missing.

Meanwhile Colonel Nicol, with the 2nd Brigade, advanced into Nepal over the Bikna Thori pass, without experiencing any opposition, and joined the headquarters of the army at Makwanpur on the 1st of March.

The 1st Brigade, under Colonel Kelly, succeeded in ascending the mountains south of the fort of Hariharpur by an undefended route, and on the 1st of March seized an important point about eight hundred yards from that fort, which the Gurkhas had neglected to occupy. The enemy, seeing the advantage which they had allowed their opponents to gain, immediately made a desperate attempt to re-take the position, but after five hours' incessant musketry firing, during which the nature 6f the ground prevented the contending forces from coming to close quarters, they were driven back with considerable loss, our own amounting to eight killed and fifty-one (including five officers) wounded. So disheartened were the Gurkhas at this repulse that they evacuated Hariharpur three days afterwards.

The intelligence of these reverses strengthened the hands of those at Khatmandu who desired peace; hostilities were immediately suspended, negotiations were resumed, and, a treaty having been concluded by which Nepal was compelled to make still greater cession of territory than had been originally demanded, the British forces were withdrawn before the end of March.

For these campaigns a silver medal was bestowed on all officers, British and native, who had served within the hills of Nepal, and on such non-commissioned officers and sepoys as were recommended by their commanding officers for conspicuous zeal or gallantry.

The Nepal War, noticeable as it was for the experience which it furnished to the Bengal Army of severe mountain fighting, and for its bitter lessons of caution, which had never been required against the semi-disciplined hordes of the Mahrattas or Mysore, was also remarkable as having given to the army the first three of those battalions of Gurkhas which have since come to be regarded as the flower of the

Indian infantry. It has already been noticed that on the fall of Malaun in 1815 numbers of Gurkhas entered the British service and were formed into three battalions. These were the 1st and 2nd Nasseri Battalions, formed at Subathu by Lieutenants Ross and MacHarg, respectively (G. G. O., 24th April 1815), and the Sirmoor Battalion, formed at Nahan by Lieutenant Young. A fourth corps was at the same time formed in Kumaon under the same General Order, and was called the Kumaon Battalion. Of the above corps the 1st Nasseri, Sirmoor and Kumaon Battalions are now the 1st Battalions of the 1st, 2nd, and 3rd Gurkha Regiments. The 2nd Nasseri Battalion was disbanded in 1829.

The speedy conclusion of the second Nepal campaign gave the Indian Government an opportunity of lightening the strain on their reduced exchequer by some much-needed economies. By G. O. C. C, 10th April, 1816, considerable reductions were made in the strength of the Bengal Army, and almost all the local corps were disbanded. Nor did anything occur in this year demanding the services of the army, except a riot at Benares, which was promptly quelled by the 2-13th and some irregular cavalry, and a disturbance in the Aligarh district, headed by one Dyaram the Taluqdar of Hathras. This man, whose aggressions in the district had been long continued, had acquired sufficient influence to be able to collect a considerable force, while his fort and town were thoroughly prepared for defence. A strong division was therefore sent against him, in February, 1817, under Major-General Marshall, comprising His Majesty's 8th and 24th Light Dragoons, the 3rd and 7th Native Cavalry, the 1st (Roberts'), and 2nd Rohilla Horse, His Majesty's 14th and 87th Foot, the 1st Battalions of the 25th and 29th, and the 2nd Battalions of the 1st, 11th, 12th, and 15th Native Infantry, the 2nd Grenadier Battalion, and a train of some 100 pieces of artillery, with which was a rocket-troop. Hathras was invested on the 12th of February ; the town was evacuated on the 23rd, but the fort held out until the 2nd of March, when a shell exploded the magazine. Dyaram, now finding further resistance impossible, cut his way through the British lines at midnight with a small party of followers clad in chain mail, and escaped. The fort was taken and dismantled.

Shortly after this (April, 1816) a serious outbreak took place at Bareilly. Beginning with a tumult about the imposition of a police tax, it soon swelled into an insurrection of a semi-religious character, and culminated in an attack by several thousand armed fanatics on the British troops stationed at the place,—the 2nd Rohilla Horse and detachments of the 2-27th Native Infantry and the Bareilly Provincial Battalion; and it was only after a severe contest (in which the troops sustained a loss of twenty-one killed and sixty-two wounded) that the insurgents were beaten off and defeated. The arrival of the 1-13th Native Infantry (which had made forced marches from Moradabad) put an entire end to the outbreak.

About the same time a rising took place in the province of Cuttack, which at one time assumed serious proportions. It was headed by a bold and active leader in the district of Khurda, named Jagbandhu, who repulsed the detachment sent against him (Ganjpura, 2nd April, 1816) and killed its commanding officer, Lieutenant Thomas Faris, 1-18th Native Infantry. Emboldened by this success, Jagbandhu advanced, seized the town of Jagarnath, and compelled the small garrison to retreat with the collector of the district to Cuttack. Captain LeFevre now marched against the insurgents with the greater part of the 1-18th Native Infantry, but Sir Gabriel Martindell had to be sent into the province with a considerable force before tranquillity was completely restored.

In this place it might also be mentioned that, in 1818, the Bhattis of Hariana broke out into insurrection, seized the town of Fatehabad, and defeated a small detachment sent to recover the place. It became necessary to send a considerable force against them, and accordingly, in September 1818, Colonel Arnold entered their country, and in the course of a few weeks restored order. The force employed on this service included a troop of horse artillery, the rocket-troop, the 1st Native Cavalry, a detachment of the 1st Local Horse, the 3rd Local Horse, Casement's Horse, the Dromedary Corps, the 2-12th, 1-17th, 2-26th, and 2-29th Native Infantry, and two battalions of Begum Samru's troops.

Meanwhile the intrigues and disturbances amongst the Mahratta princes and the consequent disorganisation of Central India, which was increased by the unrestrained violence of the bands of marauders known as Pindaris, had induced the Marquis of Hastings (to which rank and title the Earl of Moira had been raised) at the close of 1816 to make effective military arrangements, by which he intended, after the rainy season of the following year, not only to finally suppress the predatory raids of these freebooters, but also to enforce British authority over the Mahratta powers, and even, if need be, to enter on a final struggle with them for the possession of Central India. The war thus begun effected one of the greatest revolutions that modern India has witnessed; not only was the supremacy of the Mahrattas crippled, but an irretrievable blow was struck at their confederacy, which was reduced to such a state of weakness that it could regain no vigour from reunion, and with the deposition of its titular chief it lost the one link which had held it together and became disunited for ever.

The British forces, which were prepared for war during the first half of 1817, amounted to 87,951, and including native irregulars and contingents, formed the largest British Army which had ever been put into the field in India. The forces of the Mahrattas and Pindaris were estimated at two hundred and seventeen thousand. The Grand Army of Bengal, under the Marquis of Hastings, was in four principal divisions:

The Centre Division assembled at Cawnpore, and was joined there by Lord Hastings in September. It was commanded by Major-General Brown, and consisted of His Majesty's 24th Light Dragoons, the 3rd and 7th Native Cavalry and the Body-Guard, His Majesty's 87th Foot, and of Native Infantry, the 1st Battalions of the 8th, 24th, and 29th, and the 2nd Battalions of the 1st, 11th, 13th, and 25th, and a flank battalion; also detachments of horse and foot artillery, and 54 guns.

The Right Division, formed at Agra under Major-General R. S. Donkin, included His Majesty's 8th Light Dragoons, the 1st Native Cavalry, Gardner's Horse, and some native contingents, His Majesty's 14th Foot, the 1st Battalions of the 25th and 27th and the 2nd of the 12th Native Infantry, with eighteen guns.

The Left Division, commanded by Major-General D. Marshall, at Kalinjar in Bundelkhand, consisted of the 4th Native Cavalry, the 2nd and 3rd Rohilla Horse, and the 1st Battalions of the 1st, 7th, 14th and 26th, and the 2nd of the 28th, with twenty-four guns.

The Reserve Division, under Sir David Ochterlony, was composed of the 2nd Native Cavalry, two corps of Skinner's Horse, His Majesty's 67th Foot, the 1st Battalions of the 6th and 28th and 2nd Battalions of the 5th, 7th and 19th, and twenty-two guns; besides considerable numbers of contingent horse, and a detachment of the Sirmoor Battalion.

There were besides two smaller forces at Mirzapur and on the frontiers of South Bihar, for the protection of the British frontier in the south-west.

The strength of these forces amounted to about 43,000 men.

The Army of the Deccan was under the command of Lieutenant-General Sir Thomas Hislop, Commander-in-Chief of Madras, and was formed in seven divisions.

Hostilities with the Mahrattas commenced at Poona early in November, 1817, at which time Lord Hastings, with his right and centre divisions in positions to threaten the safety of Gwalior, was engaged in imposing on Sindhia a treaty by which the latter bound himself to assist the British against the Pindaris and all other bodies of freebooters. This treaty was concluded on November the 6th. Immediately afterwards the army of the commander-in-chief was attacked and rendered for the moment incapable of active measures by a violent outbreak of cholera: this is supposed to have been the first occasion on which the disease had been encountered in an epidemic form, and it spread terror amongst all ranks of the army. At length after the camp had been moved several short marches on to higher and more healthy ground, the disease disappeared, having in one week destroyed 764 fighting men and 8,000 followers.

Meanwhile the movements of the Army of the Deccan had driven the Pindaris from their haunts on the Nerbadda: two of their principal leaders, Karim Khan and Wasil Muhammad, flying from the British columns, marched towards Gwalior in the expectation of finding there shelter and aid. But a forward movement of a detachment of the centre division intercepted their communications with Gwalior and compelled them to turn off towards the north-west. Thither they were closely followed by Major-General Marshall with the left division of the Grand Army, who came up with their rear-guard at Bichi-tal, in Kotah, west of the Nimghat, on December the 14th. The cavalry under Colonel Newberry (24th Light Dragoons) charged the enemy, who broke immediately, and the pursuit was continued as far as the Parbati river.

At the same time Major-General Donkin, with the right division of the army, having advanced from the Chambal, heard that the Pindaris, flying from the left division in a north-westerly direction, were within a few miles of him. Taking a light division with him, he came up with Karim Khan at Kalana on the Western Sindh River, and the enemy on his appearance immediately fled in all directions, leaving a quantity of property in his hands. A large party was attacked and defeated by Gardner's Horse, but the main body, finding their advance towards the north-west frustrated, made good their retreat between the Parbati and the Sindh to Shergarh. Here, however, they came across a division of the Army of the Deccan, which circumstance again obliged them to hasten their retreat and change their course towards the south-west. Their numbers were reduced to little more than 2,000, while several smaller parties were scattered about the country, one of which was met and annihilated by Captain Roberts, with the 1st Rohilla Cavalry, at Taraghat. Meanwhile the Pindari leader, Chitu, who had taken refuge some twenty-five miles west of Kotah, was driven thence by Major-General Donkin and forced to fly to the thickets near Komalner, in Meywar.

While the Grand Army had thus been occupied in pursuing the bands of Pindaris, affairs had for a moment taken a serious turn for the British in Nagpur. Here the treachery or weakness of the Rajah, Apa Sahib, allowed an attack to be made on the British Residency on the 26th of November by a force of 3,000 Arab mercenaries in his employ. The British troops then at Nagpur consisted of two battalions of Madras sepoys, a few troopers of the Madras Body-Guard, three troops of the 6th Bengal Native Cavalry, and two companies of Bengal sepoys composing the Resident's Escort. These took up a position on the Sitabaldi hill, standing close to the Residency, and for nearly eighteen hours sustained, with varying fortune, the desperate attacks of the Arabs: at last about noon on the 27th, at a most critical moment, the fortunes of the day were saved by a gallant charge of the cavalry under Captain Fitzgerald. As a reward for their services on this occasion, the 6th Bengal Native Cavalry received permission (20th February, 1819) to bear on their standards the words "Seetabuldee, 27th November, 1817," in commemoration of "the brilliant and decisive charge made on that day by three troops of the regiment, headed by Captain Fitzgerald"; and *Subadar* Bhagwan Singh received, as a reward for conspicuous gallantry, a gold medal, 300 *bighas* of land, and a pension of R100 a month. The casualties of the Bengal cavalry were twenty-three killed, and twenty-five (including three British officers) wounded. On the 29th reinforcements arrived, consisting of three more troops of the 6th Bengal Native Cavalry and the 1-22nd Bengal Native Infantry, while a fortnight later the whole of Brigadier-General Doveton's division of the Army of the Deccan reached Nagpur. When intelligence of the state of affairs at Nagpur reached Lord Hastings, the division at Mirzapur under Brigadier-General Hardyman, consisting of the 8th Bengal Native Cavalry, His Majesty's 17th Foot, and the 2-8th Bengal Native Infantry, was ordered to make a forward movement to the Nerbadda. This force, having advanced as far as Jubbulpore, was opposed by the Subahdar of that place at the head of 3,000 troops. The enemy were, however, quickly dispersed (19th December, 1817) and suffered severely in their flight, while the town surrendered on the same day, and Hardyman established his headquarters there, having lost in the action no more than two men killed, and three British officers, one native officer, and six men wounded.

In the meantime, negotiations with Apa Sahib had led to no definite result, and arrangements were accordingly made by Brigadier-General Doveton for commencing hostilities against Nagpur. The Mahratta army was attacked at noon on the 16th of December, and by half past 1 the enemy were dispersed, and their camp and a great quantity of artillery captured.[1] The Arabs in the service of the Rajah now threw themselves into the citadel of Nagpur, and defended themselves there for five days, until, having repulsed a general assault of the British, in which the latter lost 301 killed and wounded, they secured for themselves favourable terms and capitulated.

The defeat of the Rajah of Nagpur and the success of the subsequent operations of the army of the Deccan against Holkar left the British Government free to prosecute the pursuit of the scattered Pindaris and to complete their annihilation, which had been the principal object of the campaign. At this time Major-General Donkin was at Ghaintaghat on the Chambal, and Major-General Brown was detached from the Grand Army with a detachment consisting of the 3rd and 4th Bengal Native Cavalry, the Dromedary Corps, some irregular horse, and the 1-18th Bengal Native Infantry. This force advanced to Suner, arriving there on the 5th of January, 1818. The Pindaris meanwhile, under Karim Khan and Wasil Muhammad, who had fought at the battle of Mahidpur, had been compelled after that defeat to retire westward towards Jawad. That place was accordingly the centre towards which the several British detachments moved. Chitu now joined the other Pindari leaders, and throughout the month of January their forces were perpetually hunted backwards and forwards until the main body was finally defeated and destroyed at Kotri by a detachment from the force of Colonel J, W. Adams of the Bengal Army. Chitu escaped and afterwards joined the Peshwa's routed army in the Deccan; the other leaders surrendered to the British. Before this event Jaswant Rao Bhao, the Jagirdar of Jawad, had been attacked by Major-General Brown on account of his conduct in aiding the Pindaris; Jawad was carried by storm (29th January), the British force losing in the attack one officer and thirty-seven men killed and wounded. The neighbouring fortress of Komalner surrendered soon afterwards.

This attainment of the great objects of the policy of Lord Hast-

---

1. This engagement was called the battle of Sukandarra by the Bengal sepoys.

ings was followed soon after by the overthrow at Ashta of the Peshwa, Baji Rao, the once formidable head of the Mahratta confederacy. The governor-general, therefore, deemed a longer maintenance in the field of his great army unnecessary, and in February, 1818, orders were issued for the return to cantonments of the larger portion of the Bengal forces. One brigade of the right division remained some time longer to assist in restoring order in the territories of Holkar, after which it joined the reserve division under Sir David Ochterlony in Rajputana, while Brigadier-General Hardyman[2] had not yet left the Nerbadda country. From the left division a strong force, augmented by several corps from the centre, remained in the field under Major-General Marshall for operations in Nagpur and the upper Nerbadda, and generally for the settlement of districts relinquished by the Rajah of Nagpur. This consisted of the 7th Bengal Native Cavalry, the 1st Battalions of the 14th and 26th, and 2nd Battalions of the 1st, 13th, and 28th Native Infantry, 3,000 of Sindhia's Contingent, 400 of Baddeley's Rohilla Cavalry, and a heavy train of artillery. These troops were concentrated at Kimlasa, in Bundelkhand, On the 5th of March, and were first employed against the *kiladars* of Dhamoni and Mandala, who, inspired secretly to resistance by the Rajah of Nagpur, refused to surrender those fortresses. Dhamoni surrendered to the troops without a struggle, but at Mandala, the town had to be carried by assault (26th April) before the garrison of the fort would come to terms: the loss on our side was three killed and fourteen wounded. Major-General Marshall[3] being now recalled to Cawnpore, Brigadier-General Watson[4] succeeded to the command; and the attention of this officer had at once to be given to the hostile attitude of Apa Sahib of Nagpur, who, having been foiled in his plan of joining the army of the Peshwa, had been deposed and despatched under escort to Allahabad, but, having managed to escape from the escort of Bengal troops who had him in charge, had now taken refuge with the Gonds in the Mahadeo hills (May, 1818), whom he shortly stirred up into insurrection.

In the meantime the Peshwa had been hotly pursued hither and

---

2. Major-General Frederick Hardyman, C.B., died on the 28th November, 1821.
3. Lieutenant-General Sir Dyson Marshall, K.C.B., died at Cawnpore on the 20th July, 1823.
4. The late General Sir James Watson, K.C.B., Colonel of the 14th Foot. For a short time (during the temporary absence of Lord William Bentinck) he was acting Commander-in-Chief in Bengal. He died on the 12th August. 1862, in the 91st year of his age and the 81st of his service.

thither after the action at Ashta. Eventually, on the 16th April, he was surprised by Colonel Adams at Seoni, in Berar, totally defeated, and his army completely dispersed. Hopeless of continuing the contest, Baji Rao made overtures to Sir John Malcolm,[5] and early in June he surrendered. He was removed as a political prisoner to Bithur, near Cawnpore.

In the month of May, Brigadier General Adams took the strong fortress of Chanda by storm, with a loss of thirteen killed and fifty-five wounded: amongst the latter was Lieutenant Fell, Commanding the Pioneers. In the following month a detachment from Brigadier-General Watson's force, reinforced by some details from that of Brigadier-General Adams, made an unsuccessful attempt on the fort of Sataniwari, the repulse costing us eleven killed (including Lieutenant Manson, Commanding the Pioneers) and seventy-five wounded.

The flight of Apa Sahib, and his reception amongst the Gonds and other wild tribes of the Vindhya and Sathpura mountains, led to a prolonged campaign in that part of the country. The unhealthiness of the season at first confined operations to desultory hostilities between bands of the enemy and small detached outposts stationed in various places with the object of checking any extension of the rising in the Rajah's favour. The first occurrence of importance was disastrous for the British. A body of Arabs assembled at Mailgha, on the Tapti river, and seized the town of Maisdi; Captain Sparkes, with a company of the 2-10th Bengal Native Infantry, marched against them from Baitul; near Multai, immediately after crossing the Tapti, he encountered the enemy, who were in force (20th July); his detachment was surrounded, but fought gallantly until their ammunition was exhausted, when the whole party was destroyed, except two *naiks* and seventeen sepoys, of whom ten were wounded, those killed being Captain Sparkes, one *subadar*, one *jemadar*, four havildars, two *naiks*, 82 sepoys and seven followers. Reinforcements were immediately sent to Baitul, but even as they advanced another detachment of thirty of the 2-10th Bengal Native Infantry was surprised and destroyed, and Multai and several other towns were seized by the Gonds and Arabs. As soon as a sufficient force was assembled, active measures were adopted to subdue the enemy. The town of Multai was retaken by Major Cumming, and the enemy, who evacuated the place, were pursued by Captain Newton, 2-10th, with a squadron of the 7th Bengal Native Cavalry and some light infantry.

---

5. Major-General Sir John Malcolm, G.C.B., Madras Army, died in London on the 30th May, 1833.

They were overtaken near Harna on the 24th of August, and 170 of them killed. Another party was attacked at Burdai by Major Bowen, with a squadron of cavalry and 100 light infantry, and 300 of them killed, while Lieutenant Cruickshank, 1-24th, doing duty with the 2-10th Native Infantry, with 180 infantry, 50 of the 7th Bengal Native Cavalry, and 80 Rohilla Horse, destroyed a large band of the enemy at Junagarhi. At the end of September Captain Newton, with the 2-10th Bengal Native Infantry, one company of the 1-23rd, and a squadron of the 7th Bengal Native Cavalry, advanced into the hills from Baitul, and made reprisals on the Gonds for their participation in the attack on Captain Sparkes. With the commencement of 1819, a concerted plan of attack was commenced on the headquarters of Apa Sahib. The ex-Rajah fled before the British advance, and being joined by the old Pindari chief, Chitu, made his way to the fortress of Asirgarh. The *kiladar* of that place gave a temporary asylum to Apa Sahib, but refused to admit Chitu, who, fleeing towards Malwa, was killed by a tiger in the jungles of the Vindhya hills. Apa Sahib only remained at Asirgarh a few days, when he again fled, disguised as a mendicant, and eventually took refuge with Ranjit Singh in the Punjab, and later with the Rajah of Jodhpur, where he died.

In July 1818, it may here be noticed, a detachment from the reserve division of the Grand Army, under the command of Lieutenant-Colonel W. A. Thompson, took the strong fort of Madhurajpura by storm, with trifling loss. The 1-27th and the 1-28th Bengal Native Infantry and a detachment of the Corps of Pioneers were employed on this service.

Early in 1819, the reduction of Asirgarh was undertaken, the *kiladar* of which place had been guilty of open acts of hostility by his reception of Apa Sahib and by his firing on the British troops in pursuit of the fugitive. The forces employed were under Brigadier-General Doveton and Sir John Malcolm; with the former were a troop of horse artillery, the 6th, and a squadron of the 7th Bengal Native Cavalry, and two Madras native cavalry regiments; the 1st and 2nd Battalions of the 15th and the 2nd of the 29th Bengal Native Infantry, five battalions of Madras native infantry, and some pioneers. Sir John Malcolm's army was composed of Bombay and Madras troops, but was joined later by the 2-1st and 2-13th Bengal Native Infantry, with some artillery, from Saugor. Operations began on the 18th of March, on which day the *pettah* was carried, and on the 30th the lower fort was abandoned by

---

6. Lieutenant-General Sir John Doveton, G.C.B., Madras Army, died on the 7th November, 1847.

the garrison and occupied by the assailants. The bombardment of the main fort meanwhile proceeded with such success that the *kiladar*, despairing of the result, surrendered unconditionally on the 7th of April. The loss of the besiegers in the three weeks' operations amounted to one officer (Lieutenant-Colonel Fraser, Royal Scots) killed and ten wounded, and 46 men killed and 256 wounded: of these the Bengal troops lost 36 killed and 108 wounded, the greater part of whom belonged to the 2-15th and were killed or injured by the accidental blowing up of an expense magazine.

The capture of Asirgarh brought to a close the operations of the war, the results of which were not only great territorial additions to the British possessions, but still greater accessions of political strength, and the final establishment of the paramount influence of the British Government in India.

For several years after the termination of the Mahratta-Pindari war, the Bengal Army enjoyed comparative rest. Nevertheless there occurred here and there local disturbances, which necessitated military action, and a few of these will now be mentioned.

In March, 1820, a small detachment under Lieutenant Chitty, of the 1st Rohilla Horse, distinguished themselves in an engagement with a rebel leader, named Bhoja Singh, on the banks of the Chuka Nala, in Rohilkhand, completely dispersing the enemy with a loss on our side of one native officer killed and five men wounded.

In February, 1821, Colonel Richards, with detachments of the Body-Guard, Cuttack Legion, and Ramgarh Battalion, was engaged for some weeks in suppressing an outbreak of the Larka Kols.

An unfortunate affair took place in 1821 in an attack on the forces of the rebel Maharao Kishor Singh, of Kotah, in Rajputana. In this, besides some native contingent troops, the 2-6th Native Infantry, two squadrons of the 4th Light Cavalry under the command of Major Ridge, and part of the 5th Light Cavalry, were engaged. An attack on the Maharao's forces was made at Mangrol on the 1st October with the result that they were beaten with considerable loss. The success, however, was marred by the conduct of the 4th Light Cavalry, who, on being ordered to charge the enemy's cavalry, suddenly reined up and left their officers unsupported, in consequence of which Lieutenants Reade and Clerk were killed, and Major Ridge severely wounded. In the course of the following year this affair was brought to the notice of Government, with the result that, by G. O. G. G. dated 30th August, 1822, three troops of the 4th Light Cavalry were dismissed the service for cowardice:[7] *Havildar*-Major Masnad Ali and Trumpet-Major Sheik Nadir Ali, however, are mentioned as being exempt from this disgrace, and were "promoted for their gallantry in support of their commanding officer, and for their honest and fearless conduct before the Court of Enquiry."

In February, 1822, a force under Major W. C. Faithful, consisting of detachments of the 1st Light Cavalry, 2-4th and 2-9th Native Infantry, four 18-pounders, and four mortars, was engaged in Oudh against a refractory chief, named Kasim Ali Khan; the fortified village of Bardgaon was bombarded on the 9th February, and several other forts reduced.

In March, 1823, it became necessary to despatch a force for the reduction of the strong fort of Lamba, in Jodhpur territory. The force was under the command of Brigadier Knox, and consisted of the 3rd Light Cavalry, the 1-18th Native Infantry, and the grenadiers and light infantry of the 1-25th and 2-29th Native Infantry, with detachments of artillery and pioneers. After some days spent in fruitless endeavours to induce the garrison to surrender, batteries were opened on the fort on the 17th March, and four hours' firing produced such an effect that the enemy evacuated the place and fled.

The preceding four years had not been productive of any very important changes in, or additions to, the Army of Bengal. Several new local and irregular corps had been raised, amongst them especially the four Gurkha battalions already noticed : also in 1817 (G. O. G. G., 16thMay), in consequence of the disturbances in Cuttack, an irregular force was raised in that province, called the "Cuttack Legion"; this consisted originally of two troops of cavalry, with two small guns, and three companies of infantry. The cavalry was afterwards disbanded, but the infantry still survives as the 42nd Bengal Infantry (Gurkha Rifles). A similar force was raised in Gorakhpur (9th February, 1818) consisting of a battalion of light infantry, with two troops of irregular cavalry attached, and to provide for contingencies throughout the Mahratta war, various levies were raised at Cawnpore, Fatehgarh, Muttra, and Dinapore, all of which were (9th and 12th March, 1818) ordered to be completed to a strength of 1,000 men.

These four battalions were, in 1823, brought into the regular army, and Major Fagan's Fatehgarh levy, which then became the 1st Battal-

---

7. It is stated that the conduct of these men was due not so much to cowardice, as to dislike of their commanding officer, whom they wished to bring to disgrace. There is more than one instance on record in which this feeling has found expression in the same way.

ion of the 32nd, is now the 9th Bengal Infantry. On the 19th of February, 1819, orders were issued for the raising of a corps of "Sappers or Miners" to be formed at Allahahad, and to be completed to a total of 816 (native ranks): they were commanded by Major Anburey, and two companies of the existing Pioneers were incorporated in the corps.

During the preparations for, and the course of, the Mahratta war, several bodies of cavalry previously in the services of various native chiefs were received into the Company's Army : thus, besides the Rohilla Horse, raised during the Gurkha war, a corps modelled on the same lines was formed of horsemen formerly in the service of Dyaram, the Taluqdar of Hathras, and of some of the chiefs of Bundelkhand (25thMay, 1817),and in the following year three corps of local horse were formed with men received from Amir Khan, whose troops also supplied the British with two battalions of local infantry, called the "Rampura Local Battalions" (G. O. C. C,, 4th May, 1818). In 1819 (G.O.C.C., 4th February) the strength of the regular cavalry was increased, each regiment being formed into eight troops of 92 men each. A month later, the great war being now practically over, all infantry regiments were augmented by ten men per company, to enable a larger proportion of the old soldiers to visit their homes.

In the autumn of 1818 (G. O. C. C., 14th July), a detachment of volunteers was called for and despatched to Ceylon to assist the local Government there; it consisted of three battalions of infantry and some native artillery; these troops remained in Ceylon some months, but do not appear to have taken part in any active operations; they returned to Calcutta late in 1819, when they were complimented in General Orders for their alacrity in volunteering, and for their good conduct while on service; a gratuity of one month's pay and full batta was granted them, and they were allowed to select the corps of the line which they might wish to join.

The period of peace which followed the Mahratta war enabled the Government to dispense with some of its more expensive auxiliary forces. Thus, in 1819 (G. O .C. C., 28th August), one regiment of Rohilla Horse, two of Rampura Local Cavalry, and one of Skinner's Horse were disbanded, and the 3rd Rohilla Horse was transferred to the service of Oudh. No other changes occurred, however, until two years later, when (20th August, 1821) the Dromedary Corps was disbanded, and the transport which had been kept up to war strength on the frontier was greatly reduced.

After a further period of two years, the Government determined to bring to some uniform level the various and nondescript irregular regiments in the service of the Company: orders were issued for all local and provincial battalions of infantry and local horse to be placed on a fixed scale in the numbers of their officers, non-commissioned officers, and men; while at the same time a detailed list was given of all these corps, showing their composition, numbers, and duties (G. O. C. C, 6th May, 1823).

The local battalions of infantry, with the present names of those which now exist, are as follow:

The Ramgarh Local Battalion.
Bhagalpur Hill Rangers.
Dinajpur Local Battalion.
Champaran Light Infantry.
1st Nasseri (Gurkha) Battalion, now the 1st Gurkha Rifles.
2nd Nasseri (Gurkha) Battalion.
Sirmoor Battalion, now the 2nd Gurkha Rifles.
Rangpur Light Infantry, formerly the "Cuttack Legion," now the 42nd Bengal Infantry.
Gorakhpur Light Infantry.
Rampura Local Battalion.

In Civil Department:
Calcutta Native Militia, now the 18th Bengal Infantry.
Kumaon Battalion, now the 3rd Gurkha Rifles,
Bencoolen Local Battalion.
Mharwara Local Battalion.

The local horse, which, as the G. O. C. C. explains, being neither clothed nor armed by the State, take rank after the infantry, were:

1st	(Skinner's) Local Horse	now the 1st Bengal Cavalry
2nd	(Gardner's) Local Horse	now the 2nd Bengal Cavalry
3rd	(Blair's) Local Horse	formerly the 1st Rohilla Cavalry
4th	(Baddeley's) Local Horse	formerly Skinner's 2nd Regiment, now the 3rd Bengal Cavalry
5th	(Gough's) Local Horse	raised by G.O.C.C. of this date for service in Malwa

Besides the above, there were thirteen corps of provincial infantry, which were practically police levies.

In June, 1823 (G. G. O. No. 65) orders were issued for the formation of four new regiments of regular infantry, to be numbered from the 31st to the 34th. Of these the first two were formed from the infantry levies raised in 1817; the remainder were newly raised. The following detail of orders were issued on the subject:

31st Regiment

1st Battalion	to be formed from Major Wood's Benares Levy
2nd Battalion	from Captain Watson's Cawnpore Levy

32nd Regiment

1st Battalion	from the Mainpuri (originally the Fatehgarh) Levy, Major Smith
2nd Battalion	from the Muttra Levy, Captain Gilman

33rd Regiment

1st Battalion	to be raised at Dinapore
2nd Battalion	to be raised at Cawnpore

34th Regiment

1st & 2nd Battalions	both to be raised at Benares

Of these, the 1st of the 32nd is now the 9th Bengal Infantry; and the 1st of the 33rd still survives as the 10th Bengal Infantry.[8]

Before proceeding to the extensive changes in the army which were executed in the following year, it will be well to notice the interior economy and equipment of the Bengal troops as they existed down to this date. In the cavalry the ever-recurring and difficult question of remounts is one which we find constantly noticed in the orders of the period. According to the earliest rules on the subject (Minutes of Council, 8th April, 1793), horses for cavalry remounts were bought by a commissariat agent, and passed into the ranks after approval by a committee of cavalry officers; the standards at that time were, of age not under three years or over eight in times of peace, and in times of war not under four or over nine years; of height not under

---

8. The 2nd of the 32nd bore the native name of *Harriat-ki-pallan*, derived from the officer who first commanded it,—Lieutenant-Colonel J. S. Harriott.

fourteen hands and-a-half. This latter rule, however, was soon modified; for in 1801 (2nd October) orders were issued that three years old of 14—1 might be received, and even horses of 14—1 and above three years old, if the Committee were satisfied that they were otherwise unexceptionable. As early as 1794 a board was appointed for promoting the improvement of country-breds; but there is little record of the improvements effected, beyond the appointment of a secretary on R250 a month, with a further R250 for rent of an office for the board and a house for himself. Early in the century the Government Stud establishments were started, notwithstanding which the supply of good-sized horses seems to have been much exceeded by the demand, so that in 1816 (18th September) we find the standard height of stud-breds and *zemindars'* horses presented to the committee by officers of the stud reduced to fourteen hands. The purchase of remounts was now effected directly by a commissariat officer, who despatched the horses to regiments, where they were passed by a regimental committee. From the Government Stud horses were assigned to regiments by lot. In September, 1816, an experiment was made in the use of geldings as troop horses in Bengal; orders were issued for the formation of one troop of such in each regiment, remounts for which were to be obtained from the Pusa stud. But after trial for three years and-a-half (G. O. C. C, 11th March, 1820) "it having been proved to the satisfaction of the commander-in-chief that the general employment of geldings would tend to the great deterioration of the efficiency of the cavalry in India," these troops were ordered to be broken up.

Definite orders were issued in September, 1818, regarding the standards of the regular Bengal cavalry: one standard was allowed per squadron, the first being dark-blue, with the Royal Arms in the centre and the Union in the upper corner; the second of crimson, with the Company's arms; the third of the colour of the regimental facings, with the number of the regiment in the centre.

In 1820 (23rd September) the system of *bargirs* in the irregular cavalry was abolished, but this order, which no doubt occasioned much dissatisfaction, was modified two months later, and native officers of the first class were allowed to keep not more than three *bargirs*, those of the second class two, and inferior ranks one: a few years later the original system of numerous *bargirs* was reverted to.

In the artillery branch an important addition was made to the Bengal Army by the institution, in 1817, of native horse artillery: this was formed in the first place by the withdrawal from native cavalry regiments of their galloper guns, which, with the men of the various regiments whence they were detached, were formed into three troops of horse artillery; the arrangement thus made as a tentative measure was confirmed two years later, when (G. O. C. C, 1st May, 1819) the cavalry soldiers doing duty with these guns were ordered to return to their regiments, unless they might wish to remain permanently in their present service, in which case they were to take rank from their first employment with the horse-artillery troops in 1817.

Some few changes are noticeable in the organisation of Bengal infantry during these years: of these the most important, in which too the cavalry was equally concerned, was the institution (28th October, 1817) of the rank of *Subadar*-Major: definite rules for the selection and the payment of these officers were published in March, 1818, and on the same date the appointment of Colour-*Havildar* was instituted in the non-commissioned ranks. On the re-organisation of the local corps, in 1823, regulations were published as to the rates of pay in those regiments, and also with regard to the nature of their equipment. From this we find that the local regiments were dressed like those of the line, except that they retained the old black leather belts and accoutrements in the place of buff. In 1818 the facings and lace of regiments were regulated, the colour of which seems to have previously varied a good deal in accordance with the taste and fancy of commanding officers.

The date is now reached of the second great re-organisation of the Bengal Army: the system which had obtained for the last thirty years was swept away, and a new order brought into force which lasted unchanged until, after a further period of thirty years, destroyed by the events of the Indian Mutiny, it in turn gave place to the present organisation.

On the 6th of May, 1824, a G.G.O. was issued, in accordance with instructions received from the Court of Directors, ordering promotions to be made to bring the strength of officers in all infantry regiments to the following scale:

| 2 | Colonels | 2 | Majors | 20 | Lieutenants |
| 2 | Lieutenant-Colonels | 10 | Captains | 10 | Ensigns |

N.B.—The rank of Captain-Lieutenant had been abolished by G. O. C. C, dated 9th January, 1819

In cavalry regiments the strength of officers was to be half the above.

This order further directed that "as soon as the above promotions are carried out, the infantry, European and native, are to be divided into two regiments each, by the final separation of battalions," and that officers were to be posted alternately to the two regiments. The regiments so formed were then to be numbered in the order in which they were first raised. The following table shows the changes which were thus effected in the numbering of corps:

Old number		New	Old number		New
1st	1st Bttn.	2nd	18th	1st Bttn.	36th
	2nd Bttn.	4th		2nd Bttn.	37th
2nd	1st Bttn.	2nd	19th	1st Bttn.	38th
	2nd Bttn.	4th		2nd Bttn.	39th
3rd	1st Bttn.	2nd	20th	1st Bttn.	40th
	2nd Bttn.	4th		2nd Bttn.	41st
4th	1st Bttn.	2nd	21st	1st Bttn.	42nd
	2nd Bttn.	4th		2nd Bttn.	43rd
5th	1st Bttn.	2nd	22nd	1st Bttn.	44th
	2nd Bttn.	4th		2nd Bttn.	45th
6th	1st Bttn.	2nd	23rd	1st Bttn.	46th
	2nd Bttn.	4th		2nd Bttn.	47th
7th	1st Bttn.	2nd	24th	1st Bttn.	48th
	2nd Bttn.	4th		2nd Bttn.	49th
8th	1st Bttn.	2nd	25th	1st Bttn.	50th
	2nd Bttn.	4th		2nd Bttn.	51st
9th	1st Bttn.	2nd	26th	1st Bttn.	52nd
	2nd Bttn.	4th		2nd Bttn.	53rd
10th	1st Bttn.	2nd	27th	1st Bttn.	54th
	2nd Bttn.	4th		2nd Bttn.	55th
11th	1st Bttn.	2nd	28th	1st Bttn.	56th
	2nd Bttn.	4th		2nd Bttn.	57th
12th	1st Bttn.	2nd	29th	1st Bttn.	58th
	2nd Bttn.	4th		2nd Bttn.	59th

13th	1st Bttn.	2nd	30th	1st Bttn.	60th
	2nd Bttn.	4th		2nd Bttn.	61st
14th	1st Bttn.	2nd	31st	1st Bttn.	62nd
	2nd Bttn.	4th		2nd Bttn.	63rd
15th	1st Bttn.	2nd	32nd	1st Bttn.	64th
	2nd Bttn.	4th		2nd Bttn.	65th
16th	1st Bttn.	2nd	33rd	1st Bttn.	66th
	2nd Bttn.	4th		2nd Bttn.	67th
17th	1st Bttn.	2nd	34th	1st Bttn.	68th
	2nd Bttn.	4th		2nd Bttn.	69th

The re-introduction of single battalions and general re-organisation of 1824 closes another chapter in the history of the Bengal Army. Whether the past thirty years had seen as great an improvement in the quality as they had in the quantity of the Bengal troops, seems in the opinion of contemporary critics to have been doubtful. The double battalion system and with it regimental promotion of officers up to the rank of Major had been introduced in the hope of strengthening the ties between British and native ranks; but this object was defeated by the defects in the position of officers of native corps: the command of one of these regiments was of less value from any point of view than staff appointments of a second class; it was attended with great anxiety and much drudgery, and carried but little influence or consideration; under these circumstances it was not a post much sought after. A second point adverse to the efficiency of the Bengal Army was the small consideration paid to the native commissioned ranks at this period; until the institution of the rank of *Subadar*-Major, a native officer could not rise above the insignificant pay of R174 a month; when, in addition to this, it is remembered that the lower ranks were liable for most trivial offences to suffer corporal punishment, that even when a commission was gained a native officer was exposed to the harshness of his British superiors, whose habits of self-restraint, as the court-martial records of the times prove, were but too little cultivated; and that consideration for the position of native officers as such was not much insisted on from British ranks, commissioned, or non-commissioned; when all these points are considered, it is only to be wondered at that the native army displayed as much devotion and zeal in times of emergency as it undoubtedly did.

That the fact of the native army being in an unsatisfactory condition was just beginning to dawn on Anglo-Indians is proved by the commencement of that stream of newspaper and serial controversy on the subject, which twenty years later swelled into such a torrent as to almost flood all the public journals of the time. Among numerous letters and essays, some of whose arguments are proved by after-events to have been prejudiced and short-sighted, a carefully written article in the *Asiatic Journal* for May, 1821, contains much useful criticism of the sepoy army of that time. "The defects of that army," says the writer (a Madras officer), "are the paucity of British officers, the ignorance of the native officers, and the worthlessness of the material." The latter he ascribes in Madras and Bombay, to poor physique, in Bengal to the encumbrance of caste prejudices, which he declares are fostered by the British officers, who set a bad example of luxuriousness and often of inefficiency. The expression of such opinions as these was received with a torrent of abuse and sarcasm; yet who will now be found to question their truth?

CHAPTER 5

The First Burma War

During a period of nearly thirty years, since 1794, the Eastern frontier of the British possessions in Bengal had been again and again disturbed by the incursions and aggressions of the Burmese. Several representations on this subject were made to Ava, but attempts to open negotiations served only to imbue that arrogant court with the idea that the unwillingness of the Indian Government to declare war was the result of fear; the insolence of the Burmese increased year by year, until at the close of 1823 it became evident that a recourse to hostilities was the only remedy. The immediate cause of rupture was a claim laid by the Burmese to the small island of Shahpuri at the mouth of the Naf river, which was occupied by a detachment of Bengal troops. Two Burmese armies invaded British territory with the avowed object of possessing themselves of Chittagong and the adjoining districts; one of these advanced from Assam, the other from Manipur; the former was attacked at Bikrampur on the 17th of January, 1824, by a small force under Major Newton, consisting of detachments of the 1-10th and 2-23rd Bengal Native Infantry, and four companies of the Rangpur Light Infantry:[1] the enemy were driven from their stockade and routed, but the British force was too small to allow of a protracted pursuit, and the Burmese soon rallied and effected a junction with the second army from Manipur. They now advanced along the right bank of the Surma river and stockaded themselves close to Bhadrapur, a small post held by Captain Johnston with a wing of the 1-10th, one company of the 2-23rd and a few of the Rangpur Light Infantry: from this position they were driven by Captain Johnston on the 13th February, and being followed by Lieutenant-Colonel Bowen, who commanded on the Sylhet frontier, one division retired into Assam and the other entrenched themselves at Dudhpatli. Here they were attacked by the Bengal troops on the 21st February, but repulsed the latter with a loss of twenty-one killed and 135 wounded, including one officer (Lieutenant A. B. Armstrong, 1-10th Bengal Native Infantry) killed, and four others wounded, amongst whom were Lieutenant-Colonel Bowen and Captain Johnston. On the 27th of February, Lieutenant-Colonel Innes arrived at Jatrapur with the 2-19th Bengal Native Infantry, and four guns, upon which the Burmese abandoned Dudhpatli and retired into Manipur. In June, however, they again advanced into Cachar, and Colonel Innes attacked them at Talain; but he was unsuccessful, and was obliged to retire to Jatrapur, and the setting in of the rains put a period to further operations for the time. Hostilities having thus commenced, the Indian Government turned their attention to the readiest method of bringing the war to a speedy and successful conclusion. The difficulties presented by a march through the swamps and jungles of Manipur and Arakan were too great to allow an attack on that side to promise favourably: it was therefore determined to send an expedition to Rangoon, whence it was believed that the Irrawaddy could be navigated in sailing vessels, and the capital reached speedily and without loss.

The aversion of the Bengal sepoys to serve across the seas prevented any but a small detachment of them taking part in this expedition; the force from Bengal consisted of His Majesty's 13th and 38th, two companies of artillery, and the 40th Bengal Native Infantry (late the 2nd Battalion of the 20th, or Marine Regiment). The remainder of the force was drawn from the Madras Presidency. Brigadier-General Sir Archibald Campbell, K.C.B., of the 38th Foot, was appointed to the command of the expedition, the troops composing which rendezvoused at Port Cornwallis in the Andamans in the early part of May 1824.

Rangoon was reached on the morning of the 11th of May, to the astonishment of the inhabitants, who never expected to be attacked in their own country; a broadside from the frigate accompanying the expedition silenced the feeble attempts of the few Burmese guns on shore, and the force, landing without opposition, found the town entirely deserted. This was the first blow to the hopes of the British, who were thus unable to procure boats in which to continue their advance up the Irrawaddy. Indeed, Sir Archibald Campbell found it sufficiently difficult to obtain supplies for his force where he was, and from this cause, and from the unfavourable season of the year in which these

---

1. Now the 42nd Bengal Infantry (Gurkha Rifles).

operations had been begun, the troops were subjected to great privations, and suffered greatly in health, large number perishing from fever, dysentery, and other diseases incidental to the climate and locality. The Burmese to some extent confined their hostilities to cutting off all supplies and to endeavouring to fire the British ships in the river, in which latter attempt, however, they were not successful; but large bodies of them not infrequently came and stockaded themselves within striking distance of our troops, and finding it impossible to advance up the river to attack the capital, Sir Archibald Campbell lost no opportunity of attacking these bands, and many sharp engagements followed at Joazoung, Kemmendine, Kamarut, Dalla, Kyklu, and other places, in which our troops sustained considerable losses; it is calculated that up to the end of November our casualties in the various engagements at Rangoon and in the vicinity amounted to not less than 100 killed and 560 wounded, of whom a large proportion were officers. Small expeditions to more distant points were also sent, and Mergui, Martaban, and other places were captured.

At length, in December, the enemy massed his troops for a vigorous attack on the invaders, and the British positions round the Shwe-Dagon Pagoda at Rangoon and at Kemmendine were completely hemmed in by stockades and entrenchments, held by 60,000 men, under Maha Bandula, the most celebrated of the Burmese generals. From the 1st to the 4th the skirmishing was incessant. On the 5th Sir Archibald Campbell delivered a vigorous attack on the enemy's left, forced their entrenchments, and drove them from the field, capturing the whole of their guns and military stores. But though thus defeated on his left, Bandula continued the attack from his right, until the 7th, when Sir Archibald again attacked him and drove him finally from his works, and dispersed the remains of his vast army. In these operations the British loss amounted to twenty-six killed (including two officers) and 240 wounded (including eleven officers). On the 8th and 9th the enemy were driven from Dalla with a loss on our side of two killed and forty-six wounded, and on the 15th a large body, whom Bandula had rallied, and who had strongly entrenched themselves at Kokein, about five miles to the north of Rangoon, were vigorously attacked and driven from their position with heavy-loss, our own being eighteen killed (including three officers) and 115 wounded (including fourteen officers). Among the troops engaged at Rangoon and Kokein in was a detachment of the Governor-General's Body-Guard, which had arrived from India a few days before.

During this period but partial success attended the British arms on the Eastern frontier. A force, commanded by Lieutenant-Colonel Macmorine, and consisting of seven companies of the 2-23rd Native Infantry, six companies of the Rangpur Light Infantry, the Dinajpur Local Infantry, a wing of the Champaran Light Infantry, six 6-pounder guns, and a small body of irregular horse, had been assembled at Goalpara, and moved forward from that place in March, 1824, with the object of expelling the Burmese from Assam, but after defeating the enemy in several encounters, the want of supplies and the commencement of the rains compelled Lieutenant-Colonel Alfred Richards, who had succeeded to the command on Colonel Macmorine dying of cholera, to retire to Gauhati and defer further operations for a time.

On the south-eastern frontier positive disaster was experienced We had at Chittagong a force under Colonel Shapland, consisting of the left wing of the 2-13th (now become the 27th), five companies of the 2-20th (now become the 40th), and the whole of the 1-23rd (now become the 45th), Bengal Native Infantry, the Chittagong Provincial Battalion, a newly raised Magh Levy, and some artillery in all about 3,000 men; of these a detachment (three companies of the 40th, 100 men, and five of the 45th, 250 men, with portion of the Provincial Battalion and the Magh Levy, and two guns) was in the exposed outpost of Ramu, under the command of Captain Noton of the 45th. A very large Burmese force advanced from Arakan early in May and attacked Ramu, where the detachment was reduced, by the flight of the irregulars, to only 350 sepoys. Captain Noton held his ground until the morning of the 17th of May, when, his flank being turned, he was compelled to retreat. The result was one of those terrible disasters which have, from time to time, overtaken the British forces, and the cause of which has generally been, as in this case, too great confidence in being able to: oppose large armies of uncivilised peoples with a mere handful of disciplined troops. Captains Noton, 45th, Trueman, 40th, and Pringle, 18th (commanding the Magh Levy), Lieutenant Grigg, 45th, Ensign Bennett, 45th, Assistant-Surgeon Maysmor, *Subadar* Harak Singh, and *Jemadar* Shaik Manulla, 40th, and *Subadar* Bachu Ram, 45th Bengal Native Infantry, were killed; two more officers were wounded and 250 sepoys were killed, wounded, or taken prisoners.

In Assam the retirement of the British to Gauhati during the rains had been the signal for a renewed advance on the part of the Burmans. At the end of the year, however, a force (the 46th and 57th Native Infantry and the Rangpur Light Infantry) moved against them under Lieutenant-Colonel Richards, which drove the Burmese before them and finally occupied Rangpur, the capital of Upper Assam, after a sharp encounter (29th January, 1825) in which we sustained a loss of two men killed and two officers and 49 men wounded. Of the officers wounded one was Lieutenant-Colonel Richards himself; the other was Lieutenant James Brooke of the 18th Bengal Native Infantry, then an officer in the Bengal Commissariat Department, but more widely known in after years as the Rajah of Sarawak.

The last months of 1824 witnessed the massing at Sylhet of a large force, of which the object was an invasion of Burma through Manipur, while a still larger army was prepared to march from Chittagong into Arakan and over the Arakan Yomas to the Burmese capital. These expeditions, so contrary to the original plan of the campaign, were arranged with the concurrence of the commander-in-chief, when the difficulties of the army at Rangoon made the success of the British force in that quarter a matter of grave doubt. In order to supply troops for all these expeditions, four flank battalions were formed in Bengal (G.G.O. No. 195 of 1824 and G.O.C.C, 12th July, 1824), for which twenty regiments contributed each a grenadier and a light company, and two light infantry and two grenadier battalions were thus formed of ten companies each: included in them were detachments from the 33rd and 43rd Bengal Native Infantry (now the 4th and 6th), which sent companies to the 1st Grenadier Battalion and the 1st Light Battalion; while in the 2nd Battalions of each were companies from the 59th and 63rd (the present 8th and 9th).

The Cachar force under Brigadier-General Shuldham was formed of the 7th, 14th, 39th, 44th, 45th, and 52nd Bengal Native Infantry, with two companies of artillery, four of pioneers, the Sylhet Local Battalion, the 3rd (Blair's) Local Horse, and some native auxiliaries. No opposition was encountered from the enemy, but the difficulties of the route and the incessant rains proved more formidable than any human foe; after struggling on with extraordinary difficulty and by dint of the greatest exertions through February and March, 1825, it became evident that to reach Manipur through such a country, and with a fully equipped army, was an impossibility, and Brigadier-General Shuldham accordingly relinquished the attempt and retraced his steps.

The preparations for the expedition into Arakan occasioned one of the most painful instances of mutiny in the records of the Bengal Army. Three regiments, the 26th, 47th, and 62nd, stationed at Barrackpore, received orders to march on active service; several causes were at work to make the men discontented and uneasy; the recent changes in the army had sent a number of officers to regiments in which they were strangers to their men,[2] and this no doubt was an indirect cause of the attitude of the sepoys on this occasion; moreover, the service was a very unpopular one; native superstition, ever too readily aroused, had endowed the Burmese with supernatural powers; while the nature of the country necessitated the use of bullock transport, which the sepoys had been ordered to procure at their own expense, at a time when the drain on Bengal for the supply of the Rangoon expedition had made those animals almost unprocurable; finally, despite assurances to the contrary, an impression prevailed amongst the men that they would be forced, against their will, to embark on shipboard. Unfortunately, there seems little doubt that no consideration was paid to the peculiarities of the native temperament; the first sign of discontent was met with harshness instead of attempts at re-assurance. The 47th Regiment was the first that was to march, and was ordered to parade on the 1st of November; on this they broke into open mutiny and refused to fall in. On the following day the commander-in-chief proceeded to the spot, and at daybreak two British regiments, a detachment of horse artillery and a troop of the Body-Guard were paraded at right angles to the sepoy lines; the 47th formed in front of their lines, and were joined by about 100 of the 62nd and twenty of the 26th; they were ordered to ground their arms but refused compliance. On this they were fired on by the artillery, and immediately broke and fled; many were killed on the spot, a number more were taken prisoners, of whom eleven were hanged and the rest sentenced to hard labour in chains: the number of the regime was effaced from the Army List and the native officers dismissed the service, although none of these openly took part with the mutineers (G. G. O. No. 335 of 1824). It is probable that these sentences were considered more severe than the occasion warranted both in India and at home; and the mutineers who remained in custody were pardoned four months later (G.O.C.C, 22nd April, 1825).

---

2. This has generally been assigned as a prominent cause of the Barrackpore mutiny, and there was possibly something in it. But at the same time it is to be remembered that changes of officers such as those referred to were, by no means unknown prior to the reorganisation of 1824. On the contrary, in the days of the double battalion regiments, the transfers of officers from one battalion to another in which they were strangers to the men were matters of every day occurrence. The reorganisation of 1824 practically put a stop to such transfers.

When finally formed, the expedition to Arakan was commanded by Brigadier-General Morrison,[3] and consisted of His Majesty's 44th and 54th, the 26th, 42nd, 49th and 62nd Bengal Native Infantry, the 1st and 2nd Bengal Light Infantry Battalions, the 10th and 16th Madras Native Infantry, a detachment of the 2nd Local Horse (Gardner's), with details of artillery and pioneers. The two Grenadier battalions joined the force towards the close of the service, and suffered terribly from sickness. The force commenced its march from Chittagong on the 1st of January, 1825, and at the end of March arrived before the town of Arakan. Actions took place on the 26th and 27th on the Padha hills and at Mahati, and Arakan was attacked on the 29th, but although the troops behaved with perfect steadiness, they were unable to obtain a footing on the steep ascent on which the place stands, exposed as they were to a continuous fire from the enemy. On the evening of the 31st the flank of the Burmese position was turned by the circuitous march of a detachment under Brigadier W. Richards, and on the 1st of April the place was taken. Our losses in these operations amounted to thirty killed and 213 wounded. It was now found to be too late in the season to make any further progress, especially as the passes over the Arakan mountains were quite unknown to the British. The whole of the monsoon season was passed at Arakan; fever of a most destructive type spread to a terrible extent; nothing but a mere skeleton of the army remained fit for work; and all thoughts of an advance against Amarapura had to be abandoned. It was not until the end of 1825 that the remains of the army were withdrawn to Bengal.

After remaining nine months at Rangoon, Sir Archibald Campbell commenced his march towards the capital of Burma on the 13th of February, 1825. The army was divided into three columns, of which the first was detached against Bassein, where it met with no resistance; the second under the commander-in-chief advanced by land towards Amarapura; the third under Brigadier-General Willoughby Cotton proceeded by water up the Irrawaddy, and reached Donabyu, the stronghold of the main Burmese Army, on the 28th of February. This place had been fortified with all the science of which the Burmese were masters, and was of very considerable strength and extent: its garrison was a large one, though

---

3. Brigadier-General J. W. Morrison was the officer who commanded in the brilliant action of Chrystler's Point, in Canada, in November, 1813. He died on the 15th February, 1826, a victim to the climate of Arakan.

the common account, which reckons it at 12,000, is probably much exaggerated. The whole force with Brigadier-General Cotton did not exceed 600 men; with this he attempted an assault on the 7th of March, but, though successful against the outworks, he was repulsed with heavy loss (19 killed and no wounded) in attacking the main position. On receiving news of this reverse the commander-in-chief returned with his column and joined Brigadier-General Cotton. Donabyu was again attacked on the 1st of April, and was shelled throughout the day; on the following morning the place was found to be evacuated, and it proved that this result had been brought about by the panic caused by the death of Maha Bandula, the Burmese General, who had been killed by a rocket.

Immediately after the fall of Donabyu, Sir Archibald Campbell pushed forward to Prome, which place he occupied, without resistance, on the 25th April, but both sides were now desirous of peace; the rains were approaching and the Indian Government saw a further period of costly inaction before their army, while the Burmese were alarmed at the defeats which had been sustained by their troops. Negotiations were commenced, but terms could not be arranged, and hostilities were renewed as soon as the rainy season had terminated. In the first engagement that took place (at Wah-tee-gaon on the 16th November) a brigade of Madras sepoys sustained a severe defeat, losing more than 200 officers and men. Encouraged by this success, the Burmese Army advanced on Prome, but here they were defeated, with great loss, by Sir Archibald Campbell, on the 1st, 2nd) and 5th of December. Sir Archibald afterwards continued his movement towards the Burmese capital, and several engagements took place, until finally the whole Burmese Army was totally defeated at Paghamyu,[4] on the 9th of February 1826, and fled in confusion to Amarapura. Sir Archibald advanced rapidly towards the capital, and the king, finding the invaders at his gates, was forced to sue for peace, and a treaty was finally concluded at Yandabu on the 24th of February. The army broke up immediately and returned to the coast, whence the Bengal division sailed to its own presidency. The flank battalions from Arakan had by this time returned to Dinapore, where they were broken up, and the men, after being allowed from six to eight months' leave to their homes, rejoined their regiments (G.O.C.C, 11th November, 1825).

Permission was given for the words "Ava," "Arracan" and "Assam"

---

4. Now known as Pagan.

to be borne on the colours of corps engaged, and a medal and six months' batta were afterwards granted to the troops by G.G.O. No. 84 of 1826.

The protracted operations and tardy success of the British forces in Burma were the cause of much disturbance in the newly subjugated territories of India, where a strong belief prevailed that the rule of the English was approaching its fall. The first serious outbreak was in the Saharanpur District, where a freebooter, named Kowar Singh, collected a considerable force of Gujars and established himself in the mud fort of Kunjawa amo: here he was attacked by a detachment of 350 of the Sirmoor Battalion and a small body of horse under Captain Young. The Gurkhas stormed the fort and killed 153 of the enemy, the loss on our side being five men killed, and Captain Young (slightly) and the Honourable F. J. Shore of the Civil Service, who served as a volunteer, four native officers, and twenty-nine men wounded, of whom six died. In the Rohtak district several disturbances occurred, the most serious being headed by a marauder, named Suraj Mal. For the better protection of this part of the country, two new regiments of local horse were raised at Delhi and Bareilly, and a third at Hansi by Colonel James Skinner (G. O. Nos. 338 and 345 of 1824). An unimportant attempt was made in Bundelkhand against the town and fort of Kalpi, but was frustrated by the garrison. In Central India serious disturbances occurred, especially in the Nerbadda valley, near Burhanpur; these were successfully quelled by a detachment of the Hyderabad Subsidiary Force and some of the Mandlesar Local Corps (raised in August, 1823) under Lieutenant A. Lermit (12th Native Infantry).

But the most marked defiance of British authority was at Bhurtpore, where Durjan Sal, a nephew of the late Rajah, usurped the throne and seized the person of the rightful prince, a boy about five years old. Sir David Ochterlony, the Resident at Delhi, prepared to take prompt measures to punish this outrage, but he was checked by the Supreme Government (1825), and the disappointment and mortification occasioned, not long after, the death of this distinguished veteran.[5] However, the ferment in Bhurtpore continued to increase, and at length (December 5th, 1825) the Commander-in-Chief, Lord Combermere, advanced against the place with an army of 21,000 men. This force was composed and arranged as shown:

---

5. Sir David Ochterlony died at Meerut on the 14th July, 1825.

Engineer Division
Brigadier T. Anburey, C.B.

15	Engineer officers
6	Companies of Sappers
2	Companies of Pioneers

Artillery Division
Brigadier A. Macleod, C.B.

6	Troops of Horse Artillery
2	Light field batteries
8	Companies of Foot Artillery

The siege ordnance consisted of 110 pieces

Cavalry Division
Brigadier-General J. W. Sleigh, C.B.

1st Brigade	Brigadier G. H. Murray, C.B	Brigadier M. Childers
	H. M.'s 16th Light Dragoons (Lancers)	H. M.'s 11th Light Dragoons
	6th Light Cavalry	3rd Light Cavalry
	8th Light Cavalry	4th Light Cavalry
	9th Light Cavalry	10th Light Cavalry
		2nd Brigade

First Infantry Division
Major-General T. Reynell, C.B.

1st Brigade	Brigadier-General J. M'Combe	H. M.'s 14th foot
4th Brigade	Brigadier T. Whitehead	23rd and 63rd Native Infantry
5th Brigade	Brigadier R. Patton, C.B.	6th, 18th, and 60th Native Infantry
		32nd, 41st and 58th Native Infantry

Second Infantry Division
Major-General J. Nicolls, C.B.

Brigade	Commander	Regiments
2nd Brigade	Brigadier G. M'Gregor*	H. M.'s 59th Foot; 11th and 31st Native Infantry
3rd Brigade	Brigadier-General J. W. Adams, C.B.	33rd, 36th, and 37th Native Infantry
6th Brigade	Brigadier-General W. T. Edwards**	15th, 21st, and 35th Native Infantry

* afterwards under Brigadier-General W. T. Edwards
** afterwards under Brigadier C. S. Fagan

In addition to the above troops, there were with the force Skinner's Irregular Horse, (about a thousand strong) and two detachments of 200 men each from the 1st Nasseri Battalion and the Sirmoor Battalion. The 1st Bengal European Regiment joined in January 1826, and was placed in the 2nd Division.

Operations were commenced by the despatch of a detachment to seize a *jhil* lying north-west of the town, whence in time of war water was carried by a canal into the ditches of the fortress. This duty was successfully accomplished (10th December), and the ditch continued dry throughout the siege. The army now encamped before the northern and eastern faces of the town, and batteries were constructed and opened fire on the 24th of December. The fire of the guns, however, did not produce sufficient effect on the fortifications to make a practicable breach and recourse was had to mining, with such success, that by the 18th of January two practicable breaches had been made. On that day the assault was arranged to take place, and the attacking force was divided into four columns, with a reserve. The main right column was composed of eight companies of His Majesty's 14th Foot, five companies of the 41st Native Infantry, and the 6th, 23rd, and 60th Native Infantry, with two companies of the 14th Foot, and the 18th and 32nd Native Infantry in reserve; in the left main column were His Majesty's 59th Foot, and the 15th, 21st, and 31st Native Infantry. On the right of the first column was a division of two companies of the Bengal European Regiment, the 58th Native Infantry, and 100 Gurkhas of the 1st Nasseri Battalion; an intermediate column was formed of two more companies of the Bengal European Regiment, the grenadier company of the 35th Native Infantry, the light company of the 37th, and 100 Gurkhas of the Sirmoor Battalion. The 36th and remaining companies of the 37th formed the reserve. The signal for the assault was the springing of a mine under the north-east cavalier, and as soon as the explosion took place the several storming parties advanced with the greatest steadiness. The assailants were encountered by a desperate resistance on the part of the garrison, but the latter were gradually forced to give way from point to point, until only the citadel held out, and that also surrendered in the afternoon. The loss of the garrison is said to have been 8,000. No complete return of the British loss during the operations appears to have been prepared, but it is roughly estimated to have been about 180 killed, 7S0 wounded, and 20 missing. The casualties in the assault amounted to 103 killed, 466 wounded, and eleven missing; three officers were killed, including Captain Brown of the 31st Native Infantry, and 36 were wounded, including Brigadier-Generals M'Combe and Edwards (mortally) and Brigadier Patton. Lieutenant Tindall, of the Engineers, attached to the Sappers, was killed during the siege, and Lieutenant Candy, of the Bengal European Regiment, died of the wounds he received in the assault.

During the siege the cavalry several times distinguished themselves in attacks on parties of the enemy's horse; one affair in particular is mentioned in G.O.C.C., 24th December, 1825, when *Jemadar* Sheik Ramzan Ali, of the 4th Light Cavalry, with only twenty men defended and saved a party of foragers from a large body of the enemy: for his conduct on this occasion he was promoted to the rank of *Subadar* on the spot. Here too, for the first time, the Gurkhas of the Nasseri and Sirmoor Battalions took a prominent part in the operations of a British Army, and won enthusiastic praise on all sides for their courage, discipline, and good temper.

The fall of Bhurtpore, so long considered impregnable, effectually restored tranquillity throughout the surrounding countries, and stilled the ferment which for some time past had disquieted India; while the relief which was experienced by the Government at the speedy and successful termination of what could not but be regarded as a hazardous enterprise, was plainly evinced in the highly complimentary order issued to the army by the Governor-General. In this, besides five other corps and detachments which have ceased to exist, special praise is bestowed on the 31st Native Infantry, the 1st Local Horse (Skinner's), and the Sirmoor Battalion: the commander-in-chief's order, the day after the assault, refers also to the local horse, artillery, sappers and miners, and pioneers. All the cavalry and regular infantry present at the siege were authorised (G O. 85 of 1826) to bear the name "Bhurtpore" on their colours and appointment; but it was not until thirty-three years later that this honour was extended to the Sirmoor Battalion, and it was not sanctioned for the Nasseri Battalion (the 1st Gurkha Rifle Regiment) until 1874.

Lord Combermere's short and brilliant campaign was the last in which the Bengal Army was destined to engage for many years. Freed from the anxieties of hostility on their frontier or disaffection in their dependencies, the Indian Government turned their attention to lightening the drains on their impoverished exchequer, and the military operations of the next eleven years may be dismissed in a few words. These were, indeed, only necessitated by occasional

demonstrations of turbulence and disaffection, none of which on this side of India reached an extent of any importance. The first of these was a religious tumult in Lower Bengal in 1831, where a colony of fanatical Mahomedans of the Wahabi sect fell foul both of their Shia co-religionists and of the Hindu population, and having proclaimed a religious war marched through the country, plundering and devastating on every side. They were pursued by the 11th and 48th Bengal Infantry, with a party of horse and two guns, and having been overtaken at Hooghly, were forced to betake themselves to the shelter of a stockade; thence, after an hour's fighting, they were dislodged and finally dispersed, but not without the loss of seventeen or eighteen sepoys. In the newly acquired provinces of the Eastern Frontier disturbances were, for several years, of frequent occurrence, but were for the most part easily suppressed. In Upper Assam an incursion was made in 1830 by the Singphos from Hukong, who were quickly driven back over the frontier by the Political Agent with a detachment of the Assam Light Infantry (the 42nd Bengal Infantry). A more serious affair took place at Nanklao in the Khasiah Hills in the preceding year. Thither two British officers, Lieutenants Bedingfield and Burlton, had gone for the benefit of their health, with a small guard of Assam Light Infantry. The place was suddenly attacked, on the 4th April, 1829, by some 500 Khasiahs: Bedingfield was murdered on the spot; Burlton, with nearly all the detachment, was killed on the following day retreating towards Assam. The Sylhet Light Infantry Battalion was sent up, under Captain F. G. Lister, who defeated the Khasiahs at Mamlu on the 14th April, re-took Nanklao, and stormed the strong position of Mogandi on the 21st May, losing there one sepoy killed and Assistant Surgeon Hugh Beadon (mortally) and five sepoys wounded. A desultory conflict was maintained for two years in the difficult jungles of the frontier, until at length tranquillity was restored in 1832.

At the further extremity of Bengal, disturbances in Chota Nagpur necessitated more extensive military operations: the insurrections of the Kols, a wild, aboriginal race of Central India, reached such a pitch that at length, in 1832, a force of considerable strength had to be sent into the country. This force consisted of a squadron of the 3rd Light Cavalry, the 34th and 50th Native Infantry, the Ramgarh Battalion, and detachments of the 2nd and 54th Native Infantry, together with some artillery and irregulars. Little opposition was met with, and that was more from ambushes than in open action, which indeed is hardly to be wondered at, seeing that the Kols were armed only with bows and arrows and battle-axes: quiet was not established for some months, the British loss during the campaign having been sixteen killed and forty-four wounded; amongst these was Ensign T. H. S. Macleod, of the 34th, who died of an arrow wound.

Simultaneous with the Kol rising, and, like it, of an agrarian nature, was the insurrection of the Chuars, a lawless race in the Jungle Mehals, headed by one Ganga Narayan. A still larger force had to be assembled (under the command of Colonel J. W. Fast) to put down this outbreak; it consisted of the 24th, 34th, and 50th Native Infantry, with detachments of the 25th, 31st, and 33rd, and some irregulars, and was styled "the Jungle Mehal Field Force." There was much harassing service in the jungles, but after overcoming the difficulties of a trying march in an impracticable country, Bandi, the head-quarters of Ganga Narayan, was captured and his following dispersed. Lieutenant R. H. Turnbull, of the 24th, was mortally wounded with an arrow during these operations. A similar outbreak occurred at the same time on the borders of Cuttack, in consequence of which the 38th Native Infantry was despatched from Midnapore; but the submission of the malcontents obviated the necessity for active measures.

In 1836, a rising in Cuttack occasioned the employment of the 10th, 19th and 24th Native Infantry.

In 1837-38, further disturbances occurred in the Kol country, in which the 31st Native Infantry, the Ramgarh Light Infantry, the 5th Local Horse, and a detachment of artillery, with four 6-pounders, were employed. The field force assembled at Seraikela on November 30th, 1837: on the 4th December a detachment of the 31st, under Captain Corfield, surprised and routed a party of the enemy; and on the 18th a large body of them was attacked and dispersed near Siringsia, with a loss on our side of one man killed and fifteen wounded. Several villages were destroyed as a punitive measure, and the troops remained in the district throughout the following spring.

In the autumn of 1834, a very considerable force (three troops of horse and seven companies of foot artillery, with a siege train; two squadrons of the 11th Light Dragoons; the 2nd, 4th, 6th and 7th Light Cavalry; the 3rd Local Horse; the 26th Foot; and the 3rd, 8th, 22nd, 23rd, 28th, 32nd, 36th, 44th, 51st, 61st and 68th Native Infantry,—with Brigadier-General Stevenson in command) was assembled at Ajmir with the object of marching against Jodhpur, the Rajah of which place had for several years been giving much trouble; its movements in that direction, however, were arrested by the timely submission of Man Singh, the Jodhpur Rajah, and several corps returned to cantonments. A force of one cavalry and two infantry brigades was detained in the field under Brigadier-General Stevenson, C.B., to proceed against the Shekhawats, a predatory tribe inhabiting a tract lying to the north-east of Jodhpur. This force was composed as follows:

Cavalry Brigade	4th and 7th Light Cavalry
	3rd Local Horse
1st Infantry Brigade	3rd, 22nd, and 61st Native Infantry
2nd Infantry Brigade	32nd, 36th, and 51st Native Infantry

The force marched on the 20th of November, 1834, and proceeded by short stages into the heart of the Shekhawat country, without encountering any opposition: the strongholds of the plundering chiefs were either occupied or destroyed, and at the end of December the force broke up and returned to cantonments. A detachment, consisting of the 61st Native Infantry, the 3rd Local Horse, and some artillery, remained under Colonel Wyatt at Patan, while a corps of irregulars, horse and foot, was organised for local work by Lieutenant Forster from among the feudatory tribes of the district; this force, known as the Shekhawati Contingent, was subsequently re-organised as a regiment of irregular infantry, and is now the 13th Bengal Infantry.

Contending claims to the succession and resulting misgovernment rendered it necessary, in 1838, for the Government of India to assume the administration of the territories of the deceased Rajah of Jhansi. This was opposed by the mother of the late Rajah's predecessor, who shut herself up in the fort of Jhansi, with several thousand armed followers, determined to resist the orders of the paramount power. It became necessary to despatch a force to reduce the fort, and in December, 1838, Major-General Sir Thomas Anburey appeared before the place with the 6th Light Cavalry, the 3rd Local Horse, the 25th, 33rd, 63rd, and 72nd Native Infantry, and Sindhia's Reformed Contingent (horse, foot, and artillery), together with a powerful battering train. While preparations were making for opening fire on the fort, preparatory to an assault, the contumacious Rani and her followers lost heart and, evacuating the place secretly during the night (5th January, 1839), made off without being discovered.

The period between the general re-modelling of the Bengal Army in 1824 and the augmentations in consequence of the Afghan War in 1838, although after the conclusion of the Burma and Bhurtpore campaigns it was devoid of stirring incident in the field, was nevertheless a memorable one for its numerous internal changes. The campaigns of 1825 and 1826 necessitated further additions to the native army, already larger than the resources of the Company could easily support. The mutiny of the 47th in 1824 was followed immediately by orders for the raising of a corps to take its place (G.O.C.C., 10th November, 1824), which was numbered the 69th and to which were sent all the British officers of the old 47th: in 1828 the latter number was given to the new corps, which now exists as the 7th (the Duke of Connaught's Own) Bengal Infantry, In 1824 also (G.G.O. No. 64) was raised the Sylhet Local Battalion, now the 44th Bengal Infantry (Gurkha Rifles). A general augmentation took place in the January following when all native infantry corps were ordered to recruit an additional twenty sepoys. Early in 1825 a still more extensive measure was resorted to; this was the raising of twelve additional regiments of regular infantry of 1,000 men each, which were called "Extra Regiments" G.G.O. No. 149 of 1825). Of these the first six were fully officered immediately, but the six remaining were regarded rather as depôt battalions and only received three officers each, who were borrowed from other corps: of the twelve extra regiments one only exists at the present day, namely, the 2nd, which afterwards became the 70th of the line regiments, and is now the 11th Bengal Infantry. This was the last augmentation of the Bengal Army which took place for many years, and from the close of 1825 until 1836 reductions on all sides were the order of the day; the first of these was the breaking up of the light infantry and grenadier Reductions. flank battalions on their return from Chittagong and Arakan (G. O. C. C, 11th November, 1825 and 29th April, 1826); the companies composing these, however, were not discharged, but returned to their various regiments, where they were absorbed. In 1826 (G.G.O. No. 43) the six un-officered extra regiments were reduced after an existence of less than a year; while a month later (G. G. O. No. 79) the whole of the army was reduced to peace establishment, or a full strength of ten non-commissioned officers and eighty-two privates per company. At the end of the year a complete and drastic reform of the local forces was commenced by Lord William Bentinck; the Dinajpur,

Champaran, Gorakhpur, and Rampurah local battalions were reduced (G. G. O. No. 231 of 1826); three years later the same course was pursued with regard to the whole (fifteen) of the provincial and three more local corps, the latter including the 2nd Nasseri Battalion, of which all sepoys, natives of Nipal, of over six years' service were drafted into the 1st Nasseri and Sirmoor Battalions. It does not appear that these provincial battalions, which were merely an expensive and very worthless form of police, were much regretted in the army, and a contemporary writer praises Lord William Bentinck for "having set to and cleared away the whole of the provincial corps, root and branch, so effectually that, with the past experience of their utter uselessness, we have no prospect of ever being so bothered again."

Similar changes had been taking place in the cavalry branch. In 1825 the irregular regiments were increased to ten troops of 100 officers and men each, while, at the same time, their native officers were so equalised that there should always be one *risaldar* with each squadron and a *ressaidar* under him in the other troop. In May of the same year two "Extra Regiments" of light cavalry of eight troops each were formed, and by G.G.O. No. 348 of 1825 were permanently added to the Native Cavalry as the 9th and 10th Regiments. In 1826 reductions were commenced; regular regiments were brought down to a peace establishment of sixty privates per troop, while at the end of the year similar orders were published about the first five irregular corps: no definite directions were given about the remaining three regiments of local horse until 1829, when they were paid up and discharged in accordance with G. G. O. No. 124.

The Bengal artillery was re-organised by G .G. O. No. 192 of 1825,

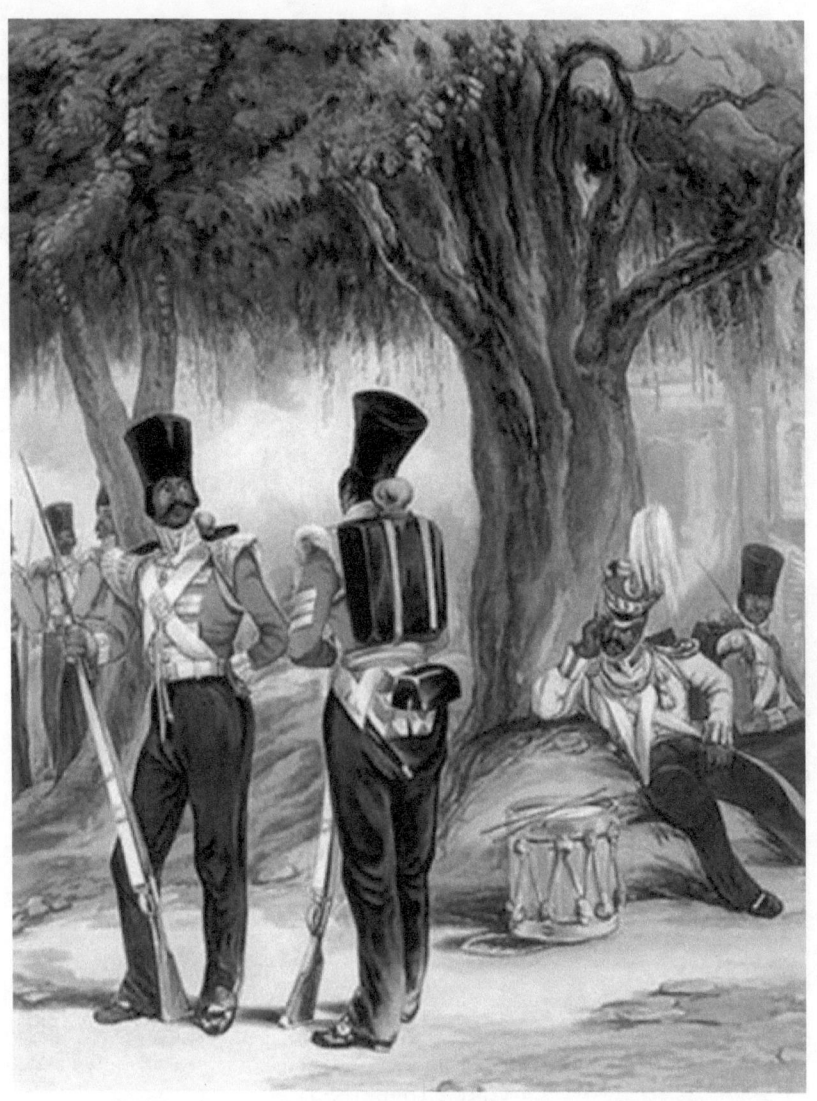

Sepoys of the Bengal Native Infantry, circa 1840

Circa 1840–1855

A British Officer of the Bengal Light Cavalry, Circa 1840

BRITISH OFFICERS OF THE BENGAL HORSE ARTILLERY

when the horse artillery was formed into three brigades of four troops each, the fourth troop in each brigade being composed of natives; the foot artillery was formed in five battalions of four companies each. By this order four companies of foot artillery were reduced, and four new European troops of horse artillery raised. Two years later (G. O. C. C, 20th June 1827) the field artillery was reduced to twelve batteries—eight British and four native—all of which were to be drawn by horses: such field ordnance as was in excess of this strength was used for independent post work and manned by *golandaz*, or native gunners.

The total strength of the Bengal Army at this period was as follows:

Horse artillery	Three brigades of tour troops each	British	1,086	
		Native	330	1,416
Foot artillery	British, five battalions of four companies each		2,250	
	Native, two battalions of eight companies		2,062	
	Gun lascars, twenty companies		1,224	5,536
Engineers	Six companies			916
Native Cavalry (regular)	ten regiments of six troops	British	260	
		Native	4,980	5,240
Native infantry (regular)	74 regiments of 8 companies	British	1,776	
		Native	55,648	57,424
European Regiment	Eight companies			781
Governor-General's Body-Guard				183
Local cavalry	Five corps of eight *rissalahs*			4,234
Local infantry	13 corps, comprising 100 companies			9,961
Miscellaneous departments				691
		Grand Total		86,382

As regards the strength of the military forces nothing remains to be noticed here except three small additions which were made towards the end of the period under review. The first of these was the "Assam Sebundy Corps," which was formed (G. G. O. No. 98 of 1835) from four companies of *sibandis* and other irregular troops maintained in Assam, with the addition of two companies transferred from the Assam Light Infantry (the strength of which was reduced from twelve to ten companies), and of two newly raised companies,—the whole making a corps of eight companies, of a strength of 756 men, with a captain in command: —this corps still survives as the 43rd Bengal Infantry (Gurkha Rifles). The second was the "Oudh Auxiliary Force," formed in 1837, and composed of a company of artillery, a regiment of cavalry and two regiments of infantry; of these, the two infantry regiments, afterwards designated the 1st and 2nd Oudh Local Battalions, were swept away in the mutiny of 1837; the mounted corps subsequently became the 6th Irregular Horse, and still survives as the 4th Bengal Cavalry. The third addition was a corps consisting of both cavalry and infantry which was raised in 1838-39 specially for service in Bundelkhand, and received the designation of the "Bundelkhand Legion." This corps will again come under notice further on.

The changes in the interior economy of the army during these years are of more immediate interest than the fluctuations in its strength. Foremost among these was the famous "half batta" measure, which it was one of the first duties of Lord William Bentinck as Governor-General to enforce, and which created almost as much discontent and indignation in the Bengal Army as the equally celebrated order of a similar nature in 1766, although on this occasion the malcontents did not proceed to such extreme measures as their predecessors in the service. Disturbed at the perilous state of their finances, the Company sought every means of economising) and with this object one of their first measures was to reduce the large military cantonments of Dinapore, Barrackpore, and Berhampore from full to half batta stations (G. G. O. No. 224 of 1828). The proceeding may have been reasonable enough, but the saving effected was comparatively very small, while the hardship inflicted by it, especially on junior officers, was great.

Early in 1825, shortly after the raising of the 69th, and when the question of foreign service was one of present importance to the Bengal troops, the 39th and 60th Regiments of Native Infantry volunteered to be placed on the list of general service corps'; this produced an order of Government complimenting these regiments for their zeal, and, after stating the advantages accruing to general service corps, giving a list of the same amounting to nine regiments, among which were the present 7th and 10th Bengal Infantry.

On the 19th of March 1827, a G.O.C.C. was issued of most vital interest to the native forces in India; it was to the following effect:— "The commander-in-chief is satisfied, from the quiet and orderly habits of the native soldiers, that it can very seldom be necessary to inflict on them the punishment of flogging, while it may be almost entirely abolished with great advantage to their character and feelings;" no native soldier, therefore, was in future to be sentenced to corporal punishment, unless for the crimes of stealing, marauding, or gross insubordination, where the individuals were deemed unworthy to continue in the native army. As may be imagined, criticism adverse to the foregoing order was not wanting, but this opposition was nothing as compared with that which greeted a G. G. O. eight years later (No. 50 of 1835) which directed "the practice of punishing soldiers of the native army by the cat-o'-nine-tails, or rattan, to be discontinued in all the presidencies; soldiers to be sentenced to dismissal from the service for any offence which might now be punished by flogging." Considering the question in the light of modern ideas and experience, it is difficult to realise the consternation created by this order, and which found expression in a flood of letters and articles addressed to every journal in the country; the arguments used were of course the same as those which were urged in more recent years with regard to a similar measure in the British Army, but while the violence engendered apparently by many years of rather uncivilized life in a trying climate caused these arguments to be expressed in more immoderate terms, the circumstances of the case deprived them of much of the cogency which they possess when applied in the later instance.[6]

---

6. At the same time the fact must not be lost sight of that the abolition of flogging did undoubtedly lead to a distinct increase in the crime of insubordination in the native army. There was much force in the remark of an old *subadar*, who had known the Bengal Army as it was in Lord Lake's time and saw the condition at which it had arrived only, four years after the abolition of flogging—"*Fauj be dar hogya,*"— "The army has ceased to fear," Apart from the abstract question whether flogging, for the maintenance of discipline, was necessary or the reverse, the abolition of this degrading punishment, so far as the native soldier was concerned, *while it was maintained in full force for his European comrade,* was an act of which the wisdom was widely questioned at the time, both in the service and out of it.

In G. G. O. No. 43 of 1829 it was notified that the names of various campaigns and actions, from Plassey to Java, were to be borne by corps engaged therein on their regimental colours and appointments; of the honours then granted the following alone now remain in the Army List:

"Delhi"	2nd Bengal Infantry
"Laswari"	1st, 2nd, and 4th Bengal Infantry
"Deig"	2nd Bengal Infantry
"Java"	The Body-Guard

To these were subsequently added "Seetabuldee," "Arakan," "Assam," "Ava," and "Bhurtpore," of which the second still survives on the colours and appointments of the 5th Bengal Infantry, and the last on those of the 1st Bengal Cavalry, the 1st, 2nd, 3rd, 4th, and 9th Bengal Infantry, and the 1st and 2nd Gurkha Regiments.

Only one noticeable change occurred about this time in the equipment of the army, namely, the substitution of fuzils for the old pikes of infantry havildars (15th August 1831). In the same year silver lace for infantry uniforms was abolished, and it was directed that the lace of every regiment should be gold (G. G. O. No. 464 of 1831).

In 1837 (G. G. O. No. 83, April 17th) another important innovation was introduced; this was the grant of good-conduct pay and the institution of the Orders of British India and of Merit. The former indulgence was granted at the rate of one rupee a month after sixteen years', and two rupees after twenty years' service, and to obtain it a sepoy should not, within the previous two years, have been convicted by a court-martial for any serious offence, nor have been twice entered in the regimental defaulter's book. The Order of British India was to be given to native officers for long and honourable service; it was divided into two classes, each having one hundred members, of whom one-half were to belong to the Bengal Army: the first class, carrying with it an extra pay or pension of two rupees a day, was granted to subadars and the corresponding grade of the irregular cavalry; the second class, with one rupee a day, was for all native officers indiscriminately. The Order of Merit, granted for conspicuous bravery in action, was divided into three classes; the third or lowest class carried with it an extra allowance to the extent of one-third of the holder's full pay or pension; the second class gave two-thirds, and the first class entitled the holder to double his full pay. These grants were followed shortly by other measures calculated to improve the position of the native soldier. By G. O. C. C. 21st June 1837, commissions were for the first time granted to native officers of irregular cavalry. In 1838 (G. G. O. No. 120, August 13th) the more important grant was made to the native commissioned ranks of pensions for wounds received in action: these, in the case of persons permanently disabled or maimed, were on the following scale :

	R
Subadar, Risaldar, or *Wurdi-*Major	25
Ressaidar	18
Naib Risaldar or *Jemadar*	12
Jemadar of Local Horse	7

Little remains to be mentioned, except an order limiting the number of *bargirs* in the irregular horse (No. 236 of 1840); having been at one time entirely forbidden, and then restricted to a very small number, the custom of keeping *bargirs* had gradually crept again into the irregular regiments, where the orders restricting it were unpopular, and if possible, evaded. The numbers now fixed were, for *risaldars* and *ressaidars* five, for *naib-risaldars* and *jemadars* two, and for *daffadars* one. These corps, hitherto officially known as "Local Horse," were, by G. G. O. No. 276 of 1840, ordered to be called in future "Irregular Cavalry"; of which the cavalry regiment of the Oudh Auxiliary Force (formed in 1838 for the service of the King of Oudh) was named the 6th Regiment.

That the measures mentioned above for the improvement of the native soldier's prospects were in the right direction, and urgently needed is amply proved by the magazine literature of the period, which teems with articles on the Bengal Army, its deficiencies, and requirements. One writer, among many others in the *United Service Magazine,* 1835, thus summarises the "points in which the condition of the native army has deteriorated: (1) Decrease of pay (as compared with the increase of expenses), (2) increase of duty, (3) decrease of consideration, (4) want in general of kindness, favour, and notice from the governing power." Probably the two last points were of far more importance than the former two; want of kindness and consideration, not only from the governing power but from regimental officers also, seems to have been but too common at the period now under notice; it was the gradual growth of years, and had become so deep-seated in a great proportion of Anglo-Indian military society that nothing short of the violent convulsion of 1857 could serve effectually to uproot it.

CHAPTER 6

Afghanistan & Scinde

After a period of twelve years of comparative tranquillity, the invasion of Afghanistan involved the Government of India in a war of four years' duration, in which the success which was at first attained was afterwards overshadowed by one great and appalling disaster, resulting in a loss of prestige and influence in Central Asia which not even the most brilliant subsequent successes served completely to repair. The proclamation which announced the determination of the Government to despatch an expedition to Afghanistan declared that it had been resolved to restore to the throne of that country the Shah Shuja-ul-Mulk, and that he would "enter Afghanistan surrounded by his own troops." Meanwhile, in anticipation of this course, a force had, about five months before, been raised for Shah Shuja, consisting of two regiments of cavalry and six of infantry, officered by British and native officers drawn from the Company's regiments: of this force the 3rd Infantry Regiment still survives as the 12th (Kalat-i-Ghilzai) Bengal Infantry.

The "Army of the Indus," as the expeditionary force was styled, was assembled at Ferozepore in November 1838, and consisted at first of between fifteen and sixteen thousand men. News, however, having been received of the withdrawal of the Persian Army which had been besieging Herat, it was determined to reduce the force, and the detailed strength of the Bengal detachment of the army was eventually as follows:

In Command	Major-General Sir Willoughby Cotton, K.C.B.	
Cavalry	Colonel Arnold	H.M.'s 16th Light Dra-
Brigade	H.M.'s 16th Lancers	goons (Lancers)
		2nd and 3rd Light Cavalry

		4th Local Horse
		Part of the 1st Local Horse (Skinner's)
Artillery	Major P. L. Pew	2nd Troop 2nd Brigade
		4th Company 2nd Battalion
		2nd Company 6th Battalion
Sappers & Miners	Captain E. Sanders, Bengal Engineers	2nd and 3rd Companies
1st Infantry Brigade	Colonel R. H. Sale, C.B., 13th Light Infantry	H.M.'s 13th Foot (Light Infantry)
		16th and 48th Native Infantry
2nd Infantry Brigade	Major-General W. Nott	31st, 42nd, and 43rd Native Infantry
4th Infantry Brigade	Lieutenant-Colonel A. Roberts, European Regiment	Bengal European Regiment
		35th and 37th Native Infantry

The Bombay column consisted of two and a half regiments of cavalry, three batteries of artillery, three regiments of infantry, and a company of sappers. The contingent with Shah Shuja-ul-Mulk amounted to about 6,000 men. A force, commanded by Lieutenant-Colonel Wade, which included a Sikh contingent of 6,000 men and 4,000 under the Shahzada Timur, eldest son of Shah Shuja, was also detailed to assemble at Peshawar and act through the Khaibar Pass: with this force were two companies each of the 20th and 21st Native Infantry, forming an escort to Colonel Wade. The total strength of the British forces employed, including reserves, amounted to about 39,000. The command of the whole was conferred upon Lieutenant-General Sir John Keane, K.C.B., of H.M's Service, then Commander-in-Chief in the Bombay Presidency.

The Bengal column marched from Ferozepore on the 10th December 1838, Sir Willoughby Cotton being in command until the force should be joined by Sir John Keane, and arrived at Rohri in Sindh on the 24th January 1839. Thence part of the force was detached to meet Sir John Keane and the Bombay troops marching from Karachi, and to hasten the Sindh chiefs in their settlement of terms of friendship with the British. This object having been attained, it was important to advance through the Bolan Pass with as little delay as possible ; the Indus was crossed by a bridge of boats, and Shikarpur reached on the 20th February. Sir John Keane was now in command of the army, while Sir Willoughby Cotton had that of the 1st (Bengal) Division of Infantry; the cavalry division was under Major-General Thackwell, and the artillery under Brigadier Stevenson of the Bombay Army. Advancing through the Bolan, Quetta was reached on the 26th March, and after a fortnight's delay the army proceeded through the Kojak Pass to Kandahar, where it arrived on the 26th April.

Up to this point no enemy had been encountered, except parties of marauding Afghans, who confined themselves to cutting off followers and stragglers, but the privations endured through want of water and scarcity of provisions were far more trying and just as destructive as would have been the most determined opposition of the Afghan Army.

At Kandahar, on May the 8th, Shah Shuja was formally installed on the *masnad,* and the army enjoyed a brief interval of comparative rest, but the difficulty in obtaining provisions still continued, as did also the annoyance of incessant robberies by the Afghans. From this place a detachment was despatched to the fort of Girishk under Brigadier Sale, consisting of detachments from the 2nd and 3rd Light Cavalry, the 13th Light Infantry, and the 16th Native Infantry, with some of the Shah's infantry and 300 of his cavalry: the chief, Kohan-dil Khan, did not, however, await the arrival of the detachment; he abandoned the fort, and fled across the Persian frontier, and Sale returned to Kandahar. At the same time unsuccessful overtures were made to the Ghilzai chiefs, who, however, showed no readiness to espouse the cause of Shah Shuja.

Leaving at Kandahar the 37th Bengal Native Infantry with some detachments and (in belief of the current reports regarding the weakness of Ghazni) the whole of the battering train, Sir John Keane resumed his march on the 27th June, and arriving before Ghazni on the 21st July, reconnoitred the place under fire the same afternoon. The fortress, which was now found to be of considerable strength, was held by Haidar Khan, son of Dost Muhammad Khan, the reigning Amir of Afghanistan. To effect a breach in its walls would have required a much more powerful battering train than had been brought from India, and as that, such as it was, had been left behind at Kandahar, no resource remained but to blow open one of the gates and endeavour to carry the place by a *coup-de-main*. After a further reconnaissance on the 22nd, the Kabul gate was selected for this purpose. The 22nd was passed in completing the necessary preparations, and was moreover enlivened by an attack on Shah Shuja's camp, which was repulsed by some of the Contingent under Captain Outram and Lieutenant Nicolson. The dispositions for the storming of Ghazni were made during the evening, and before daylight on July the 23rd the various parties were all in position. These were (1) the explosion party of engineers, under Captain Thomson of the Bengal Engineers; (2) the advance, under Colonel Dennie of Her Majesty's 13th Light Infantry, consisting of one company of that regiment and the light companies of Her Majesty's 2nd and 17th, and of the Bengal European Regiment; (3) the main storming party under Brigadier Sale, formed of the remaining companies of the 2nd Queen's, the 13th Light Infantry, and the Bengal European Regiment; (4) a false attack by three companies of the 35th Bengal Native Infantry, under Captain John Play; and (5) the reserve under Sir Willoughby Cotton, consisting of the 16th and the 48th, and remainder of the 35th Bengal Native Infantry. The operation of blowing up the gateway was completely successful, and the advance under Colonel Dennie pushed on, though met by a desperate resistance on the part of the defenders. This gave the main body of the attack time to close up with the advance, while these were closely followed by Sir Willoughby Cotton with the reserve. Within a very short time the centre square was reached, and the enemy, finding that all was lost, abandoned the citadel and fled in all directions; many of them, however, continued to fire on the troops from the houses and behind walls, until, refusing all chance of quarter, they were themselves shot down. The loss of the Afghans was very great, but the British force did not suffer as much as might have been expected, and their casualties (including the loss sustained in the reconnaissance of the 21st) amounted to no more than eighteen men killed, twenty officers and 153 men wounded, and two men missing.

On the 30th of July the army moved on towards Kabul, On its approach Dost Muhammad fled from the capital and evaded all pursuit, though a lightly equipped detachment under Captain Outram was despatched in chase of him. Shah Shuja made his public entry into Kabul on the 7th August. Three weeks later Colonel Wade, with the force of the Shahzada Timur, arrived from Peshawar, having forced the Khaibar and taken Ali Masjid with a loss of about 150 killed and wounded.

The arrival of the British force at Kabul and the installation of the Shah in his capital concluded the first phase of the Afghan war, and arrangements were soon after entered upon to withdraw a great part of the army to India. The Bombay Division left Kabul on the 18th September, and matching *via* Ghazni and Kandahar reached Quetta on the 31st October. The troops which remained in Afghanistan to strengthen the hands of the Shah were the whole of the Bengal Division of infantry, the 2nd Light Cavalry, detachments of the 1st and 4th Local Horse, and No. 6 Light Field Battery, the whole under the command of Sir Willoughby Cotton. The remainder of the Bengal troops returned to India with Sir John Keane through the Khaibar Pass, where they experienced hardships from want of water and supplies, and from the attacks of marauders, no less than in their march into Afghanistan in the earlier part of the year. They arrived at Peshawar in November, and on the 1st of January 1840 at Ferozepore, at which place, on the day following, the Army of the Indus was broken up.

In November 1839 a part of the troops which had remained in Afghanistan and Baluchistan, together with two of the British regiments which had just marched back from Kabul, were engaged under Major-General Willshire against Mehrab Khan, the Baluch Khan of Kalat, who, during the advance through the Bolan Pass in March 1839, had evinced a hostile feeling towards the British, and whom it was found necessary to chastise and render incapable of future mischief. The troops employed in this undertaking were Her Majesty's 2nd and 17th Foot, a squadron of the 4th Local Horse, and the 31st Bengal Native Infantry, with two guns, of the Bombay Horse Artillery and four of the Artillery of Shah Shuja's Contingent. The force was attacked by the enemy's horse as it approached Kalat on the 13th of November, and skirmishing continued to within a short distance of the town. There it was discovered that the fort was protected from attack by three heights before its north-western face, and which were strongly held by the enemy; these it was determined to storm immediately, and one each was assigned to the three regiments of infantry, of which half advanced to the attack, while the remaining four companies formed a reserve. The enemy were driven from their position by artillery fire before the storming parties reached them, and made good their retreat into the city, but were closely followed by the British troops; one of the gates was blown open by the fire of the Shah's artillery under Lieutenant Creed, and the town carried by storm. After some delay an entrance was also made into the citadel, where, after a brave struggle, the Khan and several Baluch *sardars* were themselves slain and the capture of the place completed. Our loss was one British and one native officer (*Subadar* Ramsahai Singh, 31st Native Infantry) and twenty-nine men killed, and eight British and two native officers and ninety-seven men wounded; among the latter being Captain Saurin and Ensign Hopper, of the 31st Bengal Native Infantry.

The objects of the expedition into Afghanistan having now been accomplished, it remained to reward the army which had been employed in the operations. All corps which advanced beyond the Bolan Pass were granted permission to bear the word "Afghanistan" on their colours and appointments, and those which were present at the capture of Ghazni and Kalat were permitted to inscribe the names of those places also; while to the whole force beyond the Bolan was issued a gratuity of six months' batta— (G.O.C.C., 22nd November, 1839, and 14th January, 1840). A medal was afterwards given for the capture of Ghazni.

The fall of Kalat and the commencement of the severe Afghan winter now produced a lull in the country, which gave reason to hope that quiet was permanently established. The troops retained in the country were divided into two commands,—the Northern under Sir Willoughby Cotton, including Kabul, Ghazni, Bamian, Jalalabad and the Khaibar, and the Southern, under Major-General Nott, comprising Kandahar, Girishk, Quetta, and Kalat. The distribution of the troops was as follows:

Kabul	H. M.'s 13th Light Infantry
	35th Bengal Native Infantry
	3 guns of No. 6 Light Field Battery
Ghazni	16th Bengal Native Infantry
	1 *rissalah* 1st (Skinner's) Local Horse
Bamian	4th (Gurkha) Infantry
	Shah Shuja's Contingent
	1 troop of horse artillery
Jalalabad	2nd Light Cavalry
	1 *rissalah* of Skinner's Horse
	3 guns of No. 6 Light Field Battery
	Detachment of Sappers & Miners
	1st Bengal European Regiment
	37th and 48th Bengal Native Infantry

Kandahar	1 *rissalah* 4th Local Horse
	1 company of foot artillery
	2 troops horse artillery of Shah Shuja's Contingent
	4 eighteen-pounders
	42nd and 43rd Bengal Native Infantry
	1 battalion infantry, Shah Shuja's Contingent
Girishk	1 battalion infantry, Shah Shuja's Contingent
	31st Bengal Native Infantry
Kalat	Detachment of artillery, Shah Shuja's Contingent
Quetta	1 battalion infantry, Shah Shuja's Contingent
	2 guns

It was not long before the distrust of Shah Shuja and the hatred of the English which was smouldering in Afghanistan betrayed itself in small and apparently unimportant outbursts, which served to portend the storm which was eventually to overwhelm the ill-fated army of occupation at Kabul. The first of these occurred early in 1840 when it became necessary to send a force against a refractory Khan named Sayyid Husain, Padshah of Kunar, who was holding out in the fort of Pashut, some fifty miles from Jalalabad. The force employed was under the command of Lieutenant-Colonel Orchard, and consisted of a wing of the 37th Bengal Native Infantry, eighty of the 1st Bengal European Regiment, a troop of the 2nd Bengal Light Cavalry, twenty sappers, the 3rd Regiment of the Shah's Infantry (now the 12th Bengal Infantry), and the 1st Regiment of the Shah's Cavalry, with three guns. On the morning of the 18th January, in pouring rain, through which the troops had been marching for several preceding days, an attack was made on Pashut. The outer gate was battered down by the fire of the guns, and Lieutenant Pigou, of the Engineers, then endeavoured to blow down the inner gate, but the only powder available was not only drenched by the rain, but also so bad as to be useless even if dry; and the storming party, who, through a mistaken bugle-call, rushed forward too soon, found themselves exposed to a heavy fire from the fort, and were obliged to retire. Another attempt was made, but with equal ill-success, and at length the troops had to be withdrawn with the loss of *Jemadar* Ganesh Tiwari (3rd Infantry) and eighteen men killed and two officers and forty-eight men wounded, many of them mortally, amongst whom was Lieutenant Collinson, 37th, who died soon after of his wounds. The attack was not, however, without result, for the fort was evacuated immediately after.

In the following August Lieutenant-Colonel H. M. Wheeler had to move out from Jalalabad, with detachments of the 1st Bengal European Regiment and the 48th Native Infantry, to punish some refractory chiefs in the Waziri Valley, and took the fort of Kajja by storm on the 19th, with a loss of one man killed and one officer (Lieutenant Parker) and eighteen men wounded.

Another affair of less importance was the attack of a small fort near Bamian by a party under Captain Garbett, where the assailants met with obstinate resistance, and did not gain possession of the place until they had recourse to burning out the garrison.

In April the wild clan of Ghilzais was in open revolt against the British and Shah Shuja, and it became necessary to take vigorous measures for their suppression. Major-General Nott, who commanded at Kandahar, contented himself at first with sending 200 cavalry to clear the road between that place and Kabul; but a stronger force being found necessary, a regiment of the Shah's infantry, 300 cavalry, and four guns of the Shah's horse artillery were despatched from Kandahar on the 7th May, under Captain William Anderson, Bengal Artillery. This detachment joined the first one on the 14th, and on the 16th, near Tazi, on the Turnak River, the enemy was encountered, some 2,000 strong, when, after an action remarkable for the gallantry displayed on both sides, the Ghilzais were driven in confusion to the refuge of their mountain fastnesses, and a British detachment occupied Kalat-i-Ghilzai.

A month later Lieutenant W. H. Clarke, 2nd Bombay Native Infantry, who, with a party of the Sindh Irregular Horse, had escorted a convoy to Kahun in the Marri hills, was, on his return, reinforced by two companies of the 5th Bombay Infantry, cut off by the Marris in the Sartof Pass (16th May, 1840) and the whole detachment destroyed. A more serious misfortune was the re-capture of Kalat by Nasir Khan, a son of the late Khan. There was no garrison in the place, beyond a small party of sepoys under Lieutenant Loveday, the Political Agent, and when it was attacked, the assailants were aided by treachery within the walls. An attempt at escalade was however repulsed, but after the defence had been protracted for some days, Lieutenant Loveday, finding resistance hopeless, capitulated (August, 1840), and was afterwards murdered by his captors. Following closely on this, another calamity overtook the troops in Sindh, when a large party of Bombay troops escorting a convoy for the relief of Kahun was driven back from the Nafusk Pass (31st August, 1840) with the loss of 179 killed (including four officers) and 92 wounded, together with its baggage, artillery and transport, and the whole of the convoy. A month later, on September 28th, Captain Brown, who commanded at Kahun, evacuated that place on honourable terms, and marched unmolested to the British post of Pulaji.

While these events were proceeding in Sindh and Baluchistan, the Northern force of the Army of Occupation was threatened by the re-appearance on the borders of Afghanistan of the ex-Amir Dost Muhammad. This prince, after fleeing from Kabul in the preceding year, had sought an asylum with the Amir of Bokhara, but driven thence by the unscrupulous cruelty of his host, he finally found an ally in the Wali of Khulum. He succeeded in raising a force, formed for the most part of Usbegs, and in August 1840 attacked a small fort, 150 miles north of Bamian, which was held by a chief friendly to the British. The outposts of Bajgah, Kamurd, and Saighan had to be recalled; Brigadier Dennie advanced by forced marches to Bamian, and with four companies of the 35th Bengal Native Infantry, four of the 4th (Gurkha) Infantry of Shah Shuja's Force, 100 of the Shah's 2nd Cavalry, 200 "Jan-baz" horse, and two guns, making a total of 880 of all ranks, attacked the enemy near Bamian on the 18th September, dispersed the Usbeg force, and compelled Dost Muhammad to fly to Nijrao. In the same month disturbances in Kohistan led to the despatch of Brigadier Sir Robert Sale into that country, with a force consisting of Her Majesty's 13th Light Infantry, two companies of the 27th[1] and two of the 37th Bengal Native Infantry, the 2nd Bengal Light Cavalry, the 2nd Cavalry, Shah Shuja's Force, and details of artillery. A successful action took place at the fortified village of Tutam-dara, near Charikar, on the 29th September, but an attempt, on the 3rd of October, to storm the fort of Julgah was repulsed with a loss of sixteen killed and thirty-one wounded. The enemy evacuated the fort the same evening. Sir Robert Sale remained in Kohistan throughout October, at the end of which month he was reinforced by the remaining companies of the 37th Native Infantry. Meanwhile every effort was made to obtain accurate information of the whereabouts of Dost Muhammad, and it at length appeared that the chief was moving towards the Ghorband Pass and was in the neighbourhood of Parwandara. Thither he was followed by the British force, which arrived at the place on the 2nd of November in time to see the enemy retreating to the hills. The two squadrons

---

1. These two companies of the 27th Native Infantry had gone up to Kabul on escort duty with stores.

of the 2nd Bengal Light Cavalry were sent on from the advance guard to endeavour to cut off the fugitives. Seeing this, the enemy's cavalry, which amounted only to about eighty ill-mounted men, turned and advanced at a slow pace towards their pursuers. Captain Fraser, commanding the squadrons, gave the order to charge, and himself, with the other officers, rode on into the midst of the enemy, but for some inexplicable reason, which has never been discovered, the troopers turned about and galloped back towards the advancing column, leaving their officers to their fate. Lieutenant and Adjutant Crispin, Lieutenant Broadfoot of the Engineers, and Assistant-Surgeon Lord, the Political Officer, were killed, and Captains Fraser and Ponsonby severely wounded.[2] Deplorable as was this affair to us, it was nevertheless Dost Muhammad's last stand; he rode into Kabul next day and gave himself up to Sir William Macnaghten, the British envoy to the Court of Shah Shuja. After remaining for a short time with the British envoy, where he charmed all who met him by his chivalrous and straightforward bearing, the ex-Amir was escorted to India by Sir Willoughby Cotton and the 1st Bengal European Regiment, who were relieved, respectively, by Major-General W. G. K. Elphinstone, C.B., and the 44th Foot. The 48th Native Infantry also returned to India at this time, as part of the escort with Dost Muhammad. With the 44th Foot there arrived from India the 5th Light Cavalry and the 27th and 54th Native Infantry., The 2nd Native Infantry had already arrived at Kabul and gone southwards to Kandahar, which place was also reinforced later on with the 38th Native Infantry. The 5th Native Infantry likewise arrived in Kabul a few months later, escorting a convoy.

While these events were happening in the north, in Baluchistan and Sindh Nasir Khan remained for some time master of the situation. Forced to move from his quarters at Mastung, he emerged from the Bolan Pass on the 28th of October, and made a vigorous attack on the post of Dadur, the repulse of which was due mainly to a splendid charge of 120 of Skinner's Horse, led by Lieutenant A. F. Macpherson, 43rd N. I., who penetrated right through the masses of the enemy and returned victorious with the loss of one *risaldar* (Mir Bahadar Ali) and two troopers killed, and Macpherson, two native

---

2. The two offending squadrons were immediately sent back to India, and by G. G. 0. No. 38 of 1841 the regiment was disbanded; the squadrons which had so disgraced themselves were dismissed the service, and the remainder were drafted into other regiments of cavalry.

officers, and twenty-five men wounded. The Baluchis made desultory attacks on the place on the two subsequent days, but finally withdrew on the arrival of reinforcements from Sukkur. On the 3rd November, Major-General Nott, with the 42nd and 43rd Bengal Native Infantry, four 18-pounders, and some cavalry and infantry of Shah Shuja's Force, arrived at Kalat from Kandahar, and re-occupied the place without opposition. Leaving the 42nd at Kalat, and garrisons at Quetta and Mastung, the General, with the 43rd, returned immediately to Kandahar. Nasir Khan still remained in arms, but his camp was attacked at Kotra, on the 1st December, by a force of Bombay troops under Lieutenant-Colonel Marshall, and he was compelled to seek safety in flight, while his army was completely dispersed with considerable loss.

The surrender of Dost Muhammad Khan and the re-establishment of British influence in Baluchistan brought the year to a satisfactory termination; but it was not long before further outbreaks disturbed the general tranquillity. The first of these was a disturbance in the Durani country, where a chief named Akhtar Khan took up arms in the Zamin-dawar, and was successful until attacked and dispersed by Captain Farrington, 2nd Bengal Native Infantry, with a detachment of native troops, at Landi-naya, on the 3rd January 1841. This was followed by an unsuccessful attack on the fort of Kajjak, near Sibi, by a detachment of Bombay troops in which two officers (one of them being Lieutenant Creed, who had so distinguished himself at the capture of Kalat) and nine men were killed, and Lieutenant-Colonel Wilson, who commanded the force, another officer, and forty men wounded; Colonel Wilson's wound proved fatal. In February it was found necessary to undertake operations against the Sangu Khel Shinwaris, inhabiting the Nazian valley, one of the eastern valleys of the Safed Koh lying to the south of Peshbolak. On this service a column was employed under Colonel Shelton of the 44th Foot, composed of his own regiment, the 27th Bengal Native Infantry, four horse artillery guns, and some details from Shah Shuja's Force, including the 3rd Infantry, and within a few days the valley was reduced to order, though not without the loss of two officers,—Captain Douglas, Assistant-Quartermasters-General, and Lieutenant Pigou, of the Engineers.

About this time General Nott, foreseeing the need of a large force at Kandahar, ordered up most of the troops from the neighbourhood of Quetta, and thus increased the force at his disposal to one regiment of cavalry, seven of infantry, two troops of horse artillery, and one company of foot artillery. This was not accomplished a day too soon, for early in April trouble again broke out with the Ghilzais, who, always disaffected towards Shah Shuja and foremost among the Afghans in their hatred of the English, were now particularly incensed by the re-building by the latter of the fort of Kalat-i-Ghilzai. They surrounded the place and attempted to obstruct the works, and threatened the force which, under Captain Macan, was located in the fort,—two regiments of infantry and part of one of cavalry (Christie's Horse) of Shah Shuja's contingent. Reinforcements were sent from Kandahar under Lieutenant-Colonel Wymer, consisting of 400 of the 38th Native Infantry, two squadrons of Christie's Horse, two horse artillery guns, and a few sappers. Wymer's force was attacked on the 29th of May, at Ilmi, about twenty miles from Kalat-i-Ghilzai, by a very large body of Ghilzais. The enemy advanced against the detachment in a solid mass, but, being received by a steady fire from the guns, they separated into three columns, which still advanced with the object of making a simultaneous attack. They were met, however, by a steady and destructive musketry fire, which their repeated rushes were not able to break through, and after an action of five hours' duration they were beaten off and dispersed. The British force, of which the 38th Bengal Native Infantry behaved with especial steadiness and courage, lost only four men killed and fifteen wounded. Scarcely was this affair brought to a successful termination than it became necessary to despatch another detachment to the Zamin-dawar, where Akhtar Khan was again in rebellion; the force employed was composed of the 5th Infantry of Shah Shuja's Force, some artillery of the same force, and two corps of Afghan Horse (called "Jan-baz"), the whole under Captain Woodburn of the 44th Bengal Native Infantry, who was also commandant of the 5th Infantry. The enemy were met with and defeated on the left bank of the Helmand, near Girishk, on the 3rd of July, but Woodburn could not follow up his success, as the "Jan-baz" would not fight. He pushed on to Girishk, where he was reinforced by Captain Griffin (24th Bengal Native Infantry) with the 1st Infantry, Shah Shuja's Force, two guns, and some cavalry. On the 17th of August, a more severe engagement took place at Sikandarabad, when Captain Griffin, with a detachment which included part of the 2nd Bengal Native Infantry, a wing of Christie's Horse, and the 1st and 5th Infantry, Shah Shuja's Force, totally defeated Akhtar Khan and dispersed his forces, his own loss being twelve killed, 102 wounded and two missing. The enemy retreated to their own valley; to attack them there a larger force was necessary, and preparations were accordingly made by Major-General Nott, Early in September he took the field in person with a considerable force, but, contrary to expectation, no resistance was met with, and Nott returned to Kandahar before the end of October.

Meanwhile, events of some importance had been occurring elsewhere. Nasir Khan of Kalat surrendered to Lieutenant-Colonel Stacy, 43rd Native Infantry, in July. In the same month a trifling outbreak occurred in Kohistan, but was easily quelled. On the 5th August Lieutenant-Colonel Chambers, with detachments of the 5th Light Cavalry, the 4th Irregular Cavalry, and the 16th and 43rd Native Infantry, gained the temporary submission of the Ghilzais by a decided success over that tribe at Karutu, near the Saighan Pass.

General Nott's short expedition against the Duranis was not concluded before the news arrived of another serious outbreak of the Ghilzais, of which the immediate cause was the reduction by the Government of the allowances paid to the tribes who held the defiles between Peshawar and Kabul. The tribesmen visited Kabul and, receiving unsatisfactory replies to their requests from the envoy and the Amir, quitted the capital, occupied the passes, and cut off all communication between Kabul and the east. Sir Robert Sale, who was about to march to India with his brigade, on relief, was ordered to clear the road. His force consisted of Her Majesty's 13th Light Infantry, a squadron of the 5th Light Cavalry, a troop of the 2nd Cavalry, Shah Shuja's Force, the 35th Native Infantry, two guns, and some sappers. The 35th, under Lieutenant-Colonel Monteath marched in advance, on the 9th October, and encamped at Butkhak; here on the same night the camp was attacked, but the assailants were repulsed. Sale, having joined the advance, attacked and forced the Khurd Kabul Pass, on the 12th, with a loss of six killed and thirty-three wounded, he himself being among the latter. From this point the 13th Light Infantry with Sale returned to Butkhak; the remainder of the force, under Monteath, was again subject to a night attack on the 17th, which, however, was unsuccessful, though it inflicted on us the loss of one officer (Lieutenant Jenkins, 35th Native Infantry) and several sepoys. Sale now decided to push on to Tezin, which was reached on the 22nd, with the loss of one officer (Lieutenant E. King 13th) and four men killed, two officers and seventeen men wounded. Marching thence on the 26th and evading the Ghilzais, who had prepared to attack his force at the Pari Dara, he forced the Jagdalak Pass, oh the 28th, and reached Gandamak on the 29th, but not without the heavy loss of 29 killed and 91 wounded. Among the former were Captain Wyndham of the 35th, who lost his life in a gallant endeavour to save that of a wounded soldier, and *Subadars* Ranjit Singh and Hardyal Singh and *Jemadar* Bhawani Singh, of the same regiment. On November 10th news reached Sale at Gandamak of the outbreak at Kabul. Unable from the weakness of his force and the want of camp equipage or supplies to return to the relief of the garrison there, he determined to occupy Jalalabad and marched into that place on November 13th.

About the same time, towards the end of October, a fresh outbreak occurred in Kohistan, which eventually resulted in one of the most painful incidents of the war. Charikar, the chief town of the district, was garrisoned by the 4th (Gurkha) Infantry of Shah Shuja's Force. On the 1st November, a strong insurgent force took up a position in the neighbourhood, cutting off the communication with Kabul. On the 3rd, Lieutenant Rattray, Assistant Political Agent, was treacherously killed at the termination of a conference with some of the insurgent chiefs, and from that date the fighting at and around Charikar was incessant. After heavy loss had been sustained (both Captain Codrington and Ensign Salusbury of the Gurkha battalion being among the slain), the utter failure of the water supply necessitated the evacuation of the place, and accordingly, on the 13th, the garrison, now reduced to 200 men, including Major Pottinger and Ensign Haughton, both wounded, Ensign Rose and Assistant-Surgeon Grant, retreated under cover of night. Dispersed, however, in the darkness, many fell by the hands of the insurgents, and many were taken prisoners and carried into slavery: Pottinger and Haughton, with one Gurkha, alone reached Kabul, though in the following year the latter officer collected 165 Gurkhas in the country round, who had escaped with their lives. All the wounded, as well as the wives and children of the sepoys, were massacred. At the same time the Kohistan Regiment mutinied and deserted, after killing their officers, Lieutenant Maule and Local-Lieutenant Wheeler.

It now remains to give a short account of the insurrection at Kabul and of the events which succeeded it, a story of defeat and disaster which make this one of the darkest pages in all the annals of the British arms in India.

On the 2nd November a tumult broke out in the city: the house of Sir Alexander Burnes (who had been nominated to succeed Sir William Macnaghten as Envoy) was attacked, and he, his brother (Lieutenant Charles Burnes, 17th Bombay Native Infantry), and Lieutenant W. Broadfoot of the 1st Bengal European Regiment, were, after a desperate defence, overpowered and slain by the insurgents. At this time the troops in Kabul were:

The 1st Troop, 1st Brigade, Bengal Horse Artillery
A battery of Artillery, Shah Shuja's Force
A detachment of the Bengal Sappers and Miners
A detachment of Sappers, Shah Shuja's Force (three companies)
Two squadrons of the 5th Bengal Light Cavalry
One *rissalah* of the 1st Irregular Cavalry
One *rissalah* of the 4th Irregular Cavalry
The 2nd Regiment of Cavalry, Shah Shuja's Force
Her Majesty's 44th Foot
The 5th Bengal Native Infantry
The 54th   ditto   ditto
The Envoy's Body-Guard
The 6th Regiment of Infantry, Shah Shuja's Force

The whole of these troops were under the command of Major-General W. G. K. Elphinstone, C.B., an officer of good repute, who had seen much service in various parts of the world (he had commanded the 33rd Foot at Waterloo), but he was at this time in an extremely bad state of health, and this interfered to a great extent with the proper performance of the onerous duties of his command: to this circumstance is to be attributed in a great measure the whole of the misfortunes which followed.

On the 3rd of November, the force was increased by the arrival of the 37th Bengal Native Infantry from Khurd Kabul.

On the following day the first misfortune occurred in the loss of the commissariat fort, with the whole of the supplies which it contained, which had to be abandoned in consequence of the delay which took place in reinforcing the small party which held it. On the 6th, Kila-i-Muhammad Sharif, which had been occupied by the enemy, was taken by storm by a detachment of three companies (one each from the 44th Foot and the 5th and 37th Native Infantry) commanded by Major Griffiths of the 37th. On the 10th the Rikabashi fort, of which the insurgents had taken possession, was retaken with the severe loss of 200 killed and wounded, amongst whom was numbered Colonel Mackrell of the 44th, an old Waterloo officer, who died the same day of his wounds. On the 13th an action was fought on the Bemaru heights, which, after a check which very nearly proved a disaster, ended in the defeat of the enemy; and the capture of their guns. Some days were now spent in fruitless discussions as to the best course to be pursued, for supplies were beginning to run low, while the enemy were increasing in numbers and boldness; but no action of any kind was taken. At length, on the 22nd November, Muhammad Akbar Khan, son of Dost Muhammad, arrived at Kabul, and on the following day the enemy again occupied the heights of Bemaru. Brigadier Shelton was sent out to dislodge them with seventeen companies of infantry (five of the 44th Foot, and six each of the 5th and 37th Native Infantry), 100 sappers, three squadrons of cavalry and one gun. The detachment was, however, mishandled, for Shelton, like Monson, though as brave a man as ever lived, was no general. The result was a disastrous defeat of the British force, which was only saved from annihilation by a charge of the cavalry and by the fall of one of the principal Afghan chiefs.

Little was now thought of but a retreat to India; supplies had failed, and cold and defeat had demoralised the remnant of the troops that still remained ; while the whole country was up in arms against us. To this end, therefore, on the 11th December, negotiations were opened with Muhammad Akbar; in the midst of which, twelve days later, December the 23rd, the British Envoy, Sir William Macnaghten, was inveigled out of cantonments to a conference and treacherously murdered. Notwithstanding the evidence this act afforded that little reliance could be placed in the good faith of the enemy negotiations were still continued, and on the 6th of January 1842, after having sustained the humiliation of giving up to the enemy all the guns but six, and although the terms, both as regarded transport and escort, had not been fulfilled by the Afghans, the Kabul garrison, amounting to 4,500 fighting men, evacuated the positions they had held, and commenced their retreat to Jalalabad. Then ensued what might have been anticipated from a knowledge of the Afghan character. Scarcely had the troops left their cantonments when the Afghans began to attack them; day after day, through the defiles of Khurd Kabul, of the Tangi Tariki, of Jagdalak, their numbers grew less and less before the bullets of the Afghan *jazels* and the cold steel of the Afghan knives, aided by the bitter cold and the deep-lying snow. The widows, married people, and children were saved by being made over to the care of Muhammad Akbar at Khurd Kabul; General Elphinstone, Brigadier Shelton, and Captain Johnson, who had gone to meet Muhammad Akbar at a conference at Jagdalak, were there taken prisoners by the Afghan chief, who detained them as hostages for the surrender of Jalalabad.[3] Reduced at Jagdalak to about 150 men, the devoted remnants of the force struggled on into that last fatal pass, where a terrible fate awaited them. Hemmed in on every side by the murderous hordes of their enemies, only some twenty officers and forty-five men survived to see another day at Gandamak: here within a few miles of Jalalabad their merciless foes fell on them again: the remnant which escaped fell one by one by the way or were cut down by the enemy, until at length one only survived,[4] grievously wounded and almost overcome with exhaustion, to reach a haven of safety and tell the fate of Elphinstone's brigade to the garrison of Jalalabad.

Sir Robert Sale, as we have seen, occupied Jalalabad on the 13th November, 1841. Aided by that excellent officer, Captain George Broadfoot, of the Madras Army, Commandant of the Corps of Sappers of Shah Shuja's Force, he immediately set about restoring the fortifications of the place, which were in a most dilapidated condition, superintending the work with unceasing vigilance, although, in consequence of the severe wound he had received in forcing the Khurd Kabul Pass, he was unable to get about without assistance, and had to be carried from point to point in a litter. By the unremitting labours of the garrison, Jalalabad was soon in a respectable state of defence, but the severity of the season and the fury of the enemy were not all that these gallant men had to contend against. Even Nature herself seemed to be arrayed against them, for the walls had not long been restored when a violent shock of earthquake once more reduced them to ruins, and in some places even levelled them with the ground. But the calamity was met with becoming fortitude; the weary work was promptly recommenced, and soon once more the walls were raised, and the place made secure against all the efforts of the enemy, who, under Muhammad Akbar Khan, were in great force in the neighbourhood.

Early in the siege the question of surrendering the place, in obedience to orders received from Major-General Elphinstone, when

---

3. Major-General Elphinstone died in captivity, at Badiabad, on the 23rd April 1842.
4. Assistant-Surgeon W. Brydon.

he capitulated at Kabul, came under the consideration of Sale and a Council of War. It has been said proverbially that "a Council, of War never fights," and in this instance there was no exception to the rule. Considering themselves abandoned, and hopeless of relief, Sale and the majority of the Council were for yielding, and notwithstanding the sterner counsels of Broadfoot, Oldfield, and Backhouse, who strongly urged the more worthy course of holding on to the place to the last, proposals for the evacuation of Jalalabad, on the condition of a safe conduct to Peshawar, were actually addressed to the enemy. An implied doubt of the sincerity with which these proposals were made afforded an opportunity of reconsidering and withdrawing them; manlier counsels prevailed and Jalalabad remained in our hands, to be defended with a tenacity which has extorted universal admiration.

From November, 1841, to April, 1842, Sale's Brigade continued straitly shut up within the walls of Jalalabad, except only when the occasional nearer approach of the Afghans afforded opportunity for a sortie. In one of these sallies (24th March, 1842) the gallant Broadfoot received a severe wound which deprived the garrison of his valuable services for the remainder of the siege.

This was now rapidly approaching its termination. A relieving force, under the command of Major-General Pollock, was on its way, but on the 7th April, a week before it reached Jalalabad, the garrison sallied forth and inflicted a crushing defeat upon the enemy and practically relieved themselves. The available force on that day was something under 1,500 men, including the 13th Light Infantry, the 35th Native Infantry, Broadfoot's sappers, and a squadron and a half of native cavalry; while that of Muhammad Akbar is described as not less than 6,000. The enemy were drawn up in a strong position to receive the attack, but they were speedily driven from it with severe loss and their army entirely dispersed. Sale's loss was eleven killed and 71 wounded; among the former being the gallant. Colonel Dennie, of the 13th Light Infantry, a distinguished officer who had served under Lord Lake in the early years of the century, had witnessed the conquest of the Isle of France, and gone through three arduous campaigns in Burma with much credit, and who had led the storming party at the capture of Ghazni three years before. The whole of the Afghan camp was captured and several British guns re-taken, together with a quantity of provisions. Of these latter it is related that when the Brigadier divided amongst his troops the sheep taken front the enemy, the 35th Native Infantry desired that their share might be given to the

13th Light Infantry, who, they said, were in more need of animal food than themselves,—a striking instance of the good fellowship which has so often existed between British and native corps, especially in times of hardship and trial.

In India, in the meantime, as soon as intelligence was received of the outbreak at Kabul, strenuous efforts were made to push up reinforcements, and before the middle of January 1842 a brigade,— consisting of a squadron of the 3rd Irregular Cavalry, and the 30th, 53rd, 60th, and 64th Native Infantry, in all about 4,300 men, with five guns (which had been borrowed from the Sikhs),—was at Peshawar under the command of Brigadier Wild. As a preparatory step to advancing to the relief of Jalalabad, Wild, on the 15th January, sent forward the 53rd and 64th, under Lieutenant-Colonel Moseley, to take possession of Ali Masjid. This was easily accomplished, and on the 19th the Brigadier himself moved forward with the remaining two regiments and four guns; but the Afridis had now risen and closed the pass, and were prepared to resist, the advance of any more troops into the Khaibar; Wild encountered them at the mouth of the pass and a severe engagement ensued, but owing to the worthlessness of the Sikh guns, which broke down at the first discharge, and to the inadequacy of the force, the attempt to get through to Ali Masjid proved a complete failure; the troops were beaten back and obliged to retire to Jamrud with considerable loss, Brigadier Wild himself and three other officers being amongst the wounded. In the meantime, Moseley, exposed to incessant attacks, had found it impossible to maintain himself at Ali Masjid, and on the 24th he was compelled to evacuate the place and retreat to Jamrud, exposed the whole way to an incessant fire from the Afridis. The loss of Moseley's detachment was heavy, as was that of another detachment sent to the entrance of the Khaibar Pass to cover his retirement. Altogether the loss amounted to thirty-seven killed (including Captain Lock, 5th Native Infantry—attached to the 60th,—Captain Wilson, 64th Native Infantry, and *Subadars* Ram Singh and Sukhlal Upadhia, 53rd Native Infantry) and 232 wounded (including six British and eight native officers). This check had a fatal effect on the force and it was not until Major-General Pollock, who had been appointed to command the forces moving into Afghanistan, arrived and assumed the command that any real progress was made in preparing for an advance. But, with all his energy, it was the 5th of April before Pollock was able to march from Peshawar. The force under his command was organised as follows:—

Artillery: Captain A. Abbott   1 troop horse artillery
     2 light field batteries
     Backhouse's Mountain Train

Cavalry: Brigadier M. White   3rd Light Dragoons
     1st Light Cavalry
     Detachment 5th Light Cavalry
     10th Light Cavalry
     3rd Irregular Cavalry
     Detachment Anderson's Horse
     late 2nd Cavalry, Shah Shuja's Force.)

Infantry: Major-General J. M'Caskill, K.H.

Major-General Sir R. H. Sale, K.C.B	13th Foot
1st Brigade	35th Native Infantry
	Broadfoot's Sappers
	The Khaibar Rangers
Brigadier W. H. Dennie, C.B.	9th Foot
2nd Brigade	26th and 60th Native Infantry
	5th Company Sappers & Miners
Brigadier C. F. Wild	
3rd Brigade	30th, 53rd & 64th Native Infantry
Brigadier T. Monteath	31st Foot
4th Brigade	6th & 33rd Native Infantry

Of these troops, however, Backhouse's Mountain Train, Broadfoot's Sappers, the detachments of the 5th Light Cavalry and of Anderson's Horse, the 13th Foot and the 35th Native Infantry were then at Jalalabad; the 31st Foot and the 6th Native Infantry had not yet arrived at Peshawar, and thus Pollock made his forward movement with only the following corps and detachments:

The 3rd Light Dragoons, the 1st and 10th Light Cavalry, and a detachment of the 3rd Irregular Cavalry. A troop of horse artillery, two light field batteries, and some siege guns. A company of Bengal Sappers and Miners. The 9th Foot, the 26th, 30th, 33rd, 53rd, 60th, and 64th Native Infantry, and a corps of Afghan riflemen styled "Ferris's *Jazelchis*."

General Pollock's advance was planned and conducted with the greatest care and circumspection. On the date above named, his force advanced in three columns, the right and left preceding the centre and crowning the heights on either side of the Khaibar Pass. The enemy (Afridis and other Khaibaris) made a determined and obstinate resistance, but after a succession of severe combats they were driven from every position they had taken up, and the pass was forced with a loss on our side of fourteen killed, 104 wounded, and seventeen missing. Pollock, pushing forward, reached Jalalabad on the 16th of April, .only to find that the garrison had already, unaided, broken up the siege of the place and effected its own relief. Here in the following month he was joined by the 31st Foot and the 6th Native Infantry.

It is now necessary to describe the doings in southern Afghanistan during the preceding six months. In November 1841, the force at Major-General Nott's disposal consisted of Her Majesty's 40th Foot, the 2nd, 16th, 38th, 42nd, and 43rd Native Infantry, the 1st, 2nd, and 5th Infantry of Shah Shuja's Force (or portions of these corps), a detachment of the 1st Irregular Cavalry, the 1st Cavalry of Shah Shuja's Force (Christie's Horse), and some details of artillery. Summoned by Sir William Macnaghten, one brigade, under the command of Colonel McLaren, marched in November for the relief of our forces at Kabul, but, being unable (so, at least, it was alleged) to overcome the difficulties of bad weather and want of food, it returned to Kandahar on the 8th December, having reinforced the garrison of Kalat-i-Ghilzai with 300 of the 43rd Native Infantry.

Ghazni was at this time held by the 27th Native Infantry, under the command of Lieutenant-Colonel Palmer. The insurgents appeared before the place on the 20th November, and on the 7th December began closely besieging it. On the 17th the defenders were compelled to abandon the city and take refuge in the fort. Here they suffered greatly from cold and want of provisions and water until the 6th of March, when the place was surrendered. The garrison were not however suffered, as they had been promised, to depart in safety; a few days after the capitulation they were furiously attacked by *ghazis*; for three days they sustained from house to house an unequal combat with their foes; at length some of the sepoys determined to cut their way out and try to make across country to Peshawar, which they believed to be only fifty or sixty miles off; on the 10th they started on their mad attempt, only to be cut down or taken prisoners in the snow-covered fields. The whole of the British officers (except one,—Lieutenant Lumsden,—who had fallen during the fighting) became prisoners, and remained in captivity for many months, subjected to the severest privations.

At Kandahar, Nott easily held his own against the insurgent gatherings that appeared in his neighbourhood. On several occasions (at Kali-Shak on the 12th January; Kanji-Kak, Panjwai and Tilu-Khan on the 7th, 8th, 9th, and 10th March; and at Baba-Wali on the 25th March) he defeated and drove off the Duranis by whom the place was threatened. During his absence on one of these expeditions, the Afghans made a furious night attack on Kandahar (10th March), evidently hoping to carry the place with a rush. Every attempt was, however, repelled by the garrison, under the command of Major Lane, 2nd Native Infantry, and eventually the enemy drew off after having sustained heavy loss. On the 10th of May Nott was joined by Major-General England, with the 41st Foot and some Bombay troops from Sindh.

The first measure now to be undertaken was the relief of the fort of Kalat-i-Ghilzai. This place had been garrisoned since November of the preceding year by the 3rd Infantry of Shah Shuja's Force, under Captain J. H. Craigie, and 40 British artillerymen; in December, as has been noticed, it had been reinforced by 300 of the 43rd Native Infantry. After sustaining a close blockade for several weeks, which was preceded by the hardships occasioned by the severity of the winter and the hostility of the surrounding country, the little garrison successfully defeated with great loss a determined attack by the enemy on the 21st of May. A week later they were relieved by Colonel Wymer from Kandahar, who withdrew the garrison and destroyed the works, and, after visiting Girishk, returned to Kandahar on the 7th June. In recognition of its gallantry, the 3rd Infantry was at a subsequent period taken into the Company's service, and is still, as the 12th Bengal Infantry, permitted to bear the name of "Kalat-i-Ghilzai," with which it is so honourably connected.

Taking advantage of the absence of Colonel Wymer and the greater part of the force, the Duranis to the number of about 8,000 men, led by Aktar Khan, came down on Kandahar on the 29th May. Nott moved out at once with a force of about 2,000 men, which included the 42nd and 43rd Native Infantry, and gave the enemy a complete overthrow, inflicting on them heavy loss, while the casualties in his own force amounted to no more than one killed and 52 wounded.

It was not until August that General Nott received permission to advance on Kabul, and on the 10th he left Kandahar with the following force:

Two troops of horse artillery, one 9-pounder foot battery, four 18-pounders, with two companies of Bengal foot artillery; the 3rd Bombay Light Cavalry, three *rissalahs* of the 1st Irregular Cavalry, five *rissalahs* of the 1st Cavalry of Shah Shuja's Contingent (Christie's Horse); the 40th and 41st Foot, the 2nd, 16th, 38th, 42nd, and 43rd Native Infantry, and the 3rd Infantry of Shah Shuja's Contingent.

The remainder of the force, including the Bombay troops not detailed to move northwards, two *rissalahs* of Christie's Horse, and three infantry regiments of Shah Shuja's Contingent, returned to India through the Bolan.

During his march towards Kabul, Nott had several engagements with the enemy. An unfortunate cavalry affair took place near Kila Azim and Karez Usman Khan, on the 28th August, in which more than seventy casualties occurred on our side, including two officers (both of the 3rd Bombay Light Cavalry) killed and three wounded. On the 30th at Karabagh, near Goaine, thirty-five miles from Ghazni, a very large force of Afghans was completely defeated and dispersed with a loss on our side of about thirty killed and wounded.[5] Ghazni was reached on September 4th and evacuated by the enemy on the night of the 5th, after an engagement in which Nott's force suffered a loss of three killed and 43 wounded: 327 of the 27th Native Infantry were here released from captivity; the walls of the citadel were demolished; and, by order of Lord Ellenborough, the famous gates of the temple of Somnath were carried off from the tomb of Sultan Mahmud. The march was resumed on the 10th September, and after further engagements with the enemy, on the 14th and 15th, near Beni Badam and Maidan (in which a loss of four killed and fifty-nine wounded was sustained, including *Subadar* Jham Singh, 43rd Native Infantry, mortally wounded), Nott reached Kabul on September the 17th.

General Pollock, however, was there before him. Leaving Jalalabad on the 20th of August, he pushed on his advance with surprising rapidity though opposed daily by the Afghans. His force included in the 1st Division the 26th and 35th Native Infantry and a company of sappers and Miners, and in the 2nd Division the 33rd and 60th Native Infantry, as well as two troops of horse artillery, one field battery,

---

5. Our losses in these two engagements are very inconveniently "lumped" together in General Nott's casualty returns. These returns show a total of 38 killed (including two officers) and 66 wounded (including four officers). The casualties at Beni Badam on the 14th and at Maidan on the 15th September are also "lumped" together in the same way.

the 1st Bengal Light Cavalry, and 600 of the 3rd Irregular Cavalry. Following, whenever opposed, his tactics of crowning the heights on either side of the pass, Pollock,—defeating the enemy at Mamu Khel on the 24th (in which action he lost seven men killed and four officers and forty-five men wounded), and again at Jagdalak on the 8th September (when his casualties amounted to six killed and fifty-eight wounded,—Captain Nugent, of the Commissariat Department being amongst the former),—drove all before him until the 12th September, when, in the Tezin Valley, his flanks were assailed in a very daring manner by the enemy, who, though repulsed and driven off, returned in the evening and kept up a series of harassing attacks throughout the night. On the morning of the 13th Pollock advanced to the mouth of the Tezin pass, where he left the 3rd Light Dragoons, part of the 1st Light Cavalry, and the 3rd Irregular Cavalry, to cover his rear, but he had no sooner quitted the valley than the Afghan horse appeared and, as had been anticipated, made a movement to fall upon the baggage train; the attempt was fatal to them, for the dragoons and the native cavalry, catching them in comparatively open ground, made a brilliant charge, completely routing them, cutting up large numbers, and capturing a standard, which was taken by Captain Goad of the 1st Light Cavalry. While this combat was proceeding in the valley, Pollock, with the main body of his force, was slowly winning his way up the Tezin pass, though obstinately opposed at every step by Muhammad Akbar Khan, who had that day brought into the field a force of 16,000 men. Infuriated by the sight of the remains of their comrades who had fallen in the retreat a few months before, the British soldier and the sepoy alike fought with irresistible spirit; the Afghans were expelled from every position they took up, and finally after a severe contest the Haft *Kotal* was surmounted and the enemy driven in headlong flight towards Kabul, with the loss of all their guns (three in number) and of probably from 1,200 to 1,500 men killed and wounded. Our own losses amounted to thirty-two killed and 130 (including four British officers) wounded, among the former being a most gallant and distinguished Native Officer, Haidar Ali, the Native Commandant of Ferris's *Jazelchis*.

This was the last effort of Muhammad Akbar. Barring a series of attacks on his rear-guard and baggage train, on the 9th, 10th and 11th, in which a loss of six killed and fifty-nine wounded was sustained, Pollock's further advance to Kabul was absolutely unopposed, and that place was reached on the 15th September, two days before the arrival of the force from Kandahar under Major-General Nott. A week later the whole of the British captives in the hands of the Afghans (those from Ghazni as well as those taken at Kabul and in the passes), having practically effected their own deliverance, arrived in Pollock's camp. On the 25th a force was detached under Major-General M'Caskill, consisting of one battery of 9-pounders and two 18-pounders, seven squadrons of cavalry, Broadfoot's Sappers, and five regiments of infantry, including the 26th, 42nd, and 43rd Native Infantry. This force marched against Istalif, in Kohistan, defeated the Afghan force which had taken refuge there (29th September), seized the town, and set fire to it in several places. The casualties in this affair amounted to one officer and five men killed, and four officers and forty-one men wounded. Prince Shahpur was now chosen to ascend the throne in the place of Shah Shuja, who had been murdered in the preceding April. The great bazaar of Kabul was blown up as a mark of British vengeance; and on October the 12th the return march to India was commenced. The rear-guard, formed by General Nott's force, was, in the retirement, several times engaged with the enemy; on the 14th, 15th and 16th October in the Haft *Kotal* Pass, where a loss, was sustained of seven killed and fifty-eight wounded; in the Jagdalak Pass on the 18th (seven killed and thirty-seven wounded); at Gandamak on the 19th (two killed and fifteen wounded), and on the 4th and 6th November near Ali Masjid, where the loss sustained was four killed and nineteen wounded; amongst the latter was Lieutenant Chamberlain of Christie's Horse (now General Sir Neville Bowles Chamberlain, G.C.B.), who was here wounded for the sixth time that year. Late in the evening of the 3rd, near Garhi Lala Beg, the rear-guard of Brigadier Wild's brigade was rushed in the darkness by a body of Afridis and sustained a loss of nineteen killed and thirty-two wounded, Lieutenant Christie, of the Artillery, Ensign Nicholson, 30th Native Infantry, and *Subadar* Siu-din Singh, 53rd Native Infantry, being amongst the former; two guns of the mountain train were also lost, but they were recovered next day. Peshawar was reached by the rear-guard on the 6th, and then the march to Ferozepore was begun.

In the meantime, in India, the Government had found it necessary to adopt measures of precaution against a new danger which had begun to develop itself. This was the hostility which for many months past the Sikhs, as a nation, had exhibited towards us, and which was, in fact, the beginning of the animosity which eventually found expression in the war of 1845-46. So marked was this hostility that apprehensions were entertained that the Sikhs would take advantage of any opportunity that might present itself of falling upon General Pollock's force during its march through the Punjab. As a support, therefore, to Pollock, and as a menace to the Sikh capital in the event of any overt act of hostility, a powerful force was assembled at Ferozepore in the autumn of 1842, under the Commander-in-Chief, Sir Jasper Nicolls, in person. This was styled "The Army of Reserve," and was organised as follows:

Artillery Brigadier C. Graham, C.B.		4 troops horse artillery 4 companies foot artillery 3 light field batteries
Engineers Major E. J. Smith		2 companies Sappers & Miners
Cavalry Major-General Sir J. Thackwell, K.C.B.	1st Bgde.	16th Light Dragoons (Lancers) 7th Light Cavalry 4th Irregular Cavalry
	2nd Bgde.	3rd Light Cavalry 6th Irregular Cavalry
1st Infantry Division Major-General J. Dennis	1st Bgde.	1st European Light Infantry 1st & 2nd Light Infantry Battalions
	2nd Bgde.	3rd Foot (the Buffs) 9th & 10th Native Infantry
2nd Infantry Division Major-General W. Battine, C.B.	3rd Bgde.	39th Foot 59th & 72nd Native Infantry
	4th Bgde.	2nd European Regiment 39th Native Infantry The Sirmoor Battalion

The precaution taken had the desired effect. Sikh turbulence was overawed for the time, and the army returning from Afghanistan was allowed to proceed unmolested. Marching across the Punjab, Pollock's force reached Ferozepore in three detachments on the 17th, 19th and 23rd December, and then after a period of general festivity, ending in a grand review of the united, forces (40,000 men, with 100 guns) before the governor-general, the army was dispersed and returned to cantonments. So ended the first Afghan War.

The satisfaction of the governor-general at the conclusion of the war is evinced by his complimentary orders to the army. For the second campaign a further donation of six months' batta, was made to all troops serving in and above the Khaibar or the Bolan Pass on the 8th September, 1842. Corps engaged in the actions around Kandahar, in the defence of Jalalabad and Kalat-i-Ghilzai, the re-capture of Ghazni and the re-occupation of Kabul, received permission to bear those names upon their colours. All ranks present in the actions at Kandahar and Ghazni and those leading to the re-occupation of Kabul, received a medal inscribed with the names of the same and the date "1842" under-written. Additional medals were given to the garrisons of Jalalabad and Kalat-i-Ghilzai, and the corps engaged in the former received permission to wear a mural crown on their appointments in commemoration of the siege. The 3rd Regiment of Shah Shuja's infantry were, in consideration of their valour and discipline in the defence of Kalat-i-Ghilzai, brought on the strength of the Bengal Army as an extra regiment, and denominated "The Regiment of Kalat-i-Ghilzai." The 2nd and 16th Native Infantry were made grenadier regiments, and the 38th, 42nd, and 43rd were made Light Infantry,—(G. O. G. G., 4th October, 1843). The corps which still exist of those thus honoured are the Sappers and Miners, the 1st Irregular Cavalry (1st Bengal Cavalry), the 33rd (4th), 42nd (5th), and 43rd (6th) Native Infantry, and the Kalat-i-Ghilzai Regiment (12th),

Embarrassed as the Indian Government was with the great and unexpected expenses of the Afghan campaigns, it was nevertheless unable to avoid taking part in another expedition at almost the opposite extremity of Asia. This was the first Chinese war, the cause of which was the forcible destruction of two and a half million pounds worth of British property by the Chinese authorities, in a violent effort to destroy the opium traffic. As in the Burmese war, however, the prejudices of the Bengal sepoys, as well as the pressing need for troops on the western frontier, prevented any but a very small contingent being despatched from this presidency, the greater part of the native soldiery employed being from Madras. Volunteers to form one regiment were called for by G. O. C. C. of the 20th January, 1840, "for service to the eastward;" and this corps, together with the 18th, 26th and 49th Foot, sailed from Calcutta in April of that year. The island of Chusan was occupied on the 5th of July, and here the British force remained during the rest of the year, in which time all the regiments suffered terribly from sickness.

Attempts at negotiation having failed, the fort of Chuenpee, situated on an island in the Canton river, was attacked and taken on January the 7th, 1841, with trifling loss. Six weeks of desultory negotiations then ensued, during which the island of Chusan was evacuated by the British. On the 19th February hostilities were resumed, and during the next fortnight some hard fighting took place in attacks on the forts at the mouth of the Canton river. On the 24th of May Canton itself was attacked, and during that and the next six days the heights above the place were occupied and several other advantages obtained, with a loss on our side of fifteen killed and 122 wounded; the city itself was, however, not entered, negotiations having been resumed, and the place ransomed for six million dollars. From Canton the force was moved to Hong-Kong, where it again suffered terribly from disease.

About this time the Bengal Volunteer Battalion (except a detachment under Major Mee, which remained in China and took part in subsequent operations up to August, 1841) returned to India, where, on their arrival they were complimented in a G. O. (No. 122 of 1841) for the alacrity with which they had volunteered for the service, and received one month's full pay and batta as a gratuity, with special leave to their homes before rejoining their several regiments.

At the end of August operations were resumed, and Amoy, Chusan, Chinhae, and Ningpo were captured by the British. During the winter operations were suspended, but were re-commenced in March, 1842, by an attack by the Chinese on the British force at Ningpo, which was repulsed with very heavy loss to the enemy.

Major Mee's detachment was sent back to India in March, 1842, previous to which, in G. O. No. 291 of 1841, another battalion of volunteers was called for in Bengal, and was formed of companies from eight different regiments,—the 3rd, 15th, 17th, 23rd, 32nd, 41st, 52nd, and 56th Native Infantry. This corps, however, was delayed at Calcutta, and did not arrive in China until June, 1842,. when it joined the expedition then about to set out for the Yang-tse-Kiang. Chin-Kiang-Foo was reached on the 15th of July and taken by storm on the 21st, with a loss on our side of thirty-four killed, 107 wounded, and three missing. On this occasion, as is recorded in a complimentary G. O. dated October 14th, three companies of the Bengal Volunteers, under Major Kent, had the good fortune to be the first engaged with the enemy. The battalion had three men wounded. The Chinese troops were scattered with great loss. This victory was the last engagement of the war, for before the British force could advance on Nankin, the Chinese sued for peace, and a treaty was concluded on August the 17th.

To the troops employed in the earlier part of the campaign, up to June, 1841, twelve months' full batta was presented; for the latter operations six months' batta was given, while all ranks received a medal, and certain honorary distinctions were granted to the British and Madras regiments.—(G. O. No. 54 of 1842).

In 1840-41-42, while the wars in Afghanistan and China were still proceeding, disturbances of a somewhat serious character occurred in Bundelkhand and in the Saugor and Nerbadda territories, which necessitated the employment of a considerable military force for their suppression. The first notable outbreak was that at Chirgaon, a small town lying about eighty miles south-west of Kalpi, the *jaghirdar* of which place went into rebellion and began committing depredations in the surrounding country: a force of nearly 2,000 men (which included the Bundelkhand Legion and part of the 13th Native Infantry) was employed in the reduction of the place, which was evacuated by the insurgents (April, 1841) after two days' operations and the capture by storm of one of the outworks; In an action near Malthone, in April, 1842, Captain Ralfe, of the 3rd Native Infantry, was mortally wounded. In June, 1842, an action took place at Panwari, in which a squadron of the 8th Light Cavalry and two companies of the 13th Native Infantry defeated a body of 3,000 Bundela insurgents, killing upwards of eighty, including their leader. In December, 1842, a smart engagement was fought at Bhagaura, near Jaitpur, in which detachments of the 40th and 57th Native Infantry defeated a considerable body of insurgents. *Subadar* Yar Khan, 51st Native Infantry, was killed in a skirmish with a body of rebels in February, 1843. Several other engagements took place in various parts of the disturbed districts, and it was not until the summer of 1843 that order was eventually restored. The troops employed from time to time in the suppression of the disturbances were the 8th Light Cavalry, the 2nd and 8th Irregular Cavalry, the 3rd, 11th, 13th, 24th, 40th, 50th, 51st, 57th and 61st Native Infantry, and the Bundelkhand Legion.

Scarcely were the campaigns in Afghanistan and China concluded when the Indian Government found themselves involved in a war with the Baluch Amirs of Sindh. A long course of intrigues and misunderstandings came to a head in a treacherous attack on the Residency of Hyderabad on the 15th February, 1843. Major-General Sir Charles J. Napier, commanding in Sindh and Baluchistan, who was then at Halla, thirty-five miles to the north-west of Hyderabad, immediately marched towards that place with such troops as were then available in that part of Sindh. His force consisted of:

9th Bengal Light Cavalry
Detail of the Poona Horse
The Sindh Horse
2 companies of artillery
1 company of Madras sappers
Her Majesty's 22nd Foot
1st, 12th and 25th Bombay Native Infantry

With these troops, amounting to less than 2,800 men, with twelve pieces of artillery, Sir Charles met and attacked the enemy (20,000 strong) at Miani, six miles from Hyderabad, on February the 17th. Rather less than 1,800 of the British troops were actually engaged in the battle which ensued, Major Outram being absent with a detachment of 200, while the detail of the Poona Horse and four companies of infantry were employed as a baggage guard. The enemy were strongly posted on and beyond the dry bed of the Fulaili *nala,* of which the high banks served as a rampart, while their flanks rested on thick jungle impassable for cavalry. Napier made a frontal attack, advancing in echelon of regiments across the plain, and our troops were met as they came to close quarters by repeated and determined charges of the Baluch infantry: for three hours a stubborn hand-to-hand fight was maintained, until at length the fortunes of the day were decided by a brilliant charge of the 9th Bengal Light Cavalry and the Sindh Horse, under Colonel Pattle, who, breaking through the enemy's right, swept across the *nala* and fell on their rear. Slowly they began to give way, and, disputing every inch of ground, they were gradually driven from the field, leaving their camp, stores, and artillery in the hands of the victors. The loss of the enemy was reckoned at 5,000, but was probably not so great; that; of the British was six British officers and fifty-six men killed, thirteen British officers, three native officers, and 178 men wounded. Among the killed was Captain Cookson, of the 9th Bengal Light Cavalry.

Sir Charles Napier entered Hyderabad on the 20th February, and on the 12th of March the annexation of the whole of Sindh was proclaimed, and the Baluch Sardars who had tendered their submission were deported to Bombay.

One powerful chief, Mir Sher Muhammad, of Mirpur, still remained in arms at the head of about 20,000 men, and posted himself at Dabba, about four miles from Hyderabad, where Sir Charles Napier, who had received reinforcements (principally Bombay troops) which had brought the strength of his force up to 5,000 men, attacked him on the 24th March. Here again the enemy were strongly posted behind a *nala,* and the resistance which they offered was, while it lasted, as firm and gallant as that they had made at Miani; but shaken by a raking cross-fire from the British artillery they began to give ground, and the advance of the infantry, led by the 22nd Foot, and the turning of both flanks by the cavalry, speedily completed their discomfiture. They gave way in utter rout and were pursued for many miles with much slaughter, and the conquest of Sindh was complete. The British loss amounted to two officers and thirty-seven men killed, and ten officers and 221 men wounded, Captain Garrett, of the 9th Bengal Light Cavalry, being numbered amongst the former.

For these successes the troops received the thanks of both Houses of Parliament; a medal was conferred on all ranks, inscribed with the names "Meeanee" and "Hyderabad;" and those names, with that of "Scinde," were authorised to be borne on the colours of all corps engaged in the two actions.

In April, 1843, a sudden outbreak took place at Kaithal, in the Karnal District. The Kaithal territories having lapsed to the British Government, Mr. Greathed, a civil officer, proceeded to the town to settle the affairs of the State, escorted by about 150 men of the 3rd Irregular Cavalry and two companies of the 72nd Native Infantry. On the 9th April the escort was suddenly attacked by the people of the place, and compelled to retire to Karnal after having sustained heavy loss. One native officer of the 3rd Irregular Cavalry, (*Ressaidar* Sarmast Khan), and all those of the two companies of the 72nd (*Subadars* Parsan Dichit and Hassan Khan, and *Jemadars* Harak Singh and Gangacharan Misser) were killed, and Lieutenant Farre of the 72nd was severely wounded in the conflict. A considerable force had to be sent to Kaithal before order was restored.

The death of the Maharajah of Gwalior (Sindhia), and the disturbances incidental to the succession of a minor, necessitated British intervention in the affairs of that State towards the close of 1843, and eventually involved the Government of India in the last of the wars with the Mahratta powers. It was at first expected that a simple demonstration would be sufficient to put an end to disturbances which had already begun to affect injuriously the peace of British districts bordering on the Gwalior territories, and accordingly with that object, in the autumn of 1843, orders were issued for the assembly of forces which were for the time designated the "Army of Exercise." The mere concentration of troops did not, however, produce the beneficial effect which had been anticipated, and eventually, in December, under the designation of the Right and Left wings of the Army of Gwalior, the forces which had been assembled at Agra and Jhansi were moved forward to attack Gwalior, respectively, from the north and the south. The composition of the two wings of the Army of Gwalior was as follows:

Right Wing	3 troops of horse artillery	
	4 companies of foot artillery	
	3 companies of sappers	
	16th Light Dragoons	
	The Body Guard	
	1st, 4th and 10th Light Cavalry and detachments of the 5th and 8th	
	4th Irregular Cavalry	
	39th and 40th Foot	
	2nd, 14th, 16th, 31st, 39th (one company), 43rd, 56th, 62nd and 70th Native Infantry	
	Regiment of Kalat-i-Ghilzai	
Left Wing	2 troops of horse artillery	
	1 company of foot artillery	
	1 company of sappers	
	9th Light Dragoons (two squadrons)	
	5th (two squadrons)	
	8th and 11th (two squadrons) Light Cavalry	
	8th Irregular Cavalry	
	3rd and 50th Foot	
	39th, 50th, 51st and 58th Native Infantry	
	The Sipri Contingent	

The cavalry were organised in four brigades, and the infantry in three divisions of two brigades each. The 1st and 2nd Brigades of Cavalry and the 1st Division (1st and 2nd Brigades) of Infantry formed, the left wing under Major-General Grey, The 3rd and 4th Brigades of Cavalry and the and and 3rd Divisions of Infantry constituted the right wing. The 2nd and 3rd Divisions were commanded respectively by Major-Generals Dennis and Littler.

The right wing, under the Commander-in-Chief, General Sir Hugh Gough, and accompanied by the Governor-General, Lord

Ellenborough, in person, crossed the Chambal river on the 22nd and 23rd December, and reached Hingona on the 26th. Advancing thence on the morning of the 29th, Sir Hugh Gough found the Mahrattas numbering about 18,000 men, with a powerful artillery, drawn up in a very strongly entrenched position in front of the villages of Maharajpur and Chaunda, about fifteen miles to the north-west of Gwalior. The 5th Brigade (39th Foot and 56th Native Infantry), under the command of Brigadier Wright, was forthwith launched against the village of Maharajpur under cover of the fire of two light field batteries, while the 3rd Brigade (40th Foot, and 2nd and 10th Native Infantry) under Major-General Valiant was directed to take the village in reverse, both movements being supported by the 4th Brigade (14th, 31st and 43rd Native Infantry) under the command of Brigadier Stacy. After a desperate contest, often hand-to-hand, these troops drove the enemy from Maharajpur; then moving on Chaunda the 5th Brigade, after a severe conflict, carried that position too, while the 3rd and 4th Brigades, cooperating, drove the Mahrattas from the villages of Shikarpur and Dompura, The cavalry at the same time were fully employed, and a spirited charge of the 4th Irregular Cavalry, resulting in the capture of two guns and two standards, was specially mentioned in the commander-in-chief's despatch. In the end the enemy were driven from the field with heavy loss, leaving in our possession fifty-six guns and the whole of their ammunition wagons. In this severe engagement the 16th and 56th Native Infantry were greatly distinguished and suffered heavily. The loss on our side was great, amounting to 106 killed, 684 wounded, and seven missing, making a total of 797. Major-General Churchill, C.B., Quarter-Master-General, Queen's troops, Lieutenant-Colonel Sanders, Deputy Secretary to the Government of India, Lieutenant Leathes, of the Artillery, Major Crommelin, 1st Light Cavalry, Lieutenant Newton, 16th Native Infantry, *Subadar*-Major Jodha Singh, *Bahadur*, 4th Light Cavalry, and *Jemadar* Khushial Singh, 16th Native Infantry, were numbered amongst the slain, and thirty-four officers were wounded, including Major-Generals Valiant and Littler. One native officer, *Jemadar* Ajudhia Singh, 16th Native Infantry—died of his wounds.

On the same day Major-General Grey, with the left wing of the Army of Gwalior, advancing from the south, gained a decisive victory over another Mahratta Army. Having crossed the Sindh river at Chandpur, that officer reached Barka-ka-Sarai on the 28th December, and there heard that the enemy, 12,000 strong, were in position at Antri, seven miles off. On the following day he made a long march to Paniar, about twelve miles from Gwalior, the Mahrattas at the same time quitting Antri and proceeding by a parallel movement until they reached the fortified village of Mangor, near Paniar, where they took up a strong position on the heights four miles to the east of the British camp, and began an attack on General Grey's long line of baggage. Detaching all the cavalry he could spare to protect the baggage, Grey attacked the enemy's centre with the 3rd Buffs, the 39th Native Infantry and a company of sappers, who carried every position before them, notwithstanding a galling fire from the enemy's guns, while the 50th Foot and a wing of the 50th Native Infantry, supported by the 58th Native Infantry, attacked and routed the enemy's left. After a conflict of two hours the Mahrattas were driven from their position with heavy loss in men and also with the loss of all their guns (twenty-four in number) and the whole of their ammunition. The loss on our side amounted to thirty-five killed (including two officers) and 182 wounded (including Brigadier Yates and six other officers). These two victories brought the campaign to a speedy termination, and order was soon restored in the Gwalior territories.

A bronze medal, made from the material of the captured guns, was issued to all ranks engaged in the campaign, and the several corps engaged in the battles of Maharajpur and Paniar were permitted to inscribe those names on their colours and appointments. Subsequently, a memorial column to those who had fallen was erected at Calcutta.

At this point it will be convenient to glance briefly at such interior changes and other matters of interest of the period as have not already been mentioned.

In October, 1840, three battalions of Light Infantry were formed at Meerut and Cawnpore from the light companies of various corps, and during the progress of the Afghan War the 1st and 2nd of these battalions were moved up to Ferozepore and Ludhiana. They were composed as follow:

1st Light Infantry Battalion	Light companies 7th, 8th, 13th, 17th, 21st, 29th & 31st Native Infantry
	Rifle company 68th Native Infantry

2nd Light Infantry Battalion	Light companies 14th, 22nd, 49th, 55th, 63rd & 66th Native Infantry
	Rifle company 72nd Native Infantry
3rd Light Infantry Battalion	Light companies 1st, 11th, 12th, 24th, 50th, 58th & 67th Native Infantry
	Rifle company 9th Native Infantry

A constant fluctuation in the strength of regiments was an inevitable result of the great demand made by the Afghan war on the resources of India, and the reductions consequent on its termination. Besides these, several more or less important additions were made to the Bengal Army between 1840 and 1845, first of which was the formation, by G. O. G. G. No. 106 of 1841, of the 7th Irregular Cavalry. This corps, which still exists as the 5th Bengal Cavalry, was raised at Bareilly, by Captain Wheler, of the late 2nd Light Cavalry. By G. G. O. No. 18 of the following year the formation of a new regular regiment of cavalry was directed, to replace the 2nd Light Cavalry, disbanded for misconduct in Afghanistan; the new corps was numbered the 11th, but eight years afterwards it received the number of the regiment whose place it was raised to supply. In January, 1842 (G.G.O. No. 25) the 8th Regiment of Irregular Cavalry was raised at Fatehgarh, under Lieutenant Ryves, 61st Native Infantry; it is now the 6th Bengal Cavalry. The 9th Irregular Cavalry was formed in February, 1844, of drafts partly from other corps of irregular cavalry and partly from Christie's Horse, one of the regiments of Shah Shuja's Force. This force had been disbanded by G .O. G. G., dated the 16th June, 1842, all the regiments, except the 3rd Infantry, which was retained as the "Regiment of Kalat-i-Ghilzai," being broken up and the men distributed throughout the infantry and irregular cavalry of Bengal. In 1844 (G.G.O. No.234) two companies were added to the "Assam Sebandy Corps" formed in 1835, which was now armed, clothed, and equipped as light infantry and designated "the 2nd Assam Light Infantry." Earlier in the same year was formed the Gwalior Contingent, numbering 10,000 men of all arms, in which the Sipri Contingent was incorporated. Volunteers from several regiments joined this force, and amongst others the 31st, 43rd, and 70th, and the Regiment of Kalat-i-Ghilzai contributed. This

Contingent, which in a short time came to be regarded as the model force of India, gained in 1857 an unenviable notoriety by the atrocities which accompanied its mutiny.

The years now under review, as well as the succeeding decade, are full of signs of the deterioration of the Bengal Army, which, as we have seen in the preceding chapters, had been growing since the early years of the century, and which was shortly to come to a head. Not the least among these symptoms was the behaviour of the sepoys of several regiments on being ordered to Sindh. The service was unpopular, especially because full batta did not accompany it, although it was, at any rate according to the notions of Hindustani soldiers, as much foreign service as the campaign in Afghanistan. The British officers, instead of repressing unreasoning complaints with a firm hand, seem in many cases to have been afraid of their men, and to have humoured them when they should have enforced the strictest discipline. Thus, when several regiments were ordered to Sindh, as many as 190 men in the 4th and 90 in the 69th applied for, and—extraordinary to relate—obtained their discharge; the 7th Light Cavalry at first refused to march, but afterwards, having expressed deep contrition for their conduct, the men were pardoned; the matter reached a climax in the 34th Native Infantry, who obstinately and in the worst spirit disobeyed its orders and refused to march, and was for this offence disbanded and the number struck out of the Army List (G. O. C. C, 20th March, 1844). The 64th at first contented themselves with writing objectionable anonymous letters to head-quarters, and was, as a punishment, ordered to Barrackpore, but, on hearing of the mutiny of the 34th, the commanding officer of the 64th represented that his corps begged to be pardoned, and to be permitted to march to Sukkur in place of the 34th; on arrival at that place, however, the 64th broke into open mutiny, and inquiry disclosed the fact that the state of the regiment had been one of utter disorganisation throughout, and that its condition had been entirely misrepresented by the commanding officer. That officer was cashiered, and the regiment was deprived of its colours until such time as it should have regained a sound state of discipline; sixty-nine men were immediately dismissed the service, and powers were vested in Sir Charles Napier to disband the corps, if necessary. This extreme measure, however, was not resorted to (G.O.C.C., 20th and 30th March 1844; G. G. O. No. 357).

To the unsoldierlike behaviour of these regiments the conduct of the Bundelkhand Legion was a bright contrast. This corps, on hearing of the mutinous refusal of the 34th Native Infantry to march to Sindh, immediately volunteered for service there; the offer was accepted with an expression of the satisfaction of the Government (G. G. O., No. 101 of 1844), and it was at the same time notified that the Legion was brought permanently on the strength of the Bengal Army: the corps immediately proceeded to Sindh, where it rendered good service and earned high praise for its conduct during a trying period of two years. The 6th Irregular Cavalry also volunteered for service in Sindh, and here it may conveniently be mentioned that during the years 1844-45 the 6th and 9th Irregular Cavalry were actively employed in protecting the northern frontier of Sindh against the incursions of the Jakranis, Bugtis, Dumkis, and other predatory tribes, with whom they had frequent engagements; on one occasion, at Uch, on the 15th January, 1845, Captain Salter, with 390 men of these two regiments, surprised and routed nearly double that number of Jakranis and Bugtis, killing a great many, including two prominent chiefs, and recapturing several thousand cattle and other plunder that they were carrying off. In the early part of 1845, the 2nd Bengal European Regiment, the Bundelkhand Legion, and detachments of the 4th, 64th, and 69th Native Infantry took an active share in the campaign against these tribes, and in the reduction (9th March, 1845) of their almost inaccessible stronghold of Trakki; their conduct earned the high commendation of Sir Charles Napier himself, who now, in recognition of the good conduct and excellent services of the regiment, directed the restoration to the 64th Native Infantry of the colours they had forfeited a year before.

The Sindh mutinies were by no means isolated instances of insubordination and bad feeling; reference to the General Orders of the commander-in-chief shows that the number of courts-martial in the native army had trebled in the last twenty years, and were steadily on the increase. It is not to be wondered at then that the Governor-General (Sir Henry Hardinge) arrived at the conclusion that this unsatisfactory state of things was in a great measure the result of Lord William Bentinck's abolition of flogging; accordingly, after long deliberation, he issued (1845) a minute repealing Lord William Bentinck's order.

The most important change in the equipment of native infantry at this time was the gradual introduction of muzzle-loading "Brunswick" rifles, the first to receive them being one company in each of the light infantry regiments (including the 42nd and 43rd), while two years later the whole of the Nasseri and Sirmoor Battalions were so armed, as well as one company each in five more regiments of the line (including the 31st and 65th). Less important, though far from trivial, changes were the substitution of canvas haversacks for the old unwieldy knapsack (G. O. C. C, 22nd March, 1844), and the introduction (12th January, 1844) of a forage cap for general duties.

CHAPTER 7

The Sikh Wars

The close of the year 1845 found the Government of India involved in a sanguinary contest with the Sikhs. Ranjit Singh, the founder of the Sikh dominion, had been on terms of friendship and alliance with the Government of India since the year 1809. He died in June, 1839, and after the death of his son and successor on the 5th November, 1840, and on the same day, of his grandson, the competition for the vacant throne, and the struggle of successive candidates for power resulted, after a series of ruthless assassinations, in the Khalsa Army becoming the real master of the state, and in the whole of the Punjab being plunged into what has been well described as a condition of "widely-spread, frantic, and sanguinary anarchy." Under such circumstances the Lahore Government, unable to control the army and dreading its power, perceived that their only hope lay in its destruction, and in this view secretly encouraged it in its desire for a contest with the English, hoping and expecting that the conflict would terminate in its overthrow and dispersion. Not much encouragement was indeed, needed, and on the 11th December, 1845, in defiance of existing treaties, a portion of the Sikh Army headed (unwillingly, it is said) by Sirdar Lal Singh (the Wazir) and Sirdar Tej Singh, crossed the Sutlej, and took up a position within a few miles of Ferozepore.

A hostile inroad of this nature had been threatening for some years, and especially during the summer and autumn of 1845, and the event consequently did not find the Government of India unprepared. It was, indeed, a fortunate circumstance that changes in the disposition of the army on our North-Western Frontier, adopted partly for sanitary reasons and partly as a reply to the menace from beyond the Sutlej, had resulted during the preceding three years in a considerable increase to the forces in the neighbourhood of the locality in which they were now most needed, and where they now proved sufficient to stem the first torrent of invasion. In addition to the old military post at Ludhiana, which had been considerably reinforced, a permanent cantonment, with a large garrison, had been established at Ferozepore. On the abandonment of Karnal, on account of excessive unhealthiness, Umballa had been adopted as a military station of the first class, with a garrison of one regiment of British dragoons, one of native regular cavalry, one of irregular cavalry, one of British infantry and three of native infantry, besides artillery. And a regiment of British infantry had been stationed at Kasauli and another at Sabathu, the battalion of Gurkhas displaced from Sabathu being removed to Jutogh, near Simla.—(G. O. G. G., 17th November, 1842).

The British forces in the upper provinces were quickly put in motion to resist the Sikh invasion. Those on the north-west frontier were first assembled, and under the designation of the "Army of the Sutlej" were arranged (G. O, C. C, 13th December, 1845) in the manner following, the whole being under the command of General Sir Hugh Gough, the Commander-in-Chief, who was accompanied into the field by the Governor-General, Lieutenant-General Sir Henry Hardinge:

Artillery Brigadier G. Brooke		7 troops Horse Artillery 7 companies Foot Artillery
Engineers		Corps of Sappers & Miners
Cavalry Brigadier D. Harriott	1st Bgde.	H. M.'s 3rd Light Dragoons 8th Light Cavalry 9th Irregular Cavalry
	2nd Bgde.	The Body-Guard 5th Light Cavalry 8th Irregular Cavalry
	3rd Bgde.	4th Light Cavalry 2nd & 3rd Irregular Cavalry

Infantry: 1st Division Major-General Sir H. G. Smith, K.C.B.	1st Bgde.	H. M.'s 31st Foot 24th & 47th Native Infantry
	2nd Bgde.	H. M.'s 50th Foot 42nd & 48th Native Infantry
Infantry: 2nd Division Major-General W. R. Gilbert	3rd Bgde.	H. M.'s 29th Foot 41st & 45th Native Infantry
	4th Bgde.	1st European Light Infantry 2nd & 16th Native Infantry
Infantry: 3rd Division Major-General Sir J. M'Caskill, K.C.B.	5th Bgde.	H. M.'s 9th Foot 26th & 73rd Native Infantry
	6th Bgde.	H. M.'s 80th Foot 11th, 27th & 63rd Native Infantry
Infantry: 4th Division Major-General Sir J. Littler, K.C.B.	7th Bgde.	H. M.'s 62nd Foot 12th & 14th Native Infantry
	8th Bgde.	33rd, 44th & 54th Native Infantry

Of these troops a small garrison was left at, Ludhiana, and the Umballa column marched as lightly equipped as possible to relieve Sir John Littler's division of 7,000 men, which was threatened at Ferozepore. The strength of the Sikh forces has been variously stated; the majority of the estimates made at the time are supposed now to have been exaggerated, and their total strength was probably not much above 40,000.

The Umballa Division and the troops from Ludhiana (which had united at Bassian) arrived on the 18th December at Mudki, eighteen miles from Ferozepore, after a long and fatiguing march, but they were scarcely encamped when intelligence was received that the Sikhs were advancing. Sir Hugh Gough immediately pushed forward to meet the enemy, and two miles from Mudki found them in position, in considerable strength and with forty pieces of cannon.

The battle commenced with heavy artillery fire on both sides, during which the British infantry advanced in echelon of brigades and deployed; the enemy's fire told severely on them in this formation, and to effect a diversion the 3rd Light Dragoons, the Body-Guard, the 5th Light Cavalry, and part of the 4th Light Cavalry (Lancers) were directed to make a movement on the enemy's left: this was effected with great gallantry, and, turning the left flank of the Sikh Army, these regiments swept along the rear of the enemy's infantry and guns, silenced the latter for a time, and put the whole of the hostile cavalry to flight. At the same time the remainder of the 4th and the 9th Irregular Cavalry assailed the Sikh right with success, and our infantry, advancing in echelon of lines, drove the Sikhs, who resisted gallantly, from one position to another at the point of the bayonet, until night put an end to the conflict. The Sikhs do not appear to have suffered very severely in men, but they lost seventeen out of their forty guns, and were obliged to fall back on their main army in the entrenched camp which they had formed at Ferozeshahr. Our losses amounted to 215 killed (including twelve officers) and 657 wounded (including forty-four officers). Among the former were Major-General Sir John M'Caskill, Captain Trower of the Artillery Lieutenant Fisher of the Body-Guard, Lieutenant Hamilton, 24th Native Infantry, and Lieutenant Spence, 42nd Native Light Infantry. Major-General Sir R. H. Sale, Brigadier Bolton, Lieutenant Munro, *Aide-de-Camp* to the Governor-General, Captain Van Homrigh, 48th Native Infantry, serving on the Staff, and Captain Dashwood and Lieutenant Pollock of the Artillery, died of their wounds within a few days of the battle. Among the native officers *Jemadar* Atar Singh, 16th Native Infantry, and *Subadar* Siu-din Tiwari, 48th Native Infantry, were killed.

On the 19th December Sir Hugh Gough was reinforced by the arrival of the 29th Foot, the 1st Bengal European Light Infantry, the 11th and 41st Native Infantry, two companies of foot artillery, and some heavy guns, and on the 21st, leaving the two native regiments to guard the wounded, he marched from Mudki for the purpose of attacking the Sikhs at Ferozeshahr.[1] After a fatiguing march of sixteen miles he was joined, as had previously been concerted, at Misriwala, about four miles from Ferozeshahr, by the Fourth Divi-

---

1. This battle has been variously styled that of "Ferozeshah," "Ferozeshuhur," "Firozeshahar," and "Pheerozshuhur." The simple unadorned name of the village round which it was fought is *Pheru*.

sion, under Major-General Sir John Littler, from Ferozepore, and at 3 p.m. the united forces, amounting to 16,700 men, with sixty-nine guns, moved forward to assail the enemy (numbering, according to their own estimate, 47,000 men, with eighty-eight guns) in the formidable position in which they had entrenched themselves.

In the arrangements for the attack, which was delivered on the western, and to some extent on the southern face of the entrenchment, the Second Division (Gilbert's) was placed on the right, the Third (now commanded by Brigadier Wallace) in the centre, and the Fourth (Littler's) on the left,—while the First Division (Smith's) was kept in reserve. The attack of the Fourth Division was entirely" under the direction of Sir John Littler: the remaining three divisions (less the 6th Brigade, of which only one regiment—the 80th Foot—was present in the field, temporarily attached to the 3rd Brigade in place of the 41st Native Infantry, left at Mudki) were divided into two wings, of which the commander-in-chief in person directed the right, while Lieutenant-General Sir Henry Hardinge (who had volunteered his services as Second-in-Command) superintended the left. The Fourth Division commenced the attack, and the "Chance of War," as Sir Hugh Gough expressed it, "placed it in opposition to the strongest part of the enemy's entrenched position": it advanced under a terrific fire of grape and canister to within 150 yards of the enemy's batteries, and the leading brigade sustained heavy losses; notwithstanding this it did not desist from its efforts to carry the position, until Colonel Reed, the Brigadier in command, perceiving that it could not get forward and "was exposed to a most destructive fire without any object," directed it to retire, which it did in almost as good order, allowing for the losses it had sustained, as that in which it had advanced. The division, with greatly reduced numbers, was thus withdrawn out of fire, and was not again brought into action.[2] In the meantime the Second and Third Divisions had advanced and, under a storm of shot and shell, "with matchless gallantry" carried the batteries opposed to them at the point of the bayonet, but the enemy were only driven as far as their camp in the immediate rear, from which they kept up a galling musketry fire. By this time the First Division, hitherto in reserve, had also come into action, and carrying the opposing guns it penetrated deep into the enemy's camp and captured the village of Ferozeshahr, which it held for several hours, while the 3rd Light Dragoons made a magnificent charge, capturing some of the most formidable batteries, sabring the gunners, and driving the enemy to the further end of the entrenchment. But night had now set in, and in the darkness terrible confusion arose; regiments and brigades became intermixed and were unable in the gloom to entirely recover their formation, while the enemy, still in possession of a large portion of the entrenchment, kept up a devastating fire. Under these circumstances a partial retirement became necessary before midnight; the hard-won ground was abandoned, and the exhausted troops, retiring to the south and south-west of the entrenchment, bivouacked for the remainder of the night, and endeavoured to snatch a little repose. But there was little repose for them; for, perished with cold and thirst and almost starving, they were still throughout the night exposed to a harassing and incessant fire whenever the moonlight or their own fires disclosed their whereabouts to the enemy. But no hardship could quell the indomitable spirit of the British soldiers; exhausted as they were, when morning dawned they were ready to complete the work begun the day before, and a general advance at daybreak, on the 22nd, carried the enemy's camp, forced them from the village of Ferozeshahr and drove them from the field. The dangers of the day did not, however, end here: Tej Singh, with the force which had menaced Ferozepore, appeared on the field at noon and threatened to overwhelm the exhausted British Army, which, without ammunition and weakened by fatigue and want of food, was now in a critical position. However, a bold front was shown by the English General, and, after an unsuccessful attempt on the position of Ferozeshahr, now occupied by the latter, Tej Singh withdrew, and the Sikhs, defeated but not demoralised, retired across the Sutlej, weakened by the loss of seventy-three pieces of artillery.

The conduct of the sepoy regiments in this battle has several times been criticised severely, but it is only fair to them to remember that the British Army was exhausted by fatigue and by long fasting

---

2. The repulse of the Fourth Division on this occasion was at the time and long afterwards attributed to the misconduct of the troops and especially of the leading regiment, the 62nd Foot; and one author (Trotter,—*History of the British Empire in India*, Vol. 1. page 53) goes to the length of asserting that "the 62nd Foot followed by the native regiments on either flank, wavered, turned, and fled in utter panic towards the rear." This assertion is apparently based on a statement which appeared in Sir John Littler's report, which was made in error and afterwards withdrawn : it is entirely without any justification in truth. The conduct of the division was enquired into at the time, and Sir Hugh Gough, in a special General Order, showed how entirely uncalled for were the aspersions which had been cast upon it. (See G. O. C. C, dated Camp Nihalki, the 28th January, 1846.)

and want of water; that under such circumstances the sepoy collapses much sooner than the British soldier; and that the sepoys fully retrieved their reputation when fighting under more favourable conditions at Sobraon. The loss of the Sikhs at Ferozeshahr is unknown, but it is probable that the killed alone amounted to two thousand: that of the British was thirty-nine British and seventeen native officers, and 664 men killed; eighty-two British officers, nineteen native officers, and 1,677 men wounded, and 379 men missing,—making a total of 2,877.[3]

Among the officers killed were Brigadier Wallace, Captains Hore (officiating Deputy Secretary to the Government of India, Military Department) and Burnett (Brigade-Major), serving on the staff; Captain Todd and Lieutenant Lambert, Bengal Artillery; Captain Box and Ensign Moxon, 1st European Light Infantry; Ensign Armstrong, 2nd Native Infantry; Major Hull, 16th Native Infantry; Major Griffin, 24th Native Infantry; Lieutenants Croly and Eatwell, 26th Native (Light) Infantry; Lieutenant Wollen, 42nd Native (Light) Infantry, and Captain Hunter, 73rd Native Infantry. Amongst the slain were also numbered two distinguished political officers,—Major Broadfoot, 34th Madras Native Infantry, whose prominent services in the glorious defence of Jalalabad have already been mentioned, and Captain Nicolson of the 28th Bengal Native Infantry. Captain Egerton, of the staff, Captain Kendall, 1st European Light Infantry, Captain Bolton, 2nd Native Infantry, and Lieutenant-Colonel Bruce, Captain Holmes, and Lieutenant Tulloch, 12th Native Infantry, died of their wounds.

The native officers killed at the battle of Ferozeshahr were *Jemadars* Raghunath and Bihari Singh, of the Artillery; *Risaldar* Mir Wazir Ali and *Jemadar* Pir Khan, 9th Irregular Cavalry; *Subadar* Shaikh Madar Bakhsh, 2nd Native Infantry; *Subadar* Bhawanilal Pande, 12th Native Infantry; *Subadar*-Major Umed Singh, 14th Native Infantry; *Subadars* Ramgulam Singh and Shaikh Rajab and *Jemadar* Sukhlal Singh and Mansaram Bajpae, 24th Native Infantry; *Subadar* Ganesh Patak, 33rd Native Infantry; *Jemadars* Rustam Patak and Din Singh, 42nd Native Infantry; *Subadars* Fakira Khan and Siu-lal Singh, 45th Native Infantry; *Subadar* Shaikh Khuda Bakhsh, 48th Native Infantry; and *Subadar* Shaikh Kadir Bakhsh, 73rd Native Infantry. *Jemadar*

---

3. This is four less than the number given in the revised official return, but that return erroneously includes four officers who had been wounded, not at Ferozeshahr, but at Mudki.

Ghulam Rasul Khan, 3rd Irregular Cavalry; *Jemadar* Jurakan Sukal, 2nd Native Infantry; *Subadar* Fateh Singh, 26th Native Infantry; *Subadar* Hanuman Tiwari, 45th Native Infantry; and *Jemadar* Bhawanidin Singh, 48th Native Infantry, died of their wounds.

Having driven the Sikhs across the Sutlej, Sir Hugh Gough advanced to Araf, and on the 27th December pushed a reconnaissance to the left bank of the river, when the enemy were found to have established themselves in great force on the opposite bank, in advance of the village of Sobraon. Having placed the First Division in a position to watch the Sikhs, with the rest of the troops at hand ready to support Sir Harry Smith in case of necessity, the commander-in-chief deferred further action until the arrival of reinforcements in men, artillery, ammunition, and stores, which were now on the way to join him. The arrival of some of these reinforcements and the approach of the rest necessitated a re-arrangement of the forces, and on the 1st January, 1846, the Army of the Sutlej was re-organized as follows:

Artillery Brigadier G. E. Gowan, C.B.		11 Troops Horse Artillery 8 Companies Foot Artillery 4 Light Field Batteries 1 Elephant Battery
Engineers Lieutenant-Colonel E. J. Smith, C.B.		Corps of Sappers & Miners
Cavalry Major-General Sir J. Thackwell, K.C.B.	1st Bgde.	3rd Light Dragoons 4th & 5th Light Cavalry 9th Irregular Cavalry
	2nd Bgde.	9th Light Dragoons (Lancers) 11th Light Cavalry 2nd & 8th Irregular Cavalry
	3rd Bgde.	16th Light Dragoons (Lancers)

		Governor-General's Body Guard
		3rd Light Cavalry
		4th Irregular Cavalry
	4th Bgde.	1st & 8th Light Cavalry
		3rd Irregular Cavalry
Infantry: 1st Division Major-General Sir H. G. Smith, K.C.B.	1st Bgde.	31st Foot
		24th & 47th Native Infantry
	2nd Bgde.	50th Foot
		42nd & 48th Native Infantry
Infantry: 2nd Division Major General W. R. Gilbert	3rd Bgde.	29th Foot
		41st & 45th Native Infantry
	4th Bgde.	1st European Light Infantry
		2nd and 16th Native Infantry
Infantry: 3rd Division Major-General Sir R. H. Dick, K.C.B.	5th Bgde.	9th Foot
		26th & 73rd Native Infantry
	6th Bgde.	80th Foot
		11th & 33rd Native Infantry
	7th Bgde.	10th Foot
		43rd & 59th Native Infantry
Infantry: 4th Division Major-General Sir J. H. Littler, K.C.B.	8th Bgde.	62nd Foot
		12th & 14th Native Infantry
	9th Bgde.	27th, 44th & 54th Native Infantry

Infantry: 5th Division Major-General Sir John Grey, K.C.B.	10th Bgde.	53rd Foot 30th and 68th Native Infantry
	11th Bgde.	6th, 9th & 38th Native Infantry
	12th Bgde.	55th & 63rd Native Infantry Nasseri Battalion Sirmoor Battalion

About the same time, as there appeared to be considerable probability of the war being prolonged, and, in that event, of the strain imposed upon the force on the north-west frontier being greater than it could endure, it was decided that a force should be despatched from Sindh to advance against the Sikhs from the south, and either assail Mooltan or join the main army under Sir Hugh Gough, as might be found most expedient. For this purpose, accordingly, about the middle of January, the following force was organized under the command of Major-General Sir C. J. Napier, with Major-General G. Hunter, of the Bengal Army, as Second-in-Command, and designated the "Sindh Field Force:"

Artillery Brigadier F. Schuler		3 Troops Horse Artillery (2 Bengal, 1 Bombay) 4 Companies Foot Artillery Light Field Batteries (2 Bengal, 2 Bombay)
Cavalry Brigadier J. B. Hearsey		6th & 7th Bengal Light Cavalry Sindh Irregular Horse
Infantry	1st Bgde.	2nd Bengal European Regiment 4th & 15th Bengal Native Infantry
	2nd Bgde.	17th Foot 7th & 12th Bombay Native Infantry
	3rd Bgde.	86th Foot

	13th & 18th Bombay Native Infantry
4th Bgde.	4th & 17th Bombay Native Infantry
	Baluch Battalion

This force began marching northwards towards the end of January, 1846, but the movement, though pushed on with great vigour, came too late, as it had not even reached Mitankot, at the confluence of the Indus and the Panjnad, when the crowning victory of Sobraon and the occupation of Lahore put an end to the war.

In this place may appropriately be mentioned an incident highly creditable to the 4th Native Infantry. A small detachment of this regiment (26 men) under the command of *Subadar* Najju Khan, was employed in escorting a party of invalids proceeding by boat from Sindh to Ferozepore. At Mitankot, on the 1st January, they were attacked by a large body of Sikhs, but undeterred by the odds against them and aided to some extent by the invalids, they boldly met the enemy and repulsed them after a sharp engagement, but with the loss of the brave *Subadar* and two men killed and several wounded and taken prisoners. The gallantry of the detachment was specially eulogised in General Orders.

On the 12th of January, Sir Hugh Gough made a slight movement in advance, and occupied a position from Hari-ki-pattan on the right to Ferozepore on the left, but, in the meantime, while he was still waiting for the heavy guns then on their way to join him, and without which he could not undertake offensive operations, the Sikhs re-crossed the Sutlej in large numbers, and began constructing an entrenchment in the neighbourhood of Chota Sobraon, on the left bank, which was connected by the existing bridge-of-boats with their camp on the right bank. Beyond a slight cannonading when they first re-appeared on the left bank, they were not molested, the advantage of allowing them to take up a position with a wide river in their rear being apparent; and so their earth-works grew daily.

About the middle of January the neighbourhood of Ludhiana, higher up the Sutlej, became the scene of important events. The Sikhs had been making several raids and excursions across the river in that vicinity, principally for the purpose of collecting supplies, a quantity of which they had stored in the fort of Dharamkot. Sir Harry Smith was despatched against this place with the 1st Brigade on the 18th

January, and easily reduced it, but while he was yet *en route* intelligence was received that *Sardar* Ranjur Singh Majithia had crossed the river with a large force of all arms, and was threatening not only Ludhiana but our line of communications at Bassian, and the siege train then moving up from Delhi. Her Majesty's 16th Lancers, the 3rd Light Cavalry, the 4th Irregular Cavalry, and two troops of horse artillery were immediately sent off to reinforce Sir Harry Smith, and joined him at Jagraon on the 20th, after two forced marches; and here, too, he was joined by the 53rd Foot, *en route* from Delhi. On the morning of the 21st Sir Harry marched from Jagraon towards Ludhiana, but *en route* he was attacked at Badowal by Ranjur Singh, who marched in a line parallel to him and furiously cannonaded the British force. Owing to the great numerical superiority of the enemy, and the pressing need for the immediate relief of Ludhiana, it was Sir Harry's object to avoid an engagement at that time; he therefore continued his march, and conducting his retirement with skill and steadiness, succeeded in extricating his force, though he suffered, heavy loss, and was unable to prevent a large portion of his baggage falling into the hands of the Sikhs. The force reached Ludhiana in the afternoon, having sustained a loss of sixty-nine killed (including Captain Campbell, 14th Foot, acting *aide-de-camp* to Sir Harry Smith, and Lieutenant Rideout, 47th Native Infantry) and sixty-eight wounded, besides an officer and several men taken prisoners. The extraordinary disproportion between the numbers killed and wounded was due to the fact that the Sikhs cruelly put to the sword all the wounded that could not be carried off by the retiring force.

At Ludhiana Sir Harry Smith was joined by the troops at that place under the command of Brigadier Godby,—the 1st Light Cavalry, the 30th and 36th Native Infantry, and the Nasseri and Sirmoor Battalions. Thus reinforced, Sir Harry Smith moved out against Ranjur Singh on the 23rd, but the Sikh *Sardar* precipitately abandoned his position at Badowal, and moved down to Talwandi, on the river, thus enabling Sir Harry to effect a junction with Brigadier Wheeler, who had been despatched by Sir Hugh Gough to reinforce him with the 2nd Brigade (less the 42nd Native Infantry, left at headquarters) and some more cavalry: these troops joined on the 26th, previous to which Sir Harry had been joined also by the Shekhawati Brigade—horse, foot, and artillery.

On the 27th Ranjur Singh received a reinforcement of 4,000 men and twelve guns, which raised his army to a strength of about 18,000 men, with sixty-seven guns. This emboldened him to advance, and on the 28th he began a movement towards Jagraon. On the same day, however, Sir Harry Smith marched out to attack him, and early in the forenoon came upon him just as he had begun to move. The Sikhs immediately faced their assailants, taking up a position close to the left bank of the Sutlej, with the village of Bundri on their right, that of Aliwal on their left, and the river in their rear. The British, almost without checking their march, formed in order of battle and advanced in line,—Hick's (the 1st) brigade on the right, Wheeler's (the 2nd) in the centre, and Wilson's (the 53rd Foot and the 30th Native Infantry) on the left, with a brigade of cavalry on either flank, and Godby's brigade (the 36th Native Infantry and the Nasseri Battalion) and the Shekhawati Infantry in direct *echelon* to the rear of the right and of the left of the line respectively. At ten o'clock the battle began with a furious cannonade from the Sikh guns, in the midst of which the British line advanced with steady gallantry. During a momentary halt Sir Harry Smith perceived that by the capture of the village of Aliwal he could operate with telling effect on the enemy's left and centre: he therefore brought up Godby's brigade to the right, and these troops and the 1st Brigade (the 31st Foot and the 24th and 47th Native Infantry), covered by the fire of a light field battery, carried the place with a rush. Almost at the same moment the cavalry on the right (the Body Guard, the 1st Light Cavalry, and the Shekhawati Cavalry) under Brigadier Cureton, charged the horse on the enemy's left and drove it back on the infantry, and when, a little later, Godby's brigade took the Sikh camp in reverse and drove the enemy through and out of it, the discomfiture of that part of the hostile force was complete. Simultaneously with these movements Brigadier Wheeler, with the 2nd Brigade (the 50th Foot, the 48th Native Infantry, and the Sirmoor Battalion) advanced on the Sikh centre under a murderous fire, drove it back and captured all the opposing guns, sustaining, however, severe loss in the conflict; and at the same time Brigadier Wilson with his brigade and Brigadier M'Dowell, with his brigade of cavalry (the 16th Lancers and the 3rd Light Cavalry) assailed the enemy's right. Here were posted the flower of the Sikh Army, the battalions disciplined by General Avitabile, and the resistance was obstinate, the Sikhs, now driven back on their left and centre, holding on tenaciously to Bundri, so as to cover the passage of the river. But soon two of these disciplined battalions, formed in square, were crumpled up and almost destroyed by daring charges of squadrons of the 16th Lancers led by

Captain Bere and Major Smyth; Bundri was carried at the point of the bayonet by the 53rd Foot, while the 30th Native Infantry charged and routed another body of the Avitabile troops. The British forces now closed in on the Sikh right and soon the enemy, routed and broken and mowed down by the deadly fire of our artillery, was in headlong flight towards the river, over which he was driven with terrible carnage and with the loss of all his guns, of which eleven were sunk in the river and fifty-six remained in our possession. In this well-fought action the Sikhs lost by their own account over three thousand men. Our own losses amounted to 151 (including four officers) killed, 413 (including twenty-five officers) wounded, and twenty-five missing,—589 in all. Among the killed was Lieutenant Smalpage, of the 4th Irregular Cavalry; and Cornet Farquhar, 1st Light Cavalry, died of his wounds. Amongst the native officers *Jemadars* Mehrwan Singh and Mustafa Khan, 3rd Light Cavalry, and *Subadar* Mehrwan Singh, 48th Native Infantry, were killed.

The proximate consequence of this victory was the evacuation by the Sikhs of all their posts on the left bank of the Sutlej except that which they had established and strengthened with so much care and labour in the vicinity of Chota Sobraon, and their expulsion from which was the next operation to be undertaken; but Sir Hugh Gough was still unable to make any movement towards the accomplishment of that object until the siege train and the reserve ammunition had arrived from the rear, and the troops detached under the command of Sir Harry Smith had rejoined. Pending these events a further re-organization of the infantry of the Army of the Sutlej was carried out in the early days of February, which affected every brigade except the Eighth. The Tenth and Twelfth Brigades were broken up, and a new Eleventh (properly Tenth) Brigade was formed, composed of the 6th, 11th and 55th Native Infantry. The 62nd Foot, the 2nd, 9th, 11th, 24th, 30th, 38th, 45th, 48th and 73rd Native Infantry were removed from the brigades to which they respectively belonged, and of these the 2nd, 24th, 30th and 48th were struck off the strength of the Army of the Sutlej altogether. Under the arrangements now made, the First Brigade was reduced to two regiments only, the 31st Foot and the 47th Native Infantry; in the Second Brigade the Nasseri Battalion was substituted for the 48th Native Infantry; in the Third, the 68th Native Infantry for the 45th; in the Fourth, the Sirmoor Battalion for the 2nd Native Infantry; in the Fifth, the 62nd Foot for the 73rd Native Infantry; in the Sixth, the 63rd Native Infantry for the 11th; and the Seventh Brigade was strengthened by the addition of the 53rd Foot.

The first portion of the siege train and the reserve ammunition for the field guns reached Sir Hugh Gough's camp on the 7th and 8th February, and at the same time the force under the command of Sir Harry Smith rejoined from the upper Sutlej. Final preparations were now made to assail the Sikhs in their entrenchments, into which the greater part of their forces had by this time been brought. The strength of these forces has been variously estimated at from 20,000 to 42,000 fighting men, but as it is known that they had no less than thirty-two regular regiments of infantry in the entrenchments, besides irregular troops and a numerous body of artillerymen, it is probable that their numbers did not fall far short of 35,000;[4] besides these the enemy had a numerous cavalry in the neighbourhood of the entrenchments, and a considerable reserve, with many heavy guns in their camp on the right bank, and there were nearly seventy pieces of artillery mounted on various parts of their works. These works themselves were described by Sir Hugh Gough and Sir Henry Hardinge immediately after their capture as being of a formidable character, and formidable enough they were found to be by those who had the task of turning the Sikhs out of them; nevertheless attempts have not been wanting to belittle the strength of the Sikh entrenchments, and with it the work accomplished by our troops that day.

The 10th of February was fixed upon as the day for the assault of the Sikh entrenchments, and at daybreak on the morning of that day, under cover of a heavy mist, our troops and batteries were silently moved into the positions assigned to them in the plan of attack. The troops engaged on this memorable occasion numbered rather more than 16,000 of all arms, and consisted of ten troops of horse artillery, ten companies of foot artillery (with forty-eight heavy guns, mortars, and howitzers), six companies of sappers and miners, three regiments of British and six and-a-half of native cavalry (including the Body-Guard, a wing of the 2nd Irregular Cavalry and the 8th Irregular Cavalry), and nine battalions of British and twelve of Native infantry (including the 33rd, 42nd, 43rd, 47th, 59th, and 63rd Native Infantry and the Nasseri and Sirmoor Battalions), most of them rather weak in numbers owing to losses in previous engage-

---

4. Hough *(Political and Military Events in British India)* says (Vol. 2, pages 298-99) that the Sikhs acknowledged that they had 37,000 men engaged at Sobraon, and that their losses amounted to between 13,000 and 14,000. But he gives no authority.

ments. As the sun rose the heavy mist disappeared, revealing the opposing forces to each other, and in a moment the engagement was opened with a single shell from the 2nd Troop, 2nd Brigade, Bengal Horse Artillery (now the 52nd Field Battery, Royal Artillery), which thus had the honour of beginning the battle of Sobraon. Presently the other batteries took up the fire, and by half past six o'clock it was fully developed; the Sikhs were not slow in responding, and soon "the thunder of one hundred and twenty pieces of ordnance reverberated in mighty combat through the valley of the Sutlej." For more than two hours a heavy and well-directed bombardment was maintained, under which the enemy, sheltered as he was behind earthworks, suffered most severely; but the rapid firing exhausted the ammunition of the heavy guns sooner than had been anticipated, and before a sufficient impression had been made on the enemy's defences it became necessary to plunge the infantry into the conflict and carry the position at the point of the bayonet. Accordingly, at nine o'clock the Third (Dick's) Division, forming the left of the British Army, moved forward to the assault of the right of the entrenchment. Advancing steadily in line, the division suffered severely from the enemy's murderous fire, under which Sir Robert Dick himself (an old and tried veteran of the Calabrian, Egyptian, Peninsular, and Waterloo campaigns) fell mortally wounded; "but soon persevering gallantry triumphed," and the leading brigade,— the Seventh,—comprising the 10th and 53rd Foot and the 43rd and 59th Native Infantry, and commanded by Brigadier Stacy, forced its way into the entrenchment without firing a shot, closely followed by the Sixth (Wilkinson's) Brigade (the 80th Foot and the 33rd and 63rd Native Infantry), and well supported by the Fifth (Ashburnham's) Brigade, the 9th and 62nd Foot and the 26th Native Infantry. But presently it became apparent that the weight of the whole Sikh Army would be thrown upon the brigades of Stacy and Wilkinson if some diversion were not effected, and to relieve the pressure on these the Second (Gilbert's) and the First (Smith's) Divisions were ordered to advance and assail the centre and left of the Sikh entrenchments. After a prolonged and desperate conflict, involving more than one repulse, these divisions also made good their footing within the defences, and then for a long hour a fierce and sanguinary struggle raged within the entrenchments; but gradually the Sikhs were forced back and out of their position to the river, where the bridge-of-boats giving way under the shot of our artillery and the pressure of the flying multitude, hundreds were drowned in trying to effect a passage, and hundreds more were destroyed by the fire of the horse artillery, which followed them up to the very margin of the stream. By noon the battle was over and the victory complete, the Sikh Army, routed and hurled headlong over the Sutlej, having lost nearly one-third of their numbers in the conflict, while sixty-seven of their guns remained in the hands of the victors. Our own losses, too, were heavy, amounting to 321 killed and 2,064 wounded, of whom thirteen of the killed and 102 of the wounded were British officers; among the former were Lieutenants Hay, of the 50th, and Rawson of the 63rd Native Infantry, both serving on the staff; Lieutenant Faithfull, Horse Artillery; Captain Shuttleworth and Ensign Hamilton, 1st European Light Infantry; Lieutenant Playfair, 33rd Native Infantry; and Captain Fisher, Sirmoor Battalion; and Brigadier McLaren, Lieutenant Lambert and Ensign Davidson, 1st European Light Infantry, Lieutenant Beatson, 14th Native Infantry (attached to the 1st European Light Infantry), and Ensign Scatcherd, 41st Native Infantry, afterwards died of their wounds. Four native officers were also killed,—*Jemadar* Pahlwan Singh, 12th Native Infantry (one company of which was in the field); *Subadar* Baijnath Pande, 33rd Native Infantry; *Jemadar* Jorawar Khan, 47th Native Infantry; and *Jemadar* Imam Khan, 68th Native Infantry. *Subadars* Bhawani Pande and Taji Singh, 26th Native Infantry; Hiraman Misr, 42nd Native Infantry; Basti Singh, 43rd Native Infantry, and Drig Sing Rana, Nasseri Battalion, died of their wounds. The behaviour of all the native corps on this occasion was admirable, and the Sirmoor and Nasseri Battalions and the 43rd and 59th Native Infantry are specially mentioned in terms of praise in Sir Hugh Gough's despatch.

No time was lost in following up the victory. The combat had indeed scarcely ceased when, in obedience to the orders of the governor-general, the troops of the Fourth Division began to cross the river at Khunda Ghat, near Ferozepore, and that night six regiments of native infantry and a troop of horse artillery were over the Sutlej under the command of Sir John Littler. On the 12th February a bridge-of-boats was completed, and on the 13th Sir Hugh Gough, with the whole force, except the heavy train and a division which had been left to collect the captured guns and the wounded and remove them to Ferozepore, was encamped at Kasur, sixteen miles from the river and thirty-two from Lahore. Here the governor-general was met by envoys from the Lahore Darbar, and to them the terms of the British Government were made known. The power of the Sikhs was for the time completely broken; the terms imposed upon them were acquiesced in, and the Maharajah made his submission in person. On the 20th February the British Army arrived at Lahore, and two days afterwards a portion of the citadel was garrisoned by English regiments.

Under the terms of the treaty, the Sikhs surrendered the remainder of the guns that they had used against us on the Sutlej,—thirty-six in number. These, added to those taken in the various engagements, made a total of 256 guns captured during the campaign, and in the course of the year they were all removed to Calcutta. Under another article of the treaty the whole of the Jullundur Doab was ceded to the Company. The towns in the plains submitted without demur, but the *kiladar* of Kot Kangra refused to surrender that place, and in April, 1846, it became necessary to send a force to turn him out. This was commanded, by Brigadier Wheeler and consisted of the 2nd, 11th, 41st, and 44th Native Infantry, and awing of the 63rd, with a siege train. Great difficulty was (experienced in dragging the guns up to the place, but once they were there the enemy gave in and surrendered the fort without fighting.

The news of the termination of the war was received with the greatest enthusiasm in England. Sir Henry Hardinge, Sir Hugh Gough, and the Army of the Sutlej were thanked by both Houses of Parliament, and both the governor-general and the commander-in-chief were raised to the peerage. The former on his own responsibility granted twelve months' batta to all the troops engaged; the inscription of "Moodkee," "Ferozeshahr," "Aliwal," and "Sobraon" on the colours of all corps which had taken part in those battles was ordered (G. O. C. C, 12th December, 1846); and a medal was granted for each of the four great battles of the campaign, those entitled to be decorated for more than one battle receiving the medal struck for the first of the four in which he was present and clasps for the subsequent engagements.

During this and the succeeding year considerable fluctuations in the strength of the Bengal Army occurred, the most important of which it will be convenient to notice here. At a very early stage of the war it became abundantly apparent that the maintenance of a large force on the Sutlej and the provision at the same time of necessary garrisons in the rear were together productive of too great a strain on the existing strength of the Bengal Army, and accordingly in January, 1846, the formation of several new corps (cavalry, artillery and infantry) was ordered.

Taking the cavalry first,—eight new corps of irregular horse were raised by G. G. O., dated 3rd, 14th, and 24th of January, 1846, and numbered from the 10th to the 17th, In the following year, however, the cavalry of the Bundelkhand Legion was brought on to the military establishment under the designation of the "10th Irregular Cavalry," in consequence of which the new regiments were all moved on one number and became the 11th to the 18th,—(G. O. G. G., dated 18th September, 1847). Of these nine regiments, two only (the 17th and 18th) survived the ordeal of the mutiny, and are now the 7th and 8th Bengal Cavalry. As regards infantry,—ten levies of a thousand men each were raised (G.G.O., 24th January, 1846) as a reserve and to act as feeders to the regiments in the field, and at the same time, in order to provide for garrison duties and for the preservation of order while so large a portion of the army was in the field, eighteen depôt battalions, of 475 men each, were formed from drafts of 165 native officers and men taken from each of the existing corps of native infantry: besides these, six levy companies and four depôt companies of native artillery were called into existence. All these corps had, however, but an ephemeral existence. The conclusion of the war and the apparent settlement of the Punjab giving hopes of a lasting peace, reductions were immediately carried out, and the first to go (March, 1846) were the levies and depôt battalions and companies referred to above, the former being disbanded and the constituent portions of the latter returned to the corps from which they had been taken. Subsequently, however, it was found necessary to provide for the needs of the newly-acquired territory and of our extended "sphere of influence," and in the summer of 1846 an important addition was made to the strength of the Bengal Army by the raising (G. G. O., dated the 30th July, 1846), on the left bank of the Sutlej, of two regiments of Sikh infantry: these corps were designated "The Regiment of Ferozepore" and "The Regiment of Ludhiana," and still survive as the 14th and 15th Regiments of Bengal Infantry. Later in the same year it was directed (G. G. O., Foreign Department, No. 2457, dated the 14th December, 1846) that "a frontier brigade" (one light field battery and four regiments of infantry) should be raised in the Trans-Sutlej and Cis-Sutlej States for police and general purposes, and also that a "Corps of Guides" should be formed for general service. The Corps of Guides and the four regiments of infantry still survive, the former under its original designation, and the latter as the 1st, 2nd, 3rd and 4th Regiments of Sikh Infantry of the Punjab Frontier Force. In the following year again extensive reductions took place; all infantry corps were reduced by twenty non-commissioned officers and 200 men, irregular cavalry regiments were brought down to a total strength of 500 each, and all the local police battalions (formed in 1844) were disbanded (G. O. G. G., 30th January, 1847). Shortly afterwards the artillery and cavalry of the Shekhawati Brigade were disbanded, the infantry alone being retained and brought upon the strength of the army (it had hitherto been a "civil" organisation) under the designation of the "Shekhawati Battalion."

A notable change in the year 1846 was the restoration of the number "34" to the Army List, the new 34th Native Infantry being the infantry of the Bundelkhand Legion, which, on the misbehaviour of the old 34th in 1844, had, as already related, volunteered to take the place of that regiment in Sindh, and had served there for two years—(G. O. G. G., 4th July, 1846).

Early in 1848 the Earl (afterwards Marquess) of Dalhousie succeeded Lord Hardinge as Governor-General. Scarcely, however, had he taken up the reins of government when the anticipations of continued peace in the Punjab were rudely dispelled by the rebellion of the Dewan Mulraj and the Sikh troops at Mooltan, the murder there of Mr. Vans-Agnew and Lieutenant Anderson, and the rapid extension of the outburst throughout the whole of the Punjab. The British officers referred to were murdered on April 20th, 1848, and by the 1st July Lieutenant Edwardes and General Van Cortlandt (of the Sikh service), with an army of irregulars from the Derajat and some troops of the Nawab of Bahawalpur (joined in July by the cavalry of the Corps of Guides,—then consisting of but a single troop under Lieutenant Lumsden) had twice (at Kineri on the 18th June, and again at Sadusam on the 1st July) beaten the troops of the rebel Mulraj, driven him to take refuge in his fortress of Mooltan, and recovered the whole of that important district except the fortress itself. After considerable delay, Lord Gough being averse to putting troops in the field during the hot weather, a force was despatched from Lahore and Ferozepore for the reduction of Mooltan—a task which was quite beyond the power of the irregular troops under the command of Lieutenant Edwardes; this force was commanded by Major-General Whish, and was composed of the following troops:

Artillery	2 Troops Horse Artillery
Major H. Garbett	4 Companies Foot Artillery
	A second class siege train
Engineers	3 Companies Sappers
Major R. C Napier	2 Companies Pioneers
Cavalry	11th Light Cavalry
Lieutenant-Colonel H. F. Salter	7th & 11th Irregular Cavalry
Infantry: 1st Brigade	H. M.'s 10th Foot
Lieutenant-Colonel A. Hervey	8th and 52nd Native Infantry
Infantry: 2nd Brigade	H. M.'s 32nd Foot
Lieutenant-Colonel F. Markham	49th, 51st & 72nd Native Infantry

Cooperating with this force was a Sikh Army, which the Lahore Durbar had despatched to Mooltan under Rajah Sher Singh, one of the most influential chiefs of the Punjab; but these troops were ill-affected, and ought never to have been allowed to proceed to Mooltan, where their presence seriously augmented the difficulties of the British commander.

It was not until the end of August that General Whish's division arrived before Mooltan. The interval was employed by Mulraj in augmenting his army and strengthening his fort, and his only reply to the British general's summons to surrender was to use every endeavour to bring about the defection of Sher Singh's army. The siege was commenced by the opening of a parallel nearly a mile from the fortifications, whence it was intended to work through the intermediate ground of gardens, brick kilns, and villages. On the night of September 9th, an attempt was made to dislodge the enemy from some houses and gardens in front of the trenches, and four companies of Her Majesty's 10th Foot, a wing of the 49th Native Infantry and one company of the 72nd, were, with some irregular artillery, told off for this duty, under the command of Lieutenant-Colonel Pattoun of the 32nd Foot. The darkness of the night and their ignorance of the locality frustrated the gallant efforts of the troops, and the attack was repulsed with a loss of fifteen killed, four offic-

---

5. Including Lieutenant Christopher, Indian Navy, who was serving as a volunteer with the irregular forces under Lieutenant Edwardes. He died of his wounds a few weeks later.

ers [5] (two mortally) and sixty-eight men wounded, and four men missing; among the killed was one native officer,—*Jemadar* Duniah Singh, 72nd Native Infantry. On the morning of the 12th the villages in front of the trenches were, after some hard fighting, cleared of the enemy by two columns under Lieutenant-Colonel Pattoun, 32nd, and Lieutenant-Colonel Franks, 10th, the whole commanded by Brigadier Hervey,—the troops engaged being one troop of horse artillery, one squadron from each of the three regiments of cavalry, five companies each of Her Majesty's 10th and 32nd Regiments, and the 8th and 49th Native Infantry. A simultaneous attack was made by some of the irregulars under General Van Cortlandt, who succeeded to some extent in diverting the attention of the enemy. The attack was made with a bravery "not surpassed during the war," and was met by an equally stubborn resistance, which, however, was at length broken down and the enemy driven into the city. Our loss was five British officers and nineteen men killed, and nine officers and 136 men wounded, the officers killed being Lieutenant-Colonel Pattoun, 32nd Foot, Major Montizambert and Quarter-Master Taylor, 10th Foot, Lieutenant Cubitt, 49th Native Infantry, and Ensign Lloyd, 8th Native Infantry. General Whish had thus secured a position within battering distance of the city walls, but it was now plainly to be seen that the force under his command was utterly inadequate for the reduction of the place: the question of continuing the operations was under anxious consideration when, on the 14th September, the matter was brought to an abrupt conclusion by the sudden desertion of Sher Singh and his whole force to the enemy. In consequence of this defection General Whish at once raised the siege, and withdrew to a position near the village of Suraj Khund, where he entrenched himself and remained threatening (though unable to blockade) the town, until he should be in a position to resume active operations; this however, did not come about for some time.

Rajah Sher Singh, distrusted by Mulraj, remained encamped under the walls of Mooltan until the 9th October, when he suddenly marched northwards. Advancing to within twenty-five miles of Lahore, he continued for some time to threaten that place, but eventually moved westwards to unite with the troops lately forming the garrison of Bannu who had mutinied and joined in the rebellion which was now fast over-spreading the Punjab, and before many weeks had elapsed he was on the Chenab at the head of a formidable force.

The rising at Mooltan had been followed by an outbreak in Hazara headed by *Sirdar* Chattar Singh, and the defection of Sher Singh and his army finally convinced the Government that it was necessary to embark once more on a regular campaign against the Sikhs. It was not, however, until October that orders were issued for the assembly of an army at Ferozepore, and in the meantime the complications on all sides had increased considerably. In the Jullundur Doab disturbances were incessant, and a serious rising took place there headed by *Sirdar* Ram Singh, who, in September, took up a strong position at the village of Bassa, on the top of a high hill near Nurpur. Here he was attacked on the 19th by a force under the command of Major Fisher, 15th Irregular Cavalry, consisting of 130 of the 15th and 16th Irregular Cavalry, two companies of the 29th and four of the 71st Native Infantry, and 300 of the 1st and 130 of the 2nd Sikh Local Infantry, and dislodged after a brief engagement, in which our loss amounted to only one sepoy killed and nine wounded. In this affair two corps of what is now the Punjab Frontier Force gained the first of that long series of successes which has made them famous among the picked troops of the Indian Army.

While these events were in progress, Chattar Singh had opened negotiations with the Amir Dost Muhammad Khan of Kabul, who accepted the-proffered alliance with readiness, and sent a considerable force into the Punjab to assist the Sikhs. Late in October the Sikh garrison at Peshawar mutinied, and Major Lawrence and the other occupants of the Residency fell into the hands of Chattar Singh, by whom they were kept in close captivity at that pace. Later on Attock was also taken by Chattar Singh, and soon the whole of the northern part of the Punjab, with the exception of Hazara (to which .Captain Abbott held on, with the assistance of local Muhammadan levies), was in the hands of the revolted Sikhs. On the 13th October a General Order was published detailing the troops which were to form the "Army of the Punjab"; these were as follow:

Artillery
Brigadier-General
J. Tennant

8 Troops Horse Artillery
3 Light Field Batteries
8 Companies Foot Artillery

Engineers
Brigadier
J. Cheape, C.B.

Corps of Sappers &
Pioneers

Cavalry

Brigadier M. White, C.B.	1st Bgde.	Her Majesty's 3rd Light Dragoons 5th & 8th Light Cavalry
Brigadier A. Pope, C.B.	2nd Bgde.	Her Majesty's 9th Light Dragoons (Lancers) 1st & 6th Light Cavalry
Brigadier H. F. Salter	3rd Bgde.	11th Light Cavalry 7th & 11th Irregular Cavalry
Brigadier J. B. Hearsey	4th Bgde.	3rd, 9th & 12th Irregular Cavalry

Infantry 1: Major General W. S. Whish, C.B.

Brigadier A. S. H Mountain, C.B.	1st Bgde.	Her Majesty's 10th Foot 8th & 72nd Native Infantry
Brigadier F. Markham	2nd Bgde.	Her Majesty's 32nd Foot 49th & 1st Native Infantry

Infantry 2: Major General W. R. Gilbert, K.C.B.

Brigadier J. Eckford	3rd Bgde.	Her Majesty's 29th Foot 31st & 56th Native Infantry
Brigadier C. Godby, C.B.	4th Bgde.	2nd European Regiment 45th & 70th Native Infantry
Brigadier A. Hervey	5th Bgde.	13th, 30th & 52nd Native Infantry

Infantry 3: Major General Sir J. Thackwell, K.C.B.

Brigadier J. Pennycuick, C.B.	6th Bgde.	Her Majesty's 24th Foot 15th & 25th Native Infantry

| Brigadier N. Penny, C.B. | 7th Bgde. | 20th, 22nd & 69th Native Infantry |

In these arrangements, however, considerable changes took place almost as soon as they were announced: the 14th Light Dragoons were added to the 1st Brigade of Cavalry; the 29th Foot were removed from the 3rd to the 5th Brigade, their place in the former being taken by the 73rd Native Infantry from the garrison of Lahore; the 15th and the 22nd Native Infantry interchanged brigades; and a fourth division, the command of which was given to Brigadier-General Colin Campbell,[6] had a brief existence of about a fortnight. This division comprised the Eighth Brigade (36th and 46th Native Infantry) and the Ninth Brigade (the 61st Foot and the 3rd Native Infantry). On its being broken up the 61st Foot were removed to the Eighth Brigade, which was then transferred to the Third Division, and the command given to Brigadier J. Hoggan, and the 3rd Native Infantry were struck off the strength of the Army of the Punjab. Of the troops above detailed, between 4,000 and 5,000 men (including most of the Sappers and Pioneers, and the 52nd Native Infantry, then belonging to the Fifth Brigade) were at Mooltan under Major-General Whish; the remainder, of which Lord Gough himself took command, numbered about 16,000.

The campaign was opened on the 22nd of November by a movement of the commander-in-chief against Sher Singh, who, with an army of 16,000, was in position at Ramnagar, on the left bank of the Chenab. Deeming it necessary to drive this force over the river, Lord Gough ordered Brigadier-General Campbell, commanding the advanced corps, to carry out this object. General Campbell accordingly moved forward from Saharan on the morning of the 22nd November with two troops of horse artillery, two light field batteries, the 1st Brigade of Cavalry and the 12th Irregular Cavalry, and the infantry brigades of Godby (less the 45th Native Infantry) and Hoggan. On arrival at Ramnagar it was found that the main body of the enemy had already crossed to the right bank; several small parties were, however, observed to be still making their way from the town to the ford, and the two troops of horse artillery were ordered to pursue and open fire on them while crossing, while a squadron of the 3rd Light Dragoons was directed to charge and clear the left bank of the river of all hostile bodies that might still remain; the charge of the dragoons was brilliant and successful, but the horse artillery, in their eagerness to over-

---

6. The late Lord Clyde, who here for the first time comes into notice in Indian warfare.

take the parties making for the ford, got into the sands of the river, and one gun became so embedded that it could not be extricated. Observing the difficulty in which the gun was placed, the enemy redoubled the artillery fire they had kept up from the right bank, and re-crossed over the whole of their cavalry. A retirement became necessary, but in an unlucky moment permission was given to the 14th Light Dragoons and the 5th Light Cavalry to charge the enemy. Exposed to a heavy and constant fire from the Sikh guns on the opposite bank, and embarrassed by the deep sand, the two regiments, after defeating and driving back the Sikh cavalry, were compelled to retire, having suffered heavy loss, not the least of which was the death of Lieutenant-Colonel Havelock, of the 14th, and of Brigadier-General Cureton, the commander of the Cavalry Division. The loss in this unfortunate and unprofitable affair, in which the 8th Light Cavalry also shared, was two British officers, one native officer, and twenty-three men killed; and eight British officers, one native officer, and forty-nine men wounded. The native officer killed was *Subadar*-Major Mir Sher Ali, *Sardar Bahadur*, of the 8th Light Cavalry—an old man of seventy-eight years, and of nearly sixty years' service.

Lord Gough remained halted at Ramnagar for several days, waiting for his heavy guns, then coming up from the rear, and during this period the Army of the Punjab was re-organised and distributed as follows (G. O. C. C, 26th November, 1848):

Artillery Brigadier-General J. Tennant		8 Troops Horse Artillery 4 Light Field Batteries 8 Companies Foot Artillery
Engineers Brigadier-General J. Cheape, C.B.		3 Companies Sappers 7 Companies Pioneers
Cavalry: Major-General Sir J. Thackwell, K.C.B.	1st Bgde.	3rd & 14th Light Dragoons 5th & 8th Light Cavalry
	2nd Bgde.	9th Light Dragoons (Lancers) 1st & 6th Light Cavalry

	3rd Bgde.	11th Light Cavalry 7th & 11th Irregular Cavalry
	4th Bgde.	3rd, 9th & 12th Irregular Cavalry
Infantry: 1st Division Major-General W. S. Whish, C.B.	1st Bgde.	10th Foot 8th & 72nd Native Infantry
	2nd Bgde.	32nd Foot 49th, 51st & 52nd Native Infantry
Infantry: 2nd Division Major-General Sir W. R. Gilbert, K.C.B.	3rd Bgde.	31st, 56th & 73rd Native Infantry
	4th Bgde.	2nd European Regiment 45th & 70th Native Infantry
	5th Bgde.	29th Foot 13th & 30th Native Infantry
Infantry: 3rd Division Brigadier-General C. Campbell, C.B.	6th Bgde.	24th Foot 22nd & 25th Native Infantry
	7th Bgde.	15th, 20th & 69th Native Infantry
	8th Bgde.	61st Foot 36th & 46th Native Infantry

This, however, was not the last of the changes made in the composition of the army, for in the middle of the following month (G.O.C.C, 14th December, 1848) the 3rd Brigade was broken up, and the five brigades junior to it re-numbered as the 3rd, 4th, 5th, 6th and 7th Brigades, respectively. Of the components of the defunct brigade, the 31st Native Infantry was posted to the new 3rd Brigade, and the 56th to the new 4th, while the 73rd was relegated to garrison duty at Lahore. At a later period some other minor changes took place, such as the removal of the 13th and the 22nd Native Infantry from the 4th and 5th Brigades, and the transfer of the 45th from the 3rd Brigade to the 5th. A Reserve Division was also formed in Sirhind, consisting of a light field battery, the 17th Irregular Cavalry, the 18th Foot, and the 17th, 19th, 58th and 61st Native Infantry, the command of which was conferred upon Major-General Sir D. St. L. Hill.

On the arrival of the siege train (27th November), Lord Gough entered on measures for effecting the passage of the Chenab and attacking the Sikh Army under Sher Singh in its position on the right bank of the river opposite to Ramnagar. With this object, on the 30th November, he detached Sir Joseph Thackwell with three troops of horse artillery, two light field batteries, two companies of pioneers, portions of the 1st and 4th Brigades of Cavalry (the 3rd Light Dragoons, the 5th and 8th Light Cavalry, and the 3rd and 12th Irregular Cavalry), and the 3rd, 6th and 8th Brigades of Infantry (less the 73rd Native Infantry and six companies of the 22nd Native Infantry), to cross the river at a ford about twelve miles above Ramnagar, and turn the left flank of the enemy on the opposite bank,—he himself, if successful in silencing Sher Singh's guns and securing the passage of the river at Ramnagar, crossing there and assailing the enemy in front. The ford was found to be too difficult and dangerous to attempt in the face of a Sikh force assembled on the opposite bank, and Thackwell therefore, in accordance with his instructions, proceeded higher up to Wazirabad, at which place Captain Nicholson,[7] Assistant to the Resident at Lahore, had secured some boats, with the aid of which the force effected the passage of the river on the 1st and 2nd of December. On the latter day Thackwell moved twelve miles down the river towards Sher Singh's position opposite Ramnagar, and resuming his march on the 3rd reached the village of Sadulapur, where he halted in consequence of the receipt of an order from the the commander-in-chief desiring him not to attack until the arrival of the 4th Brigade (the 2nd European Regiment and the 70th Native Infantry), which had been sent to reinforce him. In the afternoon, however, Sher Singh, with a large portion of his army and many guns, appeared in Thackwell's front and opened a heavy fire on the British force. The action which ensued was one principally of artillery, Thackwell, in obedience to his orders, remaining strictly on the defensive: it continued until dark, and at midnight Sher Singh silently retired towards the Jhelum, having sustained considerable loss in the cannonade. Our own loss amounted

---

7. Afterwards Brigadier-General Nicholson of Mutiny fame.

to only twenty-four killed and fifty-seven (including four British officers) wounded. *Jemadars* Thannu Ram, 25th, and Mir Amanat Ali, 36th Native Infantry, were killed, and *Jemadar* Sirdar Khan, 22nd Native Infantry, lost a leg.

On the following day Thackwell pushed on in pursuit to Jalalpur, and thence on the 5th to the village of Helan, but did not succeed in coming up with the enemy.

On the 8th the headquarters of the army crossed the Chenab by a bridge-of-boats and joined Thackwell shortly afterwards at Helan, in the vicinity of which place the whole force remained until the 12th January. On the 10th January Lord Gough was informed of the capture of Attock by Chattar Singh, who was now hastening with all his forces to effect a junction with Sher Singh on the Jhelum. Under these circumstances it became a matter of pressing necessity to attack and dispose of Sher Singh before this reinforcement should reach him,—he already having with him some 30,000 men, with sixty-two guns. Accordingly His Lordship broke up his camp and moved on the 12th to Dingi, and on the 13th towards Rasul, on the left bank of the Jhelum, in the neighbourhood of which place the Sikhs had taken up a position. The enemy's line was a most extended one, reaching from Rasul on the left to the village of Fateh-Shah-ki-Chak on the right. The original plan of attack consisted in moving on Rasul, turning the enemy's left flank, and doubling up his long, thin line in the direction of the Jhelum. But on arriving at the village of Cnota Umrao, Lord Gough, who had no intention of fighting that day, inclined to the left and moved towards the village of Chilianwala, his object being to halt there and reconnoitre the country,—which was found to be very difficult, being intersected by ravines and covered with jungle,—as well as the enemy's position, in which Sher Singh, who suspected Lord Gough's design against his left flank, had already made some change by throwing forward his right. Arrived at Chilianwala, it was found that such of the enemy as had been posted there had vacated the position and fallen back on their main line, leaving only a strong picquet, which was immediately driven off. It was now 2 p.m., and preparations were made to take up ground for encampment. Sher Singh, however, was determined to force on a battle that afternoon. With this object he opened a heavy artillery fire on the British force,—at first from such a distance as to do no execution, but after a while from the front of his position at a range of about 1,500 yards. As it was probable that the enemy would advance his guns and cannonade the encampment during the night, Lord Gough drew up his forces in order of battle, and then, ordering the troops to lie down, he opened a heavy fire of artillery on the enemy's centre. After about an hour's cannonade the fire of the enemy appeared to be sufficiently subdued to justify an advance on his position, which was accordingly ordered.

The extreme length of the position occupied by the Sikhs caused large gaps between their centre and wings. The British line, when formed for attack, did little more than oppose a front to Sher Singh's centre, and such of it as overlapped on the left faced one of the gaps mentioned above. Our troops advanced to the attack in the following order:—On the right, commanded by Sir Walter Gilbert was the Second Division, composed of the 3rd and 4th Brigades, the former of which (under Brigadier Godby) comprised the 2nd Bengal European Regiment, and the 31st and 70th Native Infantry, and the latter (under Brigadier Mountain) Her Majesty's 29th Foot, and the 30th and 56th Native Infantry. This division was flanked on the right by the 2nd (Pope's) Brigade of Cavalry (the 9th Lancers, and the 1st and 6th Light Cavalry), strengthened by the 14th Light Dragoons, with three troops of horse artillery. On the left was the Third Division, commanded by Brigadier-General Campbell; this was composed of the 5th, 6ih, and 7th Brigades (Her Majesty's 24th Foot and the 25th and 45th Native Infantry under Brigadier Pennycuick; the 15th and 69th Native Infantry, under Brigadier Penny; and Her Majesty's 61st Foot, and the 36th and 46th Native Infantry, under Brigadier Hoggan); of these the 6th Brigade (Penny's) was held in reserve. On the left flank was the 1st Cavalry Brigade (the 3rd Light Dragoons, and the 5th and 8th Light Cavalry), with three troops of horse artillery. In the centre was massed the heavy artillery; the field batteries were between the infantry brigades. The 3rd and 9th Irregular Cavalry, with the 20th Native Infantry (from the 6th Brigade), were detailed, under Brigadier Hearsey, to protect the provision and baggage train.

The British line now advanced to attack the enemy's guns in front with the bayonet, marching for that purpose for nearly a mile, through thick and unknown jungle. The right (Pennycuick's) brigade of Campbell's division was the first to engage the enemy. Emerging in some disorder from the jungle at a distance of 300 yards from the Sikh line, they were received with a storm of grape, which mowed them down by dozens before they could reach the enemy. Nothing, however, could stop their charge, and, rushing impetuously on, they threw themselves on the gunners, bayoneted them at their posts, and for a moment were masters of the position; but the Sikhs, quickly rallying and realising how small were the numbers of those who had attacked them, returned to the fight, and, aided by their cavalry, recovered the battery and drove back the British brigade almost to the point from which it had advanced to the attack. This repulse seems to have been principally owing to the 24th Foot and the 45th Native Infantry, advancing rapidly, having outpaced the 25th Native Infantry, and arrived breathless and without adequate support before the enemy. The brigade, according to Lord Gough himself, behaved heroically, and did not give way until it had lost its Brigadier (Pennycuick) and its Brigade-Major (Harris), and the 24th their Colonel (Brookes), ten other officers, and nearly a third of the whole regiment killed.

To fill the gap in the line caused by the repulse of Pennycuick's brigade, the 6th (Penny's) brigade, which had been held in reserve, was immediately pushed forward, and advanced with great gallantry; but it missed its way in the jungle, and inclining too much to the right, eventually after some severe fighting, found itself on the left of Godby's brigade.

Meanwhile, the left (Hoggan's) brigade of Campbell's division, advancing steadily through the brushwood, charged the batteries in their front, drove the Sikhs before them with great slaughter, and then wheeling to the right, recovered the ground from which Pennycuick's brigade had just been repulsed, and maintained it until the close of the engagement.

Gilbert's division, in the meantime, had undergone no less perilous experiences. Its left brigade, under Mountain, was the first to come into collision with the enemy. Advancing under a desolating fire the brigade succeeded, though not without terrible loss, in carrying the batteries in its front; but broken in its advance, the 56th Native Infantry, the left battalion of the brigade, was pierced by the Sikh cavalry, forced back in confusion and almost destroyed. The other regiments of the brigade, the 29th Foot and the 30th Native Infantry, succeeded in maintaining the ground they had captured, and held it until the end of the contest.

The right (Godby's) brigade of Gilbert's division had, in the meantime, been doing gallant service against heavy odds. Sweeping through the jungle it pressed forward under a murderous fire, and after a prolonged and sanguinary contest (at one period of which the 2nd European Regiment was obliged to change front to the rear, to repel a body of the enemy who had got behind them as they advanced), it drove the Sikhs off the field and captured ever)' gun in its front. In this contest the brigade was conspicuously aided by the fire of the field battery commanded by Captain Michael Dawes,[8] the splendid gallantry of which is said to have been the salvation not only of the brigade but of the whole of Gilbert's division.

The right flank of Gilbert's division had in the meantime been exposed by the discomfiture of the 2nd Brigade of Cavalry. Through some error on the part of the Brigadier (Pope), the brigade had got in front of the horse artillery, so as entirely to mask the fire of the latter. While endeavouring to move the brigade to the right, to get clear of the guns, Brigadier Pope was cut down by a Sikh sowar, and at the same moment an order was heard directing the brigade to turn about. By whom this order was given has never been made known, but the effect was disastrous. As the troops retired in obedience to the order, they were suddenly charged by a body of the enemy's cavalry, and the result was one of those sudden panics which are liable at times to overtake even the best of troops. Wheeling about, they dashed to the rear, riding over and disabling the horse artillery batteries, and closely followed by the Sikhs, who cut down many of the gunners and captured several guns. The disaster, however, was checked by the gallantry of two squadrons of the 9th Lancers and two of the 6th Light Cavalry, who, rallying as soon as they could get clear of the flying body of cavalry, charged the advancing enemy and stopped their onward career.

Notwithstanding this reverse, the infantry of Gilbert's division held their ground. The battle was won, but though the enemy were driven from their position, their forces were still unbroken. Lord Gough, yielding to the advice of several of his commanders, after bringing off most of the wounded, withdrew his troops from the field and fell back to the village of Chilianwala.

This movement brought back Sher Singh: with more than half of the remains of his army he had crossed the Jhelum in flight, when, late at night, he learnt that Lord Gough had withdrawn from the field of battle; he immediately re-crossed, carried off all the captured guns except twelve, massacred such of the British wounded as still lay on the field, and then returned to the heights of Rasul.

The British loss in the battle of Chilianwala amounted to 602 killed (including twenty-two British officers), 1,651 wounded (including sixty-seven British officers), and 104 missing,—making a

---

8. This was No. 17 Light Field Battery, manned by the 3rd Company, 1st Battalion, Bengal Artillery. It is now the 53rd Field Battery, Royal Artillery.

total of 2,357. Among the killed were Major C. Ekins, 7th Light Cavalry, Deputy Adjutant-General of the Army ; Lieutenant J. A. Manson, Bengal Artillery; Lieutenant A. M. Shepherd and *Jemadars* Siu-dayal Singh and Rambakhsh Singh, 6th Light Cavalry; Lieutenant A. Money, *Subadars* Chattardhari Singh, Jurawan Singh and Siu-dayal Singh, and *Jemadars* Tulsi Pande, Shaikh Dukhi and Assad Ali Khan, 25th Native Infantry; Captain W. H. Ross, Ensign A. C. de Morel, and *Jemadar* Allah-dad Khan, 30th Native Infantry; *Subadar* Kasiram Singh and *Jemadar* Kanhai Tiwari, 36th Native Infantry ; Lieutenant W. W. Warde, Ensign F. W. Robinson, *Subadars* Sewa Upadhia and Bahadur Khan and *Jemadars* Gaya-din and Mansa Ram, 56th Native Infantry; and *Subadars* Shaikh Subhani and Shaikh Niamat Ali, 70th Native Infantry.

Besides these, many afterwards died of their wounds,—including Brigadier A. Pope, C.B., 6th Light Cavalry, commanding the 2nd Cavalry Brigade; Captain (Brevet-Major) E. Christie, Bengal Horse Artillery; Lieutenant A. N. Thompson and *Jemadar* Gholam Hossain Khan, 36th Native Infantry; Captain R. Haldane, 45th Native Infantry; and Major D. Bamfield, 56th Native Infantry.

But heavy as was our loss, that of the Sikhs was treble as great. It has been estimated that in killed and wounded the fight at Chilianwala reduced Sher Singh's army by not less than 7,000 men Lord Gough himself remarked that nowhere else, except perhaps at Sobraon, had he seen "so many of the enemy's slain upon the same space."

It is necessary now to revert to the progress of the war in the other parts of the Punjab before relating the last struggle of the Sikhs at Gujerat. In the Jullundur Doab the force under Brigadier-General Wheeler was constantly engaged with parties of the enemy. At forts Rangar Nagal (October 14th) and Kalalwala (November 22nd and 23rd), at Amb (2nd December) and Budi Pind (December 28th), on the heights of Dalla (16th January) and at other places, successes were gained by various detachments formed from portions of the 7th Light Cavalry, the 3rd, 4th, 28th, 29th, and 71st Native Infantry, the 2nd, 15th, and 16th Irregular Cavalry, the 1st and 2nd Sikh Local Infantry, and the newly-raised Corps of Guides. In the action on the heights of Dalla. Cornet Christie, 7th Light Cavalry, and *Jemadar* Ramkishan Singh, 1st Sikh Local Infantry, were killed, and Lieutenant Peel, second-in-command of the latter corps, was mortally wounded. The Corps of Guides was conspicuous in many of these affairs, and with them now for the first time came prominently into public notice

Lieutenants H. B. Lumsden and W. S. R. Hodson, two officers who, in later years, arrived at high distinction in the Indian Army.

While these events were occurring in the northern and eastern parts of the Punjab, Major-General Whish, at Mooltan, lay practically inactive, awaiting the arrival of reinforcements then on the way from Bombay and Sindh. On the 1st November Mulraj, assuming the offensive, established himself on the raised banks of a dry canal which intersected the British lines, and for some days kept up a constant fire of artillery on the camp. At length, however, on the 7th, he was expelled by a detachment of the army under Brigadier Markham, his batteries destroyed, and his troops driven back into the town with the loss of five of their guns. The regiments engaged in this action, which is called that of Suraj-khund, were one troop of horse artillery, two squadrons each of the 11th Light Cavalry and the 7th and 11th Irregular Cavalry, forty sappers, six companies each of Her Majesty's 10th and 32nd Foot, and eight companies each of the 8th, 49th, 51st and 52nd Native Infantry. The casualties were three men killed, and four native officers and fifty-three men wounded. The Irregular Force under Edwardes (to whom the local rank of Major had been given) and the Bahawalpur Contingent under Lieutenant Lake were also prominently engaged, and lost, respectively, thirty-four killed and 134 wounded, and five killed and thirty-eight wounded. The total losses this day, on our side, thus amounted to forty-two killed and 229 wounded.

On the 21st of December, General Whish was joined by the reinforcements for which he had been waiting: these consisted of one troop of horse artillery, two companies of foot artillery, and two light field batteries, two companies of sappers, the 1st Bombay Light Cavalry, the Sindh Horse, Her Majesty's 60th Foot (Rifles), the 1st Bombay European Regiment (Fusiliers), and the 3rd, 4th, 9th and 19th Bombay Native Infantry,—the whole under the command of Brigadier-General the Honourable H. Dundas. The force under the command of General Whish was now increased to a total of 15,648, and preparations were pushed on for a renewal of the siege. On Christmas Day the former position before Mooltan was resumed, and on the 27th an attack was made on the enemy's position in the suburbs, which proved brilliantly successful and laid the walls of the city and fort open to our siege guns. The action was, however, attended with a loss of twenty-six killed, 172 wounded and eighteen missing, and Lieutenants Playfair, 52nd, and Gillon, 72nd Native Infantry, died of the wounds they received on this occasion.

On the 29th a sally was made by 2,000 of the enemy on the post of Sidilal-ki-Bed, which was held by Major Edwardes' Irregulars, but they were repulsed after two hours' hard fighting. Four days afterwards two breaches in the city wall were reported practicable, and simultaneous assaults were made on both (2nd January 1849), a column (32nd Foot and 49th and 72nd Native Infantry) from the Bengal Division being told off to attempt the Delhi Gate breach, and another from the Bombay Division to assail the breach at the Khuni Burj ("The Bloody Bastion"). The former was, however, found on near inspection to be quite impracticable, and all that the Bengal troops could do was to hasten round to the assistance of the column engaged at the Khuni Burj. Here the Bombay troops, after a sharp struggle, had been successful and had forced their way into the town; on which Mulraj, seeing that the city wall had been carried, took refuge in the citadel, the gates of which he closed, leaving three-fourths of his army at the mercy of their enemies. Numbers were slain in the streets of the city, and the remainder, fleeing over the walls and by the Lahori Gate, concealed themselves until nightfall in the suburbs, and then, under cover of the darkness made good their escape to their homes. The total casualties in the storm of the city of Mooltan were thirty killed, 217 wounded, and one missing.

The citadel of Mooltan was now completely invested, and Mulraj, seeing the toils closing around him, made overtures for terms; but he received the answer that nothing short of unconditional surrender would be accepted. He was not yet, however, sufficiently humbled to yield on such terms, and so continued to hold out, keeping up an undiminished fire, which occasioned many casualties amongst the besiegers; amongst others Second-Lieutenant Graham and Lieutenant Thompson, both of the Artillery, were mortally wounded during the last days of the siege. On our side the operations were pressed with vigour; under the heavy fire of the batteries the breaches in the fortifications soon became practicable, and preparations were made to storm the place. The assault was fixed for the 21st January, but on that day Mulraj, hopeless of further resistance, sent messengers to notify his desire to surrender, and at 9 a.m. on the 22nd he came out and gave himself up to General Whish. The fort was occupied on the same day, and before the departure of the army from Mooltan, the bodies of Vans-Agnew and Anderson were removed from their grave at the *Idgah* and borne through the breach which had been made by the British guns to an honoured resting-place in the citadel.

There an obelisk, visible for miles round, marks their grave, and the inscription thereon tells, in vivid and stirring words, of the treachery which compassed their death, and of the ample manner in which they had been avenged. The total casualties during the operations against Mooltan, from August 1848 to January 1849, amounted to 210 killed (including nine British officers) and 982 wounded (including fifty-five British officers).[9]

After the battle of Chilianwala, Lord Gough remained encamped between the village of that name and Mujianwala, and awaited the fall of Mooltan. That event was followed immediately by the departure of General Whish with the Bengal Division, strengthened by one Bombay brigade, to join the commander-in-chief. On the night of the 11th February, before the arrival of these troops, Sher Singh, who had been reinforced by the army of Chattar Singh, his father, and by another under one of the sons of the Amir of Kabul, began moving away from Rasul; in the course of the next few days he had withdrawn the whole of his forces, and established himself in a position near the town of Gujerat. On the 14th the position of the Sikh Army was ascertained, and on the following day Lord Gough marched from Chilianwala, and proceeding by way of Lasuria, Sadulapur, and Kunjah, he arrived on the 18th at Shadiwal, three miles from the Sikh position. At the same time a small force (the 53rd Foot, the 13th Native Infantry, and the 12th and 13th Irregular Cavalry, with four guns) under Lieutenant-Colonel Byrne, of the 53rd, was sent to Wazirabad, to prevent the Sikhs crossing the Chenab and making for Lahore, as was reported to be their intention. The whole of the troops from Mooltan had joined the main army by the 20th of February, and on the following day Lord Gough advanced to the attack. The Sikh position was about a mile south of Gujerat; their right was covered by the Dwara, a broad and dry sandy *nala;* their left rested on a rivulet, called the Katela; and their centre was formed behind the villages of Bara Kalra and Chota Kalra. Their numbers, including a body of 1,500 Afghan horse, led by Akram Khan, a son of the Amir Dost Mahommed Khan, were estimated at 60,000, with fifty-nine guns, but this was probably somewhat above the true figure. Lord Gough's plan of attack was to assail the Sikh left and centre and drive them back on their right for which purpose he advanced his right and his heavy artillery, retaining his left wing to complete the discomfiture of the enemy, after the former had done their work. His troops were arranged as follow:—

9. *London Gazette,* 3rd April, 1849.

The right, protected by one troop of horse artillery and two brigades of cavalry—Lockwood's (the 14th Light Dragoons, the 1st Light Cavalry, and two *rissalahs* each of the 11th and 14th Irregular Cavalry) and Hearsey's (3rd and 9th Irregular Cavalry),—was composed of the First (Whish's) Division, in which, besides a troop of horse artillery and a company of pioneers, were comprised two brigades,—Hervey's (Her Majesty's 10th Foot, and the 8th and 52nd Native Infantry) and Markham's (Her Majesty's 32nd Foot, and the 51st and 72nd Native Infantry),— the whole covered by two more troops of horse artillery and one (Dawes') light field battery, with two additional troops of horse artillery in reserve. On Whish's left was the Second (Gilbert's) Division, which included the brigades of Penny (the 2nd Bengal European Regiment, and the 31st and 70th Native Infantry) and Mountain (Her Majesty's 29th Foot, and the 30th and 56th Native Infantry). Next to these were the heavy guns, eighteen in number, and then the Third (Campbell's) Division, composed of the brigades of Carnegy (Her Majesty's 24th Foot, and the 25th Native Infantry) and M'Leod (Her Majesty's 61st Foot, and the 36th and 46th Native Infantry), supported by two light field batteries. On the extreme left was the Bombay brigade under Brigadier-General the Honourable H. Dundas (the 60th Rifles, the 1st Bombay European Regiment and the 3rd and 19th Bombay Native Infantry), covered by a battery of horse artillery and supported by the 1st (White's) Brigade of Cavalry (Her Majesty's 3rd and 9th Light Dragoons, the 8th Light Cavalry, the Sindh Horse, and two troops of horse artillery). The reserve was composed of the 5th and 6th Light Cavalry, the 45th and 69th Native Infantry, and a Bombay light field battery. The battle commenced at 7-30 a.m. with a furious cannonade, which was kept, up steadily for three hours; the Sikh guns replied as steadily, until, being overpowered by both number and weight of guns, the enemy were compelled to retire behind the line of the Kalra villages. The First and Second Divisions were now ordered to advance against the enemy's centre, and, though met by a determined and gallant resistance, in which they lost nearly 600 in killed and wounded, stormed the two villages, carried the position, and drove the Sikhs back on to their second line. On the left, at the same time, Campbell advanced with the Third Division and the Bombay brigade, and by skilful management of his light field batteries, which covered the advance of his infantry, with very trifling loss he forced his opponents to retire, and occupied their position without firing a musket shot. The cavalry en the flanks had, in the meantime, been actively engaged with the enemy's horse, whom they had in every instance put to flight: in particular on the left the Afghan horse and a body of Sikh cavalry were charged and routed with great loss by the Sindh Horse and a portion of the 9th Lancers.

Driven back along their line, and with their retreat to the Jhelum cut off by the British cavalry, the Sikhs made yet one more bid for victory. Urged on by some of the principal chiefs, a large body of cavalry and infantry burst forward to assail the centre of the Bombay brigade; but the readiness of Campbell frustrated their efforts; with great promptitude he turned the fire of a light field battery on the flank of the advancing host, and with such effect that in a few minutes the enemy were defeated and driven back with heavy loss. By one o'clock in the afternoon the Sikh position was entirely in the hands of Lord Gough's army, and the enemy, overthrown and routed in every direction, were in full flight, hotly pressed by the British cavalry and horse artillery. Night alone terminated the pursuit at a distance of fifteen miles from the field of battle.

Our losses in the battle of Gujerat were comparatively small, amounting to no more than 96 (including five British officers) killed, 706 (including twenty-five British officers) wounded, and four missing. Among the killed were Captain J. Anderson and Lieutenant E. W. Day, Horse Artillery; Lieutenant G. H. Sprot, 2nd Bengal European Regiment; and Lieutenant R. Cox, and *Subadar* Raghunath Singh, 8th Native Infantry. Lieutenant B. M. Hutchinson, Bengal Engineers, and *Naib-Risaldar* Mirza Kallu Beg, 3rd Irregular Cavalry, died of their wounds. Of the loss of the Sikhs no estimate appears to have been made, but it was certainly very heavy, and they lost fifty-six out of the fifty-nine guns they had in their possession at Gujerat; of these forty-two were captured in the action; the remaining fourteen were abandoned by them in their flight and subsequently brought in.

On the day after the victory two columns were despatched to follow up the flying Sikhs,—one, under Campbell, which proceeded towards Bhimbar, returned in a few days without results beyond bringing in some of the guns abandoned by the flying enemy; the other, under Sir Walter Gilbert (consisting of two troops of horse artillery, two light field batteries, four companies of foot artillery, four companies of sappers and pioneers, the 14th Light Dragoons, the 3rd, 9th, 11th, 12th and 13th Irregular Cavalry, a detachment of the Sindh Horse, the 53rd, 60th and 61st Foot, the 1st Bombay European Regiment, the 2nd Bengal European Regiment, the 13th,

22nd, 30th, 31st, 56th and 70th Bengal Native Infantry, and the 3rd and 19th Bombay Native Infantry), following closely on the enemy, pursued them with so much vigour that, on the 14th March, at Rawal Pindi, Sher Singh, Chattar Singh, thirty-five lesser chiefs, and the remains of the Sikh Army laid down their arms before the General,—forty-one guns and 20,000 stand of arms being surrendered on the occasion. It only remained to dispose of the Afghans, and Gilbert, continuing his pursuit, did not halt until he had driven them in headlong flight through the Khaibar Pass.

Thus ended the second Sikh war, which, commencing with the treacherous revolt of Mulraj, terminated with a great victory over one of the bravest of the peoples of India, gave a fine kingdom to the British Empire, and some of the best of its soldiers to the Indian Army.

Lord Dalhousie and Lord Gough each obtained a step in the peerage; the army received the thanks of Parliament; a medal was issued inscribed with the word "Punjab," and with clasps for Mooltan, Chilianwala and Gujerat, and the same names were authorised to be borne on the colours of corps engaged in those actions.

The conquest of the Punjab now brought us into contact with the warlike and semi-barbarous Pathan tribes on the north- west frontier of that province. The aggressions of these tribes led to repeated conflicts with, and expeditions against, them,—the first of these occurring in the very year of the conquest. The history of these "little wars" will, however, be more conveniently entered upon further on. It is only necessary to record here, in connection with this matter, that a few months after the conquest a noteworthy addition was made (G. G. O., dated the 18th May, 1849) to the strength of the Bengal Army. This was a force consisting of five regiments of Punjab irregular cavalry and five of Punjab irregular infantry, which were raised in the districts beyond the Sutlej for the protection of our new frontier on the north-west. About the same time the Sindh Camel Corps was transferred from the Bombay Presidency and placed on the same frontier, and at a later period three light field batteries were also formed for frontier service. These corps, with the "Frontier Brigade" raised in 1846-47, eventually constituted the "Punjab Frontier Force." The good and gallant service rendered by these troops in many a fierce encounter on the hills of the frontier and on the plains of Hindustan shall be related in due course.

The annexation of the Punjab led indirectly to a painful incident in the history of the Bengal Army. The corps located in that province had, as serving beyond the limits of the British dominions, been, since the year 1846, in the enjoyment of extra allowances on the scale formerly allowed to the troops in Sindh. With the conquest and annexation, the grounds on which alone the extra allowances had been conceded, ceased to exist, and accordingly a General Order (G. G. O., dated the 25th October, 1849) was issued notifying that as the Punjab was now a British province, the foreign service allowance would cease, except for the troops on the extreme north-west frontier, to whom, as being practically on field service, they would for the present be continued.

This announcement created profound discontent in the ranks of the corps serving in the Punjab, in many of which dangerous combinations were formed to resist the order and refuse the lower rate of pay. Serious acts of insubordination and mutiny occurred in the 13th, the 22nd, and the 32nd Native Infantry, which were visited with more or less severe punishment, but the worst case was that of the 66th Native Infantry, stationed in Fort Govindgarh, Amritsar. So mutinous was the conduct of this regiment that Sir Charles Napier felt constrained to disband the corps at once, on his own authority, and without waiting for the sanction of the Government of India. This was done by G. O. C. C, dated the 27th February, 1850, which directed that the native officers, non-commissioned officers and men of the regiment were to be marched to Umballa and there discharged from the Company's service; that the colours of the regiment were to be delivered over to "the brave and loyal men of the Nasseri Gurkha Battalion," and that the regiment was in future to be denominated "the 66th or Gurkha Regiment." The commanding officer of the Nasseri Battalion was also directed to recruit that corps at once to its full strength in place of the men transferred to the 66th.

In the spring of 1850, a wing of the 10th Native Infantry, and one of the 2nd Oudh Local Infantry, with two guns, were employed in putting down a rebellion in the district about twenty miles to the east of Lucknow. The principal occurrence connected with this affair was an attempt to take the fort of Bihta by storm on the 29th March, which was signally repulsed. Lieutenant E. D. Elderton and ten men of the 10th were killed on this occasion, and *Jemadars* Khakandi Singh and Dhaukal Singh and twenty-seven men wounded; in addition to this the 2nd Oudh Local Infantry sustained a loss of seven killed and twenty wounded. The fort was evacuated by the insurgents the same night.

The term of peace which succeeded the conquest of the Punjab was not destined to last long: in the spring of 1852 it was rudely and unexpectedly disturbed by the outbreak of a war with Burma. The lesson taught to the Court of Ava by the first war had soon been forgotten, and overweening conceit and insolence, bred of barbarian ignorance, betrayed itself in purposeless aggression and insults similar to those which had occasioned the former struggle. British merchants in Rangoon were wantonly wronged and insulted, and a demand from the Indian Government for reparation was treated with such contumely that at length, much against his will, Lord Dalhousie was forced to have recourse to arms, as the only means of obtaining redress. Having once committed himself to a war, the governor-general took every precaution that the errors of the former campaign should not be repeated, and that the business should be of as short a duration as possible. The force detailed for the expedition was taken partly from Bengal and partly from Madras, the former contributing three companies of artillery and a brigade of infantry (under the command of Brigadier Warren) composed of the 18th (Royal Irish) and 80th Foot and the 40th Native Infantry, and the latter three companies of artillery, two companies of sappers, and a brigade of infantry, consisting of the 51st Foot and three regiments of native infantry. The 38th Native Infantry was also detailed for this service, but refused to embark. The command of the expedition was conferred upon Major-General H. Godwin, C.B., who had served with Her Majesty's 41st Foot in the former war. The land forces amounted to 5,800, and were escorted by a fleet of nineteen steamships, carrying 159 guns.

General Godwin, with the Bengal brigade, reached the mouth of the Rangoon river on the 2nd April, 1852, and the same day a steamer was sent up with a flag of truce to enquire whether any communication had been received from the Court of Ava in reply to the ultimatum of the Government of India; the flag, however, was fired on from the stockades on the banks, and the last hope of a peaceful settlement was at an end. The Madras force not having arrived at the place of rendezvous, the General proceeded to Moulmein in order to make arrangements for the reduction of Martaban, situated on the opposite bank of the Salween River, where the Burmese had a considerable force. He arrived at Moulmein on the 4th, and on the 5th, after the naval squadron had bombarded the works of Martaban for two hours, the troops (a wing each of the 18th and

80th Foot and the 26th Madras Native Infantry, with detachments of Bengal artillery and Madras sappers) were landed, and, after a sharp but ineffectual resistance from the Burmese, carried the place by storm, with the trifling loss of eight men wounded. Leaving the 26th Madras Native Infantry to hold Martaban, General Godwin, with the rest of the troops returned to the mouth of the Irrawaddy on the 8th April, and the troops from Madras having now arrived, the expedition proceeded up the river on the 10th April. On the 11th the squadron arrived off Rangoon, and having been fired upon by the Burmese, replied with great power, completely silencing the enemy's batteries on the river, and blowing up and destroying most of his stockades; at the same time a detachment was landed at Dalla, opposite to Rangoon, which captured and destroyed the stockades on that side. On Monday, the 12th, the troops landed and marched at once against the enemy's position at the Shwe-dagon Pagoda; on the way, however, they were met with a heavy fire from a work known as the White House Stockade, in a very strong position and just in the way of their advance, which it was necessary to capture before further progress could be made. A battery of four guns was immediately opened upon the stockade, and when due effect had been produced, the place was carried by storm by four companies of the 51st Foot and a detachment of the Madras Sappers, though not without considerable loss. By this time, however, the troops were so exhausted by fatigue and by the intense heat of the sun (by which many, including Brigadier Warren, were struck down) that it was determined to halt and defer a further advance until the next day. On the following morning, however, it was found necessary to continue halted, and the day was occupied in bringing up the heavy guns and in further reconnoitring the enemy's position, while the ships kept up an occasional fire on various stockades. On Wednesday, the 14th April, the troops were tinder arms at 5 a.m., and advanced in a north-westerly direction through thick jungle to attack the Burmese in their position in and near the Shwe-dagon Pagoda. The enemy had assumed that our forces would advance by a road leading through the town to the southern face of the pagoda, and here every preparation had been made to receive us, the defences being armed with nearly one hundred pieces of cannon of sorts and held by a garrison of at least 10,000 men. The route taken, however, by General Godwin completely turned the Burmese position, and brought our troops opposite to the eastern face of the pagoda. After some delay, occasioned by the difficulty of bringing the heavy guns through the jungle and of finding a favourable position for placing them in battery, our artillery opened and made very effective practice on the pagoda and the town, notwithstanding a galling fire of guns and wall-pieces kept up by the enemy, which occasioned numerous casualties. At eleven o'clock, a favourable opportunity presenting itself, General Godwin determined on an immediate assault. The storming party was composed of a wing of the 80th Foot, two companies of the Royal Irish, and two of the 40th Bengal Native Infantry, the whole under Lieutenant-Colonel Coote, of the Royal Irish, who was accompanied by Captain Latter, 67th Native Infantry, to show the way. The advance to the pagoda was over a space of about 800 yards, which the troops crossed in the most steady manner and in beautiful order, notwithstanding a deadly fire under which many officers and men went down. When the steps of the pagoda were reached, the storming party made a gallant and determined rush, and with a cheer carried the upper terraces, when the enemy gave way and fled in wild confusion through the southern and western gates, leaving the British forces in possession of the Shwe-dagon Pagoda and of all Rangoon. Our casualties during these operations, from the 11th to the 14th of April, amounted in all to seventeen killed and 132 wounded, of whom four killed and eleven wounded were of the 40th Bengal Native Infantry.

The taking of Rangoon was the only important operation of the first year of the war, but several smaller engagements took place. In April an attempt was made by the Burmese to retake Martaban, but this was easily repelled. In May some reinforcements, which included the 67th Bengal Native Infantry, were received; and on the 17th of the same month an expedition was despatched against Bassein, by which that port was captured on the 19th, after a smart struggle in which we had three killed and thirty-two wounded. This was followed on the 26th by another Burmese attempt on Martaban, which was repulsed after a sharp conflict in which we sustained a loss of fourteen killed and wounded. In June an expedition (one company each of the 80th Foot and the 67th Native Infantry, with some Madras sappers) was sent up the river, by water, against Pegu, from which place the enemy were driven with little loss on our side, but the place was not retained and the expedition returned to Rangoon. In July a naval expedition was sent up the Irrawaddy, as far as Prome, but no attack was made on that place until October, when it was captured with the loss of one man killed and twelve wounded. The final military operation of the year was an expedition to Pegu, prior to the despatch of which, however, considerable reinforcements had been sent from India, and the forces in Burma reorganised in two divisions. The Bengal Division (G. G. O. No. 517 of 1852 was formed as follows:

Commanding:
Brigadier-General Sir John Cheape, K.C.B.

1st Brigade	18th Foot
Brigadier Reignolds	40th & 67th Native Infantry
18th (Royal Irish)	
2nd Brigade	80th Foot
Brigadier Dickinson	10th Native Infantry
10th Native Infantry	
3rd Brigade	4th Sikh Local Infantry
Brigadier Huish	1st Bengal European Fusiliers
37th Native Infantry	37th Native Infantry
	Regiment of Ludhiana

Of the above regiments the 4th Sikh Infantry, the 10th and 37th Native Infantry and the Ludhiana Regiment had all volunteered for service in Burma, as had also the 3rd Sikh Infantry, the Ramgarh Light Infantry (with the cavalry and artillery attached to it), and the 33rd Native Infantry, for which display of zeal and spirit the whole were complimented in G. G. O. No. 333 of 1852. The Ramgarh Irregular Cavalry at a later period proceeded on service to Burma. The 37th Native Infantry and the Regiment of Ludhiana did not leave India.

On the 18th November General Godwin embarked at Rangoon with a force of about 1,000 men, including 300 of the 1st Bengal Fusiliers, for the purpose of reducing Pegu, and on the 21st the place was taken, with a loss on our side of five killed and thirty-four wounded. Leaving there a garrison of 400 men, General Godwin returned to Rangoon, but within a few days of his departure the enemy re-assembled in great numbers and closely besieged the place, and it became necessary to send up a force to relieve it, an attempt with the boats of the squadron having failed of success. The force (which embarked at Rangoon on the 11th December and was under Godwin's personal command) consisted of 600 of the 1st Bengal Fusiliers, 300 of the 4th Sikh Infantry, 200 of the 10th Bengal Native Infantry, and 250 of the 1st Madras Fusiliers; and it was followed, by land, by a column consisting of some Madras artillery and sappers, half a troop of the Ramgarh Irregular Cavalry, and a wing of the 67th Bengal Native Infantry. Godwin landed six miles below Pegu on the 14th, and on the same day drove off the besiegers without difficulty and relieved the garrison, which had been hard-pressed from the 5th to the 14th of December and had sustained a loss of five killed and forty wounded. On the 18th General Godwin went in pursuit of the flying enemy in the direction of Shwe-gyeen, and twice came up with bodies of them, but they dispersed and disappeared as soon as the troops advanced to the attack, and within a week the failure of supplies compelled Godwin to retrace his steps to Pegu; and having left a larger garrison at this place, with the remainder of the force he returned to Rangoon.

During this period a good deal of skirmishing had taken place at Prome and in the neighbourhood of that place. In one of these affairs, at Akoktoung, on the 18th November, Captain Gardner and a *havildar* of the 40th Bengal Native Infantry were killed, and six sepoys were badly wounded in attempting to carry off the captain's body. On the night of the 8th December the Burmese made a daring attack on Prome, which was kept up until daylight on the following morning, and was eventually repelled with heavy loss to the enemy.

On the 6th January, 1853, a very creditable affair occurred at Naraghain, on the Arakan-Burma frontier, when Captain Nuthall, with 150 of the Arakan Local Battalion, surprised and captured a Burmese stockade which guarded the Aeng Pass.

About the middle of the same month a column, which included a wing of the 1st Bengal Fusiliers, a wing of the 10th Bengal Native Infantry, and a detachment of the Ramgarh Irregular Cavalry, was despatched from Martaban, under the command of Brigadier-General Steele of the Madras Army, with the object of clearing the Sitang Valley of the enemy and penetrating to Tonghoo. On the 18th a skirmish took place at Gongoh, in which we had one man killed and seven wounded. No further opposition was experienced, and on the 22nd February the column reached Tonghoo, having driven the enemy out of the whole country between that place and Martaban.

On the 4th February a very unfortunate affair occurred in the jungles to the west of Donabyu, when a naval expedition, accompanied by 300 of the 67th Native Infantry, was repulsed with heavy loss (fifteen killed and seventy-three wounded), in an attempt on the stronghold of a dacoit chief, named Myat-Toon. Captain Loch, C.B., Royal Navy, the leader of the expedition, and Captain Price, commanding the detachment of the 67th, were both mortally wounded, and the 67th sustained a further loss of five men killed and eighteen wounded. The steady gallantry with which the grenadiers and No. 1. Company of the 67th, forming the rear-guard, covered the retreat of the detachment won well-merited praise.

In consequence of this repulse it became necessary to send a considerably larger force against Myat-Toon. It was commanded by Brigadier-General Sir John Cheape, K.C.B., and consisted of 200 of the 18th, 200 of the 51st, and 130 of the 80th Foot; about 370 of the 67th Native Infantry; 200 of the 4th Sikh Local Infantry; about 70 sappers, and some guns. After making an ineffectual attempt to reach Myat-Toon's stronghold from Henzada, Sir John Cheape brought his force down to Donabyu, whence a fresh departure was made on the 7th March. From that date there was continual jungle fighting, until finally Myat-Toon's principal stronghold, at Nayoung-goun-lya, was carried by storm on the 19th, and his whole force beaten and dispersed. The gallantry of Lieutenant Johnson[10] and the detachment of the 4th Sikh Infantry in the storming of the enemy's position was specially mentioned in Sir John Cheape's despatch. Our loss during these operations amounted to twenty-two killed (including two British officers) and 108 wounded (including twelve British officers), the share of the 67th being two killed and nine wounded, and of the 4th Sikh Infantry seven killed and twenty-three wounded: amongst the killed were Ensign Boileau of the 67th, and *Jemadar* Mir Muhammad Khan of the 4th Sikh Infantry.

These were the last operations of any importance. In June, 1853, peace was concluded with the King of Burma, the province of Pegu having, in the previous December, been formally annexed to the British dominions. But notwithstanding the conclusion of peace, it was many months before the various bands of Burmese soldiery were finally driven out of the province; many small skirmishes took place, even up to the spring of 1854, and several valuable lives were lost before real pacification was effected[11]; amongst others, Captain Barry, Commandant of the Arakan Battalion, was mortally wounded in an affair near Prome, in December, 1853.

The corps engaged in the campaign, including those employed

---

10. Now General Sir Allen Bayard Johnson, K.C.B.
11. The hardship and exposure of the campaign in Burma shortly proved fatal to the Commander of the forces, Major-General Sir Henry Godwin, K.C.B., who died at Simla on the 26th October, 1853.

on the Arakan-Pegu frontier and at Moulmein, were subsequently (in 1855) authorised to inscribe the word "Pegu" on their colours and appointments, and a medal (afterwards, under the. designation of the "India Medal of 1854" adopted as the decoration for operations in India generally) and six months' batta were granted to all ranks.

The narrative of our numerous expeditions on the North-West Frontier of the Punjab may now conveniently be taken up.

After the annexation of the Punjab the people of Swat uniformly proved themselves bad neighbours, and it was against them that the first of our frontier expeditions had to be directed. This took place in December, 1849, when a force under Lieutenant-Colonel Bradshaw, C.B., moved out from Peshawar to coerce certain refractory Swati villages in the Sam Baizai district in Yusafzai, The force was composed of a troop of horse artillery, a company of sappers and miners, the 13th Irregular Cavalry, detachments of the 60th and 61st Foot, the 3rd Bombay Native Infantry, and detachments of the Corps of Guides and the 1st Punjab Infantry. Sharp fighting took place at Sanghao, Palli, Zurmandai and Sher Khana on the 11th and 14th, ending in the complete defeat of the enemy and of their allies from Upper Swat. Our losses were seven killed and forty, including two British officers, wounded; amongst the former was *Ressaidar* Pahlwan Khan of the Guides Cavalry.

The next of these expeditions was directed against the Adam Khel Afridis, who had, on the 2nd February, 1850, attacked and cut up a party of sappers employed in constructing a road in the Kohat Pass. The Commander-in-Chief, Sir Charles Napier, who was in Peshawar at the time, at once issued orders for a force, under the command of Brigadier-General Sir Colin Campbell, to move through the pass, and punish the perpetrators of this outrage, and accordingly on the 9th February, Sir Colin marched from Peshawar with a troop of horse artillery, two 5½" mortars, two companies each of the 60th, 61st, and 98th Foot, the 15th Irregular Cavalry and the 1st Punjab Cavalry, the 23rd and 31st Native Infantry, the 1st Punjab Infantry, and a detachment of the Corps of Guides. The force, which was accompanied by Sir Charles Napier in person, entered the pass on the 10th, and during its progress through to the Kohat *Kotal* it met with continuous and determined opposition ; the enemy were, however, dislodged successively from all their positions, and the villages concerned in the massacre of the sappers were taken and destroyed. The Kohat *Kotal* was reached on the 11th, and on the morning of the 12th a severe engagement took place on the heights above the camp, in the course of which a company of the 31st Native Infantry was very roughly handled and sustained considerable loss, Ensign Sitwell and *Jemadar* Dunia Singh being amongst the killed. On the 13th, the two Punjab regiments having been sent into Kohat, the force began its return march to Peshawar, which it reached on the 14th, having experienced throughout the same determined opposition as had marked its advance. The casualties during the expedition amounted to twenty killed and seventy-four wounded. Further fighting took place during the following month, in the neighbourhood of the Kohat *Kotal*, in which the 1st Punjab Infantry, under Captain Coke, distinguished themselves; and it was some time before even a semblance of peace on that part of the frontier was restored.

In October, 1851, a small expedition, under the command of Captain Coke, was sent into the Miranzai Valley, to reduce some refractory villages to order, which was effected after a little skirmishing.

To punish numerous raids and more or less serious attacks on British villages, a force, commanded by Sir Colin Campbell, was sent from Peshawar against the Mohmands in October, 1851. It was composed of a field battery, two companies each of the 61st and 98th Foot, the 2nd Irregular Cavalry, a company of sappers and miners, the 66th (Gurkhas) and a wing of the 71st Native Infantry, and a detachment of the Guides Infantry. The operations began on the 25th October, and continued until February of the following year; from time to time trifling skirmishes occurred at Banda, Matta, and other places, but little opposition was met with, and few casualties occurred. The 2nd Irregular Cavalry lost a few men, and Lieutenant Boulnois, of the engineers, was shot dead (15th January, 1852) by a party of the enemy, one of whose towers he had incautiously approached. During this expedition the Michni valley was occupied and a fort erected at that place. In March 1852, the Mohmands mustered in considerable force, and, coming out of the hills, attempted an attack on the forts built on the lands from which they had been expelled. They were first encountered in a skirmish near Shabkadar, when the misbehaviour of a half troop of the 7th Light Cavalry marred what might otherwise have proved a decisive success. On the 15th April the Mohmands again issued from the hills to the number of at least 6,000 men; they were attacked at Panjpao by Sir Colin Campbell with two horse artillery guns and detachments of the 7th Light Cavalry, 15th Irregular Cavalry, and 29th and 71st Native Infantry. The action was, on our part, confined to artillery fire, but so effective was this, that the Mohmands were completely dispersed, with a trifling loss on our side of two killed and eight wounded.

In March, 1852, it became necessary to send an expedition to coerce the Ranizais, one of the Swat clans, who had been guilty of an entirely unprovoked attack on a British detachment at Gujar-Garhi. The force employed was under the command of Brigadier-General Sir Colin Campbell and was composed of a troop of horse artillery, the 15th Irregular Cavalry, the 32nd Foot, a wing of the 29th and the whole of the 66th (Gurkha) Native Infantry. On this occasion no fighting occurred, and a fine having been imposed on the Ranizais, the force, having traversed their country, returned to Peshawar towards the end of the month. Before two months had elapsed, however, it became necessary to resume hostilities, the Ranizais having refused to pay the fine imposed upon them. Accordingly, on the 15th May Sir Colin Campbell again took the field with a force composed of one troop of horse artillery, two guns of a light field battery, the 32nd Foot, the 2nd Irregular Cavalry, the Guides Cavalry and the 1st Punjab Cavalry, a company of sappers, the 28th and 66th (Gurkha) Native Infantry, the Guides Infantry, and the 1st Punjab Infantry; and on the 18th he totally routed the Ranizais in a sharp action near the village of Skakot, which was taken and destroyed. The Ranizais, who brought 4,500 men into the field, suffered severely, while the loss on our side was only eleven killed and twenty-nine wounded. The operations were continued up to the 24th May, and a number of other villages having been destroyed, the force was withdrawn to Peshawar.

To punish a raid in which the *tahsildar* of Hashtnagar was killed, a punitive expedition, under the command of Sir Colin Campbell, was sent against the Utman Khel tribe in May, 1852. It consisted of a troop of horse artillery, a detachment of field artillery, 300 of the 32nd Foot, one squadron of the 2nd Irregular Cavalry, one squadron of the Guides Cavalry, two squadrons of the 1st Punjab Cavalry, one company of sappers, 300 each of the 28th and 66th (Gurkha) Native Infantry, the Guides Infantry, and the 1st Punjab Infantry. The first operation was the destruction of the Nawadan villages, which was effected on May 11th, with the loss of a few men wounded, and on the 13th the village of Prangarh was attacked and carried, after a gallant defence by the enemy, who stood their ground to the last though exposed to the fire of ten pieces of artillery. Our loss during the expedition amounted to three killed and fifteen wounded.

The Umarzai Waziris were, for several years after the annexation, one of the most troublesome of the border tribes. During the years 1849-50-51-52 they were guilty of repeated raids into the Bannu district, until at last it became necessary to inflict punishment. In December, 1852, an expedition against them was organised by Major John Nicholson, who, observing the utmost secrecy in all his preparations, divided his force (forty sabres of the 2nd Punjab Cavalry, and fifty of the mounted police, two companies of the 1t Punjab Infantry, the 2nd Punjab Infantry, four companies of the 4th Punjab Infantry, and the 6th Punjab Police Battalion) into three columns, which made a simultaneous entry into the Waziri country at three different points, took the tribesmen completely by surprise, and destroyed several villages almost without opposition. This success was, however, considerably discounted by twenty-three men of the 4th Punjab Infantry, who had fallen out, or remained straggling behind the column, being cut off by the enemy.

The aggressions of the Hassanzais of the Black Mountain, and the murder by them of two officials of the Customs Department, rendered it necessary to send an expedition against them in December, 1852. The troops employed were under the command of Lieutenant-Colonel Mackeson, C.B., Commissioner of Peshawar, and included a troop of horse artillery and the Mountain Train Battery[12], the 16th Irregular Cavalry, a company of sappers, the 3rd Native Infantry, the Regiment of Kalat-i-Ghilzai, the Corps of Guides, and the 1st Sikh Infantry, with some police and levies. On the 29th December, the force "advanced in three columns, two of which entered the Hassanzai country by a trying and difficult march over the heights of the Black Mountain. Some strong positions were held by the enemy on the upper spurs of the mountain, but they were carried without much resistance; and indeed the winter cold of those high altitudes was a more serious inconvenience than the opposition of the tribesmen. A number of villages Were destroyed, and the force returned across the frontier on the 2nd January, 1853, having sustained a loss of five killed and ten wounded, among the former of whom were *Subadar* Shukar Khan and *Jemadar* Jhur Singh, of the Corps of Guides.

This expedition was followed by an attack on Kotla, a small fort in the Amb territory, on the right bank of the Indus, which had been seized by the Hindustani fanatics, and whose inhabitants had aided the Hassanzais in their aggressions. The troops employed included two

---
12. Now No. 4 (Hazara) Mountain Battery.

guns of a mountain battery and the 1st and 3rd Sikh Infantry; they crossed the Indus on the 6th January, 1853, but the Hindustanis did not wait for them, having fled from the fort without firing a shot on the first appearance of danger.

In the spring of 1853 it became necessary to take measures for the punishment of the Shiranis, a Pathan tribe occupying the principal part of the Takht-i-Suliman. who had long been the terror of the Dera Ismail Khan border, and who had lately filled up the measure of their offences (raids and outrages without number) by attacking a reconnoitring party from the Draband out-post. On that occasion (14th March, 1853) they met with a total defeat from the troops at Draband (detachments of the 5th Punjab Cavalry and the Sindh Camel Corps), with a loss on our side of five killed and seventeen (including two British officers) wounded, and immediately after a force was assembled to move into the Shirani country and inflict condign punishment for the frequent violations of our territory. The force (which was under the command of Brigadier Hodgson and consisted of No. 2 Punjab Light Field Battery,[13] a squadron of the 5th Punjab Cavalry, a wing each of the 1st and 3rd Punjab Infantry, the Sindh Camel Corps, and two police battalions) entered the enemy's country by the Shekh Haidar Pass on the 31st March and occupied Drazand the same day. During the next three days the troops moved over various parts of the Shirani country, destroying the villages of the offending tribesmen without encountering any opposition worthy of the name, and on the 3rd April returned to British territory by the Draband pass, having fully accomplished the objects of the expedition without the loss of a man.

On the return of the troops from the Shirani hills. Brigadier Hodgson, with a small force (a detachment of the 4th Punjab Cavalry, the 1st Punjab Infantry, and the 6th Punjab Police Battalion) proceeded to chastise the Kasranis, a tribe which had been distinguishing itself for some years by a series of audacious raids and depredations on the Dera Ghazi Khan border. The force entered the Kasrani country on the 12th April, captured and destroyed the stockaded village of Bati after some fighting, and returned to British territory the same day, having sustained a loss of one man killed and ten wounded.

Repeated raids and outrages in the Peshawar District committed by the Jowaki Afridis of the Bori valley rendered the punishment of this clan necessary, and accordingly, in November, 1853, Colonel S. B.

---

13. Now No. 1 (Kohat) Mountain Battery.

Boileau, 22nd Foot, was sent into the valley with a force consisting of a Mountain Train Battery,[14] a squadron of the 7th Irregular Cavalry, a wing of the 22nd Foot, two companies of the 20th and a wing of the 66th (Gurkha) Native Infantry, and the Infantry of the Corps of Guides. Entering the valley by the Sargasha Pass, Colonel Boileau drove the enemy from their villages, which were then destroyed, while detachments of the Guides and Gurkhas, gallantly crowning the neighbouring heights, kept the Afridis at bay while the operations in the valley were completed, and afterwards, in the evening, covered the retirement through the Taruni pass. The steadiness and gallantry of both these corps, the former led by their intrepid Commandant, Lieutenant Hodson, and the latter by Captains Garstin and Ross, were the admiration of the whole force; indeed, the names of Hodson and the Guides are foremost in the official reports of the many frontier expeditions in which they were at this time engaged. The loss of Colonel Boileau's force was eight killed and thirty-one wounded.

In the autumn of 1854 it was found necessary to send an expedition against the Michni Mohmands, to punish them for incursions into British territory, to collect the annual tribute, which was long over-due, and to take measures to. secure the peace of the border by the destruction of the three lawless villages of Dabb, Sadin, and Shah Mansur Khel. The troops detailed for this work were under the command of Colonel S. J. Cotton, and included two horse artillery guns, the Mountain Train Battery,[15] a troop of the 10th Light Cavalry, a squadron of the 1st Irregular Cavalry, two companies of the 22nd Foot, a company of sappers, three companies of the 1st and a wing of the 9th Native Infantry, and a wing of the 1st Sikh Infantry. At daylight, on the 31st August, the force moved up against Shah Mansur Khel in two columns: the Mohmands were in some force, and made a considerable resistance, but after a sharp conflict the village was captured and destroyed and the enemy driven from the position they had taken up, with a loss on our side of one man killed and two British officers and fourteen men wounded. On the 2nd September Dabb and Sadin were also destroyed, and the force then returned to Peshawar.

Notwithstanding the destruction of these strongholds, Mohmand incursions still continued, and in March, 1855, a larger party than usual, numbering about 300, came down on a plundering expedition.

---

14. Manned by the 2nd Company, 2nd Battalion, Bengal Artillery.—(now No. 9 Mountain Battery, Royal Artillery.)
15. Idem.

They were encountered between Shabkadar and Abazai by a small force under Major Gordon, 1st Sikh Infantry, and dispersed, with a loss on our side of Ensign Bradford, 62nd Native Infantry, and four sepoys wounded. Later in the year two other slight affairs with Mohmand raiders took place in the same neighbourhood.

During the early part of 1855, the Bassi Khel section of the Aka Khel Afridis were guilty of numerous raids into British territory. Many skirmishes took place between our troops and these marauders, until at last it was found necessary to send an expedition against them, to drive them entirely out of the low hills from which they emerged on their plundering expeditions. The force detailed for this service was commanded by Lieutenant-Colonel J. H. Craigie, 20th Native Infantry, and consisted of the Peshawar Mountain Battery, two troops of the 16th Irregular Cavalry, a detachment of the 4th Native Infantry, and the 9th and 20th Native Infantry. The movement took place on the 27th March, and the enemy, to the number of a thousand fighting men, strongly posted near the villages of Alam Killi and Mir Killi, and occupying the heights in the neighbourhood, hotly disputed the advance of the column, and inflicted some loss on the British force. The sepoys, however, behaved with the greatest gallantry, and the hostile villages having been taken and destroyed, and their occupants driven some distance into the hills, the troops retired, having lost in the engagement nine men killed and one British officer, one native officer and twenty-three men wounded.

On the Kohat border the Miranzai villages were from the first hostile to the English, and the small expedition of October. 1851, did not effect much towards settling affairs. The Miranzai valley was in a very unsettled state for years, and at length, in April, 1855, an expedition had to be sent from Kohat, under Brigadier Chamberlain, to settle the country and to enforce the payment of the revenue. It consisted of the 1st and 3rd Punjab Light Field Batteries, the 4th Punjab Cavalry, a detachment of sappers, a wing of the 66th (Gurkha) Native Infantry, the 1st and 3rd Punjab Infantry, and the Sindh Rifle Corps. The expedition was at first met by no overt acts of hostility, except that shots were constantly fifed into the camp at night. However, on the 30th of April, the picquets round the camp were attacked by about 1,500 *ghazis*. The troops on picquet duty, consisting of about 130 of the 4th Punjab Cavalry and 350 of the 1st Punjab Infantry, repulsed the attack, and, following the enemy into the hills, drove them from every position they took up. The conduct of the troops was especially

The Indian Mutiny, 1857

A British Irregular Cavalry Officer
at the time of the Sikh War

A British Cavalry Officer at the time of the Sikh War

AT THE TIME OF THE SECOND AFGHAN WAR, CIRCA 1880

admirable, because they were fighting, so to speak, against their own religion, many of the *ghazis* being fellow-tribesmen, and even near relations, of the soldiers. The loss of the enemy was considerable; that of the British force was only fourteen wounded. The troops returned to Kohat on the 21st May.

In August 1855, an expedition was despatched against the Rubia Khel Urakzais, who had taken part against us in the hostilities in the Miranzai country, and had since been concerned in numerous daring raids into the Kohat district. The force employed was composed of the Peshawar Mountain Battery, No. 3 Punjab Light Field Battery, the 4th Punjab Cavalry, and the 1st, 2nd, and 3rd Punjab Infantry, and was commanded by Brigadier Chamberlain. An advance was made from Hangu on the night of the 1st September, and early in the morning on the 2nd simultaneous attacks were made on

Sangar, Nasin and Katsah, three villages on the Samana range of hills which had been most concerned in depredations in British territory, and of which the *maliks* were notorious freebooters: the arrangements were admirably carried out and the attacks perfectly successful; but on the troops beginning to retire, after the destruction of the villages, a sudden rush of the enemy cut off a party of the 2nd Punjab Infantry, of whom a native doctor and seven men were killed. The total losses of the day were eleven killed and four wounded.

In October, 1856, it became necessary to send another expedition into Miranzai, to punish the Turis, who had been guilty of many raids into British territory, and the Zaimukhts, who had been encroaching in the Miranzai Valley and had taken possession of Torawari, which had now, under their auspices, become a place of refuge for all the miscellaneous scoundrelism of the border. The force employed was under the command of Brigadier Chamberlain and consisted (besides detachments of the Punjab Mountain Train Battery, No. 1 Punjab Light Field Battery, and the 1st Punjab Cavalry) of No. 3 Punjab Light Field Battery, the 4th Punjab Cavalry, a company of sappers and miners, the 66th (Gurkha) Native Infantry, and the 1st, 2nd, 3rd, 5th, and 6th Punjab Infantry. Chamberlain moved from Kohat on the 21st October, and on the morning of the 25th completely surprised Torawari, the people of which, after some firing, were compelled to lay down their arms and surrender a number of criminals whom they were harbouring. On the 4th November the force moved into the Kuram Valley, for the purpose of dealing with the Turis, and reached Kuram Fort on the 11th, when a settlement with the Turis was effected; and after the Paiwar Pass had been visited the force returned to Thal, arriving there on the 28th. In December a detachment was employed in punishing the Miami branch of the Kabul Khel Waziris, who had murdered some followers of the force. The force returned to Kohat towards the end of December.

One more frontier expedition remains to be related in this chapter. This, which was also led by Brigadier Chamberlain, took place in March 1857 and was directed against the Bozdars, a tribe of the Dera Ghazi Khan border, who had during the preceding seven years been guilty of a most audacious series of forays into British territory. The force detailed for these operations was composed of Nos. 1, 2, and 3 Punjab Light Field Batteries, detachments of the 2nd and 3rd Punjab Cavalry, a company of Punjab sappers, a wing each of the 1st and 3rd Sikh Infantry, and the 1st, 2nd, and 4th Punjab Infantry, and was assembled at Taunsa, near Mangrotha, on the 5th of that month. Marching thence on the morning of the 6th the troops entered the Bozdar country by the Sangarh Pass at daybreak, and encamped at Dedachi Kach. That afternoon the enemy's position was reconnoitred, and on the following morning the troops advanced to the attack. Within the pass at the Khan Band defile, the enemy had taken up an exceedingly strong position, which, in former years, they had successfully held against large Sikh armies, but by skilful management, aided by the gallant behaviour of the troops, Chamberlain succeeded in forcing the position after a sharp engagement, in which he lost five men killed, and one British officer, three native officers, and forty-five men wounded. The Bozdars fled, and thereafter made no resistance during the fortnight that the force remained in their country. During that fortnight the country was traversed in various directions, and the villages of the offending tribesmen destroyed. Eventually the Bozdars tendered their submission and the troops were withdrawn, reaching Mangrotha on the 23rd March.

By G. G. O. No. 812 of 1869 the India medal, with a clasp inscribed "North-West Frontier," was granted to all survivors of the troops engaged in the following of the above operations:

1849	Expedition to Yusafzai against the Baizai Swatis
1850	Expedition against the Kohat Pass Afridis
1852	Expedition against the Utman Khels
1852	Expedition against the Ranizai Swatis
1852	Operation against the Mohmands

1852/3 Expedition against the Hasanzais of the Black Mountain
1853 Expedition against the Kasranis and Shiranis
1853 Expedition against the Jowaki Afridis of Bori
1854 Expedition to Shah Mansur Khel against the Mohmands
1855 Expedition against the Bassi Khel Aka-Khel Afridis
1855 Expedition to the Miranzai Valley
1857 Expedition to the Bozdar Hills

In the middle of 1855 serious disturbances broke out amongst the wild tribes of the Santhal Parganas. For a short time the whole country was in the hands of the insurgents, and it became necessary to place a considerable force in the field to repress the outbreak. The troops employed on this service were under the command of Major-General Lloyd, C.B., and Brigadier Bird, and comprised the following corps:—The Governor-General's Body-Guard; the 2nd and 11th Irregular Cavalry; the Ramgarh Irregular Cavalry; a detachment of the 2nd Native Infantry; the right wing of the 7th, the 13th, the 31st, a detachment of the 37th, the 40th, the 42nd, the right wing of the 50th, the 56th and the 63rd Native Infantry; the Bhagalpur Hill Rangers; and a detachment of the Shekhawati Battalion. Some desultory fighting took place, and on one occasion (at Nagor on the 27th July) the Santhals succeeded in surrounding and cutting off a detachment of the 56th Native Infantry, killing Lieutenant Toulmin, who commanded, and about twenty men, and wounding fifteen others. As a rule, however, the enemy were unable to stand their ground against even very small detachments, and eventually the leaders of the insurrection were captured, and the disturbance put down. The field force was broken up by G. G. O., dated 2nd January 1856, except one brigade which remained in the country for another year.

The long continued misgovernment of Oudh, and the hopeless anarchy resulting therefrom, led, in February 1856, to the deposition of the king and the annexation of his kingdom to the British dominions in the East. In support of the decree of annexation a small force (three light field batteries, the 1st Light Cavalry, the 5th and 15th Irregular Cavalry, the 52nd Foot, and the 22nd, 38th, 41st, 48th, 52nd and 73rd Native Infantry), under the command of Brigadier Wheler, was despatched from Cawnpore on the 1st of February and marched on Lucknow, which place was reached a few days later. No resistance was made by the king or his adherents, and within a few months the country had settled down to a condition of peace and security to which it had been a stranger for more than half a century.

This chapter may now be closed with a summary of such of the more important changes in the strength and internal economy of the Bengal Army, between the years 1848 and 1857, as have not already been noticed.

In the regular army, no augmentations or reductions took place in these years, except those consequent on the cessation or the renewal of war, and the only change was that the 11th Light Cavalry, raised in place of the old 2nd, which was disbanded for misbehaviour in Afghanistan, was, in 1850 (G. O. G. G,, 24th May), in recognition of the gallantry it had displayed before Mooltan on the 7th November 1848, appointed to fill the vacant number, and was designated "the 2nd Regiment of Light Cavalry."

The foundation of the Punjab Frontier Force, in the raising, in 1846, of the "Frontier Brigade," and in 1849 of five regiments of Punjab cavalry and five of Punjab infantry, has already been referred to. The force was remodelled in 1851 (G. G. O., 25th February), when its strength was fixed at three light field batteries, five regiments of cavalry, and five of infantry, and it was designated "the Punjab Irregular Force." In 1853 (G. G. O. No. 776, dated 27th September) the Sindh Camel Corps was re-organised "as a light infantry regiment, armed with rifles," and incorporated in the Punjab Irregular. Force as the "6th Regiment or Sindh Rifle Corps," and by G. G. O. No. 1042, dated the 4th August 1856, it was designated the "6th Punjab Infantry."

In 1854, the Nizam's disciplined force, which had been in existence for more than half a century and at one time bore a high reputation as "the Russell Brigade," was re-organized and styled the "Hyderabad Contingent," and, after forty years of honourable service, it still exists under this designation.

Two other additions were made to the Indian forces at this period, and entered in the Bengal Army List, though neither was distinctly part of the Bengal Army; the first of these was the formation (G.G.O. No. 916 of 1854) of the "Nagpur Irregular Force," consisting of one field battery, one regiment of irregular cavalry, and three regiments of infantry. The second was the raising, after the annexation of Oudh, of the "Oudh Irregular Force," consisting of three light field batteries, three regiments of cavalry and ten regiments of infantry, in which last were included the existing 1st and 2nd Oudh Local Infantry. Of these forces, the former survived the troubles of 1857, but was afterwards broken up: the latter was swept away in the torrent of the mutiny and disappeared within eighteen months of its formation.

Finally, in 1856, a Sikh corps, destined to gain fame and glory in the troublous times that were at hand, was raised for civil duties. This was the 1st Bengal Military Police Battalion, raised by Captain Rattray for service in the Santhal districts, and now known as the 45th Bengal Infantry, or "Rattray's Sikhs."

Some few interior changes and reforms are worthy of notice. In 1846 (G. O. G. G. 7th October) the remount depôt was removed from Muttra to Karnal and its establishment remodelled it was now to consist of:

1	Superintendent
1	Assistant Superintendent
1	Riding Master
1	Assistant Riding Master
2	Drill *Havildars*
2	Drill *Naiks*
50	Rough Riders

A General Order, dated 20th May 1847, directs a further experiment to be made in the use of geldings in native cavalry; a similar trial had been made between 1817 and 1820, apparently with unsatisfactory results. The G. O. C. C. under notice directs that the 11th Light Cavalry "be mounted entirely on geldings, in order that the long-contested question of their inferiority or otherwise to entire horses may be set at rest." The regiment was to be mounted, as far as possible, by exchanges with other corps, and to be completed by geldings five years old selected from the Government stud by a committee. In 1849 it was ordered that "the experiment in the 11th Light Cavalry having proved satisfactory, the 10th Light Cavalry is also to be mounted on geldings."

Amongst other minor orders, G. G. O. No. 498 of 1851 directs that Wurdi-Majors of Irregular Cavalry shall rank with Ressaidars.

In dress and equipment several small changes were introduced in both cavalry and infantry:—as, for instance, the substitution of cloth overalls in regular cavalry for the old leather breeches, which since the beginning of the century, had been a characteristic feature of Bengal cavalry and horse artillery (G. G. O. No. 57 of 1847); the introduction of a fur busby for light cavalry and Kilmarnock caps for infantry, the latter of which was a most popular head-dress amongst the sepoys, principally on account of its durability,—to which the commanding officer of one regiment rather quaintly testifies in writing the records of his corps, when, on the abolition of the Kilmarnock cap, in 1861, he remarks that many were still in wear in the regiment which had been issued on their introduction in 1847.

The irregular cavalry at this period, which seems on the whole to have shared with the horse artillery the distinction of being the most efficient service of the native army, was not free from the abuses so prevalent elsewhere. For example, the *zemindar* class, of whom it was principally composed, finding R20 a month insufficient, strove to make money by an abuse of the *bargir* system. The *asami* (literally berth or billet) in an irregular cavalry regiment was regarded as a man's property, as much as his house and land, and could on his retirement from active service be farmed out by him to the highest bidder (subject to the approval of the commandant), until such time as be had a son or a nephew of an age to put into the place.

The dress of the irregular cavalry at this time consisted of a yellow, green, or scarlet *alkhalak* tight pantaloons coloured with *Mooltani matti*, in imitation of the leather breeches of the regulars, and jack boots. Two regiments—the 1st and 4th—wore a polished steel *tawah*, or helmet, circular at the top.

An order of considerable interest at the time was published on the 14th April 1851, announcing the grant of a medal, called the "India Medal," to the surviving officers and soldiers of the Crown and the East India Company who were engaged in the several services enumerated in the following list:

1803	4th September	Storm of Aligarh
1803	11th September	Battle of Delhi
1803	23rd September	Battle of Assaye
1803	21st October	Siege of Asirgarh[16]
1803	1st November	Battle of Laswari
1803	December	Siege and storm of Gawilgarh
1804	October	Defence of Delhi

---

16. It is curious that the occupation of Asirgarh in 1803 should have been selected for the grant of the medal (the garrison having on that occasion surrendered almost without firing a shot), while the siege and capture of the same place in 1819 (which cost us more than 300 officers and men) remained absolutely unnoticed.

1804	13th November	Battle of Deig
1804	23rd December	Capture of Deig
1816		War in Nepal
1817	November	Battle of Kirki and battle and capture of Poona
1817	November/December	Battle of Sitabaldi and capture of Nagpur
1817	21st December	Battle of Mahidpur
1818	1st January	Defence of Corigaum
1824-6		War in Ava
1826		Siege and storm of Bhurtpore

Indian troops were declared to be ineligible for the decoration for Nepal and Ava, for which a medal had been already issued by the East India Company.

In 1856 (G. G. O. No. 1012) it was notified that in future no recruit for the native army would be accepted unless he consented to be enlisted for general service.

In the same year (by G. G. O. No. 1324) messes were established in all regiments of the Bengal Army.

The months of wild tumult and convulsion which followed the spring of 1857 witnessed the extinction of three-fourths of that army which it had taken exactly a century to form; many of the finest—most of the oldest—regiments succumbed to the mania of revolt, and the maintenance of the British Empire in India devolved in a great degree upon corps which were raised from amongst a people who eight years before had been our bitterest foes.

This is not a suitable work in which to enter at length into the question of the causes of the mutiny. One point at least is certain, which is often overlooked in the discussion of the question, that the canker was deeper seated than the rumours of the moment about Lord Canning's proselytising intentions, or his caste-defiling cartridges: for thirty years the *morale* of the army had been steadily deteriorating, for thirty years the evil had been growing and deepening; the grievances of the time were but the irritants which brought it to a head.

CHAPTER 8

The Great Mutiny

The events of the Indian Mutiny are so well known, and the histories which chronicle them so complete in detail, and so generally read, that nothing more than the shortest sketch of that eventful year is necessary in the present volume, even if space allowed a more detailed narrative.

Four principal causes are mentioned as having led directly to the outbreak:—first, alleged disaffection in Oudh, the principal recruiting ground of the Bengal Army, resulting, it was said, from the annexation of that province in 1856, and the consequent loss by the sepoys of old and valued privileges of precedence in the civil courts; secondly, alleged discontent amongst Musalmans, fostered and encouraged by the old royal family of Delhi, who yearned for the restoration of the ancient regal state and influence which they had long since lost; thirdly, the opportunity afforded to disaffection by the extraordinary paucity of British troops in India: and, finally, a widespread belief which had arisen, that the Government had secret designs against the caste and religion of the native soldiery. To such a belief many circumstances, upon which it is unnecessary to enter here, had combined in the early days of 1857 to lend colour, and at this point it came to be bruited about that the cartridges for the new Enfield rifles, with which the native army were to be armed, had been defiled with the fat of pigs and oxen. These unhappy rumours appealed to the most sensitive characteristics of the high-caste Bengal sepoy, and served as the breath which fanned the smouldering embers of discontent into the lurid flames of mutiny and murder.

Early in 1857 it became evident that a crisis of an extraordinary character was at hand. In March the 19th Native Infantry broke out into open mutiny at Berhampore, and was marched down to Barrackpore, and there disbanded. Seven companies of the 34th at Barrackpore displayed disaffection scarcely less culpable, and were similarly treated. On the 10th of May, the 7th Oudh Irregular Infantry met a similar fate at Lucknow; and on the same day the storm burst in earnest with the outbreak at Meerut. Here the first regiment to break into open violence against its officers was the 3rd Light Cavalry, soon followed by the 11th and 20th Native Infantry. On the same night the rebels marched to Delhi; there they were joined by the 38th, 54th, and 74th Native Infantry, and by the afternoon the city was completely in their hands, not however, without an obstinate resistance at the Magazine, the heroic defence and subsequent blowing up of which by Lieutenant Willoughby and a few of the ordnance subordinates was one of the most memorable incidents of the time.

The news of the outbreak was the signal for Lord Canning at Calcutta to send urgent messages for reinforcements from Ceylon, Bombay, and Madras, and to intercept and divert to India the troops then proceeding on service to China. The Commander-in-Chief, General the Honourable George Anson, who was at Simla, hurried down to Umballa, his movements hampered by the temporary insubordination of the Nasseri Battalion[1] at Jutogh. He had hardly time to set the small Umballa garrison in motion towards Delhi, when he was struck down by cholera and died at Karnal on the 27th May. He was succeeded in the chief command by Major-General Sir Henry Barnard, who pressed on southwards, and on the 7th June was joined by a detachment from Meerut, under Brigadier Archdale Wilson. This latter force had been victorious in two actions with the rebels at Ghaziudin-nagar, on the banks of the Hindan river, and had been reinforced by the Sirmoor Battalion under Major Charles Reid. On the 8th June, at daybreak, the enemy was attacked in a strong position at Badli-ke-Serai, six miles from Delhi, defeated, and driven back in confusion to the city, with a loss of thirteen guns and several hundred men, but our own losses were heavy too, amounting to nearly 200 officers and men, and amongst these not the least to be deplored was the death of Colonel Chester, the Adjutant General, who fell by a cannon shot, to the great loss of the Army of Bengal. On the same day the British force was established on the ridge before Delhi, that Ridge destined to become historic as the scene of so many deeds of valour and devotion in the famous fourteen weeks' siege which now began.

---

1. This was the corps formed in 1850, when the original Nasseri Battalion was transferred to the line and became the 66th Native Infantry.

Meanwhile, in the Punjab, the energy of all the talent which Lord Dalhousie had lavished upon his favourite province was-working as men like John Lawrence, Herbert Edwardes, Montgomery, and Nicholson knew how to work to save the empire. At Meean Meer, by a well planned and boldly-executed *coup-de-main* the 8th Light Cavalry and the 16th, 26th, and 49th Native Infantry, which were all known to be ill-affected, were disarmed on the morning of the 13th May by a wing of the 81st Foot and some horse artillery. At Ferozepore and Phillour the magazines were secured, and at the former place the 57th Native Infantry was disarmed by the 61st Foot; but the 45th Native Infantry there, as well as the 3rd Native Infantry from Phillour, and the 36th and 61st from Jullundur, remained in possession of their arms and eventually made their way for the most part to Delhi. Their march, however, was not undisputed, and the attack on the banks of the Sutlej on some 1,600 mutineers from Jullundur by three companies of the 4th Sikh Infantry under Lieutenant Williams and Mr. Ricketts, the Deputy Commissioner, was one of the most gallant episodes of that stirring time in the Punjab. But it was at Peshawar that the greatest danger threatened British influence in the province. There, and in the neighbourhood, were twelve native regiments, four of them cavalry, and only three of British infantry. Among the native corps were two of cavalry and two of infantry which throughout maintained their fidelity to the State: these were the 7th and 18th Irregular Cavalry, the 21st Native Infantry and the Regiment of Kalat-i-Ghilzai (now the 5th and 8th Bengal Cavalry, and the 1st and 12th Bengal Infantry). Besides these, was the Corps of Guides, raised eleven years before under the direction of Henry Lawrence, and already famous as one of the finest corps in India. On the first news of the outbreak at Meerut, the Guides were despatched to join the army before Delhi; leaving Hoti-Mardan on May 13th, they were at Delhi on the morning of the 9th of June, having completed 580 miles in twenty-seven days, at the hottest season of the year, and with only three days' halts by the way. Those who remained in the Peshawar valley proceeded with the difficult work of disarming the disaffected sepoys, with an energy which no danger could hinder. The 24th, 27th, and 51st were disarmed at Peshawar when on the point of mutiny; the news reached the 55th at Mardan and they fled with their arms, only to meet destruction from Nicholson, with his irregular levies, and from the wild tribes of the frontier. The 64th was quietly disarmed at AbazaiAbazai; the 5th Light Cavalry and 10th Irregular Cavalry were reserved for a future day.

In the North-West Provinces, where some at least of the immediate causes of the Mutiny were more keenly felt than elsewhere, the sepoy garrisons were not slow to follow the example of their comrades at Meerut and Delhi. At Lucknow, after several days of suspense, the 7th Light Cavalry, the 13th, 48th, and 71st Native Infantry, and most of the Oudh Irregulars broke into open mutiny on the 30th May- The 9th Native Infantry at Aligarh, the 10th at Fatehgarh, the 12th at Jhansi and Nowgong, the 17th at Azamgarh, the 18th and 68th at Bareilly, the 22nd at Fyzabad, the 28th and 29th at Shahjahanpur and Moradabad, and the 41st at Sitapur, together with many regiments of regular and irregular cavalry, rapidly followed suit. At Benares, on the 4th June, the 37th Native Infantry and 13th Irregular Cavalry rose, and through the deplorable hastiness and want of judgement displayed by the authorities, the Sikh Regiment of Ludhiana was to a great extent involved in the same ruin. On the next day a detachment of this regiment at Jaunpur, which had hitherto been without taint of treason, hearing that their comrades at Benares had been fired on, mutinied and murdered their adjutant. How deplorable was the blunder which turned friends into foes at such a time the services of the sister Regiment of Ferozepore at Allahabad sufficiently testify; and but for the impartial fairness of the court of enquiry on the affair in the following year, the empire would have lost the services, and India the honour, of a regiment which has crowned its splendid record with the salvation of a British Army. The Cawnpore brigade, which included the 2nd Light Cavalry and the 1st, 53rd, and 56th Native Infantry, mutinied on the 5th June; and on the next day the 6th Native Infantry at Allahabad followed the same course. Here, however, the designs of the rebels were foiled by the fidelity of the Regiment of Ferozepore, and, although the mutiny was attended with peculiarly horrible details of massacre and violence, the fort was saved until the arrival of Colonel Neill,[2] 1st Madras Fusiliers, with a small force of British soldiers, when the mutinous 6th marched off to join their comrades at Cawnpore.

Further west, in Rajputana and Malwa, the garrisons of Mhow (the 1st Light Cavalry and the 23rd Native Infantry), Neemuch (the 72nd Native Infantry and the 7th Gwalior Infantry) and Nusseerabad (the 15th and 30th Native Infantry), became infected with the same evil spirit and plunged into rebellion. On their way to Delhi, the point to which all these rebels set their footsteps, the mutineers from

---

2. This was the designation by which this officer was known and probably always will be known, but, according to Burke, his surname was actually "Smith-Neill."

Neemuch, joined by the rebels of the Mehidpur and Kotah Contingents, approached Agra, in the neighbourhood of which place, at Shahganj or Sassia, they were encountered (5th July) by a small force (part of the garrison) consisting of 500 of the 3rd Bengal European Regiment, a battery of artillery and a few volunteer horse. Though mishandled by the Brigadier in command, a brave but not very capable officer, this small force beat back the vastly superior numbers to which it was opposed, but the failure of its ammunition eventually necessitated a retirement to the fort, which was reached after a loss had been sustained of 49 killed and 92 wounded amongst the latter being Major Thomas of the 3rd European Regiment, and Captain D'Oyly and Lieutenant Lamb of the Artillery, who all succumbed to the injuries they had received. The enemy followed in hot pursuit, but without making any impression on the steadiness of the retiring force; but remaining masters of all outside of the fort, they the same evening sacked and destroyed the Agra cantonment and murdered all who had failed to escape to a place of safety.

In the Saugor District some fighting took place. There the native troops consisted of the 3rd Irregular Cavalry and the 31st and 42nd Native Infantry. The 31st remained true to their colours, but the greater part of the other two corps broke away and joined the rebels: the mutineers of the 42nd made their way northwards and, at a later date, were reported to have crossed bayonets with the 78th Highlanders in the action at Bithur. Towards the end of June a detachment, under the command of Major Gaussen, of the 42nd, took the fort of Balabet by storm, with little loss, but in destroying the place immediately afterwards a premature explosion killed Ensign Spens of the 31st and several men, and so seriously injured Lieutenant Willoughby of the Artillery (the brother of the officer who so heroically defended the Delhi magazine) that he died (three years after) from the effects. In September a detachment under Lieutenant-Colonel Dalyell, 42nd, was repulsed in an attack on Naraoli, Dalyell himself being killed in the action. Many other actions were fought during the succeeding months usually with disastrous results for the rebels, and Saugor fort was held until the spring of the following year, when it was relieved by the advance of part of the Central India Field Force under Sir Hugh Rose.

On the 30th of June a detachment under Major Renaud, Madras Fusiliers, started from Allahabad for the relief of Cawnpore; it consisted of 400 British soldiers, 300 Sikhs, 95 irregular cavalry, the faithful remnants of the 13th Bengal and the 3rd Oudh Irregular Cavalry, and two guns. Meanwhile at that city had been enacted one of the most horrible tragedies that even India had ever seen. The little garrison of 200 British officers and men, after three weeks of heroic resistance, capitulated on the 27th June, and as they embarked on country boats at Sati-chaura Ghât, on the Ganges, were massacred indiscriminately by the troops of the Nana Dundhu Pant (the adopted son and heir of Baji Rao, the last of the Peshwas), which were drawn up for the purpose on the river bank. Of the whole, only two officers (Lieutenants Delafosse and Thomson, 53rd Native Infantry) and two men escaped; a great number of the women and children were taken back to Cawnpore, there to be kept in miserable captivity until the near approach of an avenging force impelled their ruthless captor to complete the work of massacre before his victims could be torn from his grasp.

On the 10th July news of the fall of Cawnpore reached Brigadier-General Havelock, commanding the field force moving up to the relief of that place and of Lucknow, and, fearing for the safety of Renaud's little force, he sent orders to him to halt until he could join him with such additional troops as he could muster. These were only 1,000 British infantry (detachments of the 64th, 78th, and 84th Foot and of the 1st Madras Fusiliers), 130 Sikhs of the Regiment of Ferozepore, 20 volunteer cavalry, and six guns. He overtook and joined Renaud at Fatehpur on the 12th July, and with the united force, now consisting of 1,400 British and 560 Native troops, with eight guns, he met and defeated the rebel army on the same day, and marched into Fatehpur, destined now to pay the penalty of its revolt five weeks before, and of the murder by the 6th Native Infantry of the district judge, Mr. R. T. Tucker. On the 15th two more victories, at Aoung and the Pandu Naddi, were gained over the rebels, in the former of which the gallant Renaud was mortally wounded; and on the 16th, at Ahirwa, near Cawnpore, the Nana's forces were finally scattered, and Cawnpore was once more in the hands of the British.

But though the rebels were defeated, the victory had come too late to save the unhappy women and children held in captivity by the Nana, that miscreant having caused the whole of them to be massacred in the most barbarous manner on the 15th. The garrison of the Lucknow Residency, however, equally heroic and in almost equal straits, still remained to be succoured. But it was not until the 25th July that Havelock was in a position to cross the Ganges into Oudh. His troops numbered barely 1,400 and he had to traverse a country which was wholly in the hands of the revolted sepoys, who were ready to dispute every inch of his advance. On the 29th he twice defeated the enemy at Unao and Bashiratganj, but with his force weakened by cholera and sun-stroke, he was forced to fall back to Mangalwar. On the 4th August he again advanced, and on the 5th, for the second time, defeated the rebels at Bashiratganj; but difficulties were thickening around him; several thousand sepoys threatened Colonel Neill at Cawnpore; and the 7th, 8th, and 40th Native Infantry at Dinapore, having followed the course of the rest on July 25th, were said to be moving on his rear; so, once more Havelock fell back to Mangalwar, and commenced the construction of a bridge-of-boats across the Ganges. Once more the enemy re-assembled, and again Havelock marched out and defeated and dispersed them, this time at Burbia-ki-Chauki, on the 12th. Next day he re-crossed the Ganges to Cawnpore, but finding that the Nana had re-collected his forces at Bithur, he marched up to that place, and there, on the 16th, inflicted a crushing defeat on the rebels. Then, much against his will, he was compelled to return to Cawnpore, there to await the arrival of reinforcements from Calcutta.

For a month after the general mutiny at Lucknow on the 30th May, Sir Henry Lawrence, with the aid of his small British force and the native artillery, which then remained faithful, retained command of the city and cantonments. On the 30th June he marched out against the mutineers at Chinhat, but was fearfully out-numbered, and, being deserted by the native gunners in the face of the enemy, was constrained to retreat as best he could, and, weakened by losses and desertion, to confine his defensive position to the grounds of the Residency. Two days later, Sir Henry was mortally wounded by augment of a shell, and died on the 4th July, the most regretted, and perhaps the greatest, of the many victims of 1857. The command of the garrison devolved on Colonel Inglis, of the 32nd Foot, who for thirteen weeks sustained the unequal contest, until relieved by Havelock and Outram on September the 25th.

The first reinforcements of British troops from Calcutta reached Cawnpore under Sir James Outram on the 10th September: the relief column immediately started again towards Lucknow, commanded not by Outram, the senior officer, but by Havelock, to whom the former, with noble generosity, surrendered the command in order that he might have the honour of finishing the work he had so well begun. Determined resistance was encountered at Mangalwar and the

Alambagh on the 21st and 23rd, and in the city of Lucknow on the 25th and 26th, and then, after thirty-six hours of hard fighting and with a loss of 196 killed, among whom was the gallant Neill, and 339 wounded, the column entered the Residency, and the first relief of Lucknow was accomplished.

It is impossible here to notice the many Indian officers whose names appear in Colonel Inglis's despatch on the defence of Lucknow and whose gallantry aided in saving the garrison. Small share of the honour of the defence can be claimed by the native ranks of the Bengal Army; but few as were their numbers, to none is more honour due than to the faithful remnants of the 13th, 48th, and 71st Native Infantry, who vied with their British comrades in the steadfast ardour of their courage, and who well deserved the rewards bestowed on them by Government,—the Order of Merit to every man, and the honour of forming the nucleus of a corps which still bears the name of "The Lucknow Regiment."

The months of June, July, and August had been eventful ones in the Punjab and on the ridge before Delhi. Two unfortunate outbreaks occurred,—at Jhelum and Sialkot. At the former place the sepoys of the 14th Native Infantry were manifestly disaffected, and a force of sufficient strength was sent down from Rawal Pindi to disarm them. It reached Jhelum on the 7th July, but the affair was mismanaged and a conflict took place; the sepoys, beaten and driven from their lines, took refuge in the village of Samli, but in an attack on them in this position the British force was repulsed with considerable loss (44 killed and 109 wounded), and during the night most of the mutineers escaped with their arms, though they left large numbers of dead behind them. The news of this affair was the signal for the rising of the 9th Light Cavalry and the 46th Native Infantry at Sialkot, who threw open the gaol, plundered the treasury, burned the cantonments, and then marched off towards Delhi. But ready to intercept their march was John Nicholson with his moveable column. Marching from Amritsar on the 10th July, he reached Trimu Ghât, on the Ravi, on the morning of the 12th, met and defeated the insurgents there, and completed their destruction on the 16th, so thoroughly that hardly a man escaped of those who had marched from Sialkot. Returning to, Amritsar, Nicholson soon received orders to march with his force, to which the 4th Sikh Infantry from Ludhiana was added, to join the main army before Delhi; and on the 7th August he was in the camp on the Ridge, followed a week later by the moveable column. The force before Delhi was now under the command of Brigadier-General A. Wilson, Sir Henry Barnard having died of cholera on the 5th July, and his successor, Major-General Reed, C.B., having been compelled, by broken health, to retire to the hills.

All this time John Lawrence was hard at work at Lahore. Cut off from communication with Calcutta and knowing well that months must elapse before fresh British troops could arrive from that direction, he turned to the splendid material which was ready to his hand, and, profiting by the jealousy and hatred which existed between Hindustani and Punjabi, he sent regiment after regiment of Sikhs, Pathans, and Punjabi Musalmans to swell the British forces before Delhi. Hodson's Horse, the 1st Sikh Irregular Cavalry (now the 11th Bengal Lancers), eighteen new regiments of infantry (including two of Mazbi pioneers), were all raised in the Punjab between June and September 1857, and took the places there of older corps or were sent to join the forces in the field. About the same time an extra regiment of Gurkhas (now the 1st Battalion of the 4th) was raised at Petoragarh, to aid in the protection of the Kumaon Hills against the rebels of Rohilkhand. The Sirmoor and Kumaon Battalions of Gurkhas, the Corps of Guides, the 2nd and 5th Punjab Cavalry, the 4th Sikh Infantry, and the 1st, 2nd, and 4th Punjab Infantry, were fighting on the ridge in August; while, of the new levies, there were one regiment of pioneers and Hodson's Horse, the first of the Punjabi regiments of Bengal cavalry, raised in the early days of the Mutiny by the intrepid leader whose name it bears, and employed under his command in winning its first laurels in many an exciting combat under the walls of Delhi.

Since the commencement of the siege, a constant succession of attacks and sorties on the part of the enemy had worn out our army, and had placed it in the position of a besieged rather than of a besieging force. But the arrival of Nicholson with his reinforcements altered the aspect of affairs. The long-expected siege train from Ferozepore was but a few marches distant; more reinforcements were expected; and it was evident to all men that the period of waiting was approaching a termination. One more conflict was necessary before the last scene of the siege should begin. The rebels had sent out a strong force to intercept the approaching siege train, and it was imperative that their attempt should be frustrated. Nicholson was chosen for the duty. Marching out of camp with a well chosen force, including a squadron of the Guides Cavalry and the 1st and 2nd Punjab Infantry, he encountered and utterly dispersed the rebels at Najafgarh on the

25th August, sustaining, however, rather severe loss, twenty-five killed (including Lieutenant Lumsden, 1st Punjab Infantry) and sixty-seven wounded. The siege train arrived in safety on the 3rd September; for a week the city was exposed to a terrific and incessant bombardment; and then, on the morning of the 14th September, the long-looked for assault was made.

The assaulting force was divided into four columns and a reserve, as follows:

Col.			Men
1st	Brigadier-General Nicholson	H. M.'s 75th Foot	300
		1st Bengal European Fusiliers	250
		2nd Punjab Infantry	450
	Orders	To storm the breach to the left of the Kashmir Bastion, and to escalade the face of the bastion	
2nd	Brigadier W. Jones, C.B.	H. M.'s 8th Foot	250
		2nd Bengal European Fusiliers	250
		4th Sikh Infantry	350
	Orders	To storm the breach in the Water Bastion	
3rd	Colonel C. Campbell 52nd Light Infantry	H. M.'s 52nd Light Infantry	200
		Kumaon Battalion	250
		1st Punjab Infantry	500
	Orders	To assault the Kashmir Gate	
4th	Major Charles Reid Sirmoor Battalion	H. M.'s 60th Foot (Rifle's)	50
		H. M.'s 61st Foot	80
		1st Bengal European Fusiliers	160
		Sirmoor Battalion	200
		Kumaon Battalion	65
		Infantry of the Corps of Guides	200

		1st Punjab Infantry	25
		Total	780
		Kashmir Contingent	400
		Mounted Police	100
	Orders	To clear the suburb of Kishanganj and enter the Kabul Gate	
Reserve	Brigadier J. Longfield 8th Foot	H. M.'s 61st Foot	250
		4th Punjab Infantry	450
		Baluch Battalion	300
		Jhind Contingent	300
		H. M.'s 60th Rifles	200
		after covering the advance of the stormers	

The storming parties moved forward soon after daybreak on the 14th September. The first column, its advance covered by the riflemen of the 60th, having escaladed the left face of the Kashmir Bastion and carried the breach in the curtain to the left of it, moved to the right, and, in conjunction with the second column, captured the Mori Bastion and the Kabul Gate. In attempting a further advance towards the Lahore Gate, Brigadier-General Nicholson fell mortally wounded, and the remains of the column retired to the Kabul Gate. The second column, likewise covered by the fire of the 60th, carried the breach in the Water Bastion, a part diverging to the right, making their way in by the other breach to the left of the Kashmir Bastion, then turning to the right, in cooperation with the first column, it took the Mori Bastion and the Kabul Gate, and occupied the houses in the neighbourhood of the latter. The third column, after blowing in the Kashmir Gate, one of the most daring exploits recorded in military annals and a deed reflecting undying glory on the Bengal Sappers and Miners, penetrated into the city to the neighbourhood of the Jumma Masjid, but being unable to attack that point without artillery was compelled to fall back on the reserve at the church. The fourth column alone met with a repulse. It was checked in Kishanganj by barricades strongly defended by the enemy; deprived of the capable leadership of Major Reid, who was wounded early in the day, the column, after a severe conflict, was compelled to fall back, and the enemy, who pressed on its rear, were only kept in check by the firmness of the Cavalry Brigade (the 9th Lancers, and detachments of the 1st, 2nd, and 5th Punjab Cavalry, Hodson's Horse and Guides), who for two hours sat motionless on their horses, exposed to a heavy fire and suffering severe and incessant loss.

On the whole, the first day of the attack was successful, though not completely so. The 15th was devoted to securing the positions we had won. On the 16th the fighting was resumed, and the great magazine seized, and, after four more days of conflict, the British were in complete possession of the city.

Our loss in the assault was very heavy, amounting to 299 killed, 877 wounded, and ten missing. Of the Bengal Army, Lieutenant F. L. Tandy, of the Engineers, Captain G. G. McBarnet (55th Native Infantry), attached to the 1st Bengal Fusiliers, Lieutenant A. W. Murray, of the Guides, and Ensign J. T. Davidson, of the 2nd Punjab Infantry, were killed; and Brigadier-General Nicholson, Lieutenant P. Salkeld, of the Engineers, Major G. O. Jacob, 1st Bengal Fusiliers, Lieutenant E. Speke (65th Native Infantry), attached to the same regiment, Lieutenant C. H. F. Gambier (38th Native Infantry), attached to the 2nd Bengal Fusiliers, and Lieutenant R. P. Homfray, 4th Punjab Infantry, died of the wounds they received. The operations of the succeeding six days involved a further loss of 50 killed, 123 wounded, and one missing.

Thus ended the siege of Delhi. But, although the city and palace princes, were in our hands, the royal family, who represented the head of this great rebellion, though in truth they were so only in name, had escaped and were in hiding in the suburbs. On the 21st September news was brought to Lieutenant Hodson, who was chief of the Intelligence Staff, that the king and princes of Delhi were at the tomb of Humayun, some four miles from the city. Taking only fifty of his own Punjabi troopers, he galloped out to the spot, and after a delay of two hours, during which Hodson stood alone facing an angry crowd of many hundreds of the defeated monarch's followers, the last of the Moghul Emperors, preceded by his favourite wife and her son, came out in a palankin and surrendered himself. On the following day, with his second-in-command, Lieutenant McDowell, and a hundred troopers, Hodson again visited the tomb and demanded the unconditional surrender of the three shahzadahs in hiding there. Again his stern and unflinching courage prevailed over the timorous multitude before him, and he carried back his captives towards the city. But as they neared the gates the crowd, moved by the thought that the last of the monarchy of the Moghuls, "still a living influence in India," was being taken from them, began to surge with threatening murmurs round the little band of horsemen and their charge. To both the British officers it seemed that any moment might bring an attempt at rescue. Ever ready to act when necessity demanded, Hodson determined to settle the matter at once, and fearing the chance of any hesitation if the work were entrusted to one of his troopers, he himself seized a carbine and shot his captives with his own hand. Even in the midst of the thrilling story of the Indian Mutiny we must linger for a moment over this episode. Apart from the extraordinary determination and brilliant courage displayed by Hodson, the capture of the emperor and the killing of the princes were deeds of which the effects were exceptional. No individual act did so much to stem the tide of the rebellion and to deprive it of a national character; nor did any other excite such attention at the moment or such diverse criticism afterwards. For a moment no dissentient voice was heard amidst the chorus of approval which greeted the exploit, and when we read the arguments of those who have since assailed the memory of Hodson let us not forget the words of one of the fairest of them:

> Seldom, if ever, since war began had there been so much to exacerbate and infuriate an army as then inflamed the brains and fevered the blood of the men who found themselves in the bloodstained city.

The siege and capture of Delhi cost us in all 3,537 in killed and wounded—a heavy list, but productive of great results; for with the capture of the capital disappeared the trust of the people of India in the ultimate success of the revolt. But it is necessary, before proceeding with the story of the re-establishment of our influence, to glance at some of the minor details of the Mutiny in Bengal and the North-West Provinces.

At Calcutta, while the governor-general was worn out with anxiety and work, little occurred to excite the alarm of the inhabitants, except the receipt of news from the North-West, disturbing enough in itself and often exaggerated tenfold in the transit. So excited, however, did the people become by these rumours, that Lord Canning was at length induced, contrary to his own convictions, to disarm the native troops at Barrackpore. Amongst these were the 43rd and the 70th Native Infantry, both of which regiments had expressed their readiness to be led against the mutineers, and neither of which had ever shown the least signs of disaffection. They were disarmed on the 14th June, and the business was made the occasion of an ignominious panic on the part of both the Christian inhabitants of Calcutta and the sepoys themselves; the latter imagining that the seizure of their arms was a preliminary to their massacre, the former expecting momentarily to hear that the disarmament had been resisted and that the sepoys were marching against the capital.

It is useless to recapitulate the tale of mutinies and massacres of May, June, and July. In a volume which treats of the services of the Bengal Army, it would be out of place to recount the details of the ignominious end to which the old army brought its century of honourable service. Nor is it possible to relate the many brilliant actions of the Bengal officers, even were such relation necessary. Bareilly, Agra, and the North-West; Nusseerabad, Mhow, Jhansi, and Central India—none of these offer much opportunity of telling of faithful sepoys. An exception, however, may be made of the 8th Irregular Cavalry at Bareilly, where, though the men mutinied, the native officers set a splendid example of loyalty, and left their families and property to aid their English officers in their flight.

Few incidents of the Mutiny are more celebrated than the heroic defence of the house at Arrah, in Bihar, during the first week of August. The sepoys of the Dinapore brigade mutinied on July 27th, and on the same day approached the station of Arrah, in which were eleven Europeans and fifty Sikhs of Captain Rattray's police battalion (now the 45th Bengal Infantry). This little party, unequal as was the contest, determined to defend themselves where they stood, rather than seek safety in flight. Having hastily put into such a state of defence as they could the house of one of their number, they held it for seven days against all attacks of the rebels, who numbered fully 2,000 armed men, as well as a vast rabble of unarmed insurgents. Attempts to relieve them were not wanting, but an expedition despatched from Dinapore, which included detachments of the 10th and 37th Foot and Rattray's Sikhs, was ambuscaded during a night march, and had to retreat with heavy loss. At length, when the provisions of the little party were running short and there seemed no chance for them but to attempt to cut their way through the enemy under the cover of night, deliverance suddenly appeared in the person of Major Vincent Eyre, of the Bengal Artillery, who, having by great efforts collected a small force at Buxar, and defeated the rebels at Bibiganj, marched into Arrah on the 3rd August. The faithful Sikhs of the garrison received well-earned rewards and decorations.

They, with a further detachment of their regiment, were attached to Major Eyre's force; and no corps did more—few so much—towards restoring the authority of the British in the months that followed, as the gallant battalion of Rattray's Sikhs.

General Wilson was not long in following up the final success of the 20th September. On the 24th a column of 2,800 men, including 200 Punjab pioneers (now the 32nd Bengal Infantry), detachments of the 1st, 2nd, and 5th Punjab Cavalry and of Hodson's Horse, and the 2nd and 4th Punjab Infantry, marched from Delhi under Colonel Greathed of the 8th Foot. The enemy were met with and defeated at Bulandshahr, with a loss on our side of forty-seven killed and wounded. The force then proceeded by double stages to Agra, where they arrived on October 10th, having covered sixty miles in thirty-six hours. Scarcely was the camp laid out, and the men about to get some food and rest, when they found themselves suddenly assailed by the mutineers from Mhow (the 1st Light Cavalry and the 23rd Native Infantry) reinforced by fugitives from Delhi, who were advancing to the attack of Agra. The enemy, however, were not aware that any force greater than the Agra garrison was in front of them, and were as much taken by surprise as the British, and with more disastrous results to themselves. They were thoroughly beaten and dispersed, and Greathed's force moved on towards Cawnpore.

Shortly after Greathed marched from Delhi, another column set out under Brigadier-General Showers. It included detachments of Hodson's Horse and of the Guides Cavalry, the Kumaon Battalion, and the 1st Punjab Infantry. Marching westwards, as far as the edge of the Bikanir desert, it captured several leading rebels, but no organised resistance was encountered, and the column soon afterwards returned to Delhi.

Hardly had it returned, however, when the advance of the Jodhpur Legion,[3] which had mutinied at Erinpura and was making its way northwards, necessitated the despatch of a second force in the same direction. It included the 7th Punjab Infantry (now the 19th Bengal Infantry), a detachment of the Guides, and Lind's Multani Horse, and was commanded by Lieutenant-Colonel J. G. Gerrard. The column reached Rewari on the 13th November, and two days later was reinforced by the 23rd Punjab Infantry (now the 31st Bengal Infantry).

---

3. The Jodhpur Legion consisted of a detail of artillery, three *rissalahs* of cavalry and a battalion (eight companies) of sepoys. It was formed in 1835, and mutinied at Erinpura in August 1857.

The enemy were found at Narnaul on the 16th, were vigorously attacked, and completely defeated and dispersed. Our loss amounted to eight killed and 76 wounded; amongst the latter was Colonel Gerrard, who was shot through the body and died within a few hours.

At Lucknow the arrival of the force under Sir James Outram and Sir Henry Havelock was followed by a period of difficulty almost as great as that experienced during the preceding' part of the siege, the only difference being that the British position was extended, and that the increased number of the garrison allowed them to act to some extent on the offensive, instead of being confined strictly to the defensive.

In the meantime reinforcements (including the remainder of the troops intercepted *en route* to China,—a part having already come in time to take part in the first relief of Lucknow) had been arriving at Calcutta, and the forethought and energy of the new Commander-in-Chief, Sir Colin Campbell, who had arrived on the 13th August, provided means of transporting this welcome aid, with the least possible delay to the disturbed districts. On the 27th October Sir Colin himself started from Calcutta, and arrived at Cawnpore on the 3rd of November. Leaving a force to hold that place, under Major-General Windham, he pushed on towards Lucknow and arrived at the Alambagh on November 12th. Here on the 13th he made his final dispositions for the relief of our garrison in the Residency. The troops composing his force were as follow:

Cavalry Brigade		2 squadrons 9th Lancers
		1 squadron 1st Punjab Cavalry
		1 squadron 2nd Punjab Cavalry
		1 squadron 5th Punjab Cavalry
		1 squadron Hodson's Horse
Engineers		1 company Royal Engineers
		1 company Madras Sappers
		2 companies Punjab Pioneers
Infantry	3rd Brigade	5th Foot (detachment)
		8th Foot
		64th Foot (detachment)
		78th Foot (detachment)
		2nd Punjab Infantry
	4th Brigade	53rd Foot (wing)

       84th Foot (detachment)
       90th Foot (detachment)
       93rd Foot (detachment)
       1st Madras Fusiliers (detachment)
       4th Punjab Infantry
5th Brigade 23rd Foot
       82nd Foot (detachment)

  There were also a heavy battery manned by the Naval Brigade of H.M.S. *Shannon,* under Captain Sir William Peel, a field battery, and two troops and a half of horse artillery.

  On the morning of the 14th November the Dilkusha Park and the Martinière House were attacked and carried, and an attempt made by the enemy later in the day to recover their lost ground was repulsed. The 15th was occupied in preparations for a further advance and in perfecting measures for the security of the baggage, which was all left at Dilkusha. On the 16th took place the hardest fighting in the attack: a small breach, which had been made by the fire of the heavy guns in the east wall of the Sikandarabagh, was carried by a gallant rush of two companies of the 93rd Highlanders, while the remainder of that gallant regiment, the 53rd, the 4th Punjab Infantry, and a battalion made up of detachments of the 84th and 90th and the 1st Madras Fusiliers, forced their way in at other points; the post had been occupied by more than two thousand of the rebels, mostly sepoys of the 71st Native Infantry and the Oudh Irregular Force, and hardly a man escaped. The remainder of the day was occupied in an attack on a building named the Shah Najaf, which was eventually carried after we had suffered heavy loss. On the 17th a building called the "Mess House" and the Moti Mahall were carried, as well as Banks' House on the left, and the garrison at last joined hands with their rescuers. In effecting this the relieving force had sustained a loss of 122 killed, 414 wounded, and five missing; among the killed were Lieutenant-Colonel Biddulph and Captain Mayne, serving on the staff, Captain Lumsden of the 30th Native Infantry, attached to the 93rd Highlanders, and Lieutenant Frankland, 2nd Punjab Infantry; Lieutenants Halkett, Hodson's Horse, and Paul and Oldfield, 4th Punjab Infantry, died of their wounds, and the commander-in-chief was himself among the wounded. The following days were spent in reconnaissance of the roads, and in the withdrawal, on the night of the 22nd, of the garrison of the Residency, under cover of a heavy bombardment of the Kaisar-Bagh. By the 23rd November the work of withdrawal had been effected; Sir Colin Campbell fell back on Dilkusha, and the second relief of Lucknow was complete. Our further loss in the fighting at Lucknow from the 19th to the 22nd November was only one killed and fifteen wounded. The general satisfaction at the successful completion of the relief was, however, marred by the loss of Sir Henry Havelock, who died on the 24th November and was buried at the Alambagh.

It was now necessary for the commander-in-chief, having left Outram with a small force at the Alambagh, to hasten back to Cawnpore with all possible speed. The little force left at that place had, soon after the departure of the army, been threatened by the advance of the rebel Gwalior Contingent under Tantia Topi, one of the miscreants concerned in the massacre at Cawnpore, and by far the most capable native leader who appeared during the mutinies. Windham, finding that his communications with Lucknow were severed, endeavoured to gain time by aggressive measures, and attacked the Gwalior Contingent at the Pandu Nadi on the 26th November. In this unequal conflict the British were successful, and then fell back on Cawnpore. Here they were attacked by Tantia Topi on the 27th and 28th, and, overwhelmed by numbers, after severe and continuous fighting, outflanked and forced back on their entrenchments, leaving the city wholly in the hands of the rebels. A worse disaster, the destruction of the bridge-of-boats, appeared to be impending, when on the 29th, the arrival of Sir Colin Campbell and his force, from Lucknow, put a new face on the aspect of affairs and interposed to prevent the threatened calamity. After allowing some days to pass, during which the convoy of women, children, and wounded got well on the way to Allahabad, Sir Colin attacked the enemy on the 6th December, turned their right by a brilliant movement, in which the 4th Punjab Infantry were again conspicuous, seized their camp, and on the following day completed the defeat of their army and entirely dispersed them.

Whilst the commander-in-chief was compelled to remain for some time inactive for want of transport, a force under Colonel Seaton was advancing from the direction of Delhi, escorting stores for the army at Cawnpore. This column included Hodson's Horse, the 7th Punjab Infantry (now the 19th Bengal Infantry), the 1st Bengal European Fusiliers, and 120 Punjab Pioneers. The first engagement between this force and the rebels took place at Gangari, between Aligarh and Khasganj, on the 14th December, on which occasion, as well as at Patiali on the 17th and at Mainpuri on the 27th, the enemy were defeated with little difficulty. Shortly afterwards Seaton, reinforced by a party of the newly raised 1st Sikh Irregular Cavalry (now the 11th Bengal Lancers), effected a junction with the commander-in-chief at Fatehgarh.

After three weeks' detention at Cawnpore, transport having at length arrived, Sir Colin Campbell marched thence on the 24th December and met and completely defeated a rebel force at the Kali Nadi, near Fatehgarh, on the 2nd January. At the latter place he was joined by Seaton and his convoy, as already stated, and preparations were pushed on for the recapture of Lucknow. Whilst these were in progress a column, composed of the 42nd and 53rd Foot, the 4th Punjab Infantry, one troop of horse artillery and a field battery, two squadrons of the 9th Lancers, and Hodson's Horse, encountered a large force of the Oudh rebels at Shamshabad, about thirteen miles from Fatehgarh, on the 27th January, and defeated them with great loss. On the 26th February all preparations were at last completed, and the commander-in-chief again marched from Cawnpore in the direction of Lucknow.

In the meantime, at the Alambagh, Outram, with his force of 4,000 men (including the Sikh Regiment of Ferozepore), was holding his own gallantly against the rebel army, which now numbered close on 100,000. For some weeks after the relief of Lucknow the enemy were too much disheartened by their reverses to make any further hostile effort. But at length, towards the end of December, they began to take heart again, and between the 23rd of that month and the 16th of January they made several determined attacks on the British position; their ill success, however, on every occasion, soon damped their ardour, and it was not until the active preparations at Cawnpore showed the rebels that if Outram was to be overwhelmed the blow must be struck at once, ere the arrival of reinforcements made it too late, that they mustered up courage to again assail the position at the Alambagh. On the 15th, 16th, and 21st of February, they advanced to the attack, and each time were repulsed; finally, a last desperate attempt was made on the 25th, but by this time strong reinforcements had arrived at the Alambagh and the rebels were completely defeated.

About the same time the Jaunpur Field Force (which included three British battalions and an allied force of 3,000 Gurkhas of the Nepal Army) entered Oudh from the south-east under the command of Brigadier-General Franks, and moving up towards Luck-now, defeated the rebels in sharp actions at Chanda, Hamirpur, and Sultanpur, and captured the fort of Dhaurara.

Sir Colin Campbell arrived at the Alambagh on the 1st March, and on the following day the operations against Lucknow were commenced. The troops at his disposal were sufficiently numerous to allow of a carefully considered and widely extensive plan of operations being followed in the attack on Lucknow. The enemy's lines of defence were very strong except on the north side, where their position was bounded by the river GumtiGumti, and no precautions had been taken to strengthen this natural protection. It was determined, therefore, that while the main force turned the right of the rebel position, one division should cross the river and take it in reverse. Operations were commenced on the 2nd March by the seizure of Dilkusha Park; and three days later, the interval having been occupied in constructing two bridges over the river, the arrival of the force under Brigadier-General Franks placed Sir Colin Campbell in a position to proceed with the execution of his plans. Sir James Outram crossed the Gumti on the 6th, with a division which included the 2nd and detachments of the 1st and 5th Punjab Cavalry, and the 2nd Punjab Infantry; and advancing up the left bank of the river for three days he drove the enemy before him, and established batteries which enfiladed their first line of defence, and rendered it untenable. Meanwhile, the commander-in-chief had carried the Martinière on the 9th and Banks' House on the 10th; and on the following day the Sikandarabagh and the Shah Najaf were occupied without opposition, and the 93rd Highlanders and the 4th Punjab Infantry stormed the Begum Koti. Important as these operations were they were effected with comparatively small loss in point of numbers, though the death of Major Hodson, who was mortally wounded at the Begum Koti, was a great loss to the army.

Throughout the next four days the advance steadily continued, until on the 14th the Imambara was stormed by the 10th Foot and the Regiment of Ferozepore, the second and third lines of the enemy's defence were turned, and the great stronghold of the Kaisar-Bagh captured On the 16th Outram re-crossed the Gumti, and on Sunday, the 2ist, after a sharp fight in the city, in which the 4th Punjab Infantry suffered some loss, and another on the outskirts of the place, in which the commander of the 1st Sikh Irregular Cavalry was killed, the capture of Lucknow was completed and the city cleared of the rebels.

The loss of the British in the twenty days' operations was 127 killed, 595 wounded and thirteen missing. Among those who were killed or died of their wounds were Captain F Wale 1st Sikh Irregular Cavalry; Major C. A. Sanford, 5th Punjab Cavalry; Major W. S. R. Hodson, of Hodson's Horse; Captain L. G. DaCosta, Regiment of Ferozepore; Lieutenant A. J. Anderson, 2nd Punjab Infantry; and Lieutenants O. D. Thackwell, 15th, and J. Cape, 30th Native Infantry employed on the staff.

On the day after the fall of Lucknow, Sir J. Hope Grant with a force in which were included portions of the 1st and 2nd Punjab Cavalry and the 2nd Punjab Infantry, went in pursuit of a body of rebels who had retreated in a northerly direction He overtook them at Kursi and, with a trifling loss of thirteen killed and wounded, defeated and dispersed them and captured fourteen guns.

The preceding months, while all the available strength of the army had been concentrated for operations at Lucknow had been a time of some danger in other parts of India. Particularly was this the case in Eastern Bengal, where much disturbance was caused by three companies of the 34th Native Infantry, who had mutinied at Chittagong on the 18th November, endeavouring to make their way thence towards the hills of Manipur. Before they could reach those difficult jungles, however, they were pursued with forced marches by a detachment of the Sylhet Light Infantry, under Major the Honourable R. B. P. Byng, who defeated them at Latu on the 8th December, but himself unfortunately fell in the action. Thence turning their steps northwards, they were overtaken by further disaster, and finally dispersed by three separate defeats at the hands of detachments of the Sylhet Light Infantry, on the 12th, 22nd, and 26th of January 1858.

Towards the end of 1857 a force was put in the field in the Gorakhpur district under the command of Brigadier Rowcroft. It was composed at first of two battalions of the allied Gurkha forces, the Naval Brigade of H.M.S. *Pearl,* and a detachment of Rattray's Sikhs, but it was joined subsequently by the 13th Light Infantry, the Bengal Yeomanry Cavalry, and some Madras cavalry. With this force Rowcroft was in frequent conflict with the rebels, whom he defeated at Sohanpur and Phulpur, and no less than three times at Amorha.

In the meantime the troubles in the districts to the south-east of Oudh had been on the increase, and a small force under Colonel Milman, 37th Foot, was hard pressed by the rebels at Azamgarh; on the fall of Lucknow, therefore, the commander-in-chief lost no time in despatching a column under Brigadier-General Sir Edward Lugard in that direction. This force was composed of three British infantry regiments, eighteen guns, and 700 cavalry, including the 3rd Sikh Irregular Cavalry and the remains of the 12th Bengal Irregular Cavalry. Lugard marched from Lucknow on the 29th March; met and defeated a rebel force at Manihar, near Tigra, on the 11th April; drove the enemy under Kunwar Singh,[4] the rebel chief of Jagdeshpur, in Shahabad, from before Azamgarh on the 15th; and with a detachment of his column completely defeated him at Azimatgarh on the 17th, at Mannahar on the 20th April, and at Shiupur Ghât on the 21st. Sorely wounded in one of these engagements, Kunwar Singh made his way across the Ganges to Jagdeshpur, crushing on his way, on the 23rd April, a small force of Sikh and British troops, under the command of Captain Le Grand, 35th Foot, who had moved out from Arrah to intercept him. In the jungles of Jagdeshpur the rebels, under Kunwar Singh and (after that noted chief had succumbed to his wound) under his brother Umar Singh, made a prolonged and desperate stand against the force under Sir Edward Lugard, who had promptly followed them across the Ganges, and kept it continually employed throughout the hot weather and rains; during these months more than one sharp encounter took place in the recesses of the forest, and it was not until October and November, when Brigadier Douglas was in command (Lugard having been invalided), that the rebels were finally driven out of their fastnesses and defeated and dispersed, a consummation to which a body of mounted riflemen, under the command of Major Sir H. M. Havelock, materially contributed. In the operations of October 1858, in the Jagdeshpur jungles, the 20th Punjab Infantry (now the 28th Bengal Infantry) were actively employed.

Subsequent to the fall of Lucknow three columns were set in motion to clear Rohilkhand of the rebels, and ultimately to converge on Bareilly. Of these, the first was commanded by Major-General Penny, who, without meeting the rebels in any decisive encounter, fell, during a night march, into an ambush at Kakrauli, and was killed. The second column, under Brigadier-General Walpole, was composed of the head-quarters of the 9th Lancers, the 2nd Punjab Cavalry, the Highland Brigade (42nd, 79th, and 93rd Foot) and the 4th Punjab Infantry, with some artillery and a few sappers. Marching on the 7th April, little resistance was met with except at the fort of Ruiya, near

---

4. Kunwar Singh (commonly called "Kooer Singh") was the leader of all the rebels and mutineers in Shahabad and Bihar.

Rhodamau, where, on the 15th, an imprudent attack, made without adequate reconnaissance, was the cause of a check accompanied by heavy loss, of which the item most widely felt was the death of Brigadier the Honourable Adrian Hope. The third column, commanded first by Lieutenant-Colonel Coke, of the 1st Punjab Infantry, and afterwards by Brigadier Jones (60th Rifles), moved from Roorkee, and was composed of Cureton's Multani Cavalry, the 60th Rifles, the 1st Sikh Infantry, the 1st Punjab Infantry, and the 17th Punjab Infantry (now the 25th Bengal Infantry). By this force the rebels were defeated on April 17th at Bhagaula, and again on the 21st at Nagina, whence the column marched through Moradabad to Bareilly, arriving there on the 6th May, having on the preceding day defeated the rebels in a smart action on the banks of the Dojura River, in which a loss of four killed and twenty-two wounded was sustained. Here Jones' column joined the division under the commander-in-chief, on whose advance Bareilly had, after a sharp action, been evacuated by the rebels. The force with Sir Colin Campbell included Walpole's column, and besides artillery and engineers, was composed of two squadrons of the 6th Dragoon Guards, the 9th Lancers, the 2nd Punjab Cavalry, Lind's Multani Horse, and detachments of the Lahore Light Horse, the 1st and 5th Punjab Cavalry, and the 17th Irregular Cavalry; the 42nd, 64th, 78th, 79th, 82nd, and 93rd Foot, the 2nd and 22nd Punjab Infantry (the latter now the 30th Bengal Infantry), and the Baluch Battalion (now the 27th Bombay Infantry). Brigadier Jones, having subsequently been sent to relieve Shahjahanpur, where a small garrison was beleaguered, was himself attacked (15th May) by the notorious rebel, Maulvi Ahmadulla of Fyzabad; repulsing him with ease, Jones followed up the rebels and again defeated them at Mohamdi on the 25th May; and the rebels then retreated into Oudh. The Maulvi himself was shortly afterwards killed in a fight with a fellow-rebel, the Rajah of Pawayan, in the Shahjahanpur district.

In Oudh numerous bodies of rebels kept the troops fully employed. Against one of these, which had assembled near Bari, under the command of the Maulvi above-mentioned, Sir J. Hope Grant, in the month of April 1858, led a force which included a squadron of Hodson's Horse, a squadron of the 1st Sikh Irregular Cavalry, and a wing of the 5th Punjab Infantry: he encountered them on the 13th and totally defeated them, and again overthrew them at Sirsi, near Nagar, on the 12th May. In the following month a strong column, under the same officer, moved out against the rebels: it was composed of two squadrons of the 2nd Dragoon Guards, the 7th Hussars, 500 of Hodson's Horse, 150 of the 1st Sikh Irregular Cavalry, 250 mounted police, some horse artillery, the 2nd and 3rd Battalions of the Rifle Brigade, and the 5th Punjab Infantry. This force met and, after a sharp conflict, in which it sustained a loss of sixty-seven officers and men killed and wounded, inflicted a severe defeat on the rebels at Nawabganj on the 13th June. On the 22nd July, Grant with a detachment marched to the relief of Rajah Man Singh, an influential chief who, after much vacillation, had thrown in his lot with the British, and whom the rebels were now besieging in his fort of Shahganj, near Fyzabad; the enemy, however, retired without risking an action, and Fyzabad was re-occupied. A fortnight later another column started under Brigadier Horsford, and was afterwards joined by Sir J. Hope Grant and the 2nd Battalion of the Rifle Brigade. It consisted, besides artillery, of the 7th Hussars, the 9th Lancers, 300 of Hodson's Horse, the 1st Sikh Irregular Cavalry, the 53rd Foot, the 1st Madras Fusiliers, and the 5th Punjab Infantry. Without encountering any serious opposition the column reached Sultanporepore on the 20th August, and found the enemy in great force on the opposite bank of the Gumti; the passage of the river was effected on the 27th, upon which the rebels made off. No further movement of importance took place in Oudh until after the termination of the rainy season.

In other parts of the country, too, during this period, various forces were actively employed against the rebels. In the Soraon district a column under the command of Brigadier Berkeley, which included the 7th Punjab Infantry (now the 19th Bengal Infantry) and detachments of the Lahore Light Horse and the Regiment of Ferozepore, was engaged in July 1858, in the reduction of the forts of Dhainawan (miscalled "Dehaign" in the despatches) and Tiraul, from which the enemy were expelled with considerable loss. At the end of the following month a small force, consisting of detachments of the 2nd Punjab Cavalry and the 17th and 24th Punjab Infantry (now the 25th and 32nd Bengal Infantry), the whole under the command of Captain Browne, attacked a large body of rebels and mutineers at Sirpura, near Pilibhit, and after a severe contest, in which Browne was badly wounded and lost an arm, completely routed and dispersed them, killing upwards of 300 of them, including their leader. Some months later (15th January 1859), another severe action took place in this district, at Sissia-Ghât, on the Sarda or Ghagra, in which the rebels were routed and driven over the river, but not before they had inflicted on the small British detachment opposed to them a loss of thirteen killed and thirty-nine wounded, including an unusually large proportion of officers. Amongst the latter was Lieutenant Kemp, commanding a detachment of the Kumaon Levy, who was mortally wounded.

Immediately on the termination of the rainy season the Commander-in-Chief (now Lord Clyde) entered on the task for which he had for some time been preparing, of expelling the rebels and mutineers from Oudh, in which province the bulk of them, flying from various quarters before the advance of the British troops, had now taken refuge. The measures by which this object was to be accomplished were very skilfully planned, and, briefly described, consisted of the simultaneous employment of a number of independent columns, the combined movements of which were to sweep the Baiswara district (lying between the Ganges and the Gumti) and drive the rebels beyond the Ghagra, and, that accomplished, by a further series of movements to force them, across the Rapti and into the Nepal hills. These plans were carried out with great thoroughness and success by various columns commanded by Sir J. Hope Grant, Brigadiers Kelly (from Azamgarh), Wetherall (from Soraon), Pinckney, Evelegh, Horsford, Barker, Troup (from Rohilkhand), Rowcroft (from Gorakhpur), and other officers,—the whole under the direction of the Commander-in-Chief himself. To describe in detail the operations of these several columns during the months from October 1858 to March 1859 would far exceed the scope of this work, but it may not be out of place to allude to some of the most notable of the many sharp encounters which took place during this period. On the 21st October, after having defeated a numerous body of rebels at Jamo, near Sandila, Brigadier Barker took the strong fort of Birwa by storm, after a severe conflict in which his force sustained losses to the extent of fifteen men killed and seven officers and 104 men wounded. On the 3rd November the column under the command of Brigadier Wetherall (which included part of the 1st Punjab Cavalry, the 9th Punjab Infantry—now the 21st Bengal Infantry—and the Baluch Battalion) stormed the fort of Rampur Kassiah, on the Sai River, in Southern Oudh, and carried it after a prolonged contest and with the loss of 79 officers and men killed and wounded: the fort was held by 4,000 rebels, of whom half were sepoys of the 17th, 28th, and 52nd Native Infantry; 300 of these were killed and the regimental colour of the 52nd was captured. On this occasion the 9th Punjab Infantry greatly distinguished itself and sustained considerable loss. A few days later Brigadier Evelegh took the fort of Simri with trifling loss, and on the 24th of November the commander-in-chief, with the troops of two of the columns operating in Southern Oudh, completely defeated Beni Madho Singh, the most powerful of the Baiswara chiefs, at Doundiakhera and Baksar Ghât: this action was the final stroke in the clearance of the Baiswara district and opened the way to the transfer of the operations to the country lying to the north-east of the Ghagra, the tracts lying to the west of that river having already been pretty well cleared of rebel bands by the operations of Brigadiers Troup and Barker, the former of whom, advancing from the Rohilkhand side with the force under his command (which included Cureton's Multani Horse and the 66th Gurkhas) had captured Mithauli on the 9th November and advanced to Biswah on the 1st December, at which point Brigadier Barker, who had been operating in the districts to the north-west of Lucknow, also arrived on the 3rd. Sir J. Hope Grant crossed the Ghagra at Fyzabad on the 25th November, and defeated a body of the enemy on the left bank the same day: he subsequently advanced to Gonda and Sikrora and afterwards joined Brigadier Rowcroft at Tulsipur, at which place the force under the latter officer (which included part of the 1st Punjab Cavalry and the Regiment of Ferozepore) had defeated Bala Rao, the brother of the Nana, on the 23rd December. A few days later Grant routed Bala Rao's force at Kamda-Kot and captured fifteen of his guns. In the meantime Lord Clyde, who had crossed the Ghagra at Fyzabad on the 11th December, and moved northwards by Sikrora, Bahraich and Nanpara, had defeated the rebels at Barjidia and captured the fort of Masjidia, and he finally on the last day of the year routed the enemy at Sidinhia Ghât, and drove them with heavy loss into and over the Rapti, thus accomplishing the task which he had set himself and effecting the reconquest of Oudh. Subsequently permission was given to the British forces to follow the rebels into the territory of Nepal, and in February 1859 Brigadier Horsford with a force which included the 1st Punjab Cavalry and the 5th Punjab Infantry crossed the Rapti and defeated the enemy at Sitka Ghât, capturing fifteen guns. In the following month Brigadier Kelly, whose force included Murray's Jat Horse, the 3rd Sikh Infantry, and the 7th Punjab Infantry, twice defeated the rebels hear Bhutwal, in the Nepal hills; and in May Sir J. Hope Grant again overthrew them in the Jarwa Pass.

With the reconquest of Oudh the story of the War of the Indian Mutiny—so far as the Bengal Army is connected with it—comes practically to an end. Not that the rebels had then entirely ceased to trouble the land, for up to the autumn of 1859 skirmishes still occasionally took place with parties of them emerging from the hills and jungles of Nepal, and in Bundelkhand and Central India a number of small flying columns were actively employed even up to the spring of 1860 in hunting down and dispersing wandering bands; but there was nothing in these operations to call for special notice or description here. Beyond the scope of this work, too, are the campaigns of 1857-58 in Central India, for in the achievements of Sir Hugh Rose, Major-General Whitlock, and other commanders, the regiments of the Bengal Army bore no part, except the unenviable one of swelling the ranks of the enemy with their mutinous sepoys. One honourable exception, however, must be made, namely, that of the 31st Native Infantry,—now "the 2nd (the Queen's Own) Bengal (Light) Infantry," whose conduct during the trying months of the hot weather of 1857 was beyond praise—an example to other corps, which it would have been well for the latter had they copied. However, the regiment took no part in the more extensive operations which ensued, although it was constantly engaged against the rebels in the Saugor district throughout the whole of 1857 and 1858.

The general rewards granted for the mutiny were a medal, with clasps for Delhi, for the defence, the relief and the capture of Lucknow, and for Central India; and six months' batta, with extra special batta for the siege of Delhi, the defence of Lucknow, and the so-called "defence of Arrah." Every native soldier in the original garrison of Lucknow received the Order of Merit. By G. G. O. No. 4 of 1864 the regiments engaged in those operations were permitted to bear on their colours the words—"Delhi," "Lucknow," and "Central India."

Thus, after a struggle of more than two years, disappeared the last smouldering embers of this great revolt, which had at one time threatened to entirely overthrow British supremacy in Northern India, and to undo the work ,of a hundred years. To a great part of the Bengal Army of the Company the mutiny was a dishonourable and suicidal death; but from its remains arose, phoenix-like, a new army more efficient and more valuable, and destined to win a renown as glorious as that which had been gained under Adams and Munro; Goddard and Coote, and Cornwallis, and Lake, and Ochterlony.

Whilst the turmoil of the mutiny was occupying all men's minds both in India and at home, there was little time to consider the affairs of the Punjab Frontier; but any who turned their eyes in that direction must have been more and more impressed with the prudence of a policy which, by the employment of vigorous measures and capable men, had, in the short space of seven years, not only secured the faithful allegiance of the Punjab, but had even succeeded in curbing to some extent the unruly spirits on its borders.

During 1857 and 1858 only two small outbreaks occurred on the North-West Frontier, and both were occasioned by the conduct of some Hindustani fanatics who had settled amongst the Khudu Khels, and who now, in the summer of 1857, raised the standard of religious war in the villages of Shekh Jana and, on the Yusafzai border. Detachments of the Peshawar Mountain Train Battery and of the 2nd Punjab Cavalry and the 5th Punjab Infantry captured the village of Shekh Jana on the 2nd July, and on the 21st of the same month the fortified village of Narinji was taken by a force composed of detachments of the above-named corps and of the 4th Punjab Infantry, with a loss on our side of five killed and twenty-one wounded. On the 3rd of the following month a strong column of about 1,400 men, which included detachments of the Peshawar Mountain Train Battery and of the 2nd Punjab Cavalry, the 21st Native Infantry, and the 5th, 6th, and 16th Punjab Infantry, again moved against the village of Narinji, where the fanatics, aided by some of the Swat and Chamla tribes, had re-assembled in greater strength than before, and destroyed it after a little opposition, and with the loss of only one killed and eight wounded. In all these affairs the British forces were commanded by Major Vaughan.

In consequence of an outrage on the Assistant Commissioner of Yusafzai, another expedition was despatched against the Hindustani fanatics and the Khudu Khels in April 1858. The force was under the command of Major-General Sir Sydney John Cotton, K.C.B., and was composed of detachments of the Peshawar Light Horse, the 7th and 18th Irregular Cavalry, and the Guides Cavalry; of the Peshawar Light Field Battery, the Peshawar Mountain Train Battery, and the Hazara Mountain Train Battery; of the Bengal Sappers and Miners; and of the 81st and 98th Foot; the 21st Native Infantry, the Regiment of Kalat-i-Ghilzai, the 2nd Sikh Infantry, the 6th, 8th, 9th, 12th, and 18th Punjab Infantry, and the Guides Infantry;—making up a total of 4,877 men. These troops (excepting portions of the Peshawar and Hazara Mountain Train Batteries, the 2nd Sikh Infantry and the 6th and 12th Punjab Infantry, which moved up from Hazara) were assembled on the left bank of the Kabul river, opposite Nowshera, and moving forward first crossed the frontier on the 26th April. Operating in several columns, the troops took and destroyed Panjtar, Chinglai, and Mangal

Thana, the strongholds of the Khudu Khels and the fanatics, without experiencing any opposition. On the 3rd May an advance was made against SitanaSitana, where the main colony of the fanatics was located, and on the following day that place was also destroyed, after a sharp engagement in which the 21st Native Infantry, the 2nd Sikh Infantry, the Guides Infantry, and the 9th and 18th Punjab Infantry, were engaged, and in which a loss was sustained of one native officer (*Subadar* Dalu Mal, 18th Punjab Infantry) and five men killed, and one British officer, one native officer and twenty-seven men wounded. Three days later the force re-crossed the frontier, having accomplished all the objects of the expedition. The India medal was granted to the survivors of this expedition in 1869.

In December 1859 a strong expeditionary force was despatched, under Brigadier-General N. B. Chamberlain, C.B., against the Kabul Khel Waziris, to punish them for harbouring marauders who had killed Captain Mecham, of the Bengal Artillery. It included detachments of Nos. 1 and 2 Punjab Light Field Batteries, of the Peshawar and Hazara Mountain Train Batteries, of the Guides Cavalry and Infantry, and of the Sappers and Miners; the 2nd Punjab Cavalry; the 4th Sikh Infantry, and the 1st, 3rd, 4th, 6th, and 24th Punjab Infantry,—the whole amounting to nearly 4,000 men, with thirteen guns. The force entered the Waziri country by the Gandiob Pass on the 22nd December, and on the same day a column composed of the Peshawar Mountain Train Battery-, the Guides Infantry, and the 4th Sikh Infantry, encountered the Kabul Khels at Maidani; they met with a brave resistance; but the enemy, being ill armed, were soon repulsed with but small loss on our side. The Waziri encampments were destroyed, and on the succeeding days various-forays were made into the hills, resulting in the capture of some of the flocks and herds of the enemy. The tribesmen eventually made submission, and the objects of the expedition having, as far as possible, been accomplished, the force returned across the frontier, having lost one killed and eighteen wounded. The troops engaged in the operations received the India medal in 1869.

Of all the border tribes, none was more notorious for turbulence than the Mahsud Waziris. For many years the list of their offences had been increasing, until in March, 1860, they attacked the town of Tank, and were only prevented from sacking the place by the vigour and gallantry of Risaldar SaadatSaadat Khan and a detachment of 158 men of the 5th Punjab Cavalry, which was stationed there. It was recognised that the punishment of the tribe could no longer be delayed, and the formation of an expeditionary force for that purpose was therefore directed. The following troops were accordingly assembled at Tank on the 16th April, under the command of Brigadier-General Chamberlain:—Detachments of Nos. 2 and 3 Punjab Light Field Batteries, of the Peshawar and Hazara Mountain Train Batteries, and of the Guides Cavalry, the 3rd Punjab Cavalry and the Multani Cavalry; the 1st Company of Bengal Sappers and Miners; the Guides Infantry; the 4th Sikh Infantry; the 1st, 2nd, 3rd, 4th, 6th, 14th, 24th (Pioneers) and 25th (Gurkha) Punjab Infantry; and the 6th Punjab Police Battalion,—the whole numbering over 5,000 men, with thirteen guns. The force entered the Mahsud country by the Tank Zam on the 17th April, and reached Palosin on the following day. Leaving a portion of his-force at this place, under Lieutenant-Colonel Lumsden, Chamberlain advanced up the Shahur Zam on the 20th for the purpose of reconnoitring the route in that direction, and reached a point within fourteen miles of Kaniguram, the chief town of the Mahsud Waziris, on the 23rd; as he had no intention of attacking Kaniguram from this direction, he fell back on the 24th; and, retracing his steps, encamped on the 26th within a short distance of Palosin. The force left at that place had in the meantime had a sharp experience of Waziri tactics, having been suddenly attacked at *reveille* on the 23rd by a body of three thousand of the enemy, who made a desperate attempt to rush Lumsden'sLumsden's camp. The attack was delivered with determined bravery, and was not repulsed before considerable loss had been inflicted on both sides, that on ours amounting to no less than 63 killed and 166 wounded. Some days were now passed in making preparations for an advance on Kaniguram by the northern route, through the Tank Zam; during this period the Mahsuds made an offer of submission, but as our terms were unpalatable to them, the negotiations were without result. On the 2nd May Chamberlain advanced to Shingi Kot, and on the morning of the 4th he reached the Barari Pass, which the enemy were found to be holding in great strength,—variously reported at from 4,000 to 7,000 men. Two columns of attack were immediately formed to assail the heights on either side of the pass; that on the left, under Lieutenant-Colonel Lumsden, met with scarcely any resistance; that on the right, composed of the Hazara Mountain Train Battery and the 1st, 2nd, and 3rd Punjab Infantry, under Lieutenant-Colonel Green, which had to move over most difficult ground, was fiercely opposed and its first assault repulsed by the enemy, but eventually, after a severe contest, the breastworks were carried and the enemy put to flight, though not without severe loss on our side, Lieutenant Aytoun, 94th Foot, attached to the 2nd Punjab Infantry, one native officer and twenty-eight men having been killed, and Lieutenant Ruxton, 3rd Punjab Infantry, five native officers and eighty men wounded,—a total of 116 casualties. On the 5th the force continued its advance, and the same day reached Kaniguram, no further opposition having been offered. On the 9th the force marched northwards and on the following day reached Makin, the next most important town of the Mahsuds, which, as the enemy still stubbornly refused to submit, was destroyed on the 11th. The failure of supplies now rendered a further stay in the hills undesirable, and continuing his course by the Khaisora route, Chamberlain emerged from the mountains at Spinwam, in the BannuBannu Valley, on the 18th May, his force having during these operations sustained a total loss of 100 killed arid 261 wounded. For his services in these operations Brigadier-General Chamberlain was created a Knight Commander of the Order of the Bath, and all the survivors of the force received the India medal in 1869.

Nor at the same time was the North-East Frontier entirely free from the troubles arising from turbulent and savage neighbours. A small expedition, numbering some 140 fighting men, with two howitzers, the whole under the command of Captain Lowther, 1st Assam Light Infantry, was despatched in 1858 against the Abors, a predatory tribe inhabiting a range of hills on the borders of Upper Assam, but it failed to effect its object and was obliged to retire. In February of the next year another force was despatched into the same country, under the command of Lieutenant-Colonel Hannay. This was composed of sixty men of No. 4 Naval Brigade, Indian Navy; thirty-five men of the Assam Local Artillery, with two howitzers and two mortars; 166 men of the 1st Assam Light Infantry; and 150 Auxiliaries. Pashi and Rong-Kong, the principal villages of the Meyong Abors, were reached on the 27th February, and though strongly situated and defended by many stockades they were, in spite of an obstinate resistance, stormed on the same day, with a loss on our side of one man killed and one officer (Indian Navy) and forty-three men wounded.

The relations between Great Britain and China, which had been in a more or less strained and unsatisfactory condition ever since the conclusion of the first war, were openly ruptured in October 1856, in consequence of the Chinese authorities at Canton having seized a vessel under English colours, and refused redress for the outrage. Negotiations having failed to secure reparation, hostilities were begun by Sir Michael Seymour, the British Admiral, who on the 23rd October took possession of the Canton forts, and on the 29th captured a portion of the city, with a loss of two killed and eleven wounded. Hostilities continued in a desultory way for some time, and eventually led to the despatch of an expedition from England, but the outbreak of the Mutiny caused the troops (the 23rd, 82nd, 90th and 93rd Foot) to be diverted to India, and thus little was done during 1857 to settle the Chinese difficulty, though slight engagements took place from time to time. At the end of December 1857, with the assistance of a French force, Canton was stormed and captured, and a few months later reinforcements arrived from India in the shape of three faithful regiments of the old Bengal Army. The first of these was the 70th Native Infantry, which had set the example of volunteering for foreign service, while their comrades were mutinying in the North-West: they arrived in China in February 1858, and were followed in May by the 47th and the 65th Native Infantry. In June a treaty of peace was concluded at Tien-tsin, and the war was supposed to be over, but it was little regarded by the Chinese authorities at Canton, who continued as aggressive as ever, and there were consequently frequent collisions between our troops and the Chinese "braves." The 70th were engaged in the White Cloud Mountain operations in June 1858, and in the expedition to Kam-tow in August, losing on the latter occasion Lieutenant Danvers, who was mortally wounded. In an action at Shek-tsin in January 1859, a portion of the 65th was engaged and had two men wounded.

The treaty of Tien-tsin did not in any way terminate our difficulties with China: its terms were not only disregarded by the authorities at Canton but ignored all over the country; the approach of the plenipotentiaries to Fekin was barred by the closing of the mouth of the Pei-ho river, and an attempt by Rear-Admiral Hope to force a passage was disastrously repulsed (25th June 1859) with a loss of 81 killed and 345 wounded, and three vessels sunk. The allied British and French Governments had now no choice but to enforce the details of the treaty, and a force more equal to the requirements of the case was despatched to China in the early part of the following year. Hostilities were resumed in April 1860, and the island of Chusan occupied. By the 23rd of April the British force, under Lieutenant-General Sir J. Hope Grant, was collected on, the promontory of Kow-loon, adjoining Hong-Kong. It included the following Bengal troops —The 1st Sikh Irregular Cavalry (then known as Probyn's Horse), Fane's Horse (specially raised for this service), the Regiment of Lucihiana, and the 8th, 11th, 15th (Pioneers), and 19th Punjab Infantry. Of these corps, the Regiment of Ludhiana and the 11th Punjab Infantry were soon after sent to garrison Shanghai, and the 19th was detached on other duty. These corps consequently did not share in the operations of the allied forces in Northern China.

After considerable delays the allies sailed for the Pei-ho river, and disembarked on the 1st August near Peh-tang, which town was occupied without opposition. An advance was made on the 12th of the same month, when the enemy were defeated at Sinho: on this occasion the Tartar horse was driven from the field in disorder by the two regiments of Indian cavalry and two squadrons of the 1st Dragoon Guards. Two days later a further advance secured the fort of Tang-ku. In the various skirmishes up to this point our losses amounted to only three killed and twenty-seven wounded.

The way was now open for an attack on the Taku forts, and on the 21st August, at 5 a.m., a vigorous cannonade was opened on both sides and continued for three hours; after which a combined assault was made by the allies on the inner North Fort. The Chinese fought with great bravery and determination, and it was only after a severe conflict that the place was eventually carried. The outer North Fort was then attacked and taken without opposition, and the South Forts were evacuated by the enemy the same day. Our losses in the storming of the inner North Fort amounted to seventeen men killed, and twenty-one officers and 163 men wounded, while the casualties in the allied French Force reached a total of 130.

The town of Tien-tsin was entered on August 24th, and after a fortnight's halt the march was continued, and Ho-sei-wu, half-way to Pekin, reached on September 13th. Leaving that place on the 18th September, the allied force came on the Chinese Army drawn up at a place called Chang-tsia-wan on the Chow-Ho. In the battle which ensued the French force made a flank attack on the right, supported by a squadron of Fane's Horse, which gallantly charged and drove back the whole of the Tartar cavalry in that quarter. On the left the heavy masses of the enemy were charged and thrown into confusion by only 100 of the 1st Sikh Irregular Cavalry, led by Major Probyn; the 15th Punjab Infantry, pushing on after the defeated enemy with great spirit and advancing beyond Chang-tsia-wan, captured a large Chinese camp and several guns. The allied forces in this battle did not exceed 4,000 men, while those of the Chinese were estimated at

20,000, and the enemy lost 600 in killed alone, while the British loss was no more than twenty, and the French only fifteen.

On the 21st September the march was resumed and an action with the enemy took place on the same day near Tang-chow, in which the 1st Dragoon Guards and Fane's Horse distinguished themselves. The enemy were at once defeated with great loss, our own casualties amounting to no more than two men killed, and three officers and twenty-six men wounded. After a delay of about two weeks the advance towards Pekin was resumed on the 5th October, and the Summer Palace, outside the city, was reached and occupied without opposition on the 7th. On the following day some prisoners who had been treacherously captured by the Chinese near Tang-chow on the 21st of the preceding month were brought into camp, and nine more were given up on the 12th; the remainder (sixteen in number), including Lieutenant Anderson and nine sowars of Fane's Horse, had died in captivity from the barbarous ill-treatment to which they had been subjected.

Pekin surrendered on the 13th of October: the treaty of Tientsin was ratified in the course of the month, and on the 7th and 8th of November the British Army left the capital. The 1st Sikh Irregular Cavalry and the 8th, 15th and 19th Punjab Infantry returned almost immediately to India; Fane's Horse was detained at Tientsin until the following October; the Regiment of Ludhiana did not embark for India until April 1861; while the 11th Punjab Infantry was employed in and around Shanghai until May 1862, and was constantly engaged in skirmishes with the Taiping rebels.

The 1st Sikh Irregular Cavalry, Fane's Horse, and the 8th and 15th Punjab Infantry received permission in 1862 to bear the words "Taku Forts" and "Pekin" on their colours and appointments (G.G.O. No. 132 of 1862), but it was not until 1882 (G. G. O. No. 188) that the remaining regiments which had served in China (now the 7th, 10th, 11th, 15th, 22nd and 27th Bengal Infantry) were authorised to bear similarly the word "China,"—with the dates "1858-59," or "1860-62," according to the operations in which they had taken part. Medals were granted for the operations of 1857-59 and of 1860-62, with clasps for the Taku Forts and Pekin, but were not allowed to corps employed in garrison work at Chusan, Shanghai, and Canton-One more small affair requires notice; this was the Sikkim expedition, which was necessitated by an unprovoked attack on the Political Agent and his escort in November 1860. The force employed was about 1,800 strong, and was commanded by Lieutenant-

Colonel J. C. Gawler, of the 73rd Foot; it was composed of wings of the 6th Foot, the 3rd Sikh Infantry, and the 73rd Native Infantry, the head-quarters and a detachment of the Bengal Police Battalion (Rattray's Sikhs), and some other details. The expedition concentrated at Darjeeling in December 1860 and January 1861, and a forward movement was made on the 1st February. The enemy collected in force on the left bank of the Rangeet, but did not dispute the passage of the river; nor did they at any time during the operations risk a conflict with the British troops. Colonel Gawler advanced as far as the town of Tamlung, when the Sikkim rajah sued for peace, and a treaty was concluded on the 29th March.

The course of events has now brought this sketch down to the period when the Bengal Army, remodelled and re-organised after the great struggle of 1857, assumed the shape in which, with but small modifications, it has existed ever since. This chapter may be closed by a cursory survey of the changes so produced and the re-organisation which followed them.

The confusion occasioned by the outburst of the mutiny, and the isolation of the main army from the headquarters of Government afford sufficient explanation of the difficulty which attends any search after definite orders for the raising of the many regiments which were hastily formed to take the places of those which had mutinied, and to put down the rebellion. Nor in many cases were official orders published,—the only authority being a letter from the Commissioner, or even, perhaps, verbal instructions. Thus, in quick succession, sprang up Hodson's, Wale's, Murray's, Cureton's, and Lind's Horse; the 2nd, 3rd, and 4th Sikh Irregular Cavalry; Beatson's, Meade's, Robarts' and Alexander's Horse; the Benares, the Rohilkhand, and the 1st and 2nd Mahratta Cavalry. Of infantry there were the "Sikh Volunteers" (formed from the faithful Punjabis of regiments below Allahabad), the Delhi Pioneers, eighteen regiments of Punjab Infantry and a number of levies formed at various places in the North-West Provinces. All through the autumn of 1857 and the spring of 1858, as regiment after regiment of the old army joined the stream of mutiny, fresh troops succeeded to the places deserted by their faithless predecessors. It is unnecessary here to enter into the details of all these corps, nor to trace the fate of the regiments whose history ended so disgracefully in 1857. A few facts may, however, be noted, as marking the rapid development of the new army. By G. G. O. No. 736 of 1858 the formation of four regiments of European light cavalry was ordered, in substitution of eight of the regular Bengal Native cavalry corps, and the officers of the 1st, 2nd, 3rd, 4th, 6th 7th, 9th and 10th Light Cavalry were transferred to the new regiments. On the 9th September 1859, an order (G. G. O. No. 1277) was published by the governor-general detailing the regiments and parts of regiments which had shown themselves "proof against temptation, fanaticism, and threats," and mentioning the special services of all such corps. The order concludes by enumerating the regiments which would thenceforward cease to exist in the Bengal Army. In June of the same year, as active operations against the rebels became by degrees confined to a few isolated districts, the reduction of the exceptional numbers of troops in Bengal was commenced; a number of corps, including the Sikh and Gurkha regiments, were reduced to 700 sepoys, formed in ten companies of 70 men each; the newly-raised Hindustani levies were brought down to a strength of 600; and the whole of the irregular cavalry to 420 sowars per regiment.

On the 5th of January 1860 orders were issued for the disbandment of the 3rd Regiment of Hodson's Horse, while on the same date volunteers were called for to form another irregular corps for service in China. There the new regiment won distinction as "Fane's Horse," and it still exists as the 19th Bengal Lancers.

G.G.O. No. 903, dated the 11th September 1860, ordered the transfer from the control of the Punjab Government to that of the commander-in-chief of the four regiments of Sikh irregular cavalry and of the Punjab infantry regiments numbered from 7th to 24th: this order was to take effect from the 15th February 1859.

In 1861 orders were published re-organising the confused crowd of regiments, old and new, regular and irregular, which the storm of the mutiny had left to represent the Army of Bengal. The cavalry was re-organised by G. G. O. No. 494, dated 31st May 1861. In the August of the preceding year there existed seventeen native cavalry regiments under the orders of the Government of India and twenty-nine under the commander-in-chief. Of the former, the regiment of Nagpur Cavalry was disbanded; Meade's Horse was incorporated with the Central India Horse; the remainder, including the Guides Cavalry and five Punjab regiments, remained unchanged. Of the other twenty-nine, ten were disbanded,—namely, the 3rd, 9th, 12th and 16th Irregular Cavalry, Alexander's Horse, the Benares Horse, and the 1st Mahratta Horse, the 3rd Sikh Irregular Cavalry, the

Ramgarh Irregular Cavalry, and Lind's Pathan Cavalry. The remainder were numbered and designated as follows:

New name	Former name
1st Bengal Cavalry	1st Irregular Cavalry
2nd Bengal Cavalry	2nd Irregular Cavalry
3rd Bengal Cavalry	4th Irregular Cavalry
4th Bengal Cavalry	6th Irregular Cavalry
5th Bengal Cavalry	7th Irregular Cavalry
6th Bengal Cavalry	8th Irregular Cavalry
7th Bengal Cavalry	17th Irregular Cavalry
8th Bengal Cavalry	18th Irregular Cavalry
9th Bengal Cavalry	1st Regiment of Hodson's Horse
10th Bengal Cavalry	2nd Regiment of Hodson's Horse
11th Bengal Cavalry	1st Sikh Irregular Cavalry
12th Bengal Cavalry	2nd Sikh Irregular Cavalry
13th Bengal Cavalry	4th Sikh Irregular Cavalry
14th Bengal Cavalry	Murray's Jat Horse
15th Bengal Cavalry	Cureton's Multani Horse
16th Bengal Cavalry	Rohilkhand Horse
17th Bengal Cavalry	Robarts' Horse
18th Bengal Cavalry	2nd Mahratta Horse
19th Bengal Cavalry	Fane's Horse

Each regiment was to consist of 420 sowars, in six troops, as follows:

3	*Risaldars*	R300, 250 & 200 a month respectively
3	*Ressaidars*	R150, 135 & 120
1	*Wurdi*-Major	R130
6	*Jemadars*	2 each on R80, 70 and 60
6	*Kot-Daffadars*	R47
48	*Daffadars*	R38
6	*Nishanbardars*	R38
6	Trumpeters	R34
420	*Sowars*	R27

The first reorganisation of the infantry had been notified a month before—(G.G.O. No. 400, dated 3rd May 1861); by it the strength of all infantry corps was fixed at 600 privates, each regiment being divided into eight companies of the following strength:

1	*Subadar*	5	*Naiks*
1	*Jemadar*	2	Drummers
5	*Havildars*	75	Privates

Corps in possession of honorary colours were allowed to retain the special native officers already allowed for the purpose of carrying them. In August 1860 the number of infantry regiments existing was as follows:

	Regts.	Under
Regular Infantry	15	Commander-in-Chief
Irregular and extra infantry	30	Commander-in-Chief
Punjab Infantry	18	Commander-in-Chief
Punjab Infantry	7	Government of India
Sikh and Guides Infantry	5	Government of India
Hyderabad Contingent	6	Government of India
Nagpur Irregular Force	3	Government of India
Local corps	7	Government of India

The fifteen regular regiments were the 4th, 21st, 31st, 32nd, 33rd, 42nd, 43rd, 47th, 58th, 59th, 63rd, 65th, 66th (Gurkhas), 70th, and 73rd. Of these the 4th, 58th, and 73rd were now disbanded.

The 30 irregular and extra regiments were:

Regiment of Kalat-i-Ghilzai	Shekhawati Battalion
Regiment of Ferozepore	Alipore Regiment
Regiment of Ludhiana	Regiment of Lucknow
Nasseri Battalion	Loyal Purbiah Regiment
Sirmoor Rifle Regiment	Kamrup Regiment
Kumaon Battalion	1st Gwalior Regiment
Extra Gurkha Regiment	2nd Gwalior Regiment
Bhagalpur Hill Rangers	
1st Assam Light Infantry Battalion	Meerut Levy
2nd Assam Light Infantry Battalion	Agra Levy
Sylhet Light Infantry Battalion	Aligarh Levy
Arakan Battalion	Shahjahanpur Levy
Allahabad Levy	Cawnpore Levy
Fatehgarh Levy	Bareilly Levy
Mainpuri Levy	Moradabad Levy
Kumaon Levy	

Of these the Nasseri Battalion and the 2nd Gwalior Regiment and the last three of the levies were broken up. The Kamrup and Arakan Battalions and the Bhagalpur Hill Rangers were transferred to the police, and either broken up or absorbed in the general police.

Of the Punjab regiments, the first six and the last were under the Government of India. The remainder were under the commander-in-chief, and of these the 10th, 12th, 13th and 14th were broken up. The four Sikh regiments and the Corps of Guides remained unchanged. Of the local corps, the Pegu Light Infantry Battalion and one Nagpur regiment were broken up; the Mhair and Mhairwara Battalions were regarded as police. The remaining line regiments of the army were now numbered and designated as follows:

1st-12th Bengal Native Infantry	formerly the 21st, 31st, 32nd, 33rd, 42nd, 43rd, 47th, 59th, 63rd, 65th, 66th (Gurkhas) and 70th Native Infantry
13th-22nd Bengal Native Infantry	formerly the Regiment of Kalat-i-Ghitjai, the Shekhawati Battalion, the Regiment of Ferozepore, the Regiment of Ludhiana, the Sirmoor Rifle Regiment, the Kumaon Battalion, the Extra Gurkha Regiment, the Regiment of Lucknow, the Loyal Purbiah Regiment and the Alipore Regiment
23rd-36th Bengal Native Infantry	formerly the 7th, 8th, 9th, 11th, 15th, 16th, 17th, 18th, 19th, 20th, 21st, 22nd, 23rd and 24th Punjab Infantry
37th-45th Bengal Native Infantry	formerly the Allahabad, Fatehgarh, Mainpuri, Bareilly, Meerut, Agra, Aligarh, and Shahjahanpur Levies and the 1st Gwalior Infantry
46th-48th Bengal Native Infantry	formerly the 1st and 2nd Assam Light Infantry Battalions, and the Sylhet Light Infantry Battalion

Within six months, however, under instructions from the Secretary of State, this arrangement was again altered; all the Gurkha corps, including the 66th Light Infantry (the original Nasseri Battalion) were withdrawn from the line, and numbered separately from the 1st to the 4th,—the Hazara Gurkha Battalion, attached to the Punjab Irregular Force, being numbered the 5th.

The line regiments of Bengal Native Infantry were then (G. G. O. No. 990, dated October 29th, 1861) finally numbered in the following order:

New	Old Number or name
1st	21st Native Infantry
2nd	31st Native (Light) Infantry
3rd	2nd Native Infantry
4th	33rd Native Infantry
5th	42nd Native (Light) Infantry
6th	43rd Native (Light) Infantry
7th	47th Native Infantry
8th	59th Native Infantry
9th	63rd Native Infantry
10th	65th Native Infantry
11th	70th Native Infantry
12th	Regiment of Kalat-i-Ghilzai
13th	Shekhawati Battalion
14th	Regiment of Ferozepore
15th	Regiment of Ludhiana
16th	Regiment of Lucknow
17th	Loyal Purbiah Regiment
18th	Alipore Regiment (Calcutta Militia)
19th	7th Punjab Infantry
20th	8th Punjab Infantry
21st	9th Punjab Infantry
22nd	11th Punjab Infantry
23rd	15th Punjab Infantry (Pioneers)
24th	16th Punjab Infantry (Pioneers)
25th	17th Punjab Infantry (Pioneers)
26th	18th Punjab Infantry (Pioneers)
27th	19th Punjab Infantry (Pioneers)
28th	20th Punjab Infantry (Pioneers)
29th	21st Punjab Infantry (Pioneers)
30th	22nd Punjab Infantry (Pioneers)
31st	23nd Punjab Infantry (Pioneers)
32nd	24th Punjab Infantry (Pioneers)

33rd	Allahabad Levy
34th	Fatehgarh Levy
35th	Mainpuri Levy
36th	Bareilly Levy
37th	Meerut Levy
38th	Agra Levy
39th	Aligarh Levy
40th	Shahjahanpur Levy
41st	1st Gwalior Regiment
42nd	1st Assam Light Infantry Battalion
43rd	2nd Assam Light Infantry Battalion
44th	Sylhet Light Infantry Battalion

At the same time the artillery and the corps of engineers whose great deeds in the past had added so much to the glory of the Bengal Army, and whose lists had given so many honourable names to history, were transferred to the Royal Corps, and ceased to exist as separate bodies.

No notice has been made of the greatest change of all, namely, the transfer of the Indian forces to the Crown. This event, however, though of great importance politically, affected the native army in little more than name and in the conditions of service of its British officers, into the details of which it is neither necessary nor convenient to enter here. The announcement was made on the 1st November 1858, that Her Majesty had assumed the Government of India; and from that day the Honourable East India Company passed away into the pages of history.

As far as concerned the arming and equipment of the native soldiers, but few changes were made in these years, fraught with such important reforms elsewhere. The attempt to introduce the new Enfield rifle with its novel cartridge was made one of the direct causes of, or at any rate the pretext for, the mutiny; and in consequence the infantry remained for many years after with no better weapon than the old smooth-bore percussion musket. In the cavalry, however, a new weapon was introduced, called the "Victoria carbine," with which all regiments were armed (G. O. G. G. 27th April 1860). Other innovations were the introduction of khaki clothing for native regiments; and the abolition of the leather stock, a small matter seemingly, but one which made a good deal of difference in the soldier's comfort.

So ends the third great division of the military history of Bengal. With this chapter we seem to pass altogether to another epoch—to turn from ancient history to modern. The great Company which raised the fabric of the British Empire in India has passed away; the regiments it created, which won its battles and upheld its power, have disappeared; but a new army has arisen, and we turn now from the ashes of the past to tell of the living deeds of the Bengal Army of today.

CHAPTER 9

The Northwest Frontier

In the chapter which follows we must pass in review a long period of comparative inactivity for the Indian Army, although the little wars which are inseparable from a great colonial empire afford constant and sufficient incident to prove that service on the Indian frontier offers more experience of active soldiering than is to be found in any position elsewhere.

The first of these small expeditions was on the North-East Frontier, operations in in suppression of a rebellion of the tribes in the Khasiah and Hills of Assam in December 1862, and the two following months. The country had been in a disturbed state for several months and outrages had been frequent: it was not, however, until December that regular operations were commenced. The force in the disturbed districts was composed of the Eurasian Company of Artillery, the 21st, 28th, 33rd, and 44th Bengal Native Infantry, the Bengal-Military Police Battalion (Rattray's Sikhs), and some local military police, and was commanded by Colonel Dunsford. The first engagement was an attack on a convoy escorted by a party of the 21st near Jaintiapur, in which a sepoy was killed. On the 25th December a detachment of the 28th and a few of the 44th, under Lieutenant Sadleir, surprised and captured the rebel leader Ukiang Nongba. During January and February 1863 several engagements took place with the rebels, in which the 21st and 44th took the principal part, and the stockaded villages of Umkai, Umkiang and Nongbarai were captured. The losses in the operations were small, notwithstanding the difficulties of the country and the strength of some of the positions, and amounted in all to three killed and nineteen wounded: among the latter were Lieutenant-Colonel W. Richardson (at Umkiang, 5th January) and Captain A. I. Shuldham, of the 44th, and Lieutenants H. Collett (Naung-floot, 2nd February) and R. S. Robertson (Sartiong, 23rd February), of the 21st Native Infantry.

The active operations terminated in March 1863.

Towards the end of the same year the conduct of the Hindustani fanatics necessitated the despatch of an expedition against them and the tribes that were harbouring them, and this eventuated in the most severe and sanguinary conflict that had yet taken place on the North-West Frontier. .These pestilent fanatics, when expelled from Sitana in 1858, had retired to Malka, on the northern face of the Mahaban Mountain, but they had subsequently returned to Sitana and had, for a series of years, by their raids and incursions, kept the Hazara and Yusufzai borders in a constant state of unrest. Contrary to their treaty obligations, the Gaduns and Utmanzais refused to expel the fanatics, and the troubles on the border having increased during the spring and summer of 1863, a recourse to military operations at last became unavoidable. The force detailed for the purpose of expelling the fanatics from their mountain fastnesses and of punishing those who had aided and abetted them in their depredations, was placed under the command of Brigadier-General Sir N. B. Chamberlain, K.C.B., and was composed of the following corps:—Half of 'C' Battery, 19th Brigade, Royal Artillery,[1] half of No. 3 Punjab Light Field Battery; the Peshawar Mountain Train Battery; the Hazara Mountain Train Battery; detachments of the Guides Cavalry and 11th Bengal Cavalry; the 4th and 5th Companies of Bengal Sappers and Miners; the 71st Foot (Highland Light Infantry): the 101st Foot (Royal Bengal Fusiliers); the 14th (Sikhs), 20th (Punjab) and 32nd (Pioneers) Bengal Native Infantry; the Guides Infantry; the 1st, 3rd, 5th, and 6th Punjab Infantry; and the 4th and 5th Gurkha Regiments. The effective strength of the force was about 5,500 men.

The advanced column, under Lieutenant-Colonel Wilde of the Guides, entered the Ambela Pass[2] on the 20th October, and having driven back small parties of the enemy which opposed its march, was followed later in the same day by the main column under Sir Neville Chamberlain. Intelligence was at this time received that the Bunerwals had been persuaded by the fanatics to take part in the hostilities against us; and this report was confirmed on the 22nd when a reconnoitring force, which advanced as far as Kuria, in the Chamla valley, was attacked by the Bunerwals in its retirement and hard pressed by their superior numbers; the retirement was covered with great steadiness by the 20th Native Infantry, which formed the rear-guard, and

---

1. Now the 35th Field Battery, Royal Artillery.
2. Called also the Panj-dara and the Sarkhawal Pass.

the force got back to camp after dark, having sustained a loss of three killed and twenty-three wounded, amongst the former of whom was Lieutenant Gillies, Hazara Mountain Battery.

The hostility of the Bunerwals necessitated considerable alterations in the plan of the campaign, as an advance on Malka through the Chamla valley, with this powerful and warlike tribe menacing our left flank, was an operation too full of risk to be undertaken. The force, moreover, was quite inadequate for any such operation; and the only alternatives were either to abandon the expedition and retire, or else to take up a defensive position and allow the combined tribes to break their strength against it. The latter appeared to Chamberlain to be the plan best calculated to uphold the honour of our arms, and he adopted it accordingly. He therefore took up a position at the head of the pass, and this was held with slight modifications for several weeks, until the arrival of reinforcements.

On the 25th October, the picquets of the right defence being menaced by the Mahaban tribes, Major Keyes, who commanded on the spot, taking the initiative, attacked and dislodged the tribesmen from the position they had taken up on a neighbouring ridge, and following up the success, drove them, with heavy loss, from a conical hill on which they had assembled in great force. On the following day the Bunerwals made a vigorous assault on the left flank of the position, on the Guru mountain, and especially on a picquet stationed on a rocky knoll known as the Eagle's Nest. Lieutenant-Colonel Vaughan, who commanded on this side, made his arrangements with great skill, and though the fighting continued for several hours, the enemy did not succeed in making any impression on the defence; the 20th Native Infantry was again conspicuous by its steadiness, and a gallant charge was made by the 6th Punjab Infantry, which, however, suffered severely in its retirement. The attack was finally repulsed, but not before two British officers (Lieutenant Clifford, 1st Punjab Cavalry, a volunteer with the 3rd Punjab Infantry, and Lieutenant Richmond, 20th Native Infantry), *Subadar*-Major Mir Ali Shah, 20th Native Infantry, and twenty-five men had been killed, and one British officer, seven native officers, and 84 men wounded. The enemy, too, lost heavily, not less than 250 of them having been killed, and of these more than thirty were Hindustani fanatics. A simultaneous attack was made on the front of the camp, when one man was killed and one British officer and two men wounded.

On the 27th the enemy were joined by large reinforcements from Swat, Bajaur, and other parts of the country, and in fact we were now face to face with a general combination of almost all the tribes from the Indus to the borders of Afghanistan, the numbers in arms against us being not less than 15,000 men. On the 30th a united and determined attack was made on the camp in front and on the right. In the latter quarter a small but important post, known as the "Crag Picquet," held by a party of the 1st Punjab Infantry, was rushed by the enemy in force and its defenders compelled to retire; a detachment of the same regiment arriving, however, to the support of their picquet, recovered the post at the point of the bayonet, led in the most gallant manner by Major Keyes, Lieutenant Pitcher and Lieutenant Fosbery.[3]

The front attack, made by the Swat contingent, was repulsed without difficulty, as also was a feeble effort against the defences op the left. Our losses in the day's fighting amounted to fourteen killed and forty-one wounded, Major Keyes and Lieutenant Pitcher being amongst the latter.

At this period a change in the line of communications was carried out, the line of the Ambela defile having become untenable in consequence of the hostility of the Bunerwals; a new line, leading down to the plains from the right of the position, through the villages of Khanpur and Sherdara, was decided upon, and working parties employed in cutting a new road towards Ambela along the western slopes of the ridge on the right of the position, to supersede that by the gorge of the pass, which was commanded to a great extent from the Guru mountain. The next engagement with the enemy, which took place on the 6th November, began in an attack on the detachments covering the working parties on this road; the tribesmen advanced with great boldness while the working parties were being withdrawn for the day, and a sanguinary conflict ensued, in which severe losses were sustained by our troops, in. consequence of some of the covering parties having stood their ground too long after the general retirement began, and being overwhelmed by their assailants as they retreated. The casualties this day amounted to thirty-eight killed and forty wounded, among the former being Major Harding, Commandant of the 2nd Sikh Infantry, who was on the staff of the field force, Lieutenant Dougal, 79th Highlanders, attached to the 71st, and Ensign Murray, of the 71st Highland Light Infantry.

---

3. The gallant conduct of Lieutenants Pitcher and Fosbery was subsequently rewarded with the grant of the Victoria Cross.

On the evening of the 11th November it was apparent that a general attack was imminent. The enemy advanced at 10 p.m. and assaulted the Crag Picquet with great fury; they were repulsed, but returned again and again to the charge; and at one moment were so near carrying the post that it was only saved by the gallantry of a small party of five men of the 20th Native Infantry. The attacks continued until 4 a.m. on the 12th, when the enemy, having suffered severely, retired. The picquet remained constantly under arms until the morning of the 13th, when it was relieved by a detachment of the 1ist Punjab Infantry. Hardly had the change been effected when the post was again attacked in great force; Lieutenant Davidson, who was in command, was killed, and the picquet of the 1st Punjab Infantry driven out in confusion. The enemy's success did not, however, extend further, being checked by the gallantry of another party of the 1st Punjab Infantry, aided by a few of the Guides and the 14th Native Infantry under Major Ross of the latter corps; reinforcements presently arrived, and the 101st, with these detachments, stormed the crag and re-took the position. Our losses, however, were heavy, amounting to no less than 51 killed and 107 wounded.

On the 18th the position of the camp was changed, the left being withdrawn from the Guru mountain to the south of the Ambela pass. The enemy, supposing that this withdrawal was made as a preliminary tot a retreat to the plains, immediately advanced in great numbers and furiously attacked what was now the left front of the position. Every attempt was, however, repulsed and at the close of the day the tribesmen retired, having lost nearly 400 of their numbers in killed and wounded. Our own loss, too, was considerable, amounting to 43 killed and 75 wounded, among the former of whom were Captain Smith, 71st Foot, Lieutenant Jones, 79th, attached to the 71st, Lieutenant Chapman, 101st, and Lieutenant Mosley, 14th Native Infantry.

On the 19th some skirmishing took place, in which Captain Aldridge, of the 71st, was killed.

On the 20th the tribesmen again advanced in large numbers and vigorously assailed the position at various points, and in the afternoon they once more succeeded in capturing the Crag Picquet post; but it did not remain long in their possession; the 71st Highlanders and the 5th Gurkhas were promptly pushed forward, and under cover of a close and accurate fire of artillery these two regiments stormed the position and re-took it, driving the enemy over the hills in the direction of Lalu. Our losses this day amounted to twenty-seven killed, and 110 wounded, Ensign Sanderson and Assistant-Surgeon Pile, of the 101st, being amongst the former, and Sir Neville Chamberlain himself amongst the latter.

For more than three weeks after this engagement the enemy made no movement of importance. During this period Sir Neville Chamberlain was compelled, in consequence of the severity of his wound, to relinquish the command of the force and retire to the plains; he was succeeded by Major-General Garvock, who arrived on the 30th November. During this interval, too, the force was raised to a strength of nearly 9,000 men by the arrival of considerable reinforcements, consisting of the 7th and 93rd Foot (the Royal Fusiliers and the Sutherland Highlanders), the 23rd Bengal Native Infantry (Pioneers), and the 3rd Sikh Infantry. The tribesmen still continued in our front in undiminished strength, for though deserted by several clans and sections who, dispirited by repeated defeats, had gone off to their homes, they too had received powerful reinforcements, amounting to nearly 10,000 men, from Dir, Bajaur, and even Kunar. Several attempts at negotiation were made with the object of breaking up the hostile combination, but they came to nothing, and eventually General Garvock determined on making a forward movement and assailing the tribesmen in their position in his front. Accordingly on the 14th December orders were issued for an advance on the village of Lalu. The force was divided into two columns, which were placed under the command respectively of Colonel Turner, 97th Foot, and Lieutenant-Colonel Wilde; both advanced on the 15th against the enemy's position and stormed in a brilliant manner the Conical Hill on the right, driving the enemy down to Ambela; the first column then advanced and seized and destroyed Lalu. Several desultory counter-attacks were made by the enemy on the left and on the camp, all of which were repelled; and a brilliant charge by a detachment of the 1st Punjab Infantry, under Major Keyes, finally scattered the assailants in this quarter. The columns bivouacked on the ground, having lost in the day's fighting sixteen killed and sixty-seven wounded.

On the 16th the two columns moved forward into the valley. The enemy took up a strong position to resist their further advance, but being out-flanked by the first column they retired without firing a shot, and retreated slowly towards the pass leading into Buner. Colonel Turner made a movement to cut them off from this point, which was answered by a sudden and furious attack on the part of the Pathans and fanatics: the brunt of the charge fell upon 23rd and 32nd Native Infantry, who were staggered for' the moment by the violence of the onslaught, but recovering themselves they turned on their assailants and destroyed the whole of them, not one man escaping. The advance was then continued, and finally the enemy Were driven into the mouth of the pass. In this sharp affair our losses amounted to Lieutenant Alexander, of the 23rd, and seven men killed, and four officers and 76 men wounded.

This was the last engagement of the campaign. The Bunerwal chiefs tendered their submission on the following day; the Swatis retired hastily to their homes, and the Hindustani fanatics fled into the hills. A few days later Malka, the stronghold of the fanatics, was visited by some British officers escorted by the Buner tribesmen, and completely destroyed. The British force was then withdrawn to the plains, having sustained during the campaign a loss of fifteen British officers, four native officers and 219 men killed, and twenty-one British officers, twenty-seven native officers, and 622 men wounded. The India medal, with a special clasp, was afterwards granted to all survivors of the expedition (G. G. O. No. 812 of 1869).

Simultaneously with the Ambela campaign occurred a descent on the British frontier by some of the Mohmand tribes under Sultan Muhammad Khan. The garrison of the fort of Shabkadar was engaged with the enemy on the 5th December 1863, when Lieutenant Bishop, 6th Bengal Cavalry, was killed. Two days afterwards another skirmish took place, the troops engaged (detachments of the 8th Native Infantry and the 4th Sikh Infantry) sustaining a loss of two sepoys killed, and one *jemadar* and three sepoys wounded. For three weeks after this various fanatical *mullas* were engaged in stirring up the tribes and collecting adherents from the surrounding districts, until, by the 1st January 1864, their numbers amounted to 5,600. The force at Shabkadar had in the meantime been considerably increased, and now reached a total of 1,800, including half a battery of horse-artillery, detachments of the 7th Hussars and of the 2nd and 6th Bengal Cavalry, the 3rd Battalion of the Rifle Brigade, the 2nd Gurkha Regiment, and a detachment of the 4th Sikh Infantry, the whole under the command of Colonel Macdonell, of the Rifle Brigade. The enemy again came down on Shabkadar on the 2nd January: Colonel Macdonell moved out and engaged them, and in the action which followed completely routed and dispersed them, the loss on our side amounting to only two men killed, and seventeen wounded. The India medal was granted for this affair by G. G. O. No. 116 of 1884.

The history of the year 1864 again carries us to the Northern and North-Eastern Frontiers of Bengal where a long continued series of raids and incursions into British territory, culminating in an outrageous insult to a British Mission, forced on a war with the Government of Bhutan in November 1864.

The forces detailed for the operations against Bhutan were divided into four columns as follow:

Right Column,—to move from Gauhati against Dewangiri:—Half of the Eurasian Company of Artillery, one squadron of the 5th Bengal Cavalry, one company of Sibandi Sappers, and the 43rd Native Infantry (Assam Light Infantry).

Right Centre Column,—to move from Goalpara against Bissengiri:—Half of the Eurasian Company of Artillery, one squadron of the 5th and two of the 14th Bengal Cavalry, one company of Sibandi Sappers, and a wing each of the 12th and the 44th Native Infantry (Sylhet Light Infantry).

Left Centre Column,—to move from Cooch Behar against Baksa and Bala:—Half of No. 5 Battery, 25th Brigade (mountain guns) and half of No. 6 Battery, 25th Brigade Royal Artillery (mortars); one company of sappers and miners, a wing of the 11th Native Infantry, and the 3rd Gurkha Regiment.

Left Column,—to move from Jalpaiguri against Dhalimkot and Chamurchi:—Half of No, 5 Battery, 25th Brigade, (mountain guns) and half of No. 6 Battery, 25th Brigade, Royal Artillery (mortars); two squadrons of the 5th Bengal Cavalry, one company of sappers and miners, a wing each of the 11th and 18th Native Infantry, and the 30th Native Infantry.

The two columns on the right were placed under the command of Brigadier-General Mulcaster, those on the left under Brigadier-General Dunsford.

The left column, under Brigadier-General Dunsford, was the first to move. Marching from Jalpaiguri on the 28th November, it arrived before the hill fort of Dhalimkot on the 5th December, and on the following day the place was taken after a bombardment of several hours, with a loss on our side of three officers and seven men killed, and three officers and fifty-six men wounded. A considerable portion of the loss was occasioned by the premature bursting of a shell, which resulted in the death of Captain Griffin, Lieutenant Anderson, Lieutenant Waller, and several men of the artillery. No further opposition was met with, and the occupation of Dhalimkot by a detachment of the 17th Native Infantry from Darjeeling having been arranged for, the column returned to the plains and marched eastwards along the foot of the hills towards Chamurchi. In the vicinity of that place a reconnoitring party was attacked by the enemy on the 29th December, and in the skirmish which ensued the detachment had twelve men wounded. On the 31st, the post of Chamurchi was attacked and carried after a slight resistance, in which the force suffered a loss of two men killed and three wounded.

The left centre column, under Lieutenant-Colonel Watson, met with little opposition in its advance; the fort of Baksa was occupied on the 6th December, and the Bala Pass was forced, and Tazagong captured, on the 21st.

The right column, under Lieutenant-Colonel R. Campbell, 43rd Native Infantry, and accompanied by Brigadier-General Mulcaster, left Gauhati on the 2nd December, and on the 10th entered the Daranga Pass, at the top of which the fort of Dewangiri was situated. On the same day Dewangiri was captured by a party of Military Police under Captain Macdonald, who had gone up by another route, with a loss on our side of one man killed and five wounded, and on the 11th Brigadier-General Mulcaster arrived there with part of the column. On the 17th December the column was broken up and returned to the plains, Lieutenant-Colonel Campbell having been left at Dewangiri with six companies of the 43rd Native Infantry, two guns of the Eurasian Battery, a company of sappers, and some police.

The right centre column advanced from Goalpara and, on the 8th January 1865, occupied Bissengiri unopposed.

The objects of the expedition having apparently been accomplished, orders were issued for the breaking up of the field force. Suddenly however, when least expected, although warnings had not been wanting, almost simultaneous attacks were made on Dewangiri, Bissengiri, Baksa, Tazagong in the Bala Pass, and Chamurchi. In the attack on the first-named place (29th January,) one officer and five men were killed, and one officer and thirty-two men wounded. The enemy then almost surrounded the post, cut off the water-supply and the communication with the plains, and pressed the garrison so severely that Colonel Campbell, considering his force insufficient to dislodge his opponents, determined to retreat, and evacuated Dewangiri before daylight on the morning of the 5th February. The main column lost its way in the darkness and a panic set in, in which some of the wounded were abandoned and the guns (which were thrown down a ravine) and all the baggage lost.

The attacks on Bissengiri (25th January) and Baksa (26th January) were repulsed without much difficulty by the detachments of the 44th Native Infantry and 3rd Gurkha Regiment stationed at those places. That on Tazagong (27th January) was not so easily disposed of; the post there was hard pressed for several days, and even after the arrival of reinforcements it was found impossible to dislodge the enemy from the position they had taken up, an attempt to do so proving unsuccessful, with a loss on our side of one officer (Lieutenant MillettMillett, 11th Native Infantry) killed, and two officers (one mortally) and thirteen men wounded. The post at Chamurchi (which was held by a detachment of police) was also hard pressed, and it was not until a part of the 30th Native Infantry was sent up as a reinforcement that the enemy were driven off.

Reinforcements (which included the 55th and 80th Foot, a company of sappers and miners, and the 19th, 29th, and 31st Native Infantry) were quickly sent up, and two independent brigades were formed. The Left Brigade, under Brigadier-General J. M. B. Fraser-Tytler, included, besides the troops already on the spot, No. 7 Battery, 22nd Brigade, Royal Artillery, a wing of the 55th Foot, the headquarters of the 80th Foot, and the 19th and 31st Native Infantry; the Right Brigade was placed under Brigadier-General Tombs, and included No. 3 Battery, 25th Brigade, Royal Artillery, the Eurasian Battery of Artillery, a detachment of the 14th Bengal Cavalry, a company of sappers, the head-quarters wing of the 55th Foot, the 12th, 29th, and 44th Native Infantry, and a detachment of the 43rd.

The advance of the two brigades was followed by the speedy conclusion of hostilities. The enemy's stockades at Tazagong, in the Bala Pass, were captured on the 15th March by a part of the Left Brigade, with a loss of only three men killed and one officer and nineteen men wounded; and Baksa and Chamurchi were both relieved by the 24th March. On the latter date a forward movement was made by the Right Brigade from Kumrikata, and the Daranga Pass was taken the same day by detachments of the 14th Bengal Cavalry and of the 12th, 29th, and 44th Native Infantry, the whole under the command of Lieutenant-Colonel Stevens, after a smart skirmish, in which a loss was sustained of two men killed and Lieutenant Beddy, 29th Native Infantry, and thirteen men wounded. On the 1st April the final advance on Dewangiri was made, and on the following day the place was taken by storm. The storming party consisted of three companies of the 29th Native Infantry, under the command of Lieutenant Beddy (described by Brigadier-General Tombs as "a most gallant young officer, who had already distinguished himself more than once"), supported by detachments of the 55th Foot and the 12th Native Infantry. On the signal to assault being given these troops advanced with a rush and soon effected an entrance into the works: the enemy were in great strength, three thousand at least, and made a desperate but unavailing resistance; about 130 of them were killed, and they left about 120 wounded behind them. Our loss amounted to seven men killed, and four officers and 99 men wounded.

This practically concluded the war, but the Bhutiahs were not yet subdued, and it being an object of importance, moreover, to recover the guns lost at Dewangiri in February, it became necessary to keep a considerable force on the frontier until the time should arrive for the renewal of operations. During this period the troops suffered terribly from the deadly climate of the Terai. Towards the end of the year, some negotiations took place with the Bhutan Government, and the surrender of the guns was made one of the conditions of the re-establishment of peace. The guns were, however, in the hands of the Tongsoo Penlow, the leading spirit in the war against us, and as the surrender of them was delayed, Colonel Richardson, who was commanding the right column of the Bhutan Field Force, moved forward from Dewangiri into Bhutan early in February 1866, with a force consisting of a company of sappers, a wing of the 9th Native Infantry, two companies of the 12th, and the whole of the 26th Native Infantry. On the 6th February he advanced to Salika, with a loss of two men wounded, and on the 7th seized the bridge over the Monas river. Being short of transport the force had to halt for some time, and in the meantime, on the 23rd February, the Bhutiahs surrendered the guns which had fallen into their hands and the troops then returned to Dewangiri. Peace having been concluded, the field force was broken up in the spring of 1866, and the troops returned to quarters. By G. G. O. No. 86 of 1870 the India medal, with a special clasp, was granted to all troops actively engaged with the enemy in the Bhutan war.

In the autumn of 1867 insults offered to the British representative and the wanton imprisonment of British subjects by King Theodore of Abyssinia, necessitated the despatch of an expedition to that country. The nature of the undertaking, which involved a march of some hundreds of miles from the coast to the capital, through an unknown country deficient in supplies and water, and against a fortress known to be of considerable natural strength, demanded the exercise of great foresight in the arrangement of preliminaries. This received the most careful attention from the officer appointed to command,—Lieutenant-General Sir Robert C. Napier, then Commander-in-Chief of the Bombay Army,—and the event justified his selection, for seldom or never has an expedition on so large a scale been so thoroughly well prepared or so successfully carried through without a single hitch or *contretemps*.

The total force detailed for the expedition amounted to nearly 14,000 men, and consisted of four regiments and a half of cavalry; seven batteries and one native company of artillery; eight companies of engineers and sappers; and four regiments of British and ten of native infantry. Of this force Bengal contributed two regiments of native cavalry and two battalions of native infantry. These were the 10th Bengal Cavalry (Lancers) and the 12th Bengal Cavalry, the 21st Native Infantry and the 23rd Native Infantry (Pioneers).

The Bengal troops embarked at Calcutta in December and January, 1868, and the 10th Bengal Cavalry, who were the last to arrive, completed their disembarkation on the 6th March. The 23rd Native Infantry were the first at Zula, the port of disembarkation in Annesley Bay, and accompanied Sir Robert Napier's advance up the country; the 21st Native Infantry was employed in garrison duty at the base and at various posts on the road. The 12th Bengal Cavalry overtook the main column at Antalo, half-way between the coast and Magdala, the Abyssinian capital, and the head-quarters advanced with the army to the latter place. The 10th Bengal Cavalry were also ordered up in haste, but were too late to be present at the taking of Magdala.

The army advanced from Antalo on the 12th March, and arrived within a few miles of Magdala on the 7th April. Here a reconnaissance in force was commenced by the advance guard, which resulted in the first and only serious conflict of the campaign. The advance of the British troops was met by a vigorous, though scattered, attack of the enemy at Arogi (10th April); the brunt of the first charge was borne by the 4th Foot (the King's Own), whose quick-firing Enfield rifles drove the enemy back before they could get to close quarters. Another vigorous assault was made on the left, which was met and repulsed with great gallantry by the 23rd Bengal Native Infantry. The British loss was insignificant, amounting to no more than one officer and nineteen men wounded; but the enemy suffered very heavily, so much so that, rather than face a second engagement, a great proportion of Theodore's army deserted during the next two days.

Some days were spent in endeavours to induce the king to surrender, and were so far successful that the release of the British subjects who were prisoners in his fortress was accomplished. Nothing more definite, however, could be gained, and at length, after due preparation, a general advance against Magdala took place on the 13th April. As the British force advanced, the king's troops, remembering the fight at Arogi, deserted by hundreds, and fled in all directions from the fortress, so that when the storming party reached the gates the band of adherents who remained by their master's side was reduced to a mere handful. The place was taken with hardly any resistance; such of the garrison as remained surrendered; and Theodore, when he found that all was lost, discharged a pistol into his mouth and blew his brains out. Our loss in the assault amounted to only fifteen wounded, but of these no less than four were officers.

With the capture of Magdala the active operations of the campaign terminated. The retirement commenced within a few days, and by the end of May the last detachment of Bengal troops had sailed for India. Sir Robert Napier was rewarded for the complete success of the expedition with a peerage; a medal was issued to all the troops engaged, and six months' donation batta was granted; and the word "Abyssinia" was authorised to be borne on the colours and appointments of the corps employed (G. G. O. No. 1181 of 1869).

The next twelve years of the history of the Bengal Army are marked by a number of expeditions, of greater or less importance, on the North-West Frontier of the Punjab and the Eastern, North-Eastern and South-Eastern Frontiers of Bengal, as well as by two expeditions beyond sea. These will now be noticed in due order of date.

The first of these events was an affair with the Bizoti Urakzais in the Ublan Pass, about six miles from Kohat, on the 11th March, 1868. In order to repel a raid by these people, Major Jones, commanding at Kohat, moved out from that place with detachments of No. 2 Punjab Light Field Battery, the 3rd Punjab Cavalry, and the 3rd and 6th Punjab Infantry. In the engagement which ensued the enemy, though at first driven back, succeeded in repulsing two attacks on the position they had taken up, and night coming on the troops had eventually to be withdrawn, after sustaining considerable loss—eleven killed and forty-four wounded,—among the former of whom were included Captain Ruxton and *Subadar* Ram Singh of the 3rd Punjab Infantry,—the latter described as "one of the bravest officers of the Punjab Frontier Force."

In the autumn of 1868 it became necessary to send an expedition against the tribes of the Black Mountain, in Hazara. At the end of July in that year a police post at Ughi, in the Agror valley, was suddenly attacked by a mixed band of Chagarzais, Akazais, Hassanzais, and Pariari Saiads, about 500 in number. Though repulsed with some loss they still hung about the valley; presently the whole of these tribes were up, and, being joined by most of the Swati clans, the insurrection began to assume a grave aspect. On the first news of the outbreak Lieutenant-Colonel Rothney promptly moved into the Agror valley, from Abbottabad, with the Peshawar Mountain Battery and a wing of the 5th Gurkha Regiment, but, though he was subsequently joined by a wing of the 2nd Punjab Infantry, his force was inadequate to cope with the numerous bodies in his front, and he was compelled to remain almost entirely on the defensive; nor was he able to prevent the burning by the insurgents of a number of British villages. To punish the tribes concerned in the creation of these disorders, it was decided to organise an expedition forthwith which should ascend the Black Mountain and visit the settlements of the offenders, and the troops detailed for this service were collected with wonderful rapidity; in particular the 20th Native Infantry marched, in the hot month of August, 232 miles in ten days; the 31st covered 422 miles in twenty-nine days, and two companies of the Sappers and Miners nearly 600 miles in the same time.

The force was composed of the following troops, which were organised in two brigades:—"D" Battery, "F" Brigade, Royal Horse Artillery, "E" Battery, 19th Brigade, Royal Artillery, No. 2 Battery, 24th Brigade, Royal Artillery; the Peshawar and Hazara Mountain Batteries; a detachment of the 9th Bengal Cavalry; the 16th Bengal Cavalry; a detachment of the Guides Cavalry; two companies of the Sappers and Miners; the 1-6th and the 1-19th Foot; the 20th and 24th Bengal Native Infantry; the 1st, 2nd, 4th and 5th Gurkha Regiments; the 3rd Sikh Infantry, and the 2nd Punjab Infantry.

The 1st Brigade was commanded by Colonel R. O. Bright, 19th Foot, and the 2nd by Colonel J. L. Vaughan; the whole force was under the command of Brigadier-General A. T. Wilde, C.B.

On the 3rd October the operations were begun by a forward movement from Ughi. The 2nd Brigade, moving on Kilagai, met with no opposition, while the 1st Brigade experienced but faint resistance in their advance as far as Mana-ka-Dana. On the next day the position of the enemy there was carried by the 1st and 5th Gurkha Regiments, and the 1st Brigade reached Chittabut, the 2nd moving on to Mana-ka-Dana; and on the 5th October the heights of the Machai peak were carried by the 20th Native Infantry, supported by 1st and 5th Gurkha Regiments, the resistance of the enemy being still feeble and half-hearted. During the next eight or ten days, various movements were made without much opposition from the enemy, who now entered into negotiations and tendered their submission. Only the Pariari Saiads remained refractory for a while, and their villages having been destroyed, and a fine inflicted, the campaign was brought to a conclusion. The total casualties during the operations were five killed and twenty-nine wounded. By G. G. O. No. 86 of 1870 the India medal was granted for this expedition.

In February 1869, when the Bizoti Urakzais were again located in their winter settlements, an expedition was planned against their village of GaraGara, on the further side of the Ublan pass, to punish them for their raid of the previous year and tor one of which they had since been guilty. The arrangements were made with profound secrecy, and the force (two guns of No. 1 Punjab Mountain Battery, and the 1st and 4th Punjab Infantry,—the whole under the command of Lieutenant-Colonel Keyes), having left Kohat at 1 a.m. on the 25th, gained the summit of the pass without opposition; advancing into the valley beyond, they rushed the village of Gara, which was carried after a brief struggle and forthwith destroyed. The force then commenced its retirement, but the movement was one of considerable difficulty, and was not effected without loss. The casualties during the expedition amounted to three killed and thirty-three wounded.

The operations which come next in order of date occurred at the opposite extremity of the Empire, on the Eastern and South-Eastern Frontiers of Bengal. For a long series of years the Lushai clans had been guilty of predatory inroads into British territory, where they had committed numerous outrages on the inhabitants: latterly these had increased in frequency, and in the autumn of 1871 affairs had arrived at such a stage that the punishment of the offenders could no longer be delayed. For the accomplishment of this object two distinct columns were accordingly organised, to enter the Lushai country from Cachar and Chittagong, respectively.

The Cachar column (which was placed under the command of Brigadier-General G. Bourchier, C.B., and was composed of half of the Peshawar Mountain Battery, a company of sappers and miners, and 500 men each of the 22nd, 42nd, and 44th Bengal Native Infantry) left Cachar on the 21st. November, and advanced without meeting with any opposition, or being hindered in any way except by the difficulties of the country, as far as Tipai Mukh, where it arrived on the 15th of December. Thence the advance was continued across the Tawibhum stream towards the Vonpilal villages, where some opposition was met with, and the force was annoyed by being continually fired on, in consequence of which several villages were destroyed. Our loss between the 24th and 29th of December was six killed and eleven wounded. On the 9th January, 1872, a further advance was commenced through Pachui and Chipui to Kungnung, which place was defended, and was only carried with a loss of four killed and eleven wounded, Brigadier General Bourchier himself being among the latter. On the 1st February the final advance to Sellam was commenced, and thence through a very mountainous and densely-wooded country, the force moved to Champhai, the principal village of the Chief Lalburah, situated in latitude $23^0\ 26'\ 32"$ and longitude $93^0\ 21'$, which was reached on the 17th. Throughout this last advance but very slight resistance had been met with, and the people generally seemed disinclined for hostilities. The main objects, therefore, of the expedition having been attained, the column began its return march on the 21st February, and reached Cachar on the 10th of March.

The Chittagong column, under Brigadier-General C. H. Brownlow, C.B., was composed of half of the Peshawar Mountain Battery, a company of sappers, the 27th Native Infantry, and the 2nd and 4th Gurkha Regiments. Leaving Chittagong early in December, it marched to Kassalong, whence it advanced through Demagiri to Vanunah, which village was reached on the 14th December. On the 18th a slight skirmish took place between some Lushais and a party of the 2nd Gurkha Regiment; on the 30th Savunga was reached, and taken with slight opposition; and on the 4th January 1872, a detachment of the 2nd Gurkha Regiment attacked and seized the village of the Chief Lal Gnura, losing in the affair one man killed and Captain Battye and nine men wounded. The advance continued throughout January, and at the end of the month, as a proof of their readiness to treat, the child of an English planter, who had been carried off in the preceding year, was given up by the enemy. Brigadier-General Brownlow continued his advance against the Northern Howlongs, until, on the 18th February, their chiefs tendered their submission, The Southern Howlongs also submitted, peace was concluded, and the troops returned to Chittagong in March 1872.

The India medal, with a special clasp, was granted to the Lushai Expeditionary Force by G. G. O. No. 1295 of 1872.

No further disturbance occurred on the North-West Frontier until 1872, when the misbehaviour of the men of Lower Dawar, on the Bannu border, necessitated punitive measures. On the 7th March a dash was made into their country by a force under Brigadier-General Keyes, composed of two guns of No. 3 Punjab Light Field Battery and detachments of the 1st and 2nd Punjab Cavalry, 1st and 4th Sikh Infantry, and 1st Punjab Infantry. The Tochi pass, leading into the Lower Dawar valley, was traversed and the valley entered without opposition; the head-men of two villages joined the force and professed their eagerness to treat, but on the village of Haidar Khel being approached, a hot fire was opened on the troops by the inhabitants. The guns were quickly brought into action and at the same time the village was stormed with great gallantry by the 1st Sikh Infantry. More than forty of the enemy were killed; the rest surrendered, and the inhabitants of all the other villages in the valley tendered unconditional submission. The British force returned to camp at the mouth of the Tochi pass the same night, having lost only six men wounded.

At the end of 1874 an expedition was organised and despatched under Brigadier-General Stafford, C.B., against the Daphlas, a savage tribe inhabiting the hills on the borders of the Darrang district in Lower Assam, who had been guilty of plundering in British territory: the troops employed were half of the Hazara Mountain Battery and detachments of the 16th, 42nd, 43rd, and 44th Native Infantry The column advanced some distance into the hills, without meeting with any opposition; and the chiefs having tendered their submission, Brigadier-General Stafford retraced his steps, and the force was broken up early in March 1875.

In consequence of a treacherous attack on, and the massacre of, a survey party under Lieutenant Holcombe at Ninu, on the 2nd February 1875, a punitive expedition was despatched into the Naga Hills, Assam frontier, at the end of the same month. It consisted of detachments of the 42nd and 44th Native Infantry, numbering 308 in all, and was commanded by Colonel J. M. Nuttall. Leaving Dibrugarh on the 27th February, the expedition advanced by Bor Matan, across the Tesing and Desang rivers, through a thickly populated country, to the large village of Ninu, which was taken after a smart skirmish on the 19th March. A week was spent in scouring the country with detachments, and in the destruction of villages which had taken part in the massacre of February. On the 26th the column was re-united at Ninu, when the persons most directly implicated in the massacre having been captured, or given up, the troops returned to Dibrugarh, arriving there on the 11th April.

For some months after this the Nagas maintained a comparatively peaceful attitude, but in December they again displayed their hostility in an attack on another survey party, in which Captain Butler, Political Officer in the Naga Hills, was mortally wounded.

At the end of 1875 an outbreak at Perak, in the Malay Peninsula, in which the Resident, Mr. Birch, was killed, was the cause of a force of some strength being asked for from India. In a very short space of time the troops detailed to proceed from India, which included the head-quarters and 400 men of the 1st Gurkha Regiment, arrived on the scene of action, under the command of Brigadier-General John Ross. By that time, however, the disturbances had been to a great extent suppressed, and but little remained for the force from India to accomplish. Detachments were, however, twice engaged with the Malays: first, on the 20th December, when storming the Bukit Patus Pass stockades, where one man was killed and another wounded; and, secondly, at the village of Kota Lama, on the 4th January, 1876, when a detachment was surprised by a party of Malays, one officer (Major Hawkins, Brigade Major of the Indian Brigade) and two men being killed and four men wounded. After two months of jungle work, the force returned to India in March 1876.

The India medal, with a special clasp, was granted for the expedition by G. G. O. No. 242 of 1880.

Towards the end of 1877, the Naga tribes again became aggressive, and several outrages having been committed in British territory, it became necessary to adopt punitive measures against the raiders. A force of two hundred men of the 42nd Native Infantry, under Captain Brydon, was despatched in December against the important village of Mozima, which was taken and destroyed on the 8th of that month. Further than this Captain Brydon was unable to move owing to the smallness of his force; indeed, his position at Mozima was somewhat precarious until the arrival of 100 men of the 43rd Native Infantry on the 9th of January, when the Nagas sued for peace, and tranquillity was temporarily restored.

In the autumn of 1877 it became necessary to send an expedition against the Jowaki Afridis, to inflict punishment for a long series of outrages in British territory of which this tribe had been guilty. The troops engaged were No. 1 Mountain Battery and detachments of the 2nd Punjab Cavalry, 1st, 3rd, and 4th Sikh Infantry, 6th Punjab Infantry, and the Guides Infantry, the whole under the command of Colonel Mocatta, Brigadier-General C. P. Keyes, who was to have commanded, having been suddenly taken ill. The troops advanced into the Jowaki country (29th August) in three columns by different routes, destroyed several villages, and again retired by the same roads, having lost one man killed, and one officer and nine men wounded.

Colonel Mocatta's raid did not have the effect of modifying the hostile attitude of the Jowakis, who continued their forays into British territory as before, plundering several villages and murdering many of the inhabitants. As the only means of putting an end to these outrages, it was decided at last to carry out a second invasion of the Jowaki hills, and to occupy the country until the offending clans had submitted and had made due reparation. For this purpose two strong columns were detailed to enter the hills,—the one from Kohat and the other from the Peshawar side,—and to the command of these Brigadier-General C. P. Keyes and Brigadier-General C. C. G. Ross were, respectively, nominated. The former force was composed of Nos. 1 and 4 Mountain Batteries, the 29th Native Infantry, and detachments of No. 2 Mountain Battery, the 2nd Punjab Cavalry, the Guides Infantry, the 1st and 3rd Sikh Infantry, the 4th, 5th and 6th Punjab Infantry, and the 5th Gurkha Regiment; while the latter (which was divided into two brigades, commanded respectively by Colonels Doran and Buchanan) consisted of a battery of horse artillery, a heavy-battery, two companies of sappers and miners, three battalions of British infantry, and the 14th, 20th, 22nd, and 27th Native Infantry.

The force under Brigadier-General Keyes entered the Jowaki country on the 9th November, in three columns, of which, after some skirmishing, the first and second occupied Paiah, and the third Kahkto. On the 12th an attack was made on the latter column, but was repulsed by a company of the 5th Punjab Infantry; and on the following day the whole force concentrated at Paiah. For a fortnight operations were hindered by excessive rain, but at length on the 1st December an advance was made into the Jamu valley; some skirmishing took place during that and the next three days, and the column then took up a position at Bagh. On the 7th the village of Ghariba, which had long been notorious as the Alsatia of the Jowaki robbers, was captured and destroyed.

During this time Brigadier-General Ross's force had been prevented by incessant rain from starting from Peshawar, and it was not until the 4th December that it was able to move forward. On that day the two passes leading into the Bori valley were seized, the ridges above occupied, and the towers and villages in the valley destroyed.

Notwithstanding this occupation of their country, the enemy showed as yet no signs of surrender; and it was therefore decided that a simultaneous advance should be made from the north and south on the Pastaoni valley. A preliminary reconnaissance was made on the 25th December by the Peshawar force, and on the 31st Brigadier-General Ross advanced almost unopposed, and took the village of Pastaoni, where he was joined by Brigadier-General Keyes. During the next three weeks the British columns continued to move through the Jowaki country. No opposition was encountered, except by a column under Colonel Mocatta, consisting of detachments of No. 1 Mountain Battery, and of the island 3rd Sikh Infantry and the 20th Native Infantry; this column advanced from Turkai on the 15th January, into the Nara Khula defile, which was defended in some strength by the Jowakis, but it was forced without much difficulty and with little loss.

At length, on the 23rd and 24th January, the troops were withdrawn on both sides; and the movement was followed almost immediately by the complete submission of the Jowaki tribesmen. Our total loss during the ten weeks' operations amounted to eleven men killed and one officer and fifty men wounded.

The India medal, with a clasp inscribed "Jowaki," was subsequently granted for the operations between the 19th November and the 19th January. (G. G. O. Nos. .43 of .879 and 285 of 1880.)

In March 1878, shortly after the conclusion of the Jowaki campaign, an expedition was sent against the village of Skakot inhabited by the Swati tribe of Ranizais, who had lately been giving trouble on the border. The force employed was the Hazara Mountain Battery and the Guides Cavalry and Infantry, under Major R B. P. P. Campbell. Marching from Mardan on the evening of the 13th March, the detachment reached the village at 2 a.m. on the 14th and surrounded it before daybreak, when the inhabitants, finding resistance hopeless, accepted the inevitable and surrendered. The troops returned to Mardan the same day.

At the same time operations were in progress against the Utman Khels, who had made an unprovoked attack on a body of unarmed labourers employed on the Swat Canal, of whom a large number were cruelly massacred. Against the perpetrators of this outrage a detachment of the Guides (280 strong), under the command of Captain W. Battye, was sent in February, 1878, when the village of Sapri was surprised and the leader of the raiders killed. As some of the Utman Khel villages still refused to make reparation for the outrage, it became necessary to take measures to coerce them, and for this purpose, on the 20th March, a force under Lieutenant-Colonel Jenkins, commanding the Corps of Guides, marched from Mardan and crossed the Utman Khel border on the following morning. But little opposition was met with; the refractory villages submitted, and the force retired the same evening.

In 1878, the result of the Russo-Turkish war and the advance of the Russians on Constantinople was the cause of an event of considerable interest to the Indian Army,—the employment for the first time of a native force in Europe. Under instructions from the Secretary of State an expeditionary force was, on the 17th April 1878, detailed to proceed on service to the Mediterranean. It was composed Of two field batteries of Royal Artillery, two regiments of native cavalry, four companies of sappers, and six regiments of native infantry. The Bengal corps detailed were the 9th Bengal Cavalry with a squadron of the 10th Bengal Lancers attached, the 13th (Shekha-wati) and 31st (Punjab) Native Infantry, and the 2nd (the Prince of Wales' Own) Gurkha Regiment.

By G. G. O. No. 347 of 1878 these regiments of native infantry were allowed extra batta while on foreign service; while the native cavalry were authorised to draw free rations or ration money.

The force reached Malta in May, and there, in the following

month, these troops were inspected by His Royal Highness the Duke of Cambridge, Commanding-in-Chief, who afterwards issued a most complimentary order, in which he referred to the Indian Forces in the following terms:—"His Royal Highness cannot speak too highly of their soldierly qualities. Their uniform good conduct and smartness reflects the greatest credit on all ranks. Their steadiness under arms and drill and the excellent state of their camps leave nothing to be desired." The Indian troops left Malta in July and proceeded to Cyprus, where they occupied various posts until towards the end of August, when they embarked on their return to India.

An attack, in the autumn of 1879, on Mr. Damant, the Political Agent, in which that gentleman, *Jemadar* Prem Singh, and ten sepoys of the 43rd Native Infantry were killed and five sepoys wounded, there being besides many casualties among the police, compelled the Government once more to despatch an expedition against the Naga tribes.

The force detailed for this service, which was placed under the command of Brigadier-General Nation, was composed of a small party of the 34th, a detachment (300 men) of the 43rd, and the whole of the 44th Native Infantry, with two mountain guns. It was concentrated at Piphima on the 21st November, previous to which (15th November) a detachment of the 43rd, under Major Evans, attacked and took the village of Sephima, with a loss of two men killed and one officer and two sepoys wounded, while, on the 14th, a detachment of the 44th occupied the important position of Sachima. Thence, on the 22nd November, an attack was made on the Naga stronghold of Konoma. In the belief that but slight resistance would be made, the attacking force was split up into several parties, with the unfortunate result that after a whole day's fighting the artillery ammunition was found to be exhausted and the storming parties had lost a fourth of their numbers, while only a small portion of the enemy's works had been carried. Fortunately the place was evacuated during the night, and the enemy retired to an entrenched position a mile higher up the mountain. In the day's fighting one native officer (*Subadar*-Major Narbir Sahi, 44th Native Infantry) and seventeen men were killed, while the wounded amounted to four British officers (two mortally), two native officers, and twenty-seven men (three mortally,). Lieutenant R. K. Ridgeway, who was severely wounded, was awarded the Victoria Cross for distinguished gallantry in the assault.

Leaving a detachment to garrison Konoma, Brigadier-General Nation retired to Sachima. On the 27th November the village of Jotsoma was destroyed without opposition. The remainder of the month and the whole of December were passed in inaction, awaiting the arrival of supplies, transport, and reinforcements. A wing of the 42nd Native Infantry having arrived towards the end of December, active operations were immediately resumed, the village of Cheswejuma being destroyed, and Poplongmai surprised and taken, with a loss of one killed and four wounded. Further reinforcements, consisting of a wing of the 18th Native Infantry, arrived on the 12th March 1880, and the operations were prosecuted with vigour until the 28th, when the enemy sued for peace and terms were arranged. In the course of these operations our losses (including those sustained in the attack on Mr. Damant's escort) amounted to two native officers and forty-four men killed, and five British officers, two native officers and fifty-eight men wounded. Major C. R. Cock, Assistant Adjutant-General, Lieutenant H. H. Forbes, 44th Native Infantry, and twelve men died of their wounds.

The India medal, with a special clasp, was granted for the Naga Hills Expedition by G. G. O. No. 344 of 1881.

During the period under review a noteworthy event occurred in India, which may not inappropriately be mentioned in this place. This was the Imperial Assemblage at Delhi, at which, on January 1st, 1877, Her Majesty the Queen was proclaimed Empress of India, and which was attended by about 17,000 troops, consisting of eight batteries of artillery, three regiments of British cavalry, seven regiments of British infantry, six regiments of native cavalry, four companies of sappers, and thirteen regiments of native infantry, besides a representative body of the Volunteer Forces of India.

This chapter may now be brought to a close with a cursory survey of such internal changes in the Bengal Army during the eighteen years of which it treats as may seem to be of interest.

The numbering and constitution of the army remained unaltered, with the exception of the addition of one regiment to the infantry list: this was the 1st Bengal Police Battalion, which, as "Rattray's Sikhs," had rendered such excellent service in Bihar in 1857-58. In 1864, by G. G. O. No. 326, the corps was added to the Bengal Army as the "45th Bengal Native Infantry (Rattray's Sikhs)."

In other respects the period under review was remarkable for many changes in the interior economy of corps. This is readily accounted for by the fact that the re-organisation of the army was but just completed, and it was inevitable that many measures, which were but tentative, should require modification. Foremost among the changes was the new scheme for the composition of Bengal Native regiments, as notified in 1864.[4] The tabulated order was as follows:

Cavalry.

Regiments.	Mooltanis.	Hindustani Musalmans.	Trans-Indus and Border Tribes.	Punjabi Musalmans.	Hindustani Hindus.	Sikhs.	Dogras and Hillmen.	Bundelas.	Jats.	Total Troops.	Remarks.
1st Bengal Cavalry	The composition of the corps to remain as previously, *viz.*, entirely Hindustani Musalmans.										
2nd "	To be composed gradually, but eventually, of Musalmans, Dogras, Sikhs, Jats, Rajputs, Brahmans, and Mahrattas, in equal numbers, and mixed together in the several troops.										
3rd "	The same as 2nd Bengal Cavalry.										
4th "	Ditto ditto.										
5th "	Ditto ditto.										
6th "	...	1	1	...	1	1	...	1	1	6	That is, class troops.
7th "	The same as 2nd Bengal Cavalry.										
8th "	...	1	1	1	1	...	...	1	1	6	
9th "	...	...	1	2	...	2	1	...	...	6	
10th "	...	...	1	1	...	2	1	...	1	6	
11th "	...	...	1	1	...	3	1	...	...	6	
12th "	...	...	1	1	...	2	½	½	1	6	
13th "	...	...	1	2	...	2	1	...	...	6	
14th "	To remain as formerly a class regiment of Jats only.										
15th "	To remain as formerly a class regiment of Mooltanis, Duranis, Pathans, Baluchis, &c.										
16th "	...	1	1	...	2	...	1	...	1	6	
17th "	...	1	1	1	1	...	1	...	1	6	
18th "	...	1	...	1	1	1	...	...	2	6	
19th "	1	...	1	1	...	2	½	...	½	6	

---

4. Adjutant-General's Circular No. 117 N. dated 9th September, 1864.

Infantry.

Regiments.		Brahmans and Rajputs.	Hindustani Musalmans.	Jats.	Gurkhas and Hillmen.	Bundelas.	Ahirs.	Pasis.	Lodhs.	Dhanuks.	Kurmis.	Gujars.	Chumars.	Mehtars.	Hindus of inferior castes.	Punjabi Musalmans.	Trans-Indus and Border Tribes.	Dogras and Hillmen.	Trans-Sutlej Sikhs.	Cis-Sutlej Sikhs.	All races and castes.
1st Native Infantry	.	To be recruited as formerly; a predominance of Rajputs, with large numbers of Brahmans and Hindustani Musalmans, some Sikhs and low caste men.																			
2nd	,,	As formerly, chiefly of Hindustani Musalmans, Brahmans and Rajputs, a few low caste men.																			
3rd	,,	The same as the 2nd.																			
4th	,,	Do. do.																			
5th	,,	2	1	1	1	1	…	…	…	…	…	…	…	…	1	…	…	…	1	…	…
6th	,,	1	1	2	…	…	…	…	…	…	…	…	…	…	1	1	…	1	1	…	…
7th	,,	As formerly, chiefly Hindustani Musalmans, Brahmans and Rajputs, with an admixture of Cis-Sutlej Sikhs and low castes.																			
8th	,,	2	1	…	…	…	…	…	…	…	…	…	…	…	1	…	1	1	1	…	1
9th	,,	2	1	1	1	2	…	…	…	…	…	…	…	…	…	…	…	…	1	…	…
10th	,,	2	1	1	…	1	…	…	…	…	…	…	…	…	1	1	…	1	…	…	…
11th	,,	To be recruited as formerly, much the same as the 2nd.																			
12th	,,	As the 2nd, with an admixture of Punjabi Musalmans.																			
13th	,,	1	1	2	1	2	…	…	…	…	…	…	…	…	1	…	…	…	…	…	…
14th	,,	As formerly, principally Cis-Sutlej Sikhs, with a small admixture of Punjabi Musalmans and Trans-Sutlej Sikhs.																			
15th	,,	As the 14th.																			
16th	,,	As formerly, of Hindustani Musalmans, Brahmans and Rajputs, with a few Ahirs, Sikhs and low castes.																			
17th	,,	As formerly; much the same as the 2nd.																			
18th	,,	2	2	…	2	1	…	…	…	…	…	…	…	…	1	…	…	…	…	…	…

At the same time the organisation, pay, promotion, &c, of British officers under their new conditions of service formed the subject of much correspondence and of many orders during the early years of this period, into the particulars of which it is impossible to enter here. At length, on the 29th October 1863, a G. G. O. (No. 161-A)

Regiments.	Brahman and Rajputs.	Hindustani Musalmans.	Jats.	Gurkhas and Hillmen.	Bundelas.	Ahirs.	Pasis.	Lodhs.	Dhanuks.	Kurmis.	Gujars.	Chumars.	Mehtars.	Hindus of inferior castes.	Punjabi Musalmans.	Trans-Indus and Border Tribes.	Dogras and Hillmen.	Trans-Sutlej Sikhs.	Cis-Sutlej Sikhs.	All races and castes.
19th Native Infantry																				
20th ,,	\multicolumn{20}{l}{To be composed of Punjabi Musalmans and Trans-Sutlej Sikhs in nearly equal proportions, with a few Dogras.}
21st ,,																				
22nd ,,																				
23rd ,,	\multicolumn{20}{l}{A class regiment of Mazbi Sikhs.}
24th ,,																				
25th ,,																				
26th ,,																				
27th ,,	\multicolumn{20}{l}{The same as the 19th Native Infantry.}
28th ,,																				
29th ,,																				
30th ,,																				
31st ,,	\multicolumn{20}{l}{The same as the 19th Native Infantry but Cis-Sutlej Sikhs may be entertained.}
32nd ,,	\multicolumn{20}{l}{A class regiment of Mazbi Sikhs.}
33rd ,, (low caste levies)		1				3	1					1		1						1
34th ,,	1					1		1	1				1	1	1					1
35th ,,						2		2	1			2	1							
36th ,,	2		1			2					2									1
37th ,,	1	1	1			1				1	2				1					
38th ,,	2		2			2					1									1
39th ,,	1		1	1		1							1		1				1	1
40th ,,	2					3									1				1	1
41st ,,	2	1	2	1							1							1		
42nd ,,	\multicolumn{20}{l}{Chiefly of Gurkhas and Hillmen (Assamese), with a proportion, not exceeding one-fourth of its strength, of Hindustanis.}
43rd ,,	\multicolumn{20}{l}{The same as the 42nd.}
44th ,,																				
45th ,,	\multicolumn{20}{l}{As formerly, to be composed entirely of Punjabis and Sikhs.}
1st Gurkha Regiment																				
2nd ,,	\multicolumn{20}{l}{Class regiments, entirely of Gurkhas and Hillmen.}
3rd ,,																				
4th ,,																				
Sappers and Miners.	\multicolumn{20}{l}{Five-eighths Hindustanis. Two-eighths Punjabis and Sikhs. One-eighth Trans-Indus tribes.}

was published, which fixed the establishments of British officers with native regiments under the new "Irregular" system, and laid down the scale of staff salary attaching to each appointment. According to this, the British officers with a native cavalry regiment were to be a commandant, a second-in-command, two squadron officers, an adjutant and a doing-duty officer. In infantry corps there was no second-in-command; the establishment authorised included a commandant, two wing commanders, an adjutant, a quarter-master, and a doing-duty officer. On the 20th January 1864, further particulars regarding the various duties of the above-named officers were published by the commander-in-chief, and on the same date the regiments of the Bengal Army were completed with officers of all grades. Other orders of interest to the army generally were(1)the grant by G.G.O. No. 812 of 1869 of the India medal to the survivors of the troops engaged in a number of frontier expeditions since the annexation of the Punjab; (2) the alteration of the rules for good-conduct pay in 1877 (G. G. O. No. 1),—one, two, and three rupees being given to the cavalry after three, nine, and fifteen years' service, instead of, as formerly, after six, ten and fifteen years; (3) the introduction by G. O, No. 101 of 1870 of a weekly holiday on Thursday, on which no field days or parades, except musketry, should take place, nor general, district, or regimental court-martials should sit, unless the exigencies of the public service absolutely required it.

The following orders apply particularly to cavalry:—At the reorganisation in 1861 the system of Chanda Funds, involving monthly subscriptions from all ranks, was abolished; casualties were provided for by general subscriptions from the troops in which they occurred. It is obvious that such a system would place a premium on keeping horses as long as possible, however old and unfit for the service; and in 1868 the old Chanda Fund system was reverted to in most regiments, and in the course of a short time I again became universal.

In 1864 it was determined that standards should be abolished in the native cavalry regiments in possession of standards were allowed to retain them, but they were not in future to be carried on parade or in the field ; nor were any to be issued to regiments not possessing them. The appointment of *nishanbardar* consequently ceased; and all existing ones were gradually absorbed, pending which they were regarded as lance-*daffadars*.

In the same year (G. G. O. No. 278) good-conduct pay was first granted to the Bengal cavalry, the scale being, as mentioned above, one, two and three rupees after six, ten, and fifteen years' service.

In 1865, the rank of *naib-risaldar* was abolished, and those existing were absorbed, one promotion to *jemadar* being given for every two vacancies in the rank of *naib-risaldar*.

In G. O. C. C, 3rd May 1864, it was notified that the 10th, 11th, 13th, and 14th Regiments of Bengal Cavalry were to be designated "Lancers," and to these the 19th was added some five months later. Daffadars and sowars of these regiments were to be armed with lance, sword, and pistol. At the same time orders were issued that corps armed only partially with, or with various descriptions of carbine, should receive the regulation "cavalry carbine," which would be issued free to all who gave fire-arms in-exchange, and at half-price to others. Carbines were to be carried slung across the back, over the left shoulder. Lances were to be of bamboo, bayonet-shaped head, not less than ten feet long, nor more than eleven and a half feet; and the weight not over four pounds.

By G. O. No. 245 of 1866, the rank of *risaldar*-major was given to the senior *risaldar* of native cavalry regiments, with the same advantages as those enjoyed by *subadar*-majors.

G. O. No. 70 of 1875 directs the formation at Saharanpur and Hapur of an army reserve of 1,000 horses, only such animals to be received as were temporarily useless from various causes, such as bad training, tricks, obscure forms of lameness, debility, or skin diseases, but which, with careful treatment, were likely to become serviceable in the course of a few months. Turning to orders affecting infantry corps only, we find the following: G. O. No. 280 of 1864 orders that native officers of infantry shall receive pay by classes, as in the cavalry, the following being the scale of rates:

2	subadars	R100 a month
2	subadars	R80 a month
4	subadars	R67 a month
4	Jemadars	R35 a month
4	Jemadars	R35 a month

G. O. No. 515 of 1867 publishes a letter from the Secretary of State which announces that a Royal Crown shall be substituted as a device on the colours of native infantry corps, for the Lion and Crown, which was the device of the East India Company.

During the years following the re-organisation of 1861, the Enfield rifle, the introduction of which had been made the pretext for the outbreak of 1857, was gradually issued to corps of the native army. Most regiments, however, did not receive that weapon until the beginning of the next decade, when yet another change was imminent; for in 1874 the first issues of the Snider rifle were made to native corps.

In 1876 (G. O. No. 60) colours were granted for the first time to the 17th, 19th, 20th, 21st, 24th, 25th, 27th, 30th, 31st, 33rd, 34th, 35th, 36th, 37th, 38th, 39th, 40th, 41st, and 45th Native Infantry.

In the following year (G. G. O. No. 1) some important concessions and changes were made in the matter of pay, &c. A grant of R30 was authorised to every artillery-, infantry, or sapper recruit towards the provision of his kit; and a further annual allowance of R4 towards its upkeep to every non-commissioned officer and private. By the same order the pay of the commissioned ranks was raised to the following scale:

4	Subadars	R100 a month
4	Subadars	R50 a month
4	Jemadars	R80 a month
4	Jemadars	R40 a month

The matter of dress is a very prominent one in the standing orders of this period, and the following notes from the Dress Regulations for the native cavalry, published in 1863, will be found of some interest:

British Officers

In the first eight regiments, an *alkhalak*
In the last eleven regiments, a tunic
Shoulder cords of curb-chain or chain-mail
Helmet of grey felt, with bronze bars, binding, spike and chain
Pantaloons of blue or green cloth, as the case may be, with a
  double stripe, the colour of the facings Hessian boots
Forage cap the colour of the facings

Native Officers

Alkhalak, or loose frock
Pyjamas the same as the British officers' pantaloons
A native sword

The men wore in summer a white drill *alkhalak* or frock, instead of serge, and used a native saddle.

The above, however, were subject to constant change. In 1868 gilt was substituted for bronze in the helmet ornaments, white Melton pantaloons replaced the blue or green cloth for British officers, and *Multani-matti dasuti* was ordered for the pyjamas of native officers and men: jack-boots even with the top of the knee, took the place of Hessians; and the non-commissioned ranks received what was called the "Nolan saddle." In 1874 other changes were made, blue pantaloons being ordered for officers of lancer regiments and Napoleons being substituted for jack-boots.

In the native infantry too, several changes in the matter of dress took place during the period. G. O. No. 199 of 1869 introduced zouave tunics, with slashed cuffs, and serge pyjamas; No. 31 of 1871 orders native regiments dressed in green to wear helmets of that colour; and No. 188 of 1877 substituted *putties* or *jaji* trousers for white gaiters.

The chapter which we here conclude is one of no common interest to the Bengal Army; it opened on a number of raw, untrained corps, the majority of them not half-a-dozen years old, raised in an emergency, fostered under circumstances of exceptional excitement and by men of exceptional calibre. It closes on a well-trained, well-tried and well-equipped army; matured in many campaigns and improved by the careful work of many years of peace.

CHAPTER 10

The Afghan War

The course of events takes us back once more to the North-Western Frontier, where the close of the year 1878 found us involved in a war with the Government of Afghanistan: and here it may be observed that as this sketch advances, the materials at hand naturally become more voluminous, and the information derived from them more complete, and that in proportion the difficulty of keeping within the requisite bounds of a narrative like this becomes greater. The remark, however, which we made with reference to the Indian Mutiny is equally applicable to the Second Afghan War,—namely, that a subject which has been already so completely dealt with requires here nothing but a sketch of its principal outlines, and that a minute examination and criticism of its details would be both unnecessary and out of place.

The relations between the Indian Government and Sher Ali, Amir of Afghanistan and son of Dost Muhammad, had, in 1878, been for some years in a strained and unsatisfactory condition. This was due entirely to the causeless hostility and the ingratitude of the Amir himself. Sher Ali had been able to secure himself on the throne of Kabul mainly by the assistance given to him by the British Government in arms and money; by the influence of the British Government his sovereignty over Wakhan and Badakshan, till then disputed by the Government of Russia, had been admitted and made sure; and his subjects had been allowed to pass freely through the Indian Empire for purposes of trade, enjoying full protection in doing so. For these extensive favours the Amir made absolutely no return. On the contrary he requited them with active ill-will and open discourtesy, closing his territories against British subjects, maltreating British subjects who ventured within his jurisdiction, cruelly mutilating and putting to death subjects of his own on the mere suspicion that they were in communication with the British Government, and openly by word and deed, endeavouring to stir up religious hatred against the English and to incite to war against the Indian Empire. Finally he filled up the measure of his offences by receiving formally and entertaining publicly an embassy from Russia, a country with which we were then on the verge of war in connection with the affairs of Turkey, and by ignominiously repulsing at Ali Masjid, while the Russian embassy was still at his capital, an English envoy of high rank (General Sir Neville B. Chamberlain) of whose coming he had formal and timely notice from the Viceroy. The repulse of the British embassy brought matters to a crisis, and an ultimatum was addressed to the Amir, setting forth that unless reparation was made by the 20th of November, war would be declared and the British troops would cross the frontier. To this ultimatum no reply was given: war was accordingly declared and promptly begun.

The interval between the despatch of the ultimatum and the 20th of November was actively employed in organising forces for service in the field, and when the declaration of war came the preparations were practically complete. The troops detailed for the invasion of Afghanistan were formed into three distinct forces,—the Peshawar Valley Field Force, to operate on the line of the Khaibar; the Kuram Column to advance up the valley of that name; and the Kandahar Column to assail the southern part of the Amir's dominions. The operations in which these forces were severally engaged will now be noticed in order.

The Peshawar Valley Field Force was placed under the command of Lieutenant-General Sir Samuel J. Browne, K.C.B., and was composed of two divisions, the First of which; under the immediate command of Sir Samuel himself, comprised the following troops:

Cavalry	10th Hussars, 2 squadrons
	11th Bengal Lancers
	Guides Cavalry
Artillery	Royal Artillery, 4 batteries
	No. 4 Mountain Battery
	Punjab Frontier Force
Engineers	Headquarters
	Bengal Sappers and Miners, 4 companies

Infantry	1st Bgde.	4th Battalion, Rifle Brigade
		20th (Punjab) Native Infantry
		4th Gurkha Regiment
	2nd Bgde.	1-17th Foot
		Guides Infantry
		1st Sikh Infantry
	3rd Bgde.	81st Foot
		14th Native Infantry (Sikhs)
		27th (Punjab) Native Infantry
	4th Bgde.	51st King's Own Light Infantry
		6th Native (Light) Infantry
		45th Native Infantry (Sikhs)

The Second Division, which was in reserve of the first, was assembled in the first instance at Rawal Pindi under the command of Lieutenant-General F. F. Maude, C. B., V.C, and included the following troops:

Cavalry		9th (The Queen's Royal) Lancers
		10th Bengal Lancers
		13th Bengal Lancers
Artillery		2 Batteries Horse Artillery
		1 Battery Field Artillery
Infantry	1st Bgde.	1-25th Foot
		24th (Punjab) Native Infantry
		Bhopal Battalion
	2nd Bgde.	1-5th Foot
		2nd Gurkha Regiment
		Mhairwara Battalion

The forward movement into the Khaibar Pass and against the stronghold of Ali Masjid was begun on the evening of the 20th November. The 1st Brigade, under Brigadier-General H. T. Macpherson, marched from Jamrud at 2 a.m. on the 21st, with orders to occupy a position on the Rhotas heights which would command the fort. Eight hours earlier the 2nd Brigade, under Brigadier-General J. A. Tytler, had marched with orders to take post at Katakushtia, in the rear of Ali Masjid, by which the enemy's position would be turned and from which the Afghans could be cut off if they retreated. The remaining two brigades moved forward into the Khaibar Pass at 7 a.m., to make a direct attack on Ali Masjid.

These arrangements, however, were destined to attain only partial success; unforeseen difficulties of ground appeared which the necessarily imperfect reconnaissance of the country had not disclosed. The consequence was that the 1st and 2nd Brigades had not reached their positions when the general attack in front was begun by Sir Samuel Browne at midday on the 21st. The General, however, seeing how matters stood, wisely did not press the attack, but withdrew his troops to wait for a more favourable opportunity, after having lost two officers—Major Birch and Lieutenant FitzGerald, 27th Native Infantry—and fourteen men killed, one officer and thirty-three men wounded, and two men missing. On the following morning it was found that the Afghans, becoming aware of Brigadier-General Tytler's turning movement, had evacuated the fort, which was occupied without further opposition. Brigadier-General Tytler's brigade reached the enemy's line of retreat in time to take a considerable number of prisoners.

Leaving the 4th Brigade, under Brigadier-General W. B. Browne, to hold Ali Masjid, Sir Samuel Browne, with the rest of the force, advanced to Dakka, which was occupied on the 23rd. Early in December the Second Division moved up to Jamrud, in support of the First, and on the 17th of that month Sir Samuel Browne, leaving the 2nd Brigade at Dakka, moved forward to Jalalabad with the 1st and 3rd, and the cavalry and horse artillery, and occupied that place without opposition on the 20th, Lieutenant-General Maude taking charge of the Khaibar and the communications.

About the same time an expedition was undertaken against the Zaka Khel Afridis of the Bazar and Bara valleys, who had been giving trouble on the line of communications in the Khaibar; it was commanded by Lieutenant-General Maude, and was composed of two columns, which moved from Ali Masjid and Dakka respectively. The first of these consisted of three guns, a troop each of the 11th and 13th Bengal Lancers, detachments of the 5th and 51st Foot, the 2nd Gurkha Regiment and the Mhairwara Battalion; and the second, under Brigadier-General Tytler, of two guns, one company of sappers, and detachments of the 17th Foot and the 27th and 45th Native Infantry. Operating on their respective lines the two columns came into communication near the village of Walai on the 20th December, up to which time no opposition had been experienced by either. Subsequently, however, some skirmishing occurred while the troops were engaged in destroying the defensive towers of the Zaka Khel villages, and during the return march to Dakka the rear-guard of Brigadier-General Tytler's columns was hotly assailed by the Afridis. On the 22nd the two columns returned to Ali Masjid and Dakka, having accomplished the task of punishing the Zaka Khels, with a loss of only one killed, nine wounded, and one missing.

Some of the principal Afghan chiefs now declared in favour of the British, and attended a durbar held by Sir Samuel Browne at Jalalabad on the 1st of January, 1879: the year thus opened propitiously. The military operations which were undertaken in its early months were mostly of a minor character and were all thoroughly successful. On the 11th January, a small expedition under Brigadier-General Jenkins, was despatched against the Mohmands in Kama, north of the Kabul river, which met with complete success. On the 23rd the villages of Nikoti Miani and Raja Miani, near Peshbolak, which had been concerned in the murder of a *bhisti* of the 17th Foot, were visited and destroyed.

As the Zaka Khel Afridis of Bazar and Bara still continued to give trouble in the Khaibar Pass, it was decided, towards the end of January, 1879, to send a second expedition into the Bazar valley, with a view to punishing the marauders and putting a final stop to their incursions. The troops detailed for the expedition, which was under the command of Lieutenant-General Maude, were organised in three columns, which moved forward almost simultaneously from Jamrud, Ali Masjid, and Basawal, respectively. The first column included detachments of the 13th Bengal Lancers and the 24th Native Infantry; the second, portions of the 6th Native Infantry, the 2nd Gurkha Regiment, and the Mhairwara Battalion; and the third, detachments of the Guides Cavalry, Bengal Sappers, 27th and 45th Native Infantry, and 4th Gurkha Regiment. The three columns marched into Bazar on the 25th and 26th of January and, cooperating with one another, visited various parts of the valley during the next few days, blowing up the towers and destroying the fortified villages of the recalcitrant tribesmen, with whom a good deal of skirmishing took place. It was proposed to wind up the operations with the invasion of the Bara valley, but this, it was found, would have involved the Government in a war with the whole of the Afridi clans, which at that juncture would have been in the last degree inconvenient. That project was therefore abandoned, and the Afridis having tendered their submission, with promises of good behaviour for the future, the several columns were withdrawn from the Bazar valley on the 3rd February. The casualties on our side, during these operations, amounted to five killed and thirteen wounded, Lieutenant Holmes, 45th Native Infantry, being among the latter.

Early in February Jalalabad was threatened by the Mohmand who, on the 7th of that month, actually entered the Kama. A force (which included the Hazara Mountain Battery and detachments of the 11th Bengal Lancers, the 20th Native Infantry, the 4th Gurkha Regiment and the 1st Sikh Infantry) was immediately sent across the Kabul river, under Brigadier-General Macpherson, to drive the Mohmands out. Some distant firing took place, but the enemy declined a conflict, and, retiring hastily to the hills, they dispersed.

On the 28th of February, a survey party was attacked above Michni by a gathering of Mohmands, and in the conflict two men of the 24th Native Infantry were killed and three wounded. A similar outrage was committed by Shinwaris on the 17th March at Maidanak, on which occasion a *havildar* of the 45th Native Infantry was killed and Lieutenant F. M. Barclay, of the same regiment, mortally wounded. A punitive expedition was accordingly despatched against them, but the offenders made submission without attempting any resistance. Another branch of the same clan, the Shinwaris of Deh Sarak, brought punishment on themselves by an unprovoked attack (18th March) on an escort of the 27th Native Infantry. Brigadier-General Tytler was sent against them with a force consisting of two guns and detachments of the 11th and 13th Bengal Lancers, 5th and 17th Foot, 27th Native Infantry, and 2nd Gurkha Regiment, and marched from Basawal accordingly on the 24th, The enemy stood their ground near the village of Mausam, but were charged with great effect by the cavalry, who cut up large numbers of them and dispersed the rest. Mausam and other villages having been destroyed, the troops were directed to retire; in this movement they were assailed by the enemy, but, owing to the skilful manner in which they were handled, without effect, and the withdrawal was effected without difficulty. The casualties amounted to only two killed and twelve wounded.

On the 31st March intelligence was received that the Ghilzai Chief Azimatullah Khan had moved into the Lughman Valley, for the purpose of raising the people against us and of inciting the Khugianis to threaten Fatehabad, on the road to Kabul. Two columns, commanded by Brigadier-General H. T. Macpherson and Brigadier-General C. J. S. Gough, were in consequence put in motion at once, and at the same time a squadron of the 10th Hussars and another of the 11th Bengal Lancers were detached across the Kabul river to intercept Azimatullah Khan, should he attempt to move in that direction; this detachment, however, met with a singular misfortune;

starting at 10 p.m. from Jalalabad and attempting to cross the river, the squadron of the 10th Hussars missed the ford in the darkness, and one officer and forty-five men were drowned.

The column under the command of Brigadier-General Macpherson (which included the Hazara Mountain Battery, a company of sappers, and detachments of the 20th Native Infantry and 4th Gurkha Regiment) returned to Jalalabad on the 2nd April without having encountered the enemy. The force under Brigadier-General Gough, which was intended for the protection of Fatehabad, included a battery of Royal Horse Artillery, three troops of the 10th Hussars, three of the Guides Cavalry, and detachments of the 1-17th Foot and the 27th and 45th Native Infantry, and marched from Jalalabad on the 1st April. At Fatehabad, on the 2nd, this force came into conflict with about five thousand of the enemy, who after a smart engagement were defeated and driven from the field, with a loss of about 400 men. Our own loss amounted to six killed and forty wounded, among the former being Major Wigram Battye, a well known and most gallant officer of the Guides, *Ressaidar* Muhammad Khan, of the Guides Cavalry, and Lieutenant Wiseman of the 17th Foot.

Brigadier-General Tytler, with the 2nd Brigade, joined Brigadier-General Gough on the 4th April, when the combined forces marched to the village of Khugiani, nine miles beyond Fatehabad, and there took up a position. On the 12th Sir Samuel Browne, having left a suitable garrison in Jalalabad, marched thence with the remainder of the troops at the head-quarters of the First Division, and on the 14th encamped at Safed Sang, within three miles of Gandamak.

On the 21st April, the Mohmands having crossed the Kabul river for the purpose of attacking the posts in the Khaibar, two companies of the Mhairwara Battalion, under the command of Captain Creagh, were detached from Dakka for the protection of the village of Kam Dakka, the inhabitants of which had called for assistance. At this place Captain Creagh was attacked on the following morning by a large body of Mohmands, and being completely surrounded, and the ammunition running low after a long day's fighting, the detachment was in serious danger of being cut off: it was, however, relieved by the opportune arrival of a troop of the 10th Bengal Lancers and detachments of the 5th and 12th Foot, with two guns, and a gallant charge made by the troop of the 10th Bengal Lancers having driven back the enemy, the Mhairs, covered by the rest of the detachment, were brought off in safety. The casualties amounted to five killed and twenty-four wounded. Captain Creagh received the Victoria Cross for his gallantry in this affair.

The force detailed for service in the Kuram Valley was placed under the command of Major-General F. S. Roberts, C.B., V.C, and was composed of the following corps and detachments:

Cavalry		10th Hussars, 1 Squadron
Col. H. H. Gough		12th Bengal Cavalry
Artillery		1½ Batteries Royal Artillery
		Nos. 1 & 2 Mountain Batteries
		Punjab Frontier Force
Engineers		1 Company Sappers & Miners
Infantry	1st Bgde.	2-8th Foot
		29th Native Infantry
		5th Punjab Infantry
	2nd Bgde.	72nd Highlanders
		21st Native Infantry
		2nd Punjab Infantry
		5th Gurkha Regiment
		23rd Native Infantry (Pioneers)

To these troops the 5th Punjab Cavalry and the 28th Native Infantry were subsequently added.

Crossing the frontier on the 21st November, the force advanced towards the formidable position held by the Afghan troops on the Paiwar *Kotal*. A reconnaissance was made on the 28th, which though conducted as thoroughly as possible (at a cost of about a dozen casualties) was necessarily very imperfect in the information gained with regard to the interior of the enemy's position. The attack on the Afghan position was arranged for the 2nd December. Major-General Roberts' plan of operations was that the main force, under his personal command, should, by a night march, surprise and turn the enemy's left on the Spin Gawai *Kotal*, while the 8th Foot and the 5th Punjab Infantry, with the 12th Bengal Cavalry and five guns, were to remain in camp under Brigadier-General Cobbe, and assail the enemy's front as soon as the attack on the left flank had developed.

The main force started at 10 p.m. On the 1st December and attacked the Spin Gawai *Kotal* at 6 a.m. next morning, when the enemy's position was carried by a brilliant rush of the 72nd Highlanders and the 5th Gurkha Regiment. Advancing towards the centre of the position, they were checked by a precipitous ravine, the opposite side of which was held in force by the Afghan troops. It soon appeared that further movement in this direction was impossible, and General Roberts therefore decided to threaten the line of the enemy's retreat by a further turning movement towards Zabardast Kila, and thus to take the Afghan position in reverse. A vigorous attack was now made in front by the force left in camp, and the Afghans, finding themselves threatened in rear and subjected to a galling fire from the front and the left flank, retreated precipitately, abandoning their camp and a great quantity of stores and ammunition, all of which, with several guns, fell into our hands. The loss on our side was twenty-one killed, including Major A. D. Anderson, 23rd Native Infantry, and Captain J. A. Kelso, commanding No. 1 Mountain Battery, and seventy-two wounded, including Brigadier-General Cobbe.

On the 6th December General Roberts advanced to Ali Khel and on the 8th reached the Shutargardan Pass, which was reconnoitred on the following morning. In the return march towards Kuram, General Roberts determined on exploring the southern route through the Sapari or Mangiar defile, and accordingly moved in that direction from Ali Khel on the 12th, taking with him No. 1 Mountain Battery, a wing of the 72nd, the 23rd Native Infantry, and the 5th Gurkha Regiment. The main body got through the defile unmolested on the following day, but the rear-guard and baggage were attacked in force by the Mangal Pathans; the steadiness and gallantry of the 5th Gurkha Regiment on this occasion were most conspicuous: they repelled every attack made by a bold and numerous enemy during a space of five hours, and brought the baggage into camp without having lost a single load. Our loss amounted to five killed and seventeen wounded, amongst the latter being Captain F. T. Goad, Assistant Superintendent of Transport, and Captain C. F. Powell, of the 5th Gurkha Regiment, both of whom subsequently died of their wounds.

The headquarters of the column reached Fort Kuram on the 14th December, and thence, early in the following month, a flying column started under General Roberts for the reduction and occupation of the Khost district. It included a squadron of the 10th Hussars, three troops of the 5th Punjab Cavalry, Nos. 1 and 2 Mountain Batteries, a wing of the 72nd Highlanders, and the 21st and 28th Native Infantry. The fort of Matun was given up without resistance on the 6th January 1879, but on the same, day the camp was threatened by a hostile gathering of several thousand Mangals. These were attacked by General Roberts on the 7th January, and were entirely dispersed by Colonel Gough with the cavalry, No. 2 Mountain Battery and the 28th Native Infantry, on the north-west of the camp; while on the south and east Colonel Drew was equally successful with No. 1 Mountain Battery, a troop of the 5th Punjab Cavalry, the 72nd Highlanders, and the 21st Native Infantry. Three weeks were passed in exploring and surveying the district, and the column returned to Fort Kuram on the 31st January.

The remainder of the winter and early spring passed without any striking incident in the Kuram Valley.

The Kandahar Column (afterwards designated the Southern Afghanistan Field Force) was composed of two divisions, of which the First was assembled at Mooltan under Lieutenant-General D. M. Stewart, and the Second at Quetta under Major-General M. A. S. Biddulph. These two divisions included the following corps:

1st (Mooltan) Division

Cavalry
15th Hussars
8th Bengal Cavalry
19th Bengal Lancers

Artillery
10 Batteries Royal Artillery with siege-train

Engineers
3 Companies Sappers And Miners

Infantry 1st Bgde.
2-60th Rifles
15th (Sikh) Native Infantry
25th (Punjab) Native Infantry

2nd Bgde.
59th Foot
1st Gurkha Regiment
3rd Gurkha Regiment

2nd (Quetta) Division

Cavalry
1st & 2nd Punjab Cavalry
3rd Sindh Horse

Artillery
1 Field Battery
2 Mountain Batteries including No. 3 (Peshawar) Mountain Battery

Engineers		1 Company Sappers & Miners
Infantry	1st Bgde.	70th Foot
		19th (Punjab) Native Infantry
		30th Bombay Native Infantry
	2nd Bgde.	26th (Punjab) Native Infantry
		1st Punjab Infantry
		29th Bombay Native Infantry
		32nd (Punjab) Native Infantry (Pioneers)
		2nd Sikh Infantry

The Second Division, marching from Quetta, entered the Pishin Valley on the 22nd November, reached Haikalzai on the 27th, and was concentrated in the vicinity of the Kojak Pass on the 12th December. The leading troops of the First Division reached Dadar on the 5th December, and the head-quarters of the Division arrived at Quetta on the 8th, from which date Lieutenant-General Stewart assumed command of all the troops detailed for operations in Southern Afghanistan. Moving forward from these points the Second Division advanced towards Kandahar by the Kojak Pass, while the First Division moved by the Ghwaja Pass over the Khoja Amran range, both converging towards Takht-i-pul. On the 4th January the advanced guard of the field force encountered some regiments of Afghan cavalry between Saif-u-din and the Ghlo Pass, and in the skirmish which ensued eleven officers and men of the 15th Hussars and the 1st Punjab Cavalry were wounded. The united divisions then moved forward on Kandahar, which was abandoned by its garrison, and occupied without opposition on the 8th January.

From this place part of the First Division, under General Stewart, marched to Kalat-i-Ghilzai, and occupied the fort there on the 21st January; leaving a garrison there temporarily, the head-quarters, with the cavalry and the 1st Infantry Brigade, returned to Kandahar on the 11th February, and the garrison was withdrawn a few weeks later. Meanwhile part of the Second Division, under General Biddulph, marched to the river Helmand and Girishk; on the 29th January camps were formed on both sides of the river, and during the succeeding days the country beyond the river as well as that on the left bank was explored and surveyed. This position was maintained until the 23rd February, when the return march to Kandahar was commenced. The retirement was the signal for hostilities on the part of the Alizais, who on the 26th attacked the rear-guard of Bombay troops at Khushk-i-Nakhud, but were routed with heavy loss after a sharp conflict in which the casualties on our side amounted to five killed and twenty-four wounded.

The Second Division reached Kandahar on the 28th February, and was immediately afterwards broken up; a large number of the troops returning to India under General Biddulph, *via* Thal-Chotiali. During this movement one of the returning columns, composed of a squadron each of the 8th Bengal Cavalry and 2nd Sindh Horse, two guns each of the Jacobabad and Peshawar Mountain Batteries, and the 1st Punjab Infantry, the whole under the command of Major Keen, 1st Punjab Infantry, was twice attacked by local tribesmen. In the first attack (March 21st) one sepoy of the 1st Punjab Infantry was killed; in the second, at Baghao on the 24th March, which was repulsed by the 8th Bengal Cavalry and the 1st Punjab Infantry, our loss was two killed and five wounded, that of the enemy being 150 in killed alone.

About the same time (27th March) a detachment under the command of Major Humfrey, 30th Bombay Native Infantry, which included half a troop of the 1st Punjab Cavalry, was attacked at Sai-ad-Bud, in Shorawak, by a body of 1,600 Barechi insurgents, who were completely routed with the loss of nearly one hundred of their number, including several of their chiefs.

Nothing of much importance occurred in Southern Afghanistan during the remaining period of the first phase of the war.

Amir Sher Ali Khan having died at Mazar-i-Sharif on the 21st February, his son Yakub Khan succeeded to the throne of Kabul. Yakub Khan, having expressed his readiness to treat, was received by the British authorities at Gandamak, where a treaty was concluded on the 26th May. The withdrawal of the Northern Force was at once commenced, but the hot weather was then at its height and the result was most unfortunate, for cholera having broken out in the Khaibar the troops passing down the line suffered terribly, and many regiments sustained heavy losses from this cause. The Kandahar Force was fortunately kept stationary in order to avoid the unhealthiness of a march in the hot weather.

The thanks of both Houses of Parliament were voted to the Viceroy, to the commander-in-chief in India, and to all engaged in the campaign (G. G. O. No. 1085 of 1879); a special medal was granted to all troops employed in Afghanistan between the 21st November 1878 and the 26th May 1879, with clasps for the actions of Ali Masjid and Paiwar *Kotal*, which names were afterwards authorised to be borne on the colours and appointments of the corps engaged. Six months' batta was granted to all ranks by G. G. O. No. 804 of 1879.

The conclusion of peace was followed by the instalment of a British Resident, Major Sir P. L. N. Cavagnari, K.C.S.I., at Kabul, together with an escort of twenty-five sowars and fifty sepoys of the Queen's Own Corps of Guides, under Lieutenant W. R. P. Hamilton. For two months affairs seemed settled and likely to remain so, but in August it became evident that a strong feeling of hostility existed towards the British Residency on the part of a powerful section of the Afghan people. A chance *emeute* on September 3rd excited this hostile feeling into open outrage, and the consequence was an attack on the Residency, in which, after a gallant resistance, Cavagnari, his suite and escort were massacred almost to a man.

The receipt of these terrible tidings in India was the signal for the adoption of prompt and energetic measures for the re-establishment of British influence in Afghanistan, and the punishment of the treacherous Kabulis. The first order issued was that the Shutargardan Pass, leading from the Kuram valley to Kabul, should be secured ; this was followed by directions for the immediate advance, by this route, of a strong force under Major-General Sir F. S. Roberts. The first object was secured by No. 2 Mountain Battery, the 23rd Native Infantry (Pioneers), and the 5th Gurkha Regiment; while the following troops, making a total of about 6,500 of all ranks, were detailed to form a field force for an advance on Kabul from the Kuram valley:

Artillery

F Battery, A Brigade, Royal Horse Artillery
G Battery, 3rd Royal Artillery
No. 2 Mountain Battery, Punjab Frontier Force
Two Gatling guns

Cavalry
Brigadier-General
W. G. D. Massy

9th Queen's Royal Lancers, 1 squadron
12th Bengal Cavalry
14th Bengal Lancers
5th Punjab Cavalry

Engineers	7th Company, Bengal Sappers and Miners
Infantry: 1st Brigade Brigadier-General H. T. Macpherson	67th Foot 92nd Foot (Gordon Highlanders) 28th (Punjab) Native Infantry
Infantry: 2nd Brigade Brigadier-General T. D. Baker	72nd Foot (Highlanders) 5th Punjab Infantry 5th Gurkha Regiment 23rd (Punjab) Native Infantry (Pioneers)

The remainder of the troops in the Kuram valley were organised in two brigades, to the command of which Brigadier-Generals T. E. Gordon and J. A. Tytler were appointed.

At the same time the small force left at Ali Masjid. and Landi *Kotal* at the termination of the first phase of the war was rapidly augmented, and, with some changes of corps, formed into a Division under the command of Major-General R. O. Bright, to advance towards Kabul on the line of the Khaibar. This Division was organised in three brigades, commanded respectively by Brigadier-Generals C. J. S. Gough, C. G. Arbuthnot and J. Doran, and, when completed, comprised the following corps:—Four companies of sappers and miners, three batteries of Royal Artillery, No. 4 (the Hazara) Mountain Battery, the 6th Dragoon Guards, the 3rd, 10th and 17th Bengal Cavalry, the Guides Cavalry, the 2-9th, 1-12th and 51st Foot, the 8th, 24th, 27th, 30th, 31st and 45th Bengal Native Infantry, the 2nd and 4th Gurkha Regiments, the Guides Infantry, and the 4th Madras Native Infantry. The troops moving on the Kuram and Khaibar lines were designated respectively the First and Second Divisions of the Kabul Field Force, and it was decided that as soon as they came into communication, after the occupation of Kabul, the command of the whole should be vested in Sir Frederick Roberts.

Concurrently with these arrangements the Kandahar force, under Sir Donald Stewart, who was at the time actually on the move to return to India, was directed to stand fast. This force comprised six batteries of artillery, two companies of sappers and miners, the 19th Bengal Lancers, the 1st and 2nd Punjab Cavalry, the 59th and 2-60th Foot, the 15th, 19th, and 25th Bengal Native Infantry, the 3rd Gurkha Regiment, the 2nd Sikh Infantry, and the 29th Bombay Native

Infantry. Of these the 19th Bengal Native Infantry and the 2nd Sikh Infantry were in the Quetta District.

On the 24th September the advance from the Shutargardan was begun by Brigadier-General Baker, No. 1 Mountain Battery, the 21st (Punjab) Native Infantry and the 3rd Sikh Infantry having now been detailed to hold that position, under the command of Lieutenant-Colonel Money. On the 27th Sir Frederick Roberts marched from Alikhel to the Shutargardan with the head-quarters of the cavalry brigade, a squadron of the 9th Lancers, the 5th Punjab Cavalry, the 28th Native Infantry, and a detachment of the 5th Punjab Infantry; during this movement the troops were annoyed by an incessant and irritating fire from parties of Mangals and Ghilzais, which occasioned several casualties. On the same day the Amir Yakub Khan came into General Baker's camp at Kushi, in the Logar valley professing his regret for the tragedy of the 3rd and his powerlessness to have averted it. Sir Frederick Roberts himself arrived at Kushi on the 28th, and on the 1st of October the whole of the field force was assembled there. The advance from that point was continued with as much expedition as possible, though it was delayed by insufficiency of transport, the want of which was keenly felt, and on the 5th the whole force (excepting two mountain guns, a squadron of the 5th Punjab Cavalry, a wing of the 67th Foot, and the 28th Native Infantry, which were still one march in the rear, under Brigadier-General Macpherson, escorting reserve ammunition and commissariat stores), reached the village of Charasia, on the heights in advance of which, on both sides of the Sang-i-Nawishta Pass, the Afghans had taken up a formidable position.

On the following morning dispositions were made for forcing the Afghan position. The main attack, under Brigadier-General Baker, was designed to turn the enemy's right and dislodge him from his position on the heights, while a feint was made at the pass by a detachment under Major White, of the 92nd Highlanders. As soon as the real nature of Brigadier-General Baker's attack was realised by the enemy, every effort was made by them to strengthen their right and a vigorous resistance was offered to the British advance. But all opposition was borne down by the gallantry of the 72nd Highlanders, the 23rd Pioneers, the 5th Punjab Infantry, and the 5th Gurkhas, and by 3-45 p.m. the position was carried. At the same time the feint on the British right was changed into a real attack, and mainly owing to the personal gallantry of Major White, supported as it was by the bravery and dash of the Highlanders of his own regiment, the Sang-i-Nawishta was also carried, and soon the Afghans were flying in confusion towards Chardeh, with the loss of twenty guns and many hundred men.

The British casualties in the battle amounted to *Jemadar* Khanimulla, 5th Punjab Infantry, and nineteen men killed, and three British officers and sixty-four men wounded, of whom seven afterwards died.

On the 7th October the force encamped at Bini Hisar, and on the 8th the cavalry brigade advanced to Kabul. The enemy, who were in force on the Asmai heights, to the north-west of the city, were to have been attacked on the morning of the 9th, but they dispersed during the night, leaving behind their stores and artillery; on the 9th the British force encamped at Siah Sang, and on the 12th Sir Frederick Roberts formally took possession of the Bala Hisar. Vast stores of powder and ammunition of all kinds were found in the arsenal, and, notwithstanding all precautions, a considerable explosion took place on the 16th October, in which several lives were lost. Partly as a punishment of the city, partly as a precaution, orders were issued for the demolition of the fortifications of the Bala Hisar, which work was at once commenced. About this time Yakub Khan expressed his determination of abdicating, and the Government was vested temporarily in Sir Frederick Roberts, who was soon after raised to the local rank of Lieutenant-General in Afghanistan. Yakub Khan was deported to India on the 1st December.

While these events had been happening at Kabul, the little garrison at the Shutargardan had been hard pressed by the Ghilzais. The first attack was made on the 2nd October, and the second on the 14th; in both the enemy were beaten off with considerable loss, the casualties on our side being only seven wounded on the former, and two killed and eight wounded on the latter occasion. Simultaneously with the attack on the 14th an effort was made by the tribesmen against Alikhel, which was garrisoned by three guns of C-4th Brigade, Royal Artillery, and detachments of the 12th and 13th Bengal Cavalry and 5th Punjab Cavalry, and of the 8th Foot and the 11th and 29th Native Infantry: the attack was easily repulsed, with heavy loss to the enemy, our own amounting to no more than seven men wounded. During the following days considerable additions joined the enemy's forces; the Shutargardan position was completely surrounded on the 16th, and a determined attack was commenced on the 18th October. On the following day, however, reinforcements under Brigadier-General

H. H. Gough, consisting of four guns, the 5th Punjab Cavalry and the 5th Punjab Infantry, arrived at Kushi from Kabul. Colonel Money, with the Shutargardan garrison, at once assumed the offensive; the enemy were quickly defeated, and dispersed in all directions, the loss on our side amounting to no more than seven men wounded.

The Khaibar route having now been opened, the Shutargardan was abandoned for the winter and, the garrison withdrawn. The 21st Native Infantry retired to Alikhel, while No. 1 Mountain Battery and the 3rd Sikh Infantry, together with two squadrons of the 9th Lancers which had just arrived from Sialkot, accompanied Brigadier-General Gough on his return to Kabul.

Early in November the camp at Siah Sang was abandoned, and the troops moved into and occupied the fortified cantonment of Sherpur, north of the city of Kabul.

On the 1st November a mixed force under Brigadier-General Macpherson, which was afterwards joined by Sir Frederick Roberts, was despatched to establish communication with the troops moving up from the Khaibar, This having been effected (Macpherson met General Bright at Kata Sang on the 6th), several reconnaissances were undertaken in the Lughman valley, etc., after which the force returned to Sherpur, During this expedition an engagement took place at Doaba, on the 10th November, in which we had six men killed (including a sepoy of the 28th Native Infantry) and an officer and four men wounded. Later on, another force; under Brigadier-General Baker, marched into the Maidan district, where a slight collision occurred with the Ghilzais.

During the preceding two months the feeling of hostility towards the British, inflamed by their continued occupation of the country, by the destruction of the Bala Hisar, and by the deportation of the Amir to India, had been assuming more and more threatening dimensions. Aroused by their *mullas*, who everywhere were preaching a *jihad* against the foreign invaders, crowds of tribesmen were joining the standards of revolt. Mir Muhammad, an aged *mulla* of great reputed sanctity and commonly known as the Mushk-i-Alam, Muhammad Jan, a Wardak leader of some note, and Mir Bucha, a prominent Kohistaui chief, headed the insurgents; and early in December it was reported that a plan had been matured for surrounding Kabul and overwhelming the British force in Sherpur.

Measures, were immediately taken to defeat this intention; the Corps of Guides was called up from the Khaibar line, and on the 8th and 9th December two columns were sent out by Sir Frederick

Roberts to meet and disperse the Afghan forces advancing from the north and from the west, before they could unite in the vicinity of Kabul. The first, under Brigadier-General Macpherson, was composed of four guns of the Royal Horse Artillery, four guns of No. 1 Mountain Battery, a squadron of the 9th Lancers, two of the 14th Bengal Lancers, and detachments of the 67th Foot (six companies), 3rd Sikh Infantry (509 men) and 5th Gurkha Regiment (393 men). The second column, under Brigadier-General Baker, consisted of four guns of No. 2 Mountain Battery, five troops of the 5th Punjab Cavalry, and 450 each of the 92nd Highlanders and the 5th Punjab Infantry.

Macpherson, having left his cavalry (except one troop of the 14th Bengal Lancers) and horse artillery at Aushar, marched to the Surkh *Kotal*, near Karez-i-Mir, eight miles north of Kabul, and on the 10th December attacked a large body of Kohistanis who were advancing to join Muhammad Jan, drove them down the hill with heavy loss, carried their breastworks at Karez-i-Mir, and dispersed them, losing himself only seven wounded in the day's work.

During the same day Brigadier-General Baker marched round the Korogh range, south and west of the capital, and then, turning northward, advanced towards the Paghman valley, and encamped a short distance to the west of Maidan.

On the 11th Macpherson moved in a south-westerly direction from Karez-i-Mir, through the Surkh *Kotal*, towards Arghandeh, with the object of driving Muhammad Jan towards General Baker and of cutting off his retreat, and at the same time Brigadier-General W. G. Dunham Massy, with four horse artillery guns, two squadrons of the 9th Lancers, and one of the 14th Bengal Lancers, was ordered to move from Aushar towards Arghandeh, and bring himself into communication with Macpherson, with whom he was to cooperate. The combination, however, failed. Owing to an unfortunate misunderstanding, Massy moved by a shorter route than was intended, and in consequence, near the village of Kila Kazi, where Muhammad Jan had taken up a position the night before, he came face to face with an overwhelming force of Afghans (nearly 10,000 in number) while Macpherson was yet far away near the Surkh *Kotal*. The dense hordes of Afghans advanced unchecked by the fire of the four guns; the cavalry charged gallantly, but in a country cut up by watercourses and canals it was impossible that so small a body could drive a charge home with sufficient force to have any perceptible effect on the immensely superior masses opposed to them. Sir Frederick Roberts, who had arrived on the scene, and who had ordered a second charge of cavalry in the hope of saving the guns, now ordered a retreat to the village of Deh-i-Mozang, while he sent for immediate reinforcements of infantry from Sherpur. The enemy pressed hard on the retiring force; the four guns stuck in a deep ditch and had to be spiked and abandoned, and the advance of the Afghans was only checked by the timely arrival of 200 of the 72nd Highlanders, whose fire barred their passage through the Deh-i-Mozang gorge. Muhammad Jan then turned aside and occupied the Takht-i-Shah, where he was in a position to threaten the Bala Hisar.

While these events were in progress, Macpherson had continued his movement towards Arghandeh, but hearing the booming of guns he swung round his right and moved towards the point whence the sounds came, and about an hour after Massy's force had begun retiring he arrived on the ground where the action had been fought. Here he came on the rear of the enemy, whom he speedily dispersed and drove off the field. He pursued them to Kila Kazi, whence he was ordered to fall back on Deh-i-Mozang, where he arrived late in the evening. The ground where the guns had been abandoned having by these movements been partially cleared, Colonel MacGregor, the Chief of the Staff, with the assistance of Major Badcock, Captains Deane and Martin and other officers, and a few men, was able to extricate them and bring them in.

On the same day Brigadier-General Baker, moving northwards, found the road into the Chardeh valley occupied, and was obliged late in the afternoon to force a passage for his brigade. He encamped that night at Arghandeh; next morning he was informed of the enemy's movements, and was recalled to Sherpur.

Our losses on the 11th December in the two brigades of infantry were three killed and nineteen wounded. In the cavalry and artillery they amounted to twenty-seven killed and twenty-five wounded. Four officers were killed, among whom was Lieutenant Forbes, 14th Bengal Lancers.

During the night following these events, the Corps of Guides, cavalry and infantry, which had been called up from Jagdalak on the Khaibar line, arrived at Kabul, and formed a very welcome reinforcement.

On the 12th December Brigadier-General Baker marched into Sherpur, his rear-guard annoyed on the way by a running attack from the enemy, who, however, were kept well at bay by the 5th Punjab Cavalry, and the 5th Punjab Infantry. His losses were one killed and two wounded.

The position taken up by the enemy on the Takht-i-Shah was a very formidable one, and they had further increased their security by breastworks. General Macpherson received orders to dislodge them and accordingly attacked them on the morning of the 12th with detachments of the 67th and 72nd Foot, 3rd Sikh Infantry and 5th Gurkha Regiment, supported by two guns of No. 1 Mountain Battery, the assaulting force being commanded by Lieutenant-Colonel Money, of the 3rd Sikh Infantry. Notwithstanding the vigour and gallantry displayed by the force, the strength of the position rendered the attempt unsuccessful; and it was determined to wait until the co-operation of Baker's force could be obtained for a concurrent attack from the direction of Bini Hisar. Macpherson's loss in this attempt amounted to four killed and twelve wounded, one of the latter being Major Cook, V.C, of the 5th Gurkha Regiment, who afterwards died of his wounds.

On the following day, as previously arranged, simultaneous attacks were made on the Takht-i-Shah, from the north under Macpherson and from the south-east under Baker. The force under the latter included four guns of G-3rd Brigade, Royal Artillery, and four of No. 2 Mountain Battery, one squadron of the 9th Lancers, the 5th Punjab Cavalry, six companies of the 92nd Highlanders, seven of the Guides Infantry, 300 of the 3rd Sikh Infantry, and 100 of the 5th Punjab Infantry. In the course of his movement to the attack Baker found it necessary to seize the Bini Hisar ridge, which, though held by the enemy in great strength, was carried by the 92nd, but not without a fierce struggle in which that gallant regiment sustained considerable loss. Advancing thence, the 92nd and the Guides Infantry, after a stubborn resistance on the part of the enemy, stormed and carried the Takht-i-Shah position, portions of the 72nd Highlanders, the 3rd Sikh Infantry and the 5th Gurkhas, of Macpherson's force, reaching the summit at the same time from the northern side.

While these operations were proceeding on the heights, the people of the city rose and in great numbers joined the insurgent tribesmen, part of them assembling at Siah Sang and the rest seizing and occupying two strongly fortified villages situated between Siah Sang and the Bala Hisar. Leaving a detachment to hold the Takht-i-Shah, Baker, under instructions from Sir Frederick Roberts, proceeded to deal with these bodies of the enemy. The two villages were stormed and captured with little difficulty, and the cavalry under Brigadier-General Massy (one squadron of the 9th Lancers and two of the 14th Bengal Lancers) as well as the Guides Cavalry having been sent to his assistance, the enemy at Siah Sang were, after a stubborn contest, in which the 9th Lancers and the Guides Cavalry made some splendid charges, routed and driven from the field with heavy loss. This concluded the operations of the day, during which our losses amounted to two officers and twelve men killed, and two officers and forty-four men wounded.

Feeling the necessity of having more troops to face the combination against him, Sir Frederick Roberts now telegraphed to Major-General Bright to direct Brigadier-General C. J. S. Gough, with the 1st Brigade of the Second Division of the Kabul Field Force (then at Gandamak, Pezwan, and Jagdalak) to move up to Kabul as quickly as might be possible.

Foiled in their attacks from the west and south of Kabul, the enemy now made an attempt from the north of the city, and early on the morning of the 14th seized and occupied the Asmai heights in great numbers. Sir Frederick Roberts determined to dislodge them at once, and to accomplish this object despatched Brigadier-General Baker at 9 a.m., with a force consisting of four guns of G-3rd Brigade, Royal Artillery, four of No. 2 Mountain Battery, the 14th Bengal Lancers, 190 of the 72nd and 100 of the 92nd Highlanders, 460 of the Guides Infantry, and 470 of the 5th Punjab Infantry.

Baker began his operations by seizing a small conical hill forming the northern shoulder of the Aliabad *Kotal*. Leaving a small detachment to hold this point, he proceeded with the remainder of his force to expel the enemy from their position on the Asmai heights, Colonel Jenkins of the Guides heading the attack. The Afghans, favoured by the rugged nature of the ground, made a prolonged and obstinate resistance, but the forward gallantry of the Highlanders and the Guides overcame all obstacles, and by 12-30 p.m. the enemy were driven headlong from the heights, and the entire position was in our possession. Reinforced, however, by large numbers of insurgents moving up from the south-west, the Afghans rallied and returned to the encounter, and assailing the small detachment holding the conical hill they succeeded, by sheer weight of numbers, in carrying that post and capturing two mountain guns, Captain Spens of the 72nd falling covered with wounds in a heroic attempt to stem the overwhelming rush of the enemy. The lost guns were afterwards recovered.

While these events were in progress on the Asmai heights, large bodies of the enemy were found to have assembled at Siah Sang, whence they were endeavouring to make their way round the eastern flank of the Sherpur cantonment. Some cavalry and horse artillery were sent out under Brigadier-General H. H. Gough to disperse them, but they got away to the hills before they could be intercepted, except a body of about 400 who came into collision with a troop of the 5th Punjab Cavalry under Captain Vousden, who charged them with great gallantry, routed them with heavy loss, and drove them from the field.

It was now evident that the numbers combined against us were too overwhelming to admit of our holding on to isolated positions, and that concentration was becoming absolutely necessary. Roberts therefore recalled all the troops into Sherpur, and at night-fall the enemy were in possession of Kabul and the Bala Hisar.

Our losses during the operations of the 14th amounted to two British officers, two native officers and thirty men killed, and three British officers, six native officers and 99 men wounded. The native officers who were killed were *Subadar* Khaibar Singh of the Guides, and *Subadar* Raghubir Nagarkoti of the 5th Gurkha Regiment. *Subadar* Jawala Singh of the Guides, *Jemadar* Gopal Singh of the 14th Bengal Lancers, and *Jemadar* Jhanda Singh of the 5th Punjab Cavalry, afterwards died of the wounds they received this day.

The British force was now besieged in the Sherpur cantonment, a rectangular enclosure, a mile and a half long and rather more than two-thirds of a mile broad, the northern side of which was formed by the Bemaru ridge, and the other three sides by massive mud walls.

For a week no actual attack upon the cantonment was made by the enemy, though they kept up a desultory fire, which occasioned several casualties. On the 16th a body of about a thousand made an attempt or. the post of Lataband, which formed a connecting link with the forces on the Khaibar line and was held by the 28th Native Infantry and a wing of the 23rd Pioneers, but they were repulsed with considerable loss. On the morning of the 22nd the 12th Bengal Cavalry were sent out to join the troops at Lataband and return with Gough's force, which was short of cavalry: the junction was accomplished with a loss of only three killed and three wounded. On the evening of the 22nd reliable information was received in Sherpur that a determined attempt would be made on the following day to carry the position by assault, and at daybreak on the 23rd the attack began. For some hours strenuous and continued efforts were made by the Afghans to effect an entrance into the position; but enormous as were their numbers, amounting to not less than 60,000, and determined as were their assaults, they were unable to stand before the steady and continuous fire of the garrison. At length, when their attacks began to flag, they suddenly found themselves taken in flank by a detachment consisting of four guns and the 5th Punjab Cavalry, which had issued from the north side of the cantonment. Disheartened as they were by their ill-success, the sudden alarm rapidly became a panic, and the vast hordes broke and fled in all directions, pursued by the British cavalry. By 1 p.m. the firing had nearly ceased, and on the following morning not an enemy was to be seen.

From the 15th to the 23rd inclusive, the British losses amounted to two British officers and 16 men killed, and five British officers, two native officers and sixty-one men wounded; of these five were killed and 33 wounded in the final action of the 23rd December. Lieutenant Montanaro of No. 2 Mountain Battery, and *Jemadar* Jag Bahadur, of the Corps of Guides, died of their wounds. During the whole of the operations, from the 10th to the 23rd December, our casualties amounted to ten British officers, two native officers, and 91 men killed, and fifteen British officers, nine native officers, and 239 men wounded, a total of 366. The losses of the enemy during the same period were not less there 3,000 in killed and wounded.

On the 24th Brigadier-General C. J. S. Gough arrived at Kabul with his brigade, consisting of four guns of the Hazara Mountain Battery, a company of sappers and miners, the 2-9th Foot, a detachment of the 72nd Highlanders, and the 2nd and 4th Gurkha Regiments: these regiments were, however, all weak, and the total strength of the brigade scarcely reached 1,400 men. The 12th Bengal Cavalry, the 28th Native Infantry, and the wing of the 23rd Pioneers marched into Kabul with Gough.

The enemy having fled, the city and the Bala Hisar were speedily re-occupied. Comparative tranquillity was soon restored in the neighbourhood, and on the 27th December Brigadier-General Baker was detached into Kohistan with a small force (four guns of No. 4 Mountain Battery, the Corps of Guides, the 67th Foot, the 2nd Gurkha Regiment, and the 5th Punjab Infantry) to mete out punishment to Mir Bucha for his share in the late disorders. This chief's stronghold was reached on the 29th and found deserted: having destroyed it, Baker returned to Kabul on the 31st.

The operations on the Khaibar line now claim attention. While the principal interest of the war was naturally centred in the operations at Kabul, the troops at Peshawar and in posts on the Khaibar line had been constantly employed in arduous and harassing duties. Major-General Bright took command of the force at Peshawar on the 13th

September; and as troops began to arrive Brigadier-General Gough advanced with all possible speed to Dakka, and thence to Jalalabad. More trying and more destructive than a hard-fought action was the terrible sickness which now set in on the Khaibar route, several regiments being rendered unfit for even the lightest duties of garrisoning the posts on the road. The forward movement, of the division, however, continued. General Bright reached Gandamak on the 2nd November; thence he and Gough advanced and met General Macpherson at Kata Sang, as already related, after which they again returned to Gandamak. Advancing once more to Jagdalak, Gough, on the 15th December, received orders from Sir Frederick Roberts to push on to Kabul with all possible speed. For some days, however, until the arrival of further reinforcements, Gough was unable to comply with these orders, and in the meantime there were constant skirmishes with the Ghilzais on the road between Gandamak and Jagdalak, the corps principally engaged being detachments of the Hazara Mountain Battery, the 10th Bengal Lancers, the 2-9th Foot, the 24th Native Infantry, and the 2nd Gurkha Regiment. At length, having been reinforced by Colonel Norman with detachments of the 24th and the 2nd Gurkha Regiment, Gough advanced on the 21st and reached Sherpur, as we have seen, on the 24th. During these operations the force under his command sustained a loss of one man killed and eighteen wounded —two mortally.

The garrisons left at Jagdalak and Jagdalak *Kotal*, under the command of Colonel Norman, were not allowed much peace by the hostile tribesmen, who, after several vigorous attacks, made a final effort against those places on the 29th of December, under the leadership of Azimatullah Khan of Lughman; and it was only after some severe fighting that he was defeated and his following dispersed. Our casualties in these affairs amounted to four killed and eight wounded; amongst the former was Lieutenant Wright, Royal Artillery, and amongst the latter Major Thackeray, Royal Engineers. The force under the command of Colonel Norman consisted of detachments of the Hazara Mountain Battery, the 10th Bengal Lancers, the 51st Foot, and the 24th Native Infantry.

In the meantime the force on the south side of the Paiwar *Kotal* had passed the autumn without important incident, except a punitive expedition against the Zaimukhts, who had been guilty of many dastardly outrages on the line of communications in the Kuram valley. The force employed on this service was under the command of Brigadier-General Tytler, and was composed of No. 1 Battery, 8th Brigade, Royal Artillery (four screw guns), No. 1 (Kohat) Mountain Battery (two guns), a company of sappers and miners, detachments of the 1st, 13th, and 18th Bengal Cavalry, a small detachment of the 2-8th Foot, the 85th Foot, the 13th, 20th, and 29th Native Infantry, and the 4th Punjab Infantry. Marching from Balesh Khel on the 8th December, Brigadier-General Tytler entered the Zaimukht country the same day, and having destroyed a number of towers and villages *en route,* the force arrived on the 12th within a short distance of the strong fastness of Zawo. At daybreak on the 13th, General Tytler advanced to attack this place. Under cover of the fire of the two guns of No. 1 Mountain Battery, four companies of the 85th and four of the 29th Native Infantry moved forward on the right, and quickly carried several of the lower positions, while, as this attack developed, General Tytler advanced with his main column of infantry and guns up the defile leading to Zawo. The village of Bagh was reached without much resistance, but the column on the right did not succeed in occupying the ridge to the east of that place without some hand-to-hand fighting.

The troops bivouacked for the night in the positions they had occupied, and on the following morning, the advance being continued, the crest of the pass was gained after considerable resistance and the village of Zawo taken. Subsequent to this the force traversed various parts of the Zaimukht country, and having destroyed the villages concerned in the outrages in the Kuram valley and levied heavy fines in punishment, General Tytler withdrew, reaching Thal on the 23rd December. The casualties in the expedition were one man killed, and Lieutenant Renny, 4th Punjab Infantry (mortally), *Jemadar* Fazl Ahmad, 29th Native Infantry, and one man wounded.

Whilst these events were proceeding in the north, the force in Southern Afghanistan had not been altogether idle. Having recalled the troops which had already left for India and assembled the force under his command at Kandahar, Sir Donald Stewart, in accordance with his orders, proceeded to make a demonstration towards Ghazni. The force detailed for this purpose was placed under the command of Brigadier-General Hughes, and consisted of six guns of the Royal Artillery, the 2nd Punjab Cavalry, a wing each of the 59th Foot and the 3rd Gurkha Regiment, and the 29th Bombay Native Infantry. Marching from Kandahar on the 23rd September, Hughes occupied Kalat-i-Ghilzai without opposition, and having left a small force there, he advanced to Tazi, three marches further on the Ghazni road, where he remained for some weeks. Shortly after the middle of October reports began to be prevalent that the Taraki Ghilzais, incited by that fire-brand the Mushk-i-Alam, were gathering at Shahjui, under their chief, Sahib Jan, for an attack on the British camp at Tazi, and a detachment was accordingly sent forward, under the command of Colonel Kennedy, to surprise them. This small force, which consisted of three guns of the Royal Artillery, two squadrons of the 2nd Punjab Cavalry, and two companies each of the 59th Foot and the 29th Bombay Native Infantry, reached Shahjui as day broke on the 24th, drove in the picquets of the enemy, and after a sharp hand-to-hand encounter with their main body, broke and dispersed them entirely, Sahib Jan and forty-one of his men being left dead on the ground. Our own loss amounted to two men killed, and two British officers, two native officers and twenty-four men wounded.

By the end of October, Brigadier-General Hughes returned to Kalat-i-Ghilzai, and leaving a garrison there, on the 2nd November withdrew the main body of his column to Kandahar. For the rest of the winter almost complete tranquillity prevailed in the districts around that city. In the tracts, however, to the north-west of Kandahar much excitement and confusion prevailed, and reports were rife that Ayub Khan, the brother of Yakub Khan, was advancing on that place from Herat.

The new year opened quietly in and around Kabul, where the principal interest of the moment was centred in the political question of the government of Afghanistan. In March the Kabul Field Force was reorganised. The existing Second (or Khaibar) Division was broken up, and the troops, excepting those sent on to Kabul, were absorbed on the line of communications, of which Major-General Bright was now appointed Inspector-General. The force at Kabul, having been strengthened and some of the worn-out corps replaced by fresher troops from the late Khaibar Division, was now formed into two divisions, the command of the Second of which was conferred upon Major-General John Ross, Sir Frederick Roberts continuing in command of the First and of the whole force. The Kabul Field Force now consisted of the following troops:

Artillery	4 Batteries Royal Artillery
	No. 2 Mountain Battery
	No. 4 Mountain Battery
Sappers & Miners	Four companies

Cavalry		9th Lancers
		3rd & 17th Bengal Cavalry
		3rd Punjab Cavalry
Infantry	1st Bgde.	92nd Foot
		28th Native Infantry
		45th Native Infantry
	2nd Bgde.	72nd Foot
		3rd Sikh Infantry
		5th Punjab Infantry (6 companies.)
		5th Gurkha Regiment
	3rd Bgde.	67th Foot
		27th Native Infantry
		2nd Gurkha Regiment
	4th Bgde.	2-9th Foot
		24th Native Infantry
		4th Gurkha Regiment
Unattached		23rd Native Infantry (Pioneers)
		Corps of Guides

On the Khaibar line the Ghilzais continued to give trouble, and it was decided in consequence to send an expedition into Lughman as soon as the reinforcements then coming up from India should have arrived. Before this could be undertaken, however, operations had to be entered upon against the Mohmands, who had gathered on the northern bank of the Kabul river and begun crossing over. A party of them who attacked the post at Ali Boghan on the 12th January were repulsed, and a larger body was dispersed on the following day by artillery fire alone. The main body, about 1,500 strong, crossed the river near Dakka, and took up a position on the Gara heights; here they were attacked on the 15th by Colonel Boisragon (in command of a small force consisting of detachments of the 6th Dragoon Guards, 17th Bengal Cavalry, and 8th and 30th Native Infantry, with four guns) and, after a brief contest, routed and driven back over the river with considerable loss. The casualties on our side amounted to *Jemadar* Bahadur Khan, 8th Native Infantry, killed, and seven men wounded.

Towards the end of January the arrival of reinforcements at the base enabled General Bright to despatch a force into the Lughman valley. This force was under the command of Colonel Walker, of the 12th Foot, but was accompanied by General Bright himself; it consisted of four guns of the Royal Artillery, two guns of No. 4 Mountain Battery, two companies of Madras sappers, a squadron each of the 6th Dragoon Guards and the 17th Bengal Cavalry, a wing each of the 1-12th Foot, 1-25th Foot, and 27th Native Infantry, and six companies of the 30th Native Infantry. During three weeks Lughman, on both sides of the Kabul river, was traversed and explored in every direction, without any opposition from the enemy. On the 21st February the force was broken up, and the troops returned to their several posts on the line of communications.

The altered organisation of the forces holding the Khaibar line of communications has already been mentioned. Extensive changes amongst the troops employed on the line also took place at this time, many regiments and batteries having been moved on to Kabul and several sent back to India, the places of all these being taken by other corps. At the end of March the troops employed on the line were five batteries of Royal Artillery, No. 1 Mountain Battery, one company of Bengal and three of Madras sappers, the 6th Dragoon Guards, the 8th Hussars, the 4th and 5th Bengal Cavalry, a wing each of the 1st and 2nd Central India Horse, the 1-5th, 1-12th, 2-14th, 1-18th, 1-25th and 51st Foot, the 8th, 9th, 16th, 22nd, 30th, 31st, 32nd (Pioneers), and 41st Bengal Native Infantry, the 1st Gurkha Regiment, and the 1st, 4th and 15th Madras Native Infantry: Major-General Bright was in command of the whole as Inspector-General of the line of communications, Brigadier-Generals Gib, Doran and Hill being in command respectively of the three sections into which the line was divided, and Brigadier-General Arbuthnot in command of a moveable column to operate on any part of the line in which its services might be required.

The month of March in the Khaibar was marked by several attacks on small parties and on posts on the line of communications. On the 22nd Lieutenant Thurlow, 51st Foot, was shot dead, between Jagdalak and Jagdalak *Kotal*, by a band of Ghilzais from Hisarak, and on the 26th a most determined attack was made on the post of Fort Battye, near Fatehabad, by a body of Shinwaris and Khugianis. This post was held by detachments of the 4th Bengal Cavalry and the 4th Madras Native Infantry, but the garrison had fortunately been increased that evening by a detachment of the 31st Bengal Native Infantry, which had halted there for the night while in progress to a post higher up the line. The attack was pressed home with great energy, but was repulsed with heavy loss to the assailants, that of the garrison being Lieutenant Angelo, 31st Native Infantry, and six men killed, and nineteen men wounded. In consequence of these affairs two columns were sent into the Khugiani country early in April, but the enemy offered no opposition, and after some of their towers had been destroyed, they submitted and paid the fines imposed upon them. This expedition was followed a few days later by the despatch of a force into the Hisarak valley, for the punishment of a Ghilzai chief named Muizzullah Khan, who was concerned in the attack in which Lieutenant Thurlow was killed. The force, which was under the command of Brigadier-General Arbuthnot, was composed of two horse artillery and two mountain guns of the Royal Artillery, two guns of No. 1 Mountain Battery, detachments of the 6th Dragoon Guards and 4th Bengal Cavalry, two companies of sappers, one Madras and one Bengal, the 51st Foot, the 8th and 31st Native Infantry, and the 1st Gurkha Regiment. Muizzullah Khan's fort was destroyed on the 12th April; subsequently, though there was some skirmishing, and a good deal of firing into our camp at night, little opposition was encountered, except at the Auzangani defile on the 14th, where the Ghilzais made a determined stand and caused some casualties. Our losses during the expedition amounted to Lieutenant Palmer (Commissariat Department) and one man killed, and four officers and fifteen men wounded.

During the early months of 1880 nothing of importance occurred in the Kuram valley, where Major-General Watson had succeeded Brigadier-General Gordon in the command. In February Brigadier-General Newdigate was appointed to the command of a brigade, in succession to Brigadier-General Tytler, who died of pneumonia on the 14th of that month.

In January 1880, as part of a plan for the pacification of Afghanistan and our eventual withdrawal from the country, the Bengal troops under Sir Donald Stewart were ordered to move up from Kandahar to Ghazni, and thence open communication with Kabul, their place at Kandahar being taken by Bombay troops, to be moved up from Pishin and Sind. The Ghazni Field Force, as Sir Donald's command was now designated, accordingly left Kandahar on the 29th of March, and for three weeks advanced northward without meeting any opposition, although after passing Kalat-i-Ghilzai all the villages were found deserted, and it was only with much difficulty that supplies could be procured.

At length on the morning of the 19th April, about two hours after beginning the march from Mushaki, the Afghans were discovered in great force in advance of the head of the column and on a range of hills to the left of the road at Ahmad Khel, twenty-three miles south of Ghazni. Dispositions were at once made to attack the enemy and the force was arranged as follows:—In the centre were one battery of horse and one of field artillery, with a squadron of the 19th Bengal Lancers and a company of the 19th Native Infantry as escort; on the right was the greater portion of the cavalry, *viz.,* a squadron of the 19th Bengal Lancers, the 2nd Punjab Cavalry, and two squadrons of the 1st Punjab Cavalry; on the left of the guns was Brigadier-General Hughes' brigade (the 59th Foot, the 3rd Gurkha Regiment, and the 2nd Sikh Infantry) with a troop of the 19th Bengal Lancers, and on the extreme left, and slightly in rear, a heavy battery of artillery. In reserve were the 19th Native Infantry, two companies of sappers, and the headquarters escort, consisting of a troop of the 19th Bengal Lancers and a company each of the 2-60th Rifles and the 25th Native Infantry. On the road behind were the hospitals, field parks, and baggage, and in rear of all Brigadier-General Barter's brigade,—a mountain battery, the 2-60th Rifles, the 15th and 25th Native Infantry, and one squadron of the 1st Punjab Cavalry. Before the action commenced, half of Barter's brigade was moved up to the front of the baggage, and arrived in time to reinforce the right centre before the close of the fighting.

At 9 a.m. the guns took up positions, but scarcely had they opened fire, when masses of *ghazi*-led Afghans rushed furiously down the slopes from their position against the line of British infantry, while a large body of horsemen, turning the left of the British line, now reinforced by a squadron of the 19th Bengal Lancers, poured down two ravines, and, uniting at the foot of the hill, struck the Lancers before they could get up sufficient speed to meet the shock, and forced them back on the knoll occupied by Sir Donald Stewart and his staff; nor could they be rallied until they had passed to the rear of the right of the line of infantry, which was itself hard pressed and beginning to give way. The 3rd Gurkhas formed rallying squares and, throwing in a withering fire, checked for a time the reckless rush of the enemy, but the fanatic horde pressed on, enveloping both flanks, and it became necessary to bring forward every man of the reserve, the two sapper companies and a half battalion of the 19th Native Infantry reinforcing the left, while the remaining half battalion and the two companies of infantry of Sir Donald's escort supported the guns on their left.

In the centre and on the right, at this time, so impetuous was the rush of the Afghan swordsmen, that even case-shot from the guns at a distance of fifty yards was insufficient to check them; and at last, all their ammunition having been expended, the two batteries were compelled to fall back about two hundred yards.

The situation for the moment was critical; both flanks had been forced back, and all the reserves were in the front line: but the enemy's advance on the left was now effectually checked and turned back by the deadly fire of the 3rd Gurkha Regiment; the 2nd Sikh Infantry, in the centre, still maintained their position with unwavering steadiness; and on the right the enemy were charged and pushed back by the 19th Bengal Lancers and the 2nd Punjab Cavalry. All along the line the attack began to slacken; in a few minutes it ceased, and as part of Barter's brigade came up the Afghans began to fall back; soon the retirement became a rout, and the masses of the enemy, flying in all directions, were dispersed over the country. Of the 15,000 they brought into action, upwards of a thousand were left dead on the field, and the total loss could not have been less than three times that number. Our own losses amounted to seventeen killed, and one hundred and twenty-four (including nine British officers) wounded.

After a rest of two hours, the march was resumed, and Ghazni was leached on the 21st April. On the 23rd, before day-break, a strong force was despatched under Brigadier-General Palliser, against a large body of the enemy who had taken post in the villages of Shalez and Arzu, about seven miles to the south-east of Ghazni. The position was, however, found to be so strong that General Palliser considered it imprudent to attempt an assault until he was reinforced. The remainder of the troops (excepting those left to guard the camp and to hold Ghazni) arrived at 11 a.m. under Sir Donald Stewart, who immediately made dispositions to attack. In less than an hour the affair was over; the Afghans, making little or no stand, were easily expelled from the villages, and fled in confusion with a loss of 400 of their number, our own losses being no more than two killed and eight wounded.

On the 25th, at Shashgao, Sir Donald Stewart came into communication with Major-General Ross's division of Sir Frederick Roberts' force, then at Saiadabad, and on the 28th, handing over the command of the Ghazni Field Force to Brigadier-General Hughes at Haidar Khel, he left for Kabul to assume supreme command of the forces in Northern Afghanistan. The Ghazni Field Force now became the Third Division of the Kabul Field Force, and moved into the LogarLogar valley, where, on the 16th May, the command was taken over by Major-General Hills.

During the early days of April nothing of importance from a military point of view occurred at Kabul, though there were rumours of hostile gatherings in various parts of the country. The first movement of importance was the despatch to the southward of Major-General Ross with a force which was intended to meet and escort supplies to the troops moving up from Kandahar under Sir Donald Stewart. This force was composed of four guns of the Royal Artillery, No. 4 Mountain Battery, a company of sappers, a squadron of the 9th Lancers, the 3rd Bengal Cavalry, two squadrons of the 3rd Punjab Cavalry, the 2-9th Foot, the 23rd (Pioneers) and 24th Native Infantry, and the 4th Gurkha Regiment; it marched from Kabul on the 17th April, and six days later reached Saiadabad without experiencing any opposition worthy of notice. Two days after the despatch of General Ross's force, intelligence was received that an attack was to be made on it from the Logar valley, and in order to obviate any such movement a small force (two horse artillery guns, the Corps of Guides and a wing of the 92nd Highlanders) was sent to Charasia on the 20th under the command of Colonel Jenkins. On the 21st Colonel Jenkins encamped at Chihildakhtaran, near Charasia, and here he was vigorously attacked on the 25th by a body of three thousand Logaris: though hard pressed he was able to keep the enemy in check until 1-30 p.m., when Brigadier-General Macpherson arrived with reinforcements consisting of two guns of the Royal Artillery, four guns of No. 2 Mountain Battery, a troop of the 3rd Punjab Cavalry, the remaining wing of the 92nd Highlanders, six companies of the 45th Native Infantry, and two of the 2nd Gurkha Regiment. Macpherson at once assumed the offensive against the enemy's left, and having turned that flank with the Gurkhas, Highlanders and Sikhs, forced the Afghans to retire, and eventually put them to flight with heavy loss. The casualties on our side were four killed and thirty-four wounded.

On the same day (25th April) General Ross with a part of his force encountered a body of Afghans at Shekabad, near Saiadabad, and drove them from the ground with considerable loss, himself having only one man killed and four wounded in the engagement. Having established communication with the Ghazni Field Force, Ross's column (now joined by Sir Donald Stewart) moved back to Kabul, where it arrived on the 2nd May.

Nothing of much importance connected with the Kabul Field Force occurred during the months of May and June. Portions of the force moved into various parts of the surrounding country with a view to keeping open the roads and to ease the pressure on the supplies at the capital, but in no case was any opposition encountered, though Muhammad Jan, Mir Bucha, and other chiefs had in no measure relaxed their efforts to create fresh disturbances. During this period a mission was sent to Turkistan, to communicate with Abdur Rahman Khan, one of the candidates for the throne of Afghanistan, and was well received.

Towards the end of June the Third Division (late the Ghazni Field Force), under the command of Major-General Hills, after making various movements in the Logar valley, marched to Zargunshahr, where it arrived on the 30th of the month. Thence on the 1st of July, a force (under the command of Brigadier-General Palliser, and consisting of detachments of the 19th Bengal Lancers and of the 1st and 2nd Punjab Cavalry, amounting altogether to about 560 men) was detached against a gathering of 1,500 Zurmattis at the village of Patkao Shana. The enemy were overtaken while in retreat and were completely dispersed, with a loss of 200 of their number, our own loss being three killed and twenty-nine (including one officer) wounded.

All through the spring and summer negotiations had been in progress with the Kabuli sardars and Abdur Rahman Khan, with a view to establishing the latter as Amir. At last, after much intriguing, the negotiations were brought to a successful issue and the new Amir was formally proclaimed in Durbar on the 22nd of July.

During these months (April to August, 1880) affairs on the Khaibar line continued in a very unsettled state: raids and disturbances were frequent, and more than one punitive expedition had to be undertaken. During the third week in May a force under Brigadier-General Doran (two guns of No. 1 Mountain Battery, and detachments of the Central India Horse, 1-5th and 1-12th Foot, and 1st and 4th Madras Native Infantry) moved from Jalalabad into the Besud district, north of the Kabul river, and at Beninga, on the 19th; defeated and dispersed a body of Safis from Kunar, with a loss on our side of only one British officer, one native officer, and five men wounded. At the same time a column under Brigadier-General Gib (four guns of the Royal Artillery, and detachments of the 8th Hussars, 5th Bengal Cavalry, 2-14th Foot, and 32nd Native Infantry

(Pioneers) encountered and defeated a large gathering of Shinwaris at Mazina (20th May), our loss being four men killed and two officers and five men wounded. Early in June a force which was under the command of Brigadier-General Doran and included detachments of the Central India Horse and of the 9th and 32nd Native Infantry, moved into Kama, and destroyed the forts and towers of the hostile clans. In the middle of the same month an expedition was led by Brigadier-General Arbuthnot into the Lughman valley; and early in July another under Colonel Ball-Acton, which included detachments of the 4th Bengal Cavalry and the 31st Native Infantry, captured and destroyed the village of Nargashai, with a loss of only five men wounded.

In the Kuram district during these months but little of military importance occurred, though raids by the Waziris and Khostwals were frequent; in one of these the post of Chapri was rushed (1st May) by a band of Waziris and Dawaris, who succeeded in getting into the enclosure, where they killed Lieutenant Wood, of the Transport Department, and eight men, and wounded thirteen others. As the Summer advanced, however, the country quieted down to some extent, and the troops were principally occupied with preparations for the return to India, which was to be commenced in October.

At the end of July, when the principal subject of consideration was the withdrawal to India of the British troops in Northern Afghanistan, news was received of the long-threatened advance of Ayub Khan from Herat, of the terrible disaster which had befallen the Bombay force at Maiwand, and of the investment of Kandahar by the troops of Ayub Khan and the mutinous regiments of the Wali Sher Ali Khan of Kandahar. Measures for the restoration of British prestige in Southern Afghanistan and for the relief of the beleaguered garrison were promptly adopted, and on the 3rd of August orders were given for the immediate despatch from Kabul to Kandahar of a strong force under the command of Sir Frederick Roberts. At the same time instructions were issued for the formation of another strong force at Quetta (for which the 3rd, 4th, and 17th Bengal Native Infantry were detailed) to move on Kandahar from the southward under the command of Major-General Phayre. The force under the command of Sir Frederick Roberts was designated "The Kabul-Kandahar Field Force," and was composed of the following corps:

Cavalry Brigade Brigadier-General H. H. Gough		9th Lancers 3rd Bengal Cavalry 3rd Punjab Cavalry Central India Horse
Artillery Colonel A. C. Johnson		No. 6 Battery, 8th Brigade, Royal Artillery No. 11 Battery, 9th Brigade, Royal Artillery No. 2 Mountain Battery

Infantry: Major-General J. Ross, C.B., Commanding

Brigadier-General H. T. Macpherson	1st Bgde.	92nd Highlanders 23rd (Punjab) Native Infantry (Pioneers) 24th (Punjab) Native Infantry (Pioneers) 2nd Gurkha Regiment
Brigadier-General T. D. Baker	2nd Bgde.	72nd Highlanders 2nd Sikh Infantry 3rd Sikh Infantry 5th Gurkha Regiment
Brigadier-General C. M. MacGregor	3rd Bgde.	2-60th Rifles 15th (Sikh) Native Infantry 25th (Punjab) Native Infantry 4th Gurkha Regiment

By the end of the first week of August all arrangements at Kabul were complete, and on the 8th the Kabul-Kandahar Field Force was assembled at Bini Hisar; thence on the following morning it began that memorable march which has since become one of the most famous achievements of the British arms in India.[1]

The story of "Roberts' march" is interesting and instructive as an example of what can be effected by energy and careful organization. Starting with a force of picked troops, and with transport as complete

---

1. In the opinion of Sir Frederick Roberts himself the advance on Kabul from Kuram, in the autumn of 1879, was in every particular a more difficult and dangerous operation.

as could be procured under the circumstances, the undertaking was aided by the influence of the new Amir during the first part of the march, and it was not at any time impeded by open hostilities: notwithstanding these advantages the fact yet remains that to march over three hundred and twenty miles in twenty-two days with an army of 10,000 fighting men and 8,000 followers, two-thirds of the distance being through an enemy's country, was a feat which required not only energy and forethought of the first order at the head, but the most careful and competent supervision of all details, however small, and the most thorough and conscientious work in all ranks from the general commanding to the junior officer of transport.

Marching through the Logar valley, in order to gain the benefit of its fertile crops, the force reached Ghazni on the 15th August,—98 miles in seven days. Thence without a halt the march was continued through a rough and treeless country, under a scorching sun, with all the trying accompaniments of rear guard and baggage guard duties, the difficulties of which no one who has not had experience of the Indian camp-follower can fully realise; or with the almost equally wearying nights on guard, after the labours of the march and the toils of fatigue duty. Day after day the force pushed on, until on the 23rd August Kalat-i-Ghilzai was reached, 232 miles having been covered in fifteen days. Here one day was allowed for well-earned rest; and on the 25th, when the march was resumed, the force was augmented by the garrison of Bombay troops, which Sir Frederick Roberts deemed it expedient to withdraw. At length on the 27th August, at Robat, heliographic communication was established with the Kandahar garrison by the cavalry brigade, and in the evening the camp of that brigade was joined by several officers from the lately beleaguered city. It being now ascertained that the siege had been raised, and that the Afghan Army was entrenching itself in a position north-west of the town, Sir Frederick Roberts determined to give his force a day's rest at Robat, and thence to march the remaining eighteen miles to Kandahar by two easy stages, in order that his men might arrive there as fresh as possible for the work before them. The forced marches of the division therefore ended at Robat, where the main body arrived on the 28th August, and when 303 miles had been covered in twenty days.

On the 31st Kandahar was reached, and after a halt outside the Shikarpur gate, the troops encamped on the plain to the west of the city and cantonments, the 2nd and 3rd Brigades occupying Picquet

Hill, Karez Hill, and a spur of the hill above old Kandahar. On the same afternoon a reconnaissance in force (the 3rd Bengal Cavalry and the 15th Native Infantry with two guns, under Brigadier-General Gough) demonstrated that Ayub Khan was holding the village of Pir Paimal and the Baba Wali *Kotal*, north-west of the camp, in considerable strength; and that his encampment was behind (north of) these, at Mazra, but whether the latter was entrenched or not was not ascertained. Our loss in this reconnaissance amounted to three killed, and an officer and eleven men wounded.

Having thus obtained all the information he required, Sir Frederick Roberts decided on attacking Ayub Khan on the following morning, his plan of operations being briefly to threaten the enemy's left at the Baba Wali *Kotal* and to assail his right in force by the village of Pir Paimal, carry that point, and take the Baba Wali *Kotal* in reverse. For the former purpose part of the Bombay force was detailed, for the latter the whole of the infantry of the Kabul-Kandahar Force,—the 1st and 2nd Brigades to deliver the attack, while the 3rd remained in reserve, the cavalry of the Kabul-Kandahar Force meanwhile operating by the left, by the village of Gandigan, and working towards the Argandab river, so as to threaten the rear of Ayub Khan's camp and his line of retreat towards Girishk and Kakrez. To carry out these operations the troops were in position at an early hour on the morning of the 1st September, but it then became apparent that the enemy were themselves contemplating offensive measures, they having during the night occupied the villages of Gandi Mulla Sahibdad and Gandigan, at the foot of the Baba Wali range, as well as the gardens and orchards connecting these villages,—positions from which it would be necessary to expel them before any advance could be made on Pir Paimal. To secure this object Brigadier-General Macpherson was instructed to advance direct on Gandi Mulla with the 1st Brigade, take the village, and then drive the enemy from the enclosures lying between it and the low spur of the hill short of Pir Paimal, Brigadier-General Baker, with the 2nd Brigade, being ordered to advance at the same time on Macpherson's left, and clear the gardens and orchards in his immediate front. To Major-General Ross was entrusted the direction of these attacks.

Shortly after 9-30 a.m. the operations of the day were begun by a heavy battery of Royal Artillery with the Bombay force opening fire on the Baba Wali *Kotal*, and the attention of the enemy having been attracted to this point, General Ross was directed to begin the real attack, on the right of the Afghan position. Covered by the fire of two batteries, Macpherson advanced on Gandi Mulla, and after a sharp contest the village was carried by the 92nd Highlanders and the 2nd Gurkha Regiment. Baker, moving forward at the same time, encountered an obstinate resistance from the Afghans posted in the walled gardens and orchards on the left, and the 72nd Highlanders and the 2nd Sikh Infantry sustained considerable loss. At length, however, all opposition was overcome and the enemy were driven back to Pir Paimal, and the two brigades, uniting at that point and wheeling to the right, swept all before them until they reached an entrenched position on the further side of the Baba Wali *Kotal*, where the Afghans made a last desperate stand: it was, however only for a moment; a gallant rush of the 92nd, headed by Major White, broke through the opposing force, and soon the whole Afghan Army was in full flight. Owing, however, to the nature of the ground, General Ross was unable to realise the extent of the victory, and expecting the enemy to take up a fresh position further on he halted to reform his brigades. When, however, the advance was resumed a few minutes disclosed the fact that the victory was complete, and that Ayub's camp was standing deserted. The pursuit was taken up by the cavalry as effectually as possible, but owing to the extended position occupied by the enemy on the morning of the 1st Brigadier-General Gough was obliged to make such a wide detour that he did not arrive on the Afghan line of retreat in sufficient time to do as much execution as might otherwise have been effected.

Our loss on the 1st September was three British officers, one native officer and thirty-three men killed, and ten British officers, four native officers and 202 men wounded,—making a total loss on the two days of forty killed and 228 wounded,—of the latter of whom more than twenty afterwards succumbed to the injuries they had received.

Thus was brought to a worthy conclusion an undertaking which at the time was watched with breathless interest by the whole military world, and which will always rank as one of the most brilliant achievements of the British arms in India.

The battle of Kandahar not only relieved the garrison of that place, but brought the war to a speedy conclusion. The withdrawal of the remaining troops from Kabul had commenced almost immediately after the departure thence of Sir Frederick Roberts force, and the frontier, as arranged by the peace of Gandamak, was resumed. In Southern Afghanistan the field force was withdrawn, as quickly as possible, with the exception of a moderate garrison which was retained at Kandahar. Early in the following year Kandahar also was given up and the frontier, as it existed before the war, was re-established both in the north and in the south.

For the second campaign in Afghanistan the thanks of Parliament were voted to the army and the generals engaged; a medal was granted to all who were not already in possession of the first, with clasp, for the actions of Charasia, Kabul, Ahmad Khel, and Kandahar, and a special bronze star was given to the troops who took part in Roberts' march to Kandahar (G. G. O. Nos. 673 of 1880 and 472 of 1881). Regiments engaged were authorised to bear all the above names on their colours and appointments (G. G. O. No. 418 0 1881); and a second grant of six months' batta was made to all ranks (G. G. O. No. 459 of 1880).

In October 1880, during the withdrawal of the troops from Afghanistan, a punitive expedition under Brigadier-General MacGregor was despatched from the Harnai line against the Marri tribes, who, since the disaster at Maiwand, had been conspicuous for the boldness of their outrages. The force employed consisted of a mountain battery of the Royal Artillery, the 3rd Punjab Cavalry, the 2-60th Rifles, the 4th and 5th Gurkha Regiments, and the 2nd and 3rd Sikh Infantry. Very little opposition was met with, but the exceedingly difficult nature of the country rendered the expedition one of great hardship to the troops. Having traversed the country in various directions and visited Kahun, the chief town of the tribes, and the terms dictated by the British Government having been accepted, and due submission and reparation, made by the tribesmen, the force withdrew in November.

The termination of hostilities in Afghanistan left the Government of India at leisure to turn their attention to the Mahsud Waziris, who, incited thereto from Kabul, had, during the continuance of the war, been guilty of numerous raids and outrages on our borders and on the line of communications in the Kuram valley, and in the spring of 1881 an expeditionary force, under the command of Brigadier-General Kennedy, was prepared at Tank to visit them with the punishment due to their misdeeds. The force consisted of the Peshawar Mountain Battery, three guns of the Hazara and two of the Derajat Mountain Batteries, detachments of the 1st and 4th Punjab Cavalry, the 8th Company of Sappers and Miners, and a wing each of the 32nd Native Infantry (Pioneers), 1st and 4th Sikh Infantry, and 1st, 2nd, 3rd, 4th, and 6th Punjab Infantry. A reserve column was also assembled at Bannu under the command of Brigadier-General J. J. H. Gordon, comprising No. 1 Battery, 8th Brigade, Royal Artillery, No. 1 Mountain Battery (two guns), the 18th Bengal Cavalry, the 6th Company of Sappers and Miners, the 14th, 20th, 21st, and 30th Native Infantry, and the 5th Punjab Infantry. Before General Kennedy's advance, which took place on the 21st of April, the submission of most of the tribe had already been received; But the Nana Khel section still held out, and it was against them principally that the operations were directed. Passing up the Shuhur valley, the force visited various settlements of the recusant clan without experiencing much opposition until the 3rd of May, when the advance was furiously attacked, near Shah Alam Ragza, by a large force of the enemy. The charge, however, was easily repulsed by the 1st Sikh Infantry, and the enemy were driven back completely beaten; on the 5th Kaniguram was occupied, and on the 11th Makin. In the meantime, under instructions from General Kennedy, the Bannu column, under Brigadier-General Gordon, had moved into the hills, and, proceeding up the Khaisora valley, had, after some skirmishing, reached Razmak on the 9th May, when it came into communication with the Tank column. Some more skirmishing took place, but no further serious opposition was encountered, and the Nana Khels having submitted, the troops returned to British territory,—General Kennedy by the Tank-Zam and General Gordon by the Shaktu valley. The total casualties during the expedition amounted to eight killed and twenty-four wounded.

But few internal changes or points of interest are to be noted in the three years covered by this chapter; not only is the period a very short one, but it was too fully occupied by the business and excitement of active operations to leave much time for organisation or reform of details. The outbreak of the war in Afghanistan occasioned a temporary increase of regiments to a strength of 480 sowars in the cavalry and 800 sepoys (912 of all ranks) in the infantry (G. O. C. C. dated the 19th December 1878), and an attempt was made to re-enrol pensioners for garrison duty, but this proved a complete failure. On the conclusion of the first phase of the hostilities, preparations were made for a reduction by the cessation of recruiting, but the rising at Kabul soon necessitated a return to the augmented strength. An advance of Rs.15,000 was sanctioned to all silladar*silladar* regiments of cavalry thus augmented, in order to meet the expense of equipping the new men, 96 in number—the money to be repaid within two years.

The drain of the protracted operations in Afghanistan, where the great amount of sickness, rather than the severity of the fighting, occasioned a continual demand for recruits, led to the grant, in 1880, of a bounty of R50 to all recruits, R25 being paid on enlistment, and the other half on the conclusion of three years' service.

No other changes remain to be noticed, nor do any of the small alterations in the equipment of native regiments call for remark, except that contained in G. O. No. 10 of 1879, by which brown leather accoutrements took the place of buff in all infantry regiments of the line.

Circa 1880

Circa 1880

Circa 1880

Native Cavalry, Circa 1880

CHAPTER 11
Egypt & Burma

The year 1882 witnessed the commencement of a series of campaigns in Egypt, which afforded to Indian troops an opportunity of fighting and working side by side with certain British corps with which they are never brought into contact in their duties in Asia; and a special interest, therefore, attaches to the expeditions of 1882 and subsequent years such as had not existed since the force under Sir David Baird had excited the curiosity and admiration of the European troops in the same country in 1801.

The outbreak of hostilities in Egypt in July 1882 was soon followed by a call for a contingent from India. The force which, in accordance with this requisition, was despatched to take part in the operations in that country, was composed of the 2nd and 6th Bengal Cavalry, the 13th Bengal Lancers, the 7th, and 20th Bengal Native Infantry, and the 29th Bombay Native Infantry (the 2nd Baluch Battalion), the whole under the command of Major-General Sir H. T. Macpherson. The first of these regiments to disembark was the 2nd Bengal Cavalry, which landed on the 24th August and by the second week in September the whole force was collected at Ismailia, on the Suez Canal. A part of the 13th Bengal Lancers was sent on to Kassassin at the end of August and took part in a reconnaissance towards Salahieh on the 1st September, in which, however, nothing was seen of the enemy. On the 9th September, about an hour after daybreak, a general advance was made by the Egyptian Army against the British position at Kassassin. The infantry under Major-General Graham moved out to meet the attack, with their left resting on the Freshwater Canal, and the right supported by the cavalry, which, threatening the enemy's left, fell in with and defeated a separate portion of his force advancing from Salahieh. The enemy's repulse was general all along the line, the British losses being three killed and seventy-five wounded, of whom one killed and one wounded belonged to the 13th Bengal Lancers.

On the 11th September the Indian Contingent, under Sir Herbert Macpherson, arrived at Kassassin, and the infantry was then attached to the 2nd Division under Lieutenant-General Hamley, while the cavalry became the Second Brigade of the Cavalry Division. On the same day arrangements were made for an attack on the enemy's fortified position of Tel-el-Kebir on the following night, according to which the 1st Battalion of the Seaforth Highlanders (72nd Foot) and No. 9 (Mountain) Battery, 1st Brigade, Northern Division, Royal Artillery, were attached to the Indian force.

After dark on the 12th September camp was struck, and the troops moved on to their respective rendezvous. At 1-30 a.m. on the 13th, the march of the main body and of the Cavalry Division, which was slightly in rear of the right, commenced. Just as day was breaking the infantry became engaged and after a short but sharp contest carried the enemy's entrenchments, and the 2nd Cavalry Brigade moving round the extreme left of the enemy's position, harassed the retreat of the Egyptians and rapidly converted it into a headlong rout. Pushing on to the railway station, the brigade succeeded in capturing a train full of fugitives which was just leaving Tel-el-Kebir for Zag-a-zig; thence without a halt the pursuit was continued to Belbeis, which was reached soon after noon. The Indian Infantry Brigade, marching from Kassassin at 2-30 a.m., moved along the south side of the Freshwater Canal: about daybreak the batteries on the enemy's right were engaged, and in a few minutes the whole of the position south of the canal was captured. The main body of the infantry halted at Tel-el-Kebir; but the Indian Brigade, pushing on through the day, reached Zag-a-zig at 6 p.m. Sir Herbert Macpherson had meanwhile ridden on in advance, and, arriving at Zag-a-zig two hours earlier, captured ten engines and a hundred carriages, some of which were on the point of leaving the station.

The casualties of the Indian Contingent during the day were only one killed and three wounded.

On the 14th, at 3 a.m., Major-General Drury-Lowe, commanding the cavalry, taking the 2nd Brigade, with the 4th Dragoon Guards and the mounted infantry, left Belbeis; and by 4-15 p.m. arrived at Abbassieh, outside Cairo. Here he found a large portion of the Egyptian Army drawn up ready to surrender; and on the same evening Cairo was entered, the citadel occupied, and Arabi Pasha a prisoner.

By the victory of Tel-el-Kebir and the rapid pursuit to the capital all resistance was completely broken, and active military operations were brought to a close. Through the remainder of September the Indian Contingent remained in garrison at Zag-a-zig and Abbassieh, and early in October the withdrawal of the troops from Egypt commenced. By the end of that month all the Indian regiments had reached Bombay.

For services in Egypt a medal was granted to all ranks, and a bronze star was presented by the Khedive; and the words "Egypt, 1882," and "Tel-el-Kebir" were authorised to be borne on the colours and appointments of the corps engaged in the operations (G.G.O. Nos. 578 and 665 of 1882 and 325 and 341 of 1883).

In the winter of 1883-84 it was found necessary to despatch a small expedition against the Akhas, a savage tribe inhabiting the hills to the north of the Darrang district in Upper Assam, to punish them for repeated raids into British territory and to enforce the release of some captives they had carried off. The troops employed consisted of a detachment of No. 1 (Kohat) Mountain Battery, No. 2 Company, Sappers and Miners, and 200 men of the 12th and a wing of the 43rd Bengal Native Infantry, the whole under the command of Brigadier-General R. S. Hill. Diju Mukh, on the frontier, was the rendezvous; but before the arrival of all the troops an advance column of the 43rd Native Infantry and police marched (17th December) into the hills. A night attack was made on this detachment on the 23rd, with the result that two men were killed and seven wounded. Three days later, on arrival at the Tenga river, the passage was found to be opposed by the enemy in considerable force, and it was decided to concentrate the whole column before pushing on. Accordingly it was not until the 8th January that the passage of the river was effected, in the face of considerable opposition from strong stockades on the opposite bank, but as the only weapons of the enemy were bows and arrows, the casualties were not many. The Akhas, finding their position forced, fled into the hills in all directions and offered no further resistance, and the objects of the expedition having been attained, the column returned to British territory by the 23rd January. Our losses during the expedition were four killed and nine wounded. In the autumn of 1884 a small affair disturbed the tranquillity of the North-West Frontier. During the preceding eighteen months the tribes inhabiting the Zhob and Bori valleys had been guilty of repeated outrages in the neighbourhood of the Harnai pass, and it at last became necessary to send a punitive expedition against them. The expeditionary force, which moved forward from Thal-Chotiali in October, and was under the command of Major-General Sir O.V. Tanner, K.C.B., was composed of two mountain batteries, one squadron each of the 10th Bengal Lancers, the 5th Punjab Cavalry, and the 1st Bombay Lancers; a wing of the 1st Battalion, Worcestershire Regiment (29th Foot); a wing of the 1st Battalion, North Lancashire Regiment (47th Foot); the 2nd Battalion, North Staffordshire Regiment (98th Foot); two companies of the Bengal Sappers and Miners; the 1st and 45th Bengal Native Infantry; the 4th Punjab Infantry; the 2nd Bombay Infantry (Grenadiers), and a detachment of the 1st Madras Infantry (Pioneers). Advanced detachments were sent on into the Bori valley early in October, and on the 13th of that month the Political Agent, Sir Robert Sandeman, held a durbar of chiefs at the entrance to the valley, at which the submission of all except the Mena Khel, Kilzai, and Zhob tribes, was received. A standing camp having been formed at Dulai, a forward movement was made on the 18th against the fort of the chief Shah Jahan, which was occupied on the 21st. A gathering of the tribesmen was shortly after discovered at Daulatzai, on the hills north of Shah Jahan's fort, and Sir Oriel Tanner moved up to attack them on the 24th; the enemy, who were badly armed, being almost entirely without fire-arms, were quickly driven from their position with a loss of about fifty killed and several prisoners, the casualties on our side being only five wounded, including two native officers,—all of the 4th Punjab Infantry. During the next few days several villages were destroyed; but the recalcitrant tribes having now tendered their submission hostilities ceased, and about the last week in November the force was withdrawn.

Early in 1885 it became necessary to despatch another expedition to Egypt, to cooperate with the British force at Suakin. Orders on the subject were issued in G. G. O. dated the 14th February 1885, by which Major-General J. Hudson was appointed to command the Indian troops. A special scale of pay was laid down for native ranks whilst in receipt of Government rations, and the supply of grain and forage for horses was also undertaken by Government. The corps detailed were the 9th Bengal Cavalry (equipped as lancers), the 15th and the 17th Bengal Infantry,[1] and the 28th Bombay Infantry. The first detachment embarked at Bombay on the 22nd February, and by the 14th of March the whole contingent was landed at Suakin.

---

1. By an order of Government in the Military Department the designations of all regiments of native infantry were altered from the 1st January, 1885, by the elimination of the word "Native." These regiments became, therefore, from that date, "Bengal Infantry," "Madras Infantry" and "Bombay Infantry."

For the first few days but little active work was done outside the camp, but the force was subject to the annoyance of continual night attacks, in which several sentries were killed or wounded. On the 19th a reconnaissance was made by the Cavalry Brigade, supported by the Indian Contingent, through dense bush and difficult country, in the direction of Hashin; the enemy were not seen in any strength, though a few shots were exchanged at long ranges. On the following day a strong force moved out of Suakin with the object of establishing a *zariba* at Hashin; it consisted of the Guards, the 2nd Brigade, the Cavalry Brigade, the Indian Contingent, three batteries of artillery, and some engineers. As the force advanced a continuous skirmishing fire was kept up by Arabs concealed in the bush, and the hill on which it was proposed to construct the look-out post was not carried without considerable opposition and loss,—the 9th Bengal Cavalry, in a conflict in the bush, having had twelve (including *Ressaidar* Shibdeo Singh) killed and fifteen (including Major Robertson) wounded. At length the *zariba* having been established, the force retired, reaching Suakin the same evening.

On Sunday, the 22nd March, at 7 a.m., the Indian Contingent infantry, with the 1st Battalion of the Berkshire Regiment (49th Foot), some sappers, two squadrons of the 5th (Royal Irish) Lancers and on,e of the 9th Bengal Cavalry, the whole under the command of Major-General Sir J. C. M'Neill, marched from Suakin to form a *zariba* eight miles south-west of the town. At 11 a.m. only six miles had been covered, but it was determined to halt and commence the *zariba* at a place called Tofrek Tofrek. At 2-40 p.m., when the sappers and the Berkshire Regiment were cutting down the thick bush round the *zariba,* the cavalry scouts and working parties were suddenly driven in by a furious rush of a large force of Arabs. The unfinished *zariba* was defended on the west by the 15th Bengal Infantry, on the south by the 17th Bengal Infantry, and on the north by the 28th Bombay Infantry; the main attack came from the south-west, and so impetuous was the charge that the southern face of the square, which had been thrown into disorder by the cavalry picquets galloping in on the front, was broken through, and the enemy rushed into the centre in great numbers, causing great confusion amongst the baggage animals, and inflicting considerable loss on the 17th Bengal Infantry and the followers. On the first alarm the Berkshire Regiment hastened to stand to their arms and open fire, and in the meantime the 15th Bengal Infantry sustained the brunt of the attack on the west face without flinching, and by their steadiness and gallantry did much towards preserving the whole force from disaster. The enemy was at length driven off at 3-30 p.m., after having suffered terrible loss, and the *zariba* having been completed and garrisoned by the 15th and 17th Bengal Infantry, the remainder of the force returned to Suakin. The casualties amounted to seventy killed, one hundred and thirty-three wounded and thirty missing, the loss of the Bengal troops being Major Von Beverrroudt, 17th Bengal Infantry, and twenty-nine men killed, and forty-five (including Lieutenant Drury, 17th Bengal Infantry) wounded.

Throughout the rest of March the troops at Suakin were constantly employed on escort or convoy duty between that place and the various *zaribas* in the surrounding country, but no fighting took place beyond occasional long range firing in the bush; in fact, it appeared that the enemy's power was broken by his losses on the 22nd March. On the 31st of March a cavalry reconnaissance reported Tamai to be held in strength by the Arabs; and accordingly two days later a force marched in that direction, 7,200 strong, and including 1,585 men of the Indian Contingent. Passing through Tofrek, Tesselah hill was reached in the afternoon without any opposition being met with, and the force bivouacked there that night. On the 3rd April the column advanced to Tamai, and having burned all the huts there, whilst the enemy kept up a skirmishing fire from the bush, the return march to Tofrek was effected without incident. The next day the column return to Suakin.

Uneventful convoy duties were performed by the whole garrison through the month of April. On the 2nd May Lord Wolseley arrived at Suakin, and four days later a combined attack from Suakin and Otao was made on the enemy's position at Thakul, eighteen miles west of the former place, and ten miles south of Otao. The Suakin column consisted of the 9th Bengal Cavalry, some mounted infantry, and the Camel Corps; that from Otao included a company of mounted infantry, the 15th Bengal Infantry, and some native scouts. The enemy were taken completely by surprise, and were driven with considerable loss from their camp, which was destroyed. The casualties on our side were only three wounded.

The active operations of the campaign soon after came to a conclusion, but the 15th and 17th Bengal Infantry and one squadron of the 9th Bengal Cavalry were retained in garrison at Suakin, and did not return to India until November.

The Egyptian medal of 1882, with clasp inscribed "Suakin, 1885," was granted to all troops who took part in the operations in Egypt between the 26th March 1884, and the 14th May 1885, together with a special clasp for the battle of Tofrek (G. G. O. No. 655 of 1885), and by G. O. No. 849 of 1887, the Khedive's bronze star was also granted to the troops employed at Suakin. Authority was afterwards given to the corps engaged to inscribe the words "Suakin, 1885," and "Tofrek", on their colours and appointments (G. G. O. No. 478 of 1886).

We come now to the Third Burmese War, 1885, which, with the subsequent operations of 1886-89, is remarkable not so much for the breadth or brilliancy of the military operations, as for the importance of its consequences, the number of troops employed, and the harassing and arduous nature of the duties entailed.

The relations of the British Government with that of Mandalay had, ever since the accession of King Thebaw in 1879, been in a strained and unsatisfactory condition, owing to the violation of treaties by the King, to acts of aggression on the British frontier, to outrages upon British subjects and injustice to British traders, and to the intrigues of the King with a foreign European power with objects hostile to British interests. Remonstrances in connection with these matters were received with indifference and evoked nothing but insolence, the forbearance exhibited by the British Government serving only to inflate the arrogance of which two disastrous wars and the loss of large tracts of territory had failed to cure the Burmese people. Misconstruing this forbearance, King Thebaw, in 1885, filled up the measure of his offences by arbitrarily imposing on a British trading company a fine of ruinous amount, and insolently refusing to submit the matter to impartial enquiry. Under these circumstances an ultimatum was addressed to the Court of Mandalay, and this being met with an evasive reply and by the simultaneous issue of an openly hostile proclamation, war became inevitable, was declared accordingly, and orders issued (30th October, 1885) for the despatch of a field force to Burma with all speed.

The force detailed for this service was placed under the command of Major-General H. N. D. Prendergast, C.B., V.C, and was composed of six batteries of artillery, six companies of sappers and miners, three regiments of British and seven of native infantry, and a naval brigade,— out of which the Bengal Army contributed No. 4 (Hazara) Mountain Battery, two companies of sappers and miners, and the 2nd and 11th Bengal Infantry.

The whole force arrived at Rangoon between the 5th and the 11th of November, and proceeded in a fleet of the Irrawaddy Flotilla

Company's steamers to Thyetmyo; thence an advance was made on the 14th of November, and on the following day the frontier was crossed. The small towns which were first reached, such as Sinbaung-we, etc., were occupied without any opposition, the whole strength of the Burman forces in the neighbourhood of the frontier being concentrated at the forts of Gwe-gyaung-Kamyo and Minhla, which face each other on opposite sides of the river. A simultaneous attack was made on these places on the morning of the 17th November. It was expected that Gwe-gyaung-Kamyo, on the left bank, which was much the stronger position of the two, would be resolutely held; but on the approach of our troops the garrison ran off after a faint resistance, and the position was captured with a loss on our side of only two men wounded.

The brigade employed on the opposite side of the river, consisting of the 2nd and 11th Bengal Infantry and the 12th Madras Infantry, had a more arduous task to perform, and encountered considerable opposition in the attack on the village and fort of Minhla. The former was a place of some size, stretching along the river bank south of the fort, and surrounded by a bamboo stockade; the latter was a square stone structure, its walls about twenty-five feet in height, entered on the side facing the river by a narrow arch, and having on the west a double ramp, which approached the ramparts with a slope of about 25^0. The troops for the attack were landed at Malun, a large village four miles down the river, and on approaching the village of Minhla the advance was received by a smart fire from the enemy, who were concealed in thick jungle. The 11th Bengal Infantry, however, pushed on rapidly, and, supported by the 2nd, quickly carried the stockade and entered the village. The attack was now directed against the house of the Woon, which was within a further stockaded enclosure, and, in spite of a vigorous resistance, the Burmans were driven from point to point and the position carried. The fort alone remained, and it was approached by an encircling movement, the 11th Bengal Infantry making for the left or north side of the ramp, while the 2nd, extending to the right, cut off the line of retreat to the river, and at the same time advanced to the southern approach of the ramp. During the whole advance the troops were subjected to a heavy fire from the jungle round and from the fort, but, advancing steadily, the ramp was carried by a final rush from both sides, and the garrison, flying into the casemates of the fort or out of the east gate, offered no further resistance. The first to reach the *terre-plein* at the top of ramp was Lieutenant Wilkinson, of the 12th Madras Infantry, who had joined the 11th Bengal Infantry, and was closely followed by a large number of the latter regiment; as he reached the *terre-plein* he stumbled, and, falling forward, was at once set upon by the enemy and severely wounded; his life was only saved by the advance of the men of the 11th. In the day's fighting the casualties amongst the officers were heavy, Lieutenant Dury, 11th Bengal Infantry, being killed, and four officers of the 12th Madras Infantry wounded; of the rank and file three were killed and twenty-three wounded.

With the fall of Minhla the opposition of the Burman Army to the British advance was almost at an end. Two Italians, who had led and trained the enemy's forces on the frontier, surrendered on the following day, and our further advance up the river met with no serious resistance. Pagan was evacuated after a few rounds had been fired: Myingyan, where alone anything like a stand was made, was taken without loss on our side: Ava and Sagain again surrendered on the 27th November without a shot being fired: and on the 28th Mandalay was reached, the palace occupied, and the king a prisoner. On the 29th Thebaw was sent down the river under escort, and later on he was deported to India.

Intelligence having been received that the Chinese were massing troops on the frontier with a view to seizing Bhamo, Major-General Prendergast left Mandalay on the 18th December with a force of about a thousand men (which included the Hazara Mountain Battery and a company of Bengal sappers), and, proceeding up the Irrawaddy, occupied Bhamo on the 28th, without having encountered any opposition.

Thus ended the third war against the Alompra dynasty. The deportation of King Thebaw from Mandalay was followed by the annexation of Upper Burma; and throughout the remaining months of the cold weather of 1885-86, though there were repeated skirmishes with bands of insurgents, no military operations of any consequence took place, and it appeared that the country was likely in time to settle down quietly under its new rulers. But the seeds of future troubles had been sown when hundreds of Burmese soldiery, unused to any but an idle and self-indulgent life, had been allowed, on the disbandment of the king's army, to disperse armed over the country.

As the spring drew on, dacoities and outrages became more and more frequent; pretenders to the throne and local leaders arose in every quarter, whose influence and boldness increased proportionately as they perceived the inadequacy of the British force then in Burma to cope with the difficulties of the situation. To deal with these increasing disorders considerable reinforcements were sent to Burma during the winter and the succeeding spring, and amongst other corps the 7th Bengal Cavalry and the 26th, 27th, and 43rd Bengal Infantry were despatched thither on service.

General Prendergast vacated the command on the 1st April 1886, and was succeeded by Brigadier-General G. S. White, V.C, with the local rank of Major-General. Throughout the summer actions of various degrees of importance with bands of insurgents and dacoits were frequent in every district. In the neighbourhood of Pagan, Myingyan, and Meiktila, the 11th Bengal Infantry and detachments of the Sappers were continually engaged around the many posts which were established in the districts,—one officer, Lieutenant Forbes, of the former corps, being killed while on convoy duty between Meiktila and Hlaingdet on the 21st April, on which occasion also seven sepoys were wounded.

In the Bhamo district, at the same time, an expedition was despatched against Katran, close to the Chinese frontier, the stronghold of the Phonkan Tsawbwa, in which the 26th Bengal Infantry and the Hazara Mountain Battery took part. Katran, a position of considerable strength, was captured after some resistance with a loss of nine wounded, but the force was obliged to retire immediately owing to the deficiency of supplies. Another expedition marched to Katran in the following month, on which occasion no resistance was met with.

During the summer a small force, which included detachments of the 4th, 42nd, and 44th Bengal Infantry, advanced from Manipur, and, after some fighting, occupied Tammu, in the Kubo Valley. Several skirmishes took place in that neighbourhood during the summer and autumn, and eventually the enemy were driven completely out of the Kubo Valley.

But the most important operations of this period were in the Minbu district, where the 2nd Bengal Infantry were stationed. Salin, a large walled town, six miles from the right bank of the Irrawaddy and about forty miles north of Minbu, was the centre of much disturbance; the place was threatened by a large force of dacoits early in June, and in an engagement outside the walls on the 12th of that month Captain Dunsford was killed. Six weeks later the dacoits, having gathered in still .greater numbers, commenced a regular siege of the town, of which the walls were with difficulty manned by the small garrison stationed there. All the ammunition was exhausted and the defenders in serious straits, when the place was relieved on the last day of July, In the western part of the district, the Deputy Commissioner, Mr. R. Phayre, was killed at Padaing, near Magwe, on the 8th of June. This was followed by the advance of a mixed column under Major Gordon, 2nd Bengal Infantry, from Minbu, which, on the 19th June, attacked and captured Ngape, a large village at the foot of the Aeng Pass over the Arakan Yomas, thirty-seven miles west of Minbu; our loss in the affair was six killed and twenty-five wounded. The climate of Ngape, however, was found to be so terribly unhealthy at that season of the year that it became necessary to abandon the place, and the garrison retired on the 1st August.

Towards the end of the summer further reinforcements were despatched to Burma: the field force was divided into six brigades and one independent command; and early in the autumn Sir Herbert Macpherson, Commander-in-Chief of Madras, assumed command of the whole. On the 1st October 1886 the following were the Bengal troops serving in Burma:

1st Brigade	7th Bengal Cavalry
	Sappers & Miners
	43rd Bengal Infantry (Gurkhas)
2nd Brigade	No. 4 (Hazara) Mountain Battery
	Sappers & Miners
	26th Bengal Infantry
3rd Brigade	27th Bengal Infantry
4th Brigade	11th Bengal Infantry
6th Brigade	2nd Bengal (Light) Infantry
Chindwin Command	18th Bengal Infantry

These were supplemented shortly after by the 3rd Gurkha Regiment and the 5th Bengal Infantry in the 1st Brigade, and by the 1st and later by the 12th Bengal Infantry in the 2nd Brigade.

The plan of operations for the winter was to traverse the districts apportioned to these brigades with a succession of strong columns, supplemented by flying columns of cavalry- and mounted infantry; the end in every case being the capture or destruction of the local chiefs who everywhere headed the dacoit bands. Before the operations commenced, the field force and the whole Indian Army suffered a sudden and severe loss in the death of Sir Herbert Macpherson, who died of fever on the 26th October 1886, near Prome. In consequence of this misfortune, Sir Frederick Roberts, then Commander-in-Chief in India, at the special request of the Government of India, transferred his head-quarters to Burma, and assumed the command of the troops there.

The following is a brief summary of the principal events of the next twelve months in which Bengal troops were engaged:—

A column composed of the 3rd Gurkha Regiment, a detachment of Bengal sappers, and some Madras infantry, under Colonel Stedman of the first-mentioned corps, marched for the hills east of Mandalay at the end of October, and on the 26th of that month some slight skirmishing took place, in which one man was killed and three wounded. The column continued its movements in the hills for some time, during which a few unimportant skirmishes occurred. On the 20th November Captain Pulley, with a detachment of the 3rd Gurkha Regiment, marched from Lamaing, and on the 25th attacked and captured a strong position at Zibyubin, where he himself and six men were wounded. Throughout December the pursuit of the dacoit leader Hla-u was prosecuted with vigour by the 7th Bengal Cavalry. In March a mixed column, including some of the 27th Bengal Infantry, attacked and carried the stockaded position of Hmawaing,

In the Second Brigade a mixed force, under Brigadier-General Cox, consisting of detachments of the 7th Bengal Cavalry, the Hazara Mountain Battery, Bengal Sappers, Royal Welsh Fusiliers (23rd Foot), and 26th Bengal Infantry, marched to Wuntho, where a column from Shwebo cooperated; the latter was composed of detachments of artillery, of British infantry, and of the 1st and 12th Bengal Infantry. No resistance was met with, and the inhabitants of Wuntho were disarmed.

Considerable activity was exhibited in the districts of the Third Brigade during this winter, most of the operations being prosecuted by Bombay troops. In January a column assembled at Hlaingdet, under Colonel Stedman, consisting of artillery, some of the Hampshire Regiment (67th Foot), and the 3rd Gurkha Regiment from the First Brigade; this force marched into the Shan States, where little opposition was experienced and no fighting took place.

In the Fourth Brigade Captain Rose commanded a mixed column which included a detachment of the 27th Bengal Infantry. This marched in December 1886 from Wundwin against Hmawaing: several days of jungle fighting took place before the objective was reached ; Hmawaing was destroyed and the column then retired, its operations having made an excellent impression in the district.

The chief operation in the Fifth Brigade was the Ruby Mines expedition, which was organised in December and marched on the 19th of that month from Sagadaung under Brigadier-General Stewart. It consisted of four guns, 110 Bengal sappers, 96 of the King's Own South Yorkshire Light Infantry (51st Foot), and 293 of the 43rd Bengal Infantry. Occasional slight skirmishes took place, but on the whole but little resistance was experienced.

The operations of the Sixth Brigade were directed entirely against the two dacoit leaders, Boh Shwe and Oktama. A strong column advanced from Minbu under Brigadier-General Low early in December, composed of detachments of artillery and Madras cavalry, the 1st Battalion of the Rifle Brigade, the 2nd Bengal Infantry, the 3rd Hyderabad Infantry, and some mounted infantry. Little was seen of the enemy until Paeng, at the foot of the Arakan range, was reached, when a skirmish took place, in which one man was killed and seven wounded. Moveable columns were now formed, which patrolled the country, without, however, meeting many of the enemy. At the same time a column, which included some of the 11th Bengal Infantry, marched from Mitchi into the Pauk country, where a skirmish took place on the 5th January, in which one man was killed and five wounded.

On the Chindwin river the dacoit gangs were very active during the winter. On the 10th October some of the 18th Bengal Infantry had a smart skirmish on Taung-talon hill, in which three men were wounded. On the 19th of the same month Captain Sage, with a detachment of the 18th Bengal Infantry, some Bombay infantry, and Military Police, attacked and carried a dacoit position at Chauktat, with a loss of one killed and one wounded. On the 28th October the Assistant Commissioner of the district, Mr. Gleeson, was killed at Yu, and his escort of twenty men of the 18th Bengal Infantry were hard pressed; their defence, however, was so steady that they succeeded in beating off their assailants and carrying away Mr. Gleeson's body to Tandwin. Their loss was one killed and five wounded. On the 7th November a column, under Lieutenant L. C. Fryer, of the 18th Bengal Infantry, and some Madras infantry, attacked an entrenched position at Myogyi, from which they expelled the enemy with considerable loss. The casualties were three killed, and Lieutenant Fryer and two men wounded.

In the spring of 1887 Major-General White succeeded Sir Frederick Roberts in the command of the field force, which, on the 1st

April was reorganised,—the Fifth Brigade being amalgamated with the Second, and the Sixth with the Fourth. Several corps were relieved and returned to India, while the force which remained continued the work of settling the country by the operation of numerous small and rapidly moving columns.

Many engagements of more or less importance took place during the summer and autumn, in the course of which most of the dacoit leaders were either killed or captured. Of the skirmishes in which the Bengal troops were engaged, and with which alone we are now concerned, only three were of much consequence. In one, on the 5th June, detachments of mounted infantry and of the 5th Bengal Light Infantry, under Lieutenant Cuppage, attacked a strong position at Taungma, near Pyumbwin, and lost Lieutenant Darrah, Assistant Commissioner, and one man killed, and four men wounded. Four days later another detachment of the 5th had a smart skirmish in the capture of the stockaded position of Mangon, in the Second Brigade district; and on the 11th July detachments of the Royal Munster Fusiliers (104th Foot) and 5th and 10th Bengal Infantry attacked and carried Mezadaung hill, in the First Brigade district, with a loss of one killed and four wounded.

During the autumn of 1887 and the spring of 1888 detachments of the 7th Bengal Cavalry and of the 1st, 5th, 10th, and 33rd Bengal Infantry were frequently engaged in skirmishes with bands of dacoits in various parts of the country, while portions of No. 1 Bengal Mountain Battery and of the 12th Bengal Infantry were employed in operations against the Kachins in the Mogoung district, but though these services were harassing and some losses were sustained, no action took place deserving of special mention.

The operations carried out and the defeat and dispersion of dacoit bands wherever met with had the effect by the spring of 1888 of restoring order to a very great extent throughout the newly acquired territory, and it was found practicable then to make a considerable reduction in the forces in the country and to redistribute those that were retained. On the 1st of May the troops in Burma (the whole under the command of Major-General Sir George S. White) were re-arranged in three brigades (with headquarters at Mandalay Myingyan, and Meiktila respectively) and four commands (designated respectively the Bhamo, Ruby Mines, Chindwin, and Shwebo commands), the Bengal troops remaining in the country being distributed as follows:

1st Brigade	No. 1 Bengal Mountain Battery
	½ 42nd Bengal Infantry
2nd Brigade	½ 10th Bengal Infantry
	33rd Bengal Infantry
Bhamo Command	No. 2 Bengal Mountain Battery
	12th Bengal Infantry
Ruby Mines Command	½ 42nd Bengal Infantry
Chindwin Command	½ 10th Bengal Infantry

Later on in the year the Bengal troops in Burma were increased by the despatch thither of the 17th and 44th Bengal Infantry.

By G. G. O. No. 434 of 1887 the India medal, with a special clasp inscribed "Burma, 1885-87," was granted to all the troops employed between the declaration of war and the 30th April 1887, and in 1891 G. G. O. No. 64 authorised the words "Burma, 1885-87," being borne on the colours of all regiments so employed.

Though the summer of 1888 brought with it no absolute cessation of military movements in Burma and on its frontiers, it will be convenient at this point to leave that part of the country for a while, and turn to some events of importance which were in progress elsewhere.

At the end of 1887 the infringement of the treaty of 1861 by the Sikkim Rajah, and the establishment of a force of Tibetans at the fort of Lingtu, rendered military measures in-that quarter necessary, and early in 1888 a small force was concentrated on the Sikkim frontier for that purpose. It consisted of four guns of No. 9 Battery, 1st Brigade, Northern Division, Royal Artillery, 200 of the 2nd Battalion, Derbyshire Regiment (95th Foot), a wing of the 13th Bengal Infantry, and the 32nd Bengal Infantry (Pioneers), the whole under the command of Colonel T. Graham, Royal Artillery. Half the force remained at Padong, while the remainder advanced on the 16th March, and on the 20th, having attacked and carried a stockaded position at Jelaktso, near Lingtu, and a stone breastwork above, advanced towards the main position of the Tibetans. On the 21st the fort of Lingtu was occupied without resistance. The casualties in the two days were one officer and four men slightly wounded.

Early in April an entrenched camp was established at Gnathong, and here, on the 22nd of May, the garrison was attacked by the Tibetans in considerable force. The enemy were by no means wanting in courage, but the worthlessness of their weapons rendered their assault comparatively harmless, and they were beaten off with considerable loss; the casualties on our side were three killed and eight wounded.

In the middle of June the artillery and the detachment of the Derbyshire Regiment were withdrawn from Gnathong to Jalapahar; but hardly a month had elapsed before the increasing numbers of Tibetans in the Jalep pass compelled Colonel Graham to ask for reinforcements; and by the end of August his force at Gnathong amounted to 1,700 men, composed of four guns, 386 of the Derbyshire Regiment, the 32nd Bengal Infantry, and 514 of the 2nd Battalion of the 1st Gurkha Regiment.

Three weeks passed in comparative inaction, during which the Tibetans were adding to their numbers and strengthening their position in the Jalep pass. At length Graham assumed the offensive, and on the 24th of September attacked and captured the Tibetan advanced position, drove the enemy over the Nimla pass, advanced against and captured the Jalep pass after a feeble resistance, and, having crossed the pass on the 25th, advanced as far as Chambi, which place he reached on the 26th. The enemy being completely beaten and disorganised, the force returned to Gnathong, where it arrived on the 28th. The casualties in these operations were only two officers and three men wounded.

Concurrently with Graham's advance against the Tibetan position in the Jalep pass a detachment of 150 of the 13th Bengal Infantry was sent from Padong to occupy Gantok, and on the 30th a part of this detachment advanced as far as Tumlong, the capital of Sikkim; both there and on the road these troops were met with cordiality by the inhabitants. The detachment returned to Gantok on the 5th October.

Active military operations were now at an end, and, while political arrangements were in progress of settlement the troops were employed in opening out and improving the roads on both sides of the Tibet frontier. The Derbyshire Regiment and the artillery were sent back to India before the winter set in, but it was not until October in the following year that the remaining corps were withdrawn from Sikkim. The India medal, with a special clasp inscribed "Sikkim, 1888," was granted by G. G. O. No. 431 of 1889 to the troops employed in these operations.

The increasing unruliness of the tribes of the Black Mountain, Hazara, culminating (18th June, 1888) in an attack on a party of the 5th Gurkha Regiment, in which Major Battye of that regiment and Captain Urmston, 6th Punjab Infantry, were killed, resulted in the despatch against them, in the autumn of 1888, of a punitive expedition of considerable strength, under the command of Brigadier-General

J. W. McQueen. The force detailed for this service was organised in two brigades, commanded, respectively, by Brigadier-Generals Channer and Galbraith, and each brigade was formed into two columns, of which the composition was as follows:

1st Column
Colonel
J. M. Sym
Commanding

No. 4 (Hazara) Mountain Battery
Two Gatling guns
Half of the 3rd Company of Sappers and Miners
2nd Battalion, Northumberland Fusiliers (5th Foot)
3rd Sikh Infantry
1st Battalion, 5th Gurkha Regiment

2nd Column
Colonel
R. H. O'G. Haly
Commanding

No. 3 Battery, 1st Brigade, South Irish Division, Royal Artillery (4 guns)
1st Battalion, Suffolk Regiment (12th Foot)
Wing of 34th Bengal Infantry (Pioneers)
40th Bengal Infantry
45th Bengal Infantry (Sikhs)

3rd Column
Lieutenant-Colonel
M. S. J. Sunderland
Commanding

No. 3 Battery, 1st Brigade, South Irish Division, Royal Artillery (2 guns)
½ 3rd Company of Sappers & Miners
2nd Battalion, Royal Sussex Regiment (107th Foot)
14th Bengal Infantry (Sikhs)
24th Bengal Infantry

4th Column
Colonel
A. C. W. Crookshank
Commanding

No. 2 Battery, 1st Brigade, Scottish Division, Royal Artillery, and some Gatling guns
2nd Battalion, Royal Irish Regiment (18th Foot)
29th Bengal Infantry
Wing of 34th Bengal Infantry (Pioneers)
4th Punjab Infantry

A field reserve, composed of the 15th Bengal Cavalry, the 2nd Battalion of the Seaforth Highlanders (78th Foot), and the 2nd Sikh Infantry, was also formed at Abbottabad, and a contingent of the troops of the Maharajah of Kashmir was afterwards added to it. The Khaibar Rifles subsequently joined the field force, and were attached to the Third Column. The First, Second and Third Columns assembled at Ughi, in the Agror valley, on the 1st October; the Fourth concentrated at Darband on the Indus.

The Fourth Column, under the command of Colonel Crookshank and accompanied by Brigadier-General Galbraith, advanced from Darband to Chamb on the 2nd October, and thence on the morning of the 4th towards Kotkai; they were met by parties of the enemy at Shingri, and in the firing which ensued *Subadar*-Major Chattar Singh, 34th Bengal Infantry, was mortally wounded. The column proceeding on to Kotkai found the tribesmen assembled in force near that place. The 34th Bengal Infantry and the 4th Punjab Infantry, who had covered the advance, having cleared the flanks, the guns came into action, and their fire was followed by a charge of the Royal Irish Regiment. At this moment one flank was exposed to an attack by a large party of *ghazis,* mostly Hindustanis, who had concealed themselves in a ravine; these fanatics (about two hundred in number) made a desperate attempt to break our line, but their onslaught was met and in a moment repulsed by the Royal Irish and portions of the 29th and 34th Bengal Infantry, who promptly shot down or otherwise destroyed the whole gang, not a single man escaping. By 3-30 p.m. the enemy were in full flight towards Kunhar, and an hour later Colonel Crookshank seized and occupied Kotkai. The British loss amounted to four killed and twelve wounded: amongst the latter were three British officers, one of whom, Captain Beley, D.S.O., Assistant Quarter-Master-General, died next morning of his wounds. On the following day a reconnaissance was made from Kotkai towards Kunhar, in which Colonel Crookshank, commanding the column, received a severe wound, which afterwards necessitated amputation of the leg, and, eventually, on the 24th of the month, caused his death. The command of the column devolved upon Colonel Beddy, who held it until the arrival of Colonel Pratt ten days later. Several days were now spent in reconnaissances, during which some skirmishing took place, resulting in several casualties, and on the 13th General Galbraith crossed to the right bank of the Indus, and destroyed the Hindustani fort and settlement at

Maidan. The Fourth Column afterwards came into communication with the Third, but nothing of any importance occurred, and not a shot was fired after the destruction of Maidan.

The other three columns, moving up the Black Mountain from the Agror valley, also began their operations on the 4th October. The First Column, advancing to Mana-ka-dana and Chittabat, met with little opposition beyond a few stray shots, mostly directed against working parties; the Second advanced up the Barchar spur without meeting any opposition, whilst the Third moved up the Sambalbat and Chatta spurs. On the 5th the summit of the Black Mountain was reached. The advance was then continued towards Seri, skirmishing occurring each day with scattered parties of tribesmen. Seri was taken and destroyed on the 9th, and other villages of the hostile tribesmen suffered the same fate on subsequent days. On the 13th October the Third Column reached Kunhar, and came into communication with the Fourth.

The result of these operations, and of the punitive measures adopted, was that on the 19th October the Akazais tendered their submission, their example being followed on the 30th by the Hassanzais.

The efforts of General McQueen were now turned to coercing into submission the Pariari Saiads and Tikariwals, coupled with a demonstration against Thakot and the Allai country. In these operations the First Column was employed, reinforced by a wing of the 34th Bengal Infantry and assisted by a Fifth Column composed of two guns, two GatlingsGatlings, a wing each of the Seaforth Highlanders and 40th Bengal Infantry, and the Khaibar Rifles.

The Pariari Saiad country was entered on the 24th October without much opposition having been experienced. On the 28th a lightly equipped force, selected from the First and Fifth Columns, was pushed on to the village of Thakot; only a few shots were fired from a distance at the troops and the detachment soon afterwards returned to the head-quarters of the force. On the 1st November another detachment advanced into the Allai country by the Ghoraphor pass, and, after a feeble resistance, a strong position on the Chaila ridge was captured with a loss of one killed and one wounded; part of the force penetrated to Pokal on the 3rd, with a loss of one killed and four wounded.

All the tribes now tendered their submission and acceptance in full of the terms imposed upon them by Government. The objects of the expedition having thus been attained, the troops withdrew into British territory, and the field force was broken up.

The loss of the force during the operations amounted to twenty killed and fifty-seven wounded, among the latter being five British officers, two of whom died of their wounds,

The India medal, with a clasp inscribed "Hazaka, 1888," was, by G. G. O. No. 413 of 1889, granted to all troops engaged.

The cold season of 1888-89 witnessed a renewal of field operations operation in in the newly-acquired province of Upper Burma. The country was, indeed, internally quiet, and the results of the three years' occupation were satisfactory beyond the hopes of the most sanguine, but the wild tribes of the frontiers, unsettled by the change of government and by the temporary prevalence of lawlessness amongst their Burmese neighbours, began to encroach on our now comparatively peaceful subjects, and necessitated a recourse to hostilities. At the commencement of the cold weather accordingly a plan was drawn up for operations in the Chin country, and in the Mogoung, Eastern Karenni, Ruby Mines, and Bhamo districts.

The most important operations were those in the Chin country. The tribes of the Chin hills had been incessant in their depredations throughout the summer of 1888, and in September two columns moved up to the outskirts of their country, one by way of Pauk, the other by Kalewa, and occupied Thilin, Gangaw, Kan, Sihaung, Kanbale and Indin. The raids, however, continued; in December attacks were made on a working party of the 42nd Bengal Infantry near Kanbale, and on the posts of the same regiment at Sihaung and Kangyi, and in January 1889 the posts at Kan and Gangaw (where detachments of the 10th, 33rd, and 44th Bengal Infantry were engaged) were also assailed. At length a force under Brigadier-General Faunce, which included two guns of No. 1 Bengal Mountain Battery and 250 of the 42nd Bengal Infantry, moved into the Chin country, and on the 5th February, after a good deal of desultory skirmishing, occupied Tokhlaing (afterwards named Fort White), where headquarters were established. Thence General Faunce detached a column, which included 75 of the 42nd and 100 of the 44th Bengal Infantry (which had also joined the force), with two guns, to operate against the Kanhau Chins, upon whom, between the 8th and the 20th March, severe punishment was inflicted, almost all their villages having, after considerable skirmishing, been destroyed. Later, on the 4th May, a detachment, including sixty of the 42nd, was sent against the Siyin Chin village of Tartan. Here the enemy were strongly posted behind stockades, and offered such a determined resistance that the attacking force was compelled to retire with a loss of one officer and three men killed, and two officers and eight men wounded. This however was the only *contretemps* of the operations, which were on the whole eminently successful. Our losses from first to last amounted to two officers and twenty-four men killed, and six officers and forty-nine men wounded, of which the Bengal share was nine men killed and twenty-seven wounded.

In January 1889, an expedition was despatched from Mogoung for the punishment of the Lepei Kachins. This was practically a police expedition, but two guns of No. 2 Bengal Mountain Battery and a small detachment of the 1st Battalion, Hampshire Regiment (37th Foot) were attached to the police levy during the operations. Thama, the chief village of the Lepeis, was taken after a smart skirmish on the 19th February, and Wawang on the 21st, and early in March the force returned to Mogoung. On the 13th March a column was despatched against the Ithi tribe, and on the 1st April against the Sana Kachins, and a detachment was also employed against the Hlegyoman dacoits; in all these operations No. 2 Bengal Mountain Battery took part. The losses sustained during these operations were only one killed and twenty-four wounded, but of the latter no less than six were British officers, one of whom (Lieutenant Hawker, Hampshire Regiment) died of his wounds.

Two guns of No. 1 Bengal Mountain Battery took part in the operations of the Northern Column, under Brigadier-General H. Collett, which marched from Fort Stedman against the Eastern Karenni on the 29th December, 1888; and which, after some smart fighting near Lwekaw (costing us five killed and eleven wounded), occupied Sawlon on the 8th January, 1889.

In the Ruby Mines district a rising took place in January 1889, a body of eight hundred rebels threatening the town of Momeit. Several skirmishes took place, in one of which an officer of the Hampshire Regiment (37th Foot) was killed. On the 24th March a column under the command of Major Garfit, Hampshire Regiment, in which two guns of No. 1 Bengal Mountain Battery were included, was despatched from Momeit to visit the insurgent stronghold at Binbaung, which was taken on the 30th after some resistance. The column returned to Momeit on the 10th April. In February 1889, a small force, under the command of Captain E. A. Smith, Royal Artillery, composed of a detachment of the Hampshire Regiment (37th Foot), two guns of No. 2 Bengal Mountain Battery, and 150 of the 17th Bengal Infantry, was despatched from Bhamo against a body of rebels who had taken up a position at Malin in the Sinkan valley, where they had repulsed a party of police. The enemy were encountered at that place on the 7th and their stronghold captured, but not without a sharp engagement, in which a loss of five killed and eighteen wounded was sustained, including Second-Lieutenant StoddartStoddart and two men of the 17th Bengal Infantry killed, and ten men of the same regiment wounded. In the following month a detachment under the command of Major Spencer, 17th Bengal Infantry, twice defeated bodies of rebels in the neighbourhood of Mansi.

In April, 1889, a force, under the command of Brigadier-General Wolseley, was despatched from Bhamo to operate against the Paukan Kachins. The force operated in two columns, of which the northern column was under the command of Captain E. A. Smith, Royal Artillery, and the southern under that of Major St. Paul of the Rifle Brigade. In these columns were included four guns of No. 2 Bengal Mountain Battery, and 150 of the 17th and 100 of the 42nd Bengal Infantry. Little opposition was encountered by either column, and only the northern column sustained any loss,—Captain Smith and six men having been wounded, of the latter of whom two died.

On the 1st April 1889 the commands in Burma were redistributed and the force further reduced, Major-General B. L. Gordon succeeding Sir George White in the chief command. Upper Burma was now divided into two districts,—that of Mandalay, including the Bhamo, Ruby Mines and Shwebo commands, in which were Nos. 1 and 2 Bengal Mountain Batteries and the 17th Bengal Infantry; and that of Myingyan, including the Chin Field Force, with which were employed the 10th, 33rd, and 42nd Bengal Infantry.

The grant of the India medal, with a clasp for Burma, originally limited to operations up to the 30th April 1887, was by G. G. O. No. 31 of 1890 extended to all who had served in the country up to the 31st March, 1889, and an additional clasp was granted to those who were already in possession of the previous one.

In the cold weather of 1888-89 it was decided to despatch, from the Chittagong side, an expeditionary force into the Lushai country, with the combined object of inflicting punishment for past raids, in one of which a British officer employed in surveying had been murdered, and of opening out the country and establishing frontier posts. The command was given to Colonel V. W. Tregear, and the troops employed were, besides Madras and Bombay detachments, 250 men each of the 2nd and 9th Bengal Infantry and a wing of the 2-2nd Gurkha

Regiment. These troops were all assembled at Demagiri by the middle of February, 1889, and in the following month the Shendu country was visited, and the village of Howsata, the chief concerned in the murder of the British officer, taken and destroyed. The operations lasted until the middle of April, when the objects of the expedition having been fully attained, the troops were withdrawn. The only obstacles encountered were those arising from the nature of the country.

Notwithstanding the lessons taught to the wild tribes of the Chin hills during the winter of 1888-89, their depredations by no means ceased throughout the following year. This fact, coupled with the advisability of thoroughly exploring and opening out the narrow strip of country which now alone divided British Burma from India, led to the undertaking, in the cold weather of 1889-90 of military operations from Burma and Chittagong into the country of the Chins and Lushais. The Burma force was commanded by Brigadier-General W. P. Symons, South Wales Borderers, and was divided into three portions:—first, the Northern Column, which included a wing of the 10th, a detachment of the 38th, and a wing of the 42nd Bengal Infantry, to operate from Fort White under the command of Colonel Skene; secondly, the Southern Column, with which were a detachment of No. 1 Bengal Mountain Battery and a wing of the 2-4th Gurkha Regiment, to advance from Kan into the Baungshe-Baungshe Chin country under the command of Brigadier-General Symons himself; and thirdly, the garrisons on the lines of communications.

The northern column advanced at the end of November, and by the close of the year had succeeded in establishing several posts for the protection of the Burma frontier from Chin raids. During its operations it encountered considerable opposition from the Kanhau and Siyin Chins, and several casualties occurred.

The southern column, delayed by the extraordinary difficulties of the country which it had to traverse, took sixty-six days, instead of twelve, as had been estimated, to reach Haka. Throughout the operations the opposition of the Chins was of a very faint character; the malarial fever of the thickly wooded valleys through which the troops moved was the most dangerous enemy met with, and from it all the regiments engaged suffered very severely.

In March 1890 a simultaneous advance of detachments was made from Fort White and from Haka into the Tashon Chin country, which, though elaborate preparations for resistance had been made by the tribes, succeeded in reaching the Tashon Ywama, and establishing British influence without any actual fighting. The remainder of the season was occupied by the northern column in operations against the Siyins, and by the southern in numerous reconnaissances and explorations.

The losses of the two columns during these operations amounted to two British officers and seven men killed, and nine men wounded.

The force from Chittagong, under Brigadier-General V. W. Tregear, consisted of a company of sappers, the 3rd Bengal Infantry, a detachment of the 9th Bengal Infantry, the 2-2nd Gurkha Regiment, and a half battalion of the 2-4th, and a Bombay corps, and was destined to operate against the Chins, Lushais, Shendus, and other tribes occupying the hill tracts lying between the Chittagong district and the Chindwin and Kale valleys in Burma. It was divided into two columns, the northern and the Haka. The former advanced into the Lushai country, enforced the surrender of prisoners, exacted satisfaction for raids in past years, and opened the country by the construction of roads, etc. The Haka column was hindered beyond expectation by the same difficulties of country which so impeded the advance of the Southern Burma column, and was unable to complete the western section of the mule road to Haka until the 13th April. Immediately afterwards, the season being far advanced, the troops were withdrawn, and the field force broken up.

The India medal, with a special clasp inscribed "Chin-Lushai, 1889-90," was, by G.G.O. No. 275 of 1891, granted to all troops employed in these operations between the 15th November, 1889, and the 30th April, 1890.

During the winter of 1889-90, two columns were despatched (from Bhamo and Momeik) to coerce the Tonhôn Kachins, who had been giving a good deal of trouble. In the Bhamo column was included a part of the 17th Bengal Infantry, but having been left on the line of communications, this detachment was not prominently engaged in the operations, during which a good deal of fighting occurred, our losses during the expedition amounting to five killed and twenty (including two British officers) wounded

The year 1890 closed with an expedition on the North-West Frontier undertaken with the double object of exploring the Zhob Valley and of operating against the unruly sections of the Kidarzai Sherani tribe. The only Bengal troops comprised in the Zhob Valley force, which was commanded by Major-General Sir George White, were the 18th Bengal Lancers; but a force which moved from the Derajat under Colonel

A. G. Ross, and co-operated from the east, included detachments of No. 1 (Kohat) and No. 7 (Bengal) Mountain Batteries, and of the 1st and 3rd Punjab Cavalry, half battalions of the 1st and 2nd Sikh Infantry, and the whole of the 2nd Punjab Infantry. The operations entailed exertions and exposure of an exceptional kind, but little opposition was encountered from the tribesmen, and the work of the force terminated on the 3rd December, 1890. Internal The years under review are remarkable for many changes, as well in the strength as in the interior economy and conditions of service of the Indian Army. The period opens with considerable reductions. In 1882 (G. G. O. No. 210) the strength of the Bengal Army was reduced by three regiments of cavalry and six of infantry, the strength of corps retained being at the same time fixed at three squadrons, with a total strength of 550 of all ranks, for cavalry, and at eight companies, with a total strength of 832 of all ranks, for infantry. The three Assam regiments,—the 42nd, 43rd, and 44th Bengal Infantry, and subsequently the five Gurkha regiments, were, however, specially allowed to retain a total strength of 912 of all ranks. The number of British officers with every corps was at the same time increased by one, making a total of eight. The regiments selected for disbandment were the 16th and 17th Bengal Cavalry and the 4th Punjab Cavalry, the 34th, 35th, 36th, 37th, and 41st Bengal Infantry, and the 3rd Punjab Infantry.

Before many years had elapsed, however, these reductions were not only made good, but the strength of the army was raised to a higher point than that to which it had attained prior to the reductions. In the autumn of 1885 the 16th and 17th Bengal Cavalry were resuscitated, and the strength of regiments of Bengal Cavalry was increased by the addition of a fourth squadron. In the following year second battalions were added to the 1st, 2nd, 4th, and 5th Gurkha regiments, and two Bengal mountain batteries were raised. In 1887, five new battalions of Bengal infantry were raised; four (one of Mazbi Pioneers, two of Sikhs, and one of Dogras) to take the places of the disbanded 34th, 35th, 36th, and 37th Bengal Infantry, and the fifth (formed of Garhwalis) to be the second battalion of the 3rd Gurkha Regiment; at the same time the addition of a squadron to the cavalry of the Corps of Guides was ordered. In 1890 a complete re-organisation of certain regiments of Bengal infantry took place, resulting in the disappearance of the last of the old "low-caste levies" raised during the Mutiny; the old material having been mustered out, the 33rd Bengal Infantry was re-organised as a class regiment of Punjabi Musalmans, the 38th as one of Dogras, and the 40th as one of trans-frontier Muhammadans, including Baluchis; at the same time the second battalion of the 3rd Gurkha Regiment, raised three years before, became the 39th (Garhwal) Regiment of Bengal Infantry, and a new 2nd battalion of the 3rd Gurkha Regiment was formed in its place.

In addition to the above, a temporary increase of 200 men was (clause 45 of India Army Circulars, 1887) sanctioned for all corps ordered on service in Upper Burma; and (clause 44 of the Circulars of the same year) the normal strength of all infantry corps was increased to 912 of all ranks.

Nor were the changes and reforms in the interior economy of regiments less noticeable during this period. Closely affecting the British ranks were the orders concerning the tenure of regimental commands published in G.G.O. No. 209 of 1882, by which it was provided that the then holders of regimental commands should continue in that office up to the completion of a term of seven years or until fifty-five years of age, whichever should happen first, but in no case for less than five years; that their immediate successors should retain command for seven years or up to fifty-five years of age; and that thereafter the limits should invariably be seven years' command or fifty-two years of age.

Worthy of note too is the sanction given by Her Majesty, published in G. G. O. No. 592 of 1882, to the inscription of "Nagpur" on the colours of the 6th Bengal Infantry, of "China, 1858-59" on those of the 7th, 10th, and 11th Bengal Infantry, and of "China, 1860-62" on those of the 15th, 22nd, and 27th Bengal Infantry,—honours somewhat belated, perhaps, but none the less eminently merited by these corps.[2]

By G. G. 0. No. 210 of 1882 good conduct pay was granted to non-commissioned officers as follows:—one, two, three, and four rupees after two, four, six, and eight years in the grade; but in the case of naiks one and two rupees only after two and four years in that grade.

In the same year orders were published restricting the enlistment of Afridis, and naming the following corps as being alone permitted to entertain recruits of that tribe:—the 7th Bengal Cavalry, the 11th and 19th Bengal Lancers, and the 20th, 21st, 24th, 26th, and 27th Bengal Infantry. In 1885 the 17th Bengal Cavalry was added, and the 7th Bengal Cavalry and the 24th and 27th Bengal Infantry expunged from this list, nor was any more extended enlistment of Afridis encouraged until 1890 when (India Army Circulars, clauses 81, 151 and 201) the formation of extra companies of Afridis was ordered in the 21st, 24th, 26th, 27th, and 28th Bengal Infantry, and the 1st, 4th, and 5th Punjab

---

2. *Vide* earlier chapters 4 and 8.

Infantry, *vis.*, one company in each, except the 26th, in which two companies were to be formed. These extra companies were only to be a temporary increase of the established strength, and previously existing companies were in each case to be gradually reduced, in order to bring the regiment to its normal establishment.

On the 20th January, 1883, a General Order was published laying down rules as to the classes whose enlistment in the Bengal Army was permitted or otherwise, and adding a statement, such as had not been published since 1864, of the caste constitution of every corps. Of this statement the following is a *résumé*—

Corps.			Class regiment or class troop.	Muhammadans.			Hindus.				Remarks.
							Punjabi.			Hindustani.	
				Hindustani.	Punjabi.	Trans-Indus and Border.	Sikhs.	Dogras.	Rajputs.	Other Hindus.	
1st Bengal	Cavalry		C.	6	...	...	...	...	...	...	
2nd	,,	,,	C.T.	2	...	...	1	...	1	2(a)	(a) Jats.
3rd	,,	,,	C.T.	3	...	...	1	...	1	1(b)	(b) ,,
4th	,,	,,	C.T.	3	...	...	1	...	...	2(c)	(c) ,,
5th	,,	,,	C.T.	2	...	...	1	...	1	2(d)	(d) ,,
6th	,,	,,	C.T.	2	...	...	2	...	1	1(e)	(e) ,,
7th	,,	,,	C.T.	2	...	...	1	...	1	2(f)	(f) One troop of Jats and one of Brahmans.
8th	,,	,,	C.T.	3	...	...	1	...	1	1	
9th	,,	,,	C.T.	...	2	1	2	1	...	...	
10th	,,	Lancers	C.T.	...	1	1	2	2	...	...	
11th	,,	,,	C.T.	...	1	1(g)	3	1	...	...	(g) One-fourth of the troop might consist of Afridis.
12th	,,	Cavalry	C.T.	...	2	...	3	1	...	...	
13th	,,	Lancers	C.T.	...	1	1	2	2	...	...	
14th	,,	,,	C.	...	...	...	...	...	...	6(h)	(h) Jats.
15th	,,	Cavalry	C.	...	2	4	...	...	...	...	
18th	,,	,,	C.T.	...	4	...	2	...	...	...	
19th	,,	Lancers	C.T.	...	1	1	2	1	...	...	and one troop of independent trans-border tribes.

Corps	Class regiment or class company	Muhammadans				Hindus						North-East Frontier			Remarks
		Hindustani	Punjabi	Independent Trans-border	Trans-Indus and Border	Punjabi Sikhs — Jats, etc.	Mazbis	Dogras	Brahmans	Rajputs	Other Hindus	Gurkhas	Hillmen	Jarwahs of Assam	
1st Bengal Infantry	C.C.	2							2	3	1				
2nd ,, ,,	C.C.	2							2	3	–				
3rd ,, ,,	C.C.	2							3	2	–				
4th ,, ,,	C.C.	2							2	3	–				
5th ,, ,,	C.C.	2							–	2	3(a)				(a) Two of Jats.
6th ,, ,,	C.C.	2							1	2	4(b)		2		(b) Ditto.
7th ,, ,,	C.C.	2							–	2	2				
8th ,, ,,	C.C.	2							–	3	2				
9th ,, ,,	C.C.	2							–	2	2(c)				(c) Jats.
10th ,, ,,	C.C.	1	1						2	3	3(d)		1		(d) Two of Jats.
11th ,, ,,	C.C.	2							1	2	1				
12th ,, ,,	C.C.	2							–	–	2				
13th ,, ,,	C.C.	2							–	–	4(e)				(e) Two of Jats.
14th ,, ,,	C.C.	3				7(f)									(f) Cis-Sutlej Sikhs chiefly.
15th ,, ,,	C.C.					7(g)									(g) Ditto.
16th ,, ,,	C.C.	2	2						2	3	2				
17th ,, ,,	C.C.	3	1						–	3	1		1		
18th ,, ,,	C.C.	2				4(h)									(h) Cis-Sutlej Sikhs prohibited.
19th ,, ,,	C.C.		1	1.	1										
20th ,, ,,	C.C.		1	2(i)	1	2(j)		2							(i) Afridis. (j) Cis-Sutlej Sikhs prohibited.

Regiment															Notes
21st	"	"	...	C.C.	...	2	1(m)	-	3(m)	...	...	...	...	...	(m) Afridis.
22nd	"	"	...	C.	...	3	...	...	...	...	...	...	...	...	(n) Cis-Sutlej Sikhs prohibited.
23rd	"	"	...	C.	...	...	...	...	4(o)	8	1	...	...	...	(o) Ditto.
24th	"	"	...	C.	...	2	...	1	3(p)	...	...	...	...	...	(p) Ditto.
25th	"	"	...	C.	...	3	...	...	3(q)	...	...	...	...	...	(q) Ditto.
26th	"	"	...	C.	...	...	...	2	4(s)	...	2	...	...	...	(s) Ditto (r) Afridis.
27th	"	"	...	C.	2	2	...	2	3(f)	...	2	...	...	...	(t) Ditto.
28th	"	"	...	C.	2	...	...	1	3(u)	...	1	...	...	...	(u) Ditto.
29th	"	"	...	C.	2	...	...	1	4(w)	...	1	...	...	...	(w) Ditto.
30th	"	"	...	C.	2	...	...	2	4(x)	...	...	...	...	...	(x) Cis and Trans-Sutlej Sikhs.
31st	"	"	...	C.	2	...	...	2	4(y)	...	...	...	...	...	(y) Cis and Trans-Sutlej Sikhs.
32nd	"	"	...	C.	...	...	8	...	...	8	...	...	...	...	
33rd	"	"	...	C.	...	...	...	...	...	...	2	2(z)	...	...	(z) Jats, etc.
38th	"	"	...	C.	...	...	...	...	...	...	2	4(aa)	2	...	(aa) 2 of Jats.
39th	"	"	...	C.	...	...	...	...	...	...	...	4(aa)	2	...	
40th	"	"	...	C.	...	...	...	...	...	...	3	4	...	...	
42nd	"	"	...	C.	...	...	...	...	...	...	...	...	...	...	
43rd	"	"	...	C.	...	...	...	...	...	...	...	...	...	...	
44th	"	"	...	C.	...	...	...	...	...	...	...	...	7	...	
45th	"	"	...	C.	...	...	...	...	...	...	...	...	7	...	
1st Gurkha Regiment	}									6					
2nd	"	"	...	C.	...	...	...	...	...	...	...	...	...	...	
3rd	"	"	...	C.	1	...	...	...	...	...	...	...	...	8	
4th	"	"	...	C.	...	...	...	...	...	...	...	...	...	...	

The addition of a squadron to every cavalry regiment, the raising of four new infantry regiments of the line, and various minor changes, necessitated the publication in 1889 (2nd January) of a corrected table, of which the following gives the Cavalry constitution:

Corps.	Class regiment or class troop.	Muhammadans.			Hindus.					Remarks.
		Hindustani.	Punjabi.	Trans-frontier Tribes.	Trans-Indus Border Tribes.	Punjabi.		Hindustani.		
						Sikhs.	Dogras.	Rajputs.	Jats.	Other Hindus.	
1st Bengal Cavalry	C.	8	...	...	...	...	...	...	...	...	
2nd ,, ,,	C. T.	2	...	...	...	2	...	2	2	...	
3rd ,, ,,	C. T.	3	...	...	...	2	...	1	2	...	
4th ,, ,,	C. T.	4	...	...	...	2	...	...	2	...	
5th ,, ,,	C. T.	2	...	...	...	1	...	1	4	...	
6th ,, ,,	C. T.	2	...	...	...	3	...	1	1	1	
7th ,, ,,	C. T.	2	...	...	...	1	1	1	2	1(a)	(a) Brahmans.
8th ,, ,,	C. T.	3	1	...	...	1	...	1	1	1	
9th ,, Lancers	C. T.	...	3	...	1	3	1	...	...	...	
10th ,, ,,	C. T.	...	2	...	1	3	2	...	...	...	
11th ,, ,,	C. T.	...	1	...	1(b)	4	2	...	...	...	(b) ¼ Afridis allowed.
12th ,, Cavalry	C. T.	...	3	...	...	4	1	...	...	...	
13th ,, Lancers	C. T.	...	2	...	1	3	2	...	...	...	
14th ,, ,,	C.	...	...	...	...	...	...	...	8	...	
15th ,, Cavalry	C.	...	3	...	5	...	...	...	...	...	
16th ,, ,,	C. T.	...	...	...	...	4	2	...	2	...	
17th ,, ,,	C.	...	4	2(c)	2	...	...	...	...	...	(c) Such as Baluchis, Afghans, Afridis.
18th ,, Lancers	C. T.	...	5	...	...	3	...	...	...	...	
19th ,, ,,	C. T.	...	2	1(d)	1	3	1	...	...	...	(d) Afridis allowed.
Guides Cavalry	C. T.	...	1	...	2	3	...	...	...	...	
1st Punjab Cavalry	C. T.	2	...	...	2	2	2(e)	...	...	...	(e) May include Punjabi Hindus.
2nd ,, ,,	C. T.	1	1½	...	1½	3	...	...	1	...	
3rd ,, ,,	C. T.	2	1	...	1	3	1(e)	...	...	...	
5th ,, ,,	C. T.	1	1	...	1	3	1(e)	...	1	...	

The constitution of the infantry corps was, except in a few cases, almost identical with that ordered in 1883, the only difference being that the companies of "other Hindus" (exclusive of Jat companies) were entirely eliminated, and extra companies of Rajputs substituted in their place; the Assam Gurkha regiments exchanged their Jarwah companies for an eighth company of Gurkhas, while the Jarwahs were distributed throughout the regiment, fifteen to each company; the 45th became a class regiment of Sikhs only, recruiting from Cis and Trans-Sutlej; the 38th Bengal Infantry, retaining its two Rajput companies, became otherwise a class regiment, having six companies of Jats. The constitution of the new corps and of the Punjab Frontier Force was as follows:

Corps.	Class regiment or class company.	Muhammadans.			Hindus.				Remarks.
		Punjabi.	Afridis.	Trans-Indus and Border Tribes.	Sikhs.		Dogras.	Other classes.	
					Jats.	Mazbis.			
34th Bengal Infantry (Pioneers)	C.	...	...	...	...	8	...	...	
35th Bengal Infantry (Sikhs)	C.	...	...	...	8(a)	...	...	...	(a) Trans-Sutlej.
36th Bengal Infantry (Sikhs)	C.	...	...	...	8(a)	...	...	...	
37th Bengal Infantry (Dogras)	C.	...	...	...	...	...	8	...	
Guides Infantry	C. C.	1	1	1	2	...	1	2(b)	(b) One mixed company; one company of Gurkhas.
1st Sikh Infantry	C. C.	1	...	2	4	...	1	...	
2nd „ „	C. C.	2	...	1	2	...	3	...	
3rd „ „	C. C.	1	...	2	4	...	1	...	
4th „ „	C. C.	2	...	1	4	...	1	...	
1st Punjab Infantry	C. C.	2	1	1	2	...	2	...	
2nd „ „	C. C.	3	...	1	3	...	1	...	
4th „ „	C. C.	2	1	1	2	...	2	...	
5th „ „	C. C.	1	1	2	3	...	1	...	
6th „ „	C. C.	1	...	3	2	...	1	1(c)	(c) Hindustanis.

Two important changes marked the year 1886. By G. G. O. 485 of that year the Punjab Frontier Force, which had since its formation been under the control of the Government of the Punjab, was brought directly under the commander-in-chief in India. In notifying this transfer it was said that "His Excellency in Council is authorised to express the high sense entertained by Her Majesty the Queen-Empress of the loyal and brilliant services which, under the Government of the province, the Punjab Frontier Force has invariably rendered to the State from the earliest period of its creation.

The Force will continue as a separate unit and, as far as may be found practicable, its local and distinctive character will be preserved, its institutions maintained, and its existing privileges continued."

The following is extracted from the order of His Excellency the Commander-in-Chief, Sir Frederick Roberts, announcing this change (G. O. No. 58 of 1886):

> For upwards of thirty-five years the Punjab Frontier Force has been steadily adding to its laurels. Its list of casualties during that time bears testimony to the gallantry and devotion of all ranks in many a hard-fought action, while the admirable manner in which discipline has at all times been maintained has contributed materially to the high reputation for soldier-like qualities which the Brigade now so deservedly enjoys.
>
> The addition of so distinguished a force to the Bengal Army would, under all circumstances, be a matter of congratulation to the commander-in-chief in India; but, as a former Commandant of the Punjab Frontier Force, it is especially gratifying to Sir Frederick Roberts that this measure has come into operation during his tenure of office.
>
> His Excellency takes this opportunity of assuring the officers, non-commissioned officers and men of the Brigade, that it will be his special privilege, not only to watch over their interests in the future, but also to take care that the many customs and traditions which have so largely contributed to make the force what it is are interfered with as little as possible. In offering a soldier's welcome to all ranks of the Punjab Frontier Force, Sir Frederick Roberts is sure that he is only giving expression to what is the unanimous feeling throughout the Army of Bengal.

On the 13th October, 1886, an Army Circular (clause 170) was issued which closely affected the soldiers and regiments of the Bengal Army. It ordered that all native infantry regiments should be linked together in regiments of three battalions each; that enlistment should be for any one of the linked battalions; that at present the numbers of corps would remain unaltered; and that liability to transfer from one battalion to another would come into force only in the case of one or more battalions being ordered on service. At the same time a system of reserves was notified as sanctioned for the Bengal infantry, *viz.*, an active and a garrison reserve, the former composed of men transferred after not less than five or more than ten years' service with the colours; the latter of men pensioned after twenty-one years' service, or who have completed a total of colour and reserve service of twenty-one years. The active reserve was limited to 100 men per battalion; the garrison reserve was unlimited.

Further, the same circular granted pay to recruits, wherever enlisted, from date of enlistment, as well as marching batta, or free carriage for their baggage; the rates of good-conduct pay were sanctioned after three, six, and ten years' service, instead of after three, nine, and fifteen; the annual allowance for half mounting was raised from R4 to R5; and the pension rules were altered by the abolition of invalid pension after fifteen years' service, the grant of ordinary pension to all soldiers after twenty-one years' service, and of a gratuity of twelve months pay of rank to all men discharged as unfit for further service between fifteen and twenty-one years' service.

Finally, on the 13th October, 1888, an India Army Circular (clause 163) authorised fixed regimental centres for the groups of linked battalions under a territorial distribution of native infantry.

CHAPTER 12

Tribesmen

The punishment inflicted on the Chins, the Lushais, and other tribes on the frontier of Burma, during the period from 1888 to 1890, did not prove wholly effectual in putting a stop to their incursions into British territory, and during the years from 1890 to 1893 a number of expeditions took place against one or another of these savage tribes.

As early as the autumn of 1890, a sudden outbreak occurred in the Lushai Hills culminating in determined attacks on the forts of Changsil and Aijal, which were then held by bodies of military police. Reinforcements, which included a detachment of the 40th Bengal Infantry, were hurried up from Silchar; the village of Thanruma, the leading insurgent chief, was taken and destroyed on the 4th October, and Changsil and Aijal were relieved on the following day;, the village of the Chief Khalkum was destroyed on the 17th.

Of greater importance than these were the operations which it was found necessary to carry out in the Chin Hills during the winter of 1890-91, the immediate causes of which were the general restlessness of the Chin tribes and the perpetration of numerous outrages by the people of Thetta, a village in the Baungshe Chin country. On the 1st of January a small force (130 of the 2-4th Gurkhas, and a few Madras sappers) was despatched against, under the command of Captain Carnegy; an attack was made on the place on the following day, but the enemy's stockades were found to be too strong to be forced, and the detachment had to be withdrawn after Lieutenant James, of the Royal Engineers, and two men of the 2-4th Gurkhas had been killed. Notwithstanding the ill-success of this attack, the Thetta people almost immediately afterwards made their submission, and entered into an agreement to pay a fine and to desist for the future from molesting our lines of communication in the Chin Hills. Subsequently, the countries of the Baungshe and Kanhow Chins were visited by columns detailed for the purpose, and of which detachments of the newly-formed 39th Bengal Infantry (composed of Garhwalis) and of the 2-4th Gurkhas formed part; these columns met with little opposition, and indeed there was no fighting, except a skirmish with the Kanhows at Tenzaung on the 21st February. Later on (and April) a small column under the command of Lieutenant Mocatta, 39th Bengal Infantry, was engaged in a smart action with the Chins of Tlantlang, near the Sao-var stream; in this engagement a detachment of the 39th greatly distinguished itself by its steadiness and bravery under circumstances extremely trying to young soldiers, and sustained considerable loss. These operations did not, however, finally settle matters with the Chins, and the general restlessness of the tribes led, during the winter of 1891-92, to the despatch of several columns into the Southern Chin Hills. These columns, in which No. 8 (Bengal) Mountain Battery, a small detachment of the 7th Bengal Infantry, and 310 men of the 39th Bengal Infantry were included, traversed the country in various directions without meeting with much opposition, though they experienced great hardships, and they were eventually broken up at Haka and Fort White in the spring of 1892. A fresh outbreak amongst the Lushais in the early part of the same year necessitated the despatch of reinforcements, including a portion of the 18th Bengal Infantry, to Fort Aijal, in the neighbourhood of which place they were engaged in numerous skirmishes with the insurgents. At the same time a column under the command of Captain Loch, of the Military Police, in which a detachment of the 18th was included, operated in the Eastern Sonai country and captured and destroyed numerous Lushai villages. Besides these, a column under the command of Captain Rose, which included two guns of No. 8 (Bengal) Mountain Battery-and 150 of the 39th Bengal Infantry, was despatched from Fort White to Dao-khama's village, the centre of the rising, to effect a diversion in favour of Captain Shakespear, who was hemmed in at Vansanga's, and losing men daily. After a good deal of desultory fighting, the men of most of the insurgent villages took refuge in the Lieukhan and Howlong countries; the rest submitted, and in July 1892 the operations were brought to a conclusion. In October 1892 disturbances broke out afresh in the Northern Chin Hills. Troops (including a detachment of the 39th Bengal Infantry from the Southern Chin Hills) were promptly moved into the disturbed area, and punitive operations immediately undertaken against the enemy, who were defeated in numerous skirmishes and many of their villages destroyed, but it was not until the end of March 1893 that the Chins finally gave in their submission and surrendered their fire-arms. Our losses during these operations amounted to thirteen men killed, and one British officer, one native officer and thirty-three men wounded.

By Army Order No. 154 of 1893 (republished in G. O. C. C. No. 969, dated the 10th November 1893) the India medal with clasps inscribed "Burma, 1889-92," and "Lushai, 1889-92," according to the locality of the service, was granted to the troops employed on various expeditions in Burma and on its frontiers during the years named.

While these affairs were proceeding on the frontiers of Burma, events of importance were occurring in other parts of the country, and especially on the Eastern and North-Western frontiers, to which attention must now be given. Though they were not actually first in order of time, it will be convenient to give precedence to affairs on the Eastern frontier, where an unfortunate and unexpected reverse was experienced.

A revolution having occurred in Manipur in September 1890, resulting in the abdication of the Maharaja, in March 1891, Mr. Quinton, the Chief Commissioner of Assam, with an escort of 400 Gurkhas of the 42nd and 44th Bengal Infantry, under the command of Colonel Skene, proceeded to Imphal, the chief town (at which place there was already present a company of the 43rd Bengal Infantry), for the purpose of settling the affairs of the State, and of arresting and deporting Tikandrajit Bir Singh, a brother of the late Maharaja, who had been one of the leading spirits of the revolution, and now held the post of *Senapati*, or Commander-in-Chief of the Manipur Army. The attempt to arrest the *Senapati*, which was made on the 24th March, proved a lamentable failure; it was violently and successfully resisted, and open hostilities followed, desultory fighting being continued until the evening when the British force was withdrawn within the grounds of the Residency, having sustained a loss of about forty officers and men, killed and wounded, amongst the former of whom was included *Subadar* Rajbir Newar of the 43rd, and amongst the latter Lieutenant Brackenbury and *Subadar* Hima Chand Thakur, both of the 44th, who succumbed to their injuries in the course of the night. The retirement was followed by an act of sanguinary treachery on the part of the enemy. Late in the evening Mr. Quinton, Colonel Skene, and Lieutenant Simpson, 43rd Bengal Infantry, were induced to proceed to the Maharaja's palace on pretence of a conference, and there they were seized and barbarously put to death under the orders of the *Senapati* and other leaders of the insurgents, who followed up this infamous proceeding by opening a heavy fire on the troops in the Residency. These, being almost without ammunition, and the place being untenable, evacuated the position during the night and, retreating in some disorder, made their way in small parties to Kohima, Cachar and Tammu.

A detachment (33 rifles) of the 43rd Bengal Infantry stationed at Langthobal, four miles from Imphal, under the command of *Jemadar* Birbal Nagarkoti, held onto their post with considerable determination until the following day, and then retired in good order to Tammu, where (27th March) they joined Lieutenant Grant, commanding a detachment (fifty rifles) of the newly reconstituted 12th Madras Infantry (the 2nd Burma Battalion). On the following day Lieutenant Grant pushed up to Thobal in Manipur with both detachments, in the hope of saving Mr. Quinton and the other officers, the fact of whose murder was not then known, and who were believed to be prisoners in the palace at Imphal. At Thobal Lieutenant Grant and his detachment were confronted by a rabble of several thousand Manipuris, who kept up a heavy and almost ceaseless fire for several days on his entrenchment. He, nevertheless, maintained his ground without difficulty until ordered to retire to Tammu on the 9th April. The insurgents followed him in his retreat, but were met and routed by a small detachment under the command of Captain Presgrave. For his conduct in this affair Lieutenant Grant was awarded the Victoria Cross and promoted to the rank of Major, while the native officers of the detachments of the 43rd Bengal and 12th Madras Infantry were admitted to the Order of British India, and every non-commissioned officer and man was decorated with the Order of Merit.

In the meantime arrangements had been made to push forward troops on Imphal with all possible despatch from Kohima, Cachar and Tammu, and towards the end of April, after overcoming considerable difficulties with regard to the provision of transport, a column moved forward from each of those places. These columns were composed as follow:

Kohima Column Brigadier-General H. Collett, C.B.	Three guns of No. 8 (Bengal) Mountain Battery, and detachments of the 13th (100), 42nd (200), 43rd (400), and 44th (300) Bengal Infantry, and Assam Military Police (200)
Silchar (Cachar) Column Lieutenant-Colonel R. H. F. Rennick	Two guns of No. 8 (Bengal) Mountain Battery, and detachments of the 18th (370), 42nd (103), 43rd (281), and 44th (114) Bengal Infantry; the 1-2nd Gurkha Regiment; 50 of the Pioneer Company of the Calcutta Volunteer Rifles, and 207 of the Surma Valley Military Police
Tammu Column Brigadier-General T. Graham, C.B.	Four guns of No. 2 Mountain Battery, Royal Artillery; a wing of the 4th Battalion of the King's Royal Rifle Corps; the 2-4th Gurkha Regiment; and the 12th Madras Infantry

These columns reached Imphal almost simultaneously on the 27th of April, the enemy having offered little or no opposition except to the Tammu force, an advanced detachment of which, composed of parties of the 2-4th Gurkhas and the 12th Madras Infantry, had a sharp fight with a considerable body of them on the 25th April in an entrenchment at Bapam, six miles north of Palel. The Manipuris, being hemmed in, fought until nearly all were killed, the loss on our side being *Jemadar* Kiruram Gurung, 2-4th Gurkhas, and one man killed, and four British officers (including Captains Drury and Carnegy, 2-4th Gurkhas), two native officers and seven men wounded. With the occupation of Imphal the Manipur outbreak came to an end. The *Senapati* and other prominent persons fled before the arrival of our troops, but all were subsequently apprehended, and the Senapati, an official styled "the Tongal General" (said to have been an ex-mutineer of the 34th Native Infantry), and others concerned in the murder of Mr. Quinton and his companions, were executed in due course.

By G. G. 0. No. 652 of 1892 the India medal, with a clasp inscribed "North-East Frontier, 1891," was granted to the troops of the three columns engaged in the re-occupation of Manipur.

The North-West Frontier at this period was in a rather disturbed state, and the early months of 1891 witnessed the despatch of no less than three expeditions against recalcitrant tribes,—two against the Orakzais and one against the tribes of the Black Mountain in Hazara. The conduct of the Orakzai clans had for some time been so unsatisfactory, especially with regard to their repeated incursions into the Miranzai valley, that towards the end of 1890 it became apparent that a punitive expedition against them could no longer be delayed.

Accordingly in January 1891, the following force was concentrated at Kohat under the command of Brigadier-General Sir W. S. A. Lockhart, K.C.B.:

No. 3 (Peshawar) Mountain Battery
No. 4 (Hazara) Mountain Batteries
2 Squadrons 5th Punjab Cavalry
5th Company Bengal Sappers and Miners
22nd (Pioneers)
23rd (Pioneers)
29th Bengal Infantry
3rd Sikh Infantry
1st, 4th and 5th Punjab Infantry

This force, organised in three columns, advanced into the country of the hostile clans on the 26th January, traversed it in various directions, blowing up forts and towers, and having, in order to put a stop to further raids into the Miranzai valley, established posts at various points on the Samana Range, returned to Kohat about the middle of February, without having met with any opposition from the enemy, though the troops had experienced great hardships from the severity of the climate in winter. But the results obtained were not of a lasting nature, and an attack on the troops on the Samana, which took place on the 4th April, necessitated the despatch of a second expedition, for which purpose the following troops were concentrated at Hangu and Darband on the 16th April, under the command of Sir William Lockhart:

No. 3 Mountain Battery, Royal Artillery
3 Guns of No. 2 (Derajat) Mountain Battery
No. 3 (Peshawar Mountain Battery
3 Guns of Punjab Garrison Battery
19th Bengal Lancers
2 Squadrons 5th Punjab Cavalry
5th Company Bengal Sappers & Miners
1st Battalion King's Royal Rifle Corps
15th, 19th, 27th and 29th Bengal Infantry
3rd Sikh Infantry
1st, 2nd and 6th Punjab Infantry
1-5th Gurkha Regiment
A ½ battalion of the 2nd Manchester Regiment (96th Foot) was subsequently added to the force

The force advanced in three columns from Hangu and Darband on the 17th April, and during that and the following day, after a series of smart conflicts, drove the enemy off the Samana Range. Much fighting, some of it of a severe character, took place during the operations of the succeeding days, in the course of which the enemy's country was traversed in every direction, until the 16th of May, when the work entrusted to the force was finished, the offending clans having all been visited and punished and brought into complete submission. The losses sustained during these operations, from the 4th of April, amounted to twenty-eight (including *Jemadar* Hashim Ali, 19th Bengal Infantry) killed, and 73 wounded, including Major Egerton, Assistant-Adjutant-General of the Punjab Frontier Force, Captains Maisey and MacLeod, 29th Bengal Infantry, *Jemadar* Tilok Sing, 15th Bengal Infantry, and *Subadar* Mawaz Khan, 6th Punjab Infantry.

By G. G. O. No. 61 of 1892 the India medal with a clasp inscribed "Samana, 1891," was granted to the troops employed in the operations on the Samana Range in April and May 1891.

Shortly before the outbreak which brought about the second Miranzai operations, it had become necessary to despatch a punitive expedition against some of the tribes of the Black Mountain, in Hazara, in consequence of their having, contrary to the agreement entered into in 1888, violently opposed (October 1890) the march of a British detachment over the crest of the mountain. To carry out the punishment of the offending tribes, the following troops were concentrated at Darband and Oghi by the 1st March 1891, with Major-General W. K. Elles, C.B., in command:

Left (or River) Column
Brigadier-General
R. F. Williamson

No. 1 Mountain Battery, Royal Artillery
3 Guns No. 2 (Derajat) Mountain Battery
2nd Battalion, Seaforth Highlanders (78th Foot)
Wing of 32nd Bengal Infantry (Pioneers)
37th (Dogra) Bengal Infantry
Infantry of the Corps of Guides
th Sikh Infantry

Right (or Tilli) Column
Brigadier-General
A. G- Hammond

No. 9 Mountain Battery, Royal Artillery
1st Battalion, Royal Welsh Fusiliers (23rd Foot)
11th Bengal Infantry
Wing of 32nd Bengal Infantry (Pioneers)
2-5th Gurkha Regiment
Khaibar Rifles

Divisional Troops

Squadron 11th Bengal Lancers
4th Company Bengal Sappers & Miners

The advance of the two columns was begun on the 12th March, but until the 19th little opposition was experienced. Before daybreak on that day, however, a sudden and most determined attack was made on our advanced post at Ghazikot by a body composed partly of Hindustani fanatics and partly of tribesmen of the Black Mountain. The post was held by the Dogra company of the 4th Sikh Infantry, who behaved with the greatest gallantry, and after a sharp conflict repulsed the attack, though not without the loss of *Jemadar* Darshanu and three men killed, and Lieutenant Maconchy, *Subadar* Dheru, and seventeen men wounded. Slight engagements subsequently occurred at Kanhar, Diliari, Darbanai and other places, and various movements followed, but in the end the enemy made complete submission, and with the exception of a small force left to hold the Black Mountain temporarily, the troops were withdrawn to their cantonments. Our total losses during the operations amounted to six killed and forty-seven wounded.

By G. G. O. No. 258 of 1892 the India medal with a clasp inscribed "Hazara, 1891," was granted to the troops engaged in the operations on the Black Mountain.

Towards the close of the same year disturbances broke out on quite a different part of the frontier, in the remote khanates of Hunza and Nagar. With the object of restoring order, the Gilgit Agency guard (consisting of thirty men of the 20th Bengal Infantry) was reinforced by two guns of No. 4 (Hazara) Mountain Battery, and two hundred men of the 1-5th Gurkha Regiment. With this small force, together with a small party of Bengal Sappers and Miners, two battalions of the Kashmir Imperial Service Infantry, and some local levies, the whole amounting to little more than a thousand men, the British Agent, Colonel Durand, took the field on the 1st of December, effected the passage of the Hunza river into Nagar the same day, and on the 2nd, after a sharp conflict, carried the fort of Nilt by storm, with a loss of three men killed, and himself, Captain Aylmer, Bengal Sappers and Miners, Lieutenant Badcock, 1-5th Gurkha Regiment, and twenty-seven men wounded. Some further ineffective fighting occurred on the following day, in which Lieutenant Gorton, No. 4 Mountain Battery, was wounded, and on the 20th of the month, under the orders of Captain Mackenzie, Seaforth Highlanders, who was in temporary command, the almost inaccessible position of the enemy on the Hunza river, beyond Nilt, was stormed and taken with a loss of only two men wounded. The enemy were completely defeated and dispersed; on the 21st the Rajah of Nagar surrendered, and Hunza was occupied on the following day, thus bringing the operations to a conclusion.

By G. G. O. No. 986 of 1892 the India medal with a clasp inscribed "Hunza, 1891," was granted to the troops employed in these operations.

The three Isazai clans of the Black Mountain—the Hasanzai, the Akazai, and the Madda Khel—having, in 1892, in breach of engagements entered into by them after the Black Mountain campaign of 1891, received and harboured in Baio, on the right bank of the Indus, one Hashim Ali Khan, a banished chief of the Khan Khel Hasanzais, who had been a prime mover of the Black Mountain disturbances, and refused to surrender or expel him, it became necessary in the autumn of 1892 to use coercive measures, and accordingly, on the 1st October, the following force was concentrated at Darband under the command of Major-General Sir W. S. A. Lockhart:

Nos. 3, 8 and 9 Mountain Batteries, Royal Artillery
No. 1 (Kohat) Mountain Battery
4th & 6th Companies Bengal Sappers & Miners
2 Squadrons 11th Bengal Lancers
1st Battalion, Bedfordshire Regiment (16th Foot)
1st Battalion, King's Royal Rifle Corps (60th Foot)
25th & 30th Bengal Infantry
4th Sikh Infantry
2 Battalions 5th Gurkha Regiment

The force advanced on Baio on the 6th October, but the place was found to be deserted, and no opposition of any sort was experienced; and all towers and defences having been blown up and destroyed, the troops were withdrawn.

In March 1893 Chilas, on the Gilgit frontier, was the scene of a sharp engagement. The fort at that place was garrisoned at the time by 300 men of the Kashmir Imperial Service Infantry under the command of Major Daniell, 1st Punjab Infantry, and on these, on the morning of the 5th March, there came down a body of 1,200 Chilasis and Kohistanis. Some severe fighting ensued, in the course of which Major Daniell fell in a daring attempt to expel the enemy from a village from which they were keeping up a heavy fire on the fort. The tribesmen were eventually repulsed with a heavy loss of 350 men in killed alone, that on our side amounting to only twenty killed and thirty-two wounded.

The course of events now takes us back to the Eastern Frontier, where, in May 1893, a small expedition (a hundred men of the 43rd Bengal Infantry) was despatched from Manipur for the purpose of punishing the people of the Kuki village of Mongham (twenty miles east of Imphal), who had made an unprovoked raid on the Naga village of Swemi and massacred nearly three hundred of the inhabitants. Mongham was reached on the 22nd May, the leaders of the raid arrested, and the village destroyed. Other villages implicated in the raid were also punished, and the detachment returned to Manipur about the middle of June.

In January 1894 an expedition was undertaken against the Abors. The force employed was composed for the most part of police, the only regular troops consisting of 100 men of the 44th Bengal Infantry. Some desultory fighting took place, and the total losses of the force amounted, including followers, to forty-one killed and forty-five wounded.

Towards the end of 1894 a serious outbreak took place on the North-West Frontier. In accordance with the terms of a treaty entered into with the Amir of Kabul in November 1893, measures were adopted during the autumn of 1894 for the delimitation of the Waziri-Afghan Boundary from Domandi, on the Gomal river, to the Laram peak, on the borders of Khost. The attitude of the Mahsud Waziris necessitated the boundary commission being accompanied by a strong escort, and for this purpose the following troops were detailed, under the command of Brigadier-General A. H. Turner:

No. 3 (Peshawar) Mountain Battery
No. 2 Company, Bengal Sappers & Miners
Squadron 1st Punjab Cavalry
20th Bengal Infantry
1-1st Gurkha Rifles
3rd Sikh Infantry

The escort was assembled at Dera Ismail Khan on the 1st October, and moving forward *viâ* Kajuri Kach (where it was joined by the members of the Commission on the 18th), it was concentrated in a position near the Inzar *Kotal*, in Wana, on the 27th. There had during this march been many indications of Mahsud hostility, but, though no attack in force was anticipated, all needful precautions were taken to secure the camp in the event of its being suddenly assailed. It was as well that these precautions were adopted, for before daylight on the morning of the 3rd November a Mahsud Waziri *lashkar*, said to have been three thousand strong, taking advantage of the darkness and of the broken nature of the ground in the vicinity, made a sudden and desperate attempt to rush the camp, and were successful in penetrating it at several points. A severe hand-to-hand conflict ensued, ending in the enemy being driven out of the camp at the point of the bayonet, though not before they had done much damage and inflicted considerable loss. As day broke they began to retreat towards the hills; the cavalry were immediately launched in pursuit, and cut up large numbers of them before they could win their way to a place of safety. Our losses amounted to Lieutenant Macaulay, Royal Engineers, *Subadar* Padam Sing Rana and *Jemadar* Khark Sing Nagarkoti, both of the 1-1st Gurkhas, eighteen non-commissioned officers and men, and twenty-four followers killed, and six British officers, forty-seven non-commissioned officers and men, and twenty-two followers wounded, of whom Lieutenant Angelo, 1-1st Gurkhas, afterwards died of the injuries he had received. The losses of the enemy were much more severe, amounting to above 600, of whom 350 were killed or died afterwards of their wounds.

This unprovoked outrage necessitated the despatch of a punitive expedition, and for that purpose the following troops, to the command of which Lieutenant-General Sir W, S. A. Lockhart, K.C.B., was nominated, were detailed:

Nos. 1 (Kohat), 3 (Peshawar) & 8 (Bengal) Mountain Batteries
A Maxim Gun manned by Devonshire Regiment
Nos. 2 & 5 Companies Bengal Sappers & Miners
2 Squadrons 1st & 1 Squadron 2nd Punjab Cavalry
3rd Punjab Cavalry
2nd Battalion Border Regiment (55th Foot)
20th, 33rd & 38th Bengal Infantry
1-1st & 1-5th Gurkha Rifles
1st & 3rd Sikh Infantry
2nd, 4th & 6th Punjab Infantry

These troops were organised in three brigades, which were concentrated at Wana, Jandola and Mirian, respectively, on the 17th December, and the Mahsuds having failed to comply with the demands made upon them, the force moved forward on the same day, marching respectively on Kaniguram, Makin and Razmak, which points were reached on the 21st without much opposition having been experienced. In the course of the succeeding four weeks the troops, broken up into smaller and more easily handled columns, visited every part of the Mahsud Waziri country without meeting with any opposition, except from small detached bands of the enemy, whose guerilla tactics caused a few casualties. The Mahsuds themselves, on the other hand, suffered substantial losses in men and property, most of their fortified towers having been blown up and destroyed, and almost all their sheep, goats and cattle captured and driven off; they eventually made their submission on the 21st of January, and shortly afterwards complied in full with the terms imposed upon them. The losses sustained by our troops amounted to no more than two killed and twenty-two wounded.

By G. G. O. No. 1082 of 1895 the India medal, with a clasp inscribed "Waziristan, 1894-95," was granted to all the troops employed in these operations from October 1894 to March 1895.

In January 1895, while the operations against the Mahsud Waziris were still in progress, events were occurring in Chitral, which eventually led to the movement of a large force upon that place through Bajaur and Swat, and of a smaller separate force from Gilgit direct. On the 1st of that month Nizam-ul-Mulk, Mehtar of Chitral, was murdered, and his brother Amir-ul-Mulk placed upon the throne. The local disturbances which ensued reached their climax when the British Agent, Surgeon-Major Robertson, was besieged in Chitral fort with a small force consisting of no more than 99 men of the 14th Sikhs and 300 of the 4th Kashmir Rifles, the whole of which were under the command of Captain Campbell. The leaders of the hostile tribesmen were Umra Khan, Chief of Jandol, and Sher Afzal, uncle of the Mehtar.

Sher Afzal and his following arrived in the neighbourhood of Chitral fort on the 3rd of March. In the course of the same afternoon a detachment composed of 200 men of the Kashmir Rifles was sent out to observe the movements of the enemy and, if possible, to drive him back; these were not long in coming into collision with the hostile force, but the action which ensued was not successful, and the detachment was compelled to retreat into the fort with a loss of twenty-three killed and thirty-three wounded, Captains Campbell and Baird being included amongst the latter. Captain Baird, who was mortally wounded, was carried into the fort by Surgeon-Captain Whitchurch, of the Indian Medical Service, who afterwards received the Victoria Cross for the gallantry he displayed upon this occasion.

Immediately on intelligence of these events being received by the Government of India, arrangements were set on foot for the despatch of a force through Swat, Bajaur and Dir for the purpose of relieving the Chitral fort. The following troops were detailed for this service under the command of Major-General Sir R. C. Low, K.C.B.:

15th Field Battery, Royal Artillery
Nos. 3 & 8 Mountain Batteries, Royal Artillery
No. 4 (Hazara) Mountain Battery
A Maxim Gun manned by Devonshire Regiment

Nos. 1, 4 & 6 Companies, Bengal Sappers and Miners
11th Bengal Lancers
Cavalry of the Corps of Guides
1st Battalion, East Kent Regiment (3rd Foot)
1st Battalion, Bedfordshire Regiment (16th Foot)
2nd Battalion, King's Own Scottish Borderers (25th Foot)
1st Battalion, King's Royal Rifle Corps (60th Foot)
1st Battalion, Gordon Highlanders (75th Foot)
2nd Battalion, Seaforth Highlanders (78th Foot)
13th, 15th, 23rd, 25th & 37th Bengal Infantry
2-4th Gurkha Rifles
Infantry of the Corps of Guides
4th Sikh Infantry

Besides these, No. 2 (Derajat) Mountain Battery, the 1st Battalion of the East Lancashire Regiment (30th Foot) and the 29th and 30th Bengal Infantry were detailed for service on the line of communication, and a Reserve Brigade was formed at Rawal Pindi. At the same time Colonel Kelly, who, with his regiment (the 32nd Pioneers), was engaged in road-making in the Gilgit Agency, was directed to assume command there and make such arrangements as seemed to him to be possible to effect the relief of Chitral though he was prohibited from undertaking any operations which did not afford a reasonable prospect of success.

While these arrangements were in progress, collisions between detachments of our troops and bodies of the enemy had occurred in several places. At Reshun, a detachment (Bengal Sappers and Kashmir Rifles) under Lieutenants Edwardes and Fowler, proceeding from Mastuj to Chitral with a supply of ammunition, was vigorously attacked during several days, and eventually, by a gross act of treachery, captured by the enemy during an armistice. In a defile beyond Koragh a detachment of the 14th Bengal Infantry, under the command of Captain Ross, which was hastening from Mastuj to the assistance of Lieutenants Edwardes and Fowler, was surrounded by the enemy on the 7th March, and after three days' fighting had to cut its way back to Koragh and Buni, which it effected, though not without heavy loss, Captain Ross and forty-six men (besides a hospital-assistant and six followers) being killed, and Lieutenant Jones and nine men wounded. Finally, at Mastuj a detachment (48 men of the 14th Bengal Infantry,

228 of the 4th and 6th Kashmir Rifles, and 50 Paniyali levy sepoys) under the command of Lieutenant Moberly sustained for more than a fortnight a series of desultory attacks from a body of the enemy nearly three thousand in number, on whom it inflicted considerable losses.

Of the remaining operations of this campaign the first that claims notice is the defence of the fort at Chitral. After the action of the 3rd March the place was closely invested by Sher Afzal and his following, who, during the ensuing forty-six days, kept up a heavy fire, and made repeated attempts to storm the defences. In these attempts they were invariably repulsed with loss, though on one occasion (7th April) they succeeded in setting fire to one of the defensive towers, and killed and wounded several of the garrison, Surgeon-Major Robertson being amongst the latter. Finding that there was small probability of their capturing the place in this way, the enemy endeavoured to breach the wall by means of a mine, and actually succeeded in pushing a gallery up to one of the towers before they were detected. On their intentions being discovered, their plans were promptly frustrated by a daring and brilliant sortie made by a detachment composed of forty men of the 14th Sikhs and sixty of the 4th Kashmir Rifles, led by Lieutenant Harley. The enemy were taken by surprise and driven off, and the shaft of the mine blown up and entirely destroyed, with a loss on our side of twenty-one men killed and wounded. Forty-eight hours later, having heard of the approach of the force under the command of Colonel Kelly from the north and of the Khan of Dir from the south, Sher Afzal hastily raised the siege and fled. During this gallant defence of the fort from the 4th of March to the 18th of April, the losses of the garrison amounted to forty-eight killed and wounded.

Colonel Kelly, whose approach was a principal factor in the Colonel Kelly's raising of the siege of Chitral, marched from Gilgit on the 23rd March with two guns of No. 1 Kashmir Mountain Battery and nearly four hundred men of the 32nd Bengal Infantry (Pioneers); he was afterwards reinforced by forty Kashmir Sappers and a hundred and fifty levy men from Cherkila, Hunza, Nagar, and Sai, and having passed Ghizr on the 31st, he succeeded during the first days of April in getting over the Shandur Pass (12,230 feet above the level of the sea),—a truly formidable operation owing to the severity of the weather and the depth of the snow. It was not, however, until the 9th of April that he came into collision with the tribesmen. On that day they attempted to bar his advance in a formidable position at Chakalwat, but he forced his way through with a loss of only four men wounded, and relieved Lieutenant Moberly at Mastuj the same day. Reinforced by a hundred men of the 4th Kashmir Rifle, Kelly advanced from Mastuj on the 13th, and in the course of the same day drove the enemy from a formidable position at Nisa Gol, inflicting on them a loss of 160 killed and wounded, while our own casualties did not exceed twenty. Continuing his advance, he reached Chitral on the 20th April, from before which place Sher Afzal and the besieging tribesmen had already fled, and Colonel Kelly thus had the good fortune, after brief though exceedingly arduous operations, to accomplish the object for which a force had been placed in the field.

It now only remains to describe the operations of that force under the command of Sir Robert Low. Sir Robert advanced from Jalala on the 2nd April, having previously by proclamation made known to the people of Swat and Bajaur, in the most distinct terms, the objects of the expedition, informing them that we had no hostile design against them, and that if they refrained from attacking our troops and from impeding in any way our march to the relief of Chitral, no hostilities would be directed against them on our part, and no part of their territory permanently occupied by us. Notwithstanding these assurances, however, the Malakand was strongly held, and Sir Robert's advance opposed with great determination when he moved up on the 3rd of April. The pass was found to be precipitous and difficult, and the enemy who held it numbered over 12,000, though some of these were badly armed. After an engagement of over five hours' duration, the position was carried by storm with a loss on our side of eleven men killed and eight British officers (including Major Tonnochy and Lieutenant Harman of the 4th Sikhs, and Lieutenant Ommanney of the Guides Infantry), two native officers and fifty men wounded, that of the enemy being over five hundred. On the following day an advance was made into the Swat valley and the enemy defeated at Khar, with a further loss of nearly five hundred men, our own casualties amounting to no more than twenty, amongst whom were Lieutenant Baldwin, of the Guides Cavalry, and Lieutenant Wynch, of the 37th Bengal Infantry. This was followed on the 7th by the passage of the Swat river, after an action in which the 11th Bengal Lancers made a gallant charge against an immensely superior number of the enemy, killing more than a hundred of them. On the 13th and 14th an action took place on the banks of the Panjkora, in which Lieutenant-Colonel Battye, of the Guides Infantry, was killed, and Captain Peebles, commanding the Maxim detachment of the Devonshire Regiment, mortally wounded. The last engagement took place at Mamuzai on the 17th, and on the 20th a detachment of five hundred men was pushed on from Barwa towards Chitral to rescue the garrison, which was believed to be in great straits, but reassuring intelligence of its safety having been received, the detachment was halted at Ashreth on the 27th, on which day Sher Afzal was brought in a prisoner by the Khan of Dir, who had been actively cooperating with our forces, with the object of recovering his territory, of which he had been deprived by Umra Khan. Umra Khan himself effected his escape and took refuge in Afghanistan. Colonel Kelly, having already effected the relief of the Chitral Fort, the further advance of the force under the command of Sir Robert Low became unnecessary, but at a later period that officer with a small portion of one of his brigades moved up to Chitral. The total losses of the force during these operations amounted to 127 officers and men killed and wounded.

By G. G. O. No. 509 of 1896 the new India Medal, recently instituted, with clasps inscribed "Relief of Chitral, 1895," and "Defence of Chitral, 1895," was granted to the troops employed in the defence of Chitral Fort and in the operations carried out for its relief, and subsequently the several corps engaged in the operations were permitted to inscribe the word "Chitral" on their colours, the 14th Bengal Infantry being allowed at the same time to emblazon "Defence of Chitral" upon theirs.

The period from 1891 to 1895 was noteworthy for the great number of reforms that were introduced, not only in the organisation and system of administration of the army (in which some remarkable changes took place), but in matters of interior economy and in those affecting the improvement of the soldiers' position as well. The principal of these changes shall now be briefly adverted to.

Amongst the first of these reforms was the amalgamation of the Staff Corps of the three Presidencies under the general designation of "the Indian Staff Corps," which was sanctioned and notified in a Royal Warrant, dated the 28th January 1891, and announced in India in G. G. O. No. 208 of 1891. This measure, however, was one the effect of which—so far as the Bengal Army was concerned— would be felt by the British officers alone, and that only in the future; it left the Bengal Army itself unchanged.

Another important reform which was announced about the same

time was the grant of an increased rate of pay to the *silladar* cavalry (G. G. O. No. 224 of 1891). By this grant the pay of non-commissioned officers and *sowars* was raised by R4 per *mensem*, that of *sowars* thus becoming R31 instead of R27.

Four years later the pay of all non-commissioned ranks in the native artillery (including drivers of British batteries), the three corps of sappers and miners, and the native infantry, was also increased by R2 per *mensem*, and the grant of the annual half-mounting allowance of R5 was allowed from date of enlistment. This increase of pay (which was extended to the Viceroy's Body-Guard and the local corps under the Government of India) was notified in G. G. O. No. 670 of 1895.

As a step towards removing a difficulty that was said to exist in attracting recruits of good quality to the service and to facilitate recruiting for the native army generally, recruiting depots were established in 1892 at the following stations, each to form the centre of a recruiting district for the classes specified:

Peshawar	For Pathans
Rawal Pindi	Punjabi Mahomedans
Amritsar	Sikhs
Sialkot (in winter)	Kashmir Dogras
Dharmsala (in summer)	Kangra Dogras
Delhi	Jats and Hindustani Mahomedans
Lucknow	Hindustani Hindus
Gorakhpur	Gurkhas

Each centre was placed .under the direct control of an officer (styled the "District Recruiting Officer") specially selected for his knowledge of the classes with whom he would have to deal.

In 1892-93, on the introduction of the Lee-Metford magazine rifle for the British infantry, the native infantry was re-armed with the Martini-Henry rifle.

With a view to increasing their fighting value, it was proposed in June 1892 to re-organise the sixteen Hindustani regiments of native infantry as class regiments. Experience had shown that not only were recruits of a better stamp attracted to class regiments, but that all ranks were more happy and contented when serving with men of their own race and caste; the regimental system was found to work more harmoniously in such corps, while *esprit de corps* was fostered and a healthy spirit of rivalry between regiment and regiment engendered. This re-organisation was carried out early in 1893, the regiments in question being divided into five classes, as follow:

Brahmins	2 regiments	1st, 3rd
Rajputs	7 regiments	2nd, 4th, 7th, 8th, 11th, 13th, 16th
Musalmans	4 regiments	5th, 12th, 17th, 18th
Jats	2 regiments	6th, 10th
Hillmen (Khas Gurkhas)	1 regiment	9th

During this period a new and a somewhat unique departure was made in the grant of permission to volunteers from the Indian Army to take temporary service under the local authorities in British East and Central Africa. The first of these bodies of volunteers was given in 1891, when, at the request of the British Central Africa Company and with the sanction of Her Majesty's Government, a party of sixty native soldiers (principally Mazbi Sikhs and men of the Hyderabad Contingent) were permitted to proceed to Central Africa with Captain Maguire, Commandant of Police there. These men did excellent service in Central Africa, many being killed or wounded in encounters with the Arab slave hunters. Captain Maguire himself fell in one of these conflicts. Early in 1892, Captain Johnson, 36th Bengal Infantry, proceeded to Central Africa as successor to Captain Maguire, taking with him ten more men (Sikhs) to replace casualties in the Central Africa Police, and in 1893 a further reinforcement of 100 men under Lieutenant Edwards, 35th Bengal Infantry, was furnished. In the early part of 1895, two hundred Sikh volunteers from the native army were despatched to British Central Africa to relieve detachments already serving there, and in October of the same rear a body of three hundred Punjabi Mahomedans was despatched to Mombassa, for service in the British East Africa Protectorate.

In this connection it may here be mentioned that in 1892 the Government of India raised and despatched to China, for service at Hong Kong, a battalion of infantry, composed of Mahomedans of Upper India, as well as detachments of artillery for service at Hong Kong, Singapore, Ceylon and Mauritius.

In 1895, a new medal was instituted to commemorate wars in India and on the frontier, in substitution of the India Medal of 1854, which had been introduced, on the suggestion of Lord Dalhousie, to avoid the multiplication of medals, and which was first issued to commemorate the Burmese War of 1852-53. With the exception of the Mutiny and the Afghan War of 1878-80; for which special medals were issued, this medal had been granted for every Indian campaign during a period of forty years, and it had, in 1895, no less than twenty-one clasps,—some officers and native soldiers possessing as many as nine and ten. There was a wide-spread feeling among those who had earned clasp after clasp that the time had come for some better recognition of their services than the addition of more clasps to the medal already possessed by them. It was therefore determined, in connection with the grant of a medal for the defence and the relief of Chitral in 1895, that the opportunity should be taken to inaugurate a new India Medal, with a distinctive ribbon, and to grant it first to the troops who took part in those operations, which would thus be placed at the head of a new series of minor wars and expeditions for which an India Medal is granted.

Finally, in the year 1895, there came into operation the most important and far-reaching reform that had been instituted in the Armies of India since their formation during the early days of the rise of the British power in this country,—*viz.*, the abolition of the Presidential Army System, under which the Madras and Bombay Armies had been maintained on a separate footing under the control of the Governments of those Presidencies and independent of the authority of the commander-in-chief in India. This reform had been advocated by many eminent officers who had devoted their attention to matters of military administration, as well as by the Army Organisation Commission assembled in 1879. The recommendations of the Army Commission on the subject were laid before Her Majesty's Government in 1881, but it was not considered expedient at that time to ask Parliament to legislate on the subject, and the matter was for the time dropped. It was not, however, forgotten, and in 1085, in 1888, and again in 1892, this important matter was brought under the notice of Her Majesty's Government. On the last occasion, the proposals of the Government of India, somewhat modified, found acceptance, and a Bill ("Madras and Bombay Armies Act, 1893—56 and 57 Vict., Cap. 62") was passed through Parliament to give effect to them. By this Act the offices of commander-in-chief of the Armies of Madras and Bombay were abolished, and the Governors in Council of those Presidencies ceased to exercise all military control and authority.

At the same time the Bengal Army was for administrative purposes divided into two portions which were styled respectively the Punjab and the Bengal Commands.

The changes in the administration and organisation of the Army of India arising out of this Act were brought into effect on the 1st April 1895 (G. G. O. No. 980 of 1894) and were briefly as follow:—

The Bengal Army was organised as the Bengal and Punjab Commands,—the Army of India consisting of the Punjab, Bengal, Madras and Bombay Commands, each under a Lieutenant-General styled the Lieutenant-General Commanding the Forces, Punjab, Bengal, Madras and Bombay, respectively, and all under the direct command of the commander-in-chief in India and the control of the Government of India.

Details as to the powers of the lieutenant-generals commanding, the conduct of business till then transacted by the Military Department of the Governments of Madras and Bombay, the distribution of the district commands, and the composition of the several forces in each command, etc., etc., were published in G. G. O. No. 981, dated 26th October 1894, Clause No. 143 of India Army Circulars of 1894, and G. O. C. C, No. 1061, dated 36th October 1894.

The details of most of these several matters need not be entered upon here: it will suffice to mention that the forces lately composing the Bengal Army were divided between the two commands in the manner following:

Punjab Command

9th, 10th & 11th Bengal Lancers

12th Bengal Cavalry

13th & 15th Bengal Lancers

16th & 17th Bengal Cavalry

18th & 19th Bengal Lancers

14th, 15th, 19th, 20th, 21st, 22nd, 23rd, 24th, 25th, 26th, 27th, 8th, 29th, 30th, 31st, 32nd, 33rd, 34th, 35th, 36th, 37th, 38th, 0th & 45th Bengal Infantry

1st & 4th Gurkha Rifles

Punjab Frontier Force, consisting of 1st, 2nd, 3rd & 5th Punjab Cavalry

Corps of Guides

Nos. 1, 2, 3 & 4 Mountain Batteries & Punjab Garrison Battery

1st, 2nd, 3rd & 4th Sikh Infantry
1st, 2nd, 4th, 5th & 6th Punjab Infantry
5th Gurkha Rifles

Bengal Command

1st Bengal Cavalry
2nd Bengal Lancers
3rd, 4th, 5th, 6th, 7th & 8th Bengal Cavalry
14th Bengal Lancers
Nos. 7 & 8 Mountain Batteries
Corps of Bengal Sappers & Miners
1st, 2nd, 3rd, 4th, 5th, 6th, 7th, 8th, 9th, 10th, 11th, 12th, 13th, 6th, 17th, 18th, 39th, 42nd, 43rd & 44th Bengal Infantry
2nd & 3rd Gurkha Rifles

The introduction of this great change in the administration and organisation of the Indian Army presents a point at which this brief sketch of the rise and progress of the Bengal Army may fittingly be brought to a conclusion. It marks the disappearance of that army as a separate and homogeneous entity, and brings to an end the glorious record of its achievements, a record which begins with Plassey and closes only with the consolidation of the British Indian Empire. The unhappy episode of the Mutiny darkens its history, but the long roll of its victories and conquests effaces that sad chapter, and we can never forget how great a part the old Bengal Army has played in the extension of the British Empire, and in the fame of its arms. For nearly a century and a half it has borne an honourable part in all our campaigns from the Nile to the Great Wall of China, and has helped to carry our victorious standards to Kabul and Mandalay, to Cairo and Pekin. The story of the Bengal Army is ended ; but it leaves to its successors a great tradition and an inspiring example.

Appendices

Appendix I.

A Chronological List of the Corps of the Bengal Army, showing particulars of their origin, and their subsequent history.

A.—INFANTRY.

Date of raising.	Where raised.	First Commandant.	Original number and native name.	REMARKS.	Present name or date of disbandment.
Jan. 1757	Calcutta	......	1st Battalion "*Lal Paltan*"—afterwards *Gillis-ki-Paltan*.	Became the 9th Battalion in 1764, the 16th in 1775, the 10th Regiment in 1781, the 17th in 1784, the 19th Battalion in 1786, the 2nd Battalion 12th Regiment in 1796, and the 1st Regiment in 1824.	Mutinied at Cawnpore in 1857.
Aug. ,,	,,	......	2nd Battalion		Destroyed at Patna in 1763.
1758	Patna	......	3rd ,,		Destroyed at Patna in 1763.
Sep. ,,	Chittagong	Capt. Hugh Grant	4th Battalion—*Grand-ki-Paltan*.	Became the 3rd Battalion in 1764, the 2nd in 1775, the 2nd Bombay Battalion in 1781, the 2nd Bengal Regiment in 1784, the 2nd Battalion in 1786, the 1st Battalion 2nd Regiment in 1796, the 5th Regiment in 1824.	Mutinied at Umballa in 1857.
Dec. ,,	......	Lt. George Wilson	5th Battalion—*Wilson-ki-Paltan*.		
1761	Patna	Capt. Giles Stibbert	6th Battalion—*Jala-sur-ki-Paltan*.	Became the 1st Battalion in 1764, the 8th in 1775, the 2nd Regiment in 1781, the 8th in 1784, the 8th Battalion in 1786, the 1st Battalion 8th Regiment in 1796, and the 9th Regiment in 1824.	Destroyed at Patna in 1763. Mutinied at Aligarh in 1857.

A Chronological List of the Corps of the Bengal Army, showing particulars of their origin, and their subsequent history—continued.

A.—INFANTRY—*continued*.

Date of raising.	Where raised.	First Commandant.	Original number and native name.	Remarks.	Present name or date of disbandment.
Dec. 1761	Chittagong	Lt. J. Matthews	7th Battalion—*Matthews-ki-Paltan*.	Became the 15th Battalion in 1764, the 10th in 1775, and the 4th Regiment in 1781.	Disbanded for mutiny in 1784.
1762	Burdwan	Capt. L. MacLean	8th Battalion—*Burdwan-ki-Paltan*.	Became the 2nd Battalion in 1764, the 1st in 1775, the 1st Bombay Battalion in 1781, the 1st Bengal Regiment in 1784, the 8th Battalion in 1786, the 1st Battalion 1st Regiment in 1796, and the 2nd Regiment in 1824.	Disbanded at Barrackpore in 1859, for having exhibited disaffection in 1857.
1763	,,	Capt. Smith	9th Battalion—*Chota Burdwan-ki-Paltan*.	Became the 8th Battalion in 1764, the 9th in 1775, the 3rd Regiment in 1781, the 9th Regiment in 1784, the 9th Battalion in 1786, the 1st Battalion 9th Regiment in 1796, and the 8th Regiment in 1824.	Mutinied at Dinapore in 1857.
,,	Midnapore	Lieut. A. Swinton	10th—*Soolteen-ki-Paltan*.	Originally a local corps; became the 13th Battalion in 1764, the 6th in 1775, the 6th Bombay Battalion in 1781, the 6th Bengal Regiment in 1784, the 6th Battalion in 1786, the 1st Battalion 6th Regiment in 1796, and the 3rd Regiment in 1824.	Mutinied at Phillour in 1857.
,,	Chittagong	Lieut. L. Brown	11th Battalion	A local corps; became the 7th Battalion in 1764; was made a local corps at Chittagong in 1775.	Disbanded in 1786.

	Station	Commandant	Battalion	History	Remarks
"	Calcutta	......	12th Battalion—*Teerbanis-ki-Paltan*; afterwards *Duffal-ki-Paltan*.	Became the 6th Battalion in 1764, the 15th in 1775, the 9th Regiment in 1781, the 16th in 1784, the 16th Battalion in 1786, the 2nd Battalion 7th Regiment in 1796, and the 10th Regiment in 1824.	Mutinied at Fatehgarh in 1857.
Aug. "	Murshidabad	Capt. R. Campbell	13th Battalion—*Gowen-ki-Paltan*.	Became the 4th Battalion in 1764, the 3rd in 1775, the 1st Regiment in 1781, the 3rd in 1784, the 3rd Battalion in 1786, the 1st Battalion 3rd Regiment in 1796, and the 6th Regiment in 1824.	Mutinied at Allahabad in 1857.
"	Midnapore	Capt. G. Ironside	14th Battalion—*Ranseet-ki-Paltan*.	Became the 10th Battalion in 1764, the 5th in 1775, the 5th Bombay Battalion in 1781, the 5th Bengal Regiment in 1784, the 5th Battalion in 1786, the 1st Battalion 5th Regiment in 1796, and the 11th Regiment in 1824.	Mutinied at Meerut in 1857.
Oct. "	Monghyr	Capt. J. White	15th Battalion—*Hote-ki-Paltan*.	Became the 12th Battalion in 1764, the 18th in 1775, the 12th Regiment in 1781, the 12th Battalion in 1786, the 1st Battalion 12th Regiment in 1796, and the 12th Regiment in 1824.	Mutinied at Nowgong and Jhansi in 1857.
"	Midnapore	Capt. S. Hampton	16th Battalion—*Bailan-ki-Paltan*.	Became the 14th Battalion in 1764, the 19th in 1775, the 13th Regiment in 1781, the 13th Battalion in 1786, the 2nd Battalion 1st Regiment in 1796, and the 4th Regiment in 1824.	Disbanded in 1861.
"	Burdwan	Capt. T. Witchcot	17th Battalion—*Burra Crawfurd-ki-Paltan*.	Became the 5th Battalion in 1764, the 4th in 1775, the 4th Bombay Battalion in 1781, the 4th Bengal Regiment in 1784, the 4th Battalion in 1786, the 1st Battalion 4th Regiment in 1796, and the 7th Regiment in 1824.	Mutinied at Dinapore in 1857.

A Chronological List of the Corps of the Bengal Army, showing particulars of their origin, and their subsequent history—continued.

A.—INFANTRY—continued.

Date of raising.	Where raised.	First Commandant.	Original number and native name.	REMARKS.	Present name or date of disbandment.
1764	Murshidabad	Capt. T. Goddard	18th Battalion—*Gawrud-ki-Paltan.*	Became the 17th Battalion the same year, the 7th in 1775, the 7th Bombay Battalion in 1781, 7th Bengal Regiment in 1784, the 7th Battalion in 1786, the 1st Battalion 7th Regiment in 1796, and the 13th Regiment in 1824.	Mutinied at Lucknow in 1857.
Mar. 1764	,,	Capt. A. Dow	19th Battalion—*Doo-ki-Paltan.*	Became the 18th Battalion in 1764, the 12th in 1775, the 6th Regiment in 1781, the 11th in 1784, the 11th Battalion in 1786, the 1st Battalion 11th Regiment in 1796, and the 15th Regiment in 1824.	Mutinied at Nusseerabad in 1857.
,,	Jellasore	Capt. J. Scotland	20th Battalion—*Escotten-ki-Paltan.*	Became the 16th Battalion in 1764, the 11th in 1775, the 5th Regiment in 1781, the 10th in 1784, the 10th Battalion in 1786, the 1st Battalion 10th Regiment in 1796, and the 14th Regiment in 1824.	Mutinied at Jhelum in 1857.
,,	Patna	Capt. J. Morgan	21st Battalion—*Morgan-ki-Paltan.*	Became the 11th Battalion in 1764, the 17th in 1775, the 11th Regiment in 1781, the 18th in 1784, and the 18th Battalion in 1786.	Incorporated in the two battalions of the 10th Regiment in 1796.

"	Calcutta	Capt. D. Hi	19th Battalion	Became the 20th in 1775	Disbanded for mutiny in 1780, and most of the men distributed amongst the regiments which marched to Madras in 1781.
Aug. 1765	Allahabad	Capt. D. Scott	20th Battalion—*Husaini-ki-Paltan*.	Became the 13th Battalion in 1775, the 7th Regiment in 1781, the 14th in 1784, the 14th Battalion in 1786, the 2nd Battalion Regiment in 1796, and the 16th Regiment in 1824.	Disbanded in 1857 for disaffection.
"	Bankipore	Colonel Sir Robert Barker.	21st Battalion—*Barkar-ki-Paltan*.	Became the 14th Regiment in 1781, the 19th in 1784, the 19th Battalion in 1786, the 2nd Battalion 11th Regiment in 1796, and the 17th Regiment in 1824.	Mutinied at Azamgarh in 1857.
1766	...	......	22nd Battalion (Pargannah or Provincial).	......	Disbanded in 1773.
"	...	......	23rd Battalion (Pargannah or Provincial).	......	Ditto.
"	...	......	24th Battalion (Ramgarh; Pargannah or Provincial).	Became the 14th Battalion in 1775, the 8th Regiment in 1781, the 15th in 1784, and the 15th Battalion in 1786.	Disbanded for mutiny in 1795.
"	...	......	25th Battalion (Pargannah or Provincial).	......	Disbanded in 1773.

A Chronological List of the Corps of the Bengal Army, showing particulars of their origin, and their subsequent history—continued.

A.—INFANTRY—continued.

Date of raising.	Where raised.	First Commandant.	Original number and native name.	Remarks.	Present name or date of disbandment.
1766	...	.....	26th Battalion (Pargannah or Provincial).	.....	Disbanded in 1773.
,,		.....	27th Battalion (Pargannah or Provincial).	.....	Ditto.
1776		.....	22nd Battalion	Became the 15th Regiment in 1781	Disbanded for mutiny in 1784.
,,		.....	23rd Battalion—*Raje-ki-Paltan*.	Became the 16th Regiment in 1781, the 20th in 1784, the 20th Battalion in 1786, the 2nd Battalion 6th Regiment in 1796, and the 18th Regiment in 1824.	Mutinied at Bareilly in 1857.
,,		.....	24th Battalion	Became the 17th Regiment in 1781	Disbanded for mutiny in 1784.
,,	Transferred from the	Capt. Stuart	25th Battalion—*Stuart-ki-Paltan*.	Became the 18th Regiment in 1781, the 21st in 1784, and the 21st Battalion in 1786.	Incorporated in the two battalions of the 12th Regiment in 1796.

service of the Nawab of Oudh in 1777.	Capt. Young	26th Battalion—*Ung-ki-Paltan.*	Became the 10th Regiment in 1781, the 22nd in 1784, the 22nd Battalion in 1786, the 2nd Battalion 3rd Regiment in 1796, and the 19th Regiment in 1824.	Disbanded in 1857 for mutiny.
,,	Capt. Baillie	27th Battalion—*Baillie-ki-Paltan.*	Became the 20th Regiment in 1781, the 23rd in 1784, the 23rd Battalion in 1786, the 2nd Battalion 5th Regiment in 1796, and the 20th Regiment in 1824.	Mutinied at Meerut in 1857.
,,	......	28th Battalion—*Kalli-ki-Paltan.*	Became the 21st Regiment in 1781, the 27th in 1784, and the 27th Battalion in 1786.	Incorporated in the two battalions of the 3rd Regiment in 1796.
,,	Capt. J. Landeg	29th Battalion—*Landeg-ki-Paltan.*	Became the 22nd Regiment in 1781, the 28th in 1784, and the 28th Battalion in 1786.	Incorporated in the two battalions of the 2nd Regiment in 1796.
,,	Capt. T. Naylor	30th Battalion—*Neelwar-ki-Paltan.*	Became the 23rd Regiment in 1781, the 29th in 1784, the 29th Battalion in 1786, the 2nd Battalion 9th Regiment in 1796, the 21st Regiment in 1824, and the 1st in 1861.	1st (Brahmin) Bengal Infantry.
July 1778	Capt. C. Marsack	31st Battalion—*Kilpatrick-ki-Paltan.*	Became the 24th Regiment in 1781 and the 24th Battalion in 1786.	Incorporated in the two battalions of the 7th Regiment in 1796.
,,	Capt. C. Bowles	32nd Battalion—*Bole-ki-Paltan.*	Became the 25th Regiment in 1781, the 25th Battalion in 1786, the 2nd Battalion 2nd Regiment in 1796, and the 22nd Regiment in 1824.	Mutinied at Fyzabad in 1857.

A Chronological List of the Corps of the Bengal Army, showing particulars of their origin, and their subsequent history—continued.

A.—INFANTRY—continued.

Date of raising.	Where raised.	First Commandant.	Original number and native name.	REMARKS.	Present name or date of disbandment.
July 1778	Cawnpore	Capt. J. Byrn	33rd Battalion—*Baran-ki-Paltan* or *Dhobi-ki-Paltan*.	Became the 26th Regiment in 1781, and the 26th Battalion in 1786.	Incorporated in the two battalions of the 11th Regiment in 1796.
,,	Ramgarh	Capt. J. Crawford (junior).	Ramgarh Light Infantry—*Chota Crawford-ki-Paltan*.	Enrolled among the line battalions as the 31st in 1786; became the 2nd Battalion 4th Regiment in 1796, and the 23rd Regiment in 1824.	Mutinied at Mhow in 1857.
1779	Benares	Capt. William Davis	34th Battalion—*Dabi-ki-Paltan*.	Became the 27th Regiment in 1781, the 30th in 1784, the 30th Battalion in 1786, the 2nd Battalion 8th Regiment in 1796, and the 24th Regiment in 1824.	Disbanded for disaffection in 1857.
,,	,,	Capt. M. Crawford	35th Battalion	Became the 28th Regiment in 1781, and the 31st in 1784.	Disbanded in 1785.
,,	,,	Capt. J. MacGowan	36th ,,	Became the 29th Regiment in 1781, and the 32nd in 1784.	Ditto.
,,	,,	Capt. W. Roberts	37th ,,	Became the 30th Regiment in 1781, and the 33rd in 1784.	Ditto.
,,	,,	Capt. T. Nicholl	38th ,,	Became the 31st Regiment in 1781, and the 34th in 1784.	Ditto.
,,	,,	Capt. R. Burton	39th ,,	Became the 32nd Regiment in 1781, and the 35th in 1784.	Ditto.

Date	Location	Commandant	Battalion	Notes	Remarks
Nov. 1780	...	Capt. W. Clode	40th Battalion	This battalion and the two following were formed of sepoy drafts, and were originally intended to reinforce General Goddard's detachment in the west of India. Became the 33rd Regiment in 1781.	Reduced in 1784, on the return of the Bombay detachment.
,,	...	Capt. W. MacClary	41st ,,	Became the 34th Regiment in 1781.	Reduced in 1784, on the return of the Bombay detachment.
,,	...	Capt. W. Bruce	42nd ,,	Became the 35th Regiment in 1781.	Disbanded in 1782 for mutiny.
Jan. 1783	Berhampore	Capt. J. Fullarton	36th Regiment	Became the 35th Regiment on the disbandment of the above in 1782.	Disbanded in 1784, on the return of the Bombay detachment.
May 1786	...	......	32nd Battalion 33rd ,, 34th ,, 35th ,, 36th ,,	These five battalions were formed of drafts from four existing regiments, and hence were known popularly as the "Chari-Yari" or "Four Friends."	In 1796 these five corps were incorporated with the two battalions respectively of the 1st, 8th, 9th, 5th and 6th Regiments.
July 1795	Calcutta	Capt. R. Hamilton	Marine Battalion—*Murriam-ki-Paltan.*	Raised for service on the Eastern Coast of the Bay of Bengal and in the Islands; brought into the line as the 1st Battalion 20th Regiment in 1803; became the 25th Regiment in 1824. See Appendix II.	Disbanded in 1859, for having exhibited disaffection in 1857.
,,	,,	Capt. H. F. Calcraft	Calcutta Native Militia—*Castor-ki-Paltan.*		Now the 18th (Musalman) Bengal Infantry.
Nov. 1795	...	Capt. Ludovic Grant	37th Battalion	Captain Grant was commandant of the 15th, and on the mutiny of that corps he was ordered to raise another regiment to replace it.	Incorporated in the two battalions of the 4th Regiment in 1796.

A Chronological List of the Corps of the Bengal Army, showing particulars of their origin, and their subsequent history—continued.

A.—INFANTRY—*continued.*

Date of raising.	Where raised.	First Commandant.	Original number and native name.	REMARKS.	Present name or date of disbandment.
Nov. 1797	Benares	Col. G. Russell	13th Regiment, 1st Battalion—*Poel-ki-Paltan*; 2nd Battalion—*Martdeel-ki-Paltan.*	Became in 1824 the 26th and 27th Regiments.	The 26th mutinied at Meean Meer in 1857, and the 27th was disbanded, for disaffection, the same year.
,,	Dinapore	Col. T. Nicholl	14th Regiment, 1st Battalion—*Stuppar-ki-Paltan*; 2nd Battalion—*Callanjan-ki-Paltan.*	Became in 1824 the 28th and 29th Regiments.	Both mutinied in 1857,—the 28th at Shahjahanpur, and the 29th at Moradabad.
Sep. 1798	Buxar / Sasseram	Col. J. Macdonald	15th Regiment, 1st Battalion—*Macdoon-ki-Paltan*; 2nd Battalion—*Broon-ki-Paltan.*	Became in 1824 the 30th and 31st Regiments.	The 30th mutinied at Nusseerabad in 1857; the 31st is now the 2nd (Rajput) Bengal Infantry. (See Appendix II.)
Nov. 1798	Jaunpur / Baragaon	Col. R. Lucas	16th Regiment, 1st Battalion—*Guttree-ki-Paltan*; 2nd Battalion—*Hilliard-ki-Paltan.*	Became the 32nd and 33rd Regiments in 1824. See Appendix II.	Now the 3rd (Brahmin) and 4th (Rajput) Bengal Infantry.

,,	Gaya, Dinapore	Col. S. Palmer	17th Regiment, 1st Battalion — *Brad-shaw-ki-Paltan*; 2nd Battalion — *Noke-ki-Paltan*.	Became in 1824 the 34th and 35th Regiments.	The 34th mutinied in 1844; the 35th was disbanded in 1857, for disaffection.
Jan. 1799	...	......	18th Regiment, 1st Battalion — *Mar-kum-ki-Paltan*; 2nd Battalion — *Barral-ki-Paltan*. 19th Regiment, 1st Battalion — *Tittee-lee-ki-Paltan*; 2nd Battalion — *Burral-ki-Paltan*.	Formed of drafts from existing regiments for service in Mysore; brought into the line on their return, and became in 1824 the 36th, 37th, 38th, and 39th Regiments.	The 36th, 37th, and 38th mutinied at Jullundur, Benares and Delhi in 1857; the 39th was disbanded, for disaffection, the same year.
May 1802	Calcutta	Lieut.-Col. R. Hamilton.	2nd Battalion, Marine Regiment — *Hamalteen-ki-Paltan*.	Became the 1st Battalion 20th Regiment in 1803, and the 40th Regiment in 1824.	Mutinied at Dinapore in 1857.
July 1803	Fatehgarh, Cawnpore.	......	21st Regiment, 1st Battalion — *Doobye-ki-Paltan*; 2nd Battalion — *Jan-sain-ki-Paltan*.	Became in 1824 the 41st and 42nd Regiments.	The 41st mutinied at Sitapur in 1857; the 42nd is now the 5th (Musalman) Bengal Infantry. (See Appendix II.)
,,	Allahabad	Capt. Thomas Wood	Pioneers	See Appendix II.	Incorporated with the Sappers and Miners.
Nov. 1803	Fatehgarh	......	22nd Regiment — *Kyne-ki-Paltan*.	Became in 1824 the 43rd and 44th Regiments.	The 43rd is now the 6th (Jat) Bengal Infantry; the 44th mutinied at Agra in 1857.

Date	Place	Commander	Original Name	Became	Remarks
Jan. 1815	Cawnpore	......	28th Regiment, 1st and 2nd Battalions—*Ochterlony-ki-Paltan*. (The 2nd Battalion was also called *Lambroon-ki-Paltan*.)	Became in 1824 the 55th and 56th Regiments.	Both mutinied in 1857, the 55th at Hoti-Mardan, and the 56th at Cawnpore.
,,	Fatehgarh / Benares	......	29th Regiment, 1st Battalion—*Moira-ki-Paltan*; 2nd Battalion—*Biskeshwar-ki-Paltan*	Became in 1824 the 57th and 58th Regiments.	The 57th mutinied at Ferozepore in 1857; the 58th was disbanded in 1861.
,,	Dinapore / Buxar	Capt. F. Andrés	30th Regiment, 1st Battalion,—*Lahtari-ki-Paltan*; 2nd Battalion—*Kartar-ki-Paltan*.	Became in 1824 the 59th and 60th Regiments.	The 59th is now the 8th (Rajput) Bengal Infantry. (See Appendix II.) The 60th mutinied at Rhotak in 1857.
Apr. 1815	Sabathu	Lieut. R. Ross	1st Nasseri Battalion	See Appendix II	Now the 1st Battalion, 1st Gurkha Rifles.
,,	,,	Lieut. J MacHarg	2nd ,, ,,	......	Disbanded in 1829.
,,	Nahan	Lieut. F. Young	Sirmur Battalion		Now the 1st Battalion, 2nd Gurkha Rifles.
,,	Kumaon	Lieut. Sir R. Colquhoun.	Kumaon Battalion	See Appendix II	Now the 1st Battalion, 3rd Gurkha Rifles.
May 1817	Cuttack	Capt. S. Fraser	Cuttack Legion		Now the 42nd Gurkha Rifles.
Mar. 1818	Benares	Major W. H. Wood	Infantry Levy	Brought into the line as the 1st Battalion 31st in 1833; became the 61st Regiment in 1824.	Mutinied at Jullundur in 1857.
,,	Cawnpore	Capt. T. C. Watson	,, ,,	Brought into the line as the 2nd Battalion 31st in 1823; became the 62nd Regiment in 1824.	Mutinied at Mooltan in 1858.

A Chronological List of the Corps of the Bengal Army, showing particulars of their origin, and their subsequent history—continued.

A.—INFANTRY—continued.

Date of raising.	Where raised.	First Commandant.	Original number and native name.	REMARKS.	Present name or date of disbandment.
Mar. 1818	Fatehgarh	Major T. P. Smith	Infantry Levy	See Appendix II	Now the 9th (Gurkha) Bengal Infantry.
,,	Muttra	Capt. P. C. Gilman	Infantry Levy—*Harriakh-ki-Paltan*.	Brought into the line as the 2nd Battalion 32nd in 1833; became the 64th Regiment in 1824.	Mutinied at Peshawar in 1857.
Feb. 1819	Allahabad	Major T. Anbury	Sappers and Miners	See Appendix II	The Corps of Sappers and Miners.
June 1823	{Dinapore Cawnpore}	......	33rd Regiment	Became the 65th and 66th Regiments in 1824.	The 65th is now the 10th (Jat) Bengal Infantry. The 66th was disbanded for mutiny at Govindgarh, Amritsar, in 1850.
Jan. 1823	Benares	......	34th Regiment	Became in 1824 the 67th and 68th Regiments.	Both mutinied in 1857; the 67th at Agra and the 68th at Bareilly.
Nov. 1824	,,	Lieut.-Col. J. Blackney.	69th	See Appendix II	Now the 7th (Rajput) Bengal Infantry.
,,	Sylhet	Capt. P. Dudgeon	Sylhet Local Battalion.	,,	Now the 44th Gurkha Rifles.
May 1825	Fatehgarh	Lieut.-Col. C. S. Fagan.	1st Extra Regiment	Became the 69th Regiment in August 1828.	Mutinied at Mootan in 1858.
,,	Cawnpore	Major Simpson	2nd ,, ,,	See Appendix II	11th (Rajput) Bengal Infantry.

,,	Mainpuri	Major S. P. Bishop	3rd ,,	Became the 71st Regiment in 1828	Mutinied at Lucknow in 1857.
,,	Allahabad	Major E. F. Waters	4th ,,	Became the 72nd Regiment in 1828	Mutinied at Neemuch in 1857.
,,	Benares	Lieut.-Col. Short	5th ,,	Became the 73rd Regiment in 1828	Disbanded in 1861.
,,	Dinapore	Lieut.-Col. Alexander	6th ,, *Alexander-ki-Paltan.*	Became the 74th Regiment in 1828	Mutinied at Delhi in 1857.

NOTE.—Six other extra regiments of infantry were raised at the same time, but were never fully officered and were reduced in the following year.

Apr. 1835	Assam	Capt. W. Simonds	Assam Sebundy Corps.		Now the 43rd Gurkha Rifles.
1835	Shekhawat	Lieut. H. Forster	Shekhawati Contingent.	See Appendix II	Now the 13th (Rajput) Bengal Infantry.
Oct. 1838	Ludhiana	Capt. W. F. Beatson.	3rd Infantry, Shah Shuja's Contingent		Now the 12th (Musalman) Bengal Infantry.
,,	...	......	Bundelkhand Legion	Brought into the line as the 34th Native Infantry in July 1846.	Three companies mutinied at Chittagong in 1857; seven companies disbanded at Barrackpore the same year for disaffection.
1843	Transferred from Bombay Army in 1849	Capt. Fitzgerald	Sindh Camel Corps		Now the 6th Punjab Infantry.
July 1846	Ferozepore	Capt. G. Tibbs	Regiment of Ferozepore.		Now the 14th Sikhs.
,,	Ludhiana	Bt.-Major P. Gordon	Regiment of Ludhiana.		Now the 15th Sikhs.
Dec. 1846	...	......	The Punjab Frontier Brigade.	See Appendix II	Now the 1st, 2nd, 3rd and 4th Sikh Infantry, and the Corps of Guides.
1849	Peshawar	Capt. John Coke	1st Punjab Infantry		Now the 1st Punjab Infantry.

A Chronological List of the Corps of the Bengal Army, showing particulars of their origin, and their subsequent history—continued.

A.—INFANTRY—*continued.*

Date of raising.	Where raised.	First Commandant.	Original number and native name.	REMARKS.	Present name or date of disbandment.
1849	Pind Dadan Khan.	Lieut. J. C. Johnston	2nd Punjab Infantry	See Appendix II	Now the 2nd Punjab Infantry.
,,	...	Lieut. R. Moorcroft.	3rd ,, ,,		Disbanded in 1882.
,,	...	Capt. H. O. Marshall	4th ,, ,,		Now the 4th Punjab Infantry.
,,	Leiah	Lt. J. E. Gastrell	5th ,, ,,		Now the 5th Punjab Infantry.
Jan. 1856	Lahore	Capt. T. Rattray	1st Bengal Police Battalion.	See Appendix II	Now the 45th Bengal Infantry (Sikhs).
1857	...	......	7th Punjab Infantry		Now the 19th Bengal Infantry.
,,	...	......	8th ,,		Now the 20th Bengal Infantry.
,,	...	......	9th ,,	See Appendix II	Now the 21st Bengal Infantry.
,,	...	......	10th ,,		Disbanded in 1861.
,,	...	......	11th ,,	See Appendix II	Now the 22nd Bengal Infantry.
,,	...	......	12th ,,		
,,	...	......	13th ,,		Disbanded in 1861.
,,	...	......	14th ,,	See Appendix II	
,,	...	......	15th ,, (Pioneer)		Now the 23rd Bengal Infantry (Pioneers).
,,	...	Capt. G. N. Cave	16th ,,	,, ,,	Now the 24th Bengal Infantry.

Date	Location	Commander	Regiment	Became	Present designation
1857	...	...	17th "	...	Now the 25th Bengal Infantry.
"	...	...	18th "	...	Now the 26th Bengal Infantry.
"	...	...	19th "	...	Now the 27th Bengal Infantry.
"	...	...	20th "	...	Now the 28th Bengal Infantry.
"	...	...	21st "	...	Now the 29th Bengal Infantry.
"	...	...	22nd "	...	Now the 30th Bengal Infantry.
"	...	...	23rd "	...	Now the 31st Bengal Infantry.
June 1857	Madhopur	Lieut. H. W Gulliver.	Punjab Pioneers	See Appendix II	Now the 32nd Bengal Infantry (Pioneers).
Dec. 1857	Cawnpore	Col. H. Palmer	Regiment of Lucknow.	.	Now the 16th (Rajput) Bengal Infantry.
"	Allahabad	Lieut. E. H. Langmore.	Allahabad Levy	.	Now the 33rd Bengal Infantry (Punjabi Mahomedans).
"	Petoragarh	Lieut. D. Macintyre	1st Extra Gurkha Regiment.	.	Now the 1st Battalion, 4th Gurkha Rifles.
1858	Fatehgarh	......	Fatehgarh Levy	Became the 34th Native Infantry in 1861.	Reduced in 1882. (Revived in 1887 as a regiment of Punjab Pioneers).
"	Mainpuri	......	Mainpuri Levy	Became the 35th Native Infantry in 1861.	Reduced in 1882. (Revived as a Sikh regiment in 1887.)
"	Bareilly	......	Bareilly Levy	Became the 36th Native Infantry in 1861.	Reduced in 1882. (Revived as a Sikh regiment in 1887.)

A Chronological List of the Corps of the Bengal Army, showing particulars of their origin, and their subsequent history—continued.

A.—INFANTRY—*concluded.*

Date of raising.	Where raised.	First Commandant.	Original number and native name.	REMARKS.	Present name or date of disbandment.
1858	Meerut	......	Meerut Levy	Became the 37th Native Infantry in 1861.	Reduced in 1882. (Revived as a Dogra regiment in 1887.)
Feb. 1858	Aligarh	Major L. P. D. Eld	Aligarh Levy	Became 39th Native Infantry in 1861. Reconstituted as a Garhwali Regiment in 1890. See Appendix II.	Now the 39th Bengal Infantry.
June 1858	Abbottabad	Capt. H. F. M. Boisragon.	25th Punjab Infantry		Now the 1st Battalion, 5th Gurkha Rifles.
,,	Phillour	Major J. C. Innes	Loyal Purbia Regiment.	See Appendix II	Now the 17th (Musalman) Bengal Infantry.
Aug. 1858	Agra	Lieut. G. L. Fraser.	Agra Levy		Now the 38th Bengal Infantry (Dogras.)
Sep. 1858	Shahjahanpur	Capt. E. Dandridge	Shahjahanpur Levy	Became the 41st Bengal Native Infantry in 1861.	Now the 40th Bengal Infantry (Pathans).
,,	Gwalior	Major H. T. Macpherson	1st Gwalior Regiment		Reduced in 1882.
Feb. 1886	Dharmsala	Major G. W. Rogers	2nd Battalion, 1st Gurkha Regiment.		2nd Battalion, 1st Gurkha Rifles.
,,	Dehra Dun	Col. S. E. Becher	2nd Battalion, 2nd Gurkha Regiment.	See Appendix II	2nd Battalion, 2nd Gurkha Rifles.
Apr. 1886	Bakloh	Maj. M. J. King-Harman.	2nd Battalion, 4th Gurkha Regiment.		2nd Battalion, 4th Gurkha Rifles.

Date	Location	Commander	Regiment	Remarks
Oct. ,,	Abbottabad	Maj. E. Molloy	2nd Battalion, 5th Gurkha Regiment.	
Apr. 1887	Meean Meer	Col. A. C. W. Crookshank.	34th Bengal Infantry (Pioneers).	
,,	Ferozepore	Lt.-Col. D. W. Inglis	35th Bengal Infantry (Sikhs).	
,,	Jullundur	Lt.-Col. J. Cook	36th Bengal Infantry (Sikhs).	
,,	Sialkot	Lt.-Col. V. Rivaz	37th Bengal Infantry (Dogras).	See Appendix II
,,	Almora	Lieut.-Col. E. P. Mainwaring.	2nd Battalion, 3rd Gurkha Regiment.	
Dec. 1890	Lansdowne	Major H. D. Hutchinson.	2nd Battalion, 3rd Gurkha Regiment.	

B.—CAVALRY.

Date	Location	Commander	Regiment	Remarks
July 1760	Patna	Sardars Mirza Shahbaz Khan and Khan Tar Beg.	Moghal Horse	Two troops officered entirely by natives. Increased to 1,000 men in 1764. Reduced to three risalahs of 100 men each in August 1765.
1773	Calcutta	Major S. Toone	Governor General's Body Guard.	Has varied in strength from time to time, but existed continuously to the present time. (See Appendix II.)
1776	Oudh	.....	Two regiments raised by the Nawab of Oudh.	Transferred to the Company in 1777.
1777	...	.....	3rd Regiment. (Raised to form with the above a Cavalry Brigade).	Served in General Goddard's expedition to Bombay; was reduced to a troop of 78 men in 1786; converted into a regular corps in June 1796; and became the 1st Bengal Light Cavalry.

2nd Battalion, 5th Gurkha Rifles.
34th Bengal Infantry (Pioneers).
35th Bengal Infantry (Sikhs).
36th Bengal Infantry (Sikhs).
37th Bengal Infantry (Dogras).
39th Bengal Infantry (Garhwal Rifles).
2nd Battalion, 3rd Gurkha Rifles.

Disbanded in 1772.

Now the Governor-General's Body-Guard.

Disbanded in May 1783.

Mutinied at Mhow in 1857.

A Chronological List of the Corps of the Bengal Army, showing particulars of their origin, and their subsequent history—continued.

B.—CAVALRY—*continued.*

Date of raising.	Where raised.	First Commandant.	Original number and native name.	Remarks.	Present name or date of disbandment.
1778	Oudh	In the service of the Nawab.	The Kandahar Horse	Lent to the British and served in General Goddard's expedition to the west of India; reduced to a troop, 78 strong, in 1786; converted into a regular corps in June, 1796. Became the 2nd Bengal Light Cavalry.	Disbanded in 1841 for misconduct in Afghanistan.
1796	Dinapore	Lt.-Col. S. Black	3rd Bengal Native Cavalry.	......	Mutinied at Meerut in 1857.
1797	Moneah	Capt. J. P. Pigot	4th Bengal Native Cavalry.	......	Disbanded in 1858, for disaffection.
1800	Ghazipur	{Lt.-Col. Thos. Wharton. Lt.-Col. J. P. Pigot.	5th Bengal Native Cavalry.	......	Ditto.
1803	...	Major R. Frith	6th Bengal Native Cavalry. Hindustani Independent Regiment.	An irregular corps formed from General De Boigne's Body-Guard and from other independent risalahs in the employ of the Company.	Mutinied at Jullundur in 1857. Reduced on the conclusion of the Mahratta War, 1805.

Several Irregular Corps were engaged on the side of the British between the years 1803–1805, all of which were reduced at the end of the war.

,,	...	Capt. Jas. Skinner	Skinner's Horse	See Appendix II	Now the 1st Bengal Cavalry.
1805	...	......	7th Bengal Native Cavalry.	......	Mutinied at Lucknow in 1857.
,,	...	......	8th Bengal Native Cavalry.	......	Disbanded in 1858, for disaffection.

Year	Location	Commander	Regiment	Notes	Status
1809	Delhi	Major W.L.Gardner	Gardner's Horse	See Appendix II	Now the 2nd Bengal Lancers.
1815	Rohilkhand	Lt. H. T. Roberts	1st Rohilla Cavalry	Became the 3rd Local Horse in 1823, and the 3rd Irregular Cavalry in 1840.	Partially mutinied in 1857. Disbanded in 1861.
,,	,,	Capt. Cunningham.	2nd ,, ,,	......	Disbanded 1819.
,,	,,	Capt. W.C. Baddeley	3rd ,, ,,	......	Transferred in 1819 to the service of Oudh.
,,	Hansi	Maj. Jas. Skinner	2nd Regiment Skinner's Horse.	See Appendix II	Now the 3rd Bengal Cavalry.
,,	...	,,	3rd Regiment Skinner's Horse.	......	Disbanded in August 1819.
1823	...	Capt. T. Gough	5th Local Horse	......	Mutinied in 1857.
1825	...	......	1st and 2nd Extra Regiments of Light Cavalry.	Became the 9th and 10th Bengal Light Cavalry in 1826.	Mutinied in 1857,— the 9th at Sialkot, and the 10th at Ferozepore.
1838	Oudh	Capt. C. Newbery	Oudh Auxiliary Force Cavalry.	See Appendix II	Now the 4th Bengal Cavalry.
,,	...	......	Cavalry of the Bundelkhand Legion.	Brought into the line in 1847 as the 10th Irregular Cavalry.	Mutinied at Peshawar in 1857.
1841	Bareilly	Capt. F. Wheler	7th Irregular Cavalry	} See Appendix II	Now the 5th Bengal Cavalry.
1842	Fatehgarh	Lt. W. H. Ryves	8th Irregular Cavalry		Now the 6th (Prince of Wales') Bengal Cavalry.
,,	...	......	11th Bengal Light Cavalry.	Became the 2nd Light Cavalry in 1850.	Mutinied at Cawnpore in 1857.
1844	...	Lt.-Col. J. Christie	9th Irregular Cavalry	Formed from the corps of "Christie's Horse", in the service of Shah Shuja.	Disbanded in May 1861.
1846	...	......	10th Irregular Cavalry	Became the 11th Irregular Cavalry in 1847.	Disbanded in 1859.
,,	...	......	11th ,, ,,	Became the 12th in 1847	Mutinied partially in 1857. Disbanded in 1861.

A Chronological List of the Corps of the Bengal Army, showing particulars of their origin, and their subsequent history—continued.

B.—CAVALRY—*concluded.*

Date of raising.	Where raised.	First Commandant.	Original number or native name.	REMARKS.	Present name or date of disbandment.
1846	...	......	12th Irregular Cavalry	Became the 13th in 1847	Mutinied at Benares in 1857.
,,	...	......	13th ,, ,,	Became the 14th in 1847	Mutinied at Jhansi and Nowgong in 1857.
,,	...	......	14th ,, ,,	Became the 15th in 1847	Mutinied at Sultanpur, Oudh, in 1857.
,,	...	......	15th ,, ,,	Became the 16th in 1847	Disbanded in 1861.
,,	...	......	16th ,, ,,	See Appendix II	Now the 7th Bengal Cavalry.
,,	...	......	17th ,, ,,		Now the 8th Bengal Cavalry.
1849	...	......	1st Punjab Cavalry	See Appendix II	Now the 1st, 2nd and 3rd Punjab Cavalry.
,,	...	......	2nd ,, ,,		Disbanded in 1882.
,,	...	......	3rd ,, ,,		Now the 5th Punjab Cavalry.
,,	...	......	4th ,, ,,		Now the 9th and 10th Bengal Lancers.
,,	...	......	5th ,, ,,		
1857	Delhi	Lieut. W. S. R. Hodson.	Hodson's Horse		Now the 11th Bengal Lancers.
,,	Lahore	Captain F. Wale	1st Sikh Irregular Cavalry,—"Wale's Horse.";	See Appendix II	
,,	,,	,, P. R. Hockin	2nd Sikh Irregular Cavalry.		Now the 12th Bengal Cavalry.
,,	...	Captain J. I. Murray	Jat Horse Yeomanry		Now the 14th Bengal Lancers.

1858	...	Lieut. G. G. Pearse	3rd Sikh Irregular Cavalry.	.....
,,	...	Lieut. J. Watson	4th Sikh Irregular Cavalry.	Disbanded in 1861.
,,	Peshawar	Captain C. Cureton.	Cureton's Multani Cavalry.	Now the 13th Bengal Lancers.
,,	Haldwani	Major F. G. Crossman.	Rohilkhand Horse .	Now the 15th Bengal Lancers.
1857				See Appendix II
,,	Muttra	Major C. J. Robarts	Muttra Horse	Reduced in 1882, but revived again in 1885. (See Appendix II.)
,,	Gwalior	Captain F. H. Smith	1st Mahratta Horse	Reduced in 1882, but revived again in 1885. (See Appendix II.)
,,	,,	,,	2nd ,, ,,	See Appendix II
				Disbanded in 1861. Now the 18th Bengal Lancers.

NOTE.—In addition to these there were a large number of corps raised in 1857-58, which were disbanded after the suppression of the disturbances.

1860	Cawnpore	Lieut. W. Fane	Fane's Horse	10th Bengal Lancers
1885	Umballa	Colonel G. C. Ross.	16th Bengal Cavalry	16th Bengal Cavalry
,,	Meean Meer	,, E.H.E. Kauntze	17th ,, ,,	17th ,, ,,

See Appendix II

The following is a sketch of the formation of the Native artillery of the Bengal army, the whole of which was disbanded after the Mutinies of 1857-58.

Three companies of Golandaz or Native artillerymen were raised by the Nawab of Oudh in 1776, and in the following year were transferred to the Company's service, and were commanded by Major Patrick Duff. These in 1778 were increased to three battalions, and became a separate brigade. The whole were, however, except one company, reduced in 1779. Three more companies were raised in 1783, but these, together with the former one, were finally reduced in 1785.

Golandaz were again raised in 1797, but were not collected into separate companies until 1805, when a corps of five companies was formed. At the same time a corps of 400 "Irregular Golandaz" was formed of Native artillerymen who had come over from the Mahrattas; it was stationed at Delhi and was gradually absorbed.

In 1811 a troop of Native horse artillery was raised for the expedition to Java, but was reduced on the conclusion of that service.

In 1815 the Golandaz were increased to the number of 16 companies. Two years later a tentative measure was introduced, withdrawing the "Galloper guns" from Native cavalry regiments and forming them into three troops of Native horse artillery; this arrangement was made permanent in 1819 (G. O. C. C., May 1st).

The Native artillery so formed remained with some modification until 1857. In 1825 (G.G.O. No. 192) the Native horse artillery was formed into four troops, one with each of the four brigades of horse artillery, while of foot there were to be two battalions of four companies each; the latter was afterwards increased to three battalions of six companies each, and a fifth troop was added to the 1st Brigade.

For Mountain Batteries see Appendix II.

Appendix II.

Existing Corps of the Bengal Army, showing dates of raising and changes in their titles.

CAVALRY.

CORPS.	When raised.	Original name or number.	REMARKS.	Date of receiving present title.
The Governor-General's Body-Guard.	1773	The Governor's Troop of Moguls.	A small European Body-Guard was formed in 1762; this was disbanded in 1772 and not a single mounted man remained in the Bengal Army. The present Body-Guard was for some time called "the Governor's troop of Moguls;" its strength has often varied, but it has existed continuously until the present time	1774.
1st Regiment of Bengal Cavalry	1803	Skinner's Horse	Reduced in 1806 to one risalah, which was employed on police duty at Delhi; reformed in 1809; designated the 1st (Skinner's) Local Horse in May 1823; named 1st Irregular Cavalry (Skinner's Horse) in 1840. Became the 1st Bengal Cavalry in	May 1861.
2nd ,, ,, Lancers	1809	Gardner's Horse	Became the 2nd (Gardner's) Local Horse in May 1823; the 2nd Irregular Cavalry in 1840; the 2nd Bengal Cavalry in May 1861, and Lancers in	June 1890.

3rd Regiment of Bengal Cavalry	1815	2nd Regiment of Skinner's Horse.	Became the 4th (Baddeley's) Local Horse in May 1823; the 4th Irregular Cavalry in 1840, and the 3rd Bengal Cavalry in	May	1861.
4th ,, ,, ,,	1838	Oudh Auxiliary Cavalry	Became the 6th Irregular Cavalry in 1840 and the 4th Bengal Cavalry in	May	1861.
5th ,, ,, ,,	1841	7th Irregular Cavalry	Received present designation in	May	1861.
6th (The "Prince of Wales'") Regiment of Bengal Cavalry.	1842	8th ,, ,,	Became the 6th Bengal Cavalry in May 1861, and made "the Prince of Wales'" in	Oct.	1883.
7th Regiment of Bengal Cavalry	1846	16th ,, ,,	Became the 17th Irregular Cavalry in September 1847, and the 7th Bengal Cavalry in		
8th ,, ,, ,,	1846	17th ,, ,,	Became the 18th in September 1847, and the 8th Bengal Cavalry in	May	1861.
9th ,, ,, ,, (Lancers)	1857	Hodson's Horse	Became the 1st Regiment of Hodson's Horse in August 1858; the 9th Bengal Cavalry in May 1861, and Lancers in	May	1861.
10th (The Duke of Cambridge's Own) Regiment of Bengal Lancers.	1857	,, ,,	Became the 2nd Regiment of Hodson's Horse in August 1858; the 10th Bengal Cavalry in May 1861; made Lancers in May 1864, and created "The Duke of Cambridge's Own" in	Feb.	1886.
11th (Prince of Wales' Own) Regiment of Bengal Lancers.	1857	1st Sikh Irregular Cavalry, "Wales' Horse."	Became the 11th Bengal Cavalry in 1861; made Lancers in May 1864, and "Prince of Wales' Own" in	Apr.	1878.
12th Regiment of Bengal Cavalry	1857	2nd Sikh Irregular Cavalry	Received its present designation in	Feb.	1876.
13th (Duke of Connaught's) Regiment of Bengal Lancers.	1858	4th ,, ,,	Became the 13th Bengal Cavalry in May 1861; made Lancers in May 1864, and "Duke of Connaught's" in	May	1861.
				Oct.	1883.
14th Regiment of Bengal Lancers	1857	Jat Horse Yeomanry	Designated "Murray's Jat Horse," in December 1859; became the 14th Bengal Cavalry in May 1861; made Lancers in	May	1864.
15th (Cureton's Mooltani) Regiment of Bengal Lancers.	1858	Formed of a number of volunteer risalahs of Pathan Horse, named from their commandants "Cureton's," "Lind's," etc.	Formed into one regiment as the "Mooltani Regiment of Cavalry," in December 1859; renamed "Cureton's Multani Regiment of Cavalry" in February 1860; became the 15th Bengal Cavalry in May 1861 and Lancers in	June	1890.

Existing Corps of the Bengal Army, showing dates of raising and changes in their titles—contd.

CAVALRY—*concld.*

Corps.	When raised.	Original name or number.	Remarks.	Date of receiving present title.
16th Regiment of Bengal Cavalry	1857	Rohilkhand Horse	Became the 16th Bengal Cavalry in May 1861; disbanded in 1882; re-established under its present designation in	Sep. 1885.
17th " "	1857	Muttra Horse	Became the Muttra Police in 1857; the Rohilkhand Auxiliary Police Levy in 1858; "Roberts' Horse" in 1859; the 17th Bengal Cavalry in May 1861; disbanded in 1882; and re-established under its present designation in	Sep. 1885.
18th " Lancers	1858	2nd Mahratta Horse	Became the 18th Bengal Cavalry in May 1861, and Lancers in	Mar. 1886.
19th Regiment of Bengal Cavalry	1860	Fane's Horse	Became the 19th Bengal Cavalry in May 1861, and Lancers in	Sep. 1864.

ARTILLERY.

Corps.	When raised.	Original name or number.	Remarks.	Date of receiving present title.
No. 7 (Bengal) Mountain Battery	1886	No. 1 Bengal Mountain Battery.	Became No. 7 (Bengal) Mountain Battery in	Nov. 1889.
No. 8 " "	1886	No. 2 Bengal Mountain Battery.	Became No. 8 (Bengal) Mountain Battery in	Nov. 1889.

INFANTRY.

The Corps of Bengal Sappers and Miners.	1803	Corps of Pioneers	Another corps raised in 1819, in which two companies of the Pioneers were incorporated: the remaining companies of the Pioneers were incorporated with this corps in 1833. Name changed to "Sappers and Pioneers" in 1847. Again became "Sappers and Miners".	Mar. 1851.
1st Regiment of Bengal Infantry	1776	30th Bengal Native Battalion.	Called *Neelwar-ki-Paltan*; became the 23rd Regiment in 1781; the 29th in 1784; the 29th Battalion in 1786; the 2nd Battalion, 9th Native Infantry in 1796; the 21st Bengal Native Infantry in 1824; the 1st Bengal Native Infantry in May 1861; the 1st Bengal Infantry in January 1885; and the 1st (Brahmin) Regiment of Bengal Infantry in	April 1893.
2nd (The Queen's Own) Regiment of Bengal (Light Infantry).	1798	2nd Battalion, 15th Regiment.	Became the 31st Bengal Native Infantry in 1824; made Light Infantry in 1858; became the 2nd Bengal Native (Light) Infantry in May 1861; received the title of "Queen's Own" in March 1876; became the 2nd (The Queen's Own) Bengal (Light) Infantry in January 1885; and the 2nd (The Queen's Own Rajput) Regiment of Bengal (Light Infantry) in	April 1893.
3rd Regiment of Bengal Infantry	1798	1st Battalion, 16th Regiment.	Became the 32nd Bengal Native Infantry in 1824; the 3rd Bengal Native Infantry in May 1861; the 3rd Bengal Infantry in January 1885; and the 3rd (Brahmin) Regiment of Bengal Infantry in	April 1893.
4th (Prince Albert Victor's Own) Regiment of Bengal Infantry.	1798	2nd Battalion, 16th Regiment.	Became the 33rd Bengal Native Infantry in 1824; the 4th Bengal Native Infantry in May 1861; the 4th Bengal Infantry in January 1885; was made "Prince Albert Victor's Own", in August 1890; and became the 4th (Prince Albert Victor's Own Rajput) Regiment of Bengal Infantry in	April 1893.

Existing Corps of the Bengal Army, showing dates of raising and changes in their titles—contd.

INFANTRY—contd.

CORPS.	When raised.	Original name or number.	REMARKS.	Date of receiving present title.
5th Regiment of Bengal (Light) Infantry.	1803	2nd Battalion, 21st Regiment.	Became the 42nd Bengal Native Infantry in 1824; was made Light Infantry in 1843; became the 5th Bengal Native (Light) Infantry in May 1861; the 5th Bengal (Light) Infantry in January 1885; and the 5th (Masalman) Regiment of Bengal (Light) Infantry in	April 1893.
6th Regiment of Bengal (Light) Infantry.	1803	1st Battalion, 22nd Regiment.	Became the 43rd Bengal Native Infantry in 1824; was made Light Infantry in 1843; became the 6th Bengal Native (Light) Infantry in May 1861; the 6th Bengal (Light) Infantry in January 1885; and the 6th (Jat) Regiment of Bengal (Light) Infantry in	April 1893.
7th (The Duke of Connaught's Own) Regiment of Bengal Infantry.	1824	69th Bengal Infantry	Became the 47th Bengal Native Infantry in 1828; the 7th Bengal Native Infantry in May 1861; was made the "Duke of Connaught's Own" in October 1883; became the 7th (The Duke of Connaught's Own) Bengal Infantry in January 1885; and the 7th (The Duke of Connaught's Own Rajput) Regiment of Bengal Infantry in	April 1893.
8th Regiment of Bengal Infantry.	1815	1st Battalion, 30th Regiment.	Became the 59th Bengal Native Infantry in 1824; the 8th Bengal Native Infantry in May 1861; the 8th Bengal Infantry in January 1885; and the 8th (Rajput) Regiment of Bengal Infantry in	April 1893.

9th " " "	1817	Fatehgarh Levy	Brought into the line in 1823 as the 1st Battalion, 32nd Bengal Native Infantry; became the 63rd Bengal Native Infantry in 1824; the 9th Bengal Native Infantry in May 1861; the 9th Bengal Infantry in January 1885; and the 9th (Gurkha) Regiment of Bengal Infantry in	April 1893.
10th " " "	1823	1st Battalion, 33rd Regiment.	Became the 65th Bengal Native Infantry in 1824; the 10th Bengal Native Infantry in May 1861; the 10th Bengal Infantry in January 1885; and the 10th (Jat) Regiment of Bengal Infantry in	April 1893.
11th " " "	1825	2nd Extra Regiment	Became the 70th Bengal Native Infantry in 1828; the 12th Bengal Native Infantry in May 1861; the 11th Bengal Native Infantry in October 1861; the 11th Bengal Infantry in January 1885; and the 11th (Rajput) Regiment of Bengal Infantry in .	April 1893.
12th (The Kalat-i-Ghilzai) Regiment of Bengal Infantry.	1838	3rd Infantry, Shah Shuja's Contingent.	Brought into the Bengal Army as the Regiment of Kalat-i-Ghilzai in 1842; became the 13th Bengal Native Infantry in May 1861; the 12th in October 1861; the 12th Bengal Infantry in January 1885; and the 12th (Musalman) Regiment of Bengal Infantry in .	April 1893.
13th (The Shekhawati) Regiment of Bengal Infantry.	1835	The Shekhawati Brigade	Became the Shekhawati Battalion in 1847; brought into the line as the 14th Bengal Native Infantry in May 1861; renumbered the 13th in October 1861; became the 13th Bengal Infantry in January 1885; and the 13th (Rajput) Regiment of Bengal Infantry in	April 1893.
14th (The Ferozepore Sikh) Regiment of Bengal Infantry.	1846	The Regiment of Ferozepore.	Brought into the line as the 15th Bengal Native Infantry in May 1861; renumbered the 14th in October 1861; and became the 14th Bengal Infantry in "	Jan. 1885.

Existing Corps of the Bengal Army, showing dates of raising and changes in their titles—contd.

INFANTRY—contd.

CORPS.	When raised.	Original name or number.	REMARKS.	Date of receiving present title.
15th (The Ludhiana Sikh) Regiment of Bengal Infantry.	1846	The Regiment of Ludhiana	Brought into the line as the 16th Bengal Native Infantry in May 1861; renumbered the 15th in October 1861; and became the 14th Bengal Infantry in .	Jan. 1885.
16th (The Lucknow) Regiment of Bengal Infantry.	1857	The Regiment of Lucknow	Brought into the line as the 20th Bengal Native Infantry in May 1861; renumbered the 16th in October 1861; became the 16th Bengal Infantry in January 1885; and the 16th (Rajput) Regiment of Bengal Infantry in .	April 1893.
17th (The Loyal Purbiah) Regiment of Bengal Infantry.	1857	The Loyal Purbiah Regiment.	Brought into the line as the 21st Bengal Native Infantry in May 1861; renumbered the 17th in October 1861; became the 17th Bengal Infantry in January 1885; and the 17th (Musalman) Regiment of Bengal Infantry in .	April 1893.
18th Regiment of Bengal Infantry	1795	Calcutta Native Militia	Became the Alipore Regiment in 1859, and the 22nd Bengal Native Infantry in May 1861; renumbered the 18th in October 1861; became the 18th Bengal Infantry in January 1885; and the 18th (Musalman) Regiment of Bengal Infantry in .	April 1893.

19th (Punjab) Regiment of Bengal Infantry.	1857	7th Punjab Infantry	Became the 23rd Bengal Native Infantry in May 1861; the 19th in October 1861; and the 19th Bengal Infantry in	Jan. 1885.
20th (The Duke of Cambridge's Own Punjab) Regiment of Bengal Infantry.	1857	8th ,, ,,	Became the 24th Bengal Native Infantry in May 1861; and the 20th in the following October; was made "The Duke of Cambridge's Own" in October 1883; and became the 20th (The Duke of Cambridge's Own) Bengal Infantry in	Jan. 1885.
21st (Punjab) Regiment of Bengal Infantry.	1857	9th ,, ,,	Became the 25th Bengal Native Infantry in May 1861; the 21st in October 1861; and the 21st Bengal Infantry in	Jan. 1885.
22nd (Punjab) Regiment of Bengal Infantry.	1857	11th ,, ,,	Became the 26th Bengal Native Infantry in May 1861; the 22nd in October 1861; and the 22nd Bengal Infantry in	Jan. 1885.
23rd (Punjab) Regiment of Bengal Infantry (Pioneers).	1857	15th (Pioneer) Regiment of Punjab Infantry.	Became the 27th Bengal Native Infantry in May 1861; the 23rd in October 1861; and the 23rd Bengal Infantry (Pioneers) in	Jan. 1885.
24th (Punjab) Regiment of Bengal Infantry.	1857	16th Punjab Infantry	Became the 28th Bengal Native Infantry in May 1861; the 24th in October 1861; and the 24th Bengal Infantry in	Jan. 1885.
25th (Punjab) Regiment of Bengal Infantry.	1857	Lahore Punjab Battalion	Became the 17th Punjab Infantry in August 1857; the 29th Bengal Native Infantry in May 1861; the 25th in the October following; and the 25th Bengal Infantry in	Jan. 1885.
26th (Punjab) Regiment of Bengal Infantry.	1857	18th Punjab Infantry	Became the 30th Bengal Native Infantry in May 1861; the 26th in October 1861; and the 26th Bengal Infantry in	Jan. 1885.

Existing Corps of the Bengal Army, showing dates of raising and changes in their titles—contd.

INFANTRY—contd.

CORPS.	When raised.	Original name or number.	REMARKS.	Date of receiving present title.
27th (Punjab) Regiment of Bengal Infantry.	1857	19th Punjab Infantry	Became the 31st Bengal Native Infantry in May 1861; the 27th in October 1861; and the 27th Bengal Infantry in	Jan. 1885.
28th (Punjab) Regiment of Bengal Infantry.	1857	20th ,, ,,	Became the 32nd Bengal Native Infantry in May 1861; the 28th in October 1861; and the 28th Bengal Infantry in	Jan. 1885.
29th (Punjab) Regiment of Bengal Infantry.	1857	21st ,, ,,	Became the 33rd Bengal Native Infantry in May 1861; the 29th in October 1861; and the 29th Bengal Infantry in	Jan. 1885.
30th (Punjab) Regiment of Bengal Infantry.	1857	22nd ,, ,,	Became the 34th Bengal Native Infantry in May 1861; the 30th in October 1861; and the 30th Bengal Infantry in	Jan. 1885.
31st (Punjab) Regiment of Bengal Infantry.	1857	Van Cortlandt's Levy	Became the 23rd Punjab Infantry in August 1857; the 35th Bengal Native Infantry in May 1861; the 31st Bengal Native Infantry in October 1861; and the 31st Bengal Infantry in	Jan. 1885.
32nd (Punjab) Regiment of Bengal Infantry (Pioneers).	1857	The Punjab Pioneers	Became the 24th (Pioneer) Regiment of Punjab Infantry in March 1858; the 36th Bengal Native Infantry (Pioneers) in May 1861; the 32nd in October 1861; and the 32nd Bengal Infantry (Pioneers) in	Jan. 1885.
33rd (Punjabi Mahomedan) Regiment of Bengal Infantry.	1857	Allahabad Levy	Became the 37th (Allahabad) Regiment of Bengal Native Infantry in May 1861; re-numbered the 33rd in October 1861; became the 33rd Bengal Infantry in January 1885; re-organised and became the 33rd	Jan. 1885.

34th (Punjab) Regiment of Bengal Infantry (Pioneers).	1858		(Punjabi Mahomedan) Regiment of Bengal Infantry in	Dec. 1890.
		Fatehgarh Levy	Became the 38th (Fatehgarh) Regiment of Bengal Native Infantry in May 1861; renumbered the 34th in October 1861; reduced in 1882; and revived under its present designation in	Apr. 1887.
35th (Sikh) Regiment of Bengal Infantry.	1858	Mainpuri Levy	Became the 39th (Mainpuri) Regiment of Bengal Native Infantry in May 1861; renumbered the 35th in October 1861; reduced in 1882; and revived under its present designation in	Apr. 1887.
36th (Sikh) Regiment of Bengal Infantry.	1858	Bareilly Levy	Became the 40th (Bareilly) Regiment of Bengal Native Infantry in May 1861; renumbered the 36th in October 1861; reduced in 1882; revived under its present designation in	Apr. 1887.
37th (Dogra) Regiment of Bengal Infantry.	1858	Meerut Levy	Became the 41st (Meerut) Regiment of Native Infantry in May 1861; renumbered the 37th in October 1861; reduced in 1882; revived under its present designation in	Apr. 1887.
38th (Dogra) Regiment of Bengal Infantry.	1858	Agra Levy	Became the 42nd (Agra) Regiment of Bengal Native Infantry in May 1861; renumbered the 38th in October 1861; became the 38th Bengal Infantry in January 1885; re-organised as a Dogra regiment under its present designation in	Dec. 1890.
39th (Garhwal Rifle) Regiment of Bengal Infantry.	1858	Aligarh Levy	Became the 43rd (Aligarh) Regiment of Bengal Native Infantry in May 1861; renumbered the 39th in October 1861; became the 39th Bengal Infantry in January 1885; re-organised as a Garhwali regiment, taking over six companies of men of that class from the 2-3rd Gurkha regiment, in December 1890; designated the "39th (Garhwal Rifle) Regiment of Bengal Infantry" in	Jan. 1892.

Existing Corps of the Bengal Army, showing dates of raising and changes in their titles—contd.

INFANTRY—contd.

CORPS.	When raised.	Original name or number.	REMARKS.	Date of receiving present title.
40th (Pathan) Regiment of Bengal Infantry.	1858	Shahjahanpur Levy	Became the 44th (Shahjahanpur) Regiment of Bengal Native Infantry in May 1861; renumbered the 40th in October following; became the 40th Bengal Infantry in January 1885; re-organised as a Baluch and trans-frontier corps in December 1890; designated the 40th (Pathan) Regiment of Bengal Infantry in .	Jan. 1892.
42nd (Gurkha Rifle) Regiment of Bengal Infantry.	1817	Cuttack Legion	Became in February 1823, the Rangpur Local Battalion, and was made a Light Infantry corps in the following month; designation changed to 1st Assam Light Infantry Battalion in 1827; became the 46th (Assam) Regiment of Bengal Native (Light) Infantry in May 1861; renumbered the 42nd in the following October; became the 42nd Bengal Infantry in January 1885; designated "Gurkha Light Infantry" in June 1886; and received its present title of "Rifles" in	Mar. 1891.
43rd (Gurkha Rifle) Regiment of Bengal Infantry.	1835	Assam Sebundy Corps	Became the Lower Assam Sebundy Corps in 1839; the 2nd Assam Light Infantry Battalion in 1844; the 47th (Assam) Regiment of Bengal Native (Light) Infantry in May 1861; renumbered the 43rd in October 1861; became the 43rd Bengal Infantry in January 1885; designated "Gurkha Light	

44th (Gurkha Rifle) Regiment of Bengal Infantry.	Sylhet Local Battalion	1824	Infantry" in June 1886; and received its present title of "Rifles" in . . . . Became the Sylhet Light Infantry Battalion in April 1827. Brought into the line as the 48th (Sylhet) Regiment of Bengal Native (Light) Infantry in May 1861; renumbered the 44th in October 1861; became the 44th Bengal Infantry in January 1885; designated "Gurkha Light Infantry" in June 1886; and received its present designation of "Rifles" in . . . . . Mar. 1891.
45th (Rattray's Sikh) Regiment of Bengal Infantry.	Bengal Police Battalion	1856	Added to the army as the 45th Regiment of Bengal Native Infantry (Rattray's Sikhs) in May 1864; became the 45th (Rattray's Sikh) Regiment of Bengal Infantry in Jan. 1885.
1st Gurkha (Rifle) Regiment— (1st Battalion) (2nd Battalion)	The 1st Nasseri Battalion	1815 1886	Became "The Nasseri Battalion" in 1829; brought into the line as "The 66th or Gurkha Regiment" in February 1850; constituted a light infantry corps in November 1858; became the 11th Regiment of Bengal Native Infantry in May 1861; in the following October was removed from the line and became the 1st Gurkha Regiment; designated "Rifles" in . . . . . Mar. 1891.
2nd (Prince of Wales' Own) Gurkha (Rifle) Regiment (The Sirmoor Rifles). (1st Battalion) (2nd Battalion)	The Sirmoor Battalion	1815 1886	Designation changed to the "Sirmoor Rifle Regiment" in August 1858; brought into the line and designated the 17th Regiment of Bengal Native Infantry in May 1861; became the 2nd Gurkha Regiment in October 1861; created "The Prince of Wales' Own" in January 1886; designated "Rifles" in . . . . . Mar. 1891.

Existing Corps of the Bengal Army, showing dates of raising and changes in their titles—concld.

INFANTRY—concluded.

CORPS.	When raised.	Original name or number.	REMARKS.	Date of receiving present title.
3rd Gurkha (Rifle) Regiment (1st Battalion) (2nd Battalion)	1815 1891	Kumaon Provincial Battalion.	Transferred from the Civil to the Military Department, as the Kumaon Local Battalion in February 1839; brought into the line as the 18th Regiment of Bengal Native Infantry in May 1861; became the 3rd Gurkha Regiment in October 1861; designated "Rifles" in .	Mar. 1891.
4th Gurkha (Rifle) Regiment (1st Battalion) (2nd Battalion)	1857 1886	Extra Gurkha Regiment .	Brought into the line as the 19th Regiment of Bengal Native Infantry in May 1861; became the 4th Gurkha Regiment in October 1861; and designated "Rifles" in .	Mar. 1891.

PUNJAB FRONTIER FORCE.

CORPS.	When raised.	Original name or number.	REMARKS.	Date of receiving present title.
1st Punjab Cavalry .	1849	1st Punjab Cavalry .	Designated "Prince Albert Victor's Own" in .	Mar. 1890.
2nd ,, ,, .	1849	2nd ,, ,, .	......	1849.
3rd ,, ,, .	1849	3rd ,, ,, .	......	1849.
5th ,, ,, .	1849	5th ,, ,, .		1849.
Corps of Guides (The Queen's Own).	1846	Corps of Guides .	Designated "The Queen's Own" in .	Mar. 1876.
No. 1 (Kohat) Mountain Battery .	1851	No. 2 Punjab Light Field Battery.	Became No. 1 Mountain Battery in January 1877; received present designation in .	Sep. 1876.

No. 2 (Derajat) Mountain Battery	1849	No. 3 Punjab Light Field Battery.	Became No. 2 Mountain Battery in December 1876, and received the title of 'Derajat' in	Sep. 1879.
No. 3 (Peshawar) ,, ,,	1851	Peshawar Mountain Train.	Received its present designation in	Dec. 1876.
No. 4 (Hazara) ,, ,,	1848	Hazara Mountain Train	Received present title in . . .	Dec. 1876.
The Punjab Garrison Battery	1851	No. 4 or Garrison Company of Artillery, Punjab Irregular Force.	Became No. 4 or Garrison Battery in January 1876; changed to No. 5 (Garrison) Battery in December 1876; received present title in	Nov. 1889.
The 1st, 2nd, 3rd and 4th Sikh Infantry.	1846	1st, 2nd, 3rd and 4th Sikh Local Infantry.	Became part of the Punjab Irregular Force in 1851; the use of the word "Local" discontinued, and present designation introduced in	Feb. 1857.
1st, 2nd, 4th and 5th Punjab Infantry.	1840	1st, 2nd, 4th and 5th Punjab Infantry.	. . . . . .	Apr. and May 1849.
6th Punjab Infantry	1843	Sindh Camel Corps	Transferred to the Bengal establishment in October 1849; incorporated in the Punjab Irregular Force as the "6th Regiment or Sindh Rifle Corps" in September 1853; changed to the 'Sindh Rifle Corps' in November 1853; received its present designation in	Aug. 1856.
5th Gurkha (Rifle) Regiment— (1st Battalion) (2nd Battalion)	1858 1886	25th Punjab Infantry, or Hazara Gurkha Battalion.	Became 5th Gurkha Regiment, or Hazara Gurkha Battalion in October 1861; made a Rifle corps in	Mar. 1891.

Appendix III.

Commanders-in-Chief of the Bengal Army.

Name.	Period of Command. From	Period of Command. To	Remarks.
Colonel Robert Clive	December 1756	25th February 1760	(And Governor.)
Major John Caillaud	25th February 1760	31st December 1760	
Major John Carnac	31st December 1760	April 1761	
Lieut.-Col. Eyre Coote, H. M.'s 84th Regiment.	April 1761		
Major Thomas Adams, H. M.'s 84th Regiment.	1763	January 1764.	
Major John Carnac	January 1764	July 1764.	
Major Hector Munro, H. M.'s 89th Regiment.	July 1764	January 1765.	
Brigadier-General John Carnac	January 1765	April 1765	
Major-General Robert, Lord Clive	April 1765	29th January 1767	(And Governor.)
Colonel Richard Smith	29th January 1767	January 1768	(Provincial.)
Colonel Charles Chapman	18th January 1768	March 1770	
Brigadier-General Sir Robert Barker	24th March 1770	22nd December 1773	(Provincial.)
Colonel Charles Chapman	22nd December 1773	18th January 1774	
Colonel Alexander Champion	18th January 1774	2nd November 1774	
Lieut.-General Sir John Clavering, K.B.	2nd November 1774	30th August 1777	Sir John Clavering died in August 1777, and a Military Board was appointed, which carried on the duties of the chief command until October.
Brigadier-General Giles Stibbert	16th October 1777	25th March 1775	(Provincial.)
Lieut.-General Sir Eyre Coote, K.B.	25th March 1779	27th April 1783	Sir Eyre Coote was absent in Madras during the last two years of his life; he died in April 1783; during his absence, and after his death until the arrival of his successor, General Stibbert officiated in the command.

Name			Remarks
Brigadier-General Giles Stibbert	27th April 1783	21st July 1785	(Provincial.)
Lieutenant-General Robert Sloper	21st July 1785	12th September 1786	
Lieut.-General Sir Charles, Earl Cornwallis, K.G.	12th September 1786	28th October 1793	And Governor-General. From December 1790 to August 1792, and from August to October 1793, Lord Cornwallis was absent in Madras. During the first period his place was filled by Sir Alexander Mackenzie; in 1793 Colonel Achmuty officiated, and was succeeded by Sir Robert Abercromby, who also continued to hold command after the departure of Lord Cornwallis from India.
Colonel Sir Alexander Mackenzie, Bart.	6th December 1790	1st August 1794	(Provincial.)
Colonel Arthur Achmuty	15th August 1793	5th October 1793	(Provincial.)
Major-General Sir Robert Abercromby, K.B.	5th October 1793	28th October 1793	(Provincial.)
Major-General Sir Robert Abercromby, K.B.	28th October 1793	23rd January 1797	
Major-General Charles Morgan	23rd January 1797	16th March 1797	(Provincial.)
Lieutenant-General Sir Alured Clarke, K.B.	16th March 1797	25th February 1801	
Major-General Sir James Henry Craig, K.B.	25th February 1801	13th March 1801	(Provincial.)
Lieutenant-General Gerard Lake (afterwards Lord Lake)	13th March 1801	30th July 1805	
General Charles, Marquess Cornwallis, K.G.	30th July 1805	5th October 1805	From 30th July 1805 to 5th October 1805 the chief command in India was held by Lord Cornwallis, that of Bengal only being held by Lord Lake. On the death of the former Lord Lake resumed the superior office. And Governor-General.
General Gerard, Lord Lake	5th October 1805	3rd March 1807	(Provincial.)
Major-General William Dowdeswell	3rd March 1807	19th June 1807	Ditto.
Major-General Sir Ewen Baillie, Bart.	19th June 1807	4th August 1807	Ditto.
Major-General William St. Leger	4th August 1807	17th October 1807	
Lieut.-General George Hewett	17th October 1807	10th December 1811	

Commanders-in-Chief of the Bengal Army—concluded.

Name.	Period of Command.		Remarks.
	From	To	
Lieut.-General Forbes Champagné	10th December 1811	14th January 1812	(Provincial.)
Lieut.-General Sir George Nugent, Bart.	14th January 1812	4th October 1813	In October 1813 Lord Moira became Commander-in-Chief and Sir George Nugent was made head of the Military Board.
General Francis, Earl of Moira (afterwards Marquess of Hastings).	4th October 1813	13th January 1823	(And Governor-General.)
Lieutenant-General the Hon'ble Sir Edward Paget, G.C.B.	13th January 1823	7th October 1825.	
General Stapleton, Lord Combermere, G.C.B.	7th October 1825	1st January 1830.	
General George, Earl of Dalhousie, G.C.B.	1st January 1830	10th January 1832.	
General Sir Edward Barnes, G.C.B.	10th January 1832	15th October 1833.	(And Governor-General.)
General Lord William H. C. Bentinck, G.C.B.	15th October 1833	20th March 1835	(Provincial.)
Major-General James Watson, C.B.	10th March 1835	5th September 1835	
Lieutenant-General the Hon'ble Sir Henry Fane, G.C.B.	5th September 1835	7th December 1839	
Lieutenant-General Sir Jasper Nicolls, K.C.B.	7th December 1839	8th August 1843.	
General Sir Hugh Gough, Bart., G.C.B. (afterwards Lord Gough)	8th August 1843	7th May 1849.	
General Sir Charles James Napier, G.C.B.	7th May 1849	6th December 1850	
General Sir William Maynard Gomm, K.C.B.	6th December 1850	23rd January 1856.	
General the Hon'ble George Anson	23rd January 1856	27th May 1857.	(Provincial.)
Major-General Thomas Reed, C.B.	5th June 1857	17th June 1857	
Lieutenant-General Sir Patrick Grant, K.C.B.	17th June 1857	13th August 1857	(Officiating.)

General Sir Colin Campbell, G.C.B., (afterwards Lord Clyde)	13th August 1857	4th June 1860.
General Sir Hugh H. Rose, G.C.B.	4th June 1860	23rd March 1865.
General Sir William R. Mansfield, K.C.B.	23rd March 1865	9th April 1870.
General Lord Napier of Magdala, G.C.B., G.C.S.I.	9th April 1870	9th April 1876.
General Sir F. P. Haines, K.C.B.	10th April 1876	7th April 1881.
General Sir D. M. Stewart, *Bart.*, G.C.B.	7th April 1881	28th November 1885.
General Sir F. S. Roberts, *Bart.*, G.C.B., G.C.S.I., V.C., now Lord Roberts	28th November 1885	7th April 1893.
General Sir George Stewart White, K.C.B., V.C.	8th April 1893.	

Appendix IV.

Chronological List of the Services of the Bengal Native Army.

Date.	Service.	Corps engaged which still exist.	Remarks.
1757.	*War with Siraj-ud-Daulah—*		
Feb. 5th	Battle near Calcutta.		
Mar. 23rd	Taking of Chandernagore.		
Jun. 18th	Capture of Katwah.		
Jun. 23rd	Battle of Plassey.		
1758.	*Expedition to the Northern Circars.—*		
Dec. 8th	Battle of Condore.		
1759.			
Apr. 8th	Storm of Masulipatam.		
Nov. 25th	Battle of Badara (with the Dutch).		
1760.	*War with Shah Alam—*		
Feb. 9th	Battle of Masimpur.		
Feb. 22nd	Battle of Sirpur.		
Apr. 26th	Relief of Patna.		
Jun. 16th	Battle of Birpur.		
1761.			
Jan. 15th	Battle of Suan.		
1763.	*War with Nawob of Bengal—*		
Jun. 24th—Jul. 1st.	Fighting at Patna and Manji		
Jul. 19th	Battle of Katwah.		

Aug. 2nd	.	Battle of Gheriah.
Sept. 5th		Storming of the lines of Udwah-nala.
Oct. 2nd	.	Capture of Monghyr.
Nov. 6th	.	Storm of Patna.
1764.		*Campaign against the Nawabs of Bengal and Oudh—*
May 3rd	.	Battle of Patna.
Oct. 23rd	.	,, of Buxar.
Dec.		Siege of Chunargarh.
Feb. 8th 1765.		Capture of Chunargarh.
Feb. 11th		Capture of Allahabad.
May 22nd	.	Battle of Kalpi (against the Mahrattas).
1767-69.		*First Mysore War.—* Operations in the Baramahal, Chikakol and Kimedi districts.
1772-73.		*Bhutia War—*
Dec. 21st		Storming of Cooch-Behar. Capture of Dalimkot.
1772-73.	.	*Saniyasi War—* The Body-Guard.
1774.		*Rohilla War—* The Body-Guard.
Apr. 23rd	.	Battle of Miranpur Katra
1776.		*Operations in the Doab—*
Jun. 10th		Battle of Korah.

Chronological List of the Services of the Bengal Native Army—continued.

Date.	Service.	Corps engaged which still exist.	Remarks.
1778. 1780.	*First Mahratta War—* March to Western India.		
Jan. 19th	Capture of Dabhoi.		
Feb. 15th	Storming of Ahmadabad.		
Mar.	Actions at Powangarh.		
Apr. 20th	Capture of Lahar.		
Aug. 3rd	Capture of Gwalior.		
Dec. 11th	Capture of Bassein.		
1781.			
Feb.	Forcing of the Bhor Ghat.		
April	Retreat down the Bhor Ghat.		
Mar. 24th	Action at Mahatpur, Central India.		
	Second Mysore War—		
Aug. 27th.	Battle of Palilur.		
Sept. 27th.	,, ,, Sholingarh.		
Oct. 23rd.	,, ,, Virakandalur.		
1781.	*Campaigns against the Raja of Benares—*		
Aug. 16th	Outbreak at Benares.		
Aug. 20th	Action at Ramnagar.		
Sept. 4th	,, ,, Patita.		
Sept.	Capture of Patita.		
Sept. 20th	Action at Lora and the Sukrut Pass.		
Nov. 10th	Capture of Bijaigarh.		
1791.	*Expedition to Quedah—*		
April 12th	Action at Point Pria Fort.		

Date	Event	Regiment	Remarks
1791. Mar 6th—21st	*Third Mysore War*—Siege and capture of Bangalore.		Honorary standards granted to the volunteer battalions; medals to all ranks who had served in Mysore.
May 14th	Battle of Arikera.		
Sep.—Dec.	Storming of hill forts.		
1792. Feb. 6th & 7th	Taking of Seringapatam.		
1793.	*Operations in Assam.*		
1794.	*Second Rohilla War*—		
Oct. 26th	Battle of Bitaura.		
1799. March 27th	*Fourth Mysore War*—Battle of Malavelli	......	Medals granted to all ranks. "Seringapatam" to be borne on colours (G. O. G. G. dated 11th April 1822).
May 4th	Storming of Seringapatam	......	
1801.	*Expedition to Egypt*.	......	Medal granted.
1803.	*Operations in the Doáb*—Taking of Sasni, Bijaigarh and Kachaura.	2nd Bengal (Light) Infantry.	
	Attack on Tatiah	3rd Bengal Infantry.	
1803.	*Mahratta War*—	......	Medal granted by G. G. O. dated 14th April 1851, to the survivors of the actions at Aligarh, Delhi, Laswari, defence of Delhi, battle of Deig and capture of Deig. Received on honorary third color (G.O. G. G. 1st October 1803); bears the word "Delhi" on appointments (G. G. O. 43 of 1829).
Sep. 4th	Storming of Aligarh.		
Sep. 11th	Battle of Delhi	2nd Bengal (Light) Infantry	
Oct. 10th	Action before Agra	1st, 2nd, and 4th Bengal Infantry.	
Nov. 1st	Battle of Laswari	1st, 2nd and 4th Bengal Infantry	"Laswari" on colours)G. O. G. 43 of 1829).
1804. Feb. 5th	Taking of Gwalior	1st and 4th Bengal Infantry.	

Chronological List of the Services of the Bengal Native Army—continued.

Date.	Service.	Corps engaged which still exist.	Remarks.
1804.	*Mahratta War*—contd. Minor operations,—Narnaul and Kanun.		
May 16th	Taking of Rampura	5th Bengal Infantry.	
Jul. & Aug.	Monson's Retreat	1st and 5th Bengal Infantry.	
October	Defence of Delhi.		
Nov. 13th	Battle of Deig	2nd Bengal (Light) Infantry	"Deig" on colours (G. G. O. 43 of 1829).
Nov. 17th	Battle of Farakhabad	1st Bengal Cavalry.	
Dec. 24th	Capture of Deig.		
1805. Jan.—Mar.	Siege of Bhurtpore	1st Bengal Cavalry; 1st and 2nd Bengal Infantry.	
	Pursuit of Holkar to the Punjab.	1st Bengal Cavalry.	
1805-6.	Operations against forts in Bundelkhand and the Doab.	3rd Bengal Infantry.	
1807.	*Expedition to Macao*	Detachment of 2nd Bengal (Light) Infantry.	
1808.	*Operations in Bundelkhand*	4th and 5th Bengal Infantry.	
1809—1812.	Taking of Bhawani (Hariana)	1st Bengal Cavalry and 6th Bengal (Light) Infantry.	
1810.	Expedition against Mauritius	……	Gold medal bestowed by the East India Company on commissioned officers, and a silver medal on the men.
1811.	Expedition to Java	Body-Guard; detachment of 4th Bengal Infantry.	"Java" on colours and appointments (G. G. O. 43 of 1829) to the Body Guard. Medals granted to all ranks by G. O. G. G. dated 28th October 1841.

Date	Event	Unit	Remarks
1814—16.	*Nepal War*		A silver medal bestowed on all officers, British and Native, and on such of the non-commissioned ranks as were specially recommended.
1814.			
Oct. 31st	Attack on Kalanga	Light Company, 4th Bengal Infantry.	
Nov. 27th	Second attack on Kalanga	Ditto	
Nov.—Dec.	Operations against Amar Singh.	......	
Nov. 25th	Action of Barharwa	Detachment of the 2nd Bengal Lancers.	
		Detachment of the 2nd Bengal Native (Light) Infantry.	
Dec. 27th	Attack on Jaithak	Light Company, 4th Bengal Infantry.	
1815.			
Jan. 1st	Disaster at Samanpur	Detachment, 2nd Bengal Lancers.	
	Disaster at Pursa.		
Feb. to Apr.	Kumaon operations.		
Apr. 14th—16th	Taking of Malaun.		
Apr. 25th	Capture of Almora.	Wing, 2nd Bengal Infantry.	
1816.			
Feb. 28th	Battle of Makwanpur	Sappers and Miners; 1st, 2nd, and 8th Bengal Infantry.	
Mar. 1st	Action at Hariharpur	5th Bengal Light Infantry (wing).	
1817—19.	*Mahratta War—*	......	G. G. O. dated April 14th, 1851, granted a medal to all survivors of the battle of Sitabaldi and capture of Nagpur.
1817.			
Nov. & Dec.	Operations against Pindaris	Body-Guard; 1st Bengal Cavalry, 2nd Bengal Lancers.	
Nov. 26-27	Battle of Sitabaldi.		
Dec. 16th	Battle of Nagpur	6th Bengal (Light) Infantry	"Nagpur" on colours (G.G.O. No. 592 of 1882).
1818.			
December	Renewed operations against Pindaris,		
	Taking of Jawad.		
1819.	Operations against Apa Sahib		
	Capture of Asirgarh	2nd Bengal Infantry.	

Chronological List of the Services of the Bengal Native Army—continued.

Date.	Service.	Corps engaged which still exist.	Remarks.
1824—26.	First Burma War—		
1824. Jan. & Feb	Operations in Sylhet and Cachar.	......	Medals granted to the troops employed (G.G.O. 84 of 1826).
May 17th	Disaster at Ramu.	42nd Bengal Infantry.	
May to Dec.	Operations at and around Rangoon	Detachment of Body-Guard.	"Ava" on colours (G.G.O. 22nd April 1826).
December	Operations in Assam.		
1825. Jan.—April	Expedition to and taking of Arakan.	2nd Bengal Lancers, 5th Bengal (Light) Infantry, detachments 8th and 9th Bengal Infantry.	"Arakan" on colours (G.G.O. 22nd April 1826) to 2nd Bengal Lancers and 5th Bengal (Light) Infantry.
Feb. & Mar. Mar. 7th	Expedition to Manipur Attack on Donabyu.	44th Bengal Infantry. Detachment of Body-Guard.	
1825, December.	Siege and assault of Bhurtpore.	1st Bengal Cavalry. Sappers and Miners, 1st, 2nd, 3rd, 4th and 9th Bengal Infantry.	"Bhurtpore" on colours to cavalry and line regiments by G.G.O. 85 of 1826. To Sappers and Miners by G.G.O. 58 of 1852.
1826, Jan. 18th.			Medal granted to all survivors by G. G. O. dated 14th April 1851.
		Detachments of 1st and 2nd Gurkha Regiments.	To 2nd Gurkha Rifles by G. O. C. C. 25th November 1859. To 1st Gurkha Rifles by G. G. O. 580 of 1874.
1829—1831	Disturbances on the Eastern Frontier.	42nd and 44th Bengal Infantry.	

1832–1837 1834	Operations against the Kols, etc. Shekhawati Expedition	2nd and 4th Bengal Infantry. 3rd Bengal Infantry.	
1838–40.	*First Afghan War (1st Phase)*—	1st and 3rd Bengal Cavalry; Sappers and Miners, 2nd, 5th and 6th Bengal (Light) Infantry.	"Afghanistan" on colours (G.O.G.G. 19th November 1839); six months' batta (G. O. C. C. 22nd November 1839).
July 23rd 1839.	Storm of Ghazni	3rd Bengal Cavalry, Sappers and Miners.	"Ghazni" on colours (G. O. G. G. 19th November 1839).
Nov. 13th 1840.	Capture of Kalat	3rd Bengal Cavalry, 2nd Bengal Infantry.	"Kalat" on colours by G. O. G. G. of February 15th, 1840.
Jan. 18th 1840.	Attack on Pashut	Sappers and Miners, 12th Bengal Infantry.	
May Sept. 18th Sept. & Oct. Ditto	Operations against Ghilzais. Action of Bamian. Operations in Kohistan. ,, in Baluchistan	1st Bengal Cavalry, 5th and 6th Bengal Infantry.	
1840–1842 1841.	*First China War*—	......	
May 1842.	Capture of Canton		Twelve months' batta for whole campaign; six months' for the final operations; medal to all ranks— G. G. O. 54 of 1842.
July 21st 1841.	Storming of Chin-Kiang-foo. *First Afghan War (2nd Phase)*—		
February	Operations in the Nazian Valley.	12th Bengal Infantry.	
April July October	,, ,, Ghilzais. ,, ,, Duranis. Actions in the Khurd Kabul and Jagdalak Passes.	Sappers and Miners.	
Nov.–Dec.	Occupation of and defence of Jalalabad.		
Nov.–Dec. 1842.	Fighting at Kabul.		
January Jan.–April	Retreat from Kabul Defence of Jalalabad	Broadfoot's Sappers (afterwards incorporated with the Sappers and Miners).	Special additional medal and badge of a mural crown (G. G. Notification 30th April 1842).

Chronological List of the Services of the Bengal Native Army—continued.

Date.	Service.	Corps engaged which still exist.	Remarks.
1842.	*First Afghan War (2nd Phase)*—contd.		
Mar. 6th	Surrender of Ghazni.		
Nov.—May	Defence of Kalat-i-Ghilzai	Detachment 6th Bengal Infantry and 12th Bengal Infantry.	'Kalat-i-Ghilzai' on colours of 12th Bengal Infantry. (G.G.O. 4th October 1842). Special additional medal (G. G. O. October 4th, 1842). Badge of a mural crown to the 12th Bengal Infantry (G.G.O. No. 174 of 1891).
Mar.—May	Fighting round Kandahar	1st Bengal Cavalry; 5th and 6th Bengal Infantry.	'Kandahar, 1842' on colours (G.G.O. 4th October and 13th December 1842).
April 5th	Forcing of the Khaibar Pass.	Sappers and Miners; 4th Bengal Infantry.	
Aug. 24th	Action at Mamu Khel	1st Bengal Cavalry, 5th and 6th Bengal Infantry.	
Aug. 30th	Battle of Goaine		
Sept. 5th	Recapture of Ghazni	1st Bengal Cavalry, 5th and 6th Bengal Infantry.	'Ghazni, 1842' on colours (G. G. O. 4th October 1842.)
,, 8th	Action of Jagdalak	Sappers and Miners.	
,, 12th—13th	Actions at Tezin and Haft Kotal.	Sappers and Miners; 4th Bengal Infantry.	
Sept.	Occupation of Kabul	Sappers and Miners; 4th, 5th and 6th Bengal Infantry.	'Kabul, 1842' on colours (G. G. O. 4th October and 8th November 1842). Further donation of six months' batta for second campaign; medal to all ranks (G. G. O. 4th October 1842).
Sept. 29th	Capture of Istalif	5th and 6th Bengal Infantry .	
1843.	*Campaign in Sindh*—		'Sindh,' 'Meeanee' and 'Hyderabad' on colours; medal to all ranks (G.G.O. 205 of 1843).
Feb. 17th	Battle of Miani	......	
Mar. 24th	,, of Hyderabad	......	
1843.	*The Gwalior Campaign*—		Maharajpore on colours (G.G. O. 4th January 1844). Bronze star issued to all ranks.
Dec. 29th	Battle of Maharajpur	Body-Guard; 3rd Bengal Cavalry; Sappers and Miners; 2nd, 6th and 12th Bengal Infantry.	

Date	Battle	Units	Medal/Honour
Dec. 29th	Battle of Paniar	6th Bengal Cavalry; Sappers and Miners.	'Paniar' on colours (G. G. O. 4th January 1844). Bronze Star to all ranks.
1845-46.	The First Sikh War—	……	Medal with clasps for Mudki, Ferozshahr, Aliwal and Sobraon (G. G. O. 12th August 1846).
Dec. 18th.	Battle of Mudki	Body-Guard; 3rd and 6th Bengal Cavalry; 5th and 7th Bengal Infantry.	"Moodkee," "Ferozshahr," "Aliwal," and "Sobraon" on colours (G. G. O. 12th August 1846).
,, 21st–22nd	,, of Ferozshahr	Body-Guard; 3rd and 6th Bengal Cavalry; Sappers and Miners; 4th, 5th and 7th Bengal Infantry	
1846. Jan. 28th	Battle of Aliwal	Body-Guard; 3rd Bengal Cavalry; 7th and 13th Bengal Infantry; 1st and 2nd Gurkha Regiments.	
Feb. 10th	,, of Sobraon	Body-Guard; 2nd Bengal Lancers; 6th Bengal Cavalry; 4th, 5th, 6th 7th, 8th and 9th Bengal Infantry; 1st and 2nd Gurkha Regiments.	
1848-49. 1848.	Second Sikh War—		"Punjab," "Mooltan." "Chilianwallah" and "Gujerat" on colours (G. G. O. 7th October 1853); also medal, with clasps for Mooltan, Chilianwala and Gujerat.
September	Siege of Mooltan	Sappers and Miners; detachment of the Corps of Guides.	
,,	Jullundur Doab	2nd Bengal Cavalry; 1st and 2nd Sikh Infantry; detachment of the Corps of Guides.	
Nov. 22nd Dec. 3rd	Affair at Ramnagar. Action of Sadulapur	Sappers and Miners; detachment of the Corps of Guides.	
Jan. 1849.	Siege and Capture of Mooltan	5th Bengal Cavalry; Sappers and Miners; detachment of the Corps of Guides.	
,, 13th	Battle of Chilianwala	Sappers and Miners; 2nd and 11th Bengal Infantry.	
Feb. 21st	,, of Gujerat	Sappers and Miners; 2nd and 11th Bengal Infantry.	
Jan.	Jullundur Doab	2nd Bengal Lancers; detachment of the Corps of Guides; 1st and 2nd Sikh Infantry.	

Chronological List of the Services of the Bengal Native Army—continued.

Date.	Service.	Corps engaged which still exist.	Remarks.
1850. February	Kohat Pass	1st Punjab Cavalry; Corps of Guides; 2nd Bengal Infantry and 1st Punjab Infantry.	India medal granted by G. G. O., 812 of 1869.
March 29th 1851.	Attack on fort of Bihta, in Oudh.		
October 1851.	Expedition against the Mohmands	2nd Bengal Lancers; Sappers and Miners; Corps of Guides; 1st Gurkha Regiment.	Ditto ditto.
March 1852.	Operations against Swat tribes	2nd Bengal Lancers; 1st Punjab Cavalry; Corps of Guides; Sappers and Miners; 1st Gurkha Regiment; 1st Punjab Infantry.	Ditto ditto.
1852-53. *Second Burma War—*			
April 14th 1853.	Taking of Rangoon	.....	'Pegu' medal, afterwards called the 'India Medal,' granted by G. G. O. dated 22nd Dec. 1853.
March 1853.	Operations against Myat Toon	4th Sikh Infantry	'Pegu' on colours to 4th Sikh Infantry (G.G.O. 18th May 1855); six months' batta; the 'India medal' granted.
1852.	Expedition against the Utman Khels.	2nd Bengal Lancers; Sappers and Miners; 1st Gurkha Regiment; Corps of Guides.	India medal granted by G. G. O. 812 of 1869.
December	Waziri Expedition	2nd Punjab Cavalry; 1st, 2nd, 4th and 6th Punjab Infantry.	
December	Black Mountain Expedition	No. 4 Mountain Battery; Sappers and Miners; 12th Bengal Infantry; Corps of Guides; 1st Sikh Infantry.	India medal (G.G.O. 812 of 1869).
1853. November	Expedition against the Jowaki Afridis.	No. 3 Mountain Battery; detachment of 5th Bengal Cavalry; Sappers and Miners; 1st Gurkha Regiment; Corps of Guides.	Ditto ditto.

Date	Campaign	Troops	Medal
April 1853.	Expedition against the Shiranis and Kasranis.	A mountain battery; the 5th Punjab Cavalry, the 1st, 3rd and 6th Punjab Infantry.	India medal (G.G.O. No. 812 of 1869).
March 1855.	Expedition against the Aka Khel	No. 3 Mountain Battery	Ditto ditto.
April 1857.	Miranzai Expedition	No. 2 Mountain Battery; Sappers and Miners; 1st Gurkha Regiment; 1st and 6th Punjab Infantry.	Ditto ditto.
March 1857.	Bozdar Expedition	Nos. 1 and 2 Mountain Batteries; 2nd and 3rd Punjab Cavalry; Sappers and Miners; 1st and 3rd Sikh Infantry; 1st, 2nd and 4th Punjab Infantry.	Ditto ditto.
1857-58. 1857. June—Sep.	*Indian Mutiny Campaigns*— Siege and capture of Delhi	9th and 10th Bengal Lancers; Sappers and Miners; 32nd Bengal Infantry; 2nd and 3rd Gurkha Regiments; 1st, 2nd and 5th Punjab Cavalry; Corps of Guides; 4th Sikh Infantry; 1st, 2nd and 4th Punjab Infantry.	Medal (G.G.O. 363 of 1858). 'Delhi' on colours (G. G. O. 4 of 1864); six months' special batta (G. G. O. 1499 of 1857); special clasp (G. G. O. 363 of 1858).
July—Aug.	Havelock's advance from Allahabad to the relief of Lucknow: actions of Fatehpur, Aoung, Pandu Nadi, Cawnpore, Unao, Bashiratganj and Burbia-ki-Chauki. Defence of a house at Arrah.	14th Bengal Infantry.	
,,	Defence 45th Bengal Infantry	Detachment 45th Bengal Infantry	'Defence of Arrah' on colours (G. G. O. 221 of 1874).
Aug. 25th June—Sep.	Battle of Najafgarh Defence of Lucknow (first phase).	Corps of Guides; 1st Punjab Infantry. 16th Bengal Infantry	'Lucknow' on colours (G. G. O. 4 of 1864); six months' special batta (G. G. O. 1544 of 1857). 'Lucknow' on colours (G. G. O. 4 of 1864).
September	First Relief of Lucknow	14th Bengal Infantry	Special clasp for 'Defence of Lucknow'—G. G. O. 363 of 1858 and 733 of 1859.

Chronological List of the Services of the Bengal Native Army—continued.

Date.	Service.	Corps engaged which still exist.	Remarks.
1857.	Indian Mutiny Campaigns—contd.		
Sep. 28th and Oct. 10th.	Actions at Bulandshahr and Agra.	9th and 10th Bengal Lancers; 1st, 2nd and 5th Punjab Cavalry; 32nd Bengal Infantry; 2nd and 4th Punjab Infantry.	
Nov. 15th	Action of Narnaul	Guides Cavalry; 19th and 31st Bengal Infantry.	
Sep.—Nov. 18th	Defence of Lucknow (second phase).	14th and 16th Bengal Infantry.	
Nov. 14th—18th	Second Relief of Lucknow	9th and 10th Bengal Lancers; 1st, 2nd and 5th Punjab Cavalry; Sappers and Miners; 32nd Bengal Infantry; 2nd and 4th Punjab Infantry.	
December	Actions of Gangari, Patiali and Mainpuri.	9th and 10th Bengal Lancers; 32nd Bengal Infantry.	
Nov.—Dec. 1857-58.	Operations in Sylhet and Cachar	44th Bengal Infantry.	
	Operations in Bihar	15th, 28th and 45th Bengal Infantry.	'Behar,' on colours to 45th Bengal Infantry only (G. G. O. 221 of 1874).
	„ in Central India	2nd and 5th Bengal Infantry	'Central India,' on colours to 2nd Bengal Infantry (G. G. O. 4 of 1864); special clasp (G. G. O. 733 of 1859).
1858. Jan. & Feb.	Defence of Alambagh	14th Bengal Infantry.	
Mar. 2nd—21st.	Capture of Lucknow	9th, 10th and 11th Bengal Lancers; 1st, 2nd and 5th Punjab Cavalry; Sappers and Miners; 14th and 32nd Bengal Infantry; 2nd and 4th Punjab Infantry.	"Lucknow" on colours (G. G. O. 4 of 1864); special clasp (G. G. O. 733 of 1859).
April—Aug.	Rohilkhand Campaign	15th Bengal Lancers; 1st, 2nd and 5th Punjab Cavalry; 14th, 19th, 25th and 30th Bengal Infantry; 1st	

Date	Campaign	Troops Engaged	Medal
May—December 1859-60.	Oudh Campaign	Sikh Infantry; 1st, 2nd and 4th Punjab Infantry. 9th, 10th and 11th Bengal Lancers; 5th Punjab Infantry. 43rd Bengal Infantry.	
1857-60.	Abor Expedition		
1858.	*Second China War*—First Campaign	7th, 10th and 11th Bengal Infantry	'China, 1858-59' on colours (G. G. O. 592 of 1882).
	Second Campaign	11th and 19th Bengal Lancers; 15th, 20th, 22nd, 23rd and 27th Bengal Infantry.	'China, 1860-62' on colours to 15th, 22nd and 27th Bengal Infantry (G. G. O. 592 of 1882). Medal with clasp according to date (G. G. O., 136 of 1862).
	Capture of Taku Forts	11th and 19th Bengal Lancers; 20th and 23rd Bengal Infantry.	'Taku Forts' and 'Pekin' on colours (G. G. O. 132 of 1862); special clasps (G. G. O. 136 of 1862).
	Surrender of Pekin	(As above).	
1858. April—May	Expedition to Sitana	Nos. 3 and 4 Mountain Batteries; 5th and 8th Bengal Cavalry; Sappers and Miners; 1st, 12th, 20th, 21st and 26th Bengal Infantry; Corps of Guides.	India medal (G. G. O. 812 of 1869).
1859. December	Expedition against the Kabul Khel Waziris.	Nos. 1, 3 and 4 Mountain Batteries; 2nd Punjab Cavalry; Sappers and Miners; 32nd Bengal Infantry; Corps of Guides; 4th Sikh Infantry; 1st, 4th and 6th Punjab Infantry.	India medal (G. G. O. 812 of 1869).
1860. April	Mahsud Waziri Expedition	Mountain Batteries; 15th Bengal Lancers; 3rd Punjab Cavalry; Sappers and Miners; 32nd Bengal Infantry; Corps of Guides; 4th Sikh Infantry; 1st, 2nd, 4th and 6th Punjab Infantry; 5th Gurkha Regiment.	India medal (G. G. O. 812 of 1869).

Chronological List of the Services of the Bengal Native Army—continued.

Date.	Service.	Corps engaged which still exist.	Remarks.
1860-61.	Sikkim Expedition	15th Bengal Infantry; 3rd Sikh Infantry	
1862-63	Operations in Khasiah and Jaintiah Hills.	21st, 28th, 33rd, 44th and 45th Bengal Infantry.	
1863. Oct.—Dec.	Ambela Expedition—	Nos. 2, 3 and 4 Mountain Batteries; 11th Bengal Lancers; Sappers and Miners; the 14th, 20th, 23rd and 32nd Bengal Infantry; the Corps of Guides; the 3rd Sikh Infantry; the 1st, 5th and 6th Punjab Infantry; and the 4th and 5th Gurkha Regiments.	India medal with special clasp (G.G.O. 812 of 1869.
1864. January	Operations against the Mohmands.	2nd Bengal Lancers; 6th Bengal Cavalry; 2nd Gurkha Regiment; 4th Sikh Infantry.	India medal (G. G. O. 116 of 1884).
1864—1866	Bhutan War—	5th Bengal Cavalry; 14th Bengal Lancers; Sappers and Miners; 9th, 11th, 12th, 18th, 19th, 26th, 29th, 30th, 31st, 43rd and 44th Bengal Infantry; 3rd Gurkha Regiment.	India medal with special clasp (G. G. O. 86 of 1870).
1868. Jan.—May	Campaign in Abyssinia	10th Bengal Lancers; 12th Bengal Cavalry; 21st and 23rd Bengal Infantry.	'Abyssinia' on colours; six months' batta and medal (G.G.O. 1181 of 1869)
1868. October	Black Mountain Expedition	Nos. 3 and 4 Mountain Batteries; 9th Bengal Lancers; Sappers and Miners; 20th, 24th and 31st Bengal Infantry; Corps of Guides; 1st, 2nd, 3rd, 4th and 5th Gurkha Regiments; 3rd Sikh Infantry; 2nd Punjab Infantry.	India medal with special clasp (G. G. O. 86 of 1870).

Date	Expedition	Troops Engaged	Reward
February 1869. 1871-72	The Bizoti Urakzai Expedition. Lushai Expedition	1st and 4th Punjab Infantry. No. 3 Mountain Battery; Sappers and Miners; 22nd, 27th, 42nd and 44th Bengal Infantry; 2nd and 4th Gurkha Regiments.	India medal with special clasp (G. G. O. 1295 of 1872).
March 1872.	Dawar Expedition	No. 2 Mountain Battery; 1st and 2nd Punjab Cavalry; 1st and 4th Sikh Infantry; 1st Punjab Infantry.	
1874-75	Daphla Expedition	No. 4 Mountain Battery; 16th, 42nd 43rd and 44th Bengal Infantry.	
February 1875. 1875-76	Naga Expedition Perak Expedition	42nd and 44th Bengal Infantry. 1st Gurkha Regiment.	India medal with special clasp (G. G. O. 242 of 1880).
1876-80	Naga Expeditions	18th, 34th, 42nd, 43rd and 44th Bengal Infantry.	India medal with special clasp (G. G. O. 344 of 1881).
1877-78	Jowaki Expedition	Nos. 1 and 2 Mountain Batteries; 2nd Punjab Cavalry; Corps of Guides; 1st and 3rd Sikh Infantry; 2nd, 4th, 5th and 6th Punjab Infantry; 5th Gurkha Regiment.	India medal with special clasp (G. G. O. 143 of 1879 and 285 of 1880).
March 1878.	Expedition against Shakot	No. 4 Mountain Battery; Corps of Guides.	
,,	Expedition against Utman Khels	Corps of Guides.	
1878	*Second Afghan War—* 1st Campaign.	Nos. 1, 2, 3 and 4 Mountain Batteries; 8th, 10th, 11th 12th, 13th, 14th, 15th and 19th Bengal Cavalry; 1st, 2nd, and 5th Punjab Cavalry; Sappers and Miners; 6th, 12th, 14th, 15th, 19th, 20th, 21st, 23rd, 24th, 25th, 26th, 27th, 28th, 29th, 32nd, 39th, and 45th Bengal Infantry; 1st,	'Afghanistan, 1878-1880' on colours (G. G. O. 418 of 1881); medal (G. G. O. 534); six months' batta (G. G. O. 804 of 1879).

Chronological List of the Services of the Bengal Native Army—continued.

Date	Service	Corps engaged which still exist.	Remarks.
1878.	*Second Afghan War*—contd.	2nd, 3rd, 4th, and 5th Gurkha Regiments; Corps of Guides; 1st and 2nd Sikh Infantry; 1st, 2nd and 5th Punjab Infantry.	
Nov. 21st	Attack on Ali Masjid	No. 4 Mountain Battery; 11th Bengal Lancers; Corps of Guides; Sappers and Miners; 6th, 14th, 20th, 27th, and 45th Bengal Infantry; 1st Sikh Infantry.	'Ali Masjid' on colours (G. G. O. 418 of 1881) and special clasp (G. G. O. 673 of 1880).
Dec. 2nd	Forcing of the Paiwar Kotal	No, 1 Mountain Battery; 12th Bengal Cavalry; 23rd and 29th Bengal Infantry; 2nd and 5th Punjab Infantry; 5th Gurkha Regiment.	'Paiwar Kotal' on colours (G. G. O. 418 of 1881); special clasp (G. G. O. 673 of 1880).
December 1879.	First Expedition to the Bazar Valley	11th and 13th Bengal Lancers; Sappers; 27th and 45th Bengal Infantry; 2nd Gurkha Regiment.	
January	Second Bazar Valley Expedition	13th Bengal Lancers; Sappers and Miners; 6th, 24th, 27th and 45th Bengal Infantry; Corps of Guides; 2nd and 4th Gurkha Regiments.	
	Second Afghan War—Second Campaign	As above, under the heading '1878-80' omitting the 26th Bengal Infantry, the 1st Sikh Infantry, and the 1st and 2nd Punjab Infantry, and with the following additions:—1st, 3rd, 4th and 5th Bengal Cavalry; 18th Bengal Lancers; 3rd Punjab	'Afghanistan, 1879-1880' on colours (G. G. O. 418 of 1881); medal as above; six months' batta (G.G.O. 459 of 1880).

Date	Event	Units	Honours
1879. Oct. 6th	Battle of Charasia	No. 2 Mountain Battery; 12th Bengal Cavalry; 14th Bengal Lancers; 5th Punjab Cavalry; 23rd and 28th Bengal Infantry; 5th Punjab Infantry; 5th Gurkha Regiment.	'Charasia' on colours (G. G. O. 418 of 1881); special clasp (G. G. O. 673 of 1880).
,,	Fighting on the Shutargardan Pass.	No. 1 Mountain Battery; 21st Bengal Infantry; 3rd Sikh Infantry.	
Dec. 10th—23rd	Operations at and around Kabul	No. 1 and 2 Mountain Batteries; 12th Bengal Cavalry; 14th Bengal Lancers; 5th Punjab Cavalry; Sappers and Miners; 23rd and 28th Bengal Infantry; Corps of Guides; 5th Gurkha Regiment; 3rd Sikh Infantry, 5th Punjab Infantry.	'Kabul, 1879' on colours (G. G. O. 418 of 1881); special clasp (G. G. O. 673 of 1880).
,, 17th—24th	Advance from Gandmak to Kabul	No. 4 Mountain Battery; Sappers and Miners; 2nd and 4th Gurkha Regiments.	As above.
,,	Expedition against the Zaimukhts.	No. 1 Mountain Battery; 1st Bengal Cavalry; 13th and 18th Bengal Lancers; Sappers and Miners; 13th, 20th and 29th Bengal Infantry; 4th Punjab Infantry.	
,, 17th—19th	Defence of Jagdalak	Detachments of No. 4 Mountain Battery and 10th Bengal Lancers; 24th Bengal Infantry; detachments of the 2nd and 4th Gurkha Regiments.	
1880. Apr. 19th	Battle of Ahmad Khel	19th Bengal Lancers; 1st and 2nd Punjab Cavalry; Sappers and Miners; 15th, 19th and 25th Bengal Infantry; 3rd Gurkha Regiment; 2nd Sikh Infantry.	'Ahmad Khel' on colours (G. G. O. 418 of 1881); special clasp (G. G. O. 673 of 1880).
,, 23rd	Actions at Shalez and Arau.		

Chronological List of the Services of the Bengal Native Army—continued.

Date.	Service.	Corps engaged which still exist.	Remarks.
1880. Apl. 25th	Action at Chihildakteran, in the Logar Valley.	No. 2 Mountain Battery; 3rd Punjab Cavalry; 45th Bengal Infantry; 2nd Gurkha Regiment; Corps of Guides.	
August	March to Kandahar	No. 2 Mountain Battery; 3rd Bengal Cavalry; 3rd Punjab Cavalry; 15th, 24th and 25th Bengal Infantry; 2nd, 4th and 5th Gurkha Regiments; 2nd and 3rd Sikh Infantry.	'Kandahar, 1880' on colours (G. G. O. 418 of 1881); special clasp (G. G. O. 673 of 1880); bronze star (G. G. O. 534 of 1880).
Sep. 1st	Battle of Kandahar		
1881. May	Mahsud Waziri Expedition	Nos. 1, 2, 3 and 4 Mountain Batteries; 18th Bengal Lancers; 1st and 4th Punjab Cavalry; 8th Company of Sappers and Miners; 14th, 20th, 21st, 30th and 32nd (Pioneers) Bengal Infantry; 1st and 4th Sikh Infantry; 1st, 2nd, 3rd, 4th, 5th and 6th Punjab Infantry.	
1882. Aug.—Sep.	*Expedition to Egypt*	2nd Bengal Lancers; 6th Bengal Cavalry; 13th Bengal Lancers; 7th and 20th Bengal Infantry.	'Egypt, 1882' on colours (G. G. O. 341 of 1883); medal (G. G. O. 578 and 665 of 1882); bronze star (G. G. O. 325 of 1882).
Sep. 13th	Battle of Tel-el-Kebir		'Tel-el-Kebir' on colours (G. G. O. 341 of 1883); special clasp (G. G. O. 665 of 1882).
1883–84	The Akha Expedition	No. 1 Mountain Battery; Sappers and Miners; 12th and 43rd Bengal Infantry.	
1884. October	Zhob Valley Expedition	10th Bengal Lancers; 5th Punjab Cavalry; Sappers and Miners; 1st and 45th Bengal Infantry; 4th Punjab Infantry.	

Date	Event	Units	Medal
1885. Mar.–Nov.	*Suakin Expedition*	9th Bengal Lancers; 15th and 17th Bengal Infantry.	'Suakin, 1885' on colours (G. G. O. 478 of 1886); Egyptian medal (G.G.O. 655 of 1885); bronze star (G. G. O. 849 of 1887).
Mar. 20th	Reconnaissance to Hashin		
Mar. 22nd	Battle of Tofrek		'Tofrek' on colours (G. G. O. No. 478 of 1886); special clasp (G. G. O. 655 of 1885).
1885–1887	*Third Burma War—* First Phase	Nos. 7 and 8 (Bengal) Mountain Batteries; Sappers and Miners; 1st, 2nd, 4th, 5th, 10th, 11th, 12th, 16th, 18th, 26th, 27th, 42nd, 43rd and 44th Bengal Infantry; 3rd Gurkha Regiment.	'Burma, 1885–87' on colours;(G. G. O. 64 of 1891); India medal with special clasp (G. G. O. 434 of 1887).
1885. Nov. 17th	Taking of Minhla	2nd and 11th Bengal Infantry.	
1888. October	Black Mountain Expedition	No. 4 Mountain Battery; 15th Bengal Cavalry; Sappers and Miners; 14th, 24th, 29th, 34th, and 45th Bengal Infantry; 2nd and 3rd Sikh Infantry; 4th Punjab Infantry; 5th Gurkha Regiment.	India medal with special clasp (G. G. O. 431 of 1889).
1888	Sikkim Expedition	13th and 32nd Bengal Infantry; 2nd Battalion, 1st Gurkha Regiment.	India medal with special clasp (G. G. O. 31 of 1890).
1885–1889	*Third Burma War—* 2nd Phase	Nos. 7 and 8 Bengal Mountain Batteries; 10th, 12th, 33rd and 42nd Bengal Infantry.	

Chronological List of the Services of the Bengal Native Army —continued.

Date.	Service.	Corps engaged which still exist.	Remarks.
1888–1889	Lushai Expedition	2nd and 9th Bengal Infantry; 2nd Battalion, 2nd Gurkha Regiment.	India medal with special clasp (G. G. O. 275 of 1890).
1889–1890	Chin-Lushai Expedition	No. 7 Bengal Mountain Battery; 10th, 38th, and 42nd Bengal Infantry; 2nd Battalion, 4th Gurkha Regiment.	
1890 Oct.—Nov.	Zhob Valley Expedition	18th Bengal Lancers; 1st and 3rd Punjab Cavalry; Nos. 1 and 7 Mountain Batteries; 1st and 2nd Sikh Infantry; 2nd Punjab Infantry.	
1890–1893.	Expeditions against the Chins, Lushais, etc.	No. 8 (Bengal) Mountain Battery; detachments of the 3rd, 7th and 18th Bengal Infantry; the 39th Bengal Infantry; detachment of the 40th Bengal Infantry; the 2-4th Gurkha Rifles.	
1891. January	First Miranzai Expedition	Nos. 3 and 4 Mountain Batteries; two squadrons of the 5th Punjab Cavalry; the 5th Company of the Bengal Sappers and Miners; the 22nd, 23rd and 29th Bengal Infantry; the 3rd Sikh Infantry; and the 1st, 4th and 5th Punjab Infantry.	
1891. March—April	Operations in Manipur	No. 8 (Bengal) Mountain Battery; detachments of the 13th and 18th Bengal Infantry; the 42nd, 43rd and 44th Bengal Infantry; the 1-2nd and 2-4th Gurkha Rifles.	India medal with special clasp (G. G. O. No. 652 of 1892).

March—April	Black Mountain Expedition	No. 2 Mountain Battery (three guns); 11th Bengal Lancers (one squadron); the 4th Company of the Bengal Sappers and Miners; the 11th, 32nd and 37th Bengal Infantry; the Guides Infantry; the 4th Sikh Infantry; the 2-5th Gurkha Rifles; and the Khaibar Rifles.	India medal with special clasp (G. G. O. No. 258 of 1892).
April—May	Second Miranzai Expedition	No. 2 Mountain Battery (three guns); No. 3 Mountain Battery; the Punjab Garrison Battery (three guns); the 19th Bengal Lancers; two squadrons of the 5th Punjab Cavalry; the 5th Company of the Bengal Sappers and Miners; the 15th, 19th, 27th and 29th Bengal Infantry; the 3rd Sikh Infantry; the 1st, 2nd and 6th Punjab Infantry; and the 1-5th Gurkha Rifles.	India medal with special clasp (G. G. O. No. 61 of 1892).
December 1892.	Operations in Hunza and Nagar.	No. 4 Mountain Battery (two guns); party of Bengal Sappers and Miners; and detachments of the 20th Bengal Infantry and 1-5th Gurkha Rifles.	India medal with special clasp (G. G. O. No. 986 of 1892).
October 1893.	Isazai Expedition	No. 1 Mountain Battery; the 4th and 6th Companies of the Bengal Sappers and Miners; two squadrons of the 11th Bengal Lancers; the 25th and 30th Bengal Infantry; the 4th Sikh Infantry; and the 1-5th and 2-5th Gurkha Rifles.	
May .	Expedition against the Kuki village of Mongham.	Detachment 43rd Bengal Infantry	

Chronological List of the Services of the Bengal Native Army—concluded.

Date.	Service.	Corps engaged which still exist.	Remarks.
1894. January—March	Abor Expedition	Detachment 44th Bengal Infantry.	
Oct.—Nov.	Waziristan Boundary Delimitation.	No. 3 Mountain Battery; No. 2 Company, Bengal Sappers and Miners; one squadron of the 1st Punjab Cavalry; the 20th Bengal Infantry; 1-1st Gurkha Rifles; and the 3rd Sikh Infantry.	India medal with special clasp (G. G. O. No. 1082 of 1895).
1894-95. Dec.—Jan.	Waziristan Expedition	Nos. 1, 3 and 8 Mountain Batteries; Nos. 2 and 5 Companies, Bengal Sappers and Miners; the 1st (two squadrons), 2nd (one squadron) and 3rd Punjab Cavalry; the 20th, 33rd and 38th Bengal Infantry; the 1-1st and 1-5th Gurkha Rifles; the 1st and 3rd Sikh Infantry; and the 2nd, 4th and 6th Punjab Infantry.	
1895.	*Chitral Operations.*		
March—April	Defence of Chitral Fort Action at Reshan	Detachment 14th Bengal Infantry. Detachment Bengal Sappers and Miners.	
	Action near Korach Defence of Mastuj March from Gilgit to Chitral; actions at Chakalwat and Nisa Gol.	Detachment 14th Bengal Infantry. Detachment 14th Bengal Infantry. Wing 32nd Bengal Infantry.	

Forcing of the Malakand Pass; actions of Khar, Swat River, Panjkora River, and Mamuzai.	Nos. 2 and 4 Mountain Batteries; Nos. 1, 4, and 6 Companies, Bengal Sappers and Miners; the 11th Bengal Lancers; the Guides Cavalry; the 13th, 15th, 23rd, 25th, 29th, 30th and 37th Bengal Infantry; the 4th Gurkha Rifles; the Guides Infantry; and the 4th Sikh Infantry.

ALSO FROM LEONAUR
AVAILABLE IN SOFTCOVER OR HARDCOVER WITH DUST JACKET

A JOURNAL OF THE SECOND SIKH WAR by *Daniel A. Sandford*—The Experiences of an Ensign of the 2nd Bengal European Regiment During the Campaign in the Punjab, India, 1848-49.

LAKE'S CAMPAIGNS IN INDIA by *Hugh Pearse*—The Second Anglo Maratha War, 1803-1807. Often neglected by historians and students alike, Lake's Indian campaign was fought against a resourceful and ruthless enemy-almost always superior in numbers to his own forces.

BRITAIN IN AFGHANISTAN 1: THE FIRST AFGHAN WAR 1839-42 by *Archibald Forbes*—Following over a century of the gradual assumption of sovereignty of the Indian Sub-Continent, the British Empire, in the form of the Honourable East India Company, supported by troops of the new Queen Victoria's army, found itself inevitably at the natural boundaries that surround Afghanistan. There it set in motion a series of disastrous events-the first of which was to march into the country at all.

BRITAIN IN AFGHANISTAN 2: THE SECOND AFGHAN WAR 1878-80 by *Archibald Forbes*—This the history of the Second Afghan War-another episode of British military history typified by savagery, massacre, siege and battles.

UP AMONG THE PANDIES by *Vivian Dering Majendie*—An outstanding account of the campaign for the fall of Lucknow. This is a vital book of war as fought by the British Army of the mid-nineteenth century, but in truth it is also an essential book of war that will enthral.

BLOW THE BUGLE, DRAW THE SWORD by *W. H. G. Kingston*—The Wars, Campaigns, Regiments and Soldiers of the British & Indian Armies During the Victorian Era, 1839-1898.

INDIAN MUTINY 150th ANNIVERSARY: A LEONAUR ORIGINAL

MUTINY: 1857 by *James Humphries*—It is now 150 years since the 'Indian Mutiny' burst like an engulfing flame on the British soldiers, their families and the civilians of the Empire in North East India. The Bengal Native army arose in violent rebellion, and the once peaceful countryside became a battleground as Native sepoys and elements of the Indian population massacred their British masters and defeated them in open battle. As the tide turned, a vengeful army of British and loyal Indian troops repressed the insurgency with a savagery that knew no mercy. It was a time of fear and slaughter. James Humphries has drawn together the voices of those dreadful days for this commemorative book.

AVAILABLE ONLINE AT
www.leonaur.com
AND OTHER GOOD BOOK STORES

ALSO FROM LEONAUR
AVAILABLE IN SOFTCOVER OR HARDCOVER WITH DUST JACKET

WAR BEYOND THE DRAGON PAGODA by *J. J. Snodgrass*—A Personal Narrative of the First Anglo-Burmese War 1824 - 1826.

ALL FOR A SHILLING A DAY by *Donald F. Featherstone*—The story of H.M. 16th, the Queen's Lancers During the first Sikh War 1845-1846.

AT THEM WITH THE BAYONET by *Donald F. Featherstone*—The first Anglo-Sikh War 1845-1846.

A LEONAUR ORIGINAL

THE HERO OF ALIWAL by *James Humphries*—The days when young Harry Smith wore the green jacket of the 95th-Wellington's famous riflemen-campaigning in Spain against Napoleon's French with his beautiful young bride Juana have long gone. Now, Sir Harry Smith is in his fifties approaching the end of a long career. His position in the Cape colony ends with an appointment as Deputy Adjutant-General to the army in India. There he joins the staff of Sir Hugh Gough to experience an Indian battlefield in the Gwalior War of 1843 as the power of the Marathas is finally crushed. Smith has little time for his superior's 'bull at a gate' style of battlefield tactics, but independent command is denied him. Little does he realise that the greatest opportunity of his military life is close at hand.

THE GURKHA WAR by *H. T. Prinsep*—The Anglo-Nepalese Conflict in North East India 1814-1816.

SOUND ADVANCE! by *Joseph Anderson*—Experiences of an officer of HM 50th regiment in Australia, Burma & the Gwalior war.

THE CAMPAIGN OF THE INDUS by *Thomas Holdsworth*—Experiences of a British Officer of the 2nd (Queen's Royal) Regiment in the Campaign to Place Shah Shuja on the Throne of Afghanistan 1838 - 1840.

WITH THE MADRAS EUROPEAN REGIMENT IN BURMA by *John Butler*—The Experiences of an Officer of the Honourable East India Company's Army During the First Anglo-Burmese War 1824 - 1826.

BESIEGED IN LUCKNOW by *Martin Richard Gubbins*—The Experiences of the Defender of 'Gubbins Post' before & during the sige of the residency at Lucknow, Indian Mutiny, 1857.

THE STORY OF THE GUIDES by *G.J. Younghusband*—The Exploits of the famous Indian Army Regiment from the northwest frontier 1847 - 1900.

AVAILABLE ONLINE AT
www.leonaur.com
AND OTHER GOOD BOOK STORES

www.ingramcontent.com/pod-product-compliance
Lightning Source LLC
Chambersburg PA
CBHW032315230426
43666CB00032B/70